Trail Blazer
Winning Edge Series

OBJECTIVE ENGLISH

For

COMPETITIVE EXAMS

Highly recommended for:

- IBPS PO / SBI PO / Specialist Officers' Exam / RBI
- UPSC Exams: Civil Services / NDA / CDS
  Forest & Engineering Services etc.
- LIC / GIC AAO & ADO Exam
- SSC Exam for Asstt. Grade / CPO-SI / CBI / Income Tax Inspectors
- Railway Recruitment Board Exam
- CTET and STET
- CLAT
- MAT / CAT / IIFT / IGNOU / GRE / Hotel Management
- Campus Selection Tests etc.

Authors

B. B. Sinha • A. P. Sharma • Nitin Sharma

Publisher
UNICORN BOOKS
F-2/16, Ansari Road, Daryaganj, New Delhi-110002
E-mail: info@unicornbooks.in • *Website:* www.unicornbooks.in
☎ 011-23262683, 45644782, 23250704

ISBN: 978-81-7806-380-5
Objective English

Edition: 2026

Printed at : *Param Offsetters, Okhla, New Delhi-110020*

Preface

Dear student,

General English is an important component of the syllabi of various competitive examinations like banking, insurance, management, NDA etc.

No amount of practice looks enough when it comes to studying for a competitive exam, mainly because of the cut-throat competition for every seat. Therefore, we decided to create a book that will give you ample amount of additional practice for objective type and other questions asked in various tests containing a section on General English.

This book is the result of untiring effort of many experts. The book covers some of the most important topics such as *Synonyms and Antonyms, Direct and Indirect Speech, Idioms and Phrases, Sentence Correction, Active and Passive Voice, Reading Comprehension, Synthesis, One Word Substitution* and *Important Words along with their meanings.* In addition to explaining every topic with suitable examples, we have provided practice exercises at the end of each unit.

We sincerely hope that this book will help you improve your objective English score substantially.

Our special thanks go to A. P. Sharma & Mr. B. B. Sinha who have inspired & motivated us to develop this book an General English for all kinds of competitive exams.

We owe a special debt of gratitude to Ms. Padma Parupudi & Sirisha Naresh for using some of the content from their book for CLAT and LL.B entrance examinations.

We have tried our best to keep errors out of this book. We shall be grateful to the readers for all their constructive suggestions.

Some Questions You Might Want To Ask

Q. Why do I need a book on Objective English?

This question may strike some people. Since various tests that include an objective English section ask, at the most, graduation level questions, what is the need for a book on Objective English? *("Haven't I read all this in my school and college?")* Well, the answer to this question is simple: one thing can be asked in a number of ways. For instance, you might know the meaning of a word, but you might not be aware of its most accurate synonym or antonym, or maybe you can write a sentence as good as a professional writer but you can't convert it to a passive voice sentence because you never needed to do that in your school or college (*Some of them are really bewildering, believe me.*) It is a habit of test-makers to make simple things complicated because they want to test how good you are when compared with other candidates. Therefore, it becomes imperative for you to study the things as they generally appear in various exams. That's why every candidate, no matter how his/her academic record has been, needs a book on Objective English. It is even more important because taking a chance when it comes to making your career might not be a bright idea.

Q. What can I expect from this book?

'Objective English for Competitive Exams' has been created in such a way that it gives you ample practice for the questions that frequently appear in the exams (of all levels) designed to measure a candidate's knowledge of general English. Whether you want to become an I.A.S. or a manager, or secure a position in a bank, or simply wish to brush upon your knowledge of English, you will find this book useful. We have taken into account the fact that the difficulty level of questions varies according to the level of exam. Therefore, this book contains both tough as well as comparatively easier examples and questions. There are exercises and test papers to test your knowledge of the topics discussed. These exercises and test papers contain the questions similar to those frequently asked in exams. Their answers and required explanations have also been provided.

Q. When should I begin to study for my exam?

The answer to this question is quite simple: the sooner you begin the better. Since the competition is so intense, it is never too early to begin your preparations. It also depends on how good you are at English at this moment. Some candidates begin their preparations when they are still pursuing a graduation degree, while some begin even sooner. At the same time, there have been aspirants who only need a few months of preparation.

Q. I'm aiming for a great score. Apart from this book, what can I do to improve my knowledge of English?

This is an important question. It is crucial to look beyond the books available in the market if you want to obtain a great score on the English section of any exam. After all, the number of pages in a book is limited. It is impossible to include every single thing and topic in a book, no matter how good the book is. For instance, this book includes thousands of important words (along with their meanings) selected carefully for the benefit of test takers, yet the list can never be complete because English language has lacs of words and new words are added every year. Similarly, only a limited number of passages can be included in a book.However, you need not worry. Here are some of the things you can do to improve your score:

- **Read English Newspapers.** This is one of the most effective techniques adopted by the toppers. A newspaper not only gives you a pool of words that can be asked in a test, but also gives you reading speed vital for your success in 'Reading Comprehension' questions. Newspapers use formal language, and it is formal language that is tested in exams. Make it a habit to read newspapers. As soon as you encounter a word you don't understand, note it down and look for the meaning in a good dictionary. In fact, you should maintain a register in which you should write down the words you learn from newspapers and magazines.

  You could read fiction, autobiographies, sports magazines, blogs etc. Try to read a variety of topics based on your interest. As you start reading daily, you will improvise on the techniques to read faster & develop the capability to retain information.

- **Read Exam Oriented Magazines.** Read the magazines that discuss topics related to the exams you're preparing for. For instance, if you are preparing for MBA entrance tests, you should read weekly and monthly business magazines because some questions (in the GK sections of exams as well as in a GD/PI) might relate to burning topics in the field of business. If you are preparing for UPSC or state-level exams, it might be a good idea to read yearbooks as well as magazines that discuss national and global issues and topics. For GRE and GMAT, reading articles will be beneficial. It not only enhances your knowledge but also gives you an idea how to write about such topics. It also improves your reading speed significantly, and speed matters a lot in exams.

- **Surf the Net.** With the advent of internet, things have become simple (as well as complicated). Though it is not a good idea to read everything that is online, if you read news and articles, relevant e-zines (free online magazines) and visit useful websites, especially those associated with the exams you're interested in, you can definitely improve your knowledge as well as vocab. What more, some of the exams that test your knowledge of English are (GRE, GMAT, IELTS, TOEFL etc.) computer-based. If you do not practice reading articles on computer screen and if you are not well-versed with computers, you might find it awkward to take an exam using a computer. Therefore, it will be a good idea to spend some time on computer. Visit the websites related to your field, read free online content and practise using free online tests and exercises. It is bound to help you in your preparation. Moreover, many websites give you stress-management tips that you will find useful.

Also, develop your reasoning capability. You could solve cross-word puzzles, Sudoku, mathematical puzzles jumbled words. Play word based games like scrabble. This will broaden your horizon as well as develop your reasoning power & vocabulary.

The biggest challenge in any competitive exam is to read all the questions & attempt as many as possible. You would not have time to solve all the questions in the given time. Since there could be negative marking, accuracy in responses is very important. You need to develop your strategy to score as many marks as possible. So you need to figure out your strong areas & your ability to guess. You need to decide which sections take more time and which ones can be done fast. In order to build confidence, your strong areas need to be targeted first in the exam.

When it comes to preparing for a competitive exam, you should use every means available to you and leave no stone unturned. This is the only way to ensure your success. All the best!

ooo

Contents

Unit-1

Important Words and Their Meanings

English language is a fusion of words which originated from different languages like Spanish, French, Latin, German, Italian, Sanskrit etc. It is so widely spoken that it is often referred to as 'Lingua Franca'. It means a language used for communication among people of different countries. Some words in English have their origins in other languages, and some other words have been absorbed into English language as they are in vogue. It will be useful to if you understand the roots of the words.

Some words appear quite frequently in various competitive exams. If you understand these words, you can improve your score substantially. Here, we have given a list of such words along with their meanings. Though no word list can ever be called a complete list, this is one of the most exhaustive word lists available. If you encounter a word you don't understand, probably you will find it here.

The thought of learning words and their meanings is intimidating to some of us at times. Vocabulary with regard to competitive exams can be classified into two areas: (A), words and their meanings; and (B), vocabulary based questions. Both the problems can be tackled by applying a strategic approach.

Two of the many strategies are:

- **Contextual Vocabulary:** It is about understanding the meaning of an unfamiliar word based on the context or circumstance in which it is used.

Example: She was an **iconoclast** as opposed to her mother who is a conservative.

Here, the given sentence suggests that the unfamiliar word 'iconoclast' is opposite of 'conservative'. The word iconoclast means one who attacks and seeks to overthrow traditional or popular ideas or institutions.

Roots, Prefixes and Suffixes: Root word is the basic word on which a word is coined. Prefix is added at the beginning of a word, and suffix is added at the end of a word. If you could understand the meanings of these words, then it will be easy to learn words. Note that a particular spelling need not always be associated with the same root, prefix or suffix. Example: India is a country of multifarious cultures. I hope you know that 'multi' means many. So, guess the meaning of multifarious. The word 'multifarious' means diverse.

Word Roots

A

Acerb, Acri = bitter in taste

Exacerbate = to make something bitter; ° Relations between them got exacerbated ° Acrid smell of fumes ° Acrimonious argument

Acro = height

Acrobat = a person who displays physical feats on rope tied to the erect poles at both ends as in a circus.

Acronym = (nym= name) short name of something that is given by taking first or top letters of all the words mentioned in it. For example, UNESCO - acronym of United Nations Educational, Scientific, (and) Cultural Organization.

Other acronyms - AIDS, RADAR, etc.

Acrophobia = mortal fear of looking down from a height.

Acropolis = (polis = city) a fort, citadel, etc. situated at height, e.g., on a hill-top.

Acrostic = word formed by taking first letters of each sentence or word used for expressing an idea or slogon taken from top downwards.

For example,

Loyalty is a virtue.
Integrity is a way of life.
Courage is an innate quality.
And
Discipline is taught in army.
i.e., licad in army is needed.

Aero = air

Aeroplane, Aerodrome, Aerobics

Ambul = walk

Ambulance, Per-ambulator

Ami = friend

Amity = friendly relation between people.

Amiable = friendly person.

Amicable = friendly atmosphere in which talks are held or disputes are settled.

Anima = soul, alive state

Animate = to make something lively (Animation film).

Animus = hostile feeling against someone.

Animosity = Anim(us) + mosity

Un-animus (decision)

Aqua = water

Aquarium = aqua + arium = place to keep, so, it means a place (usually a tank made of glass) to keep fish in water.

Aquarius = zodiac sign which resembles water carrier pot.

Aquatic = living in water (as opposed to terrestrial (living on earth).

Aqueduct = passage constructed to allow water pass across

Aquifer = under ground source of water mass.

Archae = old, ancient, of past

Archaeology = study of ancient period.

Archaic = belonging to ancient period.

Archi = first, chief

Archive = place where first (original) documents are safely kept.

Architecture = archi + (tectus = construction) art of constructing a building first on paper as a drawing.

Arch-bishop = chief bishop.

Arch enemy = main enemy.

Aster, Astro = star

Asterisk = symbol of star, used in books.

Asteroid = star-like celestial body which moves around a planet in the sky.

Astrology = study of effects of heavenly stars on the life of human-beings.

Astronomy = (nomy = law) law of stars, planets, orbiting in their paths in the sky.

Audio = hearing

Audible = what can be heard.

Audience = people sitting together to hear someone's speech.

Audition = test of voice quality by hearing a song or dialogue of a singer or actor.

Auditorium = place where audience gathers to hear speech.

Auto = self

Autograph = (graph = writing) signature of a famous person given by himself to his admirer.

Automatic = (a machine) working by itself.

Automobile = (engine) which moves by itself.

Autocracy = (auto = self + cracy = rule, governance) system of governance by one person himself.

B

Belli = fight

Bellicose = (a person) who is inclined to pick up a fight with someone.

Belligerent = (a country) which adopts war-like posture against another country.

Biblio = book

Bible = book regarded as respected source of knowledge on a subject.

Bibliography = written list of books which have been consulted by an author in course of preparing manuscript.

Biblio mania = strong liking for reading books so, you can guess meanings of Bibliophile, Bibliomancy.

Bio = life, living-beings

Biology = science of living beings.

Bio-divesity = (diverse = variety) variety of living creatures including plants which exist in harmony in a place or ecosystem.

Biography = book written by someone on the life of a famous person.

Brevi (s) = brief, short

Brevi-loquent = (loquent = speaking) a person who speaks in a few words.

Brevity = state of being brief

C

Caco = bad,

Cacophony = harsh sound ° Cacophony of city traffic ° Air is filled with cacophony of hoots, cackles of birds.

Cacography = bad handwriting.

Calli = beautiful

Calligraphy = beautiful handwriting; ° Calligraphy of inscriptions on stone plaques in memorials are worth appreciating.

Callisthenic = (calli = beautiful, good + sthenos = strength) of beautiful body strength; ° Callisthenic exercises.

Calypso = covered, folded, concealed

Eucalyptus = a tree, the leaves of which are well folded.

Apocalypse = not concealed prophecy of oracle.

Candidus = shining brightly.

Candle = a stick of wax which burns with shining brightly.

Candid = what is brightly frank; ° His reply was candid.

Candour = quality of being candid ° Candour of his speech impressed audience.

In-candescent (bulb) = electric bulb which glows brightly to give light.

Capit = head

Capitulate = to surrender, to lower one's head before someone.

De-capitate = to cut someone's head.

Per capita income = per head income.

Carni = flesh

Carnal (pleasure) = pleasure derived from sensual feelings of body made of flesh.

Carnage = large number of killings of persons (made of human flesh).

In-carnation = coming in the shape of human body (made of flesh) as by God; ° Christ birth was the incarnation of God.

Chiro = hand

Chiromancy = reading of lines on palm of hand to predict one's future, palmistry.

Chiropodist = a person who treats a patient's foot (podi, pedi) ailments with hands.

Chiropractor = a person who practises manipulation of nerves with his hands to restore to normal position - thus relieving patient's discomfort.

Macro chira = a person having large size hands.

Chromo = colour

Mono-chromatic = having one colour; ° Monochromatic paintings.

Photochromatic = changing colour with lights (photo-) falling on; ° Photochromatic glass.

Chrono = time

Chronometer = instrument which measures time.

Chronology = arrangement of past events in order of time of occurrence.

Chronicle = record of past events in order of time of occurrence.

Chronic = existing for a longtime; ° Chronic disease.

Clemen = kind, merciful

Clemency = mercy shown by authority to enemy, offenders; ° Govt. granted clemency to rebels and released from jail ° Clement judge was lenient in awarding punishment.

In-clement = not showing mercy; ° Inclement weather.

Clude = to close, shut

Include = to take inside and shut the doors; ° His name was included in the list.

Exclude = to keep out and shut the doors; ° His name was excluded from the list.

Occlude = (ob + clude) to shut passage so as to prevent escape or entry through; ° He occluded upper and lower teeth so to prevent feeding.

Pre-clude = (pre = before) to foreclose a chance of happening; ° Physical disability precluded his chance of becoming an athlete.

Cardio / Cordio = heart

Cardiac = related to heart; ° Cardiac problems.

Cardiology = science / knowledge of diseases related to heart.

Cordial = heart-felt; ° Cordial reception ° Cordial relations.

Con-cord = harmonious relation which is joing heart to heart.

Dis-cord = loss of harmony.

Corn = horn

Unicorn = having one horn; ° Unicorn animal.

Cornet = shape of a horn given to a wafer for holding ice-cream.

Cornucopia = a horn having magical power to provide food, or anything desired in abundance.

Coron = crown

Coronation = ceremony of crowning new king.

Coronette = small crown.

Corpora = body

Corporal = related to body; ° Corporal punishment.

Corporeal = related to physical state of body as opposed to spiritual.

Corps = body of / group of troops.

Corpse = dead body.

Corpus = body of / amount of collected funds to be used for a purpose; ° Corpus of funds contributed by employees is used for pension after retirement.

Corrigare = to correct

Corrigendum = list of corrections - usually printed at the end of a book.

In-corrigible = what is beyond correction; ° Incorrigible habits.

Credi = belief of something being true; ° Credible statement ° Incredible performance.

Crypto = hidden

Cryptic = hidden; ° Cryptic message / remark.

Cryptogram = coded writing - hidden in code language.

Apo-cryphal = of hidden source of origin; ° Apocryphal story - authorship of the story is hidden / not known.

Apocrypha = a book written by unknown author.

Culp = blame, accuse.

Culprit = a person who is blamed to be guilty.

Culpable = what is blame worthy; ° Culpable action.

Ex-culpate = to clear someone from blame, to declare not guilty; ° The inquiry exculpated him of all charges against him.

Cura = care

Curator = a person who is in-charge of taking care of museum, art-collection, wild-life park; ° He is the curator of museum.

Cure = to take care of ill person by treating him with medicines so that he becomes fit; ° Doctors prescribe medicines to cure an ill person.

Sine-cure = (sine = without) an employee who gets salary without care of doing work.

Cyno = dog

Cynophile = (philo = liking) a person who likes dogs.

Cynophobe = (phobo = dislike) a person who dislikes dogs.

Cynologist = a person who is expert in subject of dogs.

Cynic = a person who does not believe in selfless motive of anyone, just as a dog does not believe in an unknown person and starts barking.

D

Dactylo = finger

Hexadactylous = (a person) having six fingers; ° A hexadactylous person.

Dactylographer = a person who is expert in matching finger-print

Dei, Deo, Theo = God

Deity = representation of God; ° Worship deity in temples.

Deify = to treat a person as God; ° Devotees of a saint deify him.

Theocracy = govt. run by saints in the name of God.

Theist = a person who believes in existence of God.

(Opposite : Atheist)

Demo, Demi = people

Democracy = rule of people.

Demagogue = (dem (o) + agogue = leader) leader of the people.

Epidemic = (disease) which afflicts people in large number; ° Epidemic disease.

Endemic = (disease) which afflicts people living in a particular locality.

Pandemic = (disease) which afflicts people all over the world.

Dermato = Skin

Dermatologist = skin specialist doctor.

Leucoderma = (leuco = white) skin disease of white patches on skin.

Pachyderm = (animal) having thick skin; ° Elephant is a pachyderm.

Dox = belief, faith

Orthodox = (ortho = straight) people who have straight faith in the religion; ° Orthodox Hindus.

Paradox = a statement, opinion, situation which is contradictory to the commonly accepted belief.

Dextro, Dexter = right hand

Dextral = right-handed (opp : sinistral); ° Dextral person.

Dexterous = skilled (in using right hand); ° A dexterous person.

F

Fac, Fic = to do, to make

Factory = place where some product is made; ° Garment factory.

Factotum = (Fac = to do + totum = total) a person who does all kinds of work for someone.; ° Factotum employed by the family does all kinds of odd jobs.

Factitious = what is artificial (made - non natural); ° Factitious laughter ° Factitious flower.

Fiction = story which is made / created by imagination.

Fictitious = what is created - not real; ° Fictitious name of a person.

Fide = faith, trust

Confide = to put one's own trust in someone and share secrets with him; ° He confides in his friend - and no one else.

Confidence = trust; ° The president has full confidance in his secretary.

Confidant = a person who enjoys confidence of someone; ° He is my confidant.

Fidelity = faithfulness, loyalty; ° Fidelity to one's country ° Wife's fidelity to her husband.

In-fidel = a person who is not faithful to one's own religion.

Diffident = (a person) lacking faith in one's ability; ° A diffident person.

Perfidy = breach of trust.

Filius = son or daughter.

Filicide = killing of one's own son or daughter.

Affiliate = (ad = to + filiate) to adopt as one's son; ° University affiliates colleges.

Flex = to fold, to bend

Flexible = which can be bent, not rigid; ° Flexible opinion.

Flex = to bend; ° He flexed his arms to show museles.

Flexuous = full of many bends / turns ° Flexuous course of a river.

Genuflect = (Genu = knee) to bend knees as in prayer or in submitting before someone ° Genuflect before deity in prayer.

Flux = to flow

Influx = flow into a place; ° Influx of tourists to hill stations increases in summer season.

Effluent = (ex = out + fluent = what flows) stream of waste which is discharged; ° Effluent of factory waste.

Influent = what flows into something; ° Influent streams of tributaries fall into river.

Confluence = place where two rivers meet and further flow together; ° Sangam is the confluence of Ganga and Yamuna.

Fracto, Fragmentus, Frang (ere) = break

Fraction = a part broken from the whole.

Fragment = a broken part of wood, stone, glass; ° Fragments of glass are scattered all over the place.

Fracture = breaking of bone, etc. ° His bone has fractured.

Infraction = breach / breaking of rules; ° Infraction of traffic rules.

Infringement = breaking into others' rights, powers; ° Infringement of others' privacy.

Fragile = What is breakable due to being delicate; ° Glass is fragile material.

Frangible = what is breakable due to excess pressure or impact; ° Frangible toys ° Our bones are frangible.

Frater = brother (soror = sister)

Fratricide = killing of one's brother.

Fraternal = of brother, brotherly; ° Fraternal relations.

Fuge (re) = to flee, escape

Fugitive = a person who flees from police arrest.

Fugacious = fleeing / disappearing soon; ° Fugaicous public attention.

G

Gamos = marriage

Monogamy = system of marrying one woman at a time.

Bigamy & Polygamy = system of marrying two women / many women at a time.

Gene = to produce

Generator = machine that produces electricity.

Generation = entire mass of people who are produced by their ancestors; ° Present generation is having broad outlook.

Progeny = children produced by same parents; ° His progenies are brilliant.

Progenitor = parents who have produced progeny.

Pathogen = bacteria which produces disease.

Geo, Terra = earth, land

Geology = science of structures below the surface of the earth.

Geography = subject which deals with the marking of different structures on the surface of the earth.

Perigee = position of the planet in its orbit which is the nearest to the earth.

Territory = land within the boundary of a country; ° Indian Territory.

Terrain = tract of land with specified features; ° Hilly terrain.

Terrestrial = living on land as opposed to aquatic, or aerial, or arboreal (= living on water, air or trees).

Terrestrial living-being.

Geri, Gero, Geronto = aged, old person

Geriatric = related with aged person; ° Geriatric problems.

Gerontologist = doctor who treats aged persons' physical problems.

Gerontrocracy = govt. run by aged persons.

Gnos = know

A-gnostic = a person who does not know whether God exists or not.

Ignorant = (a person) who does not know about a subject; ° He is ignorant of what is happening in the world.

Ignore = to pretend as if one does not know; ° He ignored me when we met.

Ignoramus = a person who does not know.

Dia-gnose = to know the nature of ailments in a person's body; ° Doctor diagnosed his ailment as malaria.

Prognose / Prognosticate = (pro = beforehand) to know beforehand the course of progress of a disease.

Gregare = flock, herd

Gregarious = living in herd; ° Elephants are gregarious animal.

Aggregate = (ad + gregate) to flock together, to bring together.

Segregate = (se = apart) remove apart from flock; ° Infected person is segregated from others to avoid spreading of infection.

Gress = walk, go, step

Progress = (pro = forward) to go forward.

Retrogress = (Retro = backwards) to go in backward direction.

Ingress = to walk into a place; ° The low-lying areas were inundated due to ingress of floodwater.

Egress = (ex = out + gress) going out of a place.

Transgress = (trans = across) to go across the limit; ° Do not transgress your authority.

Gynaeco, Gyne, Gyny = woman, female.

Gynaecologist = doctor treating females disease.

Gynaecocracy = govt run by women.

Gyro = rotate

Gyrate = to move round & round, rotate.

H

Haemo = blood

Haemorrhage = excess bleeding.

Haemoglobin = red cells in blood.

Haemopoietic = what produces blood in body.

Hagio = saint

Hagiocracy = rule of saints.

Hagiolatry = (latry = worship) worship of saints.

Hagiography = biography of saint.

Halitus = breath

Halitosis = foul smell coming from one's breath.

Exhale = expel air through breath.

Inhale = draw air through breath.

Helix = spiral shape

Helical = of spiral shape.

Helicopter = flying machine having wings (opter) which move rotate in spiral motion.

Helio = sun

Haliolatry = worshipping sun.

Heliotrope = (plants) which turn. (tropo = turn) towards the sun.

Horo = hora, hour, time

Horology = skill of making watches.

Horoscope = zodiac signs of the hour of a person's birth.

Hydro = water

Hydrometer = meter to measure quantity of water in liquid.

Hydrogen = what produces water.

Hydro phobia = morbid fear of water.

I

Iatros = Physician

Iatrogenic = what is produced by wrong treatment by physician; ° Iatrogenic ailments.

Paed(i) - iatrician = Paediatrician, Physician who treats ailments of children (paedi = child).

Icono = image

Icon = image, picture, portrait of Gods, venerated personage.

Iconoclast = (clast = breaker) a person who breaks images, traditional beliefs of a religion.

Iconolatry = worshipping of icons.

J

Ject = throw

Inject = to throw medicine into body.

Project = to throw forward; ° Missile was projected towards target ° Film is projected on the screen with the help of a projector.

Reject = to throw away a discarded ° His proposal was rejected.

Conjecture = act of throwing a wild guess.

Judic = Judge

Judiciary = institution / court of judges.

Ad-judicate = to judge a case on a matter of dispute.

Judicious = who / what is justified ° Judicious decision.

Jure(re) = swear

Abjure = to swear to desist from doing something bad; ° Abjure violence ° Abjure cigarette smoking.

Perjure = to make false statement by swearing to speak truth in court; ° Perjury is punishable .

Conjure = to swear by the name of spirit while showing magic, or producing something by magic; ° Magician conjured a miracle.

L

Liga(re) = to tie, to bind

Ligament = fibrous tissue which binds bone joints together in proper place; ° Ligature = act of tying up ° Ligature of operated body-part is done with required skill.

Ob-ligate = to bind legally or morally; ° Clause of contracts obligates the parties to fulfil it ° His help in time of need has obligated me to him.

Oblige = to bind someone morally; ° One is obliged to return loan taken from bank.

Levi(s) = to make lighter (so as to rise up / float in the air).

Alleviate = (ad = to + levi = make light) to make a suffering light so as to be bearable; ° Pain-killer medicines alleviate pain.

Levitate = to rise up in the air and float due to lightness.

Locu, Loquaci = speech

Locution = style of making speech; ° Impressive locution.

Loquacious = taking too much, talkative; ° A loquacious child.

Luci = bright, shining

Lucid = shining, clear in understanding; ° Lucid speech.

Lucifer = (Luci = shining + fer = to carry) What carries shining light; ° Lucifer planets.

Lucent = shining; ° Lucent stars in the sky.

M

Magna = large, great, big

Magnify = (magna + fic = to make) to make big in size of something; ° Microscope magnifies the size of an object ° Do not magnify a problem.

Magnate = a person who holds big influence in a specified field of activity (beware of word 'Magnet'); ° He is a literary magnate.

Magnanimous = (magna + (a) nimus = soul) (a person) who has big soul i.e., who is large-hearted, compassionate towards others; ° A magnanimous person.

Magnificent = (magni = big + fic(ent) = to make) what is made big in attraction, splendour, extra-ordinary in beauty, superb; ° Magnificent buildings ° Magnificent paintings.

Magniloquent = (magni + loqua = speak) (a person, a speech) who or which is great in style of speaking; ° A magniloquent person / speech.

Magnitude = state of / extent of something which is big / large; ° Magnitude of loss / devastation.

Male = bad, evil, harmful (opposite : Bene-)

Words formed with it are :

Malefactor = one who does harm, evil act towards others; ° Malefactors must be punished.

Malevolent = (a person) who wishes (volen = to wish); ° He is malevolent towards successful persons.

Mal(e)feasance = evil action of a public official.

Mal(e)function = (of a machine) not working properly.

Mal(e)ice = evil feelings towards someone; ° He harbours malice against me.

Mal(e)ign = to defame someone by speaking evil things; ° He maligned his opponent.

Malignant = what is harmful.

Manu(s) = hand

Manual = what is done by hands; ° Manual operation of a machine. (which is not automatic)

Manufacture = (manucs = hand + fact = to make) to make / produce something by hands.

Manuscript = (script = written) written by hands; ° Manuscript of a book is handwritten copy of the author.

Manipulate = to manage something in desired direction by handling (working with hands) skillfully; ° Manipulate a person to do what is desired of him.

Manicure = (mani = hand + cura = care) taking care of hands' nails - shaping and polishing nails.

Mater = mother

Matricide = killing of mother.

Matriarch = (matri + arch (y) = rule) mother who rules over family.

Maternity = related to motherhood; ° Maternity ward in hospital.

Memora = memory

Memory = faculty of remembering.

Memoir = recording events of one's life; ° He wrote memoir.

Memorabilia = preserved matters which are associated with event / occasion worthy of remembering; ° His room is adorned with memorabilia of his childhood.

Memento = object which is associated with a particular event; ° This is the memento of his visit to England.

Memorial = a structure which is constructed in memory of a person or an event; ° A memorial of Kargil War ° A memorial of war heroes.

Mense = to measure

Immense = (in = not + mense) vast as being beyond measurement; ° Immense grief ° Immense vastness.

Mnesi, Menti = memory

A-mnesia = (a = not + Mnesi + ia = diseased condition) deseased condition of loss of memory; ° He is suffering from amnesia.

Amnesty = official grant of pardon of offense by forgetting acts of offence; ° Rebels were granted amnnesty by the govt.

Mirari = wonder

Miracle = an event which makes people wonder over; ° His survival in accident is a miracle.

Admire = (ad + mirari) to express wonder over praise worthy performance of someone; ° People admired his work.

Miso = hate

Miso-gamist = a person who hates to marry.

Misogynist = a person who hates women.

Mit = to send

Transmit = to send across to another place.

Remit = to send money by money order.

Mori = death

Memento mori = remember that everyone has to die one day.

Morgue = place where deadbody is kept before bodies are claimed by relatives.

Mortuary = place where deadbodies are kept before funeral.

Morph = shape

A-morphous = without shape.

Meta morphose - to change the shape of something.

N

Nat, naissi = birth

Re-naissance = re-birth, revival of dead art, culture, etc.

Nascent = beginning to take birth ; ° The disease is in nascent stage.

Pre-natal = period before child-birth; ° Pre-natal care of woman is must.

Native = related to one's birth; ° This town is my native place.

Innate = (in + nat) from the time of birth; ° Innate habits die hard.

Congenital (deformity) since one's birth.

Necro = dead,

Necrophagous = (a person / insect) which feeds on dead body / carrion; ° Necrophagous insect.

Necrophobia = abnormal fear of a dead body.

Nicto, Nycto, Nocto = night

Noctilucent = (nocti + luci) shinning brightly in night.

Nocturnal = active in night; ° malaria mosquito is nocturnal insect.

Nyctambulance = habit of walking in night during sleep.

Equinox = equal night (and day).

Nomen, Nomin = name

Nominate = select name of a person for something; ° He was nominated a member on the management board.

A-nonymous = (a = not) without mentioning name; ° Anomymous caller on phone.

Nomenclature = system of naming things.

Nominal = only for the sake of name - not of any value; ° He is nominal head of the committee.

Nomo = law, rule

A-nomy = state of no rule of law; ° State of anomy.

Isonomy = (iso = equal) state of equality of all in the eyes of law.

Noxi, Nocu(us) = harm

Noxious = harmful; ° Noxious fumes.

Innocuous = not harmful; ° Innocuous insect.

Nova = new

Novel = new; ° A novel idea.

Novice = (a person) who is new and hence in-experienced in a work; ° A novice worker.

Innovate = to introduce new system in existing one.

O

Ocul, Ophthalmos = eye

Ocular = related to eyes; ° ocular drops.

Occult = (ob = away + (o)cul) hidden from eyes; ° Occult objects.

Ophthalmologist = doctor of eye's disease.

Odont, denti = tooth

Odont(o) + algia = odontalgia = toothache.

Orthodontist = dentist who has specialisation in making in irregular line of teeth straight.

Denture = set of teeth.

Omni = all

Omnipotent = (omni + potent = powerful) all powerful; ° Omnipotent person.

Omniscient = (scient = knowing) knowing all things; ° God is omniscient.

Omniphagous = (phagy = eating) eating all things; ° Omniphagous insect.

Opto = vision

Optician = one who makes spectacles.

Optometrist = one who measures power of glasses for vision of eyes.

Ortho = straight

Orthodentist = see in odonto.

Orthodox = see in dox.

Orthopaedics = doctor who treats bone problems.

P

Paedi = child

Paediatrician = doctor of child diseases.

Pano = all

Pan(o) demic = (disease) affecting people (demo-) of all places.

Panacea = cure of all ills / diseases

Panopticon = a place of which all corners are visible from a central position.

Panorama = (pano + (ho)rama = view) all view; ° Panorama of recent history.

Pantheon = temple of all gods

Pandemonium = (pan = all + demon = evil spirit) a place of evil spirits where state of chaos exists; ° Pandemonium broke out in the meeting.

Patri = father

Patricide = killing of one's father.

Patriarchy = systen of family where father rules.

Patriot = a person who is devoted to his country i.e., fatherland.

Ex-patriate = a person who has gone out of own country (fatherland) to settle in other country.

Pedi = foot

Pedicare = care of feet, its nails etc.

Pedal = device in a machine to be moved by feet; ° Pedal of a bicycle.

Peddle = to sell goods by moving on feet from place to place.

Pedestal = the foot on which a structure is supported.

Pedestrian = person who moves on foot on roads.

Impediment = obstacle in moving forward / doing something by holding the feet to prevent movement; ° Stammering is an impediment in speaking.

Expedient = (action) which removes obstacles as if the feet are taken out of hold; ° Expedient action.

Expedite = to move one's feet speedily so as to hasten the progress; ° Expedite the work.

Pend(ere) = hang

Depend = to hang from someone / something for support; ° I depend on my friend for advice.

Compendium = hanging with, a list added to the end of a report or book.

Pendulum = hanging weight in a watch.

Pendant = small ornament which hangs from a necklace or chain.

Petri = stone

Petri-dish = dish made of stone.

Petrify = to make motionless like a stone due to sudden fear; ° Encounter with a snake on the road petrified him.

Pleni, Ple(re) = full, fill

Complete = full; ° Complete success.

Deplete = to take out from filled stock; ° Excess removal of water depleted the stock in tank.

Replete = filled abundantly; ° His speech was replete with juicy anecdotes.

Replenish = to fill up a vacant, exhausted stock again; ° Replenish used-up stock.

Plenty = state of being full.

Plic, plex = fold, bend

Complicate = to fold together to make ensnared; ° Complicate a simple matter.

complex = state of complicated; ° A complex problem.

Duplicate = in two folds.

Prehendere = to catch, hold, group

Prehensile = (limb) which is used to catch/hold something; ° Elephant's trunk is a prehensile limb ° Monkey tail is a prehensile limb.

Apprehend = ad + Prehend(ere), to catch hold of; ° Police apprehended the thief.

Apprehension = state of catching a feeling of something bad to happen in one's mind; ° He is disturbed due to apprehension about his safety.

Comprehend = to catch hold of something with one's mind i.e., to understand something; ° I could not comprehend what he said.

Reprehend = to hold someone responsible for wrongdoing.

Punct = dot, to dot with piercing.

Puncture = to pierce with a pointed stick so as to take out filled air; ° Puncture a cycle tube.

Punctate = to make dots of small holes on a reciept book so as to tear it off along the dotted line.

Punctilious = (a person) who takes care of doing work with accuracy to the dot of finer details; ° A punctilious worker.

Punctual = observing time of doing work to the exact point / dot; ° Be punctual in one's work.

Q

Quarant = set of forty.

Quarrantate = to arrange in a set of forty each.

Quarrantine = to isolate a patient afflicted with contagious disease from healthy perosns for a period of 40 days to avoid others getting infected.

Quater = set of four.

Quaternate = arrange in a set of 4 each.

Quater-century = 400 years.

R

Racin, Radic = root

De-racinate = to root out from native place; ° People were deracinated for building a dam.

Radical = of roots, fundamental; ° Radical change.

Eradicate = (ex = out + radic = root) to root out, remove from the roots; ° Eradicate superstitions from the people's mind ° Malaria eradication drive.

Recti = correct, right

Rectify = to correct a defect; ° To rectify defects in machine.

Rectitude = right morality; ° Rectitude of motives.

Erect = be in upright position; ° He is sitting erect on chair.

Regi = king, rule of a king.

Regicide = killing of the king.

Regime = rule of a king or govt. of a political party; ° Congress regime.

Regimen = rule to be followed for regaining health, or recovery from illness; ° Follow the regimen of taking medicines and of regular exercise.

Rupt = split, burst

Rupture = to burst; ° Blood vessel may rupture due to high blood pressure.

Erupt = to burst out; ° Violence erupted in the town.

S

Sacra, Sancti = holy

Sacred = (something) treated as holy; ° Temples are sacred place.

Sacrament = holy ceremony.

Sacrifice = (sacra = holy + fic = to do / make) to make holy offer; ° He sacrificed his life in defending the country.

Sacrilege = (sacri = holy + lege(re) = to steal) to rob of holiness of something; ° To defile a holy place is an act of sacrilege.

Consecrate = to make something holy; ° Consecrate a place as abode of Gods.

De-secrate = to destroy the holiness of a place; ° Desecrate a holy place by defiling it.

Sanctify = to make sacred, to consecrate.

Sanctity = state of sacredness; ° Sanctity of democratic institutions must be protected.

Sanctum sanctorum = place which is the holiest; ° The room of the temple in which deities are placed in the temple's sanctum sanctorum.

Sangui = blood

Sanguinary = characterised by blood shed, blood thirsty; ° Sanguinary fight ° Sanguinary vampire.

Sanguine = full of blood which is represented by cheerfulness; ° A man of sanguine disposition.

Sanguivorous = (insect) feeding on blood; ° Mosquito is sanguivorous insect.

Scribe(re) = write

Scribe = a person who writes in newspapers.

Scribble = to write on paper quickly and carelessly; ° He scribbled his message on a piece of paper.

Script = written matter / text; ° Film script.

Scripture = sacred written text.

Pre-scribe = to write the names of medicines and other instructions in advance to be followed by a patient.

Sect = cut

Sect = a religious faith which has been cut away from the main; ° Various sects have come in existence from Hindu religion.

Sectary = member / follower of a particular sect.

Bisect = cut a line in two parts.

Sine = without

Sinecure = without care to do anything; ° Sinecures in the offices enjoy perks without doing any work.

Sine die = (sine = without + die = date) without date; ° The parliament was adjourned sine die.

Sine qua non = without whom none other, i.e., indispensable; ° His presence in the meeting is sine qua non.

Sinistro, sinister = left hand (opp of Dextro)

Sinistral = using left hand; ° A sinistral person.

Sinu(us) = curved, winding in left & right directions alternately.

Sinuate = move in sinuous path; ° The snake sinuated on the ground.

Sinuous = having many alternating curves; ° River flows in sinuous path.

In-sinuate = to insert / move into someone / something by winding or turning left and right alternately; ° Roots of a tree insinuate through crevices in the rocky ground ° He insinuated derogatory remarks against me in his speech.

Somnus = sleep

Somnambulate = to walk in sleep.

Somniloquy = habit of speaking in sleep.

In-somnia = loss of sleep.

He is suffering from insomnia.

Soror = sister

Sororicide = killing of own sister.

Sorority = (on the pattern of fraternity) sisterhood.

Spect = to see, to observe.

Spectacle = an interesting event which is worth see-ing; ° Solar eclipse is a spectacle ° Independence Day parade is a spectacle.

Spectacles = pair of eye glasses which helps one see objects clearly.

Spectacular = impressive to see; ° Spectacular performance.

Spectator= a person who sees a programme/ performance / action.

Specter = imaginary view of dreadful thing or event to happen; ° Specter of imminent disaster haunts the minds of people.

In-spect = to look into something to examine it; ° Inspect the file.

Expect = (Ex = out + (s)pect = to see) to look out in future to happen; ° He expected to succeed ° He expected my support.

Intro-spect = to look within one's own self to examine one's own actions; ° He introspected over the reasons of his failures.

Retro-spect = (retro = backwards) to look back.

Speculate = to see the possibility of profits on staking money; ° He speculates in shares of companies in the share market.

Spira(re) = to breathe

Expire = to breathe out the life i.e. to die; ° The oldman expired today ° The validity of licence has expired (i.e., its life has ended).

Inspire = In + spire, to breathe life into someone to do / to have something i.e., to fill one with feelings; ° His exhortation inspired people to act against justice.

Perspire = (per = through) to breathe i.e. to send air (or vapours, water in the form of sweating) through pores of body surface; ° He was perspiring profusely due to hot weather.

Aspire = (ad = to + spire = breathe) to breathe life into one's desire to achieve something; ° He aspires to become an engineer.

Conspire = (con = with) to breathe with one's desire to do some evil against someone; ° He conspired against me to defame me.

Transpire = trans = (from one to another place) to breathe out / emit news about what happened at a place / another place; ° Decisions taken in a meeting soon transpired in the open.

Surge(re), surrect = rise up.

Surge = rise up; ° There is a sudden surge in crimes in the town.

Insurgent = a rebel who rises up against established govt.

Resurgent = what rises up again (re = again) after becoming non-existent; ° Resurgent custom.

Resurrect = to rise up again from the grave ° It is believed that Jesus Christ resurrected from the grave after he was crucified.

T

Tacitus = silent

Tacit = silent, done silently; ° He gave tacit support to indiscipline amongst partymen.

Taciturn = (a person) who is reluctant to speak, inclined to silence; ° A taciturn person.

Tact (us), Tangere = touch

Tact = a touch of skill to handle a difficult situation appropriately; ° He is a tactful person.

Tactics = a plan to handle a complex situation skillfully.

Tactile = having power to feel something by touching it; ° Our fingers are tactile limbs.

Tactual = able to be felt by touching it; ° Tactual test is sometimes more reliable than analytical test.

Tangible = able to be felt by touching because of being real- and not imaginary; ° Tangible threat ° Tangible grief.

Taxi, taxo = to arrange

Taxonomy = (taxo + nomo = rule) rule of arrangement of organisms in order of species.

Taxidermy = (taxi = arrange + derma = skin) art of arranging the skin of dead animal in life - like shape by stuffing sawdust inside.

Epitaxy = arrangement of something in layer upon (epi-) layer.

Terra = earth (see geo)

Thanato = death (also, see Mori)

Thanatophobia = abnormal fear of death.

Eu-thanasia = (eu- = well, good) act of giving a suffering person painless death.

Theo = god (see Dei, Deo)

Toxi, Toxsico = poison

Toxemia = (tox(o) + (ha)emia = blood) blood poisoning.

Toxic = containing poison; ° Toxic food.

Tract = stretch, draw

Tractable = which can stretched.

Extract = to draw out something; ° Extract juice from lemon.

Retract = to draw back; ° The bird retracted its wings ° He retracted his words given to me.

Contract = to draw together; ° He contracted his lips.

Protract = (pro = forward) to draw forward in duration, prolong for more time; ° His illness protracted for a month.

Distract = to draw attention away; ° Noise distracted his attention from his studies.

Attract = (ad = toward + tract) to draw attention towards something.

Trude(re) = to thrust, to push

Intrude = to thrust oneself into a place; ° He intruded into my office.

Protrude = to thrust forward; ° He protruded his head out of window.

U

Usuri = exorbitant rate of interest on lending.

Usury = practice of lending money on exorbitant rate of interests.

Usurer = one who practises usury.

Uxor = wife

Uxoricide = killing of one's wife.

Uxorious = liking one's wife excessively; ° A usorious husband.

V

Vert = to turn.

Vertigo = a condition of everything turning around before eyes of a person; ° He is affected with vertigo.

Avert = to turn aside; ° An accident was averted.

Vertiginous = turning, rotating; ° Vertiginous staircase.

Advert = (ad = towards + vert = turn) to turn one's attention towards someone or something; ° He adverted to me after finishing his work.

In-advertent = (a person) who is not attentive to something; ° He committed a mistake inadvertently.

Revert = to turn towards something again; ° Revert to the old habit.

Convert = to turn into something else; ° To convert water into steam.

Pervert = to turn away from right course; ° A morally pervert person.

Advertise = (ad = to + vert = turn) to give information through newspapers / T.V. about something to turn people's attention towards it.

Divert = to turn away from right path.

Versus = opposed to, different

Reverse = opposite in direction; ° Go in reverse direction.

Perverse = opposite to what is expected; ° Perverse mood.

Converse = opposite of something.

Versatile = of performances of a person or thing which are different in nature; ° A versatile musician / writer.

Diverse = different in direction / nature / quality; ° Diverse opinion.

Adverse = opposed to someone's good or something in effect; ° To make adverse remark against someone.

Averse = opposed to something in liking; ° He is averse to joing politics.

Verb(um) = word

Verbal = of words; ° Verbal experssion ° Verbal communications ° Verbal agreement.

Verbatim = (to tell / repeat) word by word; ° Repeat his statement ad verbatim.

Verbose = full of words; ° Verbose speech.

Veri = true

Verify = (veri = true + fic = to do) to ascertain the truth of something; ° Verify the report.

Verisimilitude = (veri + similarity) the state/ condition of being similar to truth.

Veritable = to be in true sense; ° Veritable victory.

Vince(re) = to win, to overcome

convince = to win over someone's, opinion by arguments; ° To convince someone about the need of helping poor people.

In-vincible = not be able to win. Who can't be won; ° Invincible enemy.

Vise, vid(ere) = look, see

Visage = face of a person which is seen.

Visible = able to be seen; ° He is not visible from here.

Vision = eye sight, faculty to see; ° His vision has become weak.

Visionary = a person who has the capability of looking into future - what will happen in future; ° He is a visionary.

Visit = go to see someone; ° He visited his family.

Visor = transparent glass in front of face of a helmet through which driver can see ahead.

Vista = a view visible through a narrow opening; ° A vista of surroundings.

Visual = of seeing; ° Visual effect.

Visualize = to see in imagination, form mental image; ° One can visualize the consequence of rash action.

Providence = (pro = forward, ahead + videre = look) foreseeing care of God; ° He survived accident by the grace of providence.

Provident = looking forward in future, having foresight of the future needs; ° Provident fund.

Improvise = (Im = not + pro + vise = look) to make something without prior looking for preparation; ° He improvised a poem on the spot.

Viva, Vita = life

Vivacious = lively, full of life; ° A vivacious person.

Viva voce = (voce = voice), living voice, oral interview of examinee.

Vivid = lively in appearance; ° Vivid paintings.

Vital = essential for life; ° Vital needs.

Vitamin = nutrients essential for life.

Vocab, Vocare = to call, speak

Advocate = to speak in favour of; ° Advocate freedom of women folk from social thrall.

Vocabulary = stock of words needed for speaking.

Vociferous = (voci = speak + fer(ous) = to carry) with loud speech; ° Vociferous portest of crowd.

Invoke = invocate, to call for help; ° To invoke God for mercy.

Provoke = to call forth a particular feeling in someone by inciting or instigating or stimulating; ° To provoke laughter / anger in someone.

Revoke = (re = back, again) to call back an order, law, etc. as by authority, govt; ° Govt. revoked ordinance.

Volen = wish, will

Volition = will; ° He helped us on his own volition.

Bene-volent = (bene = good), (a person) who wishes good for someone; ° A benevolent person. (opp. Malevolent)

X

Xeno = foreign

Xenocide = killing of foreigners.

Xenophile = a person who loves / likes foreigners.

Xero = dry

Xerography = dry writing i.e., copying a document in xerox machine.

Xeroderma = dryness of skin.

Xerophthalmia = dryness of eyes.

Xerophyte = (phyto = tree, plant) plant which thrives in dry place / desert.

Exercise on Word Root

Write down the root words involved in the formation of the following words :

1. Extract juice of lemon
2. Revive
3. Expedient
4. Chiropractic
5. Paediatrician
6. Leucemia
7. Hydrophobia
8. Specter
9. Expire
10. Taciturn
11. Tactful
12. Distract
13. Uxorious
14. Provoke
15. Intrude
16. Incinerate
17. Insinuate
18. Eradicate
19. Erect
20. Purctual
21. Replenish
22. Apprehend
23. Depend
24. Innovate
25. Native
26. Miracle
27. Manicure
28. Magnate
29. Perjury
30. Helicopter
31. Exhale
32. Transgress
33. Segregate
34. Ignore
35. Territory
36. Progeny
37. Fugitive
38. Fragment
39. Flexible
40. Confident
41. Fiction
42. Ambidextrous

43. Panacea
44. Cynophobia
45. Curator
46. Coronation
47. Chronic
48. Carnage
49. Belligerent
50. Archive

Answers to Word Roots

(1) Tractus (2) Vivere (3) Pedi (4) Chiro (5) Paedi (6) Leuco + Haemi (7) Hydro + Phobia (8) Spect (9) Spir (10) Tacit (11) Tactere (12) Tractus (13) Uxor (14) Vocare (15) Tradere (16) Ciner (17) Sinuere (18) Radi (19) Rectus (20) Punct (21) Plenum (22) Prehendere (23) Penderu (24) Nova (25) Nat (26) Mirari (27) mani(us) (28) Magna (29) Jurere (30) Helic + opter (31) Halitus (32) Gress (33) Gregare (34) Gnos (35) Terra (36) Gene (37) Fugere (38) Fractus (39) Flexere (40) Fide (41) Fic / Fact (42) Dextro (43) Pan (44) Cyno (45) Cura (46) Coran (47) Chrono (48) Carni (49) Belli (50) Arch

List of words

A

1. **A la carte:** food items ordered separately, not as a fixed-price meal
2. **Abate:** to lessen; to become less intense
3. **Abbreviate:** to shorten
4. **Abdicate:** to resign from a position of power (esp. of a ruler)
5. **Abduct:** to kidnap
6. **Aberrant:** deviating from normal/accepted
7. **Abet:** to assist in a wrongdoing
8. **Abeyance:** suspension
9. **Abide:** follow (a rule / law etc.)
10. **Abhor:** to hate or disgust
11. **Abject:** maximum; wretched
12. **Abjure:** to renounce; disavow
13. **Abode:** home
14. **Abolish:** to end (a law, practice etc.)
15. **Abominable:** hateful; contemptible
16. **Aboriginal:** native; an original inhabitant
17. **Abound:** plenty; in large numbers
18. **Abreast:** on the same level; side by side or in a row
19. **Abridge:** to shorten
20. **Abrogate:** cancel; revoke
21. **Abrupt:** sudden (ending)
22. **Abscond:** to get away (esp. to avoid a legal punishment)
23. **Absolve:** to clear of charges; to declare free from guilt
24. **Abstain:** to avoid or refrain
25. **Abysmal:** terrible; very bad
26. **Abyss:** a bottomless pit
27. **Accede:** to agree / to take over a position or throne
28. **Accessory:**something that accompanies something more useful or important
29. **Acclaim:** to praise openly
30. **Acclimate:** to get used to; to adapt

31. **Accolade:** honour and praise
32. **Accomplice:** one who helps in a wrong-doing
33. **Accord:** harmonious; agreement
34. **Accredit:** to give credit
35. **Accrue:** to accumulate; to build up
36. **Acme:** the highest point; the summit
37. **Acquaint:** to get familiar with
38. **Acquiesce:** to agree reluctantly
39. **Acquit:** to free from charges or blames
40. **Acrid:** sharp; caustic
41. **Acrimonious:** bitter and sharp
42. **Acrophobia:** fear of heights
43. **Actuate:** to start
44. **Acumen:** ability to take decision
45. **Acute:** sharp
46. **Adage:** proverb
47. **Adamant:** inflexible; rigid
48. **Adept:** skilled
49. **Adhere:** to stick to
50. **Adjourn:** to postpone; to take a break
51. **Adjudicate:** to act as a judge
52. **Adjunct:** something added
53. **Administer:** to manage or supervise
54. **Admonish:** to reprove; to warn, but not too harshly
55. **Ado:** fuss; trouble
56. **Adroit:** skillful
57. **Adulterate:** to add something inferior to something; to corrupt
58. **Advent:** arrival; emergence
59. **Adventitious:** coincidental; not planned
60. **Adverse:** unfavourable
61. **Aegis:** protection
62. **Aerial:** related to air
63. **Aesthetic:** related to beauty
64. **Affectation:** pretentious, fake behaviour
65. **Affidavit:** a written oath, esp. for legal purposes
66. **Affiliate:** to accept as a member
67. **Affinity:** liking; closeness
68. **Affliction:** illness
69. **Affluent:** rich
70. **Affray:** a noisy fight or clash
71. **Aficionado:** a person very enthusiastic about something
72. **Aftermath:** repercussions; consequences
73. **Aggrandize:** to enhance; to exaggerate
74. **Aggravate:** to make worse
75. **Aggregate:** total
76. **Aggrieved:** in pain because of an injustice
77. **Aghast:** in shock or horror
78. **Agile:** quick and fast
79. **Agitate:** to create trouble or movement
80. **Agnostic:** not having firm belief in God
81. **Agrarian:** related to agriculture
82. **Akin:** similar to
83. **Alacrity:** readiness
84. **Alias:** an assumed name
85. **Alibi:** a defense that one was not at the place of crime when the crime occurred
86. **Alienate:** to make somebody unfriendly; to isolate
87. **Allay:** to soothe (fear, worry etc.)
88. **Allege:** to say without proof (about a crime etc.)
89. **Allegiance:** loyalty

90. **Allocate:** to distribute
91. **Allude:** to hint at something
92. **Aloof:** detached; at a distance from others
93. **Altercation:** an argument
94. **Altitude:** height
95. **Alleviate:** to lessen
96. **Altruism:** a concern for other people
97. **Amalgamation:** a combination or mixture
98. **Amass:** to gather; to collect
99. **Ambient:** related to surroundings
100. **Ambiguous:** not clear in meaning
101. **Ambivalence:** having two contradictory feelings at the same time
102. **Ameliorate:** to improve
103. **Amenable:** one who can be controlled or managed
104. **Amend:** to make changes; to correct
105. **Amenities:** facilities; features and comforts
106. **Amiable:** friendly
107. **Amiss:** faulty; out of place
108. **Amity:** friendship
109. **Amorous:** related to sexual desires
110. **Amorphous:** not having a definite form or shape
111. **Amortize:** to pay in installments
112. **Amphibious:** able to work/live in both land and water
113. **Ample:** more than sufficient
114. **Amulet:** a lucky charm against evil
115. **Anachronistic:** not in order when considered according to time
116. **Analogous:** comparable to
117. **Anarchist:** one who doesn't believe in law and order; a terrorist
118. **Anathema:** something hateful; a curse
119. **Anecdote:** a short story
120. **Angst:** a state of anxiety
121. **Animated:** lively
122. **Animosity:** hatred; strong dislike
123. **Annals:** historical records
124. **Annex:** to add
125. **Annihilate:** to destroy
126. **Annul:** to declare void; to cancel
127. **Anomalous:** deviating from normal
128. **Anonymous:** whose name is not known
129. **Antagonistic:** enemy like; hostile
130. **Antediluvian:** of ancient times; old fashioned
131. **Anthology:** a collection of works (esp. literary ones)
132. **Antipathy:** a strong dislike
133. **Antiquated:** obsolete
134. **Antithesis:** direct opposite of something
135. **Apathy:** indifference
136. **Ape:** to copy; to imitate
137. **Apex:** the highest point; the top
138. **Aplomb:** self-confidence
139. **Appall:** to shock; to horrify
140. **Appease:** to satisfy someone by agreeing to their demands; to pacify
141. **Appellation:** title
142. **Apposite:** appropriate
143. **Apprehensive:** fearful that something bad is going to happen
144. **Apprise:** to inform

145. **Approbation:** assent; approval
146. **Apt:** appropriate
147. **Arbiter:** one who acts as judge in a dispute
148. **Arbitrary:** dictatorial; unrestricted (power etc.)
149. **Arcane:** secret; mysterious
150. **Archaic:** outmoded; old-fashioned
151. **Archetype:** the original one
152. **Ardent:** passionate about something
153. **Arduous:** difficult; hard
154. **Arid:** dry or dull
155. **Aristocrat:** a member of noble class
156. **Arraign:** to bring someone to trial
157. **Array:** arrangement
158. **Articulate:** to speak clearly and fluently
159. **Artless:** without deception
160. **Ascend:** to move up; to climb
161. **Ascertain:** to make sure
162. **Ascetic:** self-denying
163. **Ascribe:** to attribute or assign
164. **Asinine:** stupid
165. **Askew:** not level
166. **Aspersion:** defamation
167. **Aspiration:** a desire or wish
168. **Assail:** to attack
169. **Assassinate:** to murder
170. **Assent:** to agree
171. **Assert:** to say forcefully and confidently
172. **Assimilate:**to absorb; to take in
173. **Assuage:** to soothe; to lessen
174. **Astringent:**sharp; causing contraction of cells of a part of body
175. **Astute:** able to take advantage of a situation; wise
176. **Asylum:** refuge
177. **Atone:** to make amends for a sin
178. **Attire:** dress
179. **Attrition:** weakening due to gradual reduction in strength or number of people (as in a company)
180. **Audacious:** bold
181. **Augment:** to increase
182. **Augur:** to foretell
183. **Aura:** atmosphere of a place (an intangible quality)
184. **Auspicious:** favourable
185. **Austere:** strict in manner
186. **Autonomous:** sovereign; free to control itself
187. **Auxiliary:** supplementary
188. **Avail:** to use
189. **Avarice:** greed
190. **Averse:** disliking something strongly
191. **Avian:** related to birds
192. **Avouch/avow:** to assert
193. **Avuncular:** behavinglike an uncle
194. **Awry:** not normal; wrong
195. **Axiom:** an accepted truth needing no evidence

B

1. **Bacchanalian:** involving a drunken festivity
2. **Badger:** to pester; to repeatedly ask for something
3. **Baffling:** puzzling
4. **Baleful:** threatening; hostile
5. **Balky:** awkward
6. **Ballistic:** related to projectiles (such as fired shells, missiles etc.)
7. **Banal:** commonplace; lacking originality

8. **Bane:** annoyance
9. **Barbarian:** not civilized; savage; brutal
10. **Bard:** a poet
11. **Bask:** enjoy in the sun
12. **Bastion:** a part of a fortification
13. **Battery:** a large number of things
14. **Beatify:** to make holy
15. **Beckon:** to make a gesture to call someone
16. **Bedlam:** unrest; confusion
17. **Befit:** to be suitable for
18. **Beget:** to cause; to generate
19. **Begrudge:** to hold grudge against someone; to envy
20. **Beguile:** to deceive
21. **Behemoth:** something huge and monstrous
22. **Behest:** command
23. **Beholden:** indebted
24. **Beleaguer:** to surround; to siege
25. **Belie:** to not tell the truth; to contradict (appearance, expressions etc.)
26. **Belittle:** to trivialize; to not regard as important
27. **Bellicose/belligerent:** hostile; warlike
28. **Bemoan:** to express regret
29. **Bemuse:** to confuse
30. **Benchmark:** a standard to measure others of similar kind
31. **Benefactor:** one who provides help (esp. financial) to someone
32. **Benevolent:** kind
33. **Benign:** harmless
34. **Bequeath:** to leave something to someone by a will
35. **Berate:** to scold
36. **Bereft:** deprived of something; lacking something
37. **Berserk:** crazy; out of control
38. **Beseech:** to plead
39. **Besiege:** to surround
40. **Besmirch:** to damage reputation
41. **Bestial:** like a beast
42. **Bestow:** to present to (an honour, award etc.)
43. **Bibliography:** list of books given as reference
44. **Bicameral:** having two branches (such as a parliament)
45. **Bicker:** to argue about petty things
46. **Biennial:** occurring every two years
47. **Bigot:** a prejudiced person not tolerating other viewpoints
48. **Bilateral:** involving two sides or parties
49. **Bilious:** having a bad temper
50. **Bilk:** to cheat
51. **Blandish:** to flatter someone
52. **Blasphemy:** doing or saying something insulting about God
53. **Bleak:** not encouraging; cheerless
54. **Blight:** something that spoils something
55. **Bliss:** great pleasure and delight
56. **Blithe:** cheerful
57. **Bode:** to predict
58. **Bogus:** fake
59. **Boisterous:** unruly; noisy
60. **Bombastic:** pompous
61. **Bona fide:** genuine; not fake
62. **Boorish:** rude; ill-mannered
63. **Booty:** loot
64. **Bovine:** like a cow
65. **Brandish:** flaunt something to threaten someone (a gun, sword etc.)

66. **Bravado:** a show of bravery intended to impress someone
67. **Brevity:** quality of being brief
68. **Brink:** edge
69. **Broach:** to bring up a topic (in a discussion, debate etc.)
70. **Brook:** tolerate
71. **Brusque:** sharp; abrupt
72. **Bulwark:** a fortification
73. **Buoyant:** that floats
74. **Burgeon:** to grow rapidly
75. **Burly:** muscular
76. **Buttress:** to support

C

1. **Cabal:** a secret group
2. **Cache:** where something is kept hidden
3. **Cacophonous:** inharmonious (noise)
4. **Cadre:** a small, trained group
5. **Cajole:** to persuade by using flattery
6. **Calamity:** a disaster, esp. natural
7. **Caliber:** merit; ability
8. **Callous:** insensitive
9. **Calumny:** defamation; slander
10. **Canard:** falsehood
11. **Candor:** openness; honesty and frankness
12. **Canine:** related to dogs
13. **Canvass:** to campaign, esp. to ask opinion of people
14. **Capacious:** spacious (having ample space)
15. **Capitulate:** to surrender
16. **Capricious:** fanciful; changeable
17. **Caption:** heading or tilte
18. **Captivating:** charming; attractive
19. **Carcinogenic:** that causes cancer
20. **Cardinal:** basic; main
21. **Carnage:** slaughter; killing
22. **Cartographer:** one who makes maps
23. **Cascade:** a waterfall that falls in stages or levels
24. **Castigate:** scold or criticise
25. **Caucus:** conference; groupe of people
26. **Caustic:** biting (remark, comment etc.)
27. **Caveat:** warning
28. **Cavil:** to quibble or complain about small things
29. **Cede:** to relinquish; to surrender (position etc.)
30. **Celestial:** related to heaven
31. **Celibate:** one who abstains from sex
32. **Censure:** to criticize strongly
33. **Cerebral:** related to brain and intellect
34. **Cessation:** ending
35. **Chagrin:** humiliation; embarrassment
36. **Charlatan:** an impostor; a quake
37. **Chary:** wary; cautious
38. **Chasten:** to punish or scold
39. **Catastrophe:** a disaster
40. **Charisma:** charm; quality of being captivating
41. **Chauvinist:** one who believes in own country, race, gender etc. to be superior to others
42. **Chicanery:** trickery
43. **Chide:** to scold
44. **Chimerical:** imaginary, not real
45. **Choleric:** bad-tempered
46. **Chortle:** laugh; chuckle

47. **Chronic:** that comes and goes and lasts for a long time
48. **Chronicle:** historical record
49. **Chronological:** sequential when arranged by time periods
50. **Circumlocution:** saying indirectly, using a lot of words
51. **Circumspect:** cautious
52. **Circumvent:** to avoid
53. **Citadel:** a stronghold; a fortress
54. **Citation:** a quote; official commendation; a summon
55. **Clamour / Clamor:** loud noise
56. **Clandestine:** covert; secret
57. **Cleave:** to slice; to split
58. **Clemency:** leniency; mercy
59. **Categorical:** clear-cut; certain
60. **Clone:** to make a copy; duplicate
61. **Coagulate:** to thicken; to form a clot
62. **Coalesce:** to combine
63. **Coercion:** force
64. **Cogent:** convincing
65. **Cohabit:** to live together
66. **Cohere:** to hold or stick together
67. **Cohort:** a unit; a group
68. **Collaborate:** to work together
69. Collateral: something one pledges as security while getting a loan
70. **Colloquial:** words in everyday conversations
71. **Collude:** to conspire against someone
72. **Comatose:** tired and sleepy; lethargic
73. **Commemorate:** to pay tribute to
74. **Commensurate:** corresponding; equal
75. **Commodious:** having ample room; spacious
76. **Commodity:** a product (raw material or agricultural)that can be sold
77. **Commute:** to travel; to lessen the punishment of a criminal
78. **Compassion:** kindheartedness; empathy
79. **Compatible:** harmonious; well-suited
80. **Compelling:** convincing
81. **Compendium:** a detailed summary
82. **Compensate:** to make up (for losses etc.)
83. **Compliant:** yielding; obedient
84. **Composed:** calm
85. **Comprise:** contain; consist of
86. **Compulsive:** habitual (that is hard to resist)
87. **Concede:** admit; yield
88. **Conciliatory:** pacifying
89. **Concise:** brief and to the point
90. **Conclusive:** decisive; final
91. **Concoct:** fabricate; devise
92. **Concord:** harmony; accordance
93. **Concurrent:** occurring simultaneously
94. **Condone:** to pardon; to forgive
95. **Conducive:** helpful; encouraging
96. **Confer:** to grant or bestow (a degree, title etc.)
97. **Confidant:** a trustable person
98. **Confide:** to tell a secret to someone trustable
99. **Confiscate:** to seize; to take possession of another's property (legally)
100. **Conflagration:** fire
101. **Confluence:** junction; meeting

102. **Confound:** to confuse
103. **Confront:** to challenge
104. **Congenial:** amiable; friendly
105. **Congregation:** a group of worshippers
106. **Congruence:** harmony; similarity
107. **Conjecture:** guess
108. **Connive:** to plot or conspire
109. **Connoisseur:** expert
110. **Conscientious:** painstaking
111. Consecutive: successive; next in a sequence
112. **Consensus:** unanimity; agreement
113. **Console:** to comfort
114. **Consolidate:** to combine; to unite
115. **Conspicuous:** noticeable
116. **Constraint:** something that restricts or limits
117. **Construe:** to interpret
118. **Consummate:** perfect; flawless
119. **Contemplate:** to consider; to plan
120. **Contempt:** disdain; scorn; disrespect
121. **Contend:** to oppose; to struggle
122. **Contented:** content; satisfied
123. **Contentious:** quarrelsome; argumentative
124. **Contiguous:** adjoining; next
125. **Contingency:** something that could possibly happen
126. **Contort:** to twist or distort
127. **Contravene:** breach; against a law, principle etc.
128. **Controversial:** that causes dispute or debate
129. **Conundrum:** puzzle
130. **Convene:** to assemble for a meeting
131. **Conventional:** in accordance with accepted norms; customary
132. **Converge:** to meet, esp. at a point
133. **Converse:** opposite
134. **Conversant:** acquainted with
135. **Convict:** one who has broken a law; a criminal
136. **Convocation:** an assembly; a gathering
137. **Convoluted:** complex; twisted
138. **Copious:** plentiful
139. **Cordial:** warm; pleasant
140. **Corollary:** outcome; result
141. **Corporeal:** related to body and physical existence
142. **Corps:** a group
143. **Corroborate:** to support and validate
144. **Cosmopolitan:** multicultural
145. **Countermand:** to revoke; to cancel
146. **Countervail:** to counter the effect of something
147. **Covenant:** a pact
148. **Covert:** secret; hidden
149. **Covet:** to long for
150. **Cower:** to shrink in fear
151. **Crave:** to desire strongly
152. **Credence:** credibility; belief
153. **Credulous:** one who easily believes; naïve
154. **Crestfallen:** disappointed; depressed
155. **Cringe:** to cower
156. **Crux:** core; gist
157. **Cryptic:** puzzling; mysterious

158. **Culinary:** related to cooking
159. **Culminate:** to terminate; to end
160. **Culpable:** guilty; one who can be blamed
161. **Cumbersome:** weighty; burdensome
162. **Curb:** to limit
163. **Cursory:** superficial; quick
164. **Curt:** rude and abrupt
165. **Curtail:** to limit
166. **Cynical:** one who doubts people; a pessimistic, distrustful person

D

1. **Dally (Dilly-dally):** to procrastinate (to postpone doing something)
2. **Dauntless:** fearless
3. **De facto:** in fact
4. **Dearth:** scarcity; severe shortage
5. **Debacle:** a total disaster; devastation
6. **Debase:** to degrade; to humiliate
7. **Debauchery:** indulgence; wickedness
8. **Debilitating:** that weakens
9. **Debonair:** refined; elegant
10. **Debrief:** to question
11. **Debunk:** to expose
12. **Decimate:** to destroy
13. **Decipher:** to decode
14. **Decommission:** to retire (esp. a ship)
15. **Decorum:** propriety
16. **Decoy:** a trap
17. **Decree:** a verdict
18. **Deduce:** to infer; to conclude
19. **Deem:** to consider; to judge
20. **Deface:** to spoil; to disfigure
21. **Deficit:** shortage
22. **Deference:** respect; polite submission
23. **Definitive:** decisive
24. **Deflect:** to turn to one side
25. **Deft:** skillful
26. **Defunct:** non-operational
27. **Deign:** to condescend; to do something below one's dignity
28. **Deleterious:** poisonous; harmful
29. **Deliberate:** thoughtful
30. **Delineate:** to outline; to define
31. **Delude:** to mislead
32. **Delve:** to explore
33. **Demean:** to debase
34. **Demeanor:** conduct; behaviour
35. **Demise:** death
36. **Demography:** statistics of human population
37. **Demoralise:** to dishearten
38. **Demur:** to object to something
39. **Denigrate:** to degrade; to defame
40. **Denizen:** inhabitant
41. **Depart:** to leave
42. **Depict:** to illustrate or show
43. **Deplete:** to diminish; to use up
44. **Deplore:** to condemn
45. **Deploy:** to position; to arrange
46. **Deprive:** to dispossess of something
47. **Deride:** to ridicule
48. **Derogatory:** insulting
49. **Desiccated:** dried
50. **Desist:** to stop
51. **Desolate:** deserted; abandoned
52. Despise: to hate
53. Destitute: very poor

54. **Detached:** not attached (esp. emotionally)
55. **Detention:** confinement; custody
56. **Deteriorate:** to worsen
57. **Deterrent:** something that prevents or discourages something else
58. **Detract:** to diminish or reduce
59. **Detrimental:** damaging
60. **Devise:** to invent; concoct
61. **Devoid:** lacking something
62. **Devout:** sincere; pious
63. **Dexterity:** skill
64. **Diabolical:** evil
65. **Diffident:** shy
66. **Digress:** to deviate
67. **Dilatory:** sluggish; slow
68. **Dilemma:** an awkward situation in which one needs to choose between two undesirable alternatives
69. **Dint:** a dent; an impression
70. **Discord:** a state of disharmony
71. **Discourse:** a speech or lecture on a subject
72. **Discreet:** not easily noticeable; subtle
73. **Discrepancy:** inconsistency
74. **Discrete:** distinct; separate
75. **Discriminate:** to differentiate; to see differences
76. **Disdain:** to show contempt; to not show respect
77. **Dishevel:** to disturb; to upset
78. **Disinclination:** unwillingness
79. **Disingenuous:** insincere
80. **Disinterested:** impartial
81. **Dismal:** miserable
82. **Dismay:** shock or panic; distress
83. **Disparage:** to ridicule
84. **Disparity:** inequality
85. **Diligent:** hard-working
86. **Dire:** dreadful; terrible
87. **Disarray:** confusion and disorder
88. **Dispassionate:** non-emotional; detached
89. **Disperse:** to scatter
90. **Dispossess:** to disinherit; to deprive of a possession
91. **Dissent:** disagreement
92. **Dissipate:** to scatter or disperse
93. **Dissolute:** immoral
94. **Dissonance:** discord
95. **Distend:** to swell or bloat
96. **Distortion:** falsehood; misrepresentation
97. **Distract:** to divert
98. **Discerning:** judicious; astute
99. **Disconcerted:** disturbed; unsettled; not composed
100. **Diurnal:** related to daytime
101. **Diverge:** to deviate
102. **Diverse:** having variety
103. **Divest:** to deprive (of powers, rights etc.)
104. **Divulge:** to reveal
105. **Docile:** submissive; tame
106. **Document:** to record
107. **Doggedly:** persistently; without giving up
108. **Dogmatic:** not flexible (in opinions etc.)
109. **Doleful:** sad
110. **Domicile:** home
111. **Dormant:** hidden; latent
112. **Draconian:** severe; harsh
113. **Dubious:** of doubtful nature
114. **Ductile:** supple; flexible
115. **Dupe:** one who is easily deceived
116. **Dynamic:** vibrant; lively

E

1. **Ebullient:** cheerful; lively
2. **Eccentric:** strange; odd
3. **Echelon:** rank
4. **Edification:** teaching; instructing
5. **Effervescence:** fizz (bubbles in a drink); enthusiasm
6. **Efficacy:** effectiveness
7. **Effigy:** dummy (of a person, esp. for the purpose of protests)
8. **Effrontery:** rude boldness
9. **Effulgence:** brilliance; radiance
10. **Egocentric:** self-centered
11. **Egregious:** very bad or wrong
12. **Egress:** the way out
13. **Elate:** to uplift (spirit etc.)
14. **Elegant:** graceful
15. **Elicit:** to provoke
16. **Elite:** the upper class of a society
17. **Eloquent:** well-spoken; well-expressed
18. **Elusive:** hard to catch; evasive
19. **Emanate:** to originate or spread from
20. **Emancipate:** to set free
21. Emasculate: to weaken (spirit etc.)
22. **Embargo:** ban
23. **Embellish:** to exaggerate
24. **Embezzle:** to misuse; to steal
25. **Embroil:** to entangle; to involve
26. **Emend:** to correct
27. **Emergence:** advent; arrival
28. **Empathise:** to sympathise; to feel what other person is feeling
29. **Emulate:** to imitate
30. **Enchanting:** charming; bewitching
31. **Encompass:** toinclude
32. **Encumber:** to restrict; to hinder
33. **Encroach:** to trespass
34. **Endemic:** found or widespread in an area
35. **Endorse:** to approve; to support openly
36. **Endow:** to give (donation, property, gift etc.)
37. **Endure:** to tolerate; to withstand
38. **Enervate:** to drain; to weaken
39. **Engaging:** captivating
40. **Engender:** to cause to happen; to generate
41. **Engrave:** to carve
42. **Engulf:** to overcome; to immerse or consume
43. **Enigma:** mystery
44. **Enjoin:** to order
45. **Enlighten:** to educate on a subject; to inform
46. **Enlist:** to enroll or recruit (esp. in army)
47. **Enmity:** hostility
48. E**normity:** wickedness; heinousness
49. **Ensue:** follow
50. **Entail:** to involve
51. **Enthrall:** to mesmerize; to captivate
52. **Entice:** to tempt; to lure
53. **Entreat:** to plead
54. **Enviable:** that causes envy
55. **Envisage:** to envision or visualise
56. **Eon:** an extremely long time period

57. **Ephemeral:** short-lived; momentary
58. **Epidemic:** wide-spread
59. Epoch: era
60. **Equanimity:** composure
61. **Equitable:** justifiable; reasonable
62. **Equivocate:** to use unclear expressions in language to mislead people
63. **Eradicate:** to destroy completely
64. **Erode:** to wear away (soil etc.)
65. **Err:** to make a mistake
66. **Erratic:** irregular and inconsistent
67. **Erroneous:** wrong
68. **Erudite:** scholarly
69. **Escalate:** to increase; to intensify
70. **Escapade:** an adventurous experience
71. **Eschew:** to avoid
72. **Esoteric:** known to only a few people
73. **Espouse:** to back; to advocate for
74. **Esteem:** honour and respect
75. **Estrange:** to alienate
76. **Eternal:** that lasts forever
77. **Ethereal:** very delicate; not of this world
78. **Ethos:** spirit of a culture
79. **Euphemism:** a mild expression for something less gentle
80. **Euphoria:** great pleasure and joy
81. **Euthanasia:** mercy-killing
82. **Eventual:** final; ultimate
83. **Evoke:** to induce; to arouse
84. **Exacerbate:** to worsen; to aggravate
85. **Exalt:** to promote and praise
86. **Exasperate:** to annoy
87. **Excerpt:** an extract from a work
88. **Exclaim:** to cry out because of surprise or a feeling
89. **Excommunicate:** to remove; to bar
90. **Excruciating:** unbearable (pain etc.)
91. **Execute:** to carry out; to put into effect
92. **Exemplary:** perfect; a model for something
93. **Exempt:** to excuse
94. **Exhaustive:** comprehensive
95. **Exigency:** emergency
96. **Exile:** banishment from own country
97. **Exodus:** emigration; departure
98. **Exonerate:** to forgive; to acquit
99. **Expedient:** beneficial
100. **Expel:** to eject; to oust
101. **Expiate:** to atone; to make amends for
102. **Explicate:** to explain
103. **Explicit:** clear and detailed
104. **Expropriate:** to seize or take
105. **Exquisite:** wonderful
106. **Extempore:** done without rehearsal
107. **Extant:** in existence
108. **Extol:** to praise
109. **Extort:** to extract using force
110. **Extradite:** to send back; to hand over
111. **Extraneous:** not important or vital
112. **Extrapolate:** to estimate using past data or trends
113. **Extricate:** to disentangle; to free
114. **Exuberant:** energetic; cheerful
115. **Exude:** radiate; emit

F

1. **Fabricated:** made-up; not genuine
2. **Facet:** aspect; side
3. **Facile:** superficial; easy to get
4. **Facilitate:** to make easy and smooth
5. **Faction:** a small group or sect within a group
6. **Factitious:** artificial
7. **Fallacious:** untrue; wrong
8. **Fallible:** not perfect; that can make mistakes
9. **Fanfare:** display
10. **Farcical:** nonsensical
11. **Fastidious:** particular; fussy
12. **Fathom:** to measure
13. **Fatuous:** foolish
14. **Faux pas:** a blunder
15. **Fealty:** loyalty
16. **Feasible:** possible; realistic
17. **Feckless:** useless; incompetent
18. **Fecund:** productive
19. **Feign:** to fake; to pretend
20. **Felony:** a crime
21. **Fend (off):** to defend against
22. **Ferment:** uproar
23. **Fertile:** productive
24. **Fervor:** enthusiasm; passion
25. **Fetid:** foul-smelling
26. **Fiasco:** a disaster
27. **Fiat:** authorisation
28. **Fickle:** changeable (one's opinions, mind etc.)
29. **Fictitious:** not real; fictional
30. **Fidelity:** loyalty
31. **Figment:** fantasy
32. **Filch:** steal in small portions
33. **Filibuster:** a delaying speech meant to obstruct
34. **Finale:** the climax
35. **Finesse:** tact; skill
36. **Fiscal:** related to finances
37. **Fitful:** irregular
38. **Flagrant:** blatant; brazen
39. **Fledgling:** young and inexperienced
40. **Fluctuate:** to change or waver; to vacillate
41. **Flux:** flow
42. **Foible:** a minor weakness
43. **Foil:** to thwart; to halt; to frustrate
44. **Foment:** to provoke
45. **Foolhardy:** risky; reckless
46. **Forage:** to search for food
47. **Foray:** to raid or attack
48. **Forbear:** to refrain from
49. **Foresight:** farsightedness; ability to predict future
50. **Forestall:** to predict and prevent
51. **Forgo:** to waive; to relinquish
52. **Forsaken:** abandoned
53. **Forthright:** straightforward; frank
54. **Fortitude:** determination and courage
55. **Foster:** to encourage; to nurture
56. **Fracas:** brawl; noisy argument
57. **Fragile:** delicate
58. **Fragmented:** broken into pieces; disjointed
59. **Frantic:** panic-stricken; distressed
60. **Fraternity:** companionship and solidarity within a group; brotherhood

61. **Fraught:** troubled; tense
62. **Frivolous:** playful; light-hearted
63. **Frolic:** play
64. **Frugal:** economical; penny-wise
65. **Fruitful:** rewarding; productive
66. **Fruitless:** futile; non-productive
67. **Fulminate:** to protest; to denounce
68. **Furor:** uproar
69. **Furtive:** secretive

G

1. **Gaffe:** a blunder
2. **Gainsay:** to deny; to refute
3. **Gait:** walk; pace
4. **Gambit:** ploy; strategy
5. **Gamut:** range; extent
6. **Garner:** to store
7. **Garrulous:** talkative
8. **Genealogy:** lineage; ancestry
9. **Genesis:** origin
10. **Genre:** category (of books etc.)
11. **Geriatrics:** related to old age and old people
12. **Germane:** relevant; appropriate
13. **Ghastly:** horrifying; shocking
14. **Gimmick:** stunt; trick
15. **Glib:** superficial; insincere
16. **Glutton:** a foodie; one who eats a lot
17. **Gnarled:** twisted
18. **Goad:** to prod and encourage to do something
19. **Gory:** gruesome; violent and bloody
20. **Gracious:** kind
21. **Grandiose:** impressive
22. **Grapple:** wrestle; handle
23. **Grasp:** grip; hold
24. **Gratis:** complimentary; free
25. **Gratitude:** gratefulness
26. **Gratuitous:** free; not deserved
27. **Gravity:** seriousness
28. **Gregarious:** sociable
29. **Grimace:** expression of pain, disgust etc.
30. **Grueling:** difficult; exhausting
31. **Grumble:** to complain
32. **Gruesome:** horrible
33. **Guile:** treachery
34. **Gullible:** one who is easily deceived
35. **Gusto:** delight

H

1. **Habituate:** to accustom
2. **Hackneyed:** commonplace; worn-out
3. **Haggard:** exhausted
4. **Haggle:** to bargain
5. **Halcyon:** calm; quiet
6. **Hallucination:** delusion
7. **Hale:** fit; healthy
8. **Hamper:** hinder; impede
9. **Haphazard:** disorganised
10. **Hapless:** unlucky
11. **Harangue:** tirade; lecture, esp. scolding
12. **Harbinger:** forerunner; omen
13. **Harbor:** dock; port
14. **Hardy:** tough; resilient
15. **Haughty:** arrogant; conceited
16. **Haven:** refuge; shelter
17. **Havoc:** destruction; chaos
18. **Hazardous:** harmful

19. **Hazy:** foggy; not clear
20. **Hearsay:** gossip
21. **Hedonism:** having seeking pleasures as the only goal in life
22. **Heedless:** reckless
23. **Hegemony:** domination
24. **Heinous:** dreadful; monstrous
25. **Herald:** announcer
26. **Herculean:** enormous
27. **Hermit:** recluse
28. **Heterodox:** not conforming to traditions; unorthodox
29. **Hidalgo:** a gentleman
30. **Hideous:** repulsive; ugly
31. **Histrionic:** dramatic; exaggerated (display of emotions etc.)
32. **Hoax:** a prank or trick; a deception
33. **Holocaust:** mass destruction; slaughter
34. **Homage:** tribute
35. **Homily:** lecture
36. **Homogenous:** uniform; same throughout
37. **Hoodwink:** to trick
38. **Horde:** crowd; mass
39. **Hubris:** too much pride; conceit
40. **Huddle:** to gather; to crowd together
41. **Humane:** kind; considerate
42. **Humility:** modesty; humbleness
43. **Humus:** a soft component of soil formed by decaying leaves and organic material
44. **Husbandry:** management and conservation
45. **Hybrid:** of mixed breed
46. **Hydrophobia:** fear of water
47. **Hygiene:** cleanliness
48. **Hyperbole:** exaggeration
49. **Hypocrisy:** state of being two-faced and insincere

I

1. **Iconoclast:** one who opposes and criticizes traditional beliefs
2. **Idiosyncrasy:** behaviour peculiar to a person
3. **Idyllic:** relaxing; peaceful and calm
4. **Ignoble:** shameful; despicable
5. **Illicit:** illegal
6. **Illusory:** deceptive
7. **Illustrious:** well-known
8. **Imbibe:** to absorb; to drink
9. **Imbroglio:** a mess; a complication
10. **Imbue:** infuse; fill
11. **Immaculate:** perfectly clean
12. **Immaterial:** unimportant
13. **Immense:** enormous; huge
14. **Imminent:** forthcoming
15. **Immobile:** not moving
16. **Immunity:** freedom from punishment
17. **Immutable:** that can't be challenged
18. **Impair:** to damage
19. **Impartial:** unbiased
20. **Impasse:** a deadlock; a bottleneck
21. **Impassioned:** fervent; passionate
22. **Impassive:** that shows no emotions
23. **Impeccable:** flawless; perfect
24. **Impecunious:** poor
25. **Impede:** block; obstruct
26. **Impediment:** an obstacle

27. **Imperative:** crucial; very important
28. **Imperceptible:** unnoticeable
29. **Imperil:** to put at risk; to endanger
30. **Impertinent:** impolite
31. **Imperturbable:** composed; not easily disturbed
32. **Impervious:** that can't be penetrated
33. **Impetus:** that motivates
34. **Implausible:** improbable
35. **Implicate:** to show that someone was involved in something
36. **Implicit:** understood
37. **Implore:** to plead
38. **Implode:** to burst inwards; to cave in
39. **Impolitic:** misguided; not wise
40. **Importune:** to pester
41. **Imposing:** impressive; striking
42. **Impregnable:** that can't be defeated or destroyed; secure
43. **Impromptu:** not planned beforehand; without rehearsal
44. **Improvise:** to perform without preparation; impromptu
45. **Impudence:** effrontery; rude boldness
46. **Impugn:** to criticise severely
47. **Impulsive:** thoughtless
48. **Impute:** to attribute; to assign
49. **Inadvertent:** not intentional
50. **Inane:** absurd
51. **Inanimate:** lifeless
52. **Inaugurate:** to open or initiate formally
53. **Inborn:** innate
54. **Incapacitate:** to disable or weaken
55. **Incarcerate:** to imprison
56. **Incarnation:** personification (esp. of God, in human form); Avatar
57. **Incendiary:** provocative; inflammable
58. **Incense:** to make angry; in infuriate
59. **Incessant:** non-stop
60. **Inchoate:** that is beginning to happen; budding
61. **Incinerate:** to burn
62. **Incipient:** beginning to happen
63. **Incisive:** insightful; keen
64. **Incite:** to provoke (unrest etc.)
65. **Inclement:** severe; harsh
66. **Inclusive:** encompassing everything / everyone
67. **Incognito:** in disguise
68. **Incomparable:** unmatched
69. **Incompatible:** not harmonious
70. **Incongruous:** not suitable; inconsistent
71. **Inconspicuous:** not very noticeable; modest
72. **Incontrovertible:** indisputable
73. **Incorporate:** to integrate or join
74. **Incorrigible:** that can't be reformed; habitual
75. **Incredulous:** disbelieving; skeptical
76. **Inculcate:** to train; to instill
77. **Incumbent:** mandatory
78. **Indecent:** impolite
79. **Indecorous:** rude; inappropriate
80. **Indemnity:** guarantee; protection (against possible losses etc.)
81. **Indigenous:** native
82. **Indigent:** poor
83. **Indiscriminate:** not selective
84. **Indispensable:** crucial
85. **Indistinct:** not clear; dim

86. **Indomitable:** that can't be defeated
87. **Induce:** to persuade
88. **Indulge:** to allow oneself to enjoy something desired
89. **Industrious:** hardworking
90. **Ineffable:** indescribable; unspeakable
91. **Inept:** not skilled
92. **Inert:** inactive
93. **Inestimable:** that can't be measured
94. **Inevitable:** that can't be avoided
95. **Infallible:** that can't fail
96. **Infamous:** disreputable; ill-famed
97. **Infer:** to conclude
98. **Infidelity:** disloyalty
99. **Infinitesimal:** tiny; insignificant
100. **Inflammatory:** provocative
101. **Influx:** inflow
102. **Insidious:** treacherous; deceptive
103. **Infringe:** to trespass; to break a law
104. **Infuriate:** to enrage
105. **Ingenious:** clever
106. **Ingrained:** deep-rooted
107. **Inherent:** intrinsic; inborn
108. **Inimical:** hostile
109. **Injunction:** order
110. **Inkling:** a clue
111. **Innate:** inborn
112. **Innocuous:** mild; harmless
113. **Inordinate:** too much
114. **Inquisitive:** meddlesome; curious
115. **Insatiable:** that can't be satisfied (thirst, hunger etc.)
116. **Inscrutable:** that can't be understood; mysterious
117. **Insinuate:** to suggest
118. **Insolent:** rude
119. **Insipid:** dull
120. **Insolvent:** one who cannot pay debt; bankrupt
121. **Instigate:** to initiate; to provoke
122. **Insubordinate:** unruly; not obedient
123. **Insular:** a narrow-minded person
124. **Insuperable:** unbeatable
125. **Intangible:** that can't be felt by touching
126. **Integrity:** honesty
127. **Intensive:** rigorous; exhaustive
128. **Inter:** to bury
129. **Intercept:** to stop in the mid-way (such as a missile etc.)
130. **Interlude:** interval; break
131. **Interpolate:** to insert
132. **Interrogate:** to question
133. **Intervene:** to interfere
134. **Intimate:** close; to tell indirectly
135. **Intractable:** stubborn; not easily managed
136. **Intransigent:** stubborn
137. **Intricate:** complicated
138. **Intriguing:** interesting
139. **Introspection:** self-examination (to think inwardly about oneself)
140. **Inundate:** to flood
141. **Invective:** criticism; insult
142. **Inveigle:** to entice
143. **Inveterate:** hardened (such as an inveterate liar)
144. **Invidious:** unpleasant; undesirable
145. **Irascible:** one who is easily irritated
146. **Irate:** angry and annoyed
147. **Irksome:** annoying; tiresome
148. **Ironic:** sarcastic
149. **Irresolute:** not sure; hesitating
150. **Itinerary:** route of journey

J

1. **Jargon:** terminology used by specific groups (esp. related to professions), not by layman
2. **Jaundiced:** cynical
3. **Jaunt:** a trip
4. **Jejune:** boring
5. **Jeopardy:** risk; danger
6. **Jilt:** to reject
7. **Jinx:** to curse (as if by using a magical spell)
8. **Jest:** joke
9. **Jingoism:** excessive patriotism
10. **Jocular:** humorous
11. **Jocund:** cheerful
12. **Jolt:** a shock; a blow
13. **Jovial:** cheerful
14. **Jubilant:** proud; rejoicing
15. **Judicious:** wise; cautious
16. **Juggernaut:** an unstoppable great force
17. **Jumble:** to mix up things untidily
18. **Juncture:** a point (in time, space etc., esp. where things join)
19. **Junk:** rubbish
20. **Jurisprudence:** law
21. **Juvenile:** one who is not an adult yet
22. **Juxtapose:** to compare by putting things next to each other

K

1. **Keen:** acute
2. **Keepsake:** a souvenir; a memento
3. **Kindle:** to ignite; to inspire
4. **Kindred:** alike
5. **Kinetic:** related to motion and speed
6. **Kinship:** relationship (by blood)
7. **Kleptomania:** a strong urge to steal something, even without need for that object
8. **Knack:** talent; ability
9. **Knave:** a dishonest person
10. **Knead:** tomassage or press
11. **Knell:** sound of a bell, esp. in a funeral
12. **Kowtow:** to behave subserviently
13. **Kudos:** praise; glory

L

1. **Labyrinth:** a maze
2. **Lachrymose:** crying
3. **Lackey:** a pawn; an assistant or servant
4. **Laconic:** using few words; brief and to the point
5. **Lacuna:** void; space
6. **Laggard:** an idler
7. **Lament:** to cry; to mourn
8. **Lampoon:** to use satire to criticise someone
9. **Languid:** lethargic; not having energy or enthusiasm
10. **Larceny:** theft
11. **Lascivious:** lustful; wanton; not moral
12. **Lassitude:** weariness; lethargy
13. **Latent:** hidden but present
14. **Lavish:** extravagant
15. **Lax:** careless; not tight

16. **Layman:** one who doesn't have professional knowledge of a subject
17. **Leery:** doubting; cautious
18. **Legerdemain:** trickery; sleight of hand
19. **Legible:** readable; understandable
20. **Legitimate:** authentic; genuine
21. **Leniency:** mercy; clemency
22. **Leonine:** of or like a lion
23. **Lethargy:** laziness; sluggishness
24. **Levity:** lightness
25. **Lewd:** lustful; vulgar
26. **Liable:** responsible and accountable for something
27. **Libel:** defamation
28. **Licentious:** immoral; lustful
29. **Lilliputian:** tiny
30. **Limpid:** easy to see through; transparent
31. **Lineage:** ancestry
32. **Linguistics:** study of language
33. **Lissome:** flexible; agile
34. **Litigation:** lawsuit
35. **Livid:** enraged; very angry
36. **Loathe:** to hate very much
37. **Lofty:** haughty; high
38. **Loquacious:** talkative
39. **Lucid:** well-spoken; simple and smooth
40. **Lucrative:** rewarding
41. **Ludicrous:** absurd
42. **Luminous:** shining; radiant
43. **Lure:** to entice
44. **Luxuriant:** lush; rich

M

1. **Machiavellian:** devious; tricky
2. **Machination:** planning; plotting
3. **Maelstrom:** turbulence
4. **Magnanimity:** generosity
5. **Magnate:** a tycoon; an important person in business
6. **Magnitude:** size or extent
7. **Maim:** to injure; to damage permanently
8. **Maladroit:** clumsy; not skillful
9. **Malady:** a disease
10. **Malaise:** a feeling of sickness or uneasiness
11. **Malediction:** a curse
12. **Malevolence:** ill will towards someone
13. **Malicious:** nasty; hateful
14. **Malign:** evil; hostile
15. **Malinger:** shirk or dodge (duty, work etc.)
16. **Malleable:** that can be shaped
17. **Mammoth:** enormous
18. **Mania:** craze for something
19. **Manifest:** apparent; obvious
20. **Manifesto:** a statement declaring policy, vision etc.
21. **Manifold:** multiple
22. **Manslaughter:** killing a person without intending to do so
23. **Manuscript:** an unpublished work
24. **Mar:** deface
25. **Marginal:** peripheral; negligible
26. **Martial:** related to war
27. **Martinet:** a disciplinarian; a perfectionist
28. **Masochist:** one who takes pleasure in pain
29. **Maternal:** related to mother
30. **Matrix:** a medium or atmosphere in which something develops

31. **Mediocre:** not special or outstanding; ordinary
32. **Medley:** a mixture; a jumble
33. **Melancholy:** sad; gloomy
34. **Mellifluous:** smoothly flowing; sweet
35. **Memento:** souvenir
36. **Memorabilia:** a collection that reminds of someone or something
37. **Memorandum:** a message; memo
38. **Menagerie:** a zoo
39. **Mendacity:** falsehood
40. **Mendicant:** a vagrant; a beggar
41. **Menial:** a work that requires no skill
42. **Mentor:** a guru; a teacher or guide
43. **Mercantile:** related to business and commerce
44. **Mercurial:** changeable; volatile
45. **etamorphosis:** transformation; change in form
46. **Mete out:** to give out; to distribute
47. **Methodical:** systematic
48. **Meticulous:** painstaking; careful
49. **Maul:** to attack and injure
50. **Maverick:** one who goes against what is traditional and accepted; a rebel
51. **Mayhem:** disorder; confusion
52. **Meager:** paltry; too little
53. **Mettle:** determination; courage
54. **Miasma:** unpleasant odour or feeling
55. **Milk:** to cash in on; to exploit
56. **Minion:** an assistant; a follower
57. **Minuscule:** very small
58. **Minutiae:** trivialities; details
59. **Mirage:** an illusion
60. **Misanthrope:** one who hates mankind
61. **Miscarriage:** a spontaneous abortion; a failure
62. **Mishap:** a misfortune; an accident
63. **Miscellaneous:** assorted; various
64. **Miscreant:** wrongdoer
65. **Misogynist:** one who hates womankind
66. **Mitigate:** to diminish; to lessen
67. **Modicum:** a little quantity
68. **Mogul / Moghul:** a very powerful person in a field
69. **Mollify:** to soothe
70. **Momentous:** very important
71. **Monologue:** a long speech, esp. by one person
72. **Monotonous:** repetitive and boring
73. **Morale:** confidence
74. **Moratorium:** a temporary suspension or postponement
75. **Moribund:** close to death
76. **Morose:** depressed; gloomy
77. **Mortify:** to embarrass very much; to humiliate
78. **Motive:** purpose
79. **Motto:** slogan
80. **Muffle:** to make quite; to stifle
81. **Multifarious:** varied; having many aspects
82. **Mundane:** routine; ordinary
83. **Munificent:** generous; magnanimous

84. **Muster:** to gather (esp. courage)
85. **Mutilate:** to maim; to injure
86. **Mutiny:** revolt
87. **Myopic:** narrow-minded
88. **Myriad:** countless; numerous
89. **Mystique:** charisma and mystery related to someone or something
90. **Mythical:** not real; imaginary

N

1. **Nadir:** the lowest of something
2. **Naïve:** one who lacks experience; immature
3. **Narcissism:** egotism; self-admiration
4. **Nascent:** budding; in early stages
5. **Natal:** related to birth
6. **Nebulous:** not clear; vague
7. **Nefarious:** evil
8. **Negate:** to cancel the effect of
9. **Negligible:** insignificant
10. **Nemesis:** archrival; the worst enemy
11. **Neophyte:** a novice; a beginner
12. **Nepotism:** favouratism towards relatives and friends
13. **Nexus:** a tie-up; a connection among people or parties
14. **Niche:** a slot or position
15. **Niggard:** a miser
16. **Nocturnal:** related to night
17. **Nomenclature:** process of naming (esp. scientific)
18. **Nonchalant:** calm and casual
19. **Nonpareil:** unequalled; matchless
20. **Noted:** famous
21. **Nuance:** subtlety; minor distinction
22. **Nuisance:** that irritates or annoys
23. **Nullify:** to cancel out
24. **Nurture:** to cherish

O

1. **Obdurate:** stubborn
2. **Obese:** overweight; fat
3. **Obeisance:** respect; submission to
4. **Obfuscate:** to complicate; to confuse
5. **Objectivity:** detachment; impartiality
6. **Obligatory:** compulsory
7. **Oblique:** sloping; not direct
8. **Obliterate:** to destroy
9. **Observant:** alert
10. **Obsolete:** out of date
11. **Obstinate:** stubborn
12. **Obtrusive:** obvious; very noticeable
13. **Obviate:** to make unnecessary
14. **Occult:** supernatural
15. **Ocular:** visual
16. **Odyssey:** a journey
17. **Officiate:** to manage; to be in-charge or supervisor
18. **Offset:** to counterbalance
19. **Olfactory:** related to the sense of smell
20. **Oligarchy:** government by a group

21. **Ominous:** menacing; warning
22. **Omnibus:** compilation (esp. of literary works)
23. **Omnipotent:** having all the power
24. **Omniscient:** one who knows everything
25. **Onerous:** heavy; burdensome
26. **Onslaught:** attack
27. **Onus:** obligation; burden
28. **Operative:** operational
29. **Opine:** to state an opinion
30. **Opportune:** favourable
31. **Oppress:** to repress; to keep down unjustly
32. **Opprobrium:** severe criticism
33. **Optimum:** best of all possible
34. **Opulence:** richness; wealth
35. **Oracle:** one who gives prophetic opinions and also predicts
36. **Orator:** speaker
37. **Orchestrated:** arranged; planned and organised
38. **Ordinance:** law
39. **Ordnance:** stock of weapons
40. **Orifice:** a slit; an opening
41. **Ornate:** decorated; ornamented
42. **Orthodox:** traditional; socially accepted
43. **Oscillate:** to hesitate; to waver
44. **Ostensible:** apparent
45. **Oust:** to expel; to eject
46. **Outset:** beginning
47. **Ovation:** applause showing approval
48. **Overwhelm:** to overcome; to submerge

P

1. **Pacify:** to soothe; to appease
2. **Pagan:** one who has different (and often unaccepted) religious views
3. **Painstaking:** meticulous; thorough
4. **Palatial:** grand; lavish
5. **Paleolithic:** related to stone age
6. **Pallid:** pale
7. **Palpable:** that can be touched and felt
8. **Palsy:** paralysis
9. **Paltry:** insignificant; too small
10. **Panacea:** a cure-all
11. **Panache:** confidence; zest
12. **Pandemic:** epidemic
13. **Panegyric:** a speech praising someone
14. **Pang:** a shooting pain; a twinge
15. **Panorama:** a wide view; a scenery
16. **Paradigm:** pattern; model
17. **Paragon:** model
18. **Paramount:** top; chief
19. **Paranoid:** unreasonably suspicious of others
20. **Paranormal:** supernatural
21. **Paraphrase:** to rephrase; to restate
22. **Pariah:** an outcast
23. **Parity:** equality
24. **Parley:** meeting
25. **Parochial:** narrow-minded
26. **Paroxysm:** a fit or convulsion
27. **Parry:** to deflect (a blow etc.)
28. **Parsimonious:** miserly; frugal
29. **Parting:** farewell
30. **Partisan:** prejudiced; supporter of something

31. **Pasteurise:** to make milk safe for consumption by using a process
32. **Pastoral:** rural; bucolic
33. **Patent:** obvious
34. **Paternal:** fatherly
35. **Pathogen:** a microbe that causes disease
36. **Pathos:** sadness
37. **Patrimony:** property inherited from father
38. **Patronise:** to look down on
39. **Pauper:** a poor person
40. **Paucity:** dearth; scarcity
41. **Peccadillo:** a minor offence
42. **Peculiar:** strange
43. **Pedagogue:** a teacher
44. **Pedantic:** finicky; very concerned with small details
45. **Pedestrian:** ordinary; common
46. **Pedigree:** lineage; descent (esp. of a dog)
47. **Peevish:** irritable
48. **Pejorative:** derogatory; harsh
49. **Penance:** atonement; punishing oneself for a wrongdoing
50. **Penchant:** fondness; liking
51. **Pensive:** meditative; thoughtful
52. **Penultimate:** second to last
53. **Penury:** poverty
54. **Per se:** by itself
55. **Percolate:** to seep into
56. **Perennial:** that lasts for years or a very long time
57. **Perfidious:** treacherous
58. **Perforated:** having many small holes
59. **Perfunctory:** routine; without thinking
60. **Peril:** danger
61. **Peripheral:** not central or main
62. **Perishable:** that decays or rots quickly
63. **Perjury:** falsehood
64. **Permeable:** that can be penetrated or passed through
65. **Perpetrator:** wrongdoer
66. **Perpetual:** everlasting
67. **Perplexed:** confused
68. **Perquisite:** privilege; advantage
69. **Persecution:** harassment
70. **Perseverance:** determination
71. **Perspicacious:** discerning; wise
72. **Pertain:** to belong to
73. **Pertinent:** relevant
74. **Pervading:** spreading through
75. **Petite:** small
76. **Petrify:** to stun with fear
77. **Petulance:** irritability
78. **Phenomenal:** extraordinary
79. **Philanthropist:** humanitarian
80. **Philately:** stamp-collecting
81. **Phlegmatic:** not easily disturbed; composed
82. **Phobia:** extreme fear
83. **Physique:** build
84. **Pilfer:** to steal
85. **Pinnacle:** the top; summit
86. **Pious:** devout (religiously)
87. **Piquant:** sharp; tart
88. **Piscine:** related to a fish
89. **Pittance:** very small amount
90. **Pivotal:** crucial
91. **Placate:** to soothe
92. **Placebo:** dummy (esp. medicine)
93. **Placid:** calm
94. **Plagiarise:** to steal others' work and call it one's own

95. **Platitude:** a much used expression or remark
96. **Plausible:** believable
97. **Plethora:** excess
98. **Pliable:** flexible
99. **Plight:** difficulty
100. **Ploy:** a trick
101. **Plummet:** to drop
102. **Plutocracy:** government by rich
103. **Poacher:** a thief (esp. of animal skins and organs)
104. **Poignant:** touching; sad
105. **Polemic:** impassioned; controversial
106. **Polygamist:** married to many people at the same time
107. **Ponder:** to think over
108. **Porcine:** of a pig
109. **Portend:** to foretell; to indicate
110. **Posterior:** rear
111. **Posthumous:** after death
112. **Potent:** forceful; effective
113. **Potpourri:** a mix (esp. of dried flowers to freshen a room's air)
114. **Pragmatic:** practical
115. **Prattle:** to chatter
116. **Preamble:** introduction
117. **Precarious:** risky
118. **Precedent:** an event that happened earlier and is now an example
119. **Precipitate:** to cause
120. **Precise:** accurate
121. **Preclude:** to prevent something
122. **Precursor:** that happens before something else; forerunner
123. **Predecessor:** one that came before; forerunner
124. **Preemptive:** pro-active; preventive (such as a preemptive strike on an enemy position)
125. **Preen:** to groom; to tidy
126. **Prelude:** introduction; prologue
127. **Premeditated:** thought-out; planned beforehand
128. **Premonition:** intuition; forewarning
129. **Preposterous:** absurd; outrageous
130. **Prerogative:** privilege
131. **Presage:** an omen or sign
132. **Prestige:** esteem; reputation
133. **Presumptuous:** presuming
134. **Pretentious:** showy; pompous
135. **Preternatural:** paranormal
136. **Pretext:** an excuse
137. **Prevailing:** predominant
138. **Prevalent:** widespread
139. **Prevaricate:** to speak evasively and dishonestly
140. **Primal:** primitive; original
141. **Pristine:** unspoiled
142. **Probity:** righteousness
143. **Proclaim:** to announce
144. **Procrastinate:** to postpone unnecessarily
145. **Procure:** to obtain
146. **Prodigal:** extravagant
147. **Profane:** blasphemous
148. **Profess:** to claim; to assert
149. **Profligate:** extravagant
150. **Profound:** deep
151. **Prognosis:** forecast
152. **Proliferate:** to multiply
153. **Prolific:** fertile
154. **Prolong:** to extend (esp. in time)
155. **Prompt:** quick
156. **Prone:** inclined to

157. **Propensity:** proclivity; inclination
158. **Propinquity:** closeness with
159. **Propitiate:** to pacify
160. **Proponent:** advocate of something (such as a cause)
161. **Proportionate:** equivalent; balanced
162. **Propriety:** decency; appropriateness of behaviour
163. **Proscribe:** to forbid
164. **Protagonist:** hero (of a story, film etc.)
165. **Provident:** farsighted; prudent
166. **Provincial:** local; rural
167. **Provisional:** temporary
168. **Provocative:** that provokes
169. **Prowess:** proficiency; expertise
170. **Proximity:** closeness
171. **Pseudo:** false
172. **Pugnacious:** argumentative; aggressive
173. **Puissant:** powerful
174. **Pulverise:** to grind
175. **Punitive:** punishing; disciplinary
176. **Purgative:** cleansing
177. **Purge:** to get rid of
178. **Purport:** to falsely appear to be
179. **Purview:** range; scope
180. **Putrefy:** to decay
181. **Pyrotechnics:** a display of fireworks

Q

1. **Quack:** a fraud
2. **Quadruped:** animals having four feet
3. **Quagmire:** quicksand; a dilemma
4. **Quail:** to cower
5. **Qualified:** not complete
6. **Quandary:** dilemma
7. **Quantum:** substantial; significant (as in 'a quantum leap')
8. **Quarantine:** to isolate
9. **Quash:** to suppress
10. **Quaver:** to tremble
11. **Queer:** strange
12. **Quench:** to satiate (thirst)
13. **Querulous:** complaining
14. **Quibble:** to argue about unimportant things
15. **Quiescent:** calm; still
16. **Quiver:** to shiver; to shudder
17. **Quixotic:** idealistic and impractical
18. **Quizzical:** puzzled

R

1. **Rabid:** fanatical; a dog having rabies
2. **Raconteur:** storyteller
3. **Rally:** to reunite; to rebound
4. **Ramifications:** consequences
5. **Rampage:** a number of individuals running wildly at a place
6. **Rampant:** widespread
7. **Rancid:** rotten; stinking
8. **Rant:** to speak angrily about
9. **Rapacious:** avid; greedy
10. **Rapport:** a good relationship and mutual understanding
11. **Rash:** careless; reckless
12. **Ratify:** to approve
13. **Rationale:** logic
14. **Ravage:** to destroy and plunder
15. **Ravenous:** very hungry

16. **Raze:** to demolish; to destroy completely
17. **Realm:** kingdom
18. **Rebuttal :** refutation; contradiction
19. **Recalcitrant:** stubborn
20. **Recapitulate:** to summarise
21. **Receding:** retreating; moving back
22. **Receptive:** open to new ideas
23. **Reciprocal:** done in return
24. **Recluse:** a loner; a solitary person who doesn't socialize
25. **Recoil:** to shrink (as in fear)
26. **Reconcile:** to restore friendly relations
27. **Reconnaissance:** surveying
28. **Rectify:** to correct
29. **Recur:** to happen again
30. **Redeem:** to cash in
31. **Redoubtable:** formidable
32. **Redundant:** jobless
33. **Referendum:** public opinion collected through voting
34. **Refined:** polished; well-mannered
35. **Refractory:** stubborn
36. **Refulgent:** shining; brilliant
37. **Refurbish:** to redocorate
38. **Regale:** to entertain
39. **Reign:** control; power; sovereignty
40. **Reimburse:** to compensate for
41. **Reiterate:** to restate
42. **Rejuvenate:** to revive
43. **Relapse:** to suffer a setback
44. **Relentless:** unyielding; not giving up
45. **Relinquish:** to abandon (a position, throne etc.)
46. **Relish:** to enjoy
47. **Remedial:** corrective
48. **Reminiscent:** that reminds of something
49. **Rendezvous:** a meeting; an appointment
50. **Renege:** to break a promise
51. **Renounce:** to abandon
52. **Renovate:** to restore
53. **Renowned:** famous
54. **Repel:** to keep away
55. **Repercussions:** consequences
56. **Replenish:** to fill again
57. **Replica:** an exact copy
58. **Reprehensible:** that cannot be forgiven; disgraceful
59. **Reprimand:** to scold
60. **Reproachful:** disapproving; critical
61. **Repudiate:** to disclaim; to renounce
62. **Repulse:** to repel; to drive back
63. **Requisite:** necessary
64. **Residue:** something that remains after the main part is gone
65. **Resolute:** determined
66. Resilient: that withstands adverse conditions and recovers quickly
67. **Resonant:** echoing; resounding
68. **Resourceful:** creative
69. **Resurgent:** reviving
70. **Resurrect:** to revive
71. **Retaliate:** to strike back
72. **Reticent:** quiet; reserved
73. **Retort:** to respond angrily
74. **Retrieve:** to recover
75. **Retrogressive:** declining
76. **Retrospective:** looking back at past
77. **Revelry:** celebrations; partying

78. **Revenue:** income
79. **Reverent:** respectful
80. **Revert:** to return to
81. **Revoke:** to cancel; to retract
82. **Ricochet:** to rebound
83. **Rigorous:** laborious; hard
84. **Rift:** split
85. **Robust:** vigorous; strong
86. **Rudimentary:** elementary
87. **Rue:** regret
88. **Ruminate:** to think over
89. **Rummage:** to search through wildly
90. **Rustic:** bucolic; rural

S

1. **Sabotage:** damage
2. **Sack:** a bag; to get rid of
3. **Sacrosanct:** holy
4. **Saga:** legend
5. **Sagacious:** learned; wise
6. **Salacious:** indecent
7. **Salient:** main; prominent
8. **Saline:** somethinghaving salt in it
9. **Salubrious / Salutary:** healthy
10. **Salvation:** rescue from; redemption
11. **Sanctify:** to make holy; to bless
12. **Sanctimonious:** one who shows oneself morally superior than the others
13. **Sanguine:** cheerful; full of positivity
14. **Sardonic:** ironic; mocking
15. **Sartorial:** related to clothing
16. **Satirical:** humorously mocking
17. **Saturated:** soaked thoroughly; flooded with
18. **Savor:** to enjoy the taste of
19. **Scanty:** meager; too little
20. **Scathing:** fierce; sharp
21. **Scintilla:** a very little amount; traces
22. **Scornful:** disrespectful
23. **Scourge:** curse; bane
24. **Scrupulous:** honourable
25. **Scrutinise:** to examine thoroughly
26. **Scurrilous:** defamatory
27. **Seclusion:** isolation
28. **Sedate:** calm
29. **Sedentary:** inactive (for instance, a sedentary lifestyle)
30. **Sedition:** treason
31. **Seething:** simmering; boiling
32. **Segregate:** to separate
33. **Sensuous:** related to senses
34. **Sentient:** responsive
35. **Sequel:** something (esp. a book or film) in continuation to something else
36. **Serendipity:** tendency to make lucky discoveries
37. **Serene:** calm
38. **Serpentine:** winding (like snakes)
39. **Servile:** submissive; obedient
40. **Sever:** to break; to cut
41. **Shambles:** chaos; disorder
42. **Shibboleth:** a tradition or custom that distinguishes a group from others
43. **Shortcomings:** faults
44. **Shrewd:** clever; astute
45. **Shun:** to avoid
46. **Sibling:** a brother or sister
47. **Sidle:** to move sideways, like some snakes

48. **Siege:** blockade
49. **Simper:** to smile foolishly
50. **Simulate:** to imitate or recreate the appearance of something real
51. **Sinister:** threatening; evil
52. **Siphon:** to drain
53. **Skeptical:** doubting others
54. **Skirmish:** a small battle
55. **Skullduggery:** mischief; cheating
56. **Slander:** defamation
57. **Slay:** to kill brutally
58. **Slew:** to turn uncontrollably; a large number of
59. **Sloth:** laziness
60. **Snare:** a trap
61. **Snob:** one who only respects socially superior people
62. **Snub:** to insult by ignoring
63. **Sobriety:** seriousness
64. **Solace:** comfort
65. **Solemn:** sincere
66. **Solicitous:** interested; concerned
67. **Solvent:** one who can pay back a debt
68. **Somber:** sober; serious; sad
69. **Sonorous:** deep and rich (voice)
70. **Soporific:** causing sleep
71. **Sorority:** an alliance or group of female students in an institute
72. **Souvenir:** remembrance; a memento
73. **Spate:** outbreak
74. **Specious:** false
75. **Spectacular:** remarkable
76. **Speculate:** to do guesswork, esp. in financial matters (such as in stock market)
77. **Spendthrift:** extravagant
78. **Spirited:** energetic; brave
79. **Splenetic:** bad-tempered
80. **Splurge:** spending lavishly
81. **Sporadic:** irregular; intermittent
82. **Spree:** a period of an unrestrained activity
83. **Spurious:** fake
84. **Squalid:** filthy
85. **Squander:** to waste
86. **Stagnant:** motionless; stationary
87. **Stalemate:** a deadlock
88. **Stalwart:** determined
89. **Startle:** to surprise
90. **Static:** motionless
91. **Statutory:** according to law
92. **Steadfast:** resolute; staunch; loyal
93. **Stealthily:** silently; without being noticed; cautiously
94. **Steeped:** immersed
95. **Stern:** strict
96. **Stifle:** to suffocate
97. **Stigma:** disgrace
98. **Stimulate:** to excite; to rouse
99. **Stint:** period
100. **Stipulate:** to add as a condition
101. **Stoic:** one who tolerates pain without complaining
102. **Striated:** striped; ridged
103. **Strive:** to try hard to do something
104. **Studious:** intentional; bookish
105. **Stunted:** hindered; retarded (growth, development etc.)
106. **Stupendous:** remarkable; astonishing
107. **Stupor:** lethargy
108. **Suave:** smooth; polite
109. **Subjugate:** to conquer and overpower

110. **Subordinate:** junior; at a lower rank
111. **Subside:** to decrease; to diminish
112. **Substantiate:** to validate; to corroborate; to support with evidence
113. **Succinct:** brief; concise
114. **Succumb:** to yield to; to give in
115. **Suffice:** to be sufficient
116. **Sullen:** gloomy and irritated
117. **Sumptuous:** extravagant
118. **Sundry:** assorted; miscellaneous
119. **Supercilious:** arrogant
120. **Superfluous:** extra; excess
121. **Superimpose:** to put over another
122. **Supplant/supersede:** to replace
123. **Surmise:** to guess intelligently
124. **Surpass:** to exceed; to outdo
125. **Surrogate:** substitute
126. **Surveillance:** scrutiny
127. **Susceptible:** vulnerable to
128. **Sycophant:** a flatterer
129. **Symbiotic:** mutually beneficial to two partners
130. **Synchronise:** to cause to occur harmoniously, at the same rate
131. **Syndicate:** an association
132. **Syndrome:** set of symptoms (such as that of a disease)

T

1. **Taboo:** something forbidden
2. **Tacit:** understood without being spoken
3. **Tactics:** maneuvers
4. **Tally:** to coincide or agree
5. **Tamper:** to meddle with
6. **Tangible:** that can be touched and felt
7. **Tantalising:** teasing (for something unobtainable)
8. **Tantamount:** equivalent to
9. **Tantrum:** sulking; fit of temper
10. **Tarnish:** to taint; to smear (reputation etc.)
11. **Tautological:** unnecessary repetition of words
12. **Tawdry:** showy; cheap
13. **Tedious:** monotonous; dull
14. **Temerity:** boldness; audacity
15. **Temperate:** moderate
16. **Tempting:** enticing; appealing
17. **Tenacious:** resolute
18. **Tensile:** stretchable
19. **Tentative:** not confirmed
20. **Tenure:** term (such as a person's tenure as principal in a school)
21. **Terminal:** deadly; lethal
22. **Terrestrial:** related to land; earthly
23. **Terse:** brief
24. **Theatrics:** dramatic behaviour or display of emotions
25. **Thorny:** prickly; spiky
26. **Thrive:** to prosper
27. **Throttle:** to choke or strangle
28. **Timorous:** nervous
29. **Tirade:** a long speech made when angry
30. **Titanic:** mighty; gigantic
31. **Titillating:** exciting; tickling
32. **Toil:** hard work; labour
33. **Topsy-turvy:** upside down; in a state of disorder
34. **Torment:** to make suffer (physically or mentally)
35. **Torpid:** sluggish; lazy
36. **Tout:** to sell;to flaunt

37. **Tractable:** that can be managed
38. **Transfigure:** to transform into something beautiful; to change
39. **Transfix:** to pierce; to mesmerise
40. **Transient:** fleeting; passing; momentary
41. **Transgress:** to break a rule or law
42. **Transient:** fleeting; passing; momentary
43. **Transitory:** fleeting; passing; momentary
44. **Translucent:** radiant; glowing
45. **Transpire:** to become obvious
46. **Trauma:** a state of shock, esp. after a horrible experience
47. **Travail:** exertion; hard effort
48. **Treason:** treachery against own country or the ruler
49. **Triad:** a triplet; a trio
50. **Tribunal:** a committee to solve an issue; a court
51. **Trite:** commonplace
52. **Truculent:** defiant; not friendly
53. **Tumble:** to lose balance; to fall
54. **Tumult:** uproar
55. **Turbid:** unclear
56. **Turbulent:** turmoil; unrest
57. **Turgid:** swollen; pompous
58. **Turmoil:** uproar; disorder
59. **Tussle:** struggle; brawl
60. **Tutelage:** guidance
61. **Tyranny:** cruel dictatorship

U

1. **Ubiquitous:** present everywhere
2. **Ulterior:** hidden
3. **Ultimatum:** a demand, usually time-bound
4. **Umbrage:** offense
5. **Unanimous:** undivided (such as a decision)
6. **Unassuming:** humble; modest
7. **Unbecoming:** not appropriate
8. **Unbridled:** not restrained
9. **Uncanny:** strange
10. **Unctuous:** flattering; sycophantic
11. **Undermine:** to weaken
12. **Underscore:** to underline (for emphasis)
13. **Undue: unjustifiable;** excessive
14. **Unequivocal:** clear (such as a statement, a stand etc.)
15. **Unfathomable:** that can't be measured or explored fully
16. **Unfazed:** not shocked or disturbed by something
17. **Unflagging:** untiring; not weakening
18. **Unleash:** to release
19. **Uniform:** constant
20. **Unilateral:** one-sided
21. **Unison:** harmony
22. **Unkempt:** messy; untidy
23. **Unobtrusive:** modest; not very noticeable
24. **Unprecedented:** never before
25. **Unravel:** to solve
26. **Unseemly:** improper; rude
27. **Unsung:** unrecognised
28. **Unswerving:** unwavering; not hesitating
29. **Unwarranted:** not deserved
30. **Unwind:** to relax
31. **Upheaval:** disorder
32. **Uproar:** noise and disorder
33. **Urbane:** refined; polished

34. **Usher:** to show (a place, seat etc.)
35. **Usurp:** to grab; to take
36. **Utilitarian:** practical and realistic, not ideal or attractive
37. **Utopian:** idealistic; perfectionistic
38. **Uxorious:** a man who has excessive fondness for his wife

V

1. **Vacillate:** to hesitate in making a decision or choice
2. **Vagaries:** moods; whims
3. **Vague:** not clear
4. **Vain (in vain):** futile
5. **Vainglory:** too much pride
6. **Valediction:** farewell
7. **Validate:** to prove the validity of
8. **Valor:** courage
9. **Vanguard:** forefront
10. **Vanquish:** annihilate; defeat
11. **Variegated:** multicoloured
12. **Vehement:** heated; full of passion
13. **Vendetta:** feud; war
14. **Veneer:** a layer; surface
15. **Venerable:** esteemed; respected
16. **Venturesome:** adventurous
17. **Veracity:** authenticity; truthfulness
18. **Verbatim:** word for word
19. **Verbose:** wordy
20. **Verdict:** judgment
21. **Verisimilitude:** credibility
22. **Vertigo:** dizziness
23. **Vestige:** remnant
24. **Vex:** to irritate or annoy
25. **Viable:** workable
26. **Vicinity:** surroundings
27. **Vicious:** violent; brutal
28. **Vicissitude:** an unpleasant change
29. **Vigilant:** alert
30. **Vilify:** to malign
31. **Vindicate:** to free someone from blame
32. **Vindictive:** malicious; mean
33. **Virile:** manly
34. **Virulent:** poisonous; lethal
35. **Visage:** appearance
36. **Vitriolic:** bitter; venomous
37. **Vituperative:** abusive
38. **Vivid:** bright; vibrant
39. **Vociferous:** voluble; vocal
40. **Vogue:** trend
41. **Void:** invalid; null
42. **Volatile:** not stable
43. **Volition:** will; choice
44. **Voluble:** talkative; able to talk fluently
45. **Voluptuous:** pleasure-seeking; attractive
46. **Voracious:** insatiable (such as a voracious reader)
47. **Vulnerable:** defenseless

W

1. **Wager:** to bet
2. **Waiver:** to renounce (a claim over something, a right etc.)
3. **Wane:** to diminish
4. **Warrant:** to deserve
5. **Wary:** cautious
6. **Wheedle:** to charm; to coax
7. **Wherewithal:** means; finances
8. **Whet:** to sharpen or stimulate
9. **Whimsical:** fanciful

10. **Wholesome:** nutritious; healthful
11. **Wield:** to use; to exercise (power etc.)
12. **Wily:** crafty; devious
13. **Winnow:** to get rid of unwanted ones and keep the best ones
14. **Winsome:** pleasant; charming
15. **Wistful:** longing; regretful
16. **Withstand:** bear; resist
17. **Woeful:** sad; anguished
18. **Woo:** to entice; to flatter
19. **Wrangle:** a dispute
20. **Wreath:** a ring of arranged flowers, often put on graves
21. **Wretched:** very bad
22. **Wreak:** to inflict; to cause
23. **Wry:** cynical

X

1. **Xenophobia:** strong dislike of foreigners

Y

1. **Yearn:** to crave; to desire badly
2. **Yoke:** a burden; something that restricts freedom

Z

1. **Zany:** crazy
2. **Zealous:** passionate
3. **Zealot:** fanatic
4. **Zenith:** top; peak

ooo

Unit- 2

Synonyms and Antonyms

SYNONYMS

A synonym is a word which is similar in meaning to the given word. So in synonyms based questions, Identify the word which is closest in meaning to the given word.

Sometimes, it could be difficult to find the correct synonym. These questions are vocabulary intensive; however, there are certain strategies that may help you in your hunt for the right answer:

Analogies

An Analogy means a similarity between two or more things. In this type of questions you will be given one pair of words (main word pair). You need to identify a precise relation between these two word pairs and then from the options identify the word pair with similar relations. These questions test you not just on the meanings of the words but relation between two given words.

1. **Create a precise relation between the two given words.**

   Analogy questions are all about relation between the given words. Establishing a relation is not the same as making a sentence using any two words.

   Example: Brush : Painting

   A. piano : guitar　　B. carpenter : saw

   C. chisel : sculpture　　D. verse : poem

   In the given example, first, you need to identify a precise relation between the given main word pair. A brush is used to do painting. Brush is a tool, painting is the purpose. Carpenter (worker) uses saw(tool). Chisel (tool) is used to do sculpture (purpose). So the answer is Option C.

2. **Reframe the relation if more than one answer choice appears to be correct.**

   Sometimes you may assume a relation between the given word pair and once you work on options, there is a possibility that more than one option have the same relation. Then, you need to reframe your relation, add more detail to your relation.

   Example: Carpenter : Saw

   A. painter : brush B. tailor : scissors

   C. doctor : stethoscope D. runner : shoes

   In the above example, if you establish the relation between the main word pair as carpenter uses saw then all the options can be fit into the relation. But, if you reframe the relation as carpenter (worker) uses saw (tool) to cut (tool-function). Then the answer is Option B.

3. **Eliminate options with no precise relation.**

   It is important to master the technique of eliminating incorrect options. In a given analogy, if there are options with no consistent relation between the given word pair, then you can eliminate those options.

   Example: Revolver : Holster

   A. emotion : passion B. matriculation : induction

   C. scooter : colour D. sword : sheath

   In the above example, other than option D, the remaining options have no precise relation between the given word pairs. Eliminate options which have no relation between the given word pair. A holster holds a revolver and a sheath holds a sword. So, the appropriate answer is Option D.

4. **Ensure the direction of relation is the same.**

   It is important to establish a parallel and consistent relation and find the same relation in options.

   Example: Fox : Vixen

   A. goose : gander B. wizard : witch

   C. mare : horse D. deer : duck

   The relation between the given main word pair is Gender based. Vixen is female fox. Gander is a male goose. Witch is female, wizard is male. Mare is a female horse. A male duck is drake. So, in the above sentences the direction of relation is incorrect in options A,C. So, the answer is Option B.

5. **Practise to identify the common relations with ease.**

   Given below are some common relations. Practise them and try to develop more of such kind.

Lawyer : Courtroom (Worker : Workplace)

Mason : Stone (Worker : Material)

Surgeon : Scalpel (Worker : Tool)

Saw : Cut (Tool : Function)

Upheaval : Turmoil (Synonym relation)

Nadir : Zenith (Antonym relation)

Simper : Smile (Mannerism : Action)

Cool : Frigid (Similar word with higher/lower intensity)

Donkey : Bray (Animal: Sound)

Pig : Piglet(Animal : Younger one)

Duck : Drake (Gender relation)

Dove : Peace (Animal : Symbol of)

For example

Renounce - The king renounced his throne and went in search of peace.

Abdicate - The king abdicated his throne and fled in exile. These two synonymous words broadly carry same meaning of leaving one's possession.

But 'renounce' is used for leaving possession for a lofty cause.

Whereas, 'Abdicate' is used for deserting or leaving possession in favour of someone else for being unable to carry on with it.

SYNONYMS

A

1. Abandon - leave someone alone and uncared

Abdicate - leave power, duty, authority **Abdicate responsibility* **King abdicated throne*

Abjure - leave something voluntarily

Desert - leave someone alone *He deserted his friends

Forsake - leave comfort, luxury, bad habit

Forswear - leave something in violation of pledge *Forswear allegiance

Renounce - leave something as a supreme sacrifice*Renounced his wealth and luxury for working for world peace

2. Abandoned - left discarded **Abandoned house*

Neglected - left out of care **Neglected child*
Discarded - left alone and got rid of due to being worthless **Discarded furniture thrown in lumber room*

3. Abase - degrade someone by shameful acts **Leaders have abased themselves*
Degrade - downgrade in rank
Deprave - morally abased (corrupt)

4. Abash - make someone ashamed by shameful acts **The son abashed his family*
Mortify - make someone acutely ashamed due to humiliation **Boss' reprimand has mortified him in the presence of colleagues.*

5. Abate - become less in intensity of fury **Anger soon abated*
Allay - become less in intensity of fear, anxiety
Alleviate - become less in intensity of pain
Assuage - become less in intensity of ego; to reprieve the hurt feeling
Mitigate - become less in intensity of harshness, severity **Mitigate harsh speech with juicy anecdotes* **Mitigate crime by repentence* **Mitigate the effect of disaster through Management.*

6. Abject - in humiliating condition **Abject poverty.*
Ignoble - lacking in dignity **Ignoble behaviour*
Sordid - degrading baseness **Corruption is rampant, which is a sordid state of affairs.*

7. Aborigine - a person belonging to original race living in a place
Indigenous - a product which is produced in a place (locally/ domestically)**Indigenously manufactured product*
Native - a person who is born in a place (own country).
Autochthon - flora and fauna which is original to a place

8. Abound (in) - be in large amount **Market abounds in*
Glut - be in large excess of demand **There is a glut of vegetables in market.*
Teem - be in large numbers in a place
Swarm - **The market teems with people*

9. Abrade - scrape soft surface by rubbing with hard surface
Excoriate - wear away skin by rubbing with hard surface
Chafe - rub skin make it painful
Fret - wear away surface by constant rubbing **Dripping water frets away hard surface beneath*

Gall	- rub surface of skin so as to make blisters due to friction **Shoes galled his toes*
10. Abscond	- to flee from getting caught
Escape	- to flee confinement
Elope	- to flee secretly with someone to marry
Elude	- to flee from someone by evading him
Skive	- to flee from a place quietly
Bunk	- play truant, flee from workplace or school
11. Absorb	- soak a liquid (by a solid surface)
Imbibe	- soak knowledge/learning through mind **Imbibe knowledge *Imbibe respect for Values*
Assimilate	- absorb and make one's own **Assimilate alien culture*
12. Abstain	- to keep off from indulging in something harmful **Abstain from smoking*
Desist	- to keep off from doing something **Desist from violence*
Eschew	- to keep off from doing something on moral or practice ground **Eschew bad companion*
Refrain	- to keep off from doing something, despite feeling urge to do so **Refrain from laughing on sombre occasion*
Shun	- to keep off from someone abhorrent or repulsive **Shun lepers*
13. Abstemiousness	- self-control on eating, drinking
Abstinence	- self-denial in indulging in sensual gratification, viz. drinking alcohol
Continence	- self-control in indulging in sex **Continence rather than abstinence is advisable in case of married people, but unmarried ones are advised abstinence*
14. Absurd	- ridiculously devoid of any sense
Bizarre	- absurd because of having incongruous combinations, e.g., of old & new, tragic and comic **A bizarre dress *A bizarre plan *A bizarre incident*
Grotesque	- having laughable quality **Grotesque face*
Preposterous	- having misplaced positions of parts **Preposterous plan; completely contrary to nature.*
15. Abundant	- present in large quantity
Excessive	- present in excess of requirement
Superfluous	- in more amount than required, which goes waste

Plenty	- sufficient in amount **Plenty of eatables*
Surfeit	- excess amount of consumption causing disgust
Legion	- a large number of troops
Host	- a great number of something **A host of people gathered there*
Plethora	- excess of something which must be reduced **Plethora of laws are existing but their implementation is tardy.*
Galore	- in plenty **Food galore is available*
16. Abysmal	- of endless depth/low **Abysmal conduct*
Fathomless	- of endless depth/low which is beyond means of measurement **Fathomless cruelty*
17. Accept	- agree to have done something **Accepted his mistake*
Acknowledge	- accept the fact **Acknowleged the presence hitherto concealed of error in the plan*
Admit	- accept the fact reluctantly **He admitted his fault*
Confess	- accept one's crime **He confessed his role in hatching a conspiracy*
18. Acclimatize	- adjust oneself to a changed climate
Accustom	- adjust oneself to a changed custom
Inure	- adjust oneself to a dangerous situation **Workers were inured to work in hazardous situation (e.g., tunnel workers)*
Habituate	- adjust oneself to follow a habit or routine **He became habituated to following hygiene*
19. Accursed	- cursed to suffer
Damed	- cursed to go to hell
Doomed	- cursed to be ruined
20. Accuse	- blame for wrong-doings
Charge	- blame for committing offence
Incriminate	- blame for criminal act
Indict	- blame for legal violation (by courts)
Impeach	- blame for abuse of office of high position (by parliament)
Arraign	- blame for wrong-doing and call for explanation
21. Acerbic	- bitter in taste **Acerbic food*
Acrid	- bitter and pungent in smell **Acrid smell*
Mordant	- bitter and corrosive **Mordant liquid*
Vitriolic	- extremely bitter (speech)
22. Adamant	- rigid in one's own opinion
Resolute	- rigid in one's own decision

23. Adjourn - stop and shift for a later day or time (meeting etc.)

Defer - stop and shift for a later day or time (decision)

Postpone - stop and shift for a later day or time (an event)

Prorogue - stop and shift for a later day or time (parliament session)

24. Admire - praise for good work/achievements

Acclaim - praise publicly with enthusiasm

Applaud - praise by clapping

Compliment - praise by showering congratulations

Commend - praise by making appreciation

Hail - praise by showing/expressing gratitude

25. Admirer - one who praises good work of art, etc. **Admirer of art works*

Aficionado - one who praises a particular sport **Aficionado of bull-fight*

Aesthete - one who praises the beauty of something **Aesthete of Nature*

Dilettante - one who praises particular music **Dilettante of classical music*

Fan - one who praises a famous person **Fan of Amitabh Bachchan*

Gourmet - one who praises good food **Gourmet of Chinese dishes*

26. Ado - excited movement or flurry without much to do worthwhile **People were abuzz with ado about nothing* * *Without any further ado, the speakers were invited by the chairman for panel discussion.*

Bustle - excited movement in great hurry around a place

Flurry - excited movement in nervous agitation **Flurry of officials on arrival of minister on the ground was was pleasing to the aggrieved public.*

27. Adroit - skillful in doing something

Adept - skillful in handling a situation

Deft - skillful in doing something quickly

Dextrous - skillful in doing something with hands

Proficient - skillful in doing something with efficiency

28. Adulterate - to mix something of lower quality with superior one for making more profit on sale

Contaminate - to mix something with impure things so as to make it injurious

Taint - to mix something in small amount to a substance so as to impart a foul smell

Tinge	- to mix something in small amount to impart colour
Pollute	- mix contaminants with natural resources, e.g., water, air etc. so as to make it harmful to health.
29. Advent	- coming to a place of someone/something important **Advent of Mahatma Gandhi on national scene gave impetus to freedom struggle*
Arrival	- coming to a place of destination
30. Affect	- to show false feelings
Feign	- to affect ignorance, injury
Malinger	- to affect illness
Pretend	- to affect emotional display **Pretend sympathy*
31. Affirm	- to say something firmly or emphatically
Assert	- to say something confidently
Aver	- to say something thought to be true
Avouch	- to say something openly
Avow	- to say something with guarantee
Declaim	- to say something passionately **He declaimed his innocence*
32. Affix	- to fix with a paste **Affix stamp on the envelope*
Adhere	- to stick to a party, religion
Cling	- to stick to the body of someone **Kid clings to the mother*
Hug	- to stick to someone by taking in one's arms
Embrace	- to stick to someone by catching shoulders
33. Afflict	- to hurt as by disease, harmful condition **Ill-fate has afflicted him*
Inflict	- to hurt by attacking with weapon **Inflict injury on someone*
34. Aggravate	- make situation worse
Intensify	- make something intense/acute
Recrudesce	- make situation worse again after improvement
35. Agitate	- disturb mentally to make one lose calm
Discomfit	- disturb mentally, making one feel uneasy **Heckling by audience discomfited the speaker*
Disconcert	- disturb mentally, making one lose composure
Rattle	- disturb mentally, making one utterly nervous **Defeat rattled the politician*
Faze	- (used in negative) disturb mentally causing shame **No amount of criticism can faze him*
36. Agitated	- mentally disturbed
Disconsolate	- mentally disturbed without something to console

Distraught - mentally disturbed, making worried

Disconcerted - mentally disturbed, losing peace of mind

37. Agnate - descendant of same male ancestor (male) **Agnate brothers*

Cognate - descendant of same female ancestor **Cognate brothers*

Consanguineous - descending from the same blood **Consanguineous brothers*

Kindred - descending from blood relations

38. Aid - help given to needy

Grant - aid given on certain condition

Subsidy - aid given in part of total expenses

Subvention - aid given to cultural or literary institution to meet expenses. Interest subvention is provided to exporters earning foreign exchange for the country.

39. Alibi - a fact mentioned as evidence to prove that one was not present at the place of occurrence of crime **He showed his absence from the town as an alibit to prove his innocence*

Excuse - a fact put forward as a ruse to avoid something **Fever came handy as an excuse to avoid work*

Plea - a fact put forward to justify failure to do something **Delay in project was justified on the plea of civil unrest*

Pretext - a fact put forward as an excuse **Use pretext of paucity of funds*

40. Alienation - loss of affection in relationship **Alienation of people from politicians*

Disaffection - loss of bondage in relationship

Estrangement - loss of bondage resulting in complete separation **Estrangement between husband and wife living separately*

41. Allegiance - firm adherence to party, group

Devotion - firm adherence to religion

Esprit de corps - firm adherence to comradeship of professionals

Fealty - firm adherence to feudal lord

Fidelity - firm adherence to faith towards someone

Loyalty - firm adherence to a person

42. Allot - distribute by apportioning something to each one **Allot quarters*

Allocate - distribute by apportioning resources for each purpose

Assign	- distribute by apportioning work/duty to a person
Apportion	- distribute by apportioning amongst claimants **Father apportioned the family's property amongst his sons*
43. Alone	- indicates physically isolated **He is alone in the house*
Solitary	- indicates without companion **The convict was kept in solitary confinement*
Lonely	- indicates longing for companionship **He is feeling lonely in a place away from home*
Forlorn	- indicates dejection due to separation**Forlorn lover*
Desolate	- indicates sad due to being left bereaved **Desolate widow*
44. Amaze	- bewilder someone with surprise
Astonish	- make one too surprised to believe
Astound	- make one surprised beyond wildest expectations
Flabbergast	- make one surprised greatly
45. Amend	- make correction for improving **Amend law*
Emend	- make correction for removing errors **Emend a text of speech (edit)*
Expunge	- make correction by removing objectionable portion of write-up. * The speaker expunged the remarks of legislative member after the debate.
46. Amends	- to compensate for wrong-doings by rectifying **Apologise to make amends*
Atone	- to compensate for wrong-doing by acts of goodness **Make charity to atone himself*
Expiate	- to compensate by inflicting self-punishment **Mahatma Gandhi frequently went on fast to expiate*
Repent	- to compensate by feeling sorry for wrong-doing
47. Anathema	- someone or something intensely disliked **Lying is anathema to me*
Bete noire	- someone/something to which one feels aversion **He is my bete noire*
Pariah	- someone who is hated, abhored like untouchable
48. Ancestor	- one from whom a person is descended
Forefathers	- is more distant in lineage from whom one has descended.
Forbear/forebear	- is distant in lineage
Progenitor	- is just preceding in lineage, e.g. father
49. Anger (noun)	- expression of displeasure

Rage - violent, uncontrollable anger
Outrage - strong anger
Fury - extremely violent anger

50. Anger (verb) - make one angry **My accusation angered him*
Enrage - make one violently and uncontrollably angry
Outrage - make someone very angry
Infuriate - make someone extremely angry
Incense - make one angry, akin to burning incense.

51. Announce - inform public of important issue **Exam results are announced*
Declare - announce officially **Declare holiday*
Herald - announce imminent arrival of someone important **Nip in the air heralded onset of winter season*
Proclaim - announce official decision **Proclaim curfew*
Promulgate - Announce official order **The ordinance promulgated by the Government is still in force*

52. Announcer - one who announces something on public address system.
Herald - one who or which announces the imminent arrival. on the scene of someone/something very special
Harbinger - one who or which announces the imminent arrival of something unpleasant **Lull in the harbinger of storm*

53. Annoy - irritate someone mentally
Exasperate - vex, irritate intensely
Chagrin - **Foolish mistakes committed by him chagrined him*
Irk - irritate because of being tiring
Irritate - agitate mentally due to discomfort

54. Annoyance - feeling of mental irritation over someone's foolishness
Chagrin - feeling of mental irritation over own foolishness **Chagrin of committing ridiculous mistake*
Huff - feeling of annoyance over petty matters
Exasperation - vexation, intense annoyance

55. Annul - cancel validity of a contract
Abrogate - cancel validity of an act, law
Countermand - cancel validity of an order
Revoke - cancel validity of a decision **Revoke arrest warrant*
Repeal - to revoke, to quesh, repress, set aside.
Rescind - to cut away, abrogate

56. Anthem - song in praise of country, school, organisation **School anthem *National anthem*

Alleluia - Hallelujah, praising song for God

Epithalamium - song of praise of bride and groom in wedding cere- mony. Epithalamion

Encomium - high commendation and eulogy

Hosannah - An exclamation of praise to God **Cry hosannah to God*

57. Anxiety - feeling of distressing uneasiness due to apprehension

Angst - unfounded feeling of fear, dread

Hypochondria - unfounded anxious feeling of affliction of diseases

Paranoia - unfounded feeling of being persecuted

Snafu - unfounded feeling chaos everywhere

Worry - show concern for something or someone

58. Apotheosis - symbol of highest state of greatness **Mahatma Gandhi became apotheosis of human-beings*

Paragon - symbol of highest quality **He is the paragon of virtue*

Non-pareil - symbol of being unparralel **He is a human-being non-pareil*

Epitome - symbol of a given quality **He is an epitome of laziness*

59. Apparent - appearing to be so **Apparent calm*

Conspicuous - clearly visible to be so **Conspicuous absence*

Distinct - sharply visible **Distinct characteristics*

Manifest - openly visible **Grief on his face is manifest*

60. Appeal - request earnestly to do something required

Plead - request arguably

Exhort - request emotionally

Urge - request insistently

61. Appease - to make one pleased by agreeing to demands **Voters are appeased by politicians by announcing freebies to people*

Placate - to make one pleased by pacifying anger

Propitiate - to make one pleased by trying to win one's favour

Assuage/Mollify - to make one pleased, who has been emotionally hurt

62. Apposite - appropriate for given occasion **Apposite quotes*

Cogent - appropriate for the topic of discussion **Cogent argument*

Germane - appropriate to the issue at hand
Relevant - appropriate to the matter at hand **Relevant informations*
Pertinent - appropriate to the question **Pertinent reply*
Apropos - Appropriate to opportunity **Appropos remark*

63. Appraise - evaluate the work of someone or something as by an expert **Experts appraise employee's performance*
Assess - evaluate quantum of gain or loss **Income is assessed for taxation *Damage is assessed for compensation*
Evaluate - decide on worth of something **Exams'answer-sheets are evaluated*
Estimate - evaluate accurately cost, number or quantity **Estimate population of a place*

64. Apprehension - fearful feeling of something bad to happen
Suspicion - feeling of something bad which might be possible to happen

65. Appropriate - suitable **Appropriate action*
Befitting - suitable to the occasion **Befitting reply*
Condign - suitable to meet demand **Condign punishment*
Cogent - (in argument) suitable logically **Cogent point*
Germane - suitable to the subject's relevance **Germane to topic*

66. Approve - permit to go ahead **Approve the plan*
Endorse - permit to do something by putting one's signature on the back of the paper **Endorsed payment on the slip*
Sanction - permit as by govt. or a person in authority

67. Aquit - discharge from accusations, criminal charges
Absolve - discharge from responsibility or guilt
Exculpate - discharge from charges by declaring not guilty
Exonerate - discharge from onus of duty-lapse

68. Archaic - belonging to old time **Archaic custom*
Antiquated - having become outdated **Antiquated fashion*
Primitive - belonging to the past, undeveloped time **Primitive technology*
Pristine - belonging to old time, but still existing in its original form **Pristine religious scriptures*

69. Aroma - distinguishing smell of something **Aroma of coffee*
Bouquet - savoury smell of wine or meat **Bouquet of meat cooked in spices*

Flavour	- savoury smell of tasty food
Fragrance	- sweet smell of flowers
Redolence	- mixed smell of flowers as in a garden
70. Arrogance	- haughtiness
Audacity	- disregard of restraint
Temerity	- open & bold disregard of restraint
Hardihood	- daring disregard of restraint
Gall	- arrogant disregard of restraint
71. Arrogant	- haughty
Audacious	- showing undue boldness in disregarding others
Impudent	- showing disrespect to others
Impertinent	- showing improper behaviour
72. Arrogate	- to snatch unjustly someone's credit for good work
Usurp	- to snatch unjustly someone's power or authority
Supplant	- to snatch unjustly someone's place and take it oneself **A whore supplanted his wife*
Pre-empt	- to snatch unjustly somene's chance before he could do it or take it
73. Ascend	- to go upward **He ascended to the top of hierarchy*
Levitate	- to go up in the air floating **The saint levitated*
Soar	- to go up in the sky continuously **The missile soared up towards moon*
74. Aspect	– specific considerable matter of a fact
Dimension	– specific considerable direction of a problem
Facet	– specific considerable side of something **We should consider all facets of a proposal*
Ramification	– specific considerable consequence arising out of a problem or fact **The problem has a serious ramification for the security of the country*
75. Assent	– agree to someone's idea or proposal
Consent	– agree to someone's request
Accede	– agree to someone's request unwillingly
Acquiesce	– agree to someone's request by keeping quiet instead of refusing it
Subscribe	– agree with open support
76. Assiduous	– continuingly and deeply engaged in work **Assiduous worker*
Diligent	– delightfully engaged in work
Persistent	– resolutely, determinedly engaged

Persevering – resolutely engaged, despite failure or difficulty

77. Assignation – a place for secret meeting **Lovers' assignation*

Rendezvous – a place for pre-fixed meeting together or assembly **Parks are popular rendezvous of retired people*

Tryst – a place for pre-fixed meeting with someone **I have to keep a tryst with him*

78. Atrabilious – depressed by ill-founded anxiety

Hypochondriac – depressed by ill-founded illness or anxiety

Melancholic – depressed by persistent sadness

79. Attempt – try to achieve goal in face of difficulty & failure **He attempted thrice to succeed*

Endeavour – try to do something with great offort **He endeavoured to keep himself composed*

Strive – try to do something/succeed with persistent effort **He strove hard to lift a heavy load*

Struggle – try with great effort to fight resistance

80. Attrition – feeling of sorrow for wrongdoing

Contrition – feeling of heart-rending sorrow for sinful acts

Compunction – feeling of sorrow while doing wrongful act

Penitence – feeling of sorrow with desire to make amends for wrongdoing

Remorse – feeling of sorrow and deep regrets

81. Augur – to indicate good outcome as by an event **Increasing terror activities do not augur well for the country*

Portend – to indicate bad outcome as by an event **Global warming portends disasters*

82. Auspicious – favourable by God and, hence, able to bring luck **Auspicious occasion to do something*

Benign – favourable by good nature of someone **Benign stars*

Benevolent – favourable by kindness of a person **Benevolent person*

Propitious – favourable by supernatural powers of something **Propitious luck*

83. Austere – strict in look **Austere face*

Harsh – strict in punishing or cruelty

Severe – strict and intense **Severe punishment*

Tough	– strict and uncompromising **Tough administrator*
84. Authorise	– to allow someone do something as by an authority **The boss authorised him to take action*
Accredit	– to allow to do something recognising someone's competence **Government's accredited press reporters are invited to the press conference*
Delegate	– to allow someone work on own behalf
Franchise	– to allow someone do business by a company on its behalf
85. Autocrat	– one who exercises power imposing one's will
Despot	– one who exercises power imperiously
Tyrant	– one who exercises power in an oppressive m anner
86. Avenge	– to take revenge, vengeance on behalf of others
Retaliate	– to take on to settle scores
Revenge	– to take revenge for oneself
87. Avert	– prevent what is unpleasant **Avert accident*
Obviate	– prevent the necessity of something
Ward off	– prevent what is dangerous
Stave off	– ward off problems temporarily
Preclude	– prevent occurrence before its possibility
Parry	– Prevent attack by turning the weapon aside
88. Avoid	– to keep away so as to remain safe **Avoid oily food*
Eschew	– to keep away from something **Eschew violence*
Avert	– to keep by taking appropriate measures beforehand **Avert student's agitation by assuaging their grievances*
Evade	– to keep away by employing tact **Evade arrest*
89. Awesome	– inspiring owe of someone great, learned etc.
Formidable	– inspiring fear of someone powerful **Formidable enemy*
Menacing	– inspiring fear of some action **Menacing flood*
Minatory	– inspiring threat
90. Awkward	– indicates lack of grace or convenience in doing something **Awkward handling*
Clumsy	– indicates lack of ease

Inept	– indicates lack of appropriateness **Inept handling of situation*
Maladroit	– indicates lack of tact

B

1. Babel	– noise made by confused people in crowd
Bedlam	– uproar and confusion
Brouhaha	– overexcited uproar
Chaos	– noisy disorder and disturbance
Commotion	– noisy hustle-buste in crowd
Melee	– noisy scuffle in crowd
Pandemonium	– noisy disorder in assembled mass of crowd
Rumpus	– noisy disturbance
Uproar	– noisy protest
Clamour	– noisy shouting of crowd
2. Backtrack	– to go back from one's taken stand on a matter
Forswear	– to go back on promise or oath **Swear today, forswear tomorrow*
Recant	– to go back from one's stated belief or opinion
Retract	– to go back on one's given words
Welsh	– to go back from honouring obligation, debt payment
3. Backward	– moving in back direction **Move backward*
Retrograde	– moving in inferior condition **Retrograde society*
Retrogressive	– opposite of progressive, going back in previous inferior state of something
Regressive	– returning to previous position
4. Bad smelling	– smelling offensive
Fetid	– smelling bad and be hazardous to health
Noisome	– bad smelling, causing revulsion, disgust
Putrid	– bad smelling due to rotting of garbage, corpse
Rancid	– bad smelling and tasting offensive (said of cooking oil)
Fusty	– due to uncleanliness of place
Musty	– due to dark, unventillated condition
5. Baffle	– confuse due to complexity
Perplex	– Bewilder

Befuddle	– confuse due to difficulty in understanding
Bemuse	– make unable to think
Bewilder	– make unable to think due to confusion
Daze	– make unable to think due to blow on head
Stun	– make unable to think due to shock
Stupefy	– make unable to think due to drunken state
6. Bait	– the thing which is used to lure prey **Earthworm is used as bait for fishing *Rebate and discount are used as bait to attract customers in shops*
Decoy	– the which is used to divert attention of prey so as to become unaware of impending danger **Dummy parachutes are dropped at a place away from the place to be attacked by troops as a decoy to divert enemy's attention*
Feint	– trick employed to divert other's attention from the real intention of the one who used trick
Ruse	– trick used to divert attention from truth
7. Ban	– official forbidding for public from doing something **Public assembly on roads has been banned *Ban on strikes has been announced*
Prohibit	– forbidding by law **Smoking in public place is prohibited*
Inhibit	– to stop one from doing something *Thyroid inhibits kids' growth
Forbid	– not allow to do something undesirable
8. Banish	– expel from a place by authority *The *criminal was banished out of town*
Excommunicate	– expel someone out of his religion for anti-religious activities
Outcaste	– expel from one's own caste
Exile	– expel from one's own country and force to take refuge in another country **The dethroned king was exiled*
Extradite	– expel from a country to another one to face trials by courts for offence committed there
9. Bark	– outer covering of a tree
Peel	– outer covering of banana or else which can easily be peeled off or stripped off
Rind	– hard outer covering on some fruits, *viz.* watermelon

10. Baron – the most powerful person in a given field of business. **He is a publishing baron*

Magnate – the biggest influential businessman in a trade. **Tata is a steel magnate*

Tycoon – the most wealthy businessman in a given trade. **A shipping tycoon*

11. Beat – to strike someone's body to injure or punish

Bash – beat thoroughly with smashing blows

Batter – beat repeatedly.

Bludgeon – beat with thick stick at its one end

Box – blow on the head or ear with the hand or first

Clobber – beat with heavy blows

Clout – beat with careless, playful strokes **Clout kids on their back*

Cuff – beat with open palm on head

Pound – beat with legs by laying in ground

Pummel – beat with fists repeatedly

Slog – beat with forceful strokes

Slug – beat with hard knock

Smite – beat with hammer

Swat – beat with a flat object as a fan or book

Thrash – beat violently and repeatedly

Thresh – beat crops in order to separate grains from chaff.

12. Beg – ask humbly for getting something **Beg for alms*

Beseech – ask by repeated persuasion **Beseeched him for help*

Entreat – ask by earnest requesting

Implore – ask with anxious urgency

Importune – ask for something so repeatedly as to annoy someone, entreat causing annoyance

Supplicate – ask for something by praying before someone **Supplicate before deity in prayer*

13. Behaviour – manner in which one treats others **His behaviour is pleasing*

Conduct – one's manner of behaving in a particular situation **He conducts himself coolly in face of provocation*

Comportment – behaviour in a specified manner akin to a class of people **Comportment of an aristocrat*

Deportment	– behaviour showing etiquette
Demeanour	– behaviour in accordance with one's status **An aristocrat's demeanour*
14. Belief	– acceptance as true **I have no belief in the rumours*
Faith	– acceptance in tenets of religion or party to which one belongs **His faith in party is unshakable*
Credence	– acceptance in what someone said **People lend credence to whatever he says*
Credit	– acceptance of someone's reputation as being worth relying upon **He is a man of unblemished credit amongst people*
15. Benumb	– deprive of physical movement due to loss of sensation **Biting cold benumbed his fingers*
Petrify	– deprive of physical movement due to sudden fright **Encountered by a ferocious dog, he was petrified*
Stun	– due to shock
Stupefy	– due to amazement
16. Bequeath	– leave property to someone by making a will
Legate	– hand over property to posterity
Demise	– leave property by transferring it to someone
17. Bias	– inclination to or against someone or something as per one's liking or disliking **He has a bias for sweets *His bias against people of other castes is well-known*
Disposition	– inclination towards something due to inherent mental tendency
Predisposition	– inculcated disposition in someone to create tendency in someone so that he behaves in specified manner
Predilection	– disposition shown in advance *i.e.*, in early stage of life
Stance	– inclination to take a specified posture in a given situation
Tendency	– inclination to feel or do something in a particular manner
Trait	– mental inclination/disposition to think or act in a specified manner
18. Bigot	– a person who is an admirer of a religion or sect, and does not tolerate contrary opinion of an opponent

Chavinist – a person who is an admirer of one's own gender or group, and looks down upon people of opposite gender or group

Fanatic – admirer of one's religion or party with excessive zeal

Zealot – admirer of one's own party, religion, etc. with excessive commitment

19. Blend – to mix ingredients to prepare an agreeable mixture

Concoct – to mix ingredients to prepare a drink

Taint – to mix ingredient in small quantity to make something foul smelling

20. Block – to stop passage by putting obstacle

Clog – to stop passage by something sticky **Silt and mud clog drains*

Hamper – to impede; to derange

Interrupt – to break in between; to stop or hinder

Hinder – to put up obstacle and impede progress

Jam – to stop traffic movement by overcrowding

Obstruct – to put up obstacle and hinder movement

21. Bogus – not genuine **Bogus claim*

Erastz – not a genuine substitute of a valueable thing **Ersatz work of art*

Placebo – (medicine) not genuine – looking like genuine and used to be given to a patient suffering from imaginary diseases

Sham – not genuine – only appearing to look genuine

22. Boredom – loss of interest in something due to excess exposure to it

Cloyness – loss of interest in something causing revulsion

Doldrums – loss of interest due to prolonged indulgence in an activity

Ennui – loss of spirit due to lack of occupation

Tedium – loss of interest in some work due to lacking variety

23. Bounce – to jump up after hitting a surface

Rebound – to return back after hitting a hard surface

Reverberate – to return back from a hard surface repeatedly to make an echo

Repercuss	– (water waves) to return after hitting shores
24. Boundary	– protective wall around a building
Rampart	– protective wall around a fort or castle
Parapet	– protective wall around edge of roof or balcony
Moat	– protective ditch around a fort or castle
Stein	– protective wall around the dug portion of a well
25. Boycott	– expel from the group and refuse to socialise with
Ostracise	– expel from society and refuse to socialise with
Excommunicate	– expel from religion
Outcaste	– expel from caste by castemen
26. Brat	– a person who habitually boasts
Braggart	– a person who brags
Braggadocio	– a boastful person
27. Breach (*n*)	– braking of a rule by failing to obey it **Breach of traffic rules*
Violation	– breaking of accepted social norms **Violation of etiquette*
Contravention	– breaking of a rule by acting against it
28. Breach (*v*)	– to break a rule by failing to observe it
Violate	– to break social norms
Contravene	– to break rule by acting against it
29. Buckle	– to bend under unbearable load
Sage	– to bend in the middle of length of a beam due to its own weight
Prolapse	– to slip down from position by becoming loose
30. Bump	– move forward so as to strike something ahead **A moving car bumped into another car ahead*
Collide	– bump into something with hard knock
Crash	– bump into something with immense force
Dash	– bump into something violently
31. Bunch	– a number of keys hung together
Cluster	– a number of grapes hung from a stem
Skein	– a length of thread wound around a reel
Tassel	– hanging decorative threads
Tuft	– hanging mass of hairs, grass from one end
32. Bundle	– tied mass of something

Bale – bundle of cotton
Faggot – bundle of dried wood or sticks
Sheaf – bundle of grass, paper, etc.
Swag – bundle of personal effects hung on shoulder of a traveller or labourer
Wad – bundle of currency notes

33. Burn – hurt in fire
Scald – hurt or injure with steam or hot liquid **Scald fingers with hot milk accidently*
Singe – hurt or injure superficial hairs on skin in open flame
Scorch – hurt or injured with extreme heat (as the surface of skin in intense sun)

C

1. Cadaverous – looking pale like a corpse due to illness and imaciated body
Careworn – looking pale due to tiredness or worry
Haggard – looking pale due to exhaustion and tiredness
Pinched – looking pale due to mental tension
Wasted – looking pale due to emaciated physique
Worn – looking pale-faced due to weariness

2. Calm – not showing mental agitation
Placid – (a person) not easily agitated, nor excited by provocation
Serene – (atmosphere etc.) without any disturbance **A serene valley – a calm and quiet area.*
Tranquil – in a state of peace **Tranquil mind*

3. Cant – language spoken by people of a particular trade which is unintelligible to others **Hawkers cant* **Thieves cant*
Argot – language spoken by a close nit group **Argot of smugglers*
Jargon – language used by people of technical profession which is full of technical words **Doctors jargon*
Lingo – language too strange to be understood

4. Caper – jump around in enjoyment **Children caper on field*
Cavort – jump around in excitement **Winning players cavorted on the ground*

Frolick	– jump around cheerfully, lively **Kids frolicked around*
Gambol	– jump around playfully
5. Caprice	– swinging mood without any pattern **Capricious mood of boss was beyond the guess of subordinates*
Vagary	– swinging of weather which is unpredictable **Vagary of climate. The farmers' hopes are subjected to the vagaries of nature.*
Vicissitude	– swinging of luck or fortune which turns unpredictably
6. Caress	– touch and strike gently and lovingly **Caressed his hairs*
Fondle	– touch and strike sexually
Pet	– touch and strike erotically
Preen	– touch and caress feathers with beak (used for birds)
7. Casual	– (event etc.) occurring without pre-meditation **Casual event/occurrence*
Accidental	– involving chance **Accidental meeting with a friend*
Fortuitous	– happening without any cause *i.e.* luckily
Incidental	– happening unforeseen **Incidental event*
8. Catch	– take hold of **Catch the ball*
Grasp	– catch firmly **He grasped my shoulders with hands to hug me*
Hold	– grasp and continue to do so **He held my hand until I pulled it off.*
Nab	– catch a person while fleeing **Nab the thief*
Sieze	– hold something by confiscating from someone **Siezed stolen goods*
Apprehend	– catch someone red-handed
Grab	– catch someone/something by hand
9. Catholic	– of wide variety **Catholic taste *Cutholic faith – not restricted to a particular one*
Cosmopolitan	– of wide variety of residents **Cosmopolitan city*
Cosmic	– of wide universe **Cosmic event*
Ecumenical	– of widespread scale **Ecumenical destruction*
Universal	– of as wide as universe **Universal appeal of non-violence philosophy *Universal truth*

10. Cautious – ready to avoid potential danger. **He stood there cautious*

Circumspect – ready to avoid danger by looking around alertly

Chary – cautious in doing something due to being harmful

Aware – ready with the knowledge of what is happening around

Wary – cautious due to possible problems

11. Cede – give up territory to another country

Demise – give up property to someone

Demit – give up post held by someone

Relinquish – give up property voluntarily

12. Celebration – observance of gaiety on the occasion of some importance **Birthday celebration*

Ceremony – observance of gaiety on the occasion of social or religious rites **Marriage ceremony*

13. Chafe – wear away surface by rubbing with something hard **Collar of shirt chafed kin of nape*

Abrade – scrape by rubbing with hard surface

Excoriate – wear away skin by whipping

Fret – wear away surface by constant rubbing

Gall – make blisters by rubbing on skin

14. Chant – recite slogan in unison

Recite – sing song, prayer, etc. loudly

Dithyramb – recital of a poem or speech passionately

Drivel – recital of meaningless speech

Harangue – recital of speech forcefully

15. Chatter – to speak incessantly

Babble – to speak foolishly

Blabber – to speak too much

Jabber – to speak rapidly and incoherently

Twaddle – to speak in a trivial manner

Drivel – to speak nonsense

Prattle – to speak too much unnecessarily

16. Cheat *(n)* – one who deceives by playing tricks

Con – one who deceives by lying to make one convinced

Fraud	– a cheat who disposseses someone of money by dishonest means
Impostor	– a cheat who deceives by assuming false identity
17. Cheat *(v)*	– to deceive someone by playing trick
Con	– to deceive by lying
Defraud	– to deceive by dishonest means
Swindle	– to cheat by imposture *i.e.* assuming identity of someone else
Dupe	– to cheat by employing tricks
Gull	– to cheat
Hoodwink	– to cheat by making a person unable to see or realise the trap
18. Chew	– grind food in mouth
Chomp	– chew noisily *i.e.* ,with making sound of chewing
Munch	– chew crisp food noisily
Ruminate	– chew cud (by animal)
19. Chide	– speak angrily for doing wrong
Scold	– chide bitterly
Berate	– scold angrily
Castigate	– scold severely
Chasten	– chide so as to discipline erring person by giving punishment
Chastise	– scold with beating
Reprehend	– scold and condemn/criticize
Hector	– scold like a bully
Remonstrate	– scold and protest against wrongdoing
20. Circadian	– (biological activities in our body) occurring on daily basis **Sleeping is a circadian process*
Diurnal	– (a process) occurring on daily basis **Diurnal earth's rotation causes day and night*
Quotidian	– (work) done on daily basis **Quotidian household chores*
21. Class	– group of persons distinct from others on the basis of status in social divisions **Aristocratic class of people*
Category	– group of things distinct on the basis of quality or characteristics
Denomination	– group of things on the basis of name assigned to the whole group

Gender – group assigned on the basis of sex of birth
Genre – group of art or literary work assigned on the basis of distinct nature
Genus – category of creatures on the basis of species

22. Classify – separate on the basis of class
Categorize – separate into categories
Segregate – separate from a group isolated from others
Sort – separate papers, documents, letters according to subject matters, titles, addresses etc.
Assort – separate bills, reeipts according to related matter

23. Clean – remove dirt and dust
Cleanse – make thorough cleaning of undesirable such as soul from sin, moral from blemish
Emunge – clean bowels of stool, secreted mass from nostrils
Flush – clean toilet with large amount of water
Lustrate – clean with holy water for ceremonial purpose
Mop – clean floors with bundle of rags soaked in water
Scour – clean something by rubbing
Swill – clean by swirling with water
Wash – clean clothes, utensils, etc. with water

24. Clever – able to see someone's attempt to befool
Shrewd – having acute sense of cleverness, cunning
Crafty – having the ability to befool others
Astute – having the ability to save oneself from being befooled
Sagacious – having the ability to take decisions with farsightedness
Perspicacious – having the ability to take decisions with farsightedness

25. Cliche – (slogan etc.) over used and, hence, uninteresting anymore
Bromide – (slogan etc.) over used and, hence, ineffective in impressing people
Platitude – (remark etc.) oft-repeated and hence, uninteresting

26. Climax – state of extreme excitement in story
Bliss – state of extreme happiness in life
Culmination – state of extreme end of a process

Orgasm	– state of extreme sexual passion
Trance	– state of extreme absorption in pleasurable enjoyment, *e.g.*, listening to music or divine song
27. Climb	– go up a slope, stairs, ladders
Clamber	– climb laboriously on a slope, using hands and feet both
Board	– to go inside a transport vehicle for travelling
Mount	– to ride on a horse, bicycle etc.
Embark	– to get in a ship for journey
28. Clique	– group of experts in specified areas of knowledge
Claque	– group of hired audience to clap the speaker
Choir	– group of singers
Panel	– group of experts for decision making/discussion
Troupe	– group of artistes
29. Closeness	– nearness in relationship
Vicinity	– nearness in space, being in the neighbourhood **His house is in vicinity of mine*
Propinquity	– nearness to almost in touching contact **Sit in propinquity with each other*
Proximity	– nearness in distance
Contiguity	– nearness with mutual touching
Intimacy	– nearness in personal relations.
30. Clot	– (liquid) form a thick, sticky mass
Congeal	– (liquid) become semi solid on cooling
Coagulate	– become semi solid by chemial process
Curdle	– (milk) change into curd
31. Cogitate	– to consider deeply over a topic
Introspect	– to consider one's own past actions to find out lapses
Retrospect	– to consider about past events to find out if anything went wrong
Ruminate	– to think about deeply
Meditate	– to think carefully about something
Mull	– to consider at length about something
32. Collect	– to pick up and keep at one place
Accumulate	– to collect and store **Accumulate water* **Accumulate wealth*

Cull	– to pick up by plucking as inferior in quality
Garner	– to pick up and keep in a storage place
Gather	– to collect in a place
Summon	– to pick up courage to face challenge
Marshall	– to collect in an orderly manner **To marshall facts before arguing a case*
Muster	– collect troops or workers for putting on job
33. Colossal	– of large in size **Colossalwaste*
Monolith	– of a large single piece as of a stone **A monolith organization*
Mammoth	– of large size physique **A mammoth elephant*
34. Commit	– hand over to other's charge **This case was committed to superior court *Commit parcel to railways*
Consign	– hand over to someone for disposal or send forward **Consign goods to transporter *Deadbody was consigned to pyre*
Confide	– hand over personal secrets to someone you have trust in
Entrust	– hand over something to someone you trust **He entrusted valuables to his neighbour*
Relegate	– hand over someone/something to inferior place **He was relegated to oblivion*
35. Companion	– one who moves in someone's company **He has gone there with his two companions*
Consort	– one who accompanies with someone, and shares common destiny **He always moves with his female consort wherever he goes*
Spouse	– one who accompanies someone, and is formally married to him
36. Compare *(with)*	– to consider both liken-ness as well as difference with something else **Compare life in Delhi with that in Mumbai*
Compare *(to)*	– to consider only liken-ness of one to another **This year summer's intensity is comparable to that in a desert*
Contrast *(with)*	– to consider only the difference **Contrast the luxury of aristocrats with the penury of the peasants*
37. Compensate	– to make up for loss or deficiency

Recompense – to make up as reward for rendering service

Indemnify – to guard gainst any possible loss, and compensate in case of damage or loss incurred

38. Complacent – well satisfied and pleased with one's own achievements

Smug – complacent with a sadist arrogance for those who are less fortunate in this matter

39. Complain – air grievance about something **Complain against water supply problems*

Carp – complain by finding fault deliberately

Cavil – complain about petty problems

Grumble – complain in muted voice and sullen face

40. Complicity – active participation in conspiration/wrongdoing

Connivance – passive participation in conspiracy by means of acquiescing in wrongdoing

Collusion – active participation in wrongdoing in secret manner **Collusion with perpetrators of crime*

Indulgence – active participation in some activity to fulfil desire **Indulgence in share marketing*

Involvement – active participation in some activity by means of grossly absorbed in it

41. Concession – privilege of paying less **Students get concession in bus fares*

Discount – deduction in price of an article on sale **Store sold articles on 10% discount in prices*

Rebate – deduction in payable amount allowed to the payee **Rebate of 5% on the bill was allowed for early payment*

Exemption – freedom allowed from fulfilling obligation or liability which others have to fulfil **Exemption in tax paymont for those earning less*

Relaxation – application of rules less strictly **Relaxation of 5 years in upper age limit was allowed to the tribal candidates for entry in jobs*

42. Confine – keep within specified limit of space, scope or time **Discussion was confined to corruption *He confined himself in the house*

Immure – keep within the boundary of a place/house **Saints immure themselves in hermitage*

Incarcerate	– keep within the four walls of a room, or prison cell **They incarcerated themselves for private talks*
Intern	– keep within a specified space without allowing to cross it **War prisoners are interned in tents surrounded by barbed fences*
43. Confiscate	– seize with legal authority **Contraband goods were confiscated*
Distrain	– seize property of someone for paying his liability
Escheat	– seize unclaimed property (by the state)
Forfeit	– seize property, privilege, etc. as a penalty for wrong doing **Property of fugitive was forfeited*
Impound	– seize something and retain in custody **His car was impounded by police after it met with an accident*
44. Confute	– prove a statement to be wrong
Refute	– prove an accusation to be wrong
Disprove	– Prove a claim to be wrong
45. Congenital	– (disease, defect) present since birth **He is suffering from congenital hernia*
Inborn	– (habit, merit) present since birth **Talent in a person in inborn*
Innate	– (quality, virtue) present since birth **Compassion is an innate virtue in human beings*
46. Conserve	– prevent wasteful use of reserved resources so as to last long **Conserve water*
Preserve	– prevent valuable things from getting damaged **Preserve heritage*
Eke out	– use/consume in less amount of resources so to last longer **Eke out a living on alms*
Stint	– use in limited amount which is available by restricted allotment **Stint on rationed foods*
47. Consult	– consider something with the advisors.
Confer	– consider with one's equals or peers **Senior executives confer on company's affairs*
Advise	– consider with someone on personal matters **He advised with his friends on matters of his career*
Parley	– consider with others on matters which are contentious **Govt. parleys with the opposition leaders on the passage of legislation*

Treat – (belligerent countries) consider on negotiating terms for truce and finalise treaty.

48. Contemporary – (two things or persons) existing during the same period of time *C*ontemporary poets/leaders/art & cultures*

Contemporaneous – existing during the same time period as the existence of something else **Our friendship was contemporaneous with the period of our college days together*

Coeval – existing during the same period in the long past **Coeval cultures which are extinct now*

Coetaneous – existing with the same time of birth or origin **Coetaneous mounains*

49. Contempt – feeling of dishonour for something

Disdain – contempt for being worthless/unworthy

Scorn – derisive contempt

Spite/spleen – a feeling of hate

50. Contingent – (something) dependent upon something else **Success is contingent upon hard work*

Incumbent – (duty, responsibility) dependent upon someone expected to discharge **Care of elderly people is incumbent upon progeny*

Recumbent – something reclining upon something else for support **He is recumbent upon the pillow*

51. Continuously – without break **He slept continuously for 6 hours*

Constantly – very often – again and again **He is constantly bothering me*

Continually – at short intervals **He lost his temper continually in the meeting*

Perpetually – endlessly **Poor people suffer perpetually*

52. Controversial – causing controversy **Controversial decision*

Contentious – likely to become a matter of arguments between contenders **Census on caste basis has become a contentious issue in the country*

53. Cooperate – work jointly to achieve common goal **They cooperate with each other*

Collaborate – to work jointly on a plan

Collude – to work jointly on a conspiracy

54. Courage – quality in character to face extreme difficulties without fear

Fortitude – quality in character to endure problems

Guts – stamina to endure or face challenges

55. Coward – lacking in courage

Timid – lacking courage to venture in unknown area or mix with unknown person *Too timid to talk to strangers *Too timid to invest in shares*

Timorous – lacking courage in taking bold action on one's own accord **Too timorous to take on a challenge*

56. Crack – narrow split in surface

Chasm – profound gap in opinions, friendship

Cleavage – wide split

Crevice – narrow split in surface which runs deep

Fissure – a long and narrow split

Gape – opening gap as in open mouth **He yawned with a gape*

Hiatus – a gap with continuity

Rent – large split as by tearing **A rent in cloth*

57. Crave – desire overwhelmingly for something **Crave for wine*

Covet – desire to possess what someone else is having **I covet his success*

Hanker – strongly desire for something

Long – strongly desire for something which is not easily achieved **Long for name and fame*

Yearn – desire impatiently or eagerly **Yearn to meet family members*

Suspire – desire strongly indicated by taking deep breath

58. Crawl – move slowly along the ground with the help of hands and knees

Creep – move slowly with the body lying on the ground

Slither – move slowly on the ground with turning and twisting the body alternately in the opposite directions

59. Craze – excessive liking for something **He has a craze for sweets*

Fad – excessive arbitrary habit of doing something

Mania	– excessive tendency to do something **He has a mania of talking*
Obsession	– excessive pre-occupation with something **Obsession for watching television*
60. Create	– to bring something into existence by using skill **God created the unverse*
Generate	– to bring into existence by producing something by using a process **Generate electricity*
Engender	– to bring into existence in someone like emotion **Engender wonder/interest/anger in someone*
Breed	– to bring offsprings into existence by giving birth by animals **Animal breeds calf*
Beget	– to bring into existence offspring by humans **He has begotten four kids*
61. Credit	– to acknowledge that someone has done something appreciable
Attribute	– to give credit for something **Success was attributed to his efforts*
Assign	– Attribute something to someone
Impute	– attribute a bad motive to someone **Imputed motive to him for helping others*
62. Cringe	– to bow before someone in flattering
Cower	– to bow before someone in fear
Grovel	– to bow before someone mighty
Truckle	– to bow before someone in submission
Crouch	– to bow one's body
Stoop	– to bow one's head and shoulder and keep rest of the body erect
63. Criticise	– speak against someone unfavourably
Harangue	– criticise single forcefully or emotionally
Inveigh	– criticise with intense hostility
Vituperate	– criticise in disparaging manner
Objurgate	– denounce, upbraid someone harshly
64. Criticism	– act of criticising
Diatribe	– criticism in bitter language
Harangue	– criticism in emotional manner
Obloquy	– strong-worded criticism
Invective	– criticise abusively

Philippic	– bitter criticism
65. Cruel	– ruthless
Ferocious	– violently cruel
Savage	– furiously cruel
Barbarian	– lacking civility in behaviour
Inhuman	– lacking pity
Truculent	– fierce and brutal
66. Cry	– weep in loud voice
Keen	– cry in grief for dead person
Wail	– cry very loudly
Weep	– shed tears
67. Curse	– wish divine punishment for wrongdoing
Anathematise	– (religious head) pronounce curse for something anti-religious **Pope anathematised violence against humanity*
Imprecate	– curse by praying God to make someone suffer

D

1. Damage	– harm something **Damage machine* **Flood damaged the standing crops*
Impair	– harm someone's or something's natural ability to do something **Impaired hearing power of ears*
Hurt	– harm to cause physical injury
2. Danger	– possibility of happening something unwelcome, unpleasant or harmful **Going out in jungle is full of danger*
Risk	– something full of danger
Hazard	– chance of suffering unwelcome consequences. **Hazard of pollution*
Jeopardy	– even chance of suffering harm as a consequence **Working without safety gears can put you in jeopardy*
Peril	– chance of exposing someone to immediate harm as a consequence **Peril of war*
3. Dazzle	– shine brightly with intense light **Sun dazzles* **Dazzling gems*
Glitter	– shine with reflecting light impressively **Gold glitters.*

Coruscate	– shine with sudden flash of light
Sparkle	– shine with flashes of light as electric spark
Gleam	– shine with a brief flash of light
4. Dead body	– body of a dead person
Mortal remains	– deadbody of an important personage
Cadaver	– corpse of a dead person
Carcass	– deadbody of an animal
Carrion	– deadbody of an animal which is decaying
5. Deadlock	– a situation of no progress in talks or negotiations due to rigid attitude
Disruption	– disturbing condition in which no progress is possible
Hindrance	– condition of delay in progress
Interruption	– breaking continuity in progress
Obstruction	– disruption due to blocking the way of progress
6. Dearth	– absence of something desirable **There is a dearth of good politicians*
Lack	– unavailability of something needed **Lack of nutrition in children affects their timely growth.*
Scarcity	– unavailability of resources in sufficient amount **Scarcity of vegetables in the market causes price rise and inflation.*
7. Depris	– broken pieces of something demolished **Debris of demolished buildings*
Rubble	– broken pieces of stones, bricks etc.
Wreckage	– broken pieces of something damaged * *Wreckage of aeroplane damaged in an accident*
Flotsam	– wreckage of a ship floating on water
Lagan	– wreckage of a ship settled on the sea-bed
8. Deceive	– befool someone by making him accept false as true
Delude	– by making someone unable to see truth
Ditch	– by getting rid of someone, and leave him in the lurch
Beguile	– by tricking into doing something **Beguile someone to lend money*
Betray	– by aiding someone's enemy, or by becoming disloyal to him

9. Declare – let people officially or formally know something important **Declare examination results*

Announce – let people know by addressing publicly

Herald – let people know of something important to happen soon by indicating an event **Chill in the morning heralds arrival of winter*

Proclaim – let people know of official decision to be implemented **Proclaim curfew in the city*

10. Decorate – to beautify something not looking attractive **Decorate tent for the wedding ceremony*

Adorn – to beautify to add on the attractive-looking

Garnish – adorn a food dish before serving to diners

Embellish – make a speech more attractive by adding on juicy anecdotes

11. Decrepit – (a thing) in worn out condition **Decrepit chair/ house*

Dilapidated – in ruined state due to neglect **Dilapidated building*

Ramshackled – in a condition of severe disrepair

Rickety – in a condition of distorted shape **Rickety furniture*

12. Defalcate – steal money by removing a part of it under one's care, and falsely reconcile the account

Embezzle – remove a part of money kept under one's control

Misappropriate – to remove a part of fund for own use un authorisedly

13. Defame – spoil someone's good reputation by spreading lies

Slander – by false statement about him

Libel – by writing false accusations in newspapers

Calumniate – by speaking false things about him

Vilify – by speaking in scurrilous manner, or by name - calling

Asperse – by indirect accusation made against him

Malign – by speaking evil things about him

14. Defeat – to win victory over someone

Rout – to defeat by making enemy retreat or flee from the scene

Vanquish – to defeat enemy thoroughly

15. Defect – lacking in perfection **Defect in a machine*

Flaw – defect impairing soundness **Flaw in proposal*
Drawback – lacking in desirable features
Shortcoming – lacking in what is required
Deficiency – lacking in completeness **Deficiency in plan*
Fault – defect in character, system
Lacuna – defect due to a part missing; gap
Handicap – defect that restricts ability to function normally

16. Defector – one who changes his party to join another one
Apostate – one who changes his party or religion without harbouring ill will against it
Renegade – one who changes his party or faith/religion with rancour against it
Proselyte – one who is converted to another faith
Turncoat – one who changes party or faith for one's convenience or selfgain instead of any principle

17. Defile – make a place dirty
Desecrate – make a sarcd place dirty – spoiling its sacredness
Contaminate – make something dirty by allowing germs or harmful things mixed up
Soil – make dress dirty as with dirt, mud

18. Degenerate – to revert to poor condition **Moral degeneration of people*
Deteriorate – to become worse than the earlier condition
Depreciate – to decline in value **Prices of buildings have depreciated*
Impoverish – to decline in richness reducing to poor state **Lavish spending impoverished a rich man* **Cultivation on land leads to impoverished fertility*

19. Delicate – too fine to distinguish or detect **Delicate touch*
Subtle – too fine to realise or describe **Subtle distinction*
Subliminal – too delicate to be sufficient to be felt or to affect
Naunce – too delicate difference to make differentiation as in colours, words' meanings

20. Deliverance – setting someone free from guilt or sin
Salvation – setting someone free from mundane/temporal life

21. Delve – search something in a heap of it **Delve out the required book from a heap on the floor*

Forage – search usable things in heap of garbage **Pigs forage for eatables in the garbage*

Frisk – search the body of a person to find anything object-ionable on him by moving hands all over him

Grope – to search for something in dark by moving hands so as to feel for it

Rummage – search for something in haphazard manner by throwing things around **He rummaged contents of almirah for a document*

Scrabble – search something by blindly moving fingers or legs' toes all over a surface as if scratching it **A hill climber scrabbles slope with his toes to find a foothold on it *He scrabbled his pocket with his fingers to find out coins in it.*

22. Demise – to give, relinquish power, property to someone by will

Bequeath – to give property to someone by will

Defray – to give money to someone to meet specified expenses, *viz.*, college fees

Bestow – give gift, shower praise on someone

Confer – give title, degree, etc. to someone

Impart – to give special quality, characteristic to someone

Endow – give money as a regular source of income to someone

Endue – give someone power or position or rights **Endue voting rights on the non-resident Indians*

23. Demolish – to break a building down **The building was demolished*

Destroy – to ruin by damaging **Destroy public property*

Raze – to knock down an erected structure by hammering

Wreck – to break a ship, vehicle etc. down to ruin by damaging **Storm wrecked the building *Vehicle was wrecked in an accident*

24. Demonstrate – to show something by practical action **Effect of gravity was demonstrated by the teacher to students*

Show – to make something visible to others

Exhibit – show something interesting by displaying publicly **Exhibit works of art*

Evince	– to make something obvious by indirect indication **His lack of interest in studies is evinced by his truancy from school*
Flaunt	– to display something proudly or boastfully **He flaunted his costly pen to his friends*
Manifest	– to make something obvious to others **Talent manifests itself in a child at early age*
Display	– show something by placing in the open to be seen by all
Parade	– to show one's possession to others by demonstrating it **He paraded his knowledge*
25. Denounce	– declare something to be wrong by openly criticising it **Denounce negligence in public works*
Objurgate	– denounce in harsh language
Deplore	– express strong disapproval **Falling snorality is deplorable*
Deprecate	– express disagreement with something wrong
Decry	– denounce publicly
Assail	– denounce severely
Execrate	– denounce something for being loathsome
26. Deny	– refuse to accept truth or existence of something **Deny involvement in crime*
Decline	– refuse to accept politely **Decline someone's offer*
Disavow	– refuse to accept being responsible
Reject	– refuse to accept suggestion, advice and counselling
Repudiate	– refuse to accept, to own up something **Repudiate loan of the bank *Repudiate one's own son. *The insurance company has repudiated the claim of the policy-holder.*
Spurn	– reject with disdain **Spurn someone's offer of help*
27. Deplete	– (stock) become less due to consumption
Diminish	– become less in intensity, size
Decrease	– become less in number, value
Dwindle	– become less gradually in stock
Wane	– become less gradually in size
28. Deprive	– take away opportunity to do or to have something **He was deprived of taking part in competition*

Deny	– to refuse to give something which is due to someone **He was denied promotion*
Disenfranchise	– to take away the voting rights
29. Deride	– express contempt
Ridicule	– express contempt by laughing at someone
Lampoon	– to ridicule publicly
Scoff	– to deride scornfully
Sneer	– to deride laughingly/contemptuously
Pillory	– to ridicule by abusing
Mock	– to ridicule by making fun of someone
30. Descend	– to come down from a height **Descend from a hill *Plane descends on the airport*
Dive	– to jump down in water, or jump down headlong
Plummet	– to come down from a height by falling rapidly **Prices of commodities plummetted*
Plunge	– to come down uncontrllably
Swoop	– come down rapidly to catch a target below **Predator bird swooped to catch its prey*
31. Descendant	– one who has descended from the lineage of an ancestor **Descendant of a noble family*
Progeny	– offspring of a progenitor *i.e.,* parents
Posterity	– person of future generation **Heirloom of a family passes on to posterity*
32. Desire	– strong liking to have something **He expressed his desire to eat something*
Will	– inner desire in one's heart **He has a strong will to achieve what he wanted*
Wish	– strong desire to see something happen **His wish to see the country prosper came true *He prayed God to grant his wish*
Conation	– desire to achieve supreme objective in life **Salvation is everyone's conation*
Volition	– strong desire to do something on one's own choice or free will
33. Destroy	– damage to ruin something **Old civilizations were destroyed*
Annihilate	– destroy to the state of making non-existent **Bombing annihilated the city*

Devastate – to ruin completely by damaging as by large scale violence, colanity disaster **War devastated country's economy*

Ravage – to ruin extensively as by disease grief, worries **Flood ravaged the area as by dieare, grief, worries*

34. Determination – quality of remaining firm in pursuing goal

Resolve – act of determination with firmness in purpose

Grit – courageous determination

Mettle – determination with the ability to cope up with the diffculties

Tenacity – determination with no sign of laxity

35. Devalue – to lower the value of something

Debase – to lower the quality, character **Adulteration debases purity *Moral depravity debases a person*

Demean – to lower dignity **Demean someone's reputation*

Degrade – to lower rank, position

Abase – to lower dignity

Belittle – to lower someone's importance

36. Deviate – go off the course/path **Deviate from the right path and go elsewhere*

Digress – go off the main topic in writing or speech

Divagate – digress

Diverge – to go off the straight line by turning aside in a different direction **The road ahead diverges in different directions*

37. Devise – to prepare a plan, contrivance, etc. using skills

Contrive – to make something using tact, trick **Contrive a plan to befool someone*

Concoct – to make something by mixing ingredients **Concoct a slanderous lie to defame*

Fabricate – to make something by joining parts **Fabricate a machine*

Fashion – to make something by giving it shape using various materials with skill **Fashion a lamp with bamboo sticks*

Forge – to make something by the process of heating, casting or other things **Forge an alliance by talking to the allies*

38. Devour – to swallow hungrily

Gorge	– to swallow food greedily in large morsels
Gobble	– to swallow quickly
Raven	– to swallow voraciously as an animal
39. Difference	– dissimilarity between two which is visible **Difference in colours of two pens*
Distinction	– difference which can be perceived, analysed but not seen **Distinction in fragrance of flowers*
Discrepancy	– difference between contents of two statements or facts
Disparity	– difference between conditions of two things expected to be similar
40. Differences	– disagreements in opinions of two persons
Dispute	– disagreement over a matter of discussion **Dispute over wage revision*
Dissent	– differences over a decision made
Discord	– differences in harmonious relations
41. Dig out	– to take out something by digging the ground
Excavate	– to dig out to remove soil
Exhume	– to dig out a grave to take out a burried deadbody
Disinter	– to dig out something that had been kept burried **Disinter items of archaeological value*
42. Dilemma	– a situation in which it is difficult to take a dicision about what to do because of two equally undesirable alternatives
Plight	– a situation which puts a person in unfavourable, sorry state of affairs
Predicament	– an unpleasantly perplexing situation about what to do under the circumstances
Quandary	– state of uncertainty about what to do
43. Dilly-dally	– to avoid a job by delaying in doing it **Govt. is dilly-dallying over the decision in tackling price inflation*
Dawdle	– to avoid doing work by doing it slowly or lazily
Procrastinate	– to avoid doing a work by deliberately postponing to a later time causing inordinate delay.
44. Din	– prolonged unpleasant noise of talking or shouting **Din in classroom*
Murmur	– loud-pitched continuous noise
Hum	– low-pitched continuous noise

Drone – low-pitched continuous noise as produced by striking a musical instrument's strings

45. Dip – to put something under water or oil **Dip a wick in oil before lighting it. Dip the tea bag in the cup containing boiled water*

Dunk – to put an eatable in liquid' *viz.* milk, to make the eatable soft **Dunk bread in milk before eating*

Immerse – dip something in water so as to disappear **Idols are immersed in the river*

Inundate – dip something in excess of or large amount of **Houses were inundated in flood water *Letters of protests inundated the office*

Submerge – dip something under overflowing water **Low-lying areas were submerged in water*

46. Disaffection – (see Alienation)

47. Disagree – to have a different opinion from that of another person

Disapprove – to have unfavourable opinion about something

Differ – to have unlike opinion

Dissent – to have different opinion at an agreed or accepted decision

48. Disappear – cease to be visible

Vanish – disappear suddenly

Evanesce – disappear gradually, fade away

49. Disappointment – loss of hope

Dejection – loss of hope causing sadness

Despair – complete loss of hope

Despondence – loss of hope causing low spirit

50. Disaster – unfortunate event/destruction causing wides - pead damage

Apocalypse – unfortunate event causing great damage

Cataclysm – ....causing great upheaval

Catastrophe – ....causing great damage

Calamity – ....causing distress, misery

51. Disbelief – mental inclination of refusing to accept as true **Disbelief in rumours*

Unbelief – disbelief due to being not fit to be accepted as true

Distrust	– disbelief due to being not fit to be trusted
Mistrust	– refusal to trust someone
Incredibility	– inclination of refusing to accept as true because of the impossibility of being true, of being beyond belief
Cynicism	– inclination to refuse to accept selfless motive of anyone
52. Discard	– throw off what is useless **Discard the peels of banana*
Dispose of	– get rid of something
Jilt	– cast off the lover by breaking relationship * *The girl jilted her lover*
Moult/Molt	– cast off feathers, horns by birds/animals before new ones grow in place naturally
Shed	– cast off leaves (by trees) before new ones grow
Slough	– to cast off dead skin (by snakes) and take on new grown skin in that place
Jettison	– to cast off goods from ship to reduce load overboard to save it from sinking
53. Discharge	– set free from accusations, hospital etc.
Absolve	– set free from duty, responsibility
Acquit	– set free from charges by courts
Deliver	– set free from burden of something, guilt, etc. **Pray god to deliver from the nightmare of guilt*
Enlarge	– set free from captivity
Enfranchise	– set free from political subjugation to decide for oneself
54. Disclose	– make a concealed information, secret known
Divulge	– dislose official secrets
Betray	– disclose internal emotional feelings through expression **He took deep breath betraying his frustration*
Reveal	– disclose something by removing veil from it
55. Discourage	– dishearten someone from doing something **Insurmountable difficulties discouraged him from doing something desirable*
Dissuade	– persuade someone to desist from doing something due to being undesirable
Daunt	– to make one lose hope by putting dificulties in the way of something done by him

Deter	– discourage from doing something by threatening with consequences
56. Disgorge	– expel from mouth something eaten
Eructate	– (volcano) expelling lava
Regurgitate	– expel ingested food back into mouth (by birds, animals) for feeding fledglings, or for chewing again (cows).
Reek	– expel billowing smokes from chimney
Ooze	– expel pus, fluid from a wound
Vomit	– expel ingested food out due to nausea
57. Disguise	– alter appearance to conceal identity **Disguised himself as a woman to escape from a place*
Impersonate	– alter identity by assuming name of another person in order to cheat someone **A thug impersonated as an income tax officer to take bribe from a business man*
Masquerade	– to alter identity by pretending to be someone else **Rich man masqueraded as a beggar*
58. Disintegrate	– to break up into small parts
Shatter	– to break up into broken fragments
Fragment	– to break up into a small piece from a large whole of something
Split	– to break up into pieces by cracking under impact
59. Disobedient	– who habitually disobeys
Contrary	– who is too self-willed to obey
Recusant	– who refuses to obey orders
Froward	– insolently disobedient
Refractory	– who openly defies command
60. Disobey	– refuse to obey
Defy	– openly refuse to obey
Rebel	– refuse to obey by challenging authority of command
Revolt	– refuse to obey by violent defiance
Baulk	– (horse) refuse to obey rider's command to go ahead
Jib	– refuse to obey by showing reluctance to obey
61. Disorderly	– without being in order or arranged manner **Books are kept in the shelf in a disorderly manner*

Dishevelled	– in disorderly appearance (hairs, dress etc.)
Untidy	– in scattered manner **Untidy room*
Unkempt	– (hairs) scattered, without combed
Ruffled	– (feathers) scattered, unpreened
62. Disperse	– (mob) spread away in different directions from a place
Diffuse	– (gas, scent etc.) spread away over a large space by passing through air **Foul smell diffused in a short time*
Dissipate	– to scatter wastefully in different forms **Youth's energy dissipates in meaningless activities.*
63. Dissatisfied	– not satisfied–causing displeasure **I am dissatisfied with his performance*
Unsatisfied	– not fully satisfied–wanting more, being inadequate **Unsatisfactory performance*
Discontented	– not contented – failing to feel fulfilment in heart, or to quench the desire
Disgruntled	– not satisfied – causing resentment
64. Dissociate	– break off association with someone
Secede	– break off from a group by withdrawing from it **Secede from an organization/alliance *Rebel state seceded from the country and declared independence*
Separate	– break off by stopping staying together **Couple separated due to differences*A hall was separated from the adjoining room*
65. Distress	– extreme mental/physical suffering due to being in dangerous situation
Dismay	– extreme mental suffering due to being disheartened **I was dismayed at his behaviour*
Anxiety	– mental suffering due to worries
66. Dodge	– to evade attack by stepping aside from the line of attack **Dodge a blow/missile*
Duck	– to evade attack by sitting, bending down
Parry	– to evade verbal attack by making counter attack
Stave off/Ward off	– to evade attack by deflecting missile aside
67. Domain	– area under rule of a ruler **Law & order comes under the domain of the state government*

Bailiwick – area under the control of a person **Everyone is the master of his house, which is his bailiwick *Regional parties are personal bailiwick of local satrap*

Jurisdiction – area under the legal authority

Ken – area of knowledge of an individual **Science is beyond my ken *His idea is beyond my ken*

Province – area of one's competence, authority *Mathematics is not my province **This decision is beyond my province*

Realm – area under the influence of supreme authority of a sovereign power **Realm of the nature is replete with wonders*

68. Dominance – commanding influence on someone

Hegemony – dominance of a country over another one

Clout – influence due to the power to control others

Influence – the effect of one's states, position, wealth over other

Sway – control over others' opinions

69. Dominate – exercise commanding influence over others

Domineer – exercise command in an overbearing manner arbitrarily

Prevail – dominate by imposing one's will, opinion on others

70. Dormant – lying inactive with possibility to become active anytime **Dormant volcano *A dormant disease*

Latent – of hidden activity which is not manifested **Talent in a child is latent In early age*

Hibernating – remaining inactive, almost lifeless in winter **Hibernating toad remains burried in mud during winter (said about cold-blooded insects)*

Aestivating – remain inactive during summer

71. Dregs – worthless remanents left at the bottom of a liquid *e.g.*, in a tea cup

Scum – worthless matters which cover upper layer of a liquid

Lees – sediments left at bottom of a barrel containing wine

72. Dress – clothes which are used to wear

Costume – dress appropriate to the role of an actor in a drama

Garment – clothings of several kinds prepared for sale **Garment factory*

Garb	– clothing for distinct identity **Garb of a priest*
Habiliment	– clothes suitable to a person's work **Habiliment of a crusader*
Regalia	– dress with attached decorative medals **He is dressed up in his regalia*
Robe	– dress suitable to a profession **Lawyers' robe*
Trousseau	– dress of bride to be worn in wedding
Weeds	– dress to be worn by mourners/widows
73. Dribble	– (saliva) run down from mouth
Drool	– (saliva) run down excessively from mouth
Drivel	– (saliva) run down from nose, mouth
Salivate	– (saliva) fill the mouth in anticipation of tasty food
74. Drink	– to swallow liquid
Sip	– drink slowly in small amount at a time
Guzzle	– drink greedily in large amount
Quaff	– drink heartily
Gulp	– drink with making sound of swallowing
75. Droop	– to hang down as from weariness
Wilt	– (plant leaves) hang down limpily due to loss of moisture
Lop	– hang down limpily as of ears of rabbits due to absence of stiffness
76. Drown	– to go under water and die due to suffocation **A boy drowned in river*
Sink	– to go under water and settle on the water bed *Ship sank in the river
77. Dull	– not stimulating, inspiring interest because of being routine work **Discussion in the meeting was a dull affair*
Dreary	– charmless and depressive **Dreary life of a poor person*
Humdrum	– dull because monotonous without change **Humdrum daily household chores*
Lackadaisical	– dull because of lacking enthusiasm
Lacklustre	– lacking vividness, vitality
Monotonous	– lacking variety
Pedestrian	– lacking quality of work–being quite general, usual **Pedestrial movie*

78. **Dwarf**	– abnormally small person than usual
Midget	– extremely small person
Pigmy	– human race of small stature

E

1. **Eager**	– strongly want to do or have something **He is eager to meet his family*
Agog	– strongly eager to know about something **We are agog with the election results*
Curious	– very eager to know something unusual or interesting **Curious to know about strange things*
Inquisitive	– very eager to know by enquiring about **Inquisitive about*
Keen	– very eager to know about something
2. **Effect**	– change brought about by something accomplished **Exposure to the sun has a bad effect on the skin*
Result	– final outcome brought about by something accom plished
Consequence	– the outcome which happens as a sequence to something accomplished
Implication	– result of some action which is inherent in the action **War has a very serious implication for the belligerent countries*
3. **Effective**	– capable of showing its effect as desired or expected **The new law is very effective in curbing lawlessness*
Effectual	– capable of achieving desired purpose **Immunization programme proved effectual in eradicating polio*
Efficacious	– capable of showing desired results **Efficacious remedy for curing tuberculosis is now available* **Efficacious solution is needed to tide over problems assuming dimensions*
4. **Effigy**	– a crudely made figure of a disliked person for ridiculing him, or for showing contempt **An effigy of the chief minister was burnt in public place by the protestors*
Mannequin	– a human figure which is erected in a shop to exhibit dresses by putting on this figure

Marionette – a figure of man, woman or animal which is attached to strings in order to manipulate it to move like a living one in an enterainment show

Puppet – a figure of man or animal which is manipulated by someone with his hand inserted into its cavity for an entertainment show

Doll – a figure of pretty girl made for a kid to play with

Toy – a figure of an animal or object made for a kid to play with *A toy dog*

Scarecrow – a terrifying object's figure clothed in tattered dress erected on cultivated land to frighten birds away to protect crops from being eaten by birds

5. Egregious – (Something) extraordinarily (ex = out, gregare = flock) bad or offending which stands it alone out of others of its kind **Egregious behaviour/liar/ mistake*

Blatant – (Something) offensively bad which hurts someone seeing or hearing it **Blatant behaviour error/noise/ coloured dress*

Flagrant – outrageously bad, which hurts someone who sees it **A flagrant crime*

Wanton – maliciously, unjustifiably bad **Wanton attack/ cruelty*

6. Elevate – to take something up in vertical height *Elevate the height of a wall *Elevate rank, standard

Raise – to make something stand erect in vertical position **Raise a pole *Raise one's hand*

Rear – to raise oneself or one's part of body **The horse reared its head*

Hoist – to lift something heavy with the help of machine **Crane hoisted cargo on to a ship*

Heave – to lift something by pushing it Supward from under its bottom **He heaved his chest by drawing air in his lungs *Waves heaved the boat up during storm in the sea*

Boost – to lift the value, morale, etc. of someone **Boost spirit/sales of products*

Enhance – to raise to a higher degree, intensity etc. **Enhance the beauty, value*

Lift – to take something upward from the ground **He lifted his luggage on to his shoulder*

7. Eject – throw forth something with a force **Pilot ejected himself from the plane before it crashed*

Ejaculate – throw forth in stream of fluid **Snake ejaculates venom into victim's body*

Spout – throw forth a fluid through a narrow opening of something in a stream of jet of liquid **He swilled his mouth with water and spouted it out of the opening of lips*

Spurt – to throw forth a fluid in a sudden gushing stream

8. Elicit – to draw out information from someone using tact **Elicit a response from someone *Elicit facts from a boy*

Educe – to draw out something latent within someone **Educe talent in a kid *He educed a reply from his memory*

Evoke – to draw out *e.g,* soul of a dead person from grave **Evoke demon lying within someone *Evoke sympathy in someone*

9. Elongate – to draw out something to increase its length **A metal piece was elongated into wire*

Lengthen – grow into length **His body has lengthened with age*

Prolong – to increase the time of, duration of something to longer duration **His stay was prolonged *His illness prolonged*

Protract – to draw out something to increased length (Pro = forward, Tract = stretch) **The bird protracted its wings before starting to fly*

10. Embrace – to draw someone close to one's chest within arms as a sign of affection **He embraced his old friend when they met*

Hug – hold someone tightly in one's arms **A bear hugged his trainer*

11. Emit – to give out light, sound, etc. from within **Fluorescent tube emits bright light*

Emanate – to come out from a source, give out as a source **Flowers emanate fragrance *His face emanates happiness*

Discharge – to send forth liquid or gas from storage **Water was discharged from a dam*

Exude – to send forth smell, confidence etc. by its source **He exudes confidence *Rotten vegetation exudes bad smell*

Transude – to send forth sweat through pores of skin, or moisture through pores of tree leaves **Skin transudes sweat*

Belch – (stomach) send forth ingested air through mouth with a loud sound **He belched loudly after taking food *He belched gas accumulated in his stomach*

Fart – to send forth/expel accumulated gas inside the intestine through the anus.

12. Emphasize – to lay importance to something significant **Emphasize on the importance of ethics in behaviour*

Accentuate – lay stress on a part of syllable of a word while pro -nouncing

Stress – lay importance on a point of argument, opinion, etc. **Stress upon the need of curbing corruption*

13. Emulate – to copy or try to copy someone's achievements **The son emulated his father in doing social service*

Ape – copy mechanically actions of someone as a monkey does

Imitate – to copy the work of art which exactly resembles original

Replicate – reproduce what has been done by someone else

Mimic – to copy the voice of someone else in order to befool, or to deride him

Mime – to copy the gesture of someone else without speaking as an entertainment

Simulate – to copy by producing similar conditions for study or experiment under the same situation as required **Simulate scenery in studio for the shooting of a film*

14. Encounter – sudden confrontation with hostile persons **Criminals were killed in encounter with police*

Confrontation – face-to-face coming in front of a problem, difficult situation **He successfully handled several confron tations with problems*

Rencontre – suddenly meet old friend face-to-face after a long time

15. Encroach – violate other's territory **The outer wall of his compound has encroached into my land adjoining his land *This law encroaches people's rights*

Infringe – violate law, rules, normal behaviour **His acts infringe upon the rules of etiquette *Infringe a business contract*

Outrage – violate someone's modesty, dignity, causing hurt feelings **Wanton acts of ruffians outraged public*

Transgress – violate by crossing over limits of one's authority, moral codes etc. **The official was accused of transgressing his authority*

Trespass – to enter into someone's house without authority **The dog jumped on the person who txespassed into his master's house*

16. Enshrine – give something a place of sacredness as an idol of worship is given in a shrine **Memory of my friend is enshrined in my heart *Right of freedom of speech is enshrined in our constitution*

Sanctify – give a place of reverence by appropriate religious rituals

Consecrate – give a place of sacredness

17. Ensnare – to catch in a snare, a trap * *The bird was ensnared in a net*

Implicate – to make someone involved in an undesirable situation **Implicate someone in an act of crime*

Entangle – to make someone enmeshed in something **The cow entangled its horns in a bush*

Entwine – to make slender thread-like things twisted together– making them unable to get separated **Locks of her hairs entwined together*

Entrap – to take someone in a trap

18. Enter – get inside something **Enter a house*

Ingress – to walk into a place **Flood water ingressed into the low-lying areas*

Intrude – to enter a place forcibly **Intrude upon others' privacy *Mob intruded into his office*

Invade – to enter others' territory with the intent to cause harm **The enemy forces invaded the* neighbouring country *Pathogens invade our body to make us ill*

Trespass – enter others' or territory property unlawfully without permission **Trespassing the prohibited area is a crime*

Infiltrate – enter into another group, area, territory and get mixed up with people there with the intent to cause harm, violence **The enemy spy infiltrates the sensitive area or protected establishments to collect information*

19. Entertain – to extend hospitality with amusements **He entertained his friends with juicy anecdotes*

Regale – to extend hospitality with choice food and drink

Treat – to extend hospitality with the intent to make the guests pleased **The visiting dignitaries were given a treat in lavish surroundings of the hill town*

20. Enthusiasm – absorbing interest in some pursuit **He evinced great enthusiasm for his studies*

Ardour – burning enthusiasm **Ardour of patriotism*

Fervour – great warmth and earnestness in enthusiasm or other feelings **Fervour of a religious devout in performing rites*

Zeal – enthusiasm for a lofty objective **Zeal of a missionary*

Passion – uncontrollable enthusiasm **Passion for reading books*

21. Entice – to mislead someone by promising exciting offer **He was enticed by the lure of big city life *Discount offered on sales is a ploy to entice customers*

Beguile – to mislead by employing tricks **Multitude of attractions beguiles the tourists *A ghost beguiles its prey to a lonely place by mimicking his friend's voice*

Inveigle – to mislead by persuasion or flattery **He inveigled me into giving loan to him*

Seduce – to mislead into committing itticit activity, or away from right path. **Seduce to indulge in corruption*

Suborn – to mislead someone by inducement to commit perjury

22. Ephemeral – lasting for just one day, *i.e.*, for a very short time **Ephemeral joy of childhood *Ephemeral flowers*

Evanescent – lasting for short duration before vanishing **Evanescent apparition of ghosts*

Fleeting – (time) passing off quickly **Fleeting moments of holidays*

Transitory – (mood, anger, etc.) lasting for a shortwhile **Transitory anger turned into compassion*

Transient – (guest) staying for a brief period **Transient hotel guests*

23. Epithet – a name given by people which is attributed to his habit, quality in a well known personality **He is famous by the epithet of Mr. Joker*

Appellation – a name given to someone by people which is based on his appealing manners/work **Gandhiji earned appellation of Mahatma*

Sobriquet – a name given to someone by people on the basis of his achievements **Bose was known as the sobriquet of Netaji*

Nickname – a name by which someone is lovingly called

24. Equality – state of being equal in magnitude rank with others **Gender equality*

Equivalence – state of being equal in value with something else **Equivalence in various currencies*

Parity – state of being equal in status **Parity in post, power, or pay with those in other services*

Resemblance – state of being equal in appearance

Analogy – state of being equal in comparison with something else **Analogy between heart and pump*

Commensuration – state of being equal in measure

25. Eradicate – root out (radi = root) something that has taken root **Eradicate malaria/superstitions*

Exterminate – (ex = out, terminate = end) end, finish something by killing **Exterminate mosquitoes by fumigation*

Extirpate – finish something by depriving its source of sustenance to exist **Deforestation extirpates wild species of flora and fauna*

26. Erect – become straight and rigid in shape **Dog's ears become erect when it is alerted*

Upright – become erect in vertical direction **He is sitting upright*

Bristled	– (hairs) become erect as in fear, excitement **His hairs bristled with excitement* **Bristled hairs of pigs are used for making brush*
27. Essential	– what is required as the very essence of something **Breathing is essential for living* **Discipline is essential for the armed forces*
Necessary	– what is required to meet the needs of something **Attending meeting is necessary* **A new law is necessary to check terrorism*
Compulsory	– what is required as compulsion **Compulsory qualification for a job*
Indispensable	– what is required as one cannot do without it **His services are indispensable to his organization* **Courage is indispensable to face challenges*
Reqisite	– what is required to meet a given situation good physique is a requisite to join the army
28. Ethics	– standards of priciples adopted in one's profession **He observes the highest norms of ethics*
Morals	– standards of principles adopted in one's character **A man of loose morals*
Morality	– standards of principles adopted by someone in his or her social conduct **His conduct is against social morality*
29. Examine	– to test knowledge, facts by question
Check	– to verify facts
Investigate	– to verify the facts, cause of an occurrence **Investigate a crime*
Inspect	– to look into something to check carefully
Audit	– inspect accounts
Scrutinize	– to check details of a problem through close observations
Vet	– to scrutinize a document, manuscript, proposal, etc. for its quality, usefulness
30. Example	– which serves as a lesson to others **Severe punishment serves as an example to prospective offenders*
Instance	– which serves as an example to show the character or intention of someone **Tough punishment awarded by the courts is an instance of judiciary's intolerance to crimes*

Paradigm – which serves as an example of a pattern in some thing **Changing allegiance for personal gains is contemporary paradigm in politics*

Precedent – (rules, judgements) which serves as an example in similar cases to follow suit **Earlier judgements serve as precedents for judging subsequent cases of similar nature*

31. Exclusive – excluding others **Exclusive school for the rich people*

Exquisite – excluding others in a group of similar things **Exquisite beauty/art*

Exotic – excluding locals – belonging to foreign origin **Exotic dress/design*

32. Exhausted – drained of energy due to excessive work **Heavy work exhausted him *Exhausted due to excessive work in office*

Fatigued – tired due to long duration of working hard **Fatigued of long drive*

Haggard – having an exhausted appearance as with prolonged tiredness, anxiety etc. **A haggard face/ eyes*

Languid – drained of vigour due to fatigue, weakness **Languid gait*

Weary – tired excessively of hard work

33. Explain – to describe in detail

Expatiate – explain at length **Expatiate on one's theme/idea*

Elucidate – to explain so as to make lucid (clear), especially with illustrations

Expound – explain something in a learned manner **Expound the secrets of the universe*

34. Exquisite – impressive in quality **Exquisite art*

Elegant – impressive in grandeur **Elegant mansion/ decolouration*

Dainty – impressive in taste, beauty **Dainty woman*

35. Extempore – (do something) on the spur of moment **Reply to questions extempore*

Extemporaneous – (do something) without preparing oneself **Extemporaneous lecture*

Impromptu – (do something) promptly **He made an impromptu speech in response to the audience's request*

Instantly	– (do something) at once **Give relief instantly*
36. Extenuate	– to make seriousness of a crime, fault less serious/ light **Extenuate seriousness of his crime*
Mitigate	– to make seriousness of something light **Mitigate punishment*
Palliate	– to make seriousness light by concealing facts of crime
Gloze/Gloss (over)	– make light of a seriousness by extending excuses
37. Extinguish	– put out fire
Douse	– put out fire by throwing water on it
Quench	– put out thirst
Quell	– put out rebellion
Quail	– put out enthusiasm, courage, spirit **Failures quailed his enthusiasm*
Snuff	– put out light **He snuffed out the candle's flame*
38. Extraordinary	– unusually extra or good **Extraordinary power/ talent*
Phenomenal	– remarkably outstanding **Phenomenal performance*
Prodigious	– outstanding in size, degree, extent **A prodigious worker*
Outstanding	– exceptional, making something different from others, above others **Outstanding performance*
39. Extravagant	– spending much more unnecessarily
Spendthrift	– wastefully extravagant
Prodigal	– recklessly extravagant
Wastred	– a person who spends wastefully

F

1. Face	– a person's frontal part of head
Muzzle	– an animal's projected part of head consisting of jaws, nose, eyes, etc., *e.g.*, of a cow, horse
Countenance	– a person's face with a specified emotional expression on it **A sad countenance of a person*
Facade	– frontal part of a building **Castle's magnificent facade*
Mien	– face indicative of a specified demeanour **Mien of an aristocrat*

Physiognomy – face with specified features indicative of person's race *A man of mongoloid physiognomy

Visage – a person's face with reference to specified shape *He has a round visage/wide visage*

Facet – one of several faces of a polygonal shape

2. Facetious – (remark) lacking serious intent *Facetious remark*

Flippant – (remark) lacking in gravity of attitude **Flippant remark about patriotism*

Frivolous – lacking in seriousness of purpose, worth or importance **Frivolous conduct/suggestion. His case has been rejected by the court as frivolous.*

Triffling – (manners) playfully non-serious **Triffling manner of dealing with a serious matter*

3. Failure – not succeeding in doing something

Futility – not succeeding in producing useful outcome

Debacle – not succeeding in attempt due to sudden collapse **Our team suffered a debacle in the tournament*

Miscarriage – not succeeding in delivering as expected **Punishment to an innocent is a serious miscarriage of justice system*

4. Fake – (something made) which is not genuine, and is prepared for fraudulent purpose **A fake report/ signature*

Counterfeit – (something) imitated to look alike genuine one for fraudulent purpose **Counterfeit currency*

Ersatz – (something) which is made or imitated to serve as a substitute for the real one **Ersatz ornaments*

Sham – (something) which Is not as it is purported to be **A sham sympathy/illness*

Spurious – (something) which is not genuine **Spurious automobile bearings have been seized by the authorities*

5. Falter – become unsteady in speaking or doing something due to losing control **He faltered in speech *The old man faltered on the stairs*

Flounder – become unsteady in walking as when passing through sticky mud or pool of water **He floundered while crossing a muddy field*

Fumble	– become unsteady in using one's hands so as to catch a ball **The fielder fumbled and dropped the ball*
Stagger	– become usteady in walking as if about to fall due to weak ness or stumbling on a rough surface **He staggered when someone pushed him from behind*
6. Famous	– widely known for good virtues or possessions **This town is famous for its forts *He is famous for his bravery*
Renowned	– widely known by one's name **He is a renowned person in this town*
Popular	– widely admired by people **He is a popular leader*
Reputed	– widely respected for having good reputation as a person **A reputed person in the society*
Eminent	– widely known for superiority in a particular field **An eminent scientist*
7. Fanciful	– beyond practicality **Fanciful ideas*
Fantastic	– extravagantly fanciful **Fantastic story/idea*
Chimerical	– absurdly impractical **Chimerical idea*
Quixotic	– beyond realisation, too ideal to be realised **Quixotic ideas*
8. Fare	– money chargeable for travelling by public transport **Train fare*
Freight	– money chargeable for transporting goods by public transport **Goods' transportation freight*
Rent	– money chargeable from tenant for house given to him to live in/from users of machinery, materials by the owner
Tariff	– listed amount of money payable for various types of hotel rooms
Charge	– money payable for hiring services **Charge of hiring a taxi *Charge of a hired carpenter*
Fee	– money payable by school, doctor, lawyer for rendering services to the beneficiaries
9. Fastidious	– (someone) very critical of imperfection in work, cleanliness, taste etc.
Fussy	– critical of minor details about work
Finnicky	– excessively fastidious

Supercilious	– habitually critical of others by raising one's eyebrows while frowning
10. Fatal	– causing death **Fatal accident*
Lethal	– liable to cause death **Lethal dose of poison* **Lethal weapons*
Deadly	– liable to kill **Deadly disease*
11. Fear	– nervous feeling of threat, danger
Awe	– nervous feeling of fear from the greatness of a person **Awe of God/learned person*
Dread	– intense feeling of fear by anticipating danger **Dread of death shook him*
Fright	– intense feeling of sudden fear **Fright of encountering a ferrocious dog*
Horror	– intense feeling of fear caused by a shocking, gruesome sight **Horror of seeing a corpse*
12. Fertile	– (land) producing abundantly
Fecund	– (woman) producing offsprings abundantly
Prolific	– (writer, free) abundantly producing books/fruits
13. Fight	– engaged in physical asaults or angry arguments **They fought over a point of discussion*
Scuffle	– engaged in pushing and jostling
Fisticuff	– engaged in trading blows with fist
Financial	– money matters of a company institution **Financial management of a company is in shambles*
Fiscal	– of government treasury **Fiscal dficit*
Pecunary	– money matters of a person **Pecuniary condition of a person*
14. Fit	– violent, uncontrollable bout of anger, epilepsy **He flew in a fit of anger.*
Attack	– violent fit of pain, melancholy etc. **Attack of pain in the stomach.*
Paroxysm	– uncontrolled bout of coughing, laughing etc. **He turned blue due to prolonged paroxysm of coughing*
Convulsion	– uncontrolled bout of involuntary spasm in body
15. Flag	– a piece of cloth which is the symbol of a country **Flag of India is a tricolour*

Colours	– a flag which is the identity of a regiment **Regimental colours*
Standard	– flag representing a sovereign power **Presidential standard*
Pennant	– long, tapered triangular-shaped flag
Banner	– flag with slogans written on it, which is carried by the demonstrators
16. Flatter	– to please someone by showering praises on him **Sycophants flatter someone for personal gains*
Fawn	– to please someone with servile demeanours towards him **Courtiers fawn on the king *His dog fawns on his master's feet in a display of affection*
17. Flexuous	– bending in alternating turns **Flexuous river*
Meandering	– bending in irregular turns **Meandering water stream*
Sinuous	– bending in frequent turns at short distances
Tortuous	– bending several times in large number of turns
Winding	– bending in turns like a coil **Winding mountain roads*
18. Flinch	– to shake one's body/to shake off what give uncomfor -table feelings **Flinch at gory right*
Wince	– to shake one's body due to being in pain or disgust **His body winced in pain*
Blench	– to shiver at the fearful thought **Blenched at the very thought of death*
Quail	– shiver/shake one's body under the threat of someone as a mark of losing courage to face him **Students quail in front of the headmaster*
19. Follower	– a person who is loyal to and always follows someone **Followers of a political leader*
Cohort	– a group of followers **She has a cohort of admirers*
Henchman	– a trusted follower of a gangster who is eveready to commit crime at his (gangster's) bidding
20. Folly	– foolish weakness in character **To act before giving a thought is his folly*
Foible	– pleasant weakness in habit **Speaking inncocent truth is kids's foible*
Fraility	– weakness in character **Yielding to temptation is our major fraility*

21. Forbid – warn someone not to be something **Workers were forbidden to leave workplace*

Inhibit – to forbid by one's inner conscience or sense of propriety **Fear of contracting cancer inhibits him from smoking*

Prohibit – to forbid by authority *Smoking in public places is prohibited

Proscribe – to announce a warning against doing something **Doctor prescribed his patient not to take fatty foods*

22. Foresight – ability to judge things to happen in distant future

Clairvoyance – ability to see or perceive events in a distant place which is beyond the range of normal vision

Vision – ablity to think or plan with imagination or wisdom about future course of action **Vision of an entrepreneur*

23. Foretell – to announce something to happening in future

Forecast – to announce weather conditions obtaining in future **Forecast rains/storm*

Augur – to foretell outcome of an omen **Sighting an owl is supposed to augur well*

Portend – foretell something bad to happen in future **Portend a disaster*

Predict – foretell future events **Predict a war to take place*

Prophesy – foretell supernatural events happening in future which requires knowledge of an oracle/ saint **Prophesy doom of this world*

Prognosticate – (doctors) foretell about the onset of a disease in near future on the basis of symptoms in a patient

24. Foster – to bring up a child who is deprived of parents **Foster a child who lost his parents*

Cherish – to take loving care of a child **Cherish one's child*

Nurture – to take care of a growing child by providing nourishment, encouragement to promote his growth and development **Nurture poor children*

Rear – to take care of a growing animal until attaining maturity for meat, milk, fur etc. **Rear farm animals for meat*

25. Free – having the ability to do what one likes to **He is free to go wherever he wants to*

Independent	– being free from others' command to manage own affairs, free from other's control **Autonomous organization is free from govt. control*
Autarky	– freedom from economic dependence
Sovereign	– having supreme authority in one's own domain **Parliament is sovereign in democracy*
26. Friend	– a person with good comradeship
Chum	– a close childhood friend
Crony	– an intimate friend
Alterego	– a close friend who is one soul, two bodies
27. Frighten	– to fill someone with fright **Encounter with a snake frightened him*
Terrify	– to fill someone with terror
Threaten	– to warn of consequences
Horrify	– to fill someone with horror **Ghastly scene of the accident horrified him*
Scare	– to fill someone with nervousness due to fear
Panic	– to fill someone with nervous agitation due to fear **Bomb scare panicked people, who began to flee from the place*
Intimidate	– to fill someone with fear by threatening to make him timid (coward)
Rattle	– to fill someone with worries due to fear **A bad news rattled him*

G

1. Garbage	– unwanted disposable matters from kitchen and household
Rubbish	– unwanted disposable matters thrown as useless
Litter	– scattered rubbish **His room was filled with waste-paper litter*
Trash	– unusable portion of something after the removal of its usable portion **Sugarcane trash after extraction of juice*
Refuse	– something discarded as worthless **Refuse of vegetables*
Sullage	– mud, silt, sediments collected in sewage
2. Gaze	– to look at something fixedly for long **Gaze the stars in the night sky*

Glance	– to look for a brief period to catch a glimpse of **He glanced at a girl furtively*
Glare	– to look in anger with wide eyes
Peer	– to look with partly-closed eyes **He peered at me in an attempt to recognize me*
Stare	– to look with wide-open eyes
Gape	– to stare with one's mouth open in disbelief, wonder
3. Genocide	– deliberate masskilling of people of a particular race
Carnage	– mass-killing of people in a battle
Butchery	– mass-killing of people or animals with wanton brutality
Massacre	– mass-killing of people indiscriminately in revenge
Pogrom	– planned massacre
Get	– to possess **Get hold of*
Obtain	– get by putting in efforts
Acquire	– get by putting in prolonged efforts
Procure	– get by caring to search
4. Get rid of	– be relieved of someone/something unwanted **Get rid of his presence with me*
Dispense with	– make oneself relieved of compulsion of having to do with something undesirable **Facility of an A.T.M. has enabled us to dispense with carrying cash*
Dispose of	– be relieved of liability of, or unwanted possession **He disposed of his old house*
5. Gorge	– overfeed oneself to the extent of chocking **He gorged himself with chocolates*
Satiate/Sate	– overfeed oneself to one's satisfaction and desiring no more
Surfeit	– overfeed oneself until felt nausea or aversion to taking anymore **He surfeited himself with sweets*
6. Gradation	– gradual/graded difference in quality
Shade	– graded & delicate/minute difference in colours, opinions etc. **There is a shade difference in meanings of synonyms *It is a shade better than others*
Nuance	– very delicate/minute subtle difference in colours, meanings etc. **Nuance of expressions changed on his face*

7. **Grind**	– to break into powdery mass
Comminute	– to break into minute particles
Levigate	– to grind in a mortar
Pulverise	– to grind to fine powdery mass
Triturate	– to grind to powdery mass by crushing or thresshing
8. **Growl**	– (animal's) produce deep guttural sound of expressing anger **The dog growled at the intruder in the house*
Snarl	– (dog's) produce loud threatening sound aggressively with exposed teeth, as if it would jump on the victim **Dog snarled viciously*
Purr	– to produce low continuous sound as a cat does
Grumble	– (person's) produce low sound of voice of expressing discontent
9. **Guess**	– to conclude on basis of incomplete knowledge
Conjecture	– to conclude on basis of insufficient information
Surmise	– to conclude without any information/knowledge
Speculate	– to make wild guess at the risk of being wrong
10. **Guide**	– who leads tourists around a place/who shows the right path to others
Pioneer	– who explores path for others to move ahead in a field of knowledge. **A pioneer in cancer research*
Trailblazer	– who shows path to others in a new field of knowledge **A trailblazer scientist*
Usher	– who shows people their seats in a hall to sit on by escorting them to that place

H

1. **Harass**	– annoy someone by constant provocation
Bother	– to annoy by constantly disturbing
Badger	– to annoy, harass persistently by ragging
Harry	– to harass by attacking repeatedly **To harry the enemy forces by repeated incursions*
Persecute	– to harass by hostile activity
Tantalise	– to harass by not allowing someone to get something present within reach
Torment	– harass by teasing **Reporters tormented him with uncomfortable questions*

2. Hasty	– (action) done in a haste – without consideration **Hasty action/decision*
Impatient	– (person) lacking patience due to eagerness for something **He is impatient to hear the news*
Impetuous	– (person, action) done quickly and rashly **Impetuous decision/person*
Rash	– without waiting for thinking about **Rash action*
Impulsive	– (action, person) involving emotional action taken in involuntary impulse **Impulsive action*
3. Healthful	– which promotes health **Healthful diet*
Hygienic	– which promotes health through cleanliness **Hygienic surroundings/habits*
Sanitary	– which promotes health through preventing infections **Sanitary precautions*
Salubrious	– which promotes health through healthy climate **Salubrious climate*
Wholesome	– which promotes health by giving helpful effects on health **Wholesome food *Wholesome exercises*
Salutary	– which promotes moral health **Salutary advice *Salutary punishment reforms an erring behaviour*
4. Herd	– a group of animals moving together
Flock	– a group of birds moving together
Drove	– a group of animals being driven together
Gaggle	– a group of geese
Bevy	– a group of young girls/women
Clutch	– a group of young chicks
Brood	– a group of newly hatched fowls
Hirsel	– a group of sheep/lambs
Litter	– a group of newly born mammals
Rabble	– a group of rats/insects
Rout	– a group of revellers
Shoal	– a group of fishes moving together
Swarm	– a group of bees
5. Hesitate	– be reluctant to do something due to indecisive mind
Balk/Baulk	– ....due to facing difficulties/obstacle **He balked at making a speech*

Demur – ....due to having doubt/objection *Students demurred at accepting new syllabus*

Dither – ....due to fear of consequences

Jib – ....due to unwillingness

Qualm – ....due to anxiety of doing wrong or feeling guilty **He has no qualm about lying*

Scruple – ....due to feeling uneasy about being unethical on moral grounds

6. Hide – to keep off others, sight, knowledge **He is hiding himself behind a bush*

Conceal – to keep off from others' knowledge **Conceal truth*

Cache' – to keep something secured in a hidden place **The thief cache'd booty in a lonely place*

Camouflage – to hide something by covering with paints or materials matching with the surroundings **Tanks were camouflaged with tree twigs*

Disguise – to conceal identity by altering appearance **The king disguised himself as peasant to walk on the streets*

Dissemble – to concel one's emotions/true intentions by behaving otherwise/feigning differently **He dissembled innocence*

Enscone – to hide something in safe, comfortable place **He ensconced himself in a closet *He ensconced himself in the armchair*

Mask – hide one's face by covering with a mask

Secrete – hide in a safe place **Rats secreted grains in burrow*

Veneer – to cover/hide an ugly or coarse surface by furniture by covering it with attractive surface **Veneer furniture's exposed surfaces with sunmica sheets*

7. Hint – indirect indication **I got a hint of his involvement in crime*

Allusion – (verb is Allude) indirect reference. **Facts allusion to his involvement made him a suspect*

Innuendo – indirect disparaging reference **His speech carried innuendo against me*

Clue – indirect hint to solve a problem, mystery

Cue	– hint from behind someone to do something needed **He gave a cue to his accomplice to flee*
Insinuation	– indirect insulting remark **Flattery turned into insinuation when his objective of gaining was not realised from his boss*
8. Hold	– to restrain from moving away by capturing **He held my hands in his arm*
Captivate	– to hold attention of someone with charm **Her beauty captivated who saw her*
Enthrall	– to hold someone as a slave **Women in households are enthralled by husbands*
Fascinate	– to hold someone in spellbinding attention **His speech fascinated audience*
Engross	– to hold attention by a work someone is doing **The task engrossed him for hours*
9. Holy	– what is revered by devotees **Holy river/saint*
Divine	– what is related to God
Sacred	– dedicated to religious purpose, revered **Sacred monument*
Sacrosanct	– inviolably sacred
10. Horrible	– (act, scene) engendering horror in others **Horrible accident*
Ghastly	– which shocks others **A ghastly murder*
Gruesome	– making someone shudder with fear
Grisly	– engendering with extreme horror **Grisly monster*
Macabre	– horrible because of being associated with death, ghost etc. **Macabre rituals*
11. Hurl	– to throw upward in air
Lob	– throw in an arc or projectile in air **Lob a ball to someone in front to catch it*
Pelt	– throw forward in air to aim at the target **Mob pelted stones on the policemen*
Toss	– throw upward in air in casual manner **Toss a coin*

I

1. Idea	– a mental impression formed about something **His idea about me is not good*

Notion – vague idea **He harbours a strange notion about life in America*

Concept – mental picture made about a subject, plan **He has a clear concept about the marketing strategy to boost sales*

Perception – idea formed in one's mind on the basis of under standing about something *Police is not people friendly in the perception of general public

2. Ignoramus – an ignorant person

Agnostic – a person who does not claim to have knowledge of God or other mystery in absence of experience

Cad – a person who is ignorant of social etiquette, or knowledge of a trade

Liaty – people who are ignorant of a subject as opposed to professional practising in that field of subject **Professional jargon is beyond the ken of laity*

3. Ignore – deliberately avoid to pay attention **He ignored me when we met in the meeting*

Disregard – ignore due to being unimportant **His suggestions were disregarded by others*

Neglect – deliberately avoid to pay attention due to being indifferent to it **He neglected his studies/duty/appearance*

4. Impassive – not reacting to stimulus, emotions

Phlegmatic – hard to be aroused, not showing emotions **Phlegmatic person*

Stoic – indifferent to pain or pleasure, cool to joy or grief both

Stolid – of blank / expressionless countenance showing no emotional expression

5. Impertinent – offensive to someone's privacy **Ask impertinent questions*

Intrusive – thrusting oneself into others' affairs unsolicited **Intrusive person*

Obtrusive – thrusting into others' affairs, which is unwelcome

Meddlesome – thrusting into others' affairs which becomes inter- ference to them

Officious – offering one's good offices to others without being asked for **Officious advice. Meddlesome *Officious neighbour becomes a nuisance*

6. Impinge – to give sharp pressure on something **His shoes impinge on his toes*

Prick – to give sharp pressure by a pointed object so as to enter into it painfully

Prickle – to give sharp tingling sensation **Skin eruptions in summer prickle*

7. Impious – not showing reverence to God

Profane – given to show irreverence in acts for sacred one **Profane acts*

Sacrilegious – given to violate sacredness, holiness **Sacrilegious person *Sacrilegious conduct*

Blasphemous – (speech) not showing reverence to God, religion **Blasphemous speech*

8. Imprison – to keep someone confined in prison

Incarcerate – to keep someone confined in a room or restricted space **They incarcerated themselves to confer*

Immure – to keep confined in a walled area **She immured herself in the house to nurse her ailing father*

Intern – to keep confined within a specified area **War prisoners were interned in a field enclosed with barbed wires*

Impound – to keep confined in an enclosure as stray animals or vehicles are kept

9. Inclination – mental tendency to do something **Inclination for acting*

Attitude – mental bent **Helping attitude*

Disposition – inherent inclination **Disposition to pick up quarrel*

Pre-disposition – made prepared to be inclined to **Pre-disposition to love for country was infused in him in his childhood*

Predilection – mental state of preferring **He has a strong predilection for sports*

Propensity – natural inclination **Propensity for earning money*

Proclivity – habitual inelination

Penchant – strong liking for

Bias – frame of mind favouring someone/something

Tendency – prevailing inclination

10. Inculcate – to fill someone with good habits, values in life by repeated instructions **Inculcate patriotism in children/respect for elders*

Indoctrinate – fill someone with the lessons, principles, ideology of a religion, group by preaching **Indoctrinate devotees in religious lessons*

Infuse (*in*) – fill someone with values by pouring these values in their mind **The team was infused in enthusiasm by the coach *Infuse loyalty in the followers*

Imbue (*with*) – fill someone with good values by soaking them with these values **Imbue the disciples with spartan living*

Instil – to fill someone with values by slowly pouring **Instil good habits in children*

Insinuate – to fill into the mind of someone with some idea, suggestions etc. using skill, by suftle means **Propaganda insinuates doubt in people's mind*

11. Indecent – in bad taste (behaviour) **Indecent behaviour*

Risque – (behaviour) very close to being indecent **Risque behaviour*

Ribald – (speech) indecent in language **Ribald speech*

Scurrilous – indencent, abusive **Scurrilous remark*

Vulgar – indecently coarse devoid of sophistication **Vulgar scene in pictures*

12. Indemnify – to make up for any loss caused by one's action, to ensure to guard against anticipated loss

Compensate – to pay back for loss, injury, or suffering **Insurance cover is taken because it compensates for any damage to the insured*

Recompense – to pay back for a service rendered, trouble taken etc. **He was adequately recompensed for the trouble he took to help someone*

Reimburse – to pay back the expenses incurred by someone, refund

Reparation (*n*) – compensation paid by a defeated country to the victor for the cost of war. Germany paid reparation to the U.S.A. after the second world war.

Repay – to pay back loan

Pay damages – pay back money to compensate for causing injury of loss to someone

13. Indiscriminate – without caring to select/choose **Kill people indiscriminately *Indiscriminate firing*

Haphazard – without caring to arrange in order **Haphazard arrangement of books on self*

Random – without taking care of aim, direction **They threw balls randomly*

14. Infamy – loss of reputation, disrepute **Outrageous conduct caused his infamy*

Ignominy – contemptuous disrepute

Odium – heteful disrepute

Opprobrium – severe disrepute earned by shameful conduct

Stigma – blot on reputation

Obloquy – disrepute resulting from public blame, deunciation

15. Infer – arrive at a conclusion/opinion on the basis of reasoning **His absence from the meeting was inferred as his displeasure*

Interpret – arrive at an opinion on the basis of explanation **Interpret hidden meaning of an omen*

Conclude – arrive at an opinion by judging/on the basis of judgement **He concluded that I was innocent*

Construe – arrive at an opinion on the basis of explanation in a specified way/particular context **His abstention from voting was construed to be diefiance of party whip*

Deduce – arrive at an opinion/conclusion on the basis of assumption **The detective deduced from the evidence that the servant was involved in crime*

16. Influence – effect on others' cast by someone's character or bahaviour **He has great influence on people*

Clout – effect on others of someone's authority

Impression – effect on others of image, behaviour of someone **His gentle conduct cast good impression on others*

17. Inform – to let someone know about something **He was informed of the arrival of his friend*

Advice of to let someone know about the situation which is prevailing **Investors were advised of the risk involved*

Acquaint	– to let someone know about situation to get familiar or conversant with it **To acquaint someone with the plan*
Apprise of	– to let someone know about something by making him understand about it **He was apprised of worker's performance*
18. Inherent	– (a quality) be present in someone inseparably **Arrogance is inherent in him*
Immanent	– be present within someone **Gold is immanent in everyone*
Intrinsic	– be present with someone associated by its very nature **Heat is intrinsic with the sun *Antique has intrinsic value*
19. Injurious	– likely to cause injury
Deleterious	– likely to cause harm, harmful in effect **Deleterious to public health*
Detrimental	– likely to cause harm to one's interest **Detrimental to our health*
Disastrous	– likely to cause great damage, loss **Disastrous war*
Inimical	– likely to cause harm as an enemy causes
Insidious	– likely to cause harm in subtle manner
Noxious	– likely to cause harm as a poison does **Noxious fumes*
Pernicious	– likely to cause harm by ruining as death destroys
20. Inkling	– vague feeling or hint about something to happen **I had an inkling of what was going to happen*
Intuition	– instinctive feeling of something to happen
Apprehension	– ominous feeling of something to happen
Anticipation	– prior feeling of something to happen **Anticipation of a favourable decision*
Foreboding	– fearful apprehension
Hunch	– feeling of suspicion about what will happen
Premonition	– uncanny feeling of what will happen **To have a premonition of imminent danger*
Presentiment	– impression of something evil to happen
Prescience	– feeling of knowing beforehand about what is to happen

21. Innovate – make changes in the existing form of something to give it a new look, to improve **Innovate the bureaucratic system*

Renovate – (building) to give it a new look again by repairing **Renovate the old house*

Retrofit – (machine) to give a new look by fitting it with extra facilities to match its latest version **Retrofit the old model car with the latest gadgets*

Revamp – to give something a new look by total overhauling. **Revamp a project*

22. Insert – push something inside a gap, hole

Insinuate – push something *viz.,* roots by plants, indirect remark against someone cleverly through the gap **Tree insinuates its roots through crevices in rocks *He insinuated himself through the crowd to reach in frontline*

Penetrate – push inside by thrusting forcefully **The enemy troops penetrated into the border*

Pierce – push a pointed object into something by tearing into it **A needle pierced his finger*

23. Instigate – (external provocation) arouse someone to commit. wrong, undesirable act **Instigate the mob to defy the orders*

Incite – (self-emotion) arouse someone to commit crime, unlawful act **Anger and discontent incite people to indulge in violence*

Foment – to arouse people to create trouble, problem. **Foment the law and order problem.*

24. Instruction – advice, direction given to be obeyed

Directive – official instruction

Injunction – authoritative instruction

Prescription – doctor's instruction given to a patient

25. Insult – loss of respect

Affront – insult as if slapped in the face

Dishonour – loss or violation of dignity

Offense – insult causing hurt feelings

Umbrage – insult causing shadow on reputation

Disgrace – insult lowering reputation

Derogate	– insult by belittling someone
Disparage	– insult by contempting as being lower in rank
26. Insulting	– causing insult
Derogatory	– causing insult by trying to belittle someone **Derogatory remark*
Disparaging	– causing contempt as if one is lower in rank **Disparaging behaviour*
27. Interject	– to insert statement/start speaking in the middle of someone speaking **An audience interjected a question to the speaker*
Intercede	– to insert oneself in a dispute on behalf of one party to use one's good offices to settle dispute **He interceded on behalf of his friend and apologised for his mistakes*
Interpose	– to insert something in between two other things **Interpose an opaque surface between light source and eyes of someone to obstruct vision* **Interpose between two quarreling persons to disengage them*
Intervene	– to come between two others forcibly. **Intervene into others' affairs.*
28. Invincible	– who cannot be defeated **Invincible enemy*
Unconquerable	– that which can't be conquerred **Unconquerable problems*
Indomitable	– which cannot be tamed, subdued **Indomitable courage, zeal*
Insurmountable	– which cannot be mounted upon **Insurmountable summit*
29. Involved	– be engaged in useful activity **To get involved in local politics*
Indulged	– be engaged in something to gratify one's desire **He is indulged in activities related to music and art*
Complicit	– be engaged in unlawful activities **He is complicit in criminal activities*
Engrossed	– be engaged with absorbing attention **Engrossed in listening music*
Embroiled	– be engaged in conflict, contentious situation **Embroiled in court cases*

30. Irritable – readily get excited, angered, annoyed **Irritable person*

Cantankerous – readily irritated and start quarrelling **Cantankerous old maid/person*

Choleric – readily get angered **A man of choleric disposition*

Fractious – easily irritated uncontrollably **Fractious person*

Irascible – easily provoked to anger

Fretful – get easily irritated and start gnashing teeth in anger

Peevish – get irritated in discontent **Get peevish on being left out*

Petulant – get irritated and sulking like a child **Petulant nature of a person*

Snappish – get irritated and start speaking or replying in acerbic tongue

Testy – irritable to acute degree

Waspish – get irritated quickly

31. Irritation – feeling of annoyance

Dudgeon – feeling of deep resentment

Huff – a fit of resentment **He left the meeting in a huff when he was not allowed to speak*

Pique – feeling of resentment due to hurt ego, pride **He was piqued at his remark.*

Resentment – feeling of displeasure **Unjust remark caused resentment in him*

J

1. Journey – act of travelling from one place to another **A journey by train*

Cruise – travelling by a ship on sea for pleasing without any destination **Patrol ships cruised along the sea shores*

Excursion – travelling a short distance for pleasure **They went on excursion to forts and musea on city outskirts.*

Expedition – travelling undertaken for a particular purpose **Scientists went on an expedition to the north pole to study environment of that area*

Jaunt	– travelling to a place for pleasure **The family went on a foreign jaunt*
Junket	– travelling for pleasure at others' expenses/ government expenses **Offiials often make a junket to foreign lands*
Pilgrimage	– travelling to religious places **He has gone on pilgrimage to Tirupati*
Tour	– travelling for official work/to discharge duty
Trip	– travelling to a given place **Trip to Delhi*
Voyage	– travelling through ship or spacecraft in sea or space for a long distance **Astronauts went on a vayage to Mars in a spacecraft*
2. Justify	– to show that action is right/just **He justified his decision*
Rationalise	– to show that an action is right by specious reasonings put forward **Rationalise one's action to convince others*
Vindicate	– to show that an action was right by subsequent evidence/facts **Subsequent events vindicated his prophesy*
3. Jut out	– extend out from a straight line **Window panes jut out of the wall*
Project	– extend outward **A part of beam projected out of the wall*
Protrude	– extend out into something else from its place **His swollen eyes protruded *An iron rod protruded through the sand layer*
Protruberate	– extend out from the surface of the body **His nose protruberates on the face *A tumour protruberates on his forehead*
Stick out	– to extend out by thrusting something **Do not stick your head out of the train's window*

K

1. Kill	– to take life of a person by violent means **Kill someone with weapon/by strangulation*
Assassinate	– to kill an important person **A leader of a prominent party was assassinated*
Murder	– to kill a person by hatching a plot **Murder the enemy by ambushing him*

Cull	– to slaughter birds/chicken selectively
Slaughter	– to kill an animal for meat
Decimate	– to murder one-tenth of people of a race/group
2. Kind	– (a person) who is considerate and generous to others **He was a kind person*
Beneficient	– who does help and good to others
Benevolent	– who wishes well of others
Benign	– who is not harmful, who does no harm to others
Humane	– who is compassionate in dealing with others
Magnanimous	– who is having a large heart towards others
3. Kneel	– to bend one's body and rest it on bent knees **Kneel down in punishment *He kneeled down to pick up something lying on the ground*
Knowtow	– to bend on the knees before someone in supplication and put forehead on the ground
Cower	– to bend on the knees in a abject fear/terror before someone
Genuflect	– to bend one's knees as in prayer

L

1. Lament	– to express sorrow **To lament over one's bad luck*
Bemoan	– to wail in grief
Grieve	– to suffer grief, sorrow and endure it alone in silence **Grieve bereavement of one's dear one*
Mourn	– to express grief **Mourn the death of a leader and wear black on the occasion of condolence meeting*
Condole	– to express sympathy with one who is grieving **Condole with a friend over his father's death*
2. Lamentation	– expression of grief over death of someone
Condolence	– expression of sympathy with someone who has suffered grief of death of his dear one
Dirge	– expression of grief in the form of a poem or composition for the funeral of a dead person **Sing dirge for the dead*
Elegy	– expression of lamentation in a poem

Requiem	– expression of grief on the occasion of public gathering for the repose of the soul of a dead person
Threnody	– lamentation for the dead
3. Laugh	– to voice happiness or amusement
Cachinnate	– to laugh loudly
Guffaw	– to laugh boisterously
Fleer	– to laugh mockingly
Chortle	– to laugh delightfully/gleefully
Giggle	– to laugh in half-suppressed manner in a silly way as and when feel embarrassed
Chuckle	– to laugh in amusement **Chuckle at someone's ridiculous gestures*
Snigger	– to laugh in half-suppressed voice in a disrespectful manner
Titter	– laugh in half-suppressed manner to express amusement
4. Lawyer	– one who practises law in courts
Advocate	– one who pleads clients' cases in courts, pleader
Advoate-General	– highest ranking govt.'s advocate
Attorney	one who represents a litigant by being appointed by him to represent on his behalf
Attorney-General	– one who is head of govt.'s law department and represents the govt. in legal matters
Barrister	– (in U.K.) a senior lawyer who practises in high courts
Jurist	– one who is an expert in law
Solicitor	– one who prepares a case for a client and represents a client in lower courts
Solicitor-General	–Govt.'s seniormost solicitor – next in rank to Attorney-General
5. Laziness	– lack of inclination to do something
Languor	– laziness due to sensuous pleasure/feeling emotional softness/soft touch **Languor felt on inhaling pleasant scent*
Lassitude	– laziness due to physical/mental weariness
Listlessness	– l aziness due to lack of enthusiasm
Sluggishness	– laziness causing to move slowly

6. Lazy – not inclined to do something

Indolent – habitually lazy (person) who does not want to take pain to do something

Languid – feeling dis-inclination to work due to fatigue

Languorous – feeling laziness due to sensuous pleasure

Languishing – lazy due to illness

Listless – lazy due to the lack of enthusiasm

Sluggish – slow to move due to laziness

Enervated – who is lazy due to luxurious style of living

7. Learned – (person) having acquired knowledge by study **A learned professor*

Scholarly – (person) highly knowledgeable

Erudite – (speech) showing full of knowledge **Erudite speech*

Pedant – a knowledgeable/learned person, who parades his knowledge

Cogniscenti – learned person in a specified field of knowledge **Cogniscenti of literature*

8. Lewd – (remark) showing vulgarity, indecent, obscene

Lascivious – (remark, look) showing sexual expression **Lascivious gesture*

Libidinous – (remark) characteristic of libido, complete surrender to sexy desire

Lustful – showing lewd desire

9. Lie down – to rest body on ground or bed

Lie prone – to lie down with chest on the ground

Lie supine – to lie down with chest upward

Lie prostrate – to lie down with limbs outstretched

Lie recumbent – to lie down with resting the body on a pillow

10. Lift – see *elevate*

Levitate – to raise oneself above the ground and stay out in the air without support

11. Limp – drooping because of not being stiff or erect

Floppy – drooping, limp as a dog's ears

Flaccid – limp and soft

Flabby – limp and loose **Flabby muscles*

Wilted	– drooping due to losing moisture as in the case of a plant's leaves
12. Lonely	– (place/people) without company **A lonely place* **A lonely person*
Deserted	– (place) without anyone to take care **A deserted house*
Desolate	– (place) without anyone to take care **A deserted house*
Desolate	– (place) devoid of people **A desolate place*
Solitary	– (living) without anyone in company **Solitary living in prison cell*
13. Look	– turn one'seyes in the direction of the object to see **Look at the map*
See	– to perceive an image of something with one's eyes' visual power by looking at it **I looked at the map, but could not see its fine prints due to weak eye-sight*
Behold	– to hold one's eyes on something and see **Behold the beauty of nature*
Watch	– to look at something with full attention **Watch the cricket match on the television.*
Glance	– to look at something for a brief period
Espy	– to look into distant space as if to detect something
Gaze	– to look at something for a long period
Gloat	– to look smugly at one's prized possession
Stare	– to look at something with wide-open eyes
Peer	– to look at something with partly-closed eyes, trying to recognize it **He peered at him from a distance*
Glare	– to stare at someone in anger
Leer	– to stare at someone lasciviously
Ogle	– to stare at someone lecherously
Glower	– to stare at someone in sullen mood
Pore	– to stare at someone with eyes fixed on it with complete concentration of mind **He pored over the book*
14. Loot	– rob, snatch possession of someone

Plunder	– loot with open violence **Plunder the travellers on the highway*
Pillage	– loot in open violence **Mob pillaged the roadside vendors*
Despoil	– loot under the guise of legality **Politicians despoil the public money*
Sack	– (victorious army) loot the conquered place and its people's properties
15. Loud	– (sound) harsh to hear **A loud noise*
Raucous	– (laughter, voice) harsh to hear
Stentorian	– (sound) exceedingly harsh **Stentorian siren*
Stertorous	– (snoring) harsh and loud
Strident	– (noise) loud and harsh **Strident traffic noise*
Shrill	– (cry) loud and piercing to ears **Shrill cry*
16. Loyalty	– faithfulness of someone towards a person
Patriotism	– faithfulness of someone towards one's own country
Devotion	– faithfulness to a cause, religion etc., dedication
Fealty	– faithfulness of a tenant to his lord **Servant's fealty to his master*
Fidelity	– faithfulness of spouse in conjugal life
Allegiance	– faithfulness towards party, group
17. Lure	– attract by tempting others **Toys lure the children* **Special offers lure the customers*
Entice	– attract by a tempting tact **Entice people to join the sect*
Inveigle	– attract by employing deceit
Seduce	– attract someone to wrong path **He was seduced to crime by the prospect of getting rich overnight*
Tempt	– attract too strongly to resist (with advantage) **The offer was tempting* **Tempt someone with bribe*

M

1. Malice	– feeling of ill-will against someone with a desire to hurt him
Malevolence	– desire of, wish of evil things about someone **Harbour malevolence towards someone*

Grudge	– feeling of resentment against someone **He holds grudge against me*
Grouse	– complaining stance against someone in resentment
Despite	– (noun of the word 'Despise') feeling of contempt, disdain
Spleen	– bad temper, resentful feeling against someone **He poured his spleen against me when I tried to explain myself.*
Spite	– feeling of a desire to hurt someone
Rancour	– feeling of bitter resentment for a long time
Resentment	– feeling of indignation due to hurt emotions
2. Malodour	– unpleasant, foul smell of something
Stink	– unpleasant smell of garbage, sullage etc.
Stench	– very unpleasant, unbearable stink as emanating from a rotting mass
3. Malodorous	– giving out malodour **Malodorous toilet*
Fetid	– giving out offensive smell
Fusty	– (place) giving out bad smell due to dampness **Musty damp room*
Noisome	– giving out bad smell which might affect health **Noisome fumes*
Putrid	– giving out bad smell due to rot/decay **Putrid vegetables*
Rancid	– giving out foul smell due to decomposed oil and fat **Rancid butter*
Rank	– giving out very bad smell **Rank cigar*
4. Mark	– a sign left by something **Mark of ink on the paper dropped off an inkpot*
Contrail	– longitudinal streak of mark left on curtains by fading due to exposure to sunlight/a long streak of white fumes left behind a jet plane passing in the sky **White contrail of a jet plane*
Aftermath	– long streak of mowed grass in a field/unpleasant consequences left as mark of disastrous event *War left a ruined town in its aftermath
Rut	– mark left by the passing vehicles' tyres on the ground

Spoor – mark left by an animal's hoofs, which is followed by hunters

Trail – mark left by the people passing across a path **Trail is made across a field by the people passing through it daily* **An tnjured animal left a trail of blood behind its escape route* **He scraped the barks on the trees to make a trail through the jungle to be followed by others of his team*

Wake – mark left on the water surface as a turbulence on the surface behind a ship passing ahead **Failed monsoon left famine in its wake*

5. Marvel – something/someone which/who arouses wonder or admiration in others **Universe is a marvel of God's creation*

Miracle – something/someone which/who arouses wonder because of being beyond human experience **This machine is a miracle in efficiency* **His surviving the accident was a miracle*

Prodigy – someone who arouses wonder because of being extraordinary in talent **He is a child prodigy showing extraordinary talent early in age*

Phenomenon – someone/something who engenders wonder because of being extraordinary in nature **Total solar eclipse is a phenomenon* **Mahatma Gandhi was a phenomenon*

6. Mash – to crush into pulp **Mash potato* **He mashed his finger with a blow of the hammer*

Squash – to crush into a flat mass as by hitting hard or pressing under a heavy object **He squashed an insect under his shoes* **Squash a tomato flat*

Crumple – to crush a cloth into irregular folds **Press a cloth to crumple into the broken creases*

7. Massacre – kill a large number of people brutally

Butcher – kill in cruel manner a large number of animals / people

Decimate – kill a large number of people belonging to a particular group or race or community

Slaughter – to kill brutally a large number of people in violent manner

Carnage – act of killing of a large number of people

Pogrom	– act of killing of a large number of people of particular ethnicity in organized plot
8. Mediator	– one who gets a dispute settled by negotiation
Arbitrator	– one who gets a dispute setted by his tact/ wisdom acceptable to both the parties
Arbiter	– one who gets a dispute settled by dictating at his will because of having supremacy **Fate is an arbiter of our destiny*
Intermediary	– one who acts as a go-between to settle dispute on the terms of a deal between the two parties
9. Memento	– small item kept to renew the past memory **Childhood mementos keep one's past memorable*
Memorabilia	– item belonging to/associated with someone or an event kept as one's memory
Remembrance	– item associated with a dead person/person living far away/an event of distant past, which is kept as a memory
Souvenir	– item kept as a memory of a place visited in the past
Token	– item which has been gifted by someone and is kept as a sign of his affection
10. Memorial	– a structure erected in the memory of an important person/event **Lincoln memorial *War memorial*
Monument	– a structure erected in commemoration of an event of historical importance **India Gate is a monument of the martyrs in the war*
Mausoleum	– structure of a tomb which is large and magnificent
Tomb	– structure erected on the grave of a dead person who has been buried elsewhere
11. Mercenary	– (troop, warrior) who takes part in war for a country, army for earning money instead of patriotism/a warrior who fights for money sake for a country, army
Hack	– a person who sells his dignity/honour of being an independent writer/artist by working on hire for someone
Hireling	– a person who works for someone on payment for services

Venal	– (person in authority) who sells his independence/ integrity for bribe paid to him **A venal bureaucrat*
12. **Mire**	– soft, sticky, muddy tract of land
Bog	– Mire covered with decayed vegetation
Marsh	– tract of wetland
Quagmire	– mire in which legs go in upon walking
Swamp	– marshy land upon which trees and bushes have grown
13. **Miser**	– (a person) who spends money very grudgingly
Frugal	– who spends money prudently – who does not spend on unnecessary things, thrifty
Penurious	– who is so miser as to live like a poor
Parsimonious	– who spends sparingly
Niggardly	– who spends too little on his own requirements, too
Stingy	– who is unwilling to spend on others
14. **Miserable**	– (condition) deserving pity **Miserable health*
Abject	– (condition) extremely undignified, in which one loses self-pride **Abject poverty*
Ignoble	– not honourable in character or purpose
Pitiable	– (condition) which engenders pity in others
Wretched	– (condition) which is extremely contemptible
15. **Mistake**	– wrong committed in judging something **He made a mistake in identifying him*
Error	– wrong committed by deviating from accuracy **Made an error in multiplication* **Grammatical error*
Blunder	– a serious nature of error which appears stupid **Calling A.P.J. Abdul Kalam as Abul Kalam Azad in speech was his blunder*
Fault	– a wrong done by someone knowingly without reck **It was my fault to go out in dead night without regard to risk involved*
Faux pas	– error in social etiquette **Shouting abuse in social gathering was a faux pas, which I inadvertently committed*
Gaffe	– a blunder which causes embarrassment

Mal-a-prop – an error in using a wrong word in place of a similarly sounding word **Using 'contiguous' for a disease in place of 'contagious' is a mal-a-prop*

16. Motivate – encourage someone to do something by showing cause, purpose and filling him with inner urge

Inspire – encourage by infusing zeal, animated feelings to do something

Encourage – fill someone with courage to do something

Induce – encourage to do something by showing gain, profit, which lures him

Suborn – encourage someone to commit perjury, *i.e.,* give wrong evidence in courts by giving bribe

17. Motive – purpose, cause which fills with inner urges to do something **Patriotism was the prime motive behind joining the army*

Inspiration – purpose etc. which fills someone with animation, zeal to do something **Social iniquities worked as inspiration to him to join social service*

Inducement – gain, greed which spurs one to do something **Pleasure of wielding power was the inducement for him to join I.A.S.*

Afflatus – divine inspiration which urges one to do something

18. Mysterious – (something) which remains unexplained and arouses curiosity and amazement **A mysterious object appeared in the sky which has never been seen before*

Mystic – (symbol, religious rite) which cannot be explained by ordinary people and, hence, arouses curiosity and amazement **Mystic rites *Mystic formula*

Arcane – (secret) which remains unexplained to persons of average understanding

Abstruse – (something) which is too complex to be understood

Enigmatic – (situation, occurrence) which is perplexing **Enigmatic circumstances surround his death*

Esoteric – (something) which remains unexplained to those who are not having special knowledge **Esoteric poetry*

Recondite	– (subject) too profound to be understood by average people

N

1. **Nap**	– a slight, short sleep or dozing
Catnap	– a nap in daytime
Siesta	– a nap in the hottest part of day in summer
2. **Nascent**	– being in the process of taking birth **Nascent rebellion should be nipped in the bud*
Inchoate	– being in process of developing imperfect
Rudimentary	– being in the state of not fully developed or not matured **Rudimentary knowledge* **Rudimentary stage of a planning*
Incipient	– being in the early stage of process/exisence **Incipient tumour is removed by surgery*
3. **Nonsense**	(talk) absurd **His nonsense is irritating*
Drivel	– nonsense of an idiot/mad person **Drivel of a mad person*
Gobbledygook	– absurd talk aimed at confusing others **Pseudo-scientific gobbledygook*
Poppycock	– absurd/senseless talking **His poppycock was aimed at impressing others*
Twaddle	– absurd talk of an ignorant-in-the-subject person **Cricket watchers indulge in twaddle about intricacy of the game as if they were experts*
4. **Novice**	– (person) who is new, inexperienced in a job **A novice carpenter*
Neophyte	– (person) who has just joined a group, party etc.**A neophyte has to master rules and procedures*
Greenhorn	– an inexperienced person
Tyro	– (person) who has begun to learn
Apprentice	– (person) who is learning a trade under the supervision of an expert **Apprentice carpenter*

O

1. **Object**	– express opposition to someone's action/ statement **They objected his proposal*

Dispute – express opposition on account of not being true or correct *He disputed my claim*

Impugn – express opposition by challenging *Impugn someone's motive of doing something*

Protest – express opposition because of being irrea - sonable *Protest undue criticism*

(Take) exception – express opposition because of being offen -ding *He took exception to his insolent behaviour*

2. Obstacle – something which blocks passage or progress *Wooden bollards are erected on road as obstacle to prevent traffic *Disunity is an obstacle for the party to win elections*

Barrier – something put up in the way to block a passage

Blockage – obstruction blocking passage *Blood clot creates blockage in the blood circulation*

Blockade – obstruction which prevents ingress & egress from a place *Police barricading put up blockade around the office building*

Hindrance – obstruction causing delay in progress *Econo - omic slowdown is a hindrance in country's progress*

Obstruction – something that obstructs progress *Mob's shouting caused obstruction in the meeting*

Hurdle – barrier put up in the way which has to be jumped over in order to go ahead

Impediment – difficulty which prevents progress *Lacking in vocabulary is impediment in fluent speech*

3. Occurrence – an incident which just takes place without apparent connection with anything else *His arrival was an unexpected occurrence*

Event – an important occurrence which has a special bearing *A historical event *Total solar eclipse is a rare celestial event*

Happening – an occurrence which just takes place

Happenstance – a happening which takes place by chance

Incident – an occurrence of minor nature in connection with something else *An incident of hostility took place on the border*

Incidence – an undesirable occurrence *Incidence of theft in the train shook the passengers *High incidence of heart diseases is caused by faulty food habits*

Instance – a specific occurrence which serves as an example to prove a point **It was an instance of oppression against the weaker section of the society*

4. Omen – an occurrence which is indicative of something good or bad to happen soon **End of war is a good omen for the counry *Howling of dogs is a bad omen*

Augury – an occurrence which is indicative of good outcome **Good monsoon is augury of good harvesting season*

Portent – occurrence which is indicative of bad outcome **Seeing a bright object falling from the sky is a menacing portent*

5. Ominous – (an event) which gives worry about what bad may happen **Ominous dark clouds*

Inauspicious – which gives fear of unfavourable consequences **An inauspicious event*

Portentous – which gives threatening impression about what may happen **Portentous celestial event*

Unpropitious – what can't be appeased to be favourable or helpful **Unpropitious luck*

6. Opposite – Situated at the other end of something **He is sitting opposite to me *Opposite end of the room *He took stance opposite to mine*

Contrary – (a fact, proposition) which is in opposition to another one **Contrary views of members on a matter made it difficult to take decision*

Contradictory – (counter + diction) a statement which is opposite to another one **Contradictory statements of witnesses about what happened makes it obvious that one of them is untrue*

Antithesis – (two things or qualities) which are directly opposite to one another **Water is antithesis of fire *Hell is antithesis of heaven*

7. Order – authoritative instruction given to someone

Behest – earnest command **He filed a complaint against me at the behest of my detractor*

Command – order which must be obeyed **Military command*

Diktat	– order which is imposed on someone by a superior which is unfair **Boss's diktat*
Edict	– authority's proclamation – order pronounced publicly
Decree	– Court's order to litigants
Fiat	– arbitrary order **A dictator rules by fiat*
Canon	– religious order of codes of conduct to be observed by the devotees **He violated the canons of etiquette*
Injunction	– order requiring a person to do or not to do a particular act **Doctor's injuction to refrain from smoking has to be faithfully obeyed by the patient*
Mandate	– order/command given by people to their representatives to manage affairs of the state **The party got the mandate to form government in the election*
Ordainment	– order prescribed by the destiny for deciding someone's fate in advance **He is ordained to suffer*
8. Outdated	– belonging to the past – no more now **Outdated fashion*
Antiquated	– very old, of the past **Antiquated machine*
Ante-diluvian	– primitive, belonging to very old period **Ante-diluvian civilization*
Archaic	– of old time and now rarely used **Archaic language*
Obsolete	– gone out of vogue, no more in use **Obsolete models of cars*
9. Overture	– initial move towards starting a dialogue, negotiation, relationship **A shy person rarely makes an overture of friendship* **My overture to old foe was requited with cold response*
Approach	– initial move/advance made to an unknown person for friendship **He made a timid approach to his fellow passenger in the journey*
Advance	– initial move to show one's intention of starting amorous relationship with a person of opposite sex **She rebuffed his advances*
Bid	– initial move to getting something from some *He made a bid for others' sympathy

Tender	– initial move in the form of indirect hint by actions to show one's intention towards someone **He made several tenders of his attraction towards her in the past, but she did not take the cue*

P

1. Paradox	– (a fact, truth) which is contrary to accepted belief, norms
Anomaly	– (fact) which is contrary to general rule, expectations **A reticent person that he is, is anomaly in his family of garrulous persons* **People in a free country yet to get freedom from social iniquities is an anomaly*
Antimony	– (conclusion) which is contrary to another conclussion – though both are derived from the same premise
Irony	– (expression) which is contrary to what was intended to convey **Nominating criminals for election, even as proclaiming not to do so, is a stark irony*
2. Passion	– intense emotional longing **His passion for reading books drew him to the book fair*
Fervour	– intentional emotional devotion **He prays with fervour*
Ardour	– intense emotional zeal like a leaping flame **Ardour of a neophyte*
3. Peak	– the highest point as of a mountain, summit
Apex	– the highest point of a pointed object, Acme **Apex of a tree leaf*
Vertex	– the highest point of a rock, career of a person
Zenith	– the highest point in the sky over one's head (opposite Nadir) **His popularity is on the zenith*
4. Peep	– to look through a narrow slit at something **He peeped into the room*
Peek	– to look at something furtively **He peeked into the room to know what was happening there*
Pry	– to look into others' private life intrusively **Prying into someone's private affairs is a bad habit*
Voyeur	– (a person) who furtively looks at others engaged in sexual activity to derive passive pleasure

5. Perplex – to mentally disturb to throw into confusion **Difficult questions in exams perplexed him*

Agitate – to disturb mentally

Discomfit – to mentally disturb to make someone feel uneasy **Hooting and catcalls discomfitted the speaker*

Disconcert – to mentally disturb so as to lose composures

Perturb – to mentally disturb acutely

Rattle – to mentally disturb so as to make one nervous **Sudden explosion rattled people*

Upset – to mentally disturb to bewilder **Bad news about the family upset him*

Vex – to mentally disturb due to annoyance

Faze – to mentally disturb so as to feel ashamed or discouraged **No amount of insult fazed him*

6. Persuade – to make one agree to do something by reasoning to convince him **He persuaded me to change my decision*

Coax – to make one agree by gentle persuasion **He was coaxed to agree to the suggestion*

Cajole – to make one agree by flattery

Inveigle – to make one agree by using artful tact **To inveigle someone to accompany to the market*

Wheedle – to make one agree by misleading words or acts **Wheedle someone persistently to consent to the request*

7. Pierce – to thrust a pointed object so as to enter into someone's body **Pierce the skin with a needle*

Stab – to thrust sharp weapon into a body **Stab someone with a knife*

Gore – thrust animal's horn or tusker's teeth into someone **A wild bull gored a person*

Impale – pierce a pointed object and keep fixed or unable to move **A snake was impaled on the ground with a bident*

8. Pillar – tall, vertical structure to support load

Beam – long, horizontal structure to support load

Pole – long piece of wood, steel or such material

Mast	– long pole upon which sails, flag are supported **Flag is hoisted on a mast*
Stake	– long piece of wood or steel pointed at one end of it, which is used for fencing.
Pylon	– very long, tower-like pole, which is used for supporting high–tension electric wires
Prop	– long pole which is used as a support for something to prevent it from falling from down
9. Politic	– (action, decision) which is sensible in a given circumstance **It is politic to keep away from dispute*
Pragmatic	– (action, decision) which is based on practical consideration
Provident	– (action, decision) which is based on concern for future **Saving money is a provident decision*
Prudent	– (action, decision) which is based on thought for consequences
Sagacious	– (action etc.) based on careful considerations, or good judgement
10. Poor	– (person) lacking in the means of living
Penurious	– extremely poor
Destitute	– completely devoid of the means of living
Impecunious	– a poor who lacks in money for sustenance, penniless
Impoverished	– poor because of losing wealth **Impoverished landlords*
Indigent	– poor because of lacking means to meet stet
11. Pot pourri	– collection of miscellaneous items of entertainment
Melange	– collection of miscellaneous items
Medley	– collection of miscellaneous songs, which are sung in continuity as a single song
Montage	– collection of miscellaneous photographs placed together to look like a single photograph
Collage	– collection of miscellaneous newspaper clippings, photographs etc. pasted on the same surface as a work of art
12. Poverty	– state of being poor
Penury	– state of being penurious

Indigence	– state of being indigent
Destitution	– state of being destitute
Privation	– state of being deprived of means of living
13. Powerful	– having great power **Powerful engine*
Potent	– having great effect **A potent drug*
Potentate	– a powerful person having great influence
Mighty	– having great might/physical strength **Mighty army*
Puissant	– having great ability (to jump on a horse in a race)
14. Praise	– express admiration
Laud	– praise by singing or shouting slogans **People lauded their leader*
Extol	– highly praise someone
Eulogize	– praise a deceased person in a condolence meeting
Commend	– praise by naming a person for good work **Commend a soldier for his bravery*
Panegyrize	– praise in an oration, writing in paper etc.
Approbate	– public praise approving one's good work **Approbate government's policy*
15. Prayer	– spiritual communion with God
Matins	– morning prayer
Vespers	– evening prayer
Paternoster	– prayer recitation to the (Pater–) of the universe – supreme father
16. Precedence	– preceding another in order of importance, rank in privilege **The President of India takes precedence of all others in official protocol*
Precedent	– preceding event/instance which serves as an example to follow in subsequent cases **Precedent of earlier court's judgement helps subsequent decisions*
Antecedent	– preceding circumstances of one's life which helps forming an opinion about him **Antecedent of a person is unblemished*
Priority	– preceding circumstances of one's life which help forming an opinion about him **Antecedent of a person is unblemished*

17. Pretend – to give false impression by insincere action *Pretend sympathy for someone in trouble*

Profess – to give false impression by insincere speech *Profess loyalty to someone*

Feign – to give false impression by insincere posture *Feign death by lying motionless *Feign ignorance*

Malinger – to give false impression of being ill in order to avoid duty

Play possum – (insects) to give false impression of death by lying motionless to save itself from the predators

18. Prevaricate – to speak in a round about manner so as to evade speaking the truth

Equivocate – to speak ambiguously so that it can be interpreted in equally two meanings to evade truth

Palter – to speak insincerely so as to be able to deny later

Fib – to speak lie in order to save oneself from embarrassment at that moment and get rid of the situation

19. Pride – unjustified opinion of one's own worth

Conceit – excessive pride which is exaggerated

Hubris – excessive pride which becomes the cause of downfall *Hubris of Hitler led to his downfall and death*

Vanity – excessive pride in one's ability which is worthless *i.e.*, of no value *Vanity of being a noble descendant*

Vainglory – boastful vanity *Vainglory of being a minister/actor*

20. Principle – fundamental belief governing action *Principle of a party*

Doctrine – fundamental belief of a religion/sect which is taught to the followers

Dogma – doctrine which is considered inviolable and sacrosanct

Tenet – principle held by a group or party truthfully

21. Prize – thing given to a winner of competition or lottery

Award – thing given in recognition of achievement *Award of the best actor*

Reward – thing given for services rendered *Loyal partyman was rewarded with the governor -ship*

Wages – the thing given for bad acts in return *He is suffering as a wages of sin *Ruined economy of the country was the wages of bad policies*

Largesse – thing given in generosity *The government gives largesse to the poor people*

Bounty – thing/money given for helping capture a culprit

Bonus – thing given to workers for good productivity

Incentive – thing given to motivate or encourage

22. Profession – occupation for which knowledge is a must **Medical profession of a doctor *Teaching profession*

Occupation – activity/work in which one is engaged *Writing books is the reired person's occupation*

Vocation – main job/employment *His vocation is govern ment service*

Avocation – side occupation apart from vocation, which one pursues as hobby

Metier – occupation in which one is specially trained and expert in doing it *Marketing is his metier*

Business – occupation of commercial nature

Trade – occupation in which specific skill is acquired *His trade is carpentry*

23. Property – things owned by a person *This house is his sole property*

Asset – property such as house, land etc. owned by a person who can convert into money by selling if need arises *He has accumulated assets in various towns*

Chattel – personal property other than land or money – such as cattles

Personalty – personal properties

Realty – real estate properties of a person

Fortune – great stock of wealth of a person *He spent fortune for his son's education*

Wealth – valuables possessed by someone *He lost his wealth*

24. Puzzle – (game, question) which carries tricky answer/solution requiring mental agility to solve **Cross-word puzzle*

Riddle – question etc. requiring skill to solve because of being full of contradictions

Enigma – (something) which is beyond common understanding, giving rise to speculation **He is an enigma to his friends*

Conundrum – puzzle or riddle, which is too complex to be solved

Q

1. Quack – a person, who practises a profession and pretends to have qualifications for that **Quack physician* **Quack psychologist*

Charlatan – a person who pretends to have knowledge more than he actually possesses

Humbug – a person who pretends to be important more than he actually is, a fraud **A humbug in politics* **A humbug politician*

2. Quarrel (*v*) – to engage in verbal argument over differences

Altercate – to engage in heated arguments

Squabble – to engage in petty quarrel

Wrangle – to engage in noisy quarrel

3. Quarrel (*n*) – noisy argument over a dispute **Domestic quarrel*

Brawl – quarrel which disturbs the neighbours **A brawl on thc road*

Broil – quarrel which annoys others

Fracas – quarrel with uproarious noise

Melee – quarrel which hand-to-hand fighting

Row – angry quarrel which attracts others' attontion

Scrap – quarrel with jostling

Scuffle – quarrel with trading blows

4. Quarrelsome – a person who is predisposed/inclined to pick up fight with others

Pugnacious – predisposed to engage in fisticuff

Belligerent – (nations) engaged in actual fighting

Bellicose – (a person) who is eager to fight

5. Quibble – argue on irrelevant points so as to avoid the real issue

Pettifog – un–necessarily argue on petty points

R

1. Reason (*with*) – to argue with someone to convince him of his fault

Expostulate – to argue with someone to object to his fault **Expostulate with someone of his bad habit of gambling*

Remonstrate (with) – to argue to show one his fault in protest

2. Rebound – to spring back after hitting a surface

Boomerang – (a plan, plot) come back on the originator instead of the intended target to harm

Repercuss – (something like action, event) rebound as a bad consequence **A war repercusses on nation's economy*

Reverberate – (sound) rebound several tunes after hitting walls of a hall to make echo **Her shriek reverberated through the hall*

Ricochet – (a flat object thrown forward) rebound by deflecting from the surface several times after hitting it **A flat stone was thrown horizontally, which ricocheted on the smooth surface*

Rebound – to rebound as a credit or discredit someone's good or bad act upon him **Good acts rebound to his credit *Good upbringing rebounds on one's behaviour*

3. Rebuff – bluntly refuse to entertain someone's advances, attempt to come close **The girl rebuffed his advances*

Snub – rebuff disdainfully

Spurn – bluntly refuse to entertain someone's proposal, request

4. Rebuke – express sharp disapporoval of someone's wrong action **Rebuked him for disobeying his orders*

Chide – scold for a wrong done

Admonish – scold in a mild manner/goodwill manner **Admonished him to remind him of obligations to his family*

Objurgate	– rebuke sharply/harshly, to berate
Upbraid	– rebuke sharply **He was upbraided for his cowardice*
5. Recede	– to go back to a distant position from the point where an observer is looking at **Flood water receded gradually from the inundated road *His hairline is receding back from his forehead*
Retreat	– to go back from a place of trouble to a safe place **Troops retreated from the war zone to safety*
Retrogress	– to go back again to earlier inferior condition from a superior one **Religious fundamentalism makes a society retrogressive*
6. Recrimination	– return accusation with a counter accusation
Repartee	– witty reply in return of a witty remark
Riposte	– counter-strike to a strike as in the game of fencing **A befitting riposte to an insult*
Retort	– quick return in the form of retaliatory reply to a remark
Retaliation	– return attack for an attack
7. Regard	– to consider as a point of view **I regard him useless *I regard him as my friend*
Recon	– to consider as a point of loss or gain on the basis of calculation **Recon the loss*
Deem	– to consider as a point of judgement **I deem it fit for selection*
8. Regret	– to express sorrow for wrong act **He regretted his harsh reply to his elder*
Repent	– to feel sorrow for committed sin with change of heart to become the same person **He repented cruelty he had perpetrated on others*
Rue	– express sorrow on a past event or action with a wish that it had not happened at all **I rue the day I made friendship with him*
Lament	– to express sorrow for something bad that had happened **He lamented his death *He lamented the falling standard of politics*
9. Rehabilitation	– action of restoring lost ability to live on one's own **Rehabilitation of those who have been uprooted from their native place enables them*

to live as before *Rehabilitate amputated persons by prosthetics

Re-instatement – action of putting a person in the same post he had earlier been removed *The court ordered his re-instatement*

Rapprochement – action of restoring harmonious relations earlier to hostility

Status quo ante – restoration of earlier condition

10. Reject – do not agree to accept due to deficiency *He rejected the bad quality goods *His application was rejected*

Refuse – do not agree because of one's unwillingness *He refused the party ticket for contesting the election *He refused to help him*

Decline – refuse politely *He declined to accept help*

Deny – do not agree to accept because of being untrue *He denied allegations against him *He denied that the earth is flat*

11. Relevant – (matter, argument, etc.) connected with the issue at hand *Relevant remark*

Apposite/Apt – which is suitable for the purpose at hand *Apposite reply *Apt quotation*

Germane – which is significant to the subject *Facts are germane to the issue at hand*

Pertinent – (things) related to the subject matter, which holds good for the topic *Pertinent question *Files pertinent to the case*

12. Relic – remains of a dead person preserved as an object of reverence

Relict – surviving part of something which has become instanct *Relict of instinct civilization*

Reliquiae – fossil remains of animal/plant

Remains – left-over part of something which does not now exist *Dead body is the remains of a deceased person *Remains of a ruined fort*

13. Relief – removal of pain, distress, sufferings *Medicine gave relief from pain *Food, shelter were provided to the flood victims as relief*

Reprieve – removal of sufferings by means of temporary postponement of punishment, temporary relief, respite

*Rains brought reprieve from sweltering summer heat *Suspension of tax collection was a reprieve to the people facing financial hardship*

Riddance – removal of the situation causing annoyance, annoying or unbearable suffering **Unwanted guest's departure is a good riddance to a host*

14. Relieve – to give relief, romove suffering **To relieve tension*

Mitigate – to lessen punishment, grief etc. by making it milder **Mitigate punishment *Mitigate seriousness of accusation.*

Assuage – to lessen hurt feelings

15. Repair – set right a broken or damaged thing **Repair machine/building*

Rectify – set right a mistake

Mend – set right what is torn **Mend shoes*

16. Repentance – feeling of sorrow for sinful acts with change of heart

Penance – feeling of sorrow with self–punishment

Penitence – feeling of sorrow by expressing regret without intent to make amends

Compunction – feeling of sorrow due to hurt conscience while doing sinful act **He had no compunction in deceiving his friend*

Contrition – feeling of sorrow with painful heart and intending to confess, so as to unburden his guilt feeling

Remorse – feeling of sorrow for sinful acts with intent to do expiation–self-punishment

17. Replace – to change a defective thing with a right one of the same thing **Replace the fused bulb *The inefficient officer was replaced*

Substitute – to change something with another kind **Computer has substituted the typewriters *Card payment has substituted the cash payment*

Supersede – to change a deficient or obsolete thing with more suitable one by setting the former aside **Supersede old law with a new one *Supersede the inefficient officer with another one*

18. Reprimand – (superior authority to subordinate) blame a subordinate in disapproval of his conduct or decision

Reprove – disapprove someone's wrong action by speaking to him

Reproach – censure/blame someone in disapproval of his conduct

19. Request – to beg someone for something

Entreat – request earnestly

Implore – request anxiously due to urgency

Solicit – request repeatedly so as to annoy the person requested

Plead – request by pleading for something

Beseech – request fervently

Importune – request persistently so as to cause harassment to the person requested

Supplicate – request humbly by bending with folded hands before the person requested

20. Restore – bring back to normal condition or former level **Restore peace/lost glory*

Restitute – bring back property, rights which had been taken away **Restitute his conjugal life by reuniting him with his wife*

Retrieve – bring back something which is likely to be lost or destroyed, or from ruin **Retrieve valuable articles from a house on fire* **Retrieve one's business*

Replenish – bring back stock to make up what has been consumed **Replenish food stock*

Reclaim – bring back waste/marshy land for use or in a condition of being able to be used for good purpose

Recover – bring back stolen goods, what has been lost **Recover stolen watch* **Recover loss in business* **Recover sense*

Recuperate – recover lost health due to illness

Rejuvenate – recover youthful vigour which has been lost due to age, weakness **Rejuvenate youthfulness*

Redeem – recover pawned article, sold shares etc. by buying back again **Redeem mortgaged house*

Ransom – bring back a captured person by paying demand money for his release **He ransomed his kidnapped son*

21. Resurrect – to bring back to life from a grave **Resurrect the ancient culture*

Resurge – to bring back to activity after lying dormant or from virtual extinction **Resurge economy*

Revive – to bring back to life which has ceased to exist **Revive old feud *Revive relationship*

Resuscitate – to bring back breathing from asphyxiated state **Mouth–to–mouth blowing air resuscitated stopped breathing in a victim*

22. Retaliate – return harmful action of someone with harmful action *i.e.,* return in the same coin **He retaliated his hostility in equal measure*

Reciprocate – return good gesture/action of someone with similar gesture **Reciprocate favour*

Requite – return good action with bad one or vice versa, *ie.,* bad action with good one **He requited my friendship with deceitful action against me*

23. Retract – withdraw, take back something spread out **Retract the spread wings (by a bird) *Retract one's given statement*

Recant – to withdraw statement formally made earlier

Renege – withdraw a promise given earlier **He reneged on his promise*

Backtrack – withdraw, go back by stepping back from the position, or an undertaking.

24. Retrench – remove employees in order to reduce expenditure, to ward off financial loss

Cashier – remove employees by revoking job contract

Dismiss – remove an employee due to his indicipline

Lay off – remove employees temporarily because of the shortage of work

25. Revenge – action of exacting or inflicting punishment on someone for a harm done by the person who has suffered **He took revenge for his insult*

Retribution – action of exacting condign punishment on someone for evil doings in the form of divine judgement **Natural calamity is a retribution for neglecting environmental protection *A just retribution of wickedness*

Vengeance – furious, wrathful, vindictive revenge **Police killed the criminal in vengeance for his killing innocent policemen*

Reprisal – retaliatory attack on someone to take revenge for hostile action despite warning to desist **Attack in reprisal* **Shops were sealed in reprisal to continued black marketing in essential goods despite repeated warnings*

26. Reverence – gesture of deep devotion **Show reverence to saints*

Deference – gesture of courteous regard **Yield to elders in deference to their wishes.*

Esteem – gesture of giving high regard **I hold him in high esteem*

Homage – gesture of respect **Pay homage to a person in high position*

Obeisance – gesture of reverence by supplication **Supplicate in obeisance to deity*

Tribute – gesture of regard by acknowledging **Erecting statue of a person is a tribute to him*

Veneration – gesture of reverence due to age, wisdom **Show veneration to old persons*

27. Revolt – raising voice of dissent against authority **People's revolt against government's unfair decision*

Coup d'etat – sudden overthrow of established rule

Insurgency – armed rebellion

Insurrection – attempt to overtake government by force

Lese majeste – Treason, crime against a ruler

Sedition – act or speech which incite rebellion

Mutiny – uprising of troops against their own establishment

Putsch – sudden uprising

Rebellion – armed struggle in defiance to the authority of the government

Uprising – rising of people in revolt against established rule

28. Rich – (person) who possesses enough wealth.

Affluent – who is having increasing source of earning money

Opulent – who indulges in ostentatious display of one's wealth

Wealthy – who possesses enough income–generating property

29. Ridicule – laugh at someone to make fun of him **Ridicule a pretentious person *They ridiculed him for his ugly look*

Deride – make fun of someone by scornful, contemptuous laughter **They derided him for his foolishness*

Mock – make fun of someone by doing his caricature **He mocked my serious thoughts*

Taunt – make fun of someone in a humiliating manner **To taunt someone for his defeat or failure*

Lampoon – make fun of someone by satirical drama, writing articles, etc. **The drama lampooned the political leaders/society for practising absurd customs*

Pillory – make fun of someone by exposing his deeds publicly **He pilloried his opponent*

Scoff – deride scornfully **Scoff him at his attempt to do something brave*

Fleer – deride someone by laughing mockingly

Sneer – make fun of/deride someone by curling lips in smile **They sneered at him when he told some jokes*

Jeer – make fun of someone by shouting/heckling **Crowd jeered the speaker*

30. Ridiculous – which induces laughter due to being absurd **Ridiculous plan*

Risible – which induces laughter due to being contemptible

Ludicrous – which induces laughter due to being preposterous **Ludicrous acts of a jester.*

Droll – which induces laughter due to being amusing in an odd way

Funny – which induces laughter due to being comical **Funny act/remark*

31. Risk – chance of getting harmed/injured **Jumping in turbulent water involves risk*

Hazard – chance of facing problems **A journey full of hazards*

Jeopardy	– chance of getting harmed due to exposing one to dangerous situation **Working without safety gears put workers in jeopardy*
Peril	– chance of getting harm due to imminent danger **Landslide puts people in peril*
32. Rude	– (person) having offensive behaviour
Insolent	– extremely rude
Impolite	– having offensive manners
Impudent	– showing open defiance boldly
Brash	– having overbearing manners
Impertinent	– rude towards respectable persons
Churlish	– having bad temper/arrogant behaviour
33. Ruse	– trick, artifice to divert attention from reality **Employ ruse by pretending illness to avoid work*
Ploy	– trick employed to turn situation in own favour **Use clever ploys to get others' support*
Feint	– trick to divert opponent's attention before attacking him **Feint of skilled fencer*
Gimmick	– trick like a magician employs to hoodwink others
Subterfuge	– ruse to evade consequences (subter = under, fuge = flee)
Stratagem	– trick to deceive enemy or to gain advantage over adversary
Trick	– crafty artifice to deceive **Magicians' tricks*

S

1. Sacrilege	– irreligious act of violating sacredness of what is sacred like a temple, for example **Desecration of a holy place is a sacrilege*
Blasphemy	– irreligious act of speaking evil about what is sacred **Blasphemy of criticising others' religion*
Heresy	– irreligious act of believing in the principles contrary to accepted orthodoxy **Not believing in doing religious rites is heresy*
Profanity	– irreligious act of showing contempt or irreverence for what is holy/sacred **Treating sacred thing irreverently is profanity*
2. Sad	– feeling unhappy, sorrowful **The bad news made him sad*

Desolate	– sad due to lonely feeling
Disconsolate	– unconsolably sad
Forlorn	– sad due to loss of hope
Doleful	– sad due to grief
Gloomy	– sad with depressed mood
Lugubrious	– mournfully sad **Lugubrious mood*
Melancholic	– habitually sad **A melancholic person is averse to anything cheerful*
3. Sarcastic	– (remark) which is in the form of taunting **The sarcastic remark hurt him*
Satirical	– (denunciation, riducule) which is taunting on vice, social aberrations etc. **Satirical play on social vices*
Sardonic	– (expression) which is disdainfully taunting characterised by bitter smile **Sardonic grin*
Ironic	– (statement) which is taunting characterised by speaking opposite to what is intended to say **What a wonderful person you are!*
4. Satire	– (literary piece of writing) intended to ridicule human follies, social vices **This film was a satire on human pettiness and selfishness*
Skit	– (literary writing, play/drama) intended to ridicule in humorous manner
Squib	– (a short literary work) intended to ridicule in sarcastic/malicious manner
Lampoon	– (a work, writing) intended to ridicule in a virulent manner **A lampoon on social vices*
5. Scatter	– throw all around at random **scattering seeds in the field is technically known as 'broadcasting'*
Spread	– move a liqid so as to cover space on ground all around **Spread liquid on the floor*
Disperse	– move something in all directions at random **Disperse the crowd *Wind dispersed the fog*
Diffuse	– disperse gaseous matter through the air **Diffuse fume/scent throughout the room*
Dissipate	– disperse wastefully **Dissipate youth's energy *Plot surface dissipates heat and becomes cool*
Disseminate	– disperse by distributing amongst others all around **Disseminate knowledge*

6. Scrap – small pieces of paper, metals torn or cut from large size **Metal scraps are lying all around this place*

Fragment – small piece of broken mass/disintegrated mass **Fragments of broken glass*

Shard – fragment of earthenware, crockery

Shrappel – fragment of a shell, exploded bomb

Sliver – long piece of wood, cloth, metal torn from a large size portion **Sliver of wood*

Splinter – small piece of wood, cloth, metal etc., taken out of a large portion

7. Scrape – rub a surface with a rough material so as to remove dirt on it, or its superficial outer layer **Scrape grime off the kitchen wall *Scrape paint from the surface. *A hard stone rubbed his hand to crape its skin*

Graze – (a bullet) rub a surface lightly while passing along it. **A bullet strayed off the course and grazed the arm of a person standing by*

Grate – rub a surface of something with a toothed surface so as to scrape into pieces **Grate the potato into chips*

Scratch – rub a smooth surface with a sharp object so as to tear it off at several places **Nails scratched his face *He scratched his name on the wall with a knife*

8. Scream – loud, piercing sound of a cry as in fear, anger **Scream in fear*

Shriek – loud high–pitched sound as of a cry in pain **Shriek in pain*

Shrill – loud harsh sound of crying

Screech – loud grating sound as produced on applying sudden brakes on a running vehicle. **Vehicle screeched to a sudden halt*

Hoot – loud piercing sound as of a siren, horn.

9. Seclude – to separate from others by keeping away to avoid contact **Aggressive prisoner was secluded from other prisoners*

Segregate – to separate a group of persons or things from other group on the basis of title, nomenclature etc.

*Books are segregated on the basis of author's title *Minority communities segregate themselves in ghetto away from the majority community*

Quarantine – to separate an infected person with contagious disease from others, who may get infected (usually for a period of forty days (quarant = forty)

Isolate – separate by taking away from the company **Nitrogen is isolated from the mixture of gaseous elements in the air by cooling *He has been isolated from his group of friends*

Assort – separate things/goods in various sizes, qualities **Assort oranges in various sizes*

Sort – separate the letters according to their destinations **Sort the letters to be sent to different places*

10. Serious – not triffling, sincere in attitude **Serious person*

Grave – having calm or cheerless disposition **Grave mood*

Somber – gloomy, depressed, sad **Sombre occasion of mourning *He is sitting in somber mood*

Staid – devoid of levity in mood **A staid person*

Solemn – mirthless person, face, mood, occasion **Prayer time is a solemn occasion*

11. Servile – (attitude) of submitting before someone as a servant **Servile bureaucrats*

Subservient – of serving others of important position as an obedient subordinate

Slavish – (attitude) like that of a slave **Slavish obedience*

Obsequious – (attitude) of flattering others in ostentatious submission **Obsequious politeness*

12. Shake – move to and fro **Shake hands *Shake the tree branch*

Convulse – shake the body uncontrollably and involuntarily as in epilepsy, laughter etc. **He convulsed with laughter*

Rock – shake something violently as in storm **The sea waves rocked the boat*

Teeter – shake the body as if about to fall in drunk condition **The inebriated person teetered home*

Totter	– teeter due to weakness **The old man tottered while walking*
Toddle	– shake body as when a child begins to learn walking **A child toddled*
Sway	– to shake with slight movements as tree leaves and branches do in gentle breeze
Wobble	– to shake as does rickety furniture due to loose joints
13. Shameless	– (person, act) lacking sense of shame or modesty
Brazen	– arrogantly shameless **Brazen denial of having done anything wrong*
Brash	– rudely shameless
Impudent	– misbehaving shamelessly
Unabashed	– unembarrassingly shameless
14. Shelter	– place of protection from hostile conditions **A shelter to protect people from rains*
Asylum	– place to provide shelter to mentally ill persons or orphans
Harbour	– place of protection for ships in the sea, or where the criminals are concealed **A cave is the harbour of fugitives *Dark corners in the kitchen provide harbour to insects*
Haven	– place which is a natural protection from hostile conditions **Mother's lap is the ultimate haven for a kid from his or her father's wrath*
Lee	– (a rock, wall) which provides shelter from storm **Lee of a huge rock protects people from storm or rains*
Refuge	– place which provides protection and shelter for people who have fled their houses/homeland **Refuge for people from the war–affected*
15. Shine	– to glow with light **The sun shines*
Dazzle	– to shine brilliantly **Polished shoes dazzled*
Glare	– to glow with intense light **Sun glares in mid–day in summer*
Gleam	– shine with sudden flash of light
Glimmer	– shine with faint light
Glisten	– shine with faint intermittent light

Glitter	– shine brilliantly with reflected light **Gold ornaments glitter*
Scintillate	– shine with flashes of light
Shimmer	– shine with tremulous light
Sparkle	– shine with sparkling light
Twinkle	– shine like stars
Show	– to put/place something in open for other to see
Display	– to show in order to attract attenttion **Display skill*
Parade	– to show something which is impressive * *To bring into others' knowledge.*
Flaunt	– to show prized possession proudly
Flourish	– to show something by waving in air to attract attention
Exhibit	– to show attractlive things in public place. **Art.*
Brandish	– to show by waving in air, gun, weapon etc., to scare away
16. Shrink	– to contract to become less in size **The cloth shrinked on washing*
Shrivel	– (leaf) to contract in size with wrinkles on it due to loss of moisture **Dried leaf shrivels*
Wither	– to shrink on losing freshness **Plucked flowers soon wither*
Wizen	– (skin) shrink with wrinkles due to old age **Wizened skin of old man*
17. Shy	– feeling nervous and hesitant in company with others
Coy	– affectedly shy
Demure	– shy in mixing with strangers **Demure woman*
Modest	– shy of speaking high of oneself **Modest scholar*
18. Similarity	– state of likenness in a particular aspect between two or more **There is no similarity in his behaviour with that of his brother*
Analogy	– similarity for comparison between two different things **There is striking analogy between heart and pump*
Commensuration	– Similarity in measurement **There is no commensuration between his work and salary, which should justifiably be commensurate with each other*

Conformity – similarity in forms or shapes

Correspondence – similarity in response **My affection for him is not in correspondence with his affection for me*

Parity – similarity in status, level **Salary in a company is in parity with another one in the public sector*

Resemblance – similarity in appearance **Resemblance between the twins in toto*

Equivalence – similarity between two different things in value **An ideal consumer, driven by economically rational mind, always tries to gain equivalent to the money paid by him*

19. Sink – go down under the surface of water **The ship sank in the river*

Drown – go down the surface of water and suffocate **Boys drowned in the river*

Dip – put something in a liquid **Dip a wick in oil before lighting it *Dip the nib of this pen in the ink*

Dunk – put solid etable in a liquid eatable so as to make it soft to eat **Dunk bread in milk *Dunk biscuit in tea*

Immerse – plunge something by throwing under water *Image of the Goddess is immersed in the river after the Puja celebration

Overwhelm – to cover something under a mass of something **A huge number of problems have overwhelmed me*

Inundate – to put something under the surface of water by spreading over **Flood water inundated the low–lying areas*

Submerge – to put under the surface of something by lowering it down **A water pump is submerged down the bore to pump up water*

20. Slap – strike someone's side–face with the open palm

Box – strike someone's side–face – below the ears with the fist

Cuff – strike someone's head or face with the back of the open palm

21. Smell – property of a substance which is perceived by olfactory sense, *i.e.*, nose

Odour	– bad, unpleasant odour
Stink	– offensively bad smell
Stench	– very offensive smell
Aroma	– distinctive good smell of something **Aroma of coffee.*
Bouquet	– tasty smell of something being cooked **Bouquet of cooked meat*
Flavour	– savoury smell of tasty food
Fragrance	– sweet smell of flower **Rose fragrance*
Redolence	– sweet smell of mixed fragrance of several flowers **Redolence of flower garden*
Incense	– sweet smell of burning stet (agarbatti)
22. Smile	– to broaden one's lips in happiness
Grin	– to broaden one's lips wide open, exposing teeth
Grimace	– to smile affectedly in disgust/embarrassment with wry face
Simper	– smile affectedly in order to please someone
Smirk	– smile in self–satisfactory expression
23. Speech	– public lecture **Election speech*
Address	– speech delivered to a particular class of audience. **Address to the nation by the President. * The President addressed the joint session of both the houses of Parliament.*
Oration	– eloquent speech **He gave a brilliant oration in the conference*
Talk	– informal speech
Harangue	– vehemently passionate speech
Philippic	– critical speech against a public person or way of life
Sermon	– religious or moral speech
Homily	– speech giving practical advice
Discourse	– speech on a topic by a scholar
Tirade	– abusive speech against someone
24. Spin	– to rotate something on its axis as a top
Whirl	– spin rapidly
Whorl	– rotate on spiral path
Rotate	– turn around on its axis as a wheel

Revolve	– to turn around a circular path **Earth revolves around the sun*
Twirl	– to spin rapidly **Twirl a coin*
Gyrate	– to spin on a base/fixed point
Pirouette	– to spin on one foot or its toe as a dancer
Swivel	– to turn around a fixed base as a swivel chair
25. Spoils	– looted goods **A child brought toffees as spoils from a party *Sleuths discovered huge amounts of currency notes stashed as spoils of office by the corrupt official*
Booty	– stolen goods **They apportioned their booty*
Swag	– stolen goods taken away in bundles
26. Spontaneous	– (coming or happening) without pre–meditated effort **Spontaneous laughter/reaction*
Impromptu	– (to do something) promptly/without taking time to prepare **He delivered an impromptu speech*
Extempore	– (to do something) quickly at the spur of the moment **He replied to the question extempore*
Improvised	– (to do) without looking forward for preparation, without the required provisions **He improvised a poem*
27. Spot	– patch of something undesirable on clean surface **Mud spots on immaculate dress*
Mottle	– irregular patches of circular shape in various colours on animal's skin **Variegated mottles on cow's skin*
Speckle	– small–sized patches of colour different from that of the surface **Stars speckled the blue sky*
Spangle	– patches of glittering circular–sized matter strewn all over the surface., *viz,* glittering glass or metal pieces sewn on a cloth, tiny drops of dews on grass, tiny drops of sweat on the skin of the body **Cold perspiration bespangled his forehead*
Stipple	– patches of small dots scattered all over a surface **Stipples of ink on shirt *Stipples of sunrays coming through trees' leaves dotted the side walk of the road*
28. Spread	– the area to which a folded material can be unfolded **Spread of the carpet covers the whole room*

Extent – the area to which scope of something covers *Extent of the scope of discussion is limited*

Expanse – vast area of space **Expanse of the universe is infinite*

Tract – the area which a land extends to **A large tract of land*

29. Stay – remain in a place **He stayed in the meeting until it ended*

Linger – remain in a place for longer than expected as if reluctant to leave **Foul smell lingered in the room even after opening the doors and windows*

Torry – remain in a place for longer than intended due to compulsion **He had to tarry in a distant town for few days because of suspended trains due to flood *He tarried on the station due to delay in the arrival of the train*

Stagnate – remain in a place and rot due to obstruction in moving ahead **His career stagnated in the absence of the scope of promotions *Pool of water stagnated in the ditches*

30. Steal – to take away someone's possession surreptitiously

Pilfer – to steal in small portions, in instalments **Cashier pilfered cash totalling lakhs*

Filch – to steal through the window in a quick move as in snatching **He filched my bag and fled*

Purloin – to steal by quietly lifting and pocketing **He purloined my watch kept on the table*

Burgle – to steal by breaking into a house at night **A thief burgled my house at night*

Plagiarize – steal a portion of the written text authored by someone else and claim to have written oneself **Plagiarize data from the journals and include in one's own writing*

Embezzle – misappropriate money kept under own custody

31. Stimulate – cause sensitive part of the body to arouse **Stimulate the taste by savoury food*

Impel – cause to move forward by pushing forward **Impel someone to do as desired*

Actuate – cause to move forward by using force to drive *Machine is actuated by mechanical force

Arouse – cause passion to awaken

Goad – spur, prod, provoke to move by poking with spikes *Goad the animal to drag the cart

Provoke – cause to stir anger, annoyance, laughter *Provoke someone to angry retaliation

32. Stoop – to come down below one's dignity to do something mean and selfish **I cannot stoop to lying to my friend *He can stoop to do anything for selfish reason*

Condescend – to come down from one's exalted status to mix socially with people of lower status **The noble person does not mind to condescend with commoners*

Deign – (used always in negative sentence) coming down below one's status to do something which is not befitting one's status **He does not deign to reply to my accusations *He does not deign to argue with lowly persons*

33. Stop – to prevent someone/something from doing some thing **Stop him from speaking*

Arrest – prevent someone from moving freely by taking into custody by police

Check – prevent from spreading further **Check epidemic*

Curb – prevent horse/animal from moving ahead by controlling with rein **Curb horse/dog*

Detain – to prevent someone/something from leaving a place **Police detained a suspect for questioning him *The train was detained at the station for searching luggages*

Restrain – stop someone from doing something under pressure, threat **He was restrained from entering the election fray*

Staunch – stop flow of blood from wound **Tourniquet staunched bleeding*

Stem – stop something/condition from worsening **Stem the rot in the education system*

Stymie – stop progress by hindering **Divisive tendencies stymie the progress of the country*

Stunt – stop the growth of or development of *Luck of nutrition stunts physical development of a child*

34. Strange – surprisingly unusual **Strange customs/behaviour*

Absurd – logically unsual **Absurd reply*

Antic – amusingly unusual **Antic gesture*

Bizarre – horribly absurd **Bizarre idea*

Fantastic – fancifully unusual – devoid of reality **Fantastic idea*

Grotesque – ridiculously unusual **Grotesque shape*

Preposterous – foolishly absurd–like head of an animal in its back, and tail in the front **Preposterous suggestion*

Queer – obliquely unusual **Queer notion of life in America*

35. Strict – uncompromising in observance or enforcement of rules or principles **Strict laws *Strict judge*

Austere – (appearance, face) frighteningly strict **Austere face of a strict teacher*

Stern – firmly uncompromising in observance **Stern disciplinarian*

Stringent – (action, rules) severely uncompromising **Stringent punishment*

Rigorous – uncompromising in applying rules **Rigorous observance of rules*

36. Strike – to hit forcefully **Strike ball*

Smite – hit hard **He smote on the back of someone*

Slug – hit with weapon such as rod etc. **Batsman slugged the ball to the boundary*

Slog – hit at random **Slog the haystack*

Swat – hit with a flat weapon **Swat a bee with a flat cardboard*

Clout – hit softly with open palm **Clout a child to reprimand*

Knock – hit by colliding **Knock door *Car knocked down a cyclist*

37. Struggle – to make efforts to tide over adversity **He struggled the whole life to survive*

Contend – to make efforts to succeed **Sport's participants contended to win*

Cope – to make efforts to deal with difficulties **One has to cope with problems in life*

38. Stub – disposable small part at the end of something usable **Stub of cigarette or pencil*

Stubble – left–over part at the end of something wich is cut above the left over part **Stibble of paddy stalk is left in the ground along with the roots after harvesting the crop *Stubble of beard wich is crropped above it*

Stump – remaining part of a felled tree **Stump of felled tree remains standing there*

39. Suffocate – deprive breathing due to access of fresh air **Suffocated in closed room*

Asphyxiate – deprive breathing by lack of oxygen in body

Choke – deprive breathing as by pressing or obstructing windpipe

Stifle – deprive breathing as by pressing mouth and nose

Strangle – deprive breathing by squeezing throat

Smother – deprive breathing as by fumes, smoke

40. Suggest – to mention an idea, proposal etc. for consideration **I suggested him to go home.*

Advise – to give counsel **He advised me to be cautious*

Recommend – to suggest something to be worthy of acceptance **I recommended his name for job*

41. Surprise – strike someone with wonder **His sudden arrival surprised me*

Amaze – to greatly surprise someone

Astound – to surprise someone beyond wildest expectation **My friend's testimony against me astounded me*

Astonish – to surprise beyond belief

42. Surrender – to give up resisting someone **Surrender to the will of God.*

Capitulate – give up unconditionally or at agreed terms before the enemy **Capitulate under pressure*

Concede – give up fight and accept defeat **The team conceded defeat*

Defer – give up objecting and surrender before someone out of respect **Defer to the wishes of elders*

Submit – give up resistance and surrender reluctantly **Submit before unjust demand*

Succumb – give up resistance when one becomes unable to keep fighting, especially illness/injury **He succumbed to his illness and died*

Yield – give up resistance due to intense pressure **He yielded to his persistent demand*

43. Surround – to encircle a place **This city is surrounded by hills*

Beleaguer – to surround someone to harass him **Seniors beleaguered a fresher in the college*

Besiege – to surround a person or place to make it impossible to escape away **Beggars besiege pilgrims for alms *Troops besieged the town*

Cordon – to surround a person or place to make someone unable to approach or enter **The leader is cordoned by his bodyguards *The meeting place was cordoned off by the police to prevent any outsider from entering*

Maroon – to surround a place/person to isolate or leave helpless **The village was marooned by flood*

Checkmate – to surround a person so as to be unable to make counter attack **Checkmate one's rival*

44. Swell – to become larger in size **His knee has swelled due to injury*

Bloat – to become larger in size due to accumulation of fluid inside **The animal's carcass has bloated*

Distend – to become larger due to pressure inside hollow forcing outer cover outward **Over–eating distended his belly*

Dilate – to become larger in size due to expansion **Medicine dropped in eyes dilated the eyes to facilitate internal examination by the ophthalmist*

Inflate – to become larger in size by pumping air inside **Cyclo tryos inflate with air pumped inside the tubes*

Bulge – to become larger in size by protruding from the surface in round shape **A tumour bulged on his forehead*

45. Sycophant – a person who behaves servilely to someone to please him

Flatterer – a person who praises someone insincerely to please him

Toady – a person who is eveready in service of someone to please him

Lackey – a person who follows someone behind servilely *A lackey walks behind a person moving in a vehicle*

46. Sympathy – (sympathise is verb) feeling of sorrow for a sufferer **His sympathy for the oppressed people drove him to fight injustice*

Empathy – feeling of vicarious suffering to realise how a sufferer must be feeling by imagining himself to be in his place

Compassion – deep sympathy

Condolence – expressing sympathy with a person who has lost his near kin who had died **Condole with the son who has lost his father*

Commiseration – feeling of pity for the sufferer **Commiserate with someone in poor health*

T

1. Talkative – (person) who talks too much **A talkative child*

Loqnacious – who indulges in continuous talking

Garrulous – excessively talkative without much sense or on trivial matters

Glib – who talks non-stop, fluently speaks

2. Tarnish – to make a shining surface dull by smearing dirt **Tarnished glass panes of windows*

Besmear – to make dirty by smearing something

Besmirch – to make dull by discolouring

Blemish – to make a surface dirty by making or marking with spots **Blemish a clean surface by sprinkling ink or colours*

Defile – to make a sacred place dirty

Sully – to make a surface dirty by smearing mud, sullage

3. Tasty – pleasantly agreeable to taste

Delicious – delightfully agreeable to taste

Luscious – juicy and sweet

Delectable – highly delightful **Delectable food*

Succulent – full of juice **Succulent fruit*

4. Tear – to force apart a surface of something **A nail tore his shirt*

Rend – tear into pieces **An explosion rent the body of the victim*

Sunder – tear apart

Split – to tear apart lengthwise from a large piece **Split a log with an axe into two parts*

Cleave – to spearate joint pieces along the joining line **Cleave the cloves of a garlic bulb*

Rive – tear apart from seam, Rip

5. Tempt – (*see lure*)

6. Terrible – causing terror due to being extremely bad, depressing **Terrible news*

Awful – causing fear due to being extremely bad **Awful behaviour*

Enormous – causing fear due to being extremely excessive **Enormous wickedness*

Ghastly – causing shock due to being extremely unpleasant **Ghastly murder*

Horrible – causing disgust due to being so unpleasant **Horrible living condition in slums*

Horrendous – inspiring shudden due to being extremely **Horrendous crime*

Horrid – inspiring horror due to being extremely unpleasant

7. Terrific – inspiring fear due to being extra ordinarily excellent **Terrific performance*

Tremendous – inspiring tremour due to being extraordinarily huge **Tremedous mountain peak*

Immense – inspiring wonder, fear due to being extremely large **Immense vastness of sky*

8. Terrifying – inspiring terror/violent fear caused by being dangerous

Frightening – inspiring fright/sudden fear

Horrifying – inspiring horror/shocking fear as by a gruesome sight **Horrifying sight*

Awesome – inspiring awe

Appalling – inspiring horror causing paleness of face

Dreadful – inspiring dread/fear caused by anticipation of danger

9. Theft – an act of stealing by a thief **A thief committed a theft in this house*

Burglary – an act of stealing by silently entering someone's house

Heist – an act of stealing by forcibly entering **Heist in a bank*

Larceny – an act of stealing someone's property for own use **He is driving a car obtained by larceny*

Piracy – act of stealing something produced, created by someone and sell it as genuine **Piracy of song records (or C.D. tape) *Pirated print of a new cinema.* Also, *robbery on ships sailing in sea by pirates*

10. Thrash – (see Beat)

11. Threat – statement of intention to harm someone as retribution **He received a threat on phone*

Coercion – threat given to someone who is unwilling to do something desired and force him to do it

Duress – threat of cruel treatment to compel someone do as desired

12. Throw – to send out something with a force in a direction **He threw stones in the pond*

Fling – to throw casually so as to fall on the ground **He flung the note–book in anger*

Hurl – throw missiles upon someone in an attempt to hurt someone **He hurled a shoe on the speaker addressing the meeting*

Jettison – throw materials overboard so as to reduce load on aircraft or ship to prevent from falling down or sinking **Jettison goods to keep aeroplane keep flying*

Lob – throw something on a trajectory **He lobbed the ball towards me*

Pelt – throw missile towards someone so as to hit him **Mob pelted stones on the policemen*

Toss – fling a coin in the air to make head or tail

13. Tie – to bind things together with a rope or cord **Tie the hands of the thief*

Fasten – to tie firmly

Gird – to tie a cloth/loin around waist with a belt

Ligate	– tie wound, ruptured skin with surgical cord
Tether	– to tie an animal with a longer rope attached to a stake in the ground so as to limit the movement of the animal upto a limited distance from the stake
Yoke	– tie animals to a horizontal bar attached to a cart so as to drag it
Harness	– tie a horse with the long belts to a vehicle to be dragged by the horse
14. Tolerate	– to put up with without reacting against someone's unpleasant behaviour, thing's harmful effect **I can't tolerate his arrogance anymore *One can tolerate a small amount of poison/bitter taste of capsicum*
Bear	– to put up with something painful or inconvenient with patience **Bear acute pain *Please bear with me until the programme concludes*
Brook	– to put up with something objectionable by taking it as usual occurrence **I can't brook factionalism and indiscipline in party*
Endure	– to put up with something inconvenient, or unpleasant patiently for a long time **I can't endure his gaffe anymore*
15. Tradition	– norms of doing something which has been follow -ed by people from generation to generation **To treat the guest as God is our tradition*
Custom	– norms of doing something conventionally **It is our custom to exchange gifts on festivals*
Practice	– norms of doing something habitually **Daily walking is his practice*
16. Treasure	– wealth of gold and other precious possession accumultatod **Treasure of Nizam of Hyderabad*
Treasure-trove	– a hidden treasure which is dicovered accidently **He chanced upon an attic which turned out to be a treasure-trove*
17. Treasury	– a place where funds of the government are kept deposited
Coffer	– a place where funds of an institution, person are kept stored **Company's coffer depleted in the period of lean season of business*

Fisc – place where public funds are stored *Unclaimed property returns to the fisc*

Exchequer – Nation's treasury *Pension is paid to the employees of the government from the exchequer*

18. Tremble – shaking of body as in fear in quick short movements *He stood there trembling *He began to tremble when confronted by a ferocious dog*

Shiver – shake body due to extreme cold. *He was shivering in winter night*

Shudder – shake with convulsive movement due to horror

Quake – shake violently due to shock *Earth suddenly began to quake due to loud explosion*

Quaver – shaking of one's voice as in fear or excitement *His voice quavered in excitement*

Quiver – shaking to and fro as of trees in light breeze; or lips up and down in excitement *His lips quivered*

Flicker – shaking of flame *Candle's flame flickered in the wind*

19. Trick – (see Ruse)

20. Trifle – to treat something in frivolous manner–that is, in non-serious manner *Trifle with one's own career*

Toy – to treat playfully

Flirt – to treat in casual manner–without serious intent *Flirt with future plan*

Dally – to treat in careless manner *Dally with one's duty*

21. Trim – to cut down irregular branches to smooth shape *Trim garden hedges *Barber trimmed hairs*

Truncate – to cut something short *Truncate a long stick*

Lop – to cut off branches, *viz,* of a tree

Pare – to cut outer layer to remove *Pare potato*

Dock – to cut short the tail of an animal

Poll – cut the horn of an animal

Prune – to cut superfluous part of something *Prune stem off the flower*

Crop – to cut away end protion of something *Crop edges of a photograph*

Clip	– to cut with scissors **Clip the wings of a bird *Clip wool from the sheep*
22. Try	– to make attempt to do something **He tried to run fast to catch up with others*
Endeavour	– to try hard to accomplish something **Endeavour to achieve success*
Strive	– to try laboriously to accomplish **Strive hard to lift a heavy stone*
Persevere	– to try continuously, in spite of failures, to accomplish **He persevered to get selected for the professional course*
23. Turning point	– a stage in time when important changes take place in one's life, history etc.
Climacteric	– a stage in one's life when important changes in physical conditions take place **Climacteric age marks the changes like menopause in women*
Epoch	– a turning point in time of history when important events take place **The treaty ushered in an era of peace *Advent of Gandhi in the freedom struggle marked the epoch-making event in the history of India*
Watershed	– turning point, point of time which divides tow phases of events/distinct histories. **Year 2005 was the watershed in Bihar politics which marked the end of lawlessness and beginning of development.*
24. Twist	– to turn obliquely **He twisted someone's arm*
Wrench	– to turn around by pulling forcefully **Wrench a tight screw*
Wrest	– to twist someone's hand or fist to snatch something he had held firmly **Wrest his arm to snatch a pen from his grip*
Wring	– to twist a bird's neck, clothes to drain water off **Wring wet clothes *Wring fowl's neck to kill it*
Distort	– twist something out of its shape **Collision distorted the vehicle badly*
Contort	– twist lips, face to show cotempt, pain etc. **He contorted his lips in disgust*

U

1. Ubiquitous	– (something ominous) present everywhere **On May Day, the labour movement/demonstration*

*is ubiquitous in the country *Policemen are ubiquitous in the town on a day of disturbed law and order*

Omnipresent – (God, something divine) present everywhere **God is believed to be omnipresent*

Universal – (something applicable) present everywhere **Universal truth *Universal law of gravity*

2. Uncommuncative– not prone to talking

Laconic – prone to talking in few words

Reticent – not inclined to talking about one's own affairs

Taciturn – prone to be cautious in talking by remaining silent. Taciturn approval of the powerful politician is evident in the serious labour agitations.

3. Understanding – mutually tolerant relationship in joint activities **They enjoy perfect understanding *They have an understanding about who would do which part of the work*

Nexus – mutually helping relationship for unfair purpose **Nexus between the politicians and the criminals is well known*

Coordination – mutual understanding in working together in harmony or tandem **Coordination between various agencies helps smooth progress in work*

4. Unrestrained – (activity) without restraint **Unrestrained violence*

Libertine – (immoral activity) unrestrained indulgence **Libertine lecher*

Licentious – unrestrained indulgence in immoral activity without regard to accepted norms **Licentious activities*

Dissolute – unrestrained indulgence in immoral activity without regard to/concerned with the need for control **Dissolute activity.*

Extravagant – unrestrained indulgence in spending, praising etc.

Profligate – recklessly unrestrained indulgence in immoral activity

Rampant – growing unrestrained/unrestricted activity **Rampant corruption*

Wanton – willful indulgence in unchecked wrong activity **Wanton cruelty*

5. Untidy	– (a place) with scattered articles, strewn all around **An untidy room*
Unkempt	– (hairs) not combed to look smooth **Unkempt hairs*
Dishevelled	– (hairs) in disorderly condition **Wind dishevelled his hairs*
Ruffled	– (feathers of bird) in disorderly condition, **Ruffled feathers*
Sloppy	– (dress) loose and unfitting **Sloppy dress.*
Slipshod	– (work, workmanship) ill-cared, lacking in details **Slipshod arrangements*
Slovenly	– (person) with dirty habits/appearance **Slovenly person*
Slatternly	– (woman) with dirty habits/appearance **A slatternly woman*
6. Untiring	– (effort) not to get tired of making efforts to achieve something **Make untiring effort*
Unflagging	– (courage, morale) not to give up or become unvigorous **Unflagging courage*
Indefatigable	– (person) not to get fatigued **Indefatigable warrior*
7. Upheaval	– state of violent disorder turning everything agitated **Political upheaval has gripped the nation*
Turmoil	– state of agitation/disorder
Turbulence	– (river) the state of agitation in the flowing water **Turbulence in the river capsized a boat*
Topsy-turvy	– state of agitation turning everything upside down
8. Upset	– disturbed mentally or emotionally **He is upset because of being badly treated by his friends*
Disconcerted	– disturbed due to confusion
Disconsolate	– disturbed emotionally without or beyond consolation **Disconsolate victim of accident*
Distraught	– Disturbed mentally from grief or worries

V

1. Vacant	– (a place) devoid of its usual occupant **A vacant house is available to let *A vacant niche/seat/ chair*

Vacuum	– a place devoid of air or contents
Void	– a vacuum caused by departure of someone **His demise caused a void in politics*
Empty	– (a place) devoid of its usual contents **Empty bottle/jar/wagon*
Vacuous	– (mind) devoid of ideas **A vacuous mind*
2. Vagabond	– (person) wandering from place to place in the absence of means of livelihood or home
Vagrant	– (person) who wanders idly **Vagrant beggars*
Tramp	– (person) who wanders from place to place by travelling in search of job and means of livelihood
Rogue	– (animal/person) wandering and doing mischief **A rouge elephant on the city roads caused havoc*
3. Verify	– to confirm the truth of something **Events verified his prediction *Verify the spelling of a word*
Certify	– to confirm to genuineness **Certify a document*
Vouch	– to confirm as by practical evidence **His conducts vouch for his being a gentleman*
Attest	– to confirm something to be true
Authenticate	– to confirm something to be genuine
4. Violation	– breach of law/rule
Infraction	– breach of rule by mere failure to adhere to it
Infringement	– breach of other's rights or privileges
Contravention	– breach of rule by going or acting against it **Party defection is in contravention of parliamentary democracy*
Transgression	– breach of limits of own authority or propriety **He indulges in occasional transgression in drinking wine.*

W

1. Wander	– move about aimlessly
Roam	– wander for delight
Prowl	– (animal) wander in search of prey
Gad	– wander even as expected to stay at home **Housewives gad around the marketplace*

Gallivant	– wander in search of pleasure or amusement **Gallivant in park, fair*
Traipse	– wander from place to place for specific purpose **Leaders traipse around for convassing in the elections*
Rove	– wander aimlessly around a place **Rove in the woods*
Loaf	– wander lazily to pass time **Loaf along the river*
2. Warning	– act of making someone aware of danger **He shouted a warning to flee from the house afire*
Caution	– act of making someone circumspect of impending danger
Caveat	– warning to be wary of something suspect
Caveat emptor	– warning to the purchaser to be wary of being duped
Caveat venditor	– warning to the seller against indulging in a malpractice
3. Waver	– change one's opinion/decision repeatedly due to hesitation in remaining firm
Vacillate	– change one's opinion/decision repeatedly due to hesitation in remaining firm
Dither	– change one's opinion/decision due to being indecisive
4. Weird	– fearsome due to being supernatural **Weird stillness of jungle at night*
Uncanny	– fearsome due to being strangely supernatural **Uncanny feeling*
Eerie	– fearsome due to being ghostly **Eerie moaning from a deserted house*
Macabre	– fearsome due to being related to death **Macabre rituals of Tantrik*
5. While away	– to pass time leisurely **While away the day gossiping*
Beguile	– to pass time by doing some meaningful work **Beguile time by reading books or coaching the neighbourhood kids*
Fleet	– to pass time by doing nothing **Fleet one's time sitting in the balcony*

Idle away	– to pass time by walking around without purpose **Idle away time wandering in the sun*
Lounge	– pass time by reclining a on support **Lounge by the roadside lamp-post and talk to the passers-by*
Loll	– to pass time by sitting in laziness **Passengers loll supine on their seats in the train coach*
6. Wicked	– an evil (person)
Iniquitous	– devoid of just and fair attitude **Iniquitous person*
Nepharious	– denunciable iniquity **Napharious neglect of the parents*
Flagitious	– shameful wickedness **Flagitious propaganda*
7. Will	– desire **He has lost his will to fight adversity*
Conation	– ultimate desire **Salvation from mundane world or one's soul is everyone's conation*
Volition	– free will **He did it on his own volition*
8. Worry	– (see anxiety)
9. Wreckage	– broken parts of a ship, aeroplane, train destroyed in an accident
Flotsam	– broken parts of a ship which remain floating on the sea
Jetsam	– broken parts of a ship or jettisoned goods which are washed ashore and salvaged
Lagan	– broken parts of a ship which sink to the bottom of the sea
10. Writhe	– to roll or twist one's body in pain **Writhe in pain*
Squirum	– to roll one's body in embarrassment **He squirmed in his seat due to embarrassment caused by insinuation directed against him by the speech -maker*
Wriggle	– to twist one's body as in an attempt to pass through a narrow passage
Wallow	– to roll one's body in something pleasurable **The buffalow wallows in mud *The rich man wallows in the luxury of his richness*
Welter	– to roll one's body in something difficult to endure **Welter in poverty *Welter in sweltering summer*

ooo

Multiple Choice Question Answers

Choose the correct option out of the given options which can replace the word (marked in bold) in the sentence:

1. He is quite **meticulous** in his dealings with others.
   (A) reserved (B) haughty (C) indifferent (D) careful
2. He committed **heresy** by speaking against the religious orthodoxy.
   (A) offence (B) blasphemy (C) sin (D) crime
3. He is **writhing** in pain.
   (A) rolling (B) wresting (C) squirming (D) twisting
4. His **sardonic** grin was quite offending.
   (A) sneering (B) satisfying (C) nicious (D) caustic
5. His **iniquitous** behaviour hurts me.
   (A) unjust (B) unequal (C) uneven (D) unusual
6. He **segregated** bills and vouchers collected over a period.
   (A) assembled (B) filed (C) sorted (D) separated
7. **Vagabond** urchins loiter all day on the street.
   (A) Tramp (B) Stray (C) Astray (D) Discarded
8. He wore a **somber** expression on his face.
   (A) gloomy (B) shadowy (C) sleeping (D) sorrowful
9. **Rampant** corruption has gripped the nation.
   (A) unchecked (B) furious (C) raging (D) running
10. He squandered money in **wanton** manner.
    (A) willful (B) unjust (C) malicious (D) heedless
11. The wild animal **glared** at its prey.
    (A) glowered (B) stared (C) gloated (D) ogled
12. He **abandoned** his old home and shifted to a new one.
    (A) Renounced (B) Demised (C) Deserted (D) Forsake
13. She indulges in flirtations with reckless **abandon**.
    (A) enjoyment (B) unrestraint
    (C) carelessnes (D) involvement
14. He **abased** his dignity with his questionable deeds.
    (A) degraded (B) lowered (C) reduced (D) depreciated
15. Adulteration **debased** the quality or purity of precious gold.
    (A) devalued (B) depreciated
    (C) lowered (D) enhanced
16. His son's unbecoming conduct has **abashed** him.
    (A) insulted (B) degraded (C) ashamed (D) humbled
17. His fever has started to **abate** after one week.
    (A) worsen (B) improve (C) decrease (D) vanish
18. A kid was **abducted** for ransom from the kid's family.
    (A) kidnapped (B) seduced (C) taken away (D) allured

19. The President of a country **abdicated** to take refuge in another country.
(A) abducted (B) fied (C) renounced (D) resigned
20. He tried to **adduce** a forgotten matter by jogging his forehead with his finger.
(A) deduce (B) to take out from memory
(C) recollect (D) recall
21. He is **adept** in the art of origami.
(A) ignorant (B) clumsy (C) expert (D) recall
22. He earns **adequate** to meet his expenses.
(A) sufficient (B) superfluous
(C) enough (D) just equal to the requirement
23. Mud **stuck** to his shoes.
(A) adhered (B) clung (C) attached (D) affixed
24. Long time **adherent** to the party changed his loyalty in the latter stage of his life.
(A) believer (B) supporter (C) stickler (D) attachment
25. His house is **adjacent** to mine.
(A) contiguous (B) added (C) attached (D) beside
26. The parliament session was adjorned **sine die**.
(A) suspended (B) postponed
(C) deferred (D) without fixing the date of reconvening
27. The position of the political leaders is now a days a **sine cure**
(A) without work (B) cosy
(C) earning income without any care to do something in return
(D) careless
28. The rich man died **sine prole**.
(A) without medicine (B) without money
(C) without offspring
(D) without anyone to care about him
29. The father **admonished** his son for wayward activities.
(A) reproved (B) cautioned (C) rectified (D) apprised
30. The **adonis** was the cynosure of all eyes in the party
(A) aphrodite (B) very handsome young man
(C) narcissus (D) don
31. The grand old man **adored** his grandchildren.
(A) loved (B) liked fervently
(C) worshipped (D) disliked
32. The drawing hall was **adorned** with bric-a-brac.
(A) decorated (B) arranged (C) beautified (D) painted
33. He is an **adroit** sculptor.
(A) clever (B) ingenious (C) adept (D) clumsy

34. The **advent** of Mahatma Gandhi on the horizon of freedom struggle gave a shot in the arm of the struggle.
(A) adventure (B) arrival (C) rise (D) return

35. He is my bitter **adversary**.
(A) enemy (B) antagonist (C) critic (D) adviser

36. He takes **adversities** in life in his usual strides.
(A) enemies (B) antagonists
(C) hardships (D) annoyance

37. The official **adverted** to the complainant and heard his grievances.
(A) turned his attention (B) turned his face
(C) turned his chair (D) turned his eyes

38. The investors were **advised** of the risk involved in the share market.
(A) cautioned (B) informed (C) suggested (D) consulted

39. The programme was organized under the **aegis** of a voluntary organisation (NGO).
(A) age-old experience (B) shield
(C) arrangement (D) routine activity

40. Mount Everest came into existence **acons** ago.
(A) pre-historic period (B) medieval period
(C) indefinitely long period (D) a few centuries ago

41. The accused **acknowledged** his involvement in the crime.
(A) accepted (B) admitted (C) confessed (D) conceded

42. They **acquainted** the boss with their plans.
(A) informed (B) made conversant
(C) made known (D) familiarised

43. The fighter aircraft displayed brilliant **feats** in the air.
(A) aerobics (B) acrobatics (C) aerobatics (D) aeronautics

44. Their **acrimonious** dispute vitiated the relationship.
(A) acrid (B) harsh (C) sharp (D) bitter

45. He is **actuated** by selfish motives.
(A) incited (B) motivated (C) impelled (D) driven

46. He is endowed with remarkable **acumen** in business matters.
(A) acuteness (B) discernment
(C) insight (D) sharpness

47. He lacked the ability to **adapt** to the changed situations.
(A) adjust (B) adopt (C) reconcile (D) conform

48. The parliament was **addressed** by a visiting foreign dignitary.
(A) visited (B) attended (C) lectured (D) advised

49. He is an **affable** and courteous gentleman.
(A) friendly (B) benign (C) pleasant (D) favourable

50. He **affected** ignorance.
(A) feigned (B) adopted (C) preferred (D) assumed

51. He has great **affinity** for sweets.
(A) adherence (B) predilection
(C) affectation (D) attraction

52. He **protested** that the newspaper account is misleading.
(A) objected (B) asserted (C) confirmed (D) denied

53. The old man is **afflicted** with crippling gout.
(A) inflicted (B) affected (C) distressed (D) lashed

54. His insinuation was an **affront** to me.
(A) attack (B) criticism (C) directed (D) offence

55. Epidemic struck the people in the **aftermath** of flood.
(A) resultant event (B)consequence
(C) disaster (D) calamity

56. Advance age has **aggravated** his ailments.
(A) annoyed (B) irritated (C) worsened (D) aggrieved

57. The gory sight of the accident left us **aghast**.
(A) amazed (B) frightened (C) horrified (D) shocked

58. The aeroplane was **airborne** on schedule.
(A) afloat (B) aloft (C) flying (D) soaring

59. The door of the room was **ajar**.
(A) shut (B) open (C) wide open (D) partly open

60. He did his job with **alacrity**.
(A) bitter feelings (B) regretfully
(C) unwillingly (D) liveliness

61. He has **alienated** his entire family.
(A) estranged (B) deserted
(C) antagonised (D) annoyed

62. He **alighted** from the aeroplane with his hand-bag.
(A) descended (B) disembarked
(C) dismounted (D) boarded

63. Gossipping is the **ailment** of idle persons.
(A) nutrient (B) food
(C) pastime (D) entertainment

64. The court ordered a handsome **alimony** to the divorcee.
(A) maintenance (B) alms
(C) sustenance (D) allowance

65. The minister's assurance **allayed** the people's fear of draconian law.
(A) mitigated (B) mollified (C) soothed (D) moderated

66. He often **alludes** to his yeoman's services.
(A) insinuates (B) refers (C) reminds (D) hints

67. The adviser of the president acts as his **alter ego** during his absence.
(A) another self(B) confidant (C) alternative (D) deputy

68. He always takes an **altruistic** approach.
(A) unselfish (B) truthful (C) charitable (D) generous

69. He is **alumnus** of a prestigious college.
(A) student (B) graduate (C) admirer (D) pass-out
70. His personality is a strange **amalgam** of contradictory traits.
(A) alloy (B) combination
(C) merger (D) blend
71. He is an **ameteur** of cricket.
(A) aficionado (B) novice (C) dabbler (D) expert
72. The **ambiguities** of modern poetry render it difficult to comprehend.
(A) equivocations (B) complexities
(C) uncertainties (D) explicitness
73. Nomads are **ambulatory** tribes.
(A) walking (B) prehensile (C) moving (D) roving
74. Robbers lurked behind a bush in **ambush**.
(A) waiting to attack (B) concealed
(C) hiding (D) waiting
75. Masters like to hire **amenable** servants.
(A) manageable (B) docile
(C) tractable (D) stubborn
76. The offender was **amerced** for traffic violation.
(A) punished (B) mulcted (C) penalised (D) fined
77. I think something is **amiss** in your plan.
(A) missing (B) wrong (C) astry (D) offending
78. The government offered **amnesty** if the rebels lay down arms.
(A) permission (B) pardon
(C) forgetfulness (D) ignorance
79. He became **amorous** of her on the very first look.
(A) enamoured (B) infatuated (C) passionate (D) loving
80. He is bubbling with **amour patriae**.
(A) love (B) loyalty (C) patriotism (D) fatherhood
81. He refused to compromise with his **amour propre**.
(A) first love (B) self-esteem (C) love affair (D) love
82. People want to get **ample** supply of tap water in their houses.
(A) adequate (B) abundant (C) overflowing (D) profuse
83. She was **amused** by the children's conversation.
(A) excited (B) pleased (C) aroused (D) happy
84. Using modern sports car in a historical film is **anachronism**.
(A) wrong time reference (B) time matching
(C) obsolete (D) disorder
85. Calmpose tablet is used as an **analgesic**.
(A) pain reliever (B) febrifuge
(C) antipyretic (D) tranquiliser
86. I don't see any **analogy** between our problems.
(A) comparison (B) agreement (C) similarity (D) difference

87. His misdemeanour earned his father's **anathema**.
(A) loath (B) hate
(C) dislike (D) imprecation

88. Her presence **animated** the party.
(A) enlivened (B) stimulated (C) energized (D) fortified

89. A deep-seated **animosity** between the two sisters was a problem for the family.
(A) opposition (B) hostility (C) enmity (D) antagonism

90. The victorious country **annexed** part of a territory of the defeated country.
(A) appended (B) added
(C) attached (D) supplemented

91. The ruling party was **annihilated** in the election.
(A) defeated (B) destroyed (C) decimated (D) vanquished

92. The deity was **anointed** by the priest.
(A) smeared (B) desecrated
(C) rubbed with oil (D) annoyed

93. A quiet person was an **anomaly** in his exuberant family.
(A) odd (B) incongruous
(C) inconsistency (D) deviation

94. Little is known about his **antecedents**.
(A) precedence (B) anti activities
(C) events (D) character

95. He meets his guests in his house's **anterior** hall.
(A) backside (B) internal (C) front (D) posterior

96. Antiquated machines are lying idle in the factory.
(A) old (B) obsolete (C) antique (D) archaic

97. Hot is **antithesis** of cold.
(A) contrast (B) against
(C) opposed (D) direct opposite

98. The government seems to be **apathetic** to controlling corruption.
(A) unsympathetic (B) unconcerned
(C) against (D) concerned

99. Many **apocryphal** stories about him are doing rounds.
(A) false (B) spurious (C) doubtful (D) unauthentic

100. He is a rowed **apologist** of the government policies.
(A) critic (B) demanding apology
(C) defender (D) analyst

101. Movie stars are **apotheosis** of glamour to the fans.
(A) god (B) icon
(C) deified symbol (D) symbol

102. He was terrified by ghostly **apparitions** in sleep.
(A) appearance (B) phantom
(C) wraith (D) spirit

103. Politicians have unsatiated **appetite** for power.
(A) desire (B) need (C) hunger (D) craving

104. He gave his critics an **apposite** reply.
(A) opposite (B) apt (C) irrelevant (D) adapted

105. The police did not **apprehend** violent mood of the mob.
(A) catch (B) grasp (C) anticipate (D) perceive

106. A huge fund was **appropriated** in the budget for primary education.
(A) made suitable (B) provided
(C) justified (D) set aside

107. God is the sole **arbiter** of our fate.
(A) mediator (B) decision-maker
(C) arbitrator (D) judge

108. He is my **arch** rival.
(A) cunning (B) sly (C) mischievous(D) chief

109. **Archaic** social traditions have become irrelevant.
(A) antique (B) antiquated (C) old (D) medieval

110. **Ardent** devotees thronged the congregation.
(A) earnest (B) fervent (C) passionate (D) fierce

111. He cunningly **arrogated** the credit of someone who did the job.
(A) appropriated (B) claimed
(C) assumed (D) snatched

112. He filed the documents **arsy-varsy**.
(A) topsy-turvy (B) preposterous
(C) haphazardly (D) reverse

113. The orator **articulated** his ideas.
(A) jointed (B) enunciated
(C) expressed clearly (D) spoke

114. The author **ascribed** innocence to the wife of her cruel husband in the novel.
(A) described (B) imputed (C) indicated (D) attributed

115. He looked **askance** at me.
(A) doubtfully (B) distrustfully
(C) disapprovingly (D) obliquely

116. He vehemently **aspersed** on his opponents.
(A) sprayed (B) traduced (C) sprinkled (D) attacked

117. He is an **assiduous** student.
(A) diligent (B) vehement (C) arduous (D) acerbic

118. The neophyte **assimilated** the party doctrines quickly.
(A) learnt (B) imbibed (C) arduous (D) acerbic

119. He passed the evening **assorting** collected bills and vouchers.
(A) arranged (B) sorted (C) distributed (D) classified

120. He **assumed** the style of an aggressive go-getter.
(A) pretended (B) supposed (C) adopted (D) expected

121. He **assured** us that everything would be well.
(A) ensured (B) promised (C) confirmed (D) insured

122. He is an **astute** politician.
(A) arrogant (B) shrewd (C) pragmatic (D) keen

123. One should **atone** for committing sinful deeds.
(A) expiate (B) pardon (C) amend (D) reconcile

124. He attributed his bad temper to his ill health.
(A) allocated (B) contributed
(C) assigned (D) credited

125. The student's **audacity** shocked the teacher.
(A) temerity (B) arrogancy
(C) recklessness (D) boldness

126. He works overtime to **augment** his income.
(A) add (B) increase (C) enlarge (D) eke out

127. Good monsoon **augurs** bumper harvest.
(A) prognosticates (B) predicts
(C) interprets (D) indicates

128. His stoic **aura** crumbled at the slightest provocation.
(A) halo (B) atmosphere
(C) character (D) greatness

129. A marriage is solemnised on an **auspicious** day.
(A) opportune (B) favourable (C) propitious (D) holy

130. The principal's **austere** face was enough to quail them.
(A) fiery (B) grave (C) stern (D) strict

131. The harsh punishment **avenged** the crime.
(A) retributed (B) revenged (C) requited (D) reciprocated

132. He is not **averse** to extending amnesty to the rebels.
(A) repugnant (B) disgusted (C) loath (D) opposed

133. Our plan to stage protest against the government went **awry**.
(A) askew (B) distorted (C) lopsided (D) crooked

134. His non-stop **babble** is annoying.
(A) utterance (B) chatter (C) murmur (D) humming

135. The **babel** in the meeting made it impossible to understand who is telling what.
(A) noisy confusion (B) noisy uproar
(C) chattering (D) noise

136. The dissidents' plan to attack the policies of the party **backfired**.
(A) rebounded (B) boomeranged
(C) recoiled (D) returned

137. The **background** of one's upbringing shapes one's character.
(A) situation (B) milieu
(C) environment (D) experience

138. The seats in the coach were **back-to-back**.
(A) front-to-front (B) dos-a-dos
(C) round robin (D) face-to-face

139. The dispute engendered **bad blood** between rivals.
(A) enmity (B) hostility (C) animosity (D) bloody war

140. Offers of discount are favourite **baits** to lure customers employed by sellers.
(A) ploys (B) traps (C) ruse (D) hooks

141. The cart-pulling horse suddenly **baulked** at moving ahead.
(A) jibbed (B) stopped (C) refused (D) hesitated

142. They **bamboozed** us into joining their team.
(A) pushed (B) shoved (C) hoodwinked (D) bambooed

143. They were **bandying** accusations upon each other.
(A) trading (B) exchanging (C) throwing (D) bowling

144. He **banged** the door open in anger.
(A) stroke (B) blew (C) slammed (D) threw

145. The guests were **banqueted** to sumptuous menu.
(A) honoured (B) feasted (C) regaled (D) partied

146. His acerbic **barbs** were pinching.
(A) thorns (B) pointed edges
(C) carping remarks (D) beards

147. An inebriate suddenly **barged** into my room.
(A) broke (B) entered (C) forced (D) intruded

148. The vote-seekers **barnstorm** countryside soliciting votes.
(A) raid (B) campaign (C) tour (D) visit

149. The reporters overwhelmed the minister with **barrage** of questions.
(A) volley (B) barrier (C) flood (D) obstruction

150. The police **barricaded** the meeting ground.
(A) blocked (B) obstructed (C) surrounded (D) barred

151. Venal officials **barter** their pride for material gains.
(A) exchange (B) swap (C) trade (D) bargain

152. Nobody **bats** an eye on outrageous behaviour of the present-day politicians.
(A) opens (B) flutter (C) closes (D) casts

153. The spectators **bated** their breaths at the nip-and-tuck race.
(A) held (B) restrained (C) lessened (D) drew

154. A pioneer does not tread on a **beaten** path.
(A) thrashed (B) trodden (C) used (D) defeated

155. This gown **becomes** your personality.
(A) comes for (B) attracts (C) fits (D) befits

156. I warn you stop **badgering** me.
(A) pestering (B) worrying (C) baiting (D) disturbing

157. I **beaconed** him to come near me.
(A) light house (B) warned (C) signalled (D) guided

158. Stop **befudding** the public with misleading propaganda.
(A) muddling (B) stupefying (C) meddling (D) fudgeing

159. He **begrudged** his friend getting the award.
(A) envied (B) reluctantly accepted
(C) resented (D) coveted

160. He is used to **beguile** lazy afternoon with reading good books.
(A) pass pleasantly (B) while away
(C) fleet (D) waste away

161. Tourists amusingly **behold** marching sentries on the Wagah border.
(A) catch (B) look (C) regard (D) witness

162. A maverick is **beholden** to no one.
(A) obligated (B) attached (C) responsible (D) look at

163. It does not **behoove** you to be rude to others.
(A) honour (B) suit (C) appropriate (D) honourable

164. The volcano suddenly became active and began to **belch** smoke and fire.
(A) eructate (B) blow out (C) eject (D) emit

165. His trembling hands **belied** his calm voice.
(A) lied down (B) falsified (C) contrasted (D) controlled

166. A peace treaty was formalised by the **belligerent** countries.
(A) hostile (B) bellicose (C) pugnacious (D) warring

167. The injured animal **bellowed** in pain.
(A) roared (B) cried (C) howled (D) wailed

168. The rich man was solicited **benefaction** for earthquake victims.
(A) benefit (B) charity (C) goodness (D) kindness

169. A small **bequest** of a testator made him live comfortably.
(A) donation (B) charity
(C) disposition by will of property (D) will

170. A serious illness **bereaved** them of their mother.
(A) deprived (B) survived (C) killed (D) snatched

171. They **beseeched** him to come home at once.
(A) castigated (B) solicited (C) begged (D) appealed

172. Propaganda was aimed at **besmirching** his good reputation.
(A) smearing (B) tarnishing (C) spoiling (D) besotting

173. Nobel prize is **bestowed** on the renowned achievers.
(A) gifted (B) awarded (C) stowed (D) conferred

174. "Woe **betide** you," He cursed.
(A) gifted (B) awarded (C) stowed (D) conferred

175. He inadvertently **betrayed** a secret.
(A) exposed (B) revealed (C) misled (D) deceived

176. The boy and the girl were **betrothed** recently.
(A) engaged (B) married (C) tied in knots (D) united

177. His **tearful** plea was designed to bias the judge.
(A) prejudice (B) incline (C) favour (D) bend

178. The couple used to **bicker** as a matter of habit.
(A) flicker (B) quiver (C) argue (D) quarrel

179. He bade **adieu** to his friend going abroad.
(A) good bye (B) bon voyage (C) farewell (D) good wishes

180. He does not earn even to meet his **bare** needs.
(A) naked (B) open (C) minimal (D) bald

181. He expects us to do his **bidding** all the time.
(A) command (B) summons
(C) performing (D) subordination

182. He **bided** his time until right opportunity to take revenge on me.
(A) called (B) waited (C) wasted (D) sought

183. Villages agreed to **billet** visiting students from the town.
(A) let enter (B) allow stay
(C) provide requested lodging (D) chase out

184. He is an annoying **blab**.
(A) blabbermouth (B) bore
(C) idiot (D) egoist

185. He suddenly **blacked out** due to acute weakness.
(A) became black (B) became unconscious
(C) fell down (D) became dark faced

186. Long illness has **blanched** her face.
(A) dried (B) whitened (C) bleached (D) tanned

187. The loudspeaker **blared** cheap songs all night.
(A) emit (B) sounded loudly
(C) shrieked (D) roared

188. He remained **blase** throughout the programme.
(A) bored (B) annoyed (C) cloyed (D) surfied

189. He was **blasphemed** by the critics for airing his frank opinion.
(A) blasted (B) slandered (C) applauded (D) abused

190. Their faces **blazed** with enthusiasm.
(A) fired (B) gleamed (C) burnt (D) glowed

191. His pioneering research **blazed the trail** in the field of space science.
(A) fired (B) triggered
(C) showed the new path (D) led

192. His eyes became **bleary** with tears.
(A) blurred (B) filled (C) dim (D) blotted

193. One-year discontinuity in his studies became a **blemish** on his career.
(A) blame (B) blot (C) defect (D) flaw

194. Sky and sea seemed to **blend** in the horizon.
(A) mix (B) combine (C) mingle (D) combine

195. Pests **blighted** the crops in the field.
(A) wilted (B) crippled (C) withered (D) blasted

196. Career promotion has **bloated** his ego.
(A) expanded (B) distended (C) puffed (D) inflated

197. Campaign against corruption proved to be **blockbuster**.
(A) explosive (B) highly effective
(C) deadly (D) useful

198. The child has **bloomed** into a handsome youth.
(A) blossomed (B) flowered (C) developed (D) grown

199. A bully **blusters** to cow down others.
(A) threatens (B) flusters
(C) rebukes (D) utters empty menaces

200. The spectators **bolstered** the morale of their respective teams with shouting encouraging slogans.
(A) propped (B) raised (C) supported (D) enhanced

201. Bonafides of this person is suspect.
(A) good behaviour (B) goodness
(C) faithfulness (D) truth

202. Reduction in the rates of income tax was a **bonanza** granted by the government to the tax payers.
(A) bonus (B) good gain (C) windfall (D) favours

203. He is a minister and a litterateur **to boot**.
(A) bargain (B) help (C) besides (D) extra

204. The dog **bounded** across the field.
(A) leashed (B) tied (C) bolted (D) ran

205. He gave the boy a **box** on his ear.
(A) spar (B) slap (C) strike (D) blow

206. Conceited people use to **brag**.
(A) bark (B) boast (C) shout (D) yell

207. He **braided** strands of twigs in a rope.
(A) twisted (B) branded (C) weaved (D) plaited

208. The desparado **brandished** his gun to scare the people away.
(A) aimed (B) flourished (C) fired (D) shook

209. A midnight **brawl** disturbed the sleeping neighbours.
(A) noise (B) shouting (C) squabble (D) fighting

210. His **brazen** arrogance shocked everyone around.
(A) impudent (B) bold (C) shy (D) brassy

211. The tree's branches swayed in the **breeze**.
(A) whiff (B) slow wind (C) storm (D) gale

212. **Brevity** made his speech impressive.
(A) duration (B) boldness (C) briefness (D) fearlessness

213. A law and order crisis is **brewing** in the town.
(A) concocting (B) fomenting (C) developing (D) steeping

214. Tea was filled in the cup to its **brim**.
(A) edge (B) rim (C) brink (D) top

215. The enraged animal **bristled** up.
(A) ran briskly (B) raised its hairs erect
(C) brushed (D) became stiff

216. I won't **brook** interference in my work.
(A) suffer (B) tolerate (C) allow (D) brood

217. He quickly **browsed** the shelf for something to read.
(A) looked cursorily (B) inspected
(C) searched (D) peeped

218. Stormy sea waves **buffeted** ships around aimlessly.
(A) feasted (B) ate (C) pushed (D) blew

219. He used to **bully** his classmates.
(A) intimidate (B) beat
(C) pushed around (D) butted

220. His friend always stood by him as a **bulwark**.
(A) bull (B) defence
(C) rampart (D) protecting wall

221. A ferocious bull **bunted** a man down on the ground.
(A) chased (B) butted
(C) pushed with its head (D) hanged on its horns

222. A small town **burgeoned** into a city within a decade.
(A) bloomed (B) spurted (C) grew (D) became big

223. The company could not cope with the tough market competition and went **bust**.
(A) broke (B) burst (C) bankrupt (D) ruined

224. The ingenuous boy usually becomes the **butt** of ridicule in the group.
(A) head (B) handle (C) point (D) target

225. She **cached** her valuables in a safe place.
(A) kept (B) enclosed (C) catched (D) hided

226. She is in a habit of **cadging** groceries from the neighbours.
(A) stealing (B) catching (C) begging (D) borrowing

227. A government tends to become **callous** after staying in power for a long time.
(A) hard (B) insensitive
(C) apathetic (D) exposed

228. He takes every opportunity to **calumniate** his rivals.
(A) challenge (B) slander (C) insult (D) call upon

229. It has become a trend in films to cast famous actors of the past in **cameo** role.
(A) engraved (B) short scene
(C) gem (D) superfluous

230. Military tanks are painted green to **camouflage**.
(A) beautify (B) disguise (C) colour (D) make visible

231. He gave a **candid** reply to the query.
(A) brilliant (B) shining (C) honest (D) frank

232. The **candour** of his speech impressed the audience.
(A) candidness(B) openness (C) fairness (D) impartiality

233. The wrecked car was **cannibalised** of its working parts to fit into another car which needed these parts.
(A) eaten (B) deprived
(C) strengthened (D) rehabilitated

234. He is a **canny** businessman.
(A) astute (B) skilled (C) thrifty (D) cautious

235. He violated the basic **canons** of good behaviour.
(A) mortars (B) armours
(C) rules (D) fundamentals

236. **Cants** of hawkers are difficult to comprehend.
(A) lingo (B) speech (C) call (D) shouting

237. **Cantankerous** maid was a bane to housewife.
(A) cruel (B) peevish (C) shouting (D) idiotic

238. The auditorium has a large **capacity**.
(A) ability to receive (B) power
(C) capability (D) ability

239. Smaller nations **capitulate** to the degemony of America.
(A) buckle (B) sag (C) yield (D) capture

240. A **capricious** person acts to the dictates of his fancy.
(A) unpredictable (B) changing
(C) vicarious (D) whimsical

241. Her stunning beauty **captivated** the beholders.
(A) captured (B) fascinated (C) imprisoned (D) caught

242. The **carcass** of once-thriving industrial town is lying desolate now due to the closure of industry.
(A) dead remains (B) deadbody
(C) cadaver (D) skeleton

243. Probity in one's personal life is of **cardinal** value.
(A) important (B) fundamental
(C) prime (D) cordial

244. The moving car suddenly **careened** besides the road.
(A) turned (B) tilted (C) overturned (D) broke down

245. The train **carriered** towards the destination.
(A) hurtled (B) ran (C) speeded (D) departed

246. The lover **caressed** beloved hairs.
(A) preened (B) tidied (C) petted (D) combed

247. He is fond of **carnal** pleasure.
(A) corporal (B) corporeal (C) sensual (D) human

248. Stinking **carrion** lying on the road nauseated the passers-by.
(A) garbage (B) deadbody (C) rot (D) vegetables

249. He was handed over a **carte blanche** in a deal for his piece of land.
(A) signed document (B) signed blank cheque
(C) white paper (D) full authority

250. Oligopoly is fraught with **cartel** formation to fleece the consumers.
(A) association (B) group
(C) business nexus (D) pricing

251. Petrol price-rise has **cascading** effect on the market.
(A) waterfall (B) successive
(C) head long (D) falling

252. **Cassandras** of doom of the world are destined to be belied.
(A) prophetesses (B) fortune-tellers
(C) prediction-mongers (D) announcers

253. **Castor** wheels enable the trolley move in all the directions.
(A) rotating (B) swivelling (C) casted (D) small

254. He went out to the market dressed in his **casuals**.
(A) occasional dress (B) irregular dress
(C) informal dress (D) usual dress

255. A missile was **catapultated** in space.
(A) hurled (B) captured (C) launched (D) shot

256. An earthquake caused **catastrophe** in the area.
(A) misfortune (B) deluge (C) triumph (D) calamity

257. Cheap films **cater** for the popular taste of cinegoers.
(A) pander (B) supply (C) provide (D) satisfy

258. He is a man of **catholic** taste.
(A) christian (B) liberal
(C) broad-minded (D) whole

259. Boatman **caulked** the seams between jointed planks.
(A) watertight (B) closed
(C) filled the gap (D) nagging

260. We all detested his **cavalier** manners.
(A) gallant (B) domineering
(C) supercilious (D) nagging

261. Art galleries are **caviar** to the general public.
(A) distasteful (B) detasted
(C) unappreciated by the ignorant (D) unpopular
262. He could not find anything to **cavil** about the arrangements.
(A) object (B) find faults (C) oppose (D) appreciate
263. Newspapers were unanimous in **censure** of the government policy
(A) censor (B) reproach (C) consensus (D) support
264. Orderly meeting suddenly broke into **chaos**.
(A) disorder (B) chasm (C) battle (D) jumble
265. Boiling milk **charred** her fingers.
(A) singed (B) grilled (C) boiled (D) ruined
266. A **charlatan** pretends to be knowledgeable.
(A) pedant (B) quack (C) impostor (D) fraud
267. She is excessively **chary** of her friends.
(A) suspicious (B) trustful (C) confident (D) wary
268. His effort to escape was **checkmated**.
(A) defeated (B) prevented
(C) completely checked on all sides (D) manoeuvred
269. She **chicaned** him into marrying her.
(A) coerced (B) cheated (C) cajoled (D) tricked
270. He is a **chronic** smoker.
(A) habitual (B) constant (C) inveterate (D) incorrigible
271. Arrange the bills and vouchers in **chronological** order.
(A) fixed (B) definite
(C) in sequence of time (D) periodical
272. The policeman received a **citation** for bravery.
(A) award (B) quotation
(C) censure (D) commendation
273. He **cited** the rules in his defence.
(A) saw (B) quoted (C) censure (D) commendation
274. They **clamoured** their demands in the meeting.
(A) shouted (B) claimed (C) forced (D) announced
275. **Clandestine** meeting of rebels took place in jungle.
(A) underhand (B) secret (C) hidden (D) illicit
276. The doors **clattered** in the wind.
(A) rattled (B) clashed (C) closed (D) collapsed
277. This costume designer has the patronage of wealthy **clientele**.
(A) witnesses (B) customers (C) franchisees (D) followers
278. His career has reached its **climax**.
(A) pinnacle (B) plateau (C) climacteric (D) zenith
279. He was happy to have **clinched** a business deal.
(A) grasped (B) clasped (C) secured (D) bit

280. He conducts his affairs in a **cloak** of secrecy.
(A) caper (B) pretext (C) mask (D) cover

281. The thieves **clobbered** the inmate when he resisted them from collecting the booty.
(A) battered (B) defeated
(C) closed in a room (D) pushed

282. The cars **clogged** the road due to heavy traffic.
(A) hindered (B) impeded (C) stuck (D) choked

283. The recluse leads a **cloistered** life.
(A) enclosed (B) confined (C) quiet (D) secluded

284. Over-indulgence in anything soon **cloys** you.
(A) gluts (B) satiates
(C) causes aversion (D) disgusts

285. The whole **clutch** of kittens invaded the kitchen.
(A) bevy (B) ensemble (C) brood (D) hatch

286. A loud thunderbolt **curdled** my blood.
(A) congealed (B) clogged (C) coagulated (D) stopped

287. He **cocooned** himself in blankets.
(A) sheltered (B) protected (C) ensconced (D) warmed

288. Family members **coddle** elderly persons who are unable to care for themselves.
(A) ignore (B) molly coddle
(C) ameliorate (D) mollify

289. The police resort to **coercive** measures to quell the riot.
(A) corrective (B) forcible (C) compelling (D) intimidating

290. These two mountains are **coeval** in existence.
(A) ancient (B) of same age
(C) contemporaneous (D) very old

291. **Coffers** of corrupt officials overflow with slush money.
(A) lockers (B) purse (C) vaults (D) almirah

292. A **cog** of the motor's gear wheel got broken.
(A) clab (B) nail (C) tooth (D) slot

293. The court took **cognizance** suo motu of police atrocity on innocent people.
(A) recognition (B) consideration
(C) complaint (D) notice

294. There is no **coherence** in his argument.
(A) sticking together (B) cohession
(C) consistency (D) glue

295. A dictionary is an output of long-time **collaboration** of many minds.
(A) nexus (B) connivance
(C) combined labour (D) alliance

296. One has to **collate** someone's statement with that of another to know the truth.
(A) arrange (B) inspect (C) attach (D) corroborate

297. The surgeon **colligated** two ends of incision.
(A) collected (B) tied (C) cut (D) combined

298. They **colluded** in hatching a conspiracy.
(A) combined (B) conspired (C) agreed (D) contracted

299. Commit a **colossal** fraud on public.
(A) humongous(B) unusual (C) big (D) nasty

300. The soldier was **commended** for bravery.
(A) recommend (B) mentioned
(C) mention with praise (D) commented

301. Payment was not **commensurate** with the quantum of work I do.
(A) equal in measure (B) measurable
(C) equal (D) adequate

302. We **commiserated** with him over the demise of his wife.
(A) felt sorry (B) condoled (C) repented (D) empathised

303. A **complaisant** person will never antagonise anyone.
(A) satisfied (B) complaining
(C) inclined to please (D) obliging

304. He **comports** himself with utmost dignity.
(A) reports (B) supports (C) deports (D) conducts

305. His **comprehension** of physics is amazing.
(A) doubt (B) understanding
(C) dislike (D) vast knowledge

306. He **conceded** defeat in the election even as the counting was halfway.
(A) counted (B) agreed (C) surrendered(D) admitted

307. A brief spell of good performance filled the player with **conceit**.
(A) humility (B) arrogance
(C) vanity (D) over-estimation

308. Their **concerted** efforts won them success.
(A) continuous (B) done in collaboration
(C) combined (D) laborious

309. You can **conciliate** the respect of your associates with sincerity of intent.
(A) win over (B) appease (C) restore (D) antagonise

310. He is quick to **concoct** an excuse for not fulfilling his commitment.
(A) mix up (B) juggle (C) imagine (D) cook

311. The teacher **condescended** to the student's intellectual level, in order to enable them to comprehend the subject.
(A) stoop (B) compromised
(C) lowered his level (D) assented

312. He **confected** a home remedy from herbs.
(A) contrived (B) concocted
(C) sold (D) sweetened

313. The culprit **confessed** his complicity in the crime.
(A) surrendered (B) revealed
(C) admitted (D) conceded

314. She **confides** in no one but her husband.
(A) believes (B) reveals (C) trusts (D) commits

315. He **confined** himself in the house the whole day.
(A) limited (B) enclosed (C) immured (D) restricted

316. His property was **confiscated** so that the banks' loans could be cleared.
(A) seized (B) appropriated
(C) distrain (D) forfeited

317. Complicated court's jargons **confound** the litigants.
(A) perplex (B) surprise
(C) bewilder (D) increase the confusion

318. He successfully **confuted** his opponent's charges.
(A) denied (B) confounded
(C) disputed (D) refuted

319. Devotees **congregate** on the banks of the holy rivers on the religious occasions.
(A) flock (B) assemble (C) throng (D) crowd

320. Spectators of the match could merely **conjecture** the outcome.
(A) speculate (B) surmise (C) project (D) conclude

321. The policeman on duty **connived** at the traffic violations.
(A) winked (B) ignored (C) complied (D) conspired

322. He **consigned** unpleasant thoughts to oblivion.
(A) set apart (B) delivered (C) devoted (D) banished

323. He came to the party with his **consort**.
(A) spouse (B) escort (C) group (D) associate

324. He was **conspicuous** by his booming laughter.
(A) seen (B) evident (C) visible (D) noticeable

325. The dais was abuzz with **constellation** of great orators.
(A) brilliance (B) stars (C) group (D) assemblage

326. His moral conscience **constrained** him to abstain from wrongdoings.
(A) curbed (B) forced (C) obliged (D) held

327. He **contemplates** buying a new car.
(A) plans (B) thinks (C) ponders (D) proposes

328. His misdeeds were **contemptible**.
(A) mean (B) pardonable(C) abject (D) admirable

329. He is **contemptuous** of people of lower ranks.
(A) disregardful (B) disdainful
(C) condemnable (D) averse

330. This locality is dotted with **contiguous** houses.
(A) closely situated (B) continuous
(C) touching (D) dirty

331. He **contorted** his lips in disgust.
(A) bent (B) stretched
(C) mangled (D) twisted

332. He is the most **contrary** child I have ever seen.
(A) adverse (B) willful
(C) contradictory (D) discordant

333. The threat of dire consequences was **couched** in his police speech.
(A) cushioned (B) folded (C) rapped (D) convoluted

334. Indiscipline should not be **countenanced.**
(A) approved (B) encouraged (C) abetted (D) patronized

335. Condole with someone aggrieved with **counterfeit** grief.
(A) mock (B) fraudulent (C) ersatz (D) sham

336. It was a **crass** misrepresentation of facts.
(A) gross (B) delicate (C) shameless (D) boorish

337. The soldier **crawled** towards the enemy post in darkness.
(A) slithered (B) squirmed (C) creeped (D) strode

338. We did not lend **credence** to the wild rumours.
(A) support (B) belief (C) claim (D) credit

339. Problems **crop** up every now and then in his life.
(A) appear (B) manifest (C) surface (D) grow

340. Fearful of a loud thunderbolt, a boy **crouched** under the table.
(A) crawled (B) hide (C) kneeled (D) covered

341. An argument **culminated** in fisticuff.
(A) concluded (B) developed (C) climaxed (D) grew

342. Workers took up **cudgels** for wage revision.
(A) fight (B) club (C) weapons (D) arguments

343. The director raised his finger to give the actor **cue to start** his dialogue.
(A) clue (B) stimulus (C) suggestion (D) hint

344. The hall is adorned with **curios**.
(A) curious decorations (B) objects of art
(C) precious objects (D) valuable objects

345. He hurled **curses** on his adversary.
(A) malediction (B) swear
(C) profanity (D) accusation

346. **Cute** mannerism of the baby was pleasing.
(A) curt (B) pretty (C) cunning (D) keen

347. He is **crazy** about the cricket game.
(A) mad (B) cool (C) sane (D) shaky

348. He is temperamentally a **credulous** person.
(A) suspicious (B) creditable
(C) unsuspecting (D) crude

349. It is a very **critical** moment in his life.
(A) hazardous (B) crucial (C) precarious (D) unimportant

350. He was censured for his **culpable** act.
(A) criminal (B) heinous (C) blameworthy(D) praiseworthy

351. He is trying to **cultivate** friendship with me.
(A) till (B) grow (C) neglect (D) improve

352. He is crazy about **accumulating** wealth.
(A) amassing (B) gathering (C) filling (D) squandering

353. Police used force to **curb** violence.
(A) quell (B) check (C) block (D) encourage

354. He is very **curious** about his neighbours.
(A) desirous (B) inquisitive (C) indifferent (D) excited

355. **Current** practice of endogamous marriages is crumbling now.
(A) prevalent (B) running (C) obsolete (D) modern

356. He gave a very **curt** reply to my query.
(A) rude (B) brief (C) abrupt (D) polished

357. He followed **customary** practice of visiting the neighbours occasionally.
(A) habitual (B) conventional
(C) uncommon (D) regular

358. He is **cynical** about his colleagues' motives.
(A) insane (B) contemptuous
(C) distrustful (D) trusting

359. He deliberately **dallies** with his duties.
(A) procrastinates (B) fondles
(C) hastens (D) loiters

360. There is a **dearth** of doctors in the hospitals.
(A) famine (B) abundance (C) plethora (D) scarcity

361. Health gradually **decays** in old age.
(A) rots (B) degenerates
(C) decomposes (D) flourishes

362. She has acquired reputation for **deceit**.
(A) deception (B) fraud (C) honesty (D) distortion

363. **Deciduous** trees take on new leaves annually.
(A) permanent (B) shedding
(C) evergreen (D) eternal

364. He is a man of **decisive** actions
(A) determining (B) determined
(C) conclusive (D) prevaricat

365. He **affirmed** his intention to resign his job.
(A) offended (B) averred (C) denied (D) asserted

366. A **decrepit** old man could hardly walk.
(A) weak (B) infirm (C) emaciated (D) vigorous

367. **Dedicated** workers are the assets of a company.
(A) devoted (B) sacrificing (C) dallying (D) triffling

368. He is a scholar of **deep** knowledge.
(A) profound (B) abysmal (C) shallow (D) drowning

369. The **defective** machine hampered the progress of the work.
(A) imperfect (B) faulty (C) flawless (D) abnormal

370. The meeting was **deferred** due to the lack of quorum.
(A) postponed (B) put off
(C) held on schedule (D) yielded

371. He was in a **defiant** mood.
(A) defeating (B) obedient (C) rebellious (D) decorous

372. **Deficit** in money withheld the work on the project.
(A) flaw (B) shortage (C) want (D) surplus

373. The **defiled** house was stinking.
(A) impure (B) sullied (C) impured (D) immaculate

374. He felt **degraded** with their remarks.
(A) defeating (B) obedient (C) rebellious (D) decorous

375. The defeated team members wore a **dejected** expression.
(A) rejected (B) sad (C) despirited (D) elated

376. The guests were treated with **delectable** dinner.
(A) delightful (B) tasteful (C) charming (D) disagreeable

377. Factory chimney spewed **deleterious** fumes.
(A) harmless (B) pernicious (C) stinking (D) unpleasant

378. It was a **deliberate** action.
(A) careful (B) intentional
(C) premeditated (D) impulsive

379. He has a **delicate** sense of smell.
(A) crude (B) exquisite (C) fragile (D) delightful

380. She takes great **delight** in teasing me.
(A) charm (B) joy (C) satisfaction (D) distress

381. Oh! God, **deliver** me from these boring people.
(A) throw (B) liberate (C) enthrall (D) save

382. He **demurred** to accept the post offered to him.
(A) wavered (B) hesitated (C) refused (D) agreed

383. The **demure** girl sat aloof.
(A) sober (B) hesitant (C) indecorous (D) arrogant

384. People **denounce** the politicians as morally corrupt.
(A) declare (B) announce (C) condemn (D) commend

385. He **denied** me what was my due.
(A) refused (B) withheld (C) allowed (D) repudiated

386. We all wshould **deplore** the present state of morality.
(A) bemoan (B) denounce (C) rejoice (D) applaud

387. One earnestly **desires** to join family get-together in festivals.
(A) yearns (B) craves (C) solicits (D) loathes

388. Polar regions are **desolate** places.
(A) sad (B) uninhabited
(C) populous (D) barren

389. Rescuers made a final **desperate** attempt to save the child.
(A) reckless (B) hopeless (C) hopeful (D) intolerable

390. He has become **despondent** about his failing health.
(A) dependent (B) despairing (C) happy (D) encouraged

391. He is now **destitute** of resources due to reckless squandering.
(A) deprived (B) needy
(C) impoverished (D) affluent

392. He could not get a job yet due to his **desultory** attempt.
(A) distressing (B) fitful (C) consistent (D) pertinent

393. He **detected** a theif lurking behind the house in the dark.
(A) descried (B) discovered (C) overlooked (D) missed

394. He is a devout Hindu.
(A) sincere (B) holy (C) pious (D) irreverent

395. He is a **dextrous** artist.
(A) deft (B) clever (C) inept (D) righthanded

396. This creeper is **dextrorse**.
(A) right-handed (B) climbing from right to left
(C) climbing straight up (D) sinistrorse right

397. **Diffident** person shirks from taking the responsibility.
(A) confused (B) defiant
(C) unconfident (D) self-confident

398. Narrow arteries are **dilated** to all blood flow.
(A) expanded (B) expatiated (C) spread (D) constricted

399. The government adopts **dilatory** tactics in taking unpalatable decision.
(A) procrastinating (B) deferring
(C) prompt (D) widening

400. He **discarded** the old hat.
(A) rejected (B) cast aside (C) threw (D) retained

401. Hooting by audience **disconcerted** the orator.
(A) ruffled (B) discomfitted
(C) calmed (D) confused

402. Bereaved of elder brother, he was **disconsolate**.
(A) unhappy (B) inconsolable
(C) soothed (D) sad

403. There is stark **discrepancy** in what you preach and what you practise.
(A) gap (B) contrariness
(C) consistency (D) discreetnee

404. He brought **disgrace** on his family with his misdeeds.
(A) insult (B) ignominy (C) respect (D) honour

405. His petty quibblings **disgusted** me.
(A) delighted (B) relished (C) offended (D) annoyed

406. A gust of wind **dishevelled** his hairs.
(A) tidied (B) disarrayed (C) hanged (D) loosened

407. Stashed pot of valuables was **disintered** from the courtyard's underground.
(A) burried (B) exhumed (C) dug out (D) extracted

408. He is **disinterested** in their dispute.
(A) impartial (B) un-interested
(C) having selfish motive (D) indifferent

409. He was in **dismal** mood.
(A) sinister (B) melancholic
(C) gay (D) annoyed

410. He **dismantled** the machine's parts for packing.
(A) broke (B) knocked down
(C) separated (D) assembled

411. Deadlock in negotiation **dismayed** both sides.
(A) grieved (B) disheartened
(C) encouraged (D) pained

412. Wind **dispersed** the cloud in the sky.
(A) dispelled (B) gathered (C) blew (D) drove away

413. His **disposition** towards meticulousness in work is appreciable.
(A) inclination (B) proclivity
(C) unwillingness (D) mental

414. He **disregarded** my advice.
(A) ignored (B) heeded (C) disrespected (D) mistreated

415. She **dissembled** crookedness with ingenuous pretention.
(A) betrayed (B) concealed (C) dispersed (D) dismantled

416. **Dissuated** him from leaving the job.
(A) persuaded (B) deterred (C) discouraged (D) dissipated

417. His stomach **distended** with flatulence.
(A) extended (B) protruded (C) bloated (D) shrunk

418. **Distinction** in height helps us identify the twins.
(A) clarity (B) confusion (C) difference (D) resemblance

419. The boy was reading the story of a damsel in **distress**.
(A) agony (B) comfort (C) danger (D) safety

420. **Diurnal** cacophony on city roads subsides in late evening.
(A) daytime (B) nocturnal (C) daily (D) morning

421. Social and cultural **diversity** is the uniqueness of our countery.
(A) divergence (B) dis-similarity
(C) difference (D) uniformity

422. Compassion is **divine** virtue in a person.
(A) supreme (B) sacred (C) mundane (D) religious

423. Docile workers readily follow the instructions.
(A) submissive(B) meek (C) intractable (D) stubborn

424. Pet is a d**omesticated** animal.
(A) domestic (B) tamed (C) household (D) wild

425. He is sitting with **dreary** face.
(A) fearful (B) gloomy (C) dreaded (D) cheerful

426. He is a **droll** person.
(A) comically humorous (B) serious
(C) boring (D) whimsical

427. He is a person with **dusky** complexion.
(A) shadowy (B) swarthy (C) blond (D) twilight

428. He made an **earnest** appeal to people to help him.
(A) urgent (B) arrogant (C) fervent (D) triffling

429. It is our weakness to run after **earthly** pleasure.
(A) divine (B) mundane (C) ordinary (D) worthless

430. His **egotism** has alienated all his friends.
(A) egoism (B) self-conceit(C) humility (D) selfishness

431. The sun **emerged** from behind the clouds.
(A) cam out (B) emanated (C) immerged (D) mixed up

432. Hordes of technocrats **emigrate** to U.S.A. every year.
(A) leave own country to settle in a foreign country
(B) immigrate (C) move (D) flee

433. He soon rose to **eminence** in his field of expertise.
(A) exclusiveness (B) prominence
(C) reputation (D) obscurit

434. He is **encumbered** with numerous obligations.
(A) enmeshed (B) burdened (C) hampered (D) disburden

435. His arrogant behaviour **infuriated** me.
(A) incensed (B) pacified (C) fired (D) provoked

436. Social system has still **enslaved** womenfolk.
(A) bonded (B) imprisomed
(C) emancipated (D) suppressed

437. Toys of childhood are **ephemeral**.
(A) temporary (B) permanent (C) shortlived (D) long lasting

438. **Epicurean** leaders of present time are in sharp contrast of Gandhian leaders.
(A) indulgent in luxury (B) sensuous
(C) ascetic (D) licentious

439. We **esteem** him for his honesty.
(A) commend (B) respect (C) disdain (D) support

440. The universe is **eternal**.
(A) unchanging (B) perpetual
(C) enduring (D) transitory

441. Griffing with patients' treatment is against the professional **ethics**.
(A) beliefs (B) honesty
(C) immorality (D) principles of morality

442. The minister tried to **evade** reporter's questions.
(A) dodge (B) confront (C) escape (D) elude

443. Adversaries always tend to **exaggerate** one's weakness.
(A) extenuate (B) magnify (C) overstate (D) extend

444. He was **exzalted** to venerable position by the people.
(A) elevated (B) depreciated
(C) downgraded (D) praisesd

445. The boy is endowed with **exceptional** intellect.
(A) special (B) peculiar (C) average (D) outstanding

446. He is reputed to be easily **excitable**.
(A) stimulated (B) placid (C) infuriated (D) provoked

447. The old woman began to **execrate** all those who were teasing.
(A) denounce (B) imprecate (C) damn (D) bless

448. Cool breeze **exhilarated** the morning walkers.
(A) inspired (B) exhorted (C) cheered up (D) depressed

449. Moneylenders charge **exorbitant** interests on loans.
(A) prevailing (B) usurious (C) fair (D) unusual

450. He ordered his staff to **expedite** the work.
(A) hasten (B) move
(C) procrastinate (D) ensnare

451. He is an **expert** in this field.
(A) experienced (B) greenhorn
(C) knowledgeable (D) connoiss

452. He expressed his **explicit** opinion.
(A) open (B) unequivocal
(C) confused (D) ambiguous

453. His remark was **extraneous** to the topic at hand.
(A) extrinsic (B) extra (C) impertinent (D) rare

454. He is an **extravagant** person.
(A) expensive (B) spendthrift
(C) immoderate (D) thrifty

455. This the story of **fabulous** exploits of an adventure.
(A) marvellous (B) fictitious
(C) factual (D) historical

456. The hall is adorned with **factitious** flowers.
(A) fictional (B) artificial (C) real (D) factual

457. Fiction writer needs a fecund mind.
(A) prolific (B) fruitful (C) effete (D) lazy

458. He made a **fervent** appeal for support.
(A) feverish (B) fiery (C) burning (D) dispassionate

459. He is a person of exteremely **fickle** mind.
(A) capricious (B) stable (C) capacious (D) fictitious

460. The servant's **fidelity** towards his master is perfect.
(A) fealty (B) belief (C) disloyalty (D) confidence

461. He extended a **flimsy** excuse for his failure.
(A) thin (B) shoddy (C) loose (D) convincing

462. He is my bitter **foe**.
(A) adversary (B) feud (C) friend (D) fiend

463. Lack of generosity is his notable **foible**.
(A) failing (B) character (C) forte (D) flaw

464. Speeches shall be **followed** by dinner.
(A) accompanied (B) succeeded
(C) preceded (D) ensued

465. He is feeling **forlorn** of own people in this distant city.
(A) sad (B) in company of
(C) desolate (D) hopeless

466. The **former** of the two suggestions was acceptable.
(A) prior (B) past (C) latter (D) ancient

467. A **fortuitous** incident changed his life.
(A) fortunate (B) incidental (C) accidental (D) deliberate

468. He is a man of **frail** body constitution.
(A) fragile (B) brittle (C) delicate (D) robust

469. Fresh vegetables are available in abundance.
(A) new (B) raw (C) unfaded (D) stale

470. She is worried about her **froward** daughter.
(A) contrary (B) arrogant (C) tractable (D) frowing

471. He is very **frugal** in spending money.
(A) miser (B) prudent (C) penurious (D) lavish

472. He made a **futile** attempt to appease his foe.
(A) vain (B) fruitless (C) effectual (D) frivolous

473. **Gallant** soldier captured the enemy post singlehanded.
(A) galloping (B) chivalrous (C) valorous (D) cowardly

474. Clouds are **gathering** in the sky indicating rainfall.
(A) accumulating (B) collecting
(C) dispersing (D) fritteri

475. **Gaudy** decor looks vulgar.
(A) showy (B) garish (C) immodest (D) sober

476. Kids were frolicking in **gay** spirit.
(A) miserable (B) jolly (C) wanton (D) showy

477. **Germane** facts were collected to reach the conclusion.
(A) genuine (B) relevant (C) inept (D) inapt

478. **Giant** stature of a woman makes her unattractive.
(A) great (B) monstrous (C) huge (D) petite

479. His carrer prospect seems to be gloomy.
(A) shady (B) dark (C) bright (D) hopeless

480. He is sitting with **glum** face.
(A) morose (B) dark (C) sorrowful (D) cheerful

481. His social service brought **glory** to her.
(A) wonder (B) fame (C) grace (D) obloquy

482. Human beings are generally **gregarious** people.
(A) reclusive (B) seclusive (C) social (D) unsocial

483. He **grieves** over the loss in business.
(A) laments (B) weeps (C) rejoices (D) keens

484. Ordinary people **hallow** the saints.
(A) honour (B) venerate (C) consecrate (D) desecrate

485. Bad weather **hampered** the progress of the work.
(A) hindered (B) furthered (C) interfered (D) delayed

486. The group, though looked cohesive, lacked **harmony**.
(A) symmetry (B) melody (C) concord (D) discord

487. A **hasty** decision usually makes one repentant.
(A) precipitate (B) testy (C) deliberate (D) quick

488. He never **heeds** sane advice.
(A) listens (B) cares (C) worries (D) ignores

489. He was punished for his **heinous** offence.
(A) sinful (B) feral
(C) irreprehensible (D) admirable

490. He is **humble** despite high rank.
(A) arrogant (B) polite (C) meek (D) submissive

491. He is **ignorant** of what is happening around him.
(A) oblivious (B) unknown (C) aware (D) illiterate

492. He was censured for his **ignoble** conduct.
(A) honuorable (B) ignominious
(C) inferior (D) infamous

493. Breaking out of war with hostile country is **imminent**.
(A) impending (B) possible (C) remote (D) impossible

494. Innoculation renders a child **immune** from diseases.
(A) impune (B) exempt (C) resistant to (D) susceptible

495. His **impassionate** appeal moved people.
(A) emotional (B) impassive (C) tranquil (D) inflamed

496. An **impecunious** person was unable to procure basic needs.
(A) penniless (B) poor (C) wealthy (D) indigent

497. He was feared due to his **imperious** behaviour.
(A) unnecessary (B) perilous
(C) overbearing (D) submissive

498. His **impertinent** behaviour annoyed me.
(A) irrelevant (B) brazen (C) insane (D) polite

499. He is known to always take **impetuous** decisions.
(A) rash (B) emotional (C) careful (D) studied

500. A country is left **impoverished** by war it fights.
(A) reduced to poverty (B) bereft
(C) enriched (D) poor

501. The boy got punishment for his **impudent** behaviour.
(A) bold (B) arrogant (C) brazen (D) courteous

502. His habit of lying is **acquired** since childhood.
(A) inherent (B) natural (C) cultivated (D) congenital

503. Dissatisfaction **incites** anger.
(A) stimulates (B) instigates (C) subsides (D) encourages

504. The crowd was **instigated** by inflammatory speech to resort to violence.
(A) provoked (B) exhorted (C) deterred (D) urged

505. The police **inculpated** him with unlawful activity.
(A) exonerated (B) incriminated
(C) ensnared (D) indicted

506. He is **indifferent** towards politics.
(A) attracted (B) unconcerned
(C) concerned (D) similar

507. This plant is **indigenous** to India.
(A) autochthonous (B) aboriginal
(C) alien (D) natural

508. The **implacable** creditor refused to give more time to return money despite entreaties.
(A) cruel (B) inexorable (C) merciful (D) flexible

509. He **improvised** his act directly on the stage.
(A) extemporize (B) rehearsed
(C) provided (D) prepared

510. Rain water **ingressed** into the houses in the low-lying areas.
(A) immersed (B) entered (C) egressed (D) progressed

511. People somehow got rid of **iniquitous** despot.
(A) unjust (B) cruel (C) hostile (D) righteous

512. **Inordinate** delay in the train's arrivals irked the passengers.
(A) disorderly (B) excessive
(C) unreasonable (D) moderate

513. **Inquisitive** mind keeps on asking why.
(A) prying (B) peeking (C) curious (D) uninterested

514. An **intrepid** person des not hesitate to venture.
(A) anxious (B) fearless (C) shaky (D) timid

515. The **irascible** old man was easily provoked to anger.
(A) testy (B) irritating (C) calm (D) rash

516. The spy was in **jeopardy** of being discovered.
(A) danger (B) hazard (C) chance (D) safety

517. He is in **jolly** mood.
(A) sportive (B) jovial (C) melancholy (D) playful

518. She **ravelled** the knot like a Gordian knot.
(A) tangled (B) unravelled (C) revolved (D) complicated

519. They pursued their goal in a **lackadaisical** manner.
(A) lacking (B) listless
(C) unconcerned (D) lively

520. Spectators **lauded** their home team for winning the game.
(A) extolled (B) celebrated (C) lamented (D) shouted

521. She **lavished** praise on him.
(A) lashed (B) heaped (C) grudged (D) reserved

522. **Lax** laws engenders a sense of impunity in the offenders.
(A) rigid (B) strict (C) lenient (D) loose

523. He **leeched** his friend until the entire fortune was exhausted.
(A) sucked (B) sponged on
(C) treated (D) befooled

524. A **libertine** person is despicable.
(A) free (B) licentious (C) prudish (D) pure

525. It was **lifeless** performance.
(A) dead (B) animate (C) dull (D) living

526. Gymnast's daily practice keeps his muscles **limber**.
(A) stiff (B) lithe (C) bending (D) loose

527. His body was **limp** with exhaustion.
(A) loose (B) drooping (C) tired (D) erect

528. One can see the bottom of the **limpid** pool.
(A) pellucid (B) lucid (C) calm (D) opaque

529. **Lineage** of a race horse determines its worth.
(A) age (B) pedigree (C) posterity (D) performance

530. In the absence of meaningful engagements, time **lingers**.
(A) fleets (B) lengthens (C) tarries (D) stays

531. An incompetent person becomes **malevolent** towards successful people.
(A) injurious (B) malicious (C) benevolent (D) selfish

532. **Malign** people in high position without substance.
(A) vilify (B) abuse (C) praise (D) despise

533. He is suffering from **malignant** tumour.
(A) malevolent (B) malicious (C) pernicious (D) benign

534. The holiday was **marred** by bad weather.
(A) damaged (B) impaired (C) spoilt (D) enhanced

535. The lawyer **marshalled** facts before arguing the case in the court.
(A) ordered for (B) arranged in order
(C) combined (D) scattered

536. He is a **mendacious** person.
(A) false (B) veracious (C) lying (D) untrue

537. Mostly the non-government organizations, though they profess to work for poor people, yet are **mercenary**.
(A) profit-seeking (B) venal
(C) voluntary (D) dishonest

538. He is **meticulous** about his physical appearance.
(A) finical (B) fearful (C) methodical (D) careless

539. A **moderate** change in the existing law is required.
(A) mild (B) excessive (C) radical (D) harsh

540. He leads a **modest** life.
(A) modern (B) moderate (C) pretentious (D) unassuming

541. Need to take tough stand against corruption is a **moot** point.
(A) doubtful (B) debatable (C) indisputable (D) major

542. **Morbid** condition of the economy is a cause of concern.
(A) deadly (B) bad (C) sick (D) healthy

543. Rejected by voters in the election, many small parties are in **moribund** state.
(A) discarded (B) dying (C) vivacious (D) closure

544. His death was **mourned** by his colleagues.
(A) deplored (B) lamented (C) remembered (D) rejoiced

545. He **mumbled** his views on the subject of discussion.
(A) articulated (B) muted (C) muttered (D) uttered

546. She is so **naive** as to believe in anyone.
(A) novice (B) simpleton (C) crafty (D) non-sense

547. His wife keep on **nagging** at him all day.
(A) pricking (B) hectoring (C) comforting (D) complaining

548. He **nibbled** at the apple he was eating.
(A) bite (B) gorged (C) gulped (D) scratched

549. He gave the restaurant waiter a **niggardly** tip.
(A) poor (B) stingy (C) miser (D) generous

550. The accused was pronounced guilty, defence lawyer's brilliant arguments **notwithstanding**.
(A) failure (B) despite (C) due to (D) without

551. He is a **novice** in politics.
(A) tyro (B) experienced
(C) fool (D) new

552. **Obnoxious** smell forced us to cover our nose.
(A) annoying (B) odious (C) offensive (D) delightful

553. New models of cars become **obsolete** in a few years.
(A) old (B) outdated (C) in vogue (D) antique

554. **Ominous** dark clouds look **ominous**.
(A) portentous (B) threatening (C) propitious (D) harmful

555. Public anger against price-rise of petrol is **palpable**.
(A) obvious (B) evident
(C) perceptible (D) imperceptible

556. An amount of one rupee is a **paltry** sum these days.
(A) petty (B) contemptible
(C) significant (D) inconsiderable

557. He **paraded** his medal and prizes proudly.
(A) marched (B) flaunted
(C) concealed (D) promenaded

558. Checking corruption in the country is **paramount**.
(A) supreme (B) most important
(C) unimportant (D) superior

559. Grief is **patent** on her face.
(A) unconcealed (B) latent
(C) dim (D) obscure

560. The old man was sitting in **pensive** mood.
(A) sorry (B) grieving
(C) thinking (D) thoughtless

561. It is a **perennial** fruit bearing plant.
(A) throughout the year (B) seasonal
(C) perpetual (D) eternal

562. His **perfidious** friend ditched him.
(A) faithful (B) disloyal (C) perfect (D) false

563. He does his job in **perfunctory** manner.
(A) professional (B) functional

(C) indifferent (D) diligent

564. Mountaineering is a **perilous** adventure.
(A) injurious (B) risky
(C) safe (D) disadvantageous

565. The building **perished** in the earthquake.
(A) ruined (B) survived (C) decayed (D) disappeared

566. The shrine witnesses **perpetual** stream of pilgrims.
(A) unending (B) discontinuous
(C) permanent (D) temporary

567. **Persistent** incidents of violence in the city make people afraid of moving out freely.
(A) insistent (B) steady (C) sporadic (D) tenacious

568. A **perspicacious** person does not easily get befooled.
(A) astute (B) transparent
(C) imperceptive (D) dim

569. The import of what he said in his speech was **perspicuous**.
(A) indistinct (B) lucid (C) opaque (D) bright

570. He was **persuaded** to perjure in the court.
(A) agreed (B) induced (C) dissuaded (D) coaxed

571. Do not try to **pervert** my statement.
(A) distort (B) correct (C) mislead (D) misuse

572. A hypochondriac in suffering from **phantom** feeling of pain in the abdomen.
(A) real (B) imaginary (C) ghost (D) illusory

573. He is a man of **phlegmatic** disposition.
(A) humorous (B) placid (C) passionate (D) passive

574. The devotee leads a life full of **piety**.
(A) pain (B) devotion (C) veneration (D) irroverence

575. His **piteous** cry for help moved us.
(A) reverent (B) pathetic (C) delightful (D) pious

576. The political leaders **pillory** each other in public fora.
(A) push (B) ridicule publicly
(C) approbate (D) laugh at

577. His slogans are full of **platitudes**.
(A) cliche (B) novelty (C) repetitions (D) trivial

578. He gave a **plausible** explanation of his failure to accomplish the assigned task.
(A) applaudable (B) truthful
(C) specious (D) untrue

579. People of **plebeian** taste can't appreciate abstract art works.
(A) sophisticated (B) vulgar
(C) popular (D) trite

580. The power breakdown **plunged** the whole city into darkness.
(A) stooped (B) submerged(C) emerged (D) soared
581. His **poignant** remorse was cathartic.
(A) severe (B) pricking (C) sincere (D) mild
582. She was walking carefully **poising** a water jug on her head.
(A) balancing (B) controlling
(C) disbalancing (D) stabilizing
583. **Polemical** views of bigots are a threat to social harmony.
(A) uncompromising (B) controversial
(C) eirenic (D) argumentative
584. To joust with a potent person is not a **politic** act.
(A) shrewd (B) expedient (C) tactless (D) clever
585. People's outrage over rising hardships due to high inflation **portends** doom for the government.
(A) augurs (B) forebodes (C) threatens (D) foretells
586. Judgment of this age should be left to **posterity**.
(A) descendants(B) ancestry (C) priority (D) future
587. Several **potent** arguments were put forward to prove the point.
(A) weak (B) powerful (C) cogent (D) useful
588. His plan was unacceptable because it was not **practicable**.
(A) practical (B) feasible (C) unattainable (D) worth
589. He is a **practical** politician.
(A) sensible (B) unwise (C) practising (D) practicable
590. Job tenure in private companies is **precarious**.
(A) secure (B) unsure because of depending on other's mercy
(C) unsteady (D) dangerous
591. Many a tribal society is still mired in **primitive** traditions.
(A) primary (B) pristine (C) old (D) modern
592. He is highly regarded because of his impeccable **probity**.
(A) venality (B) rectitude (C) obediency (D) sincerity
593. A **prodigal** person is likely to be impoverished in due course of time.
(A) improvident (B) frugal
(C) proud (D) extraordinary
594. A precocious child possesses **prodigious** talent.
(A) extra-ordinarily marvellous
(B) commonplace (C) proven (D) progressing
595. Harsh retort by the son **ruffled** his father.
(A) upset (B) untidied (C) smoothed (D) soothed
596. Tyrants are **ruthless**.
(A) compassionate (B) cruel
(C) adamant (D) ferocious

597. Holy shrines are **sacred** to the devotees.
(A) pious (B) blasphemous
(C) pure (D) venerable

598. **Sagacious** patriarch is a source of prudent advice.
(A) sapient (B) practical (C) illustrious (D) foolish

599. **Salient** features of a machine determine its price.
(A) solid (B) outstanding
(C) basic (D) unimportant

600. The chief organizer delivered his **salutatory** speech.
(A) valedictory (B) welcoming
(C) favourable (D) beneficial

601. The criminals committed the crime with complete **sangfroid**.
(A) composure (B) discomfiture
(C) confusion (D) easiness

602. The boy passed **scurrilous** remarks on the girls passing by.
(A) obscene (B) jocular (C) decent (D) crude

603. He has **queer** notion about life in U.S.A.
(A) different (B) odd (C) usual (D) questionable

604. **Radical** change in polity is needed to check rampant corruption.
(A) root (B) basic (C) superficial (D) drastic

605. He failed to **redeem** his pawned watch due to want of money.
(A) reclaim (B) ransom (C) forfeit (D) abandon

606. It is very difficult to handle a **refractory** child.
(A) hard (B) obstinate (C) obedient (D) rude

607. The party refused the return of the **renegades** into party fold.
(A) apostates (B) adherents (C) sticklers (D) traitors

608. **Repentance** cleanses the sinner's soul.
(A) remorse (B) sorrow (C) impenitence(D) regret

609. He **repudiated** the charges made against him.
(A) disowned (B) enforced (C) accepted (D) contradicted

610. Dispersal of clouds **revealed** the sun in the sky.
(A) shrouded (B) divulged (C) unveiled (D) concealed

611. The river takes a **sinuous** path through the valley.
(A) side (B) straight (C) flexuous (D) circuitious

612. People are **skeptical** about government's sincerity to curb corruption.
(A) shaky (B) confident (C) doubtful (D) cynic

613. A **somber** passage way led to the large hall.
(A) gloomy (B) doleful (C) dusky (D) bright

614. The **voluble** spokesman kept on speaking to the chagrin of the listeners.
(A) succinct (B) verbose (C) strident (D) loud

615. Only a few lucky ones could **survive** in the disaster.
(A) succour (B) remain alive
(C) succumb (D) win

616. It is not wise to **squander** the precious resources.
(A) spend (B) preserve (C) dissipate (D) splurge

617. He is **steadfast** in his faith.
(A) staunch (B) firm (C) wavering (D) constant

618. He unleashed a vicious campaign to **tarnish** my reputation.
(A) blacken (B) blemish (C) brighten (D) exalt

619. His position in the team is **tenuous**.
(A) slender (B) strong (C) attenuated (D) tender

620. She took out frozen stuff from the refrigerator and kept on the table to let it **thaw**.
(A) warm (B) deliquesce (C) melt (D) freeze

621. It is not good to **traduce** someone's character.
(A) malign (B) abuse (C) praise (D) expose

622. **Treason** is an unforgivable crime.
(A) loyalty (B) sedition (C) treachery (D) patriotism

623. He was forgiven for **venial** offence.
(A) vicious (B) pardonable (C) felonious (D) serious

624. His **wanton** disregard of others' sentiments is not appreciable.
(A) willful (B) reckless (C) lewd (D) unintentional

625. This town has **warm** climate throughout the year.
(A) hot (B) moderately hot
(C) cold (D) cool

626. The wet log got **warped** on getting dried up.
(A) bent (B) straightened
(C) twisted (D) flat

627. His **wayward** son has become incorrigible.
(A) willful (B) obedient (C) astray (D) capricious

628. He looked **weary** after long hours of work.
(A) tired (B) interested (C) energetic (D) sad

ooo

Exercises on Synonyms

Test-1

Use the most appropriate meaning of the words out of the given options:

1. Archaic
   (A) Archive (B) Abysmal (C) Antiquated (D) Pristine
2. Assignation
   (A) Tryst (B) Assignment
   (C) Secret meeting (D) Secrecy
3. Assent
   (A) Accede (B) Acquiesce (C) Subscribe (D) Disagree
4. Aborigine
   (A) Indigenous (B) Native
   (C) Original (D) Imported
5. Abandon
   (A) Desert (B) Forsake (C) Abjure (D) Renounce
6. Abate
   (A) Alleviate (B) Mitigate (C) Stop (D) Assuage
7. Abstain
   (A) Refrain (B) Abscond (C) Elude (D) Assert
8. Confess
   (A) Admit (B) Surrender (C) Affirm (D) Approve
9. Apposite
   (A) Opposite (B) Appropriate (C) Germane (D) Opposing
10. Appraise
    (A) Apprise (B) Evaluate (C) Appease (D) Approve
11. Exhort
    (A) Criticize (B) Urge (C) Abuse (D) Rebuke
12. Conspicuous
    (A) Manifest (B) Secret (C) Conspiring (D) Clear
13. Anthem
    (A) Praise (B) Requiem (C) Admiration (D) Alleluia
14. Aroma
    (A) Bouquet (B) Flavour (B) Arrogance (D) Malodour
15. Obstinate
    (A) Audacious (B) Obscure (C) Obvious (D) Austere
16. Avert
    (A) Convert (B) Revert (C) Advert (D) Evade
17. Indict
    (A) Impeach (B) Indicate (C) Infuriate (D) Dictate

18. Abject
(A) Ignoble (B) Objectionable
(C) Abominable (D) None of these

19. Usurp
(A) Arrogate (B) Soak (C) Use up (D) Unusual

20. Aquit
(A) Quit (B) Exple (C) Exonerate (D) Remove

21. Levitate
(A) Float in air (B) Soar (C) Ascend (D) Make lavish

22. Franchise
(A) Delegate (B) Emancipate (C) Incriminate (D) Chafe

23. Abscond
(A) Skive (B) Abstain (C) Discard (D) Forfeit

24. Vitriolic
(A) Virtuous (B) Verify (C) Mordant (D) Habituated

25. Deft
(A) Skilled (B) Deaf (C) Dumb (D) Very fast

26. Hug
(A) Defile (B) Cling (C) Humiliate (D) Honour

27. Adjourn
(A) Prorogue (B) Resume (C) Applaud (D) Inflict

28. Distraught
(A) Disturbed (B) Disconcerted
(C) Startled (D) Amazed

29. Fealty
(A) Allegiance (B) Dirty (C) Befitting (D) Augur

30. Minatory
(A) Minaret (B) Menacing
(C) Mean-minded (D) Minimal

Choose the word pairs out of the given options which resemble in meanings:

31. (A) Chafe (B) Ignoble (C) Clumsy (D) Excoriate
32. (A) Impeach (B) Arraign (C) Obviate (D) Indicate
33. (A) Ancestor (B) Progeny (C) Offspring (D) Forebears
34. (A) Despot (B) Tyrant (C) Dreadful (D) Dreaded
35. (A) Bizarre (B) Blizzard (C) Plethora (D) Preposterous
36. (A) Galore (B) Glare (C) Abundant (D) Grotesque
37. (A) Autochthon (B) Aborigine
(C) Automatic (D) Automation

38. (A) Discard (B) Dispose (C) Desert (D) Forsake

39. (A) Abysmal (B) Fathomless
(C) Zenith (D) Shun

40. (A) Dextrous (B) Doomed (C) Deft (D) Lazy

41. (A) Avow (B) Avid (C) Avouch (D) Devout

42. (A) Dilettante (B) Gourmet (C) Dissatisfied (D) Alienated

43. (A) Atone (B) Petrify (C) Expiate (D) Intrepid

44. (A) Herald (B) Harbinger (C) Exasperate (D) Outrage

45. (A) Cogent (B) Condign (C) Pristine (D) Tough

46. (A) Audacious (B) Audible
(C) Obstinate (D) Harsh

47. (A) Facet (B) Ramification
(C) Facade (D) Feature

48. (A) Imbibe (B) Assimilate
(C) Reject (D) Avert

49. (A) Feign (B) Malinger (C) Defunct (D) Defend

50. (A) Maladroit (B) Malignant (C) Clumsy (D) Malodorant

Choose the odd one out from the options in each set of 4 words:

51. (A) Aficionado (B) Fan (C) Kindred (D) Dilettante

52. (A) Cling (B) Inflict (C) Affix (D) Adhere

53. (A) Cognate (B) Rattle (C) Faze (D) Agitate

54. (A) Bunk (B) Elope (C) Elude (D) Outrage

55. (A) Commend (B) Fealty (C) Hail (D) Acclaim

56. (A) Esprit d' corps (B) Fidelity
(C) Devotion (D) Auspicious

57. (A) Parry (B) Imbibe (C) Obviate (D) Stave off

58. (A) Deserted (B) Solitary (C) Lonely (D) Forlorn

59. (A) Surfeit (B) Legion (C) Host (D) Cloy

60. (A) Toddle (B) Taint
(C) Tinge (D) Contaminate

61. (A) Teem (B) Swarm (C) Glut (D) Taint

62. (A) Chomp (B) Eschew (C) Shun (D) Refrain

63. (A) Inure (B) Accustom (C) Aver (D) Habituate

64. (A) Alibi (B) Plea (C) Pretext (D) Plead

65. (A) Chagrin (B) Charge (C) Exasperate (D) Annoy

66. (A) Rage (B) Fury (C) Outrage (D) Demolish

67. (A) Arrogant (B) Paragon (C) Nonpareil (D) Epitome

68. (A) Harsh (B) Severe (C) Austere (D) Fret

69. (A) Menacing (B) Benign (C) Awesome (D) Formidable

70. (A) Severe (B) Melancholic
(C) Atrabilious (D) Hypochondriac

Test-2

Select Synonyms of the given words out of the options mentioned:

1. Bequeath
(A) Benumb (B) Bludgeon (C) Demise (D) Bemuse

2. Box
(A) Cuff (B) Bait (C) Faint (D) Clog

3. Ersatz
(A) Zealot (B) Ennui (C) Sham (D) Placebo

4. Scald
(A) Berate (B) Chide (C) Scorch (D) Brat

5. Prolapse
(A) Progress (B) Proceed (C) Sag (D) Bump

6. Swag
(A) Boast (B) Bundle (C) Wad (D) Faggot

7. Dash
(A) Bump (B) Breach (C) Bale (D) Tuft

8. Parapet
(A) Moat (B) Stein (C) Rampart (D) Doldrums

9. Pandemonium
(A) Credence (B) Demeanour
(C) Uproar (D) Tedium

10. Retract
(A) Recant (B) Retrogress
(C) Extradite (D) Stun

11. Fetid
(A) Placebo (B) Musty (C) Blend (D) Cloy

12. Doldrums
(A) Unsteady (B) Obstruction
(C) Tedium (D) Tuft

13. Clog
(A) Jam (B) Stop (C) Cluster (D) Crash

14. Braggart
(A) Bigot (B) Fanatic (C) Brat (D) Batter

15. Stun
(A) Petrify (B) Beat (C) Pound (D) Thress

16. Peel
(A) Rind (B) Slog (C) Perplex (D) Stupefy

17. Ruse
(A) Rancid (B) Rot (C) Faint (D) Faith

18. Exile
(A) Expel (B) Excommunicate
(C) Extradite (D) Ban

19. Slog
(A) Smite (B) Flay (C) Slobber (D) Thress

20. Importune
(A) Fate (B) Beseech (C) Supplicate (D) Bias

Choose a pair of words having similarity in meanings out of the four given options:

21. (A) Comportment (B) Deportment
(C) Credit (D) Faith

22. (A) Credit (B) Entreat (C) Conduct (D) Implore

23. (A) Forswear (B) Forgo (C) Welsh (D) Abuse

24. (A) Commotion (B) Bedlam
(C) Bias (D) Demise

25. (A) Demeanour (B) Behaviour
(C) Mean-ness (D) Meaningless

26. (A) Predilection (B) Predisposition
(C) Credence (D) Brouhaha

27. (A) Chauvinist (B) Sham (C) Braggart (D) Fanatic

28. (A) Tassel (B) Tuft (C) Skein (D) Faggot

29. (A) Rancid (B) Ruse (C) Putrid (D) Retrograde

30. (A) Bait (B) Baffle (C) Banish (D) Befuddle

Choose the odd one out from the following options:

31. (A) Melee (B) Rumpus (C) Malignant (D) Babel

32. (A) Wad (B) Bale (C) Sheaf (D) Fad

33. (A) Boycott (B) Ostracize (C) Buckle (D) Outcaste

34. (A) Bounce (B) Collide (C) Rebound (D) Reverberate

35. (A) Tedium (B) Ennui (C) Boredom (D) Ostracize

36. (A) Contaminate (B) Adulterate
(C) Taint (D) Clog

37. (A) Stance (B) Trait (C) Tendency (D) Stare

38. (A) Thrash (B) Thress (C) Trash (D) Pound

39. (A) Magnate (B) Magnet (C) Baron (D) Tycoon

40. (A) Prohibit (B) Inhibit (C) Forbid (D) Protest

Test-3

Choose the synonymous words for the given words out of the following options:

1. Anathematise
(A) Hate (B) Dislike (C) Imprecate (D) Criticize

2. Preen
(A) Caress (B) Praise (C) Pinch (D) Ruminate

3. Compensate
(A) Compare (B) Complete (C) Rebate (D) Indemnify

4. Haggard
(A) Haggler (B) Careworn (C) Vagary (D) Drivel

5. Universal
(A) Catholic (B) Christian
(C) Omnipresent (D) Worldly

6. Wory
(A) Weary (B) Sorrowful (C) Chary (D) Cliche

7. Prattle
(A) Practise (B) Avoid (C) Blabber (D) Condemn

8. Keen
(A) Interested (B) Anxious (C) Care (D) Wail

9. Cant
(A) Lingo (B) Limbo (C) Catch (D) Caper

10. Disdain
(A) Fearless (B) Spite (C) Diatribe (D) Decry

11. Placid
(A) Lazy (B) Dupe (C) Tranquil (D) Complacent

12. Cull
(A) Gather (B) Muster (C) Accumulate (D) Waste

13. Invective
(A) Investment (B) Curse (C) Philippic (D) Impute

14. Vicissitude
(A) Vacillate (B) Adventure
(C) Vagary (D) Luck

15. Chant
(A) Recite (B) Shout (C) Call (D) Chatter
16. Cringe
(A) Prostrate (B) Tremble (C) Crowl (D) Cower
17. Hoodwink
(A) Huddle (B) Dupe (C) Drivel (D) Excoriate
18. Clique
(A) Panel (B) Troupe (C) Crook (D) Claque
19. Creep
(A) Sip (B) Impound (C) Pleat (D) Slither
20. Yearn
(A) Craze (B) Fad (C) Long (D) Gape
21. Impute
(A) Insert (B) Condemn (C) Attribute (D) Insult
22. Nab
(A) Wink (B) Sleep (C) Apprehend(D) Frolick
23. Cavort
(A) Jump (B) Hold (C) Gambol (D) Grab
24. Imposter
(A) Prosper (B) Chant (C) Fret (D) Con
25. Ruminate
(A) Rue (B) Row (C) Chew (D) Rumble
26. Reprehend
(A) Comprehend (B) Apprehend
(C) Castigate (D) Munch
27. Circadian
(A) Actor (B) Diurnal
(C) Approximate (D) Colossal
28. Bliss
(A) Trance (B) Bless (C) Beautiful (D) Chasm
29. Savage
(A) Ruin (B) Ferocious (C) Tyrant (D) Curse
30. Hiatus
(A) Sorrow (B) Disaster (C) Depression (D) Chasm
31. Lustrate
(A) Cleanse (B) Mop (C) Scour (D) Wash
32. Flush
(A) Flood (B) Swill (C) Emunge (D) Sort
33. Sort
(A) Category (B) Sport (C) Assort (D) Reduce

34. Sagacious
(A) Shrewd (B) Smug (C) Congenital (D) Timid

35. Vicinity
(A) Vainglory (B) Vanity (C) Propinquity (D) Venture

36. Congeal
(A) Hide (B) Concoct (C) Curdle (D) Solidify

37. Mall
(A) Smear (B) Clot (C) Entrust (D) Meditate

38. Incarcerate
(A) Exempt (B) Confiscate
(C) Immure (D) Refute

39. Distrain
(A) Detatch (B) Separate (C) Escheat (D) Confiscate

40. Parley
(A) Parlay (B) Confer (C) Cooperate (D) Collude

Choose the pair of given words with similar meanings out of the four in each set:

41. (A) Continuously (B) Perpetually
(C) Continually (D) Constantly

42. (A) Contemporary (B) Coeval
(C) Coetaneous (D) Pristine

43. (A) Coward (B) Crazy (C) Timorous (D) Courageous

44. (A) Grovel (B) Truckle (C) Breed (D) Long

45. (A) Worn (B) Torn (C) Pinched (D) Tranquil

46. (A) Jargon (B) Janket (C) Lingo (D) Frolick

47. (A) Fondle (B) Like (C) Reject (D) Pet

48. (A) Blow (B) Babble (C) Curse (D) Blabber

49. (A) Generate (B) Engender (C) Spoil (D) Ruin

50. (A) Generated (B) Congenital
(C) Progenitor (D) Innate

Choose the odd one out from the four options given in each set:

51. (A) Crevice (B) Rent (C) Fissure (D) Craze

52. (A) Vituperate (B) Vilify (C) Inveigh (D) Objurgate

53. (A) Twaddle (B) Prattle (C) Drivel (D) Wail

54. (A) Cavort (B) Grasp (C) Nab (D) Grab

55. (A) Swindle (B) Grab (C) Defraud (D) Dupe

56. (A) Claque (B) Choir (C) Troupe (D) Criticize

57. (A) Segregate (B) Secede (C) Sort (D) Assort

58. (A) Nomination (B) Denomination
(C) Genre (D) Genus

59. (A) Astute (B) Sagacious
(C) Thrifty (D) Perspicacious

60. (A) Summon (B) Marshall (C) Muster (D) Order

Test-4

Choose the most suitable synonym of the given word out of the four suggested options :

1. Fabricate
(A) Fashion (B) Imagine (C) Figment (D) Repair

2. Raven
(A) Shout (B) Rout (C) Devour (D) Shatter

3. Pedestrian
(A) Walker (B) Pedlar (C) Humdrum (D) Hawker

4. Impair
(A) Damage (B) Imply (C) Pare (D) Risk

5. Lacklustre
(A) Shine (B) Monotonous
(C) Sticky (D) Darkness

6. Jeopardy
(A) Risk (B) Calamity (C) Distrust (D) Vanish

7. Guzzle
(A) Dazzle (B) Dribble (C) Quaff (D) Adorn

8. Cadaver
(A) Greedy (B) Garnish (C) Debris (D) Carcass

9. Wilt
(A) Sag (B) Droop (C) Crumple (D) Slump

10. Coruscate
(A) Crash (B) Guzzle (C) Glitter (D) Crack

11. Confer
(A) Talk (B) Discuss (C) Endue (D) Denounce

12. Grope
(A) Gap (B) Dark (C) Fizzle (D) Frisk

13. Debris
(A) Stone (B) Scum (C) Fragment (D) Rubble

14. Dominance
(A) Dormancy (B) Hegemony
(C) Jurisdiction (D) Courage

15. Proclaim
(A) Decide (B) Deny (C) Herald (D) Support

16. Embellish
(A) Garnish (B) Delude (C) Garner (D) Embolden

17. Dilapidated
(A) Damaged (B) Loose (C) Ruined (D) Rickety

18. Lees
(A) Clout (B) Weeds (C) Dregs (D) Forge

19. Vilify
(A) Defile (B) Asperse (C) Vanquish (D) Validate

20. Turncoat
(A) Deceive (B) Overhaul (C) Proselyte (D) Rectify

21. Handicap
(A) Lacuna (B) Disabled (C) Weakness (D) Delicate

22. Impoverish
(A) Improper (B) Degenerate
(C) Impair (D) Dull

23. Hibernating
(A) Dormant (B) Domineering
(C) Swaying (D) Revealing

24. Predicament
(A) Importance (B) Prediction (C) Dilemma (D) Dispute

25. Exhume
(A) Burry (B) Resume (C) Confiscate (D) Disinter

26. Discrepancy
(A) Discredit (B) Disparity (C) Demerit (D) Discord

27. Dunk
(A) Immerse (B) Prick (C) Drone (D) Murmur

28. Procrastinate
(A) Crush (B) Swat (C) Dawdle (D) Accuse

29. Apocalypse
(A) Divulge (B) Eucalyptus
(C) Calamity (D) Dispair

30. Cynicism
(A) Foolishness (B) Patriotism
(C) Mistrust (D) Dejection

Choose pairs of words with similar meanings out of the given options:

31. (A) Masquerade (B) Lampoon (C) Disguise (D) Eructate

32. (A) Jib (B) Balk (C) Split (D) Reek

33. (A) Disgorge (B) Ooze (C) Coruscate (D) Dazzle
34. (A) Jettison (B) Jetsam (C) Jilt (D) Absolve
35. (A) Betray (B) Cheat (C) Hoodwink (D) Divulge
36. (A) Dault (B) Deter (C) Threaten (D) Challenge
37. (A) Recusant (B) Rude (C) Cruel (D) Froward
38. (A) Unkempt (B) Disgruntled
(C) Dishevelled (D) Shed
39. (A) Parry (B) Duck (C) Secede (D) Drool
40. (A) Costume (B) Custom (C) Trousseau (D) Garnish

Choose the odd one out from the given options:

41. (A) Gleam (B) Sparkle (C) Coruscate (D) Impair
42. (A) Lackadaisical (B) Dreary
(C) Dull (D) Glittering
43. (A) Ken (B) Province (C) Realm (D) Dominance
44. (A) Execrate (B) Manifest (C) Decry (D) Deprecate
45. (A) Invoke (B) Evince (C) Flaunt (D) Parade
46. (A) Scoff (B) Sneer (C) Pillory (D) Repudiate
47. (A) Curse (B) Conation (C) Volition (D) Wish
48. (A) Grit (B) Mettle (C) Fret (D) Resolve
49. (A) Moult (B) Mould (C) Shed (D) Slough
50. (A) Despair (B) Despondence
(C) Dejection (D) Disaster

Test-5

Choose the most appropriate synonym of the given words out of the suggested options:

1. Instance
(A) Occurrence (B) Example
(C) Accident (D) Event
2. Inquisitive
(A) Curious (B) Enquiring
(C) Careful (D) Investigating
3. Gloze
(A) Shining (B) Glaze (C) Mitigate (D) Glare
4. Protract
(A) Prolong (B) Lengthen (C) Elongate (D) Lengthy
5. Spout
(A) Fat (B) Rotund (C) Spit (D) Spurt

6. Prodigal
   (A) Outstanding (B) Talented
   (C) Spendthrift (D) Marvellous
7. Efficacious
   (A) Efficient (B) Effective (C) Effluent (D) Affluent
8. Fervour
   (A) Passion (B) Flow (C) Raging (D) Fire
9. Expatiate
   (A) Spotless (B) Praise (C) Expound (D) Partition
10. Indispensable
   (A) Essential (B) Disposable
   (C) Likable (D) Acceptable
11. Equivalence
   (A) Balanced (B) Equilibruim
   (C) Valid (D) Parity
12. Snuff (out)
   (A) Sniffle (B) Snuffle (C) Extinguish (D) Snore
13. Puppet
   (A) Marionette (B) Doll
   (C) Mannequin (D) Statue
14. Scarecrow
   (A) Effigy (B) Scaring object to frighten crows/birds
   (C) Ugly (D) Crow
15. Flagrant
   (A) Flag bearer (B) Flagitious
   (C) Outrageous (D) Flowing
16. Phenomenal
   (A) Universal (B) Egregious
   (C) Phantom (D) Prodigious
17. Vet
   (A) Veteran (B) Validate (C) Scrutinize (D) Virtue
18. Indispensable
   (A) Essential (B) Rejectable
   (C) Intolerable (D) Useless
19. Parity
   (A) Pare (B) Pruning (C) Purity (D) Equality
20. Transitory
   (A) Transit (B) Touring (C) Ephemeral (D) Eternal
21. Educe
   (A) Deduce (B) Provoke (C) Produce (D) Evoke

22. Heave
(A) Sigh (B) Swing (C) Hoist (D) Cry

23. Exude
(A) Fart (B) Belch
(C) Ooze out (sweat) (D) Expel

24. Stress
(A) Accentuatc (B) Straln
(C) Press (D) Defy

25. Ape
(A) Ancestor (B) Forebears
(C) Imitate (D) Infringe

26. Mime
(A) Mimic (B) Deride (C) Amuse (D) Entertain

27. Transgress
(A) Translate (B) Tranfer (C) Encroach (D) Travel

28. Infiltrate
(A) Filter through/into (permeate) (B) Purify
(C) Intrude (D) Invade

29. Eradicate
(A) Radicalise (B) Extirpate
(C) Suffocate (D) Remove

30. Extempore
(A) Impromptu(B) Expire (C) Extra (D) Timely

Choose pair of words out of the given options, which are similar in meaning:

31. (A) Keen (B) Cry (C) Sharp (D) Agog
32. (A) Fleecing (B) Fluent (C) Fleeting (D) Transient
33. (A) Elope (B) Beguile (C) Benign (D) Inveigle
34. (A) Lift (B) Crane (C) Escalator (D) Boost
35. (A) Belch (B) Fart (C) Eructate (D) Expel
36. (A) Enshrine (B) Holy (C) Reverence (D) Consecrate
37. (A) Paradigm (B) Example (C) Parable (D) Comparison
38. (A) Weary (B) Bleary (C) Weird (D) Languid
39. (A) Quail (B) Quack (C) Quell (D) Tremble
40. (A) Blatant (B) Clamourous
(C) Flagrant (D) Arrogant

Choose the odd one out from the given options:

41. (A) Extravagant (B) Prodigal
(C) Spendthrift (D) Thrift

42. (A) Artificial (B) Mannequin
(C) Effigy (D) Toy

43. (A) Query (B) Audit (C) Vet (D) Check

44. (A) Hoist (B) Elicit (C) Rear (D) Elevate

45. (A) Clash (B) Encounter
(C) Confrontation (D) Encroachment

46. (A) Entwine (B) Ensnare (C) Entangle (D) Intrude

47. (A) Deduce (B) Seduce (C) Suborn (D) Beguile

48. (A) Indispensable (B) Compulsory
(C) Disposable (D) Necessary

49. (A) Morale (B) Morality (C) Ethics (D) Morals

50. (A) Effect (B) Consequence
(C) Results (D) Affect

Test-6

Choose the closest synonym of the given words below:

1. Triffling
(A) Joking (B) Terrorising(C)Frivolous (D) Flitting

2. Augur
(A) Portend (B) Omen (C) Forecast (D) Accuse

3. Facade
(A) Main door (B) Main front
(C) Physiognomy (D) Fraud

4. Rattle
(A) Shake (B) Scare (C) Panic (D) Shout

5. Muzzle
(A) Gun (B) Face (C) Pipe (D) Suffocate

6. Autonomous
(A) Automatic (B) Sovereign
(C) Authority (D) Authorised

7. Prophesy
(A) Prophet (B) Oracle (C) Rare (D) Predict

8. Chum
(A) Crony (B) Sycophant
(C) Spoon (D) Slave

9. Counterfeit
(A) Illegal (B) Contrary (C) Fake (D) Encounter

10. Cherish
(A) Charge (B) Accuse (C) Vivid (D) Nurture

11. Proscribe
    (A) Prescribe (B) Describe (C) Forbid (D) Write
12. Sinuous
    (A) Meandering (B) Sensitive
    (C) Serious (D) Soaring
13. Sham
    (A) Shameful (B) Spurious (C) Shy (D) Superior
14. Stagger
    (A) Spread (B) Stump (C) Flounder (D) Stay
15. Fare
    (A) Charge (B) Fee (C) Tariff (D) Freight
16. Henchmen
    (A) Cohort (B) Follower (C) Criminals (D) Today
17. Debacle
    (A) Debate (B) Difference
    (C) Miscarriage (D) Downfall
18. Fussy
    (A) Noisy (B) Leaking (C) Fused (D) Finnicky
19. Fawn
    (A) Deer (B) Today (C) Lick (D) Favour
20. Standard
    (A) Upright (B) Quality (C) Colours (D) Banner
21. Fisticuff
    (A) Fists (B) Scuffle (C) Fright (D) Horror
22. Eminent
    (A) Exceptional (B) Arrogant
    (C) Renowned (D) Great
23. Lethal
    (A) Lazy (B) Late (C) Languid (D) Fatal
24. Vision
    (A) Foresight (B) Clarity (C) Visuals (D) Eyes

Choose the pair of words, out of given options, which bear the same meaning:

25. (A) Muzzle (B) Visage (C) Face (D) Countenance
26. (A) Freight (B) Tariff (C) Fee (D) Rent
27. (A) Frighten (B) Intimidate (C) Horrify (D) Fawn
28. (A) Portend (B) Portly (C) Round (D) Prognosticate
29. (A) Facet (B) Facetious (C) Factitious (D) Frivolous
30. (A) Rear (B) Nurture (C) Posterior (D) Nullify

31. (A) Autarky (B) Autonomy (C) Autocracy (D) Automatic
32. (A) Alter ego (B) Alternative (C) Friend (D) Egocentric
33. (A) Torturous (B) Tortuous (C) Painful (D) Sinuous

Choose the odd one out from the given options:

34. (A) Colours (B) Standard (C) Banner (D) Flag
35. (A) Winding (B) Sinuous (C) Flexuous (D) Torturous
36. (A) Flatter (B) Inhibit (C) Prohibit (D) Forbid
37. (A) Renowned (B) Famous (C) Popular (D) Nominated
38. (A) Stumble (B) Flounder (C) Fumble (D) Falter
39. (A) Sham (B) Humiliating (C) Ersatz (D) Fake
40. (A) Fitful (B) Fisticuff (C) Scuffle (D) Fight

Test-7

Choose the appropriate word to be filled in the blank space of the sentence out of the four suggested options in the following:

1. The .... from every household is to be thrown at a specified place, from where municipal trucks collect it for disposal.
   (A) Refuse (B) Sullage (C) Rubbish (D) Garbage
2. Getting annoyed, he .... at me in anger.
   (A) Looked (B) Stared (C) Glared (D) Peered
3. A large number of sikhs were .... in the wake of the assassination of Indira Gandhi.
   (A) Massacred (B) Butchered (C) Killed (D) Murdered
4. A large number of sikhs lost their lives in .... post Indira Gandhi's assassination.
   (A) Pogrom (B) Genocide (C) Carnage (D) Revenge
5. The drainage was choked with ....
   (A) Refuse (B) Trash (C) Sullage (D) Rubbish
6. The plastic tea cups are .... after use.
   (A) Dispensed with (B) Got rid of
   (C) Disposed of (D) Thrown
7. He .... himself with sweets in the party until felt aversion.
   (A) Surfeited (B) Sated (C) Satiated (D) Gorged
8. He earned the fame as .... of research in cancer treatments.
   (A) Guide (B) Trailblazer (C) Usher (D) Pioneer
9. An atheist does not hesitate to .... religion in speech.
   (A) Blaspheme (B) Profane (C) Insult (D) Criticize

10. An expressionless countenance of a .... person does not betray his emotions.
(A) Impassive (B) Phlegmatic (C) Stolid (D) Stoic

11. A person of .... courage is called a brave person.
(A) Indomitable (B) Unconquerable
(C) Invincible (D) Unwavering

12. He was cautious in speaking to women to avoid being blamed of .... behaviour.
(A) Indecent (B) Scurrilous (C) Risque (D) Vulgar

13. The boys standing on the road-side .... at the girls passing by furtively.
(A) Stared (B) Gazed (C) Peered (D) Glanced

14. Festering grievances against the government ...... people to revolt.
(A) Instigate (B) Arouse (C) Foment (D) Incite

15. It is very difficult to distinguish the .... of synonymous words.
(A) Nuances (B) Differences (C) Gradation (D) Shades

16. A boy .... himself through the crowd to the frontline near the dais.
(A) Inserted (B) Pushed (C) Insinuated (D) Penetrated

17. Teeth .... food in the mouth before being swallowed.
(A) Grind (B) Triturate (C) Comminute(D) Pulverise

18. The .... at the insulting remark hurt him deeply.
(A) Resentment (B) Pique (C) Dudgeon (D) Annoyance

19. A student .... a question in the class much to the annoyance of the lecturer.
(A) Intervened (B) Interceded (C) Interjected (D) Asked

20. The cat .... at me when I tried to chase it.
(A) Grumbled (B) Snarled (C) Purred (D) Growled

21. The patient's condition worsened because he ignored doctor's .... to desist from taking oily food.
(A) Injunction (B) Directive (C) Instruction (D) Prescription

22. He .... the boy by showing a chocolate but not giving him.
(A) Persecuted (B) Tormented (C) Tantalised (D) Harried

23. He has no .... of where his friend has gone without informing him.
(A) Intuition (B) Anticipation (C) Hunch (D) Inkling

24. He was upset with the .... of ghost's apparitions in the darkness of night.
(A) Apprehension (B) Premonition
(C) Presentiment (D) Prescience

25. An old model car was .... so to look like a new model.
(A) Innovated (B) Renovated (C) Revamped (D) Retrofitted

26. Unhygienic condition is .... to our health.
(A) Injurious (B) Disastrous (C) Deleterious (D) Inimical

27. Kids would do good to themselves by heeding to .... advices of their elders.
(A) Salutary (B) Salubrious (C) Sanitary (D) Wholesome

28. .... of bees invaded the person who stoked their beehive.
(A) Shoal (B) Drove (C) Swarm (D) Flock

29. He.......... his malevolence behind his affected geniality towards me.
(A) Dissembled (B) Disguised (C) Ensconced (D) Masked

30. I have no .... as to how to solve this problem.
(A) Cue (B) Hint (C) Clue (D) Allusion

31. The horse suddenly .... at dragging the cart, despite goading.
(A) Hesitated (B) Jibbed (C) Balked (D) Dithered

32. A temple is .... for the devotees.
(A) Holy (B) Divine (C) Sacrosanct (D) Sacred

33. The mob .... stones on policemen.
(A) Lobbed (B) Hurled (C) Pelted (D) Tossed

34. We have strange .... about aliens.
(A) Notion (B) Idea (C) Perception (D) Concept

35. He is in the habit of giving unsolicited .... advice to others.
(A) Officious (B) Meddlesome (C) Obtrusive (D) Intrusive

36. His new shoes .... on his toes.
(A) Pricked (B) Prickled (C) Impinged (D) Hurt

37. A nail .... his finger.
(A) Impinged (B) Prickled (C) Punctured (D) Pricked

38. Wrongly parked vehicles were towed to be .... by traffic police.
(A) Intered (B) Imprisoned (C) Interned (D) Impounded

39. Patriotism makes us .... to feel happy over our national team's victory in international games.
(A) Biased (B) Inclined (C) Pre-disposed (D) Tend

40. His hobnobbing with an opposition leader was .... to be an act of disloyalty to the party.
(A) Inferred (B) Deduced (C) Interpreted (D) Construed

41. The rich man adequately .... the person who saved his life from an assailant.
(A) Indemnified (B) Compensated
(C) Recompensed (D) Repaid

42. A gunman fired shots ....
(A) Haphazardly (B) Randomly
(C) All around (D) Indiscriminately

43. Propaganda .... doubt about someone's probity in people's mind.
(A) Inculcates (B) Instils (C) Infuses (D) Insinuates

44. Investors were .... of the risks involved in investing in stocks.
(A) Informed (B) Acquainted (C) Advised (D) Aprised

45. Arrogance is .... in him.
(A) Immanent (B) Inherent (C) Innate (D) Intrinsic

46. A chemical factory's chimney spewed .... fumes.
(A) Obnoxious (B) Noxious (C) Poisonous (D) Injurious

47. Politicians are infamous for being .... in shady deals with criminals.
(A) Involved (B) Indulged (C) Engrossed (D) Complicit

48. The host himself .... each guest to his seat in the hall.
(A) Led (B) Guided
(C) Ushered (D) Accompanied

49. The tigers .... at the circus ringmaster even as they meekly followed his command.
(A) Purred (B) Grumbled (C) Snarled (D) Growled

50. Beggars in streets .... him for alms.
(A) Harassed (B) Tormented (C) Badgered (D) Bothered

Test-8

Choose the correct word out of the given options, which would fit in the blank.

1. He is a person of .... character.
(A) Impeccable (B) Immaculate
(C) Consummate (D) Divine

2. His action is not .... with requirement.
(A) Congruous (B) Compatible
(C) Consistent (D) Consonant

3. .... kids are frolicking joyously.

(A) Animate (B) Vivacious (C) Active (D) Energetic

4. The accused was finally .... by the enquiry committee.

   (A) Exonerated (B) Exculpated (C) Acquited (D) Released

5. He was .... in a case of bribery.

   (A) Accused (B) Indicted (C) Arraigned (D) Incriminated

6. He has .... enormous wealth.

   (A) Amassed (B) Acquired (C) Gained (D) Gathered

7. One has to overcome .... in one's life.

   (A) Adversity (B) Affliction (C) Ordeal (D) Disaster

8. A .... deliberately parades his knowledge.

   (A) Quack (B) Charlatan (C) Pedant (D) Hypocrite

9. He .... his ignorance in this matter.

   (A) Vouched (B) Avouched (C) Avowed (D) Averred

10. He played a hoax of bomb scare for a ....

    (A) Lark (B) Amusement

    (C) Racreation (D) Entertainment

11. The police earned .... for timely recovery of a bomb planted in the marketplace by a terrorist.

    (A) Kudos (B) Approbation

    (C) Admiration (D) Appreciation

12. Ice hockey is played on a ....

    (A) Turf (B) Playground

    (C) Rink (D) Gymnasium

13. Police .... the criminal's hideout to apprehend.

    (A) Raided (B) Invaded (C) Attacked (D) Assaulted

14. His aggressive nature is .... to his upbringing.

    (A) Ascribed (B) Imputed (C) Attributed (D) Assigned

15. He was .... to the criminal activity of corruption by the lure of lucre.

    (A) Seduced (B) Enticed (C) Allured (D) Attracted

16. America's .... over weaker nations enables it to cast its influence to further its interests.

(A) Preponderance (B) Hegemony

(C) Dominance (D) Command

17. The boy is wont to .... illness to avoid going to school.

(A) Malinger (B) Feign (C) Pretend (D) Affect

18. Chimney of chemical factory spews .... fumes.

(A) Noisome (B) Noxious (C) Abnoxious(D) Foul

19. An elderly person, who wishes well of others, is a ....

(A) Benevolent person (B) Benefactor

(C) Samaritan (D) Altruist

20. Devotees .... their hands and feet with holy water before entering sanctum sanctorum of holy place.

(A) Clean (B) Cleanse (C) Lustrate (D) Anoint

21. He reached the .... of his career in a short span of time.

(A) Climax (B) Peak (C) Zenith (D) Pinnacle

22. The doctor .... the patient to follow the regimen of treatment.

(A) Ordered (B) Decreed (C) Ordained (D) Enjoined

23. His conscience .... him to confess his crime.

(A) Coerced (B) Constrained

(C) Restrained (D) Exacted

24. He .... his hatred against me by pretending to be friendly.

(A) Dissembled (B) Concealed

(C) Cloaked (D) Camouflaged

25. She .... my offer of help by ignoring it.

(A) Snubbed (B) Scoffed (C) Sneered (D) Scorned

26. He earned fame as a .... of research in cancer treatment.

(A) Guide (B) Trailblazer (C) Usher (D) Pioneer

27. He is a person of .... courage.

(A) Indomitable (B) Unconquerable

(C) Invincible (D) Unwavering

28. He was upset with the .... of ghost's apparitions.

(A) Premonition (B) Presentiment

(C) Apprehension (D)Prescience

29. Unhygienic conditions are .... to our health.

(A) Injurious (B) Disastrous (C) Deleterious (D) Inimical

30. I have no .... as to how to solve this problem.

(A) Cue (B) Clue (C) Hint (D) Allusion

31. Beggars in streets .... people for alms.

(A) Harass (B) Badger (C) Bother (D) Torment

32. The rich man adequately .... the person who saved his life.

(A) Indemnified (B) Compensated

(C) Recompensed (D) Repayed

33. The circus tigers .... at the ringmaster even as they meekly follwed his command.

(A) Purred (B) Grumbled (C) Snarled (D) Growled

34. The host himself .... each guest to his seat in the reception hall.

(A) Led (B) Guided

(C) Ushered (D) Accompanied

35. The horse suddenly .... at dragging the cart despite goading.

(A) Hesitated (B) Balked (C) Jibbed (D) Dithered

36. He is in the habit of giving unsolicited .... advice to others.

(A) Officious (B) Meddlesome

(C) Obtrusive (D) Intrusive

37. Patriotism makes us .... to feel happy over the victory of our cricket team.

(A) Pre-disposed (B) Inclined

(C) Biased (D) Disposed

38. His hobonobbing with the opposition leaders was .... to be an act of disloyalty to his own party.

(A) Inferred (B) Deduced (C) Interpreted (D) Construed

39. It is good to heed .... advice of elders.

(A) Salubrious (B) Sanitary (C) Wholesome(D) Salutary

40. .... of bees invaded the person who stoked the beehive.

(A) Shoal (B) Drove (C) Swarm (D) Flock

41. He has no .... of where has his friend has gone.

(A) Intuition (B) Anticipation

(C) Hunch (D) Inkling

42. He .... the boy by showing a chocolate but not giving it to him.

(A) Harried (B) Tormented (C) Annoyed (D) Tantalised

43. The boy .... himself through the crowd to the front line near the dais.

(A) Pushed (B) Penetrated

(C) Insinuated (D) Inserted

44. Festering grievances against the government .... people to revolt.

(A) Instigate (B) Incite (C) Arouse (D) Foment

45. An expressionless countenance of a ....person does not betray his emotions.

(A) Impassive (B) Phlegmatic (C) Stolid (D) Stoic

46. Plastic tea cups are .... after use.

(A) Dispensed with (B) Disposed of

(C) Got rid of (D) Discarded

47. The drainage was choked with ....

(A) Refuse (B) Trash (C) Sullage (D) Rubbish

48. A large number of sikhs lost life in ....post Indira Gandhi's assassination.

(A) Pogrom (B) Genocide (C) Carnage (D) Killings

49. The boys standing on the roadside .... at the girls passing by furtively.

(A) Stared (B) Gazed (C) Peered (D) Glanced

50. Teeth .... food in the mouth before being swallowed.

(A) Grind (B) Triturate (C) Comminute (D) Pulverise

Test-9

Choose the most appropriate synonym of the words out of given options:

1. Abandon
   (A) Desert (B) Jilt (C) Abundant (D) Decontrol
2. Rate
   (A) Evaluate (B) Value (C) Run (D) Repeat
3. Fashion
   (A) Blase (B) Dandy (C) Vogue (D) Beauty
4. Look
   (A) Pore (B) Pour (C) Askance (D) Browse
5. Gaze
   (A) Peer (B) Glare (C) Gloat (D) Glower
6. Behaviour
   (A) Demeanour (B) Mien (C) Action (D) Delinquency
7. Complacent
   (A) Calm (B) Cool (C) Smug (D) Compliment
8. Acclimatise
   (A) Inure (B) Adapt (C) Adopt (D) Satisfy
9. Order
   (A) Judgement (B) Diktat
   (C) Arrange (D) Serialise
10. Refuse
    (A) Baulk (B) Denial (C) Disorder (D) Admit
11. Disobedient
    (A) Rude (B) Recusant (C) Docile (D) Dormant
12. Native
    (A) Autochthon (B) Birthplace
    (C) Resident (D) Endemic
13. Protest
    (A) Avoid (B) Contest
    (C) Declaration (expressing disagreement, disapproval or opposition)
    (D) Contravene
14. Calamity
    (A) Apocalypse (B) Earthquake
    (C) Enemity (D) Flood

15. Disaster
(A) Monster (B) Accident (C) Catastrophe (D) Contest
16. Premonition
(A) Foreboding (B) Admonition
(C) Denomination (D) Guess
17. Lazy
(A) Languorous (B) Slow
(C) Inactive (D) Dormant
18. Criticism
(A) Critical judgement (B) Inveigh
(C) Vituperate (D) Excoriate
19. Earmark
(A) Assign (B) Necessary (C) Spot (D) Point out
20. Surprise
(A) Wonder (B) Annoy (C) Astound (D) Apprehend
21. Compulsory
(A) Compelling (B) Optional
(C) Sine qua non (D) Composite
22. Deny
(A) Repudiate (B) Surrender (C) Refuse (D) Negate
23. Hint
(A) Refer (B) Allude (C) Remark (D) Indication
24. Insinuation
(A) Insult (B) Accuse (C) Innuendo (D) Reference
25. Desire
(A) Conation (B) Pray (C) Lust (D) Greed
26. Anthologize
(A) Apologize (B) Cull
(C) Amass
(D) Gathering selected literaryworks and poems
27. Accumulate
(A) Accommodate (B) Fill
(C) Amass (D) Overflow
28. Vomit
(A) Throw out (B) Disgorge (C) Ooze out (D) Expel
29. Ascend
(A) Levitate (B) Soar (C) Lift (D) Heave

30. Boost
(A) Stoop (B) Condescend
(C) Raise (D) Burst

31. Rear
(A) Back (B) Lift (C) Forward (D) Retreat

32. Surfeited
(A) Surplus (B) Blase (C) Glut (D) Overflow

33. Maverick
(A) Trick (B) Transient (C) Docile (D) Intractable

34. Dive
(A) Swoop (B) Jump (C) Fall (D) Swim

35. Plunge
(A) Flight (B) Soar (C) Plummet (D) Dip

36. Justify
(A) Explain (B) Decide (C) Rationalise (D) Adjudicate

37. Toss
(A) Throw (B) Project (C) Roll (D) Lob

38. Zeal
(A) Jealousy (B) Envy (C) Fervour (D) Vagary

39. Vicissitude
(A) Luck (B) Vagrant (C) Vagary (D) Sway

40. Foment
(A) Froth (B) Incite (C) Impel (D) Goad

41. Provoke
(A) Goad (B) Poke (C) Prick (D) Promote

42. Inquisitive
(A) Curious (B) Enquiring (C) Insisting (D) Questioning

43. Topsy-Turvy
(A) Top heavy (B) Topple
(C) Turmoil (D) Turning around

44. Impolite
(A) Hard (B) Impertinent
(C) Unpolished (D) Angry

45. Herald
(A) Fore runner (B) Shining

(C) Hamper (D) Impudent

46. Instance
(A) Insistence (B) Precedent (C) Incident (D) Attempt

47. Sadist
(A) Gloomy (B) Unhappy (C) Cruel (D) Depressed

48. Forlorn
(A) Sad (B) Ebulient (C) Upset (D) Agitated

49. Disinterested
(A) Uninterested (B) Indifferent
(C) Distraught (D) Gloomy

50. Upset
(A) Unhappy (B) Discomfited
(C) Annoyed (D) Unconcerned

51. Breach
(A) Void (B) Boost (C) Coast (D) Violation

52. Sobriquet
(A) Sober (B) Epithet
(C) Nom de plume (D) Denomination

53. Designation
(A) Design (B) Post
(C) Denomination (D) Nomenclature

54. Boredom
(A) Doldrums (B) Cloyness (C) Blase (D) Sadness

55. Ennui
(A) Unique (B) Disinclined (C) Tedium (D) Gloom

56. Adamant
(A) Rude (B) Insolent (C) Resolute (D) Reckless

57. Wonderful
(A) Exceptional (B) Superb
(C) Phenomenal (D) Magnificent

58. Transgress
(A) Transpire (B) Transit (C) Infringe (D) Transport

59. Glut
(A) Plethora (B) Rot (C) Dearth (D) Transport

60. Authorise
(A) Empower (B) Allow (C) Franchise (D) Entitle

61. Baron
(A) Prince (B) Don (C) Tycoon (D) Laity

62. Realm
(A) Reality (B) Truth (C) Domain (D) Cosmos

63. Construe
(A) Interpret (B) Construct (C) Restrain (D) Constrain

64. Exude
(A) Expel (B) Emit (C) Transmit (D) Intrude

65. Inherent
(A) Innate (B) Immanent (C) Congenital (D) Inherited

66. Intrude
(A) Trespass (B) Invade (C) Insert (D) Penetrate

67. Conjecture
(A) Wonder (B) Guess (C) Imagine (D) Fluke

68. Compatible
(A) Compact (B) Commensurate
(C) Conforming (D) Compressible

69. Solicit
(A) Beseech (B) Solitary (C) Affirm (D) Lament

70. Assert
(A) Consent (B) Agree (C) Profess (D) Advise

71. Affront
(A) Afraid (B) Push (C) Umbrage (D) Regret

72. Repent
(A) Rue (B) Curse (C) Damn (D) Reject

73. Disparage
(A) Discourage (B) Insinuate (C) Disperse (D) Lampoon

74. Discard
(A) Remove (B) Garbage (C) Molt (D) Dampen

75. Segregate
(A) Degrade (B) Congregate (C) Quarantine (D) Dissociate

76. Relic
(A) Antique (B) Remains (C) Extant (D) Obsolete

77. Cynicism
(A) Madness (B) Distrust (C) Unreliability (D) Arrogance

78. Pride
(A) Ego (B) Hubris (C) Egoism (D) Egotism

79. Controvert
(A) Contravene (B) Decline (C) Refuse (D) Dismiss

80. Enervate
(A) Debilitate (B) Nervous (C) De-energize (D) Castrate

81. Miser
(A) Thrifty (B) Frugal
(C) Parsimonious (D) Austere

82. Chauvinist
(A) Zealous (B) Patriot (C) Jealous (D) Tough

83. Predicament
(A) Pre-decided (B) Prediction (C) Quandary (D) Addiction

84. Vitriolic
(A) Bitter (B) Blue (C) Shining (D) Rotten

85. Slaughter
(A) Decimate (B) Kill (C) Murder (D) Assassinate

86. Pogrom
(A) Decorum (B) Fury (C) Carnage (D) Atrocity

87. Emaciate
(A) Attenuate (B) Extenuate (C) Weaken (D) Discourage

88. Dwindle
(A) Exhaust (B) Deplete (C) Wane (D) Deficit

89. Shudder
(A) Hudle (B) Shut down (C) Quake (D) Shiver

90. Demean
(A) Draw meaning (B) Devalue
(C) Debase (D) Abase

91. Sullage
(A) Garbage (B) Refuse (C) Rubbish (D) Sewage

92. Incarcerate
(A) Curse (B) Immure (C) Enclose (D) Arrest

93. Coax
(A) Cajole (B) Cogitate
(C) Enrage (D) Contemplate

94. Strident
(A) Cacophonous (B) Stringent
(C) Striving (D) Studious

95. Bolland
(A) Pylon (B) Pole (C) Prop (D) Stake

96. Defile
(A) Scrape (B) Defalcate (C) Ruin (D) Desecrate

97. Flexuous
(A) Flexible (B) Flowing (C) Sinuous (D) Rigid

98. Crafty
(A) Artist (B) Expert (C) Cunning (D) Clever

99. Grind
(A) Chew (B) Ruminate (C) Triturate (D) Crush

100. Sycophant
(A) Obsequious (B) Survivor
(C) Obedient (D) Toady

101. Ploy
(A) Plight (B) Bait (C) Decoy (D) Ruse

102. Retrench
(A) Reduce (Staff/workersfor economising) (B) Dig
(C) Punish (D) Cashier

103. Comouflage
(A) Subterfuge (B) Cover (C) Dissemble (D) Deprive

104. Veneer
(A) Ensconce (B) Vent (C) Mask (D) Paint

105. Bark
(A) Rind (B) Cuticle (C) Scurf (D) Hide

106. Truncate
(A) Trim (B) Turn away (C) Relinquish (D) Concise

107. Itinerate
(A) Iterate (B) Scour (C) Intimidate (D) Sojourn

108. Rickety
(A) Decrepit (B) Thin (C) Emaciated (D) Dislocated

109. Cache
(A) Catch (B) Care (C) Store (D) Conceal

110. Reprimand
(A) Resent (B) Irritate (C) Censure (D) Quarrel

111. Pugnacious
(A) Pug marked (B) Quarrelsome
(C) Cruel (D) Huffy

112. Scrap
(A) Fracas (B) Waste (C) Litters (D) Tear

113. Prolapse
(A) Prolong (B) Elongate (C) Relapse (D) Sag

114. Disposition
(A) Displacement (B) Dispersal
(C) Tendency (D) Scattering

115. Brood
(A) Drove (B) Clutch (C) Flock (D) Litters

116. Singe
(A) Charm (B) Soothe (C) Scald (D) Languish

117. Ricochet
(A) Rebound (B) Crook (C) Curved (D) Collide

118. Delve
(A) Dip (B) Insert (C) Grope (D) Bounce

119. Drool
(A) Devil (B) Fool (C) Dump (D) Drivel

120. Obviate
(A) Observe (B) Avert (C) Disobey (D) Rebound

121. Dilly-dally
(A) Dandle (B) Hurry (C) Dawdle (D) Hamper

122. Contort
(A) Retort (B) Distort (C) Fraud (D) Diffuse

123. Imposter
(A) Defraud (B) Swindle (C) Cheat (D) Timid

124. Stagnate
(A) Rot (B) Stink (C) Linger (D) Swindle

125. Swat
(A) Perspirate (B) Slog (C) Satiate (D) Bat

126. Eerie
(A) Calm (B) Macabre (C) Timid (D) Tranquil

127. Hector
(A) Berate (B) Heckle (C) Bully (D) Hamper

128. Dunk
(A) Dubious (B) Scold (C) Drown (D) Slug

129. Congeal
(A) Curdle (B) Thaw (C) Freeze (D) Melt

130. Haggard
(A) Tired (B) Careworn (C) Torn (D) Unhappy

131. Smother
(A) Asphyxiate (B) Smoothen (C) Sway (D) Clean

132. Turncoat
(A) Paint (B) Torn (C) Apostate (D) Refund

133. Abject
(A) Ignoble (B) Absurd (C) Abominate (D) Benign

134. Hiatus
(A) Plateau (B) Peak (C) Cleavage (D) Charm

135. Grit
(A) Scrape (B) Scrap (C) Mettle (D) Grated

136. Confine
(A) Refined (B) Contain (C) Incarcerate (D) Arrest

137. Ersatz
(A) Razzmatazz (B) Sham
(C) Coruscate (D) Polish

138. Daze
(A) Bewilder (B) Dazzle (C) Faze (D) Polish

139. Inculcate
(A) Calculate (B) Calcify (C) Instil (D) Insert

140. Stink
(A) Rancid (B) Fetid (C) Rankle (D) Rot

141. Treat
(A) Regale (B) Behave (C) Punish (D) Threaten

142. Officious
(A) Officiating (B) Rude
(C) Meddlesome (D) Hard-working

143. Nepharious
(A) Nephrological (B) Obnoxious
(C) Naive (D) Wicked

144. Behold
(A) Catch (B) Look (C) Oblige (D) Accuse

145. Exonerate
(A) Acquit (B) Exaggerate (C) Feign (D) Treat

146. Raze
(A) Anger (B) Chide (C) Wreck (D) Ruin

147. Debris
(A) Rubble (B) Ruin (C) Raze (D) Damage

148. Tarnish
(A) Tear (B) Frazzle (C) Tatter (D) Besmirch

149. Pound
(A) Sterling (B) Surround (C) Thrash (D) Ditch

150. Opulent
(A) Fatty (B) Rotund (C) Rich (D) Opaque

151. Vicinity
(A) Propinquity (B) Visual (C) Vices (D) Cauge

152. Retrofit
(A) Retreat (B) Revamp (C) Counterfeit (D) Misfit

153. Greenhorn
(A) Immature (B) Tyro (C) Greenery (D) Revoke

154. Fathom
(A) Depth (B) Bottom
(C) Measure the depth (D) Froth

155. Extirpate
(A) Annihilate (B) Uproot (C) Eradicate (D) Terrorize

156. Deprave
(A) Dissolute (B) Deprived (C) Snatch (D) Denounce

157. Raven
(A) Voracious (B) Greedy (C) Devour (D) Rude

158. Injunction
(A) Diktat (B) Order (C) Directive (D) Advice

159. Latent

(A) Dormant (B) Live (C) Active (D) Dull

160. Humdrum

(A) Doldrums (B) Noise (C) Hollow (D) Dreary

161. Excommunicate

(A) Banish (B) Extradite (C) Exile (D) Contact

162. Fealty

(A) Fidelity (B) Patriotism (C) Morality (D) Mimicry

163. Trail

(A) Pursue (B) Follow (C) Contrail (D) Trim

164. Apprehend

(A) Comprehend (B) Reprehend
(C) Nab (D) Refuge

165. Riposte

(A) Repose (B) Resume (C) Repartee (D) Relax

166. Sanctum sanctorum

(A) Shrine (B) Sanctify
(C) Sanctity (D) Sanctimonious

167. Continence

(A) Abstinence (B) Self-restraint (in sexual urge)
(C) Abstention (D) Control

168. Conundrum

(A) Doldrum (B) Connivance
(C) Puzzle (D) Trick

169. Prolific

(A) Copious (B) Lavish (C) Profuse (D) Fecund

170. Vendetta

(A) Revenge (B) Vend (C) Venality (D) Revolt

171. Demise

(A) Bestow (B) Endow (C) Bequeath (D) Confer

172. Evince

(A) Convince (B) Manifest (C) Evict (D) Influence

173. Corroborate

(A) Prove (B) Substantiate
(C) Correspond (D) Relate

174. Applaud
(A) Commend (B) Clap (C) Uproar (D) Shout

175. Nurture
(A) Tender (B) Rear (C) Rupture (D) Nurse

176. Atone
(A) Tone down (B) Tend (C) Expiate (D) Amend

177. Redeem
(A) Restore (B) Recuperate (C) Rejuvenate (D) Retrieve

178. Largesse
(A) Largeness (B) Bounty (C) Bonus (D) Incentive

179. Recede
(A) Concede (B) Retreat (C) Secede (D) Proceed

180. Recant
(A) Chant (B) Repeat (C) Revert (D) Renege

181. Vintage
(A) Distillary (B) Viticulture (C) Vignette (D) Primitive

182. Rend
(A) Rent out (B) Rendition (C) Split (D) Hire

183. Distend
(A) Extend (B) Bulge (C) Attenuate (D) Project

184. Prorogue
(A) Inveigle (B) Provoke (C) Protract (D) Adjourn

185. Rampant
(A) Scatter (B) Disseminate
(C) Wanton (D) Unkempt

186. Quail
(A) Quake (B) Quiver (C) Gore (D) Quell

187. Divagate
(A) Wander (B) Gad (C) Digress (D) Diffuse

188. Execrate
(A) Exculpate (B) Denounce (C) Dread (D) Excuse

189. Skive
(A) Bunk (B) Elope (C) Skuttle (D) Scoot

190. Faux pas
(A) Failure (B) Mistake (C) Gaffe (D) Awe

191. Betray
(A) Cheat (B) Deceive (C) Befool (D) Hamper

192. Philippic
(A) Philander (B) Philanthrope
(C) Philately (D) Tirade

193. Wring
(A) Crush (B) Mash (C) Twist (D) Squash

194. Concoct
(A) Blend (B) Brew (C) Taint (D) Tinge

195. Jaunt
(A) Expedition (B) Cruise (C) Junket (D) Junk

196. Stymie
(A) Stem (B) Arrest (C) Curb (D) Stanch

197. Squirm
(A) Wallow (B) Writhe (C) Squirt (D) Welter

198. Preposterous
(A) Grotesque (B) Fantastic (C) Antic (D) Strange

199. Malice
(A) Malign (B) Spite (C) Malignant (D) Malediction

200. Pandemonium
(A) Uproar (B) Harmony (C) Panic (D) Distrust

Choose the odd word out of the set given below:

201. (A) Brat (B) Braggart
(C) Braggidocio (D) Bereft

202. (A) Bedlam (B) Babble (C) Brouhaha (D) Malee

203. (A) Indemnify (B) Recompense
(C) Subsidize (D) Compensate

204. (A) Stubborn (B) Astute (C) Audacious (D) Obstinate

205. (A) Arrogate (B) Usurp (C) Supplant (D) Urge

206. (A) Lynch (B) Slay (C) Flay (D) Assassinate

207. (A) Deter (B) Dissuade (C) Discourage (D) Desperate
208. (A) Defeat (B) Rout (C) Route (D) Vanquish
209. (A) Brandish (B) Flaunt (C) Flounder (D) Flourish
210. (A) Intrude (B) Meddle (C) Obtrude (D) Ingress
211. (A) Laugh (B) Guffaw (C) Leer (D) Fleer
212. (A) Deleterious (B) Delectable (C) Detrimental (D) Insidious
213. (A) Prone (B) Liable (C) Susceptible (D) Disposed
214. (A) Impair (B) Damage (C) Weaken (D) Improve
215. (A) Capitulate (B) Concede (C) Capture (D) Succumb
216. (A) Domination (B) Hegemony (C) Supremacy (D) Bully
217. (A) Demur (B) Jib (C) Dim (D) Baulk
218. (A) Teeter (B) Totter (C) Sway (D) Temper
219. (A) Harry (B) Tantalise (C) Hamper (D) Badger
220. (A) Adorn (B) Garnish (C) Embellish (D) Cartel
221. (A) Patent (B) Manifest (C) Latent (D) Conspicuous
222. (A) Mop (B) Swill (C) Flush (D) Expunge
223. (A) Jargon (B) Lingo (C) Limbo (D) Argot
224. (A) Prudent (B) Prurient (C) Pragmatic (D) Politic
225. (A) Parity (B) Analogy
(C) Plurality (D) Correspondence
226. (A) Acquiesce (B) Acquit (C) Assent (D) Consent
227. (A) Sympathy (B) Ruth
(C) Commiseration (D) Apathy
228. (A) Doctrine (B) Dogma (C) Nurture (D) Tenet
229. (A) Bouquet (B) Fragrance (C) Buffet (D) Redolence
230. (A) Introspect (B) Cogitate (C) Retrospect (D) Prospect
231. (A) Commit (B) Demit (C) Confide (D) Entrust
232. (A) Shy (B) Coy (C) Demure (D) Brash
233. (A) Haven (B) Harbour (C) Hovel (D) Refuge
234. (A) Serene (B) Tranquil (C) Serenade (D) Placid
235. (A) Zenith (B) Pinnacle (C) Apex (D) Peek
236. (A) Propitious (B) Proprietary (C) Auspicious (D) Benign

237. (A) Requiem (B) Elegy (C) Dirge (D) Encomium
238. (A) Transient (B) Transitory (C) Ephemeral (D) Eternal
239. (A) Pedant (B) Charlatan (C) Erudite (D) Omniscient
240. (A) Malinger (B) Malignant (C) Feign (D) Pretend
241. (A) Clairvoyance (B) Foresight (C) Foresee (D) Vision
242. (A) Apostate (B) Proselyte (C) Renegade (D) Appease
243. (A) Finicky (B) Feverish (C) Fussy (D) Fastidious
244. (A) Lackadaisical (B) Pedestrian (C) Lacklustre (D) Lampoon
245. (A) Cringe (B) Cram (C) Cower (D) Crunch
246. (A) Flounder (B) Fumble (C) Falter (D) Flunk
247. (A) Swag (B) Booty (C) Spoils (D) Sag
248. (A) Vocation (B) Avocation (C) Avouch (D) Metier
249. (A) Stupendous (B) Enormous (C) Immense (D) Immeasurable
250. (A) Distraught (B) Dismantle (C) Disconcerted (D) Disconsolate
251. (A) Mammoth (B) Monster (C) Monolith (D) Colossal
252. (A) Germane (B) Cogent (C) Absurd (D) Apropos
253. (A) Credence (B) Credibility (C) Credit (D) Debit
254. (A) Teem (B) Abound (C) Tamper (D) Swarm
255. (A) Predict (B) Prophesy (C) Prophecy (D) Augur
256. (A) Redoubtable (B) Formidable (C) Dubious (D) Menacing
257. (A) Reveal (B) Betray (C) Divulge (D) Dissemble
258. (A) Eke (B) Stint (C) Conserve (D) Compensate
259. (A) Odium (B) Oddity (C) Opprobrium (D) Ignominy

Test-10

Choose the word which is the closest in meaning to the given word:

1. Junket
   (A) Junk (B) Jaunt (C) Worthless (D) Rusted
2. Ruse
   (A) Gimmick (B) Red (C) Insolent (D) Jeer

3. Benevolent

(A) Violent (B) Well-wisher

(C) Benign (D) Magnanimous

4. Lewd

(A) Greed (B) Irritating (C) Lascivious (D) Listless

5. Impertinent

(A) Impatient (B) Unsuitable (C) Imprudent (D) Insolent

6. Jut out

(A) Protuberate (B) Lob (C) Throw (D) Remove

7. Peril

(A) Push (B) Pre-empt (C) Jeopardy (D) Protrude

8. Decimate

(A) Decimal (B) Droll (C) Pillory (D) Recant

9. Lampoon

(A) Laugh (B) Declare

(C) Laughter (scornful) (D) Decant

10. Bemoan

(A) Grieve (B) Cry (C) Grumble (D) Groan

11. Chortle

(A) Guffaw (B) Ogle (C) Pore (D) Flirt

12. Vengeance

(A) Retribution (B) Vindication

(C) Contrary (D) Threat

13. Jurist

(A) Lawyer (B) Juror (C) Judge (D) Journalist

14. Lassitude

(A) Disinclination (B) Listlessness

(C) Lasciviousness (D) Desolate

15. Reciprocate

(A) Rationalise (B) Retaliate (C) Requite (D) Revive

16. Flabby

(A) Sluggish (B) Limp (C) Wilted (D) Lewd

17. Opulent
   (A) Fluffy (B) Swollen (C) Affluent (D) Rude

18. Leer
   (A) Ogle (B) Lecher (C) Lewd (D) Lascivious

19. Cashier
   (A) Castrate (B) Count (C) Retrench (D) Restore

20. Stentorian
   (A) Musty (B) Shrill (C) Rank (D) Tempting

21. Mend
   (A) Criticize (B) Remind (C) Retrench (D) Rectify

22. Allegiance
   (A) Allegation (B) Criticism (C) Fealty (D) Alleviation

23. Reprove
   (A) Reproach (B) Prove (C) Repent (D) Repay

24. Rancour
   (A) Pain (B) Repentance (C) Spleen (D) Stink

25. Remains
   (A) Remainder (B) Dividend (C) Relic (D) Dead body

26. Rut
   (A) Spoor (B) Rot (C) Rancid (D) Putrid

27. Rehabilitation
   (A) Relocation (B) Re-instatement
   (C) Return (D) Relapse

28. Phenomenon
   (A) Marvel (B) Trailblazer (C) Fundamental (D) Essence

29. Expostulate
   (A) Propose (B) Expound (C) Remonstrate (D) Expatiate

30. Carnage
   (A) Carnality (B) Corporal (C) Incarnate (D) Pogrom

31. Quagmire
   (A) Quaint (B) Quid (C) Bog (D) Quilt

32. Pugnacious

(A) Potent (B) Bellicose (C) Belligerent (D) Bully

33. Gaffe

(A) Hook (B) Gobble (C) Faux pas (D) Gap

34. Quack

(A) Cheat (B) Novice (C) Charlatan (D) Pedant

35. Afflatus

(A) Affairs (B) Suborn (C) Flatulence (D) Inspiration

36. Riddle

(A) Puncture (B) Hole (C) Conundrum (D) Fracture

37. Gobble dygook

(A) Gambling (B) Poppycock (C) Ogle (D) Inchoate

38. Greenhorn

(A) Unicorn (B) Tyro (C) Impugn (D) Montage

39. Gore

(A) Bloody (B) Impale (C) Coax (D) Stake

40. Overture

(A) Overboard (B) Overwhelm

(C) Tender (D) Ordain

41. Inchoate

(A) Coax (B) Incipient (C) Innocent (D) Intent

42. Impugn

(A) Spin (B) Fight (C) Dispute (D) Decide

43. Happenstance

(A) Chance (B) Instantly (C) Incidence (D) Omen

44. Portent

(A) Augury (B) Bad omen (C) Archaic (D) Outdated

45. Antiquated

(A) Ante-diluvian (B) Antic

(C) Antique (D) Neophyte

46. Unpropitious

(A) Improper (B) Unlucky

(C) Portentous (D) Unimportant

47. Antithesis
   (A) Opposite   (B) Synthesis
   (C) Synchronous   (D) Annex
48. Edict
   (A) Edit   (B) Adopt   (C) Diktat   (D) Bid
49. Pragmatic
   (A) Provident   (B) Indigent   (C) Potent   (D) Contrary
50. Zenith
   (A) Zeal   (B) Zest   (C) Sky   (D) Pinnacle

Choose the pair of words out of the given options which resembles in meanings:

51. (A) Pilgrimage (B) Excursion (C) Devotion (D) Caravan
52. (A) Deem (B) Trim (C) Recon (D) Recant
53. (A) Humane (B) Humid (C) Kind (D) Human-being
54. (A) Lascivious (B) Sticky (C) Greedy (D) Libidinous
55. (A) Churlish (B) Churning (C) Brash (D) Creaking
56. (A) Vindicate (B) Vent (C) Justify (D) Vend
57. (A) Risible (B) Risque (C) Drill (D) Ludicrous
58. (A) Kowtow (B) Cower (C) Decimate (D) Stickout
59. (A) Jeer (B) Scoff (C) Jaunt (D) Deny
60. (A) Mourn (B) Maim (C) Mount (D) Condole
61. (A) Laugh (B) Ridicule (C) Mute (D) Cachinnate
62. (A) Renege (B) Revenge (C) Recant (D) Ridicule
63. (A) Indolent (B) Pedant (C) Languid (D) Lustful
64. (A) Languid (B) Sluggish (C) Lonely (D) Desolate
65. (A) Revive (B) Resuscitate (C) Redeem (D) Recuperate
66. (A) Venal (B) Desolate (C) Deserted (D) Strident
67. (A) Mutiny (B) Musty (C) Opulent (D) Uprising
68. (A) Spy (B) Espy (C) Peer (D) Intent
69. (A) Solicit (B) Request (C) Suite (D) Dismiss
70. (A) Glance (B) Glee (C) Gaze (D) Pour
71. (A) Supersede (B) Overlay (C) Substitute (D) Obsolete

72. (A) Pillage (B) Despoil (C) Profit (D) Protrude
73. (A) Assuage (B) Assure (C) Mitigate (D) Reject
74. (A) Spite (B) Despite (C) Spit (D) Alternative
75. (A) Regret (B) Sorry (C) Deny (D) Rue
76. (A) Tail (B) Contrail (C) Tally (D) Trail
77. (A) Retaliate (B) Recede (C) Retreat (D) Secede
78. (A) Miracle (B) Prodigy (C) Pogrom (D) Mystic
79. (A) Snub (B) Snore (C) Spurn (D) Snuff
80. (A) Mercenary (B) Mariner (C) Venal (D) Arbiter
81. (A) Souvenir (B) Remembrance
(C) Reminder (D) Showbiz
82. (A) Quibble (B) Quiz (C) Queer (D) Pettifog
83. (A) Abject (B) Ignoble (C) Object (D) Abstract
84. (A) Extol (B) Enigma (C) Fervour (D) Approbate
85. (A) Absurd (B) Abstruse (C) Recondite (D) Neophyte
86. (A) Realty (B) Personalty (C) Profession (D) Metier
87. (A) Hubris (B) Horror (C) Vainglory (D) Fib
88. (A) Impediment (B) Hurdle (C) Manacle (D) Eminent
89. (A) Penury (B) Palter (C) Privation (D) Secrecy
90. (A) Rattle (B) Faze (C) Rout (D) Defunct
91. (A) Pry (B) Prick (C) Voyeur (D) Peer
92. (A) Discomfit (B) Disconcert (C) Doubt (D) Dubious
93. (A) Conman (B) Canon (C) Cannon (D) Injunction
94. (A) Mast (B) Pylon (C) Bolard (D) Obelisk
95. (A) Poverty (B) Pot pourri (C) Medley (D) Palter
96. (A) Puissant (B) Potent (C) Privation (D) Collage
97. (A) Prayer (B) Song (C) Anthem (D) Paternoster
98. (A) Precedence (B) Priority (C) Preceding (D) Prior
99. (A) Palter (B) Patter (C) Equivocate (D) Prefer
100. (A) Fortune (B) Wealth (C) Incentive (D) Prize

Choose the odd one out from the given options:

101. (A) Journey (B) Voyage (C) Expedition (D) Erand

102. (A) Ploy (B) Subterfuse (C) Pillory (D) Feint
103. (A) Benign (B) Benevolent
(C) Magnanimous (D) Mourn
104. (A) Erudite (B) Pedant (C) Scholar (D) Charlatan
105. (A) Insolent (B) Intolerant (C) Impertinent (D) Impudent
106. (A) Dirge (B) Elegy (C) Requiem (D) Downcast
107. (A) Hazard (B) Hamper (C) Risk (D) Jeopardy
108. (A) Kneel (B) Genuflect (C) Bend (D) Kowtow
109. (A) Fleer (B) Sneer (C) Flail (D) Jeer
110. (A) Lament (B) Laugh (C) Bemoan (D) Grieve
111. (A) Giggle (B) Titter (C) Snigger (D) Totter
112. (A) Reverence (B) Veneration (C) Obeisance (D) Repentance
113. (A) Advocate (B) Attorney (C) Arbitrator (D) Solicitor
114. (A) Languor (B) Lassitude (C) Listlessness (D) Lewd
115. (A) Retrieve (B) Restore (C) Restitute (D) Destitute
116. (A) Limp (B) Flaccid (C) Levity (D) Flabby
117. (A) Sedition (B) Pillory (C) Putsch (D) Insurgency
118. (A) Hold (B) Behold (C) Peer (D) Pore
119. (A) Supplicate (B) Entreat (C) Importune (D) Curtsy
120. (A) Raucus (B) Strident (C) Arrogant (D) Stertorous
121. (A) Vanity (B) Penitence (C) Remorse (D) Contrition
122. (A) Entice (B) Inveigle (C) Lure (D) Attract
123. (A) Apposite (B) Opposite (C) Germane (D) Pertinent
124. (A) Noisome (B) Fetid (C) Foul (D) Rancid
125. (A) Repartee (B) Riposte (C) Retort (D) Retrench
126. (A) Pogrom (B) Aftermath (C) Trail (D) Contrail
127. (A) Retract (B) Repercuss (C) Boomerang (D) Recochet
128. (A) Mash (B) Squash (C) Powder (D) Crumple
129. (A) Admonish (B) Objurgate (C) Upbraid (D) Punish
130. (A) Memento (B) Mentality
(C) Memorabilia (D) Token
131. (A) Cenotaph (B) Mousoleum (C) Tomb (D) Sensitive
132. (A) Fracas (B) Fracture (C) Scrap (D) Melee

133. (A) Frugal (B) Parisimonious (C) Stingy (D) Prudent

134. (A) Panegyrise (B) Eulogize (C) Laud (D) Euphoria

135. (A) Induce (B) Encourage (C) Poke (D) Suborn

136. (A) Wage (B) Largesse (C) Reward (D) Bounty

137. (A) Doctrine (B) Dogma (C) Tenet (D) Reward

138. (A) Profess (B) Malinger (C) Fein (D) Malign

139. (A) Prevaricate (B) Fabricate (C) Palter (D) Fib

140. (A) Caper (B) Cajole (C) Wheedle (D) Inveigle

Test-11

Choose the closest word out of the given options, which has the same meaning as the word suggested:

1. Heresy
   (A) Hearsay (B) Hermit (C) Blasphemy (D) Hermetic
2. Writhe
   (A) Wrest (B) Wring (C) Squirm (D) Twist
3. Forlorn
   (A) Sarcastic (B) Doleful (C) Crazy (D) Solemn
4. Flotsam
   (A) Levitate (B) Flat (C) Prostrate (D) Jetsam
5. Sardonic
   (A) Satirical (B) Bitter (C) Caustic (D) Sardine
6. Iniquitous
   (A) Unequal (B) Flagitious (C) Ubiquitous (D) Unkempt
7. Skit
   (A) Slip (B) Squat (C) Squib (D) Irony
8. Caveat
   (A) Cavern (B) Callous (C) Caution (D) Cater
9. Segregate
   (A) Assemble (B) Sort (C) Aggregate (D) Sway
10. Vagabond
    (A) Vagary (B) Tramp (C) Vacuous (D) Stray

11. Somber
(A) Amber (B) Ember (C) Soar (D) Staid

12. Wanton
(A) Upheaval (B) Arrogant (C) Rampant (D) Upset

13. Shimmer
(A) Simmer (B) Incense (C) Glimmer (D) Glean

14. Ubiquitous
(A) Unique (B) Omnipresent
(C) Reticent (D) Untidy

15. Wizen
(A) Shrivel (B) Wizard (C) Conform (D) Aroma

16. Wrench
(A) Turn (B) Mangle (C) Wring (D) Nexus

17. Coy
(A) Cozy (B) Caring (C) Demure (D) Gyrate

18. Watershed
(A) Flow (B) Epoch (C) Water colour (D) Spill over

19. Parity
(A) Paring (B) Peer (C) Analogy (D) Semblance

20. Dock
(A) Lop (B) Detour (C) Dais (D) Tumble

21. Homily
(A) Humility (B) Humanity (C) Sermon (D) Honour

22. Purloin
(A) Pilfer (B) Pruriance (C) Besiege (D) Besmirch

23. Coercion
(A) Coarse (B) Cruelty (C) Duress (D) Crude

24. Goad
(A) Impel (B) Trot (C) Burgle (D) Choke

25. Stub
(A) Stab (B) Stamp (C) Stomp (D) Stubble

Choose the pair of words out of the given options, which have the same meanings:

26. (A) Conation (B) Cheating (C) Volition (D) Reconning
27. (A) Welter (B) Swelter (C) Sweat (D) Wriggle
28. (A) Lugabrious (B) Melancholic (C) Laborious (D) Mournful
29. (A) Loll (B) Lull (C) Lounge (D) Lug
30. (A) Profuse (B) Dissipate (C) Diffuse (D) Defer
31. (A) Weird (B) Wind (C) Wound (D) Macabre
32. (A) Sharp (B) Shred (C) Shrapnel (D) Fragment
33. (A) Turmoil (B) Trouble (C) Topsyturvy (D) Distress
34. (A) Objectionable (B) Obsequious (C) Staid (D) Slavish
35. (A) Licentious (B) Dissolute (C) Turbulent (D) Eerie
36. (A) Simper (B) Pilfer (C) Teeter (D) Totter
37. (A) Upset (B) Distraught (C) Terrible (D) Sully
38. (A) Commensuration (B) Correspondence (C) Commendation (D) Condemnation
39. (A) Drown (B) Dowse (C) Douse (D) Dunk
40. (A) Nefarious (B) Nexus (C) Nascent (D) Coordination
41. (A) Train (B) Box (C) Cuff (D) Trigger
42. (A) Frolick (B) Fraud (C) Fisc (D) Coffer
43. (A) Buffet (B) Bouquet (C) Redolence (D) Buffer
44. (A) Legate (B) Ligate (C) Lever (D) Tether
45. (A) Philippic (B) Tirade (C) Gyrate (D) Tamper
46. (A) Imprompt (B) Extempore (C) Instant (D) Instense
47. (A) Long (B) Linger (C) Tarry (D) Tract
48. (A) Hoist (B) Heist (C) Gird (D) Larceny
49. (A) Besmirch (B) Sully (C) Besot (D) Bespecle
50. (A) Rend (B) Rent (C) Sunder (D) Thrash

Choose the odd one out form the given options in each set of words:

51. (A) Desolate (B) Disconsolate (C) Doleful (D) Doubtful
52. (A) Waver (B) Waiver (C) Vacillate (D) Dither
53. (A) Scatter (B) Scare (C) Disseminate (D) Disperse
54. (A) Gallivant (B) Gad (C) Fad (D) Loaf
55. (A) Graze (B) Grate (C) Scrape (D) Grunt
56. (A) Prove (B) Attest (C) Authenticate (D) Vouch
57. (A) Shrill (B) Shriek (C) Screech (D) Sharp
58. (A) Toddle (B) Wobble (C) Totter (D) Trip
59. (A) Unnerve (B) Uncanny (C) Eerie (D) Weird
60. (A) Brazen (B) Brash (C) Impudent (D) Redolent
61. (A) Slatternly (B) Slovenly (C) Slum (D) Dishevelled
62. (A) Port (B) Harbour (C) Haven (D) Refuge
63. (A) Educe (B) Strive (C) Endeavour (D) Persevere
64. (A) Immerse (B) Emerge (C) Inundate (D) Submerge
65. (A) Laconic (B) Reticent (C) Lacuna (D) Taciturn
66. (A) Trip (B) Truncate (C) Prune (D) Clip
67. (A) Quirk (B) Smirk (C) Simper (D) Grin
68. (A) Quiver (B) Shiver (C) Shudder (D) Tether
69. (A) Whirl (B) Whine (C) Whorl (D) Twirl
70. (A) Brook (B) Tolerate (C) Bear (D) Cataract
71. (A) Spoil (B) Spoils (C) Booty (D) Swag
72. (A) Toss (B) Pelt (C) Lob (D) Gird
73. (A) Cleave (B) Rive (C) Rend (D) Bulge
74. (A) Loquacious (B) Garrulous (C) Glib (D) Blemish
75. (A) Slug (B) Lug (C) Slog (D) Swat

ooo

Antonyms

An antonym means a word which is opposite in meaning to the given word. So in antonym based questions you need to find a word opposite to the given word. Sometimes you may not find a clear opposite then find the word that is the closest option. We can use the strategies similar to that of synonyms to find the antonyms.

1. **Think of a word which is opposite to the given word before looking at options.**
   In this approach look at the given word and then think of an opposite word to it. After that go through the options and
   find an answer. By doing this you can avoid falling into the trap of ambiguous answers.

   Example: Concise

A. Vague	B. Piquant
C. Genuine	D. Prolix

   The word 'concise' means expressing content in few words. The opposite of it could be lengthy, wordy, long winded, prolix, verbose. So, the antonym for Concise is Option D.

2. **If more than one option appears to be opposite, define the word more precisely.**

   Sometimes, you may have a dilemma between two options, in such a situation, define both of them more precisely. Think how the two options differ from each other in their word usage.

   Example: Obstinate

A. Wavering	B. Rigid
C. Good	D. Cultured

   The word 'obstinate' means stubbornly adherent to an attitude, difficult to manage. The word opposite can suggest manageable easily, not rigid. The word 'cultured' means refined, enlightened. So, the antonym for the given word is Option A. The word 'wavering' means uncertain in purpose or action.

3. **If you cannot recollect the word, think of a sentence or phrase.**

   It is easy to learn words and their meanings if you focus on their usage. Try to build sentences in which you can use the word. So, if you encounter a new word, think whether you have read it in a sentence.

Example: Adulteration

A. Purification B. Approximation

C. Normalization D. Rejuvenation

You might have heard your dad saying that the fuel used in the automobile is adulterated and, hence, it is giving black smoke. The word 'adulterate' means to make impure. So, the antonym is Option A.

4. **Use the knowledge of suffix, prefix and root words to determine the meanings of the given word.**

As mentioned earlier, another effective way to learn words is by studying roots, prefixes and suffixes. So, try if you can find the meaning of the word by analyzing it.

Example: Hyperbole

A. Exaggeration B. Commensuration

C. Understatement D. Moderation

The word 'hyperbole' means an exaggerated statement. The word 'hyper' means beyond. Option A is a synonym to the given word. The word 'understatement' and 'moderation' may appear to be close. But, they are different. The word 'moderation' means to be within reasonable limits. The word 'understatement' is less than complete. So, answer is Option C.

5. **If a word is given in a sentence, and you have to find its antonym.**

This will be comparatively easy one as you can guess the meaning of the word based on surrounding information. You may find clues like antonym, synonym, definition, example related to unfamiliar word. From this you can interpret the meaning of the unknown word. And then find its antonym.

Example: After washing the stain on her apron with the new detergent soap, she found it **immaculate**.

A. radiant B. clean

C. dirty D. ghostly

Basic general knowledge says that after washing, the apron becomes clean. So, the meaning of the word is clean. Now the antonym of it is dirty.

ANTONYMS

A

Abandon = *leave alone* .... : Adopt = *to take up on one's own*

Abashed = *ashamed* .... : Honoured = *highly respected, esteemed*

Abate = *lose intensity* .... : Intensity = *the quality of being intense*

Aberration = *unwelcome deviation from right course* .... : Rectitude = *right path as of morlity*

Abet = *help in wrong doing* .... : Deter = *discourage from wrong doing*

Ability = *skill of doing* .... : Inability = *absence of skill to do something*

Abhor = *hate* .... : Adore = *like*

Abject = *degrading* .... : Honourable = *respectful, exalted*

Abjure = *swear not to do* .... : Indulge = *involve in doing; keep on doing*

Abolish = *scrap a rule/act* .... : Implement = *to enforce a rule or a project*

Abominate = *hate* .... : Like

Aboriginal = *belonging to a place from beginning* .... : Exogenous, Alien = *coming from outside*

Abridge = *make short* .... : Expand, Enlarge = *make large*

Abrogate = *do away with rule* .... : Promulgate = *enforce rule with official proclamation*

Abrupt = *suddenly* .... : Gradual = *slowly*

Abscond = *flee away from custody/ justice; hide away* : Surrender = *to submit*

Absence = *being away from a place* : Presence = *be in a place*

Absolute = *not subject to limitation* : Qualified = *subject to conditions*

Absolve = *free from charge* .... : Incriminate = *put charge against*

Abstain = *keep away from indulgence* .... : Indulge = *get oneself involved in undesirable activity*

Abstemious = *keep away from excessive eating*	Gluttonous = *eating without restraint*
Absurd = *not sensible, illogical*	Logical = *sensible*
Abundance = *excessiveness*	Scarcity, Dearth = *insufficient availability*
Abundant = *excessive in amount*	Scarce = *not sufficient*
Accede = *to agree*	Reject = refuse to agree
Accelerate = *increase speed*	Decelerate = *reduce speed*
Accept = *agree to receive*	Decline = *refuse to accept*
Acclaim = *praise*	Denounce = *criticize*
Accomplish = *to complete task*	Abort = *terminate before completion*
Accord = *agreement*	Discord = *disagreement*
Accumulate = *to store*	Deplete, Dissipate = *to exhaust*
Accusation = *blame*	Approbation = *praise*
Acerbic = *bitter; sour*	Meltiferous = *sweet like honey*
Acknowledge = *accept to have knowledge of responsibility*	Deny = *refuse to, repudiate responsibility on a claim*
Acquiesce = *keep quiet instead of protesting*	Protest = *to raise voice*
Acquit = *declare not guilty*	Convict = *declare guilty*
Acrimony = *bitter feeling*	Harmony = *concord*
Active = *capable to act*	Passive = *not active*
Acute = *severe*	Mild = *not severe*
Adamant = *refusing to yield; unrelenting*	Relenting = *yield*
Adequate = *sufficient*	Inadequate = *not sufficient*
Adjourn = *postpone a meeting*	Convene = *to call a meeting*
Admire = *to praise*	Censure = *criticize*
Adroit = *skillful*	Unskilled, Clumsy
Advance = *move forward*	Retreat = *move backward*
Avenge = *punish in return for a wrong act*	Forgive = *excuse for offence*
Adverse = *unfavourable*	Favourable

Aeons = *very long period of time* : Trice = *a moment, very short period*

Affectation = *pretentious behaviour*: Sincerity = *unpretentious behaviour*

Affection = *fond feeling* : Disaffection = *loss of affection*

Affinity = *spontaneous liking* : Aversion = *spontaneous disliking*

Affirm, Affirmative, Afford = *provide* : Deprive = *deny to provide, negate, deny negative*

Affluence = *floor of wealth* : Penury = *lacking in wealth, poverty*

Affluent = *wealthy* : Indigent = *poor*

Agitated = *disturbed* : Quiescent = *Calm, Tranquil*

Agnostic = *unknowledgeable person*: Gnostic = *knowlegeable person*

Agoraphobia = *morbid fear of open space* : Claustrophobia = *morbid fear of closed space*

Aggresive = *attacking without provocation* : Defensive = *protecting oneself from attack*

Aggravate = *to make a situation worse* : Alleviate = *Assuage, Mitigate*

Albino = *person with white skin and hair* : Brunette = *woman with dark skin and hairs*

Alert = *attention directed to pick up danger* : Distracted = *attention diverted; mentally drawn in different directions*

Alien = *belonging to another place & hence unknown* : Familiar, Native = *well known*

Alight = *to dismount from a horse's back or a vehicle* : Board = *to ride on a vehicle*

Alike = *having likeness* : Unlike = *not alike*

Alleviate = *to lessen intensity of pain, problem* : Aggravate = *make intensity of pain*

Allow = *permit* : Disallow = *not allow*

Allure = *entice, attract* : Repulse, Disinterest = *to keep away*

Alto = *highest pitch of male voice* : Soprano = *highest pitch of female voice*

Altruism = *selfless concern for*	Egoism = *concern for self others; self-cntredness; self-opinionatedness*
Amateur = *inexperienced in art*	Connoisseur = *experience knowledgeable person in art*
Ambiguous = *not clearly understood*	Obvious, clear = *clearly understood*
Ameliorate = *make better*	Exacerbate = *make worse*
Ancestor = *a person more remote than a grandparent*	Descendant = *progeny*
Analogy = *similarity between two things*	Anomaly = *deviation from one another; irregularity of condition or behaviour*
Ancestry = *generation of ancestors*	Posterity = *generation of progenies, succeeding generation*
Annex = *to add something else to something*	Cede = *to separate something to give to someone else*
Anorexia = *loss of appetite*	Bulimia = *increase in appetite; ravenous hunger*
Antagonist = *opposite to lead pole in cinema*	Protagonist = *lead actor in cinema*
Antagonize = *cause to become hostile*	Appease = *to please, make one to be pleased*
Anterior = *frontal part of something*	Exterior, Posterior = *back part*
Antipathy = *hostile feeling*	Sympathy = *compassionate feeling*
Applaud = *praise by clapping*	Heckle, Hoot, Denounce = *disapprove by hooting*
Appreciate = *recognize the value of*	Depreciate = *make something lose value*
Approbation = *praise in approval* ..	Disapproval = *disapprove by expressing it*
Apt = *suitable*	Inapt = *not suitable*
Armaggedon = *fierce war*	Skirmish = *minor scuffle*
Aristocracy = *upper class of society*	Plebeian = *lower class of society*
Arouse = *excite emotion*	Pacify = *calm the passion/emotion*
Arranged = *ordered*	Haphazard = *disordered*

Word	Antonym
Arrive = *to come to destination*	Depart = *to leave for arriving a place*
Arrogant = *exaggerated sense of self-importance*	Modest = *moderate sense of self importance*
Arrogate = *usurp other's credit*	Credit = *give someone his due credit*
Articulate = *speak clearly*	Babble = *speak incomprehensively*
Artificial = *not genuine*	Genuine
Ascend = *to go up*	Descend = *to come down*
Ascetic = *one who lives simple life*	Epicure = *one who lives luxurious enjoyable life*
Ashamed	Proud
Assemble = *to gather in a place*	Disperse = *get scattered from a place*
Ashore	Adrift
Assent = *express approval*	Dissent = *express disapproval*
Asset = *something which is usable with positive value*	Liability = *something which is burdensome and with negative value if not invested properly*
Assuage = *lessen unpleasant feelings*	Aggravate = *worsen*
Atonement = *make amends for sins*	Impenitent = *unregretful for sins committed*
Atrabilious = *ill tempered*	Genial = *pleasantly warm tempered; pertaining to natural disposition*
Attention	Distraction
Attentive	Inattentive
Attract	Repel, Distract
Attraction	Repulsion
Audacity = *arrogance*	Humility = *devoid of arrogance*
Audible = *which can be heard*	Inaudible = *which cannot be heard*
Auspicious = *indicating favourable chance*	Ominous = *indicating harmful results*
Austere = *strict in manners*	Lax = *lenient*
Authentic = *genuinely true*	Dubious = *doubtful*
Avant garde = *front runner in a field, trailblazer*	Follower = *running behind; laggard*

Avarice = *greed* .... : Lustless = *devoid of greed*

Avenge = *punish in return for a wrong act* ..... : Forgive = *excuse for offence*

Averse = *not inclined* .... : Disposed = *inclined*

Aversion .... : Affinity, predilection

Avert = *turn away* .... : Confront = *to face headlong*

Avoid = *to ignore* .... : Indulge = *to become involved*

Awake = *get up from sleep* .... : Asleep = *in state of sleep*

Aware = *be alert* .... : Unaware = *not alert*

Awkward = *clumsy; predicament* ... : Elegant = *graceful*

B

Babble .... : Articulate

Backwards = *towards back* .... : Forward = *towards ahead*

Bait = *something used to allure, attract towards the trap* .... : Spy = *secret agent; one who works covertly to distract attention from the trap laid by the authorities*

Balkanise = *to separate people into hostile groups* .. : Confederate = *to bring together separate people*

Ban = *to prohibit* .... : Permit = *to allow*

Banal = *uninteresting* .... : Stimulating = *inciting interest*

Bane = *cause of distress, curse* ..... : Boon = *cause of gain, blessings to people*

Benevolence = *well-wishing for others* ...... : Malevolence = *malignant towards others*

Bankrupt = *go without money by way of losing it in business* .... : Prosperous, Flourishing = *be wealthy*

Barbaric = *uncivilized as brabarians* : Civilized

Barren = *unable to produce yields* . Fertile = *able to produce yields*

Basement = *area of a building before ground floor* .... : Pent-house = *area/floor at the top of a building*

Bass = *lowest pitch of male voice* .. : Contalto = *lowest pitch of female voice*

Belie = *fail to achieve as hoped* ..... : Realise = *achieve as hoped*

Belief = *firmly held opinion* .... : Disbelief = *firmly rejected opinion*

Benediction = *speaking good to others, belessings* .... : Malediction = *speaking evil for others, curse*

Benefaction = *doing good to others*: Malefaction

Benevolence .... : Malevolence

Benignant = *not harmful in effect; favourable; kind* .. : Malignant = *harmful in effect*

Bequeath = *to hand over property to descendant* .... : Inherit = *to get properly left by an ancestor*

Bete noire = *one who is hated most by someone* .... : Cynosure = *one who is the star attraction of all*

Betray = *to disclose internal feelings as by facial expressions* .... : Dissemble = *to hide internal emotions*

Bias = *unjust inclination* .... : Impartial, Disinterested

Bibliophile = *book lover; collector* .. : Bibliophobe *of books*

Bigot = *intolerant to contrary opinion of others* .... : Broad-minded, Secular

Bland, Insipid = *state, tasteless* ..... : Delectable = *tasty*

Blaspheme = *speak irreverently* ..... : Revere = *to show profound respect*

Blend = *mix with something else* ... : Separate = *remove from a mix*

Bless .... : Curse, Anathematise

Blessed .... : Damned, Cursed

Bliss = *highest level of pleasure* .... : Melancholy = *profound sadness*

Blitho = *cheerful* .... : Dejected = *disheartened*

Blunt = *without sharpness* .... : Sharp

Blunt, Rude = *harsh* .... : Humble, Polite = *not harsh*

Bold = *daring* .... : Timid, Timorous, Coward = *lacking courage*

Bonafide = *sincere intention* .... : Malafide = *bad intention*

Boost = *to enhance* .... : Depress = *to lower*

Board = *enter into vehicle* .... : Alight = *come out of a vehicle*

Boon .... : Bane

Brave, Intrepid .... : Pusillanimous

Brazen = *shameless* .... : Shy

Brief = *concise, short* .... : Lengthy

Bright = *shining* .... : Dull = *lacking shine*

Brilliant = *brightly colourful* .... : Lacklustre = *lacking lustre/shine*

Brisk = *energetic* .... : Lethargic = *sluggish, lacking energy*

Broad = *wide* .... : Narrow = *not wide*

Brook = *tolerate opposition* .... : Resent = *not tolerate opposition or such behaviour*

Brunette .... : Albino

Brutal = *cruel* .... : Dainty = *small and delicate body, merciful*

Build = *to construct* .... : Demolish = *pull down*

Bury = *to put underground* .... : Disinter, Exhume = *to dig out of ground*

Bulimia .... : Anorexia

Bustle = *move around excitedly around* ..... : Quiet, Unhurried = *move quietly*

C

Cacophony = *bitter and harsh sound to ears* ..... : Symphony = *pleasant sound to hear*

Cadaverous = *like deadbody* .... : Vivacious = *like full of life*

Callow = *inexperienced* .... : Expert

Calm = *undisturbed* .... : Agitated = *disturbed*

Candour = *open and honest* .... : Duplicity = *not open and showing double character*

Capacitate = *make capable* .... : Incapacitate = *make incapable*

Capitulate = *surrender under pressure* .... : Resist, challenge = *fight to overcome release*

Caprice = *sudden change of mood without reason* : Stoicism = *remain without change of mood in pleasure of pain*

Capture = *catch hold of* .... : Release

Careful .... : Careless

Cascade = *fall down in stages headlong* ...... : Precipitate = *fall down steeply*

Casual = *not according to norms, relaxed* . : Formal = *according to accepted norms*

Catholic = *of wide attitude/outlook* : Parochial = *of narrow attitude*

Caustic = *causing burn* .... : Soothing = *causing comfortable feeling*

Cautious = *alert from danger/ dangerous situation* .... : Reckless = *not caring for effects*

Celebrity = *celebrated person, famous* ...... : Neophyte, Tyro = *newcomer in a field*

Celibate = *abstaining from sex* ..... : Lecher = *excessively indulging in sex*

Censure = *criticize* .... : Admire

Central = *near centre* .... : Peripheral, Fringe = *near outer limit*

Centrifugal = *moving away from centre* ... : Centripetal = *moving towards centre*

Chary = *cautious* .... : Negligent, Careless

Cheerful .... : Doleful, Sad, Depressed

Claim .... : Forego

Clairvoyance = *ability to see distant objects or actions beyond the power of natural viewing; sagacious* .... : Myopia = *near sightedness*

Clamorous = *shouting* .... : Quiet = *making no noise*

Clarity = *state of being clear* .... : Obscurity = *state of being unclear*

Classic = *of high quality* .... : Kitsch = *of cheap quality; inferior*

Claustrophobia = *abnormal fear of enclosed or narrow places* .... : Agoraphobia = *an abnormal fear of being in an open space*

Cleanse = *to clean* .... : Defile = *to make dirty*

Clement = *kind (weather); merciful; kind* .... : Inclement = *stormy (weather); severe; harsh*

Clinche = *stale due to repeating* ... : Novel = *new*

Climax = *highest point of excitement*: Anticlimax = *sudden end of excitement*

Cogniscenti = *knowledgeable group* : Ignoramous = *ignorant group*

Coherent = *logically consistent* ..... : Incoherent = *logically inconsistent*

Collosal = *huge in size; gigantic* ... : Tiny = *very small in size*

Comfort = *feeling of ease* .... : Discomfort = *feeling of unease*

Comfortable = *in state of comfort*.. : Uncomfortable

Commence = *to begin a meeting* .. : Conclude = *to end meeting after completing deliberations*

Commend = *to praise for good work;* entrust : Criticize

Commit = *send a case to higher court of judicature* ... : Remit = *send a case to lower court*

Commodious = *Comfortably spacious causing discomfort* : Incommodious = *not spacious*

Commonplace = *usual, not extraordinary* .... : Outstanding = *extraordinary*

Commensurate = *equal in measure or expert; in due proportion* : Incommensurate

Compassionate = *showing pity* ..... : Cruel = *causing pain or torture*

Competent = *able to succeed* .... : Incompetent = *not able to succeed; unfit*

Complexity .... : Simplicity

Comply = *act according to the command or complete the requirements* ...... : Defy = *refuse to act according to the command*

Conceal = *to hide something* .... : Reveal = *to remove veil on something*

Concern = *worry* .... : Indifference = *without concern, aloof*

Conclude = *come to end* .... : Commence = *start*

Condemn = *to denounce* .... : Commend, Approbate = *to praise; laud*

Confess = *to accept one's wrong deed* : Refute = *to deny accusation*

Confidence = *feeling of trust* .... : Mistrust = *lack of trust*

(Self) Confidence .... : Diffidence = *lack of self-confidence*

Confident = *to be sure of achieving something* : Diffident = *lacking in confidence*

Conflict = *lack of aggreement in opinion* ... : Accord = *agreement in opinion*

Word	Antonym
Conformist = *one who acts according to norms*	Iconoclast, Non-conformist
Confront	Skip, Avert
Congeal = *to coagulate; curdle*	Thaw = *to melt or transform into liquid*
Congenial = *pleasant*	Hostile = *showing dislike*
Congested = *crowded so as to hinder movement*	Spacious = *having free space*
Congregate = *to assemble in a place*	Segregate = *to remove apart*
Congruent = *identical in form*	Incongruent
Connoisseur = *expert in intricacies of art*	Dilettante = *lover of art without having expert knowledge*
Consensual	Contentious, Dissentious
Consent = *give approval*	Dissent = *express disapproval*
Consecrate = *to treat as sacred*	Desecrate = *to violate sacredness; to defile*
Conservative = *averse to change*	Liberal = *open to change*
Conserve = *to avoid misuse of resources*	Squander = *waste recklessly*
Considerate = *careful about other's interests*	Inconsiderate = *not caring for other's interests*
Consistent = *not changing over time*	Inconsistent = *changing over time*
Constrain = *compel someone to do something*	Restrain = *compel someone not to do something*
Constrict = *make narrow*	Dilate = *make wider*
Contemptible = *deserving contempt*	Admirable = *deserving praise*
Contemptuous = *showing hatred*	Respectful = *showing respect*
Contest = *challenge*	Surrender = *submit*
Continent = *able to self-control*	Incontinent = *unable to exercise control over desires*
Continuous = *continuing without break*	Sporadic = *resuming or happening at periodic intervals*
Contradict = *oppose mother's viewpoint*	Corroborate = *to confirm statement*
Conventional = *meeting norms*	Unconventional = *deviating from norms*

Contentious = *causing controversy* : Uncontentious = *not causing controversy*

Controversy = *disagreement* .... : Unanimity = *one opinion*

Converge = *meet at a point* .... : Diverge = *go away in different directions from a point*

Convict = *declare guilty* .... : Exonerate = *declare not guilty*

Copse = *small bunch of trees forming jungle* .... : Glade = *small space without trees in jungle*

Corporeal = *related to body* .... : Spiritual = *related to spirit, non-physical*

Corpulent = *of hefty body; obese* .. : Emaciated = *of thin (without flesh) body = a state of body health caused by either flesh-water or lack of nutrition*

Corrigible = *that can be corrected or reformed* ...... : Incorrigible = *that cannot be corrected*

Corroborate .... : Contradict

Cosmopolitan = *belonging to all places* ... : Provincial = *concerned with locality cowardice, timidity*

Counterfeit = *forged to cheat* .... : Genuine = *truly real*

Couth = *well mannered* .... : Uncouth = *ill-mannered*

Covert .... : Overt

Covet = *long to possess* .... : Renounce = *give up; abandon*

Coward = *lacking courage* .... : Brave, Intrepid

Cowardice .... : Courage

Crafty, Cunning .... : Ingenuous = *simpleton*

Credible = *believable* .... : Incredible = *unbelievable*

Credit (v) .... : Arrogate

Credit (n) = *trust in someone* .... : Discredit = *distrust*

Credulous = *inclined to believe* ..... : Sceptic, Incredulous

Cressendo = *gradually increasing music* : Diminuendo

Crest = *top of a wave* .... : Trough = *lower part between two crests*

Criticize .... : Commend = *praise*

Critical = *of decisive importance* ... : Uncritical

Crude = *unrefined* .... : Refined

Cruel .... : Compassionate

Cunning .... : Simpleton, Ingenuous

Curious = *eager to know* .... : Indifferent = *unconcerned*

Curse .... : Bless

Curtail = *cut short* .... : Prolong, Protract

Cynic, Sceptic .... : Credulous

Cynosure .... : Bete noire

D

Dainty .... : Burly

Damned = *cursed or sentenced to eternal punishment* .... : Blessed = *a person upon whom divine powers/favours are invoked*

Dandy = *excessively fashionable;. keeping oneself in vogue to a .... remarkable degree* .... : Sloven = *person who is habitually untidy or dirtily dressed*

Dawn = *sunrise period* .... : Dusk = *sunset period*

Debit .... : Credit

Deciduous = *(plant) which sheds its leaves once every year* .... : Perrenial, Evergreen = *tree which does not annually shed its leaves*

Decipher = *to uncode a coded* ...... *language or message* : Encrypt = *write into code*

Decline = *fail to be inclined to do .. something; disinclined* .... : Incline = *to lean towards; to dispose; to land*

Decry – *publicly denounce* .... : Laud = *publicly praise*

Deep .... : Shallow

De facto = *by the fact itself; actually* : De jure = *by dirt of law; rightful*

Defensive .... : Aggresive, offensive

Deficient = *lacking sufficiency* .... : Sufficient

Deficit = *amount by which falling short* : Surplus = *amount in excess*

Defile = *befoul; pollute* .... : Cleanse = *purify*

Deflate = *make flat by taking out air* .... : Inflate = *distend or swell by filling with air*

Word	Opposite
Deft = *skilled in doing something; clever*	Inept = *unskilled; unfit*
Defy = *challenge; resist*	Comply = *yield or defer to the wishes of another*
Degenerate = *decay*	Flourish = *grow*
Dejected = *depressed in spirits; disheartened; low spirited*	Blithe = *joyous; merry or gay in disposition*
Deleterious = *injurious*	Salutary = *beneficial*
Delete = *remove something from written*	Insert, Enter = *incorporate*
Delectable = *pleasing; delightful; tasty; dainty*	Insipid = *tasteless* Insipid person = *dull; devoid of intelligence*
Delegate = *transfer power to someone in authority*	Usurp = *to arrogate to oneself an individual or authority*
Deliberate = *intentionally (do something); by design*	Inadvertent = *unintentionally*
Deliver = *to hand over*	Receive
Demean = *to lose dignity*	Dignify = *to gain dignity*
Demise = *hand over by will*	Inherit = *receive from ancestor*
Demure = *shy and modest (woman)*	Coy = *pretend to be shy*
Denounce	Acclaim = applaud; to solute with shouts or sounds of joy and approval
Denouement = *end part of a film*	Exordium = *beginning part; introduction*
Dense = *thick*	Sparse = *thinly dispersed*
Deny	Acknowledge
Depreciate = *become less in value*	Appreciate = *increase in value*
Depressed = *feel dejected*	Cheerful
Desecrate	Consecrate
Desist = *abstain from doing something*	Insist = *persistently try to do something (upon)*
Deplete (adj.) = *reduced stock*	Replete = *filled with stock*
Deplete (v) = *reduce quantity of stock*	Replenish = *restore the reduced stock*

Deprive = *take away from someone* : Afford, Provide

Descend = *come down from a height* : Ascend = *go up*

Descendant = *progeny* .... : Ancestor = *forefathers*

Desecrate .... : Consecrate

Despair = *be without hope* .... : Hope

Despairing = *without hope;* .... : Sanguine = *cheerfully optimistic;*
despondent .... *hopeful; confident*

Despondent = *in state of losing hope* : Euphoric = *in state of happy feeling*

Desultory = *not serious in intent* ... : Fastidious = *serious in intent*
about .... *doing work in perfect manner*

Deteriorate = *worsen* .... : Improve = *get better*

Deter = *discourage from doing wrong* : Abet = *help in doing wrong*

Dextrous = *skilled in doing work* ... : Maladroit = *inefficient in doing*
work with hands

Devolve = *roll down; transmit* .... : Evolve = *develop in succesion*
.... *of processes*

Diatribe = *bitter verbal attack* .... : Encomium = *verbal praise*

Difficulty .... : Facility

Diffident = *wanting in confidence* .. : Confident

Dignify .... : Demean

Dignity .... : Indignity

Dilate = *enlarge* .... : Constrict

Dilettante = *one who loves the fine* : Connoisseur = *well informed arts*
but in a superficial way and .... *judge in the arts*
without serious purpose

Diminish = *reduce* .... : Enhance = *increase*

Dirigisme = *policy of government* .. : Laissez faire = *policy of granting*
control over economic and social .. *freedom/non-interference*
spheres

Disaffection = *loss of affection* ...... : Affection = *fondness for, or*
.... *devotion to, a person or thing;*
.... *emotion; sentiment; love*

Disclose = *reveal* .... : Conceal = *hide a secret*

Discord = *disagreement; strife* ...... : Accord

Discredit .... : Credit

Discreet = *carefully considered (action)* : Indiscreet, Rash = *hasty (action)*

Discrete = *distinctly separate from each other* : Indiscrete = *homogeneous; not separated or distinguishable in parts*

Discretion = *prudence* : Indiscretion = *want of discretion; rashness*

Disdainful = *undeserving respect* : Respectful

Disenfranchise = *take away voting rights* : Enfranchise = *grant voting rights*

Disgorge = *to expel from mouth (food)* : Gorge = *to eat greedily*

Dishevelled = *disorderly* : Spruced = *neatly arranged*

Disinter = *digout* : Bury = *put in ground*

Disinterest = *impartiality; from bias* : Bias = *unjustly inclined in free favour of another/others*

Disparity = *inequality in comparison* : Parity = *equality in comparison*

Dispensable = *which can be disposed* : Indispensable = *which is required and can't be disposed*

Disperse = *scatter* : Assemble

Disrepute = *loss of repute* : Repute

Dissatisfy = *not satisfy* : Satisfy

Dissemble = *hide* : Betray

Disseminate = *spread widely* : Garner = *collect*

Dissent : Consent

Dissuade = *discourage from doing by convincing* : Persuade = *encourage to do something by convincing*

Distract = *divert attention* : Attract = *full attention*

Diurnal = *of day time (activity)* : Nocturnal = *of night time (activity)*

Diverge = *spread in different directions from a point* : Converge = *to come from different directions to a point*

Divest = *dispossess someone of power, authority* : Invest (with) = *put power or authority in someone*

Divine = *devoted to God, spiritual* : Mundane = *of earthly matters*

Docile = *who can be taught to do independent as desired* : Maverick, Intractable = *minded*

Dogmatic = *asserting a thing as ... were a dogma* : Pragmatic = *practical in doing if it*

Doleful .... : Cheerful

Doyen = *seniormost person of a ... family* .... : Scion = *youngest person of a family*

Drooping = *hanging down* .... : Erect

Dubitable = *doubtful* .... : Indubitable = *incapable of being doubted*

Duffer = *stupid* .... : Genius = *exceptionally intelligent*

Dull = *lacking brightness or energy* : Ebulient = *full of enthusiasm*

Duplicity = *double behaviour by .... way of being dishonest* .... : Candour = *honest & open behaviour*

Dusk = *sunset time* .... : Dawn = *sunrise time*

E

Eager = *Interested to know* .... : Indifferent = *not interested*

Early .... : Late

Earthly, Mundane = *worldly* .... : Divine, Spiritual = *godly*

Ebullient = *enthusiastic* .... : Dull

Ecstasy = *feeling of great happiness* : Dolefulness

Effectual = *effective in accomplishing* .... *desired purpose* : Ineffectual

Effeminate = *having womanly* .... *characteristics* .... : Virile = *having manly characteristics*

Effete = *no longer capable of* .... *producing offspring or being effective* : Fecund = *capable of producing many offsprings*

Efficacious = *effective in producing good results* : Inefficacious

Effluent = *flowing out* .... : Influent = *flowing in*

Egoism .... : Altruism

Egotism = *quality or habit of being excessively conceited and talks only about oneself* : Modesty = *quality of being self-effacing or unassuming*

Egress = *go out of a place* .... : Ingress

Eirenic/Irenic = *promoting peace* .. : Polemic = *controversial*

Eject = *throw out*	: Inject = *push in*
Elaborate = *detail*	: Sketchy = *imperfect/inadequate*
Elastic = *resilient*	: Inelastic
Eligible = *satisfying required* .... *conditions for something*	: Ineligible = *not fulfilling the* : *required conditions*
Elder = *of more age than someone*. *else*..	: Younger = *of lower age than someone's*
Elevation = *height above surface*	: Depression = *depth below surface*
Elicit = *draw out response from*..... *someone*	: Insinuate = *insert a suggestion or hint or remark, etc. in speech*
Elite, Aristocrat	: Plebeian
Eliminate = *remove from* .... *consideration*	: Incorporate = *include in something as its part*
Eloquent = *speaking fluently*	: Taciturn = *uncommunicative; reticent*
Emaciated	: Corpulent
Emancipate = *free from bondage* .	: Enthrall, Enslave
Embark = *go on board a ship or* ... *aircraft for voyage or travel*	: Dis-embark = *alight from a ship/flight*
Embarrass = *disconcert* .... *awkward or ashamed*	: Plim = *cause to swell with pride*
Emerge = *come out of a place*	: Immerge = *to go in*
Emerse = *emerge; standing out of water*	: Immerse = *dip under the surface of a liquid*
Emigrate = *to leave or go out of* .... *one's own country to migrate to* .... *another country*	: Immigrate = *to come into another (foreign) country*
Eminent = *outstanding*	: Unknown
Empty (adj.) = *unoccupied place by usual contents*	: Full = *occupied fully*
Empty (v) = *to remove usual* .... *contents from a place or container*	: Fill = *to make it full by pouring into container*
Enchant = *to charm, bewitch*	: Disenchant
Encomium = *praise*	: Diatribe = *a continued discourse or disputation*
Encrypt = *to put electronic* .... *information in a code form which* ..	: Decipher = *to discover the meaning of something written*

can only be interpreted with a .... special purpose equipment	*badly or in a difficult or hidden way; interpret the code word*
Endogamy = *practice of marrying . within the same community ....*	: Exogamy = *marrying out of own community*
Endogenous = *growing from within*	: Exogenous = *growing by successive additions to the outside*
Enervate = *cause to lose vigour ...*	: Invigorate = *to give vigour; to strengthen*
Enfranchise = *give political freedom*	: Subjugate, Enslave
Enhance = *increase, improve, raise to higher degree*	: Reduce, Diminish
Enmity = *hatred*	: Amity = *friendship*
Enormous = *vast*	: Normal = *usual; common*
Enrage = *make one angry, infuriate*	: Pacify = *to calm; to appease*
Enrich = *make rich*	: Impoverish = *make poor*
Enthrall = *enslave*	: Emancipate = *set free*
Enthusiastic = *filled with zeal or.... interest; zealous*	: Reluctant = *devoid of zeal, interest; hesitant*
Entitle = *give someone a claim*	: Forfeit = *make one lose claim*
Entrance = *way to enter*	: Exit = *way to come out*
Envigorate = *fill with vigour*	: Enervate = *cause to lose vigour*
Ephemeral = *shortlived*	: Eternal = *lasting forever*
Equitable = *just, fair*	: Inequitable = *unfair*
Equity = *fairness & just*	: Inequity = *lack of fairness & just*
Erect = *tightly straight*	: Prostrate, Drooping = *bending downward*
Erratum = *list of errors in print*	: Corrigendum = *list of amendments made in print*
Escalate = *increase to higher level*	: De-escalate = *drop to lower level*
Esoteric = *not openly admitted; .... private knowledgeable persons*	: Exoteric = *understood by all*
Esteem = *respect*	: Disdain = *contempt; scorn*
Eternal = *everlasting; without .... beginning or end*	: Ephemeral = *lasting for a very short time*
Euphoria = *feeling of well-being*	: Despondence, Dysphoria

Evade = *to escape from doing or happening something*	Pursue = *to follow, chase*
Evitable = *that can be avoided*	Inevitable = *that cannot be avoided; something bound to happen*
Evince = *show indirectly, manifest by indication*	Hide = *conceal*
Evolve = *develop (e.g. policy plan)*	Devolve (upon) = *to pass on; transmit*
Exacerbate = *make bitter or worse*	Ameliorate = *make less painful, better*
Exaggerate = *to make something excessively described*	Underestimate = *to underplay*
Excision = *Act of cutting out/off, as in a surgical operation; extirpation*	Incision = *A slit or opening mode with a cutting instrument as in an operation*
Exclude = *keep out of consideration*	Include = *take into consideration*
Exculpate = *to declare free from accusation/blame; prove innocent.*	Inculpate = *frame charges/ accusation*
Exempt = *free from liability*	Liable = *be under obligation*
Exhale = *breathe out*	Inhale = *breathe in*
Exhaust = *to consume something completely*	Replenish = *to fill again what has been exhausted*
Exhume = *dig out what is burried*	Bury
Exist = *be in living condition*	Disappear = *cease to be in existence*
Existent = *be present in living state*	Extinct = *cease to be present in living state*
Exit	Entrance
Exogenous	Endogenous
Exonerate = *set free from charges*	Convict
Exorable = *that/who can be made to yield by entreaty*	Inexorable
Expedient = *desirable step under the circumstance*	Inexpedient = *foolish step in a given situation*
Expedite = *to speed up a process progress*	Delay, Impede = *to hinder of a process = defer*

Expel = *remove out of a place* ...... : Admit = *allow to come in a place*

Expert = *very skillful* .... : Callow, Greenhorn = *unskilled*

Explicable = *capable of being* .... : Inexplicable = *not capable of*
explained by unfolding facts .... *being explained*

Explicate = *to unfold* .... : Implicate = *to involve/ensnare*
.... *within fold of something*

Explicit = *clearly expressed* .... : Implicit = *implied – not directly*
.... *expressed*

Explode = *to burst suddenly*.......... : Implode = *to burst internally*

Expropriate = *take possession of* . : Impropriate = *take possession*
land/money for public use .... *for own private use*

Exterior = *external part of* .... : Interior = *internal part of*
something .... *something*

Extinct .... : Existent

Extinguish = *put out fire* .... : Kidle = *start a fire, make*
.... *something burn*

Extraneous = *not related to topic* .. : Relevant, Pertinent = *related to a*
.... *topic*

Extravagant = *of expressively* .... : Thrifty, Frugal = *of spending*
wasteful spending.......................... *judiciously*

Extrinsic .... : Intrinsic

Extrovert .... : Intrinsic

Extrovert = *expressing one's mind* : Introvert = *not expressing one's*
freely .... *thoughts*

Extrude = *to force out which has* .. : Intrude = *to enter somewhere*
entered somewhere unwantedly ... *unwelcomed*

Extrusive = *tending to extrude* ...... : Intrusive = *tending to intrude*

Exuberant = *effusive*...................... : Subdued = *repressed, quiet*

F

Facilitate = *to make easy* .... : Hinder = *to make difficult*

Factious = *tending to encourage*... : Unanimous = *without diversity*
factions .... *of opinions*

Fascination = *attraction* .... : Revulsion = *a sudden change*
.... *of feeling; complete disgust or*
.... *aversion*

Word	Opposite
Fictitious = *imaginary; feigned*	Genuine = *original, pure & real*
Fade = *to become dull*	Brighten = *to make shining*
Fallible = *liable to error or mistake; liable to be erroneous or false in or action*	Infallible = *incapable of fallacy or error; reliable; certain judgment*
Familiar = *well known*	Unfamiliar
Famous = *renowned for good deeds; renowned*	Infamous, Notorious = *for bad reasons*
Fanatic = *intolerant to one who differs, zealot*	Liberal
Fastidious = *aweful/intolerant to deficiency; hard to please in matters of taste; overly delicate or sensitive*	Slipshod, Desultory = *slovenly; sloppy; untidy and careless in appearance; imperfect in work habits*
Faux pas = *blunder in etiquette; breach of tact or manners*	Savoir faire = *conduct suitable to etiquette*
Facility	Difficulty
Fecund = *faithful; fertile*	Efette = *incapable of further production; barren*
Felicitate = *to congratulate for good deed*	Loath = *to hate for misdeeds, abhor*
Felony = *serious crime (punishable with forfeiture of lauds or chattels)*	Peccadillo = *trifling fault*
Ferocious = *violently, cruel, savage*	Innocuous = *unharming*
Fidelity = *trustfulness, faithfulness*	Infidelity = *unfaithfulness*
Finale = *final part of performance*	Premiere = *first performance*
Flaccid = *not rigid, loose*	Tight = *close fitting*
Flatterer = *one who pleases by praising*	Detractor = *one who belittles another; diminish reputation defame*
Fledgling = *immature like a bird which is yet to learn flying; inexperienced person*	Mature; fully developed
Flexible = *capable of bending*	Rigid = *not bending due to stiffness*
Flippant = *frivolous, lacking seriousness*	Meticulous = *careful to the minute details in working*
Foe = *enemy*	Friend

Forbid = *order not to do* .... : Permit = *allow to do*

Foresight = *ability to see ahead* .... : Hind-sight = *ability to see in the back*

Forfeit .... : Entitle

Forgo .... : Claim

Formal .... : Informal, Casual

Former = *first of the two* .... : Latter = *second of the two*

Forte = *strong point of someone's ability* .... : Handicap = *weak point of someone's ability*

Fortify = *to make strong by providing strength* .... : Undermine, Subvert = *to make weak by digging at the root*

Fortuitous = *happening by chance* .... : Pre-meditated = *happening as a sequel to after careful considerations*

Fractions = *irritable* .... : Calm

Fragile = *capable of breaking* .... : Unbreakable

Franchise = *empower with voting rights* .. : Disenfranchise = *take away voting rights*

Frank = *open-minded* .... : Cunning, Wily = *crafy*

Fraternal twins .... : Identical twins

Frantic = *wild with panic* .... : Patient = *calm in diffcult time*

Freedom .... : Subjection

Frequent = *too often at regular* ..... : Infrequent, Sporadic = *not often intervals*

Fresh .... : Stale = *not fresh*

Friend .... : Foe

Fringe = *outer border* .... : Mainstream = *main part*

Frivolous = *lacking seriousness, one frivols* : Solemn = *serious as warranted who by the occasion*

Front = *foremost part* .... : Rear = *back portion*

Froward = *doing against suggestion; willed*: Docile = *submissive; easily self-managed*

Fructuous = *producing results* ...... : Infructuous = *not producing expected results*

Frugal, Thrifty .... : Extravagant, Spendthrift

Fulminate = *to appear or come upon suddenly as sudden explosion* .... : Evanesce = *to disappear suddenly*

Funereal = *mournful, gloomy as on the occasion of a funeral* : Sanguine = *cheerful*

Furl = *to fold by rolling up* .... : Unfurl = *to spread open a rolled up length of cloth or sheet*

Futile = *producing no result* .... : Fruitful = *producing result*

Futility = *quality or state of being useless as an effort* : Utility = *quality of being useful*

G

Gain = *advantage* .... : Loss = *disadvantage*

Gall = *irritate* .... : Soothe = *give comfort feeling*

Garner = *to collect* .... : Disseminate = *to scatter, spread widely*

Garrulous = *excessively speaking as habit, using too many words* .... : Laconic = *expressing in too few words*

Gather = *collect* .... : Disperse, Scatter

General = *not particular* .... : Specific = *particular*

Generalize = *make general; common* .... : Specify = *particularise*

Genius = *superbly intelligent* .... : Duffer = *lacking intelligence; dull*

Generous = *munificent, liberal in giving* .. : Niggardly = *stingy, miserly*

Genial = *of cordial nature* .... : Querulous, Sullen = *of complaining nature*

Genuine .... : Artificial, Sham

Gigantic = *very large in size* .... : Tiny = *very small in size*

Glade = *an open space in a wood* : Copse = *a small wood; coppice*

Glance = *to look briefly* .... : Stare = *to look fixedly*

Glare = *to shine intensely* .... : Gleam = *to shine softly*

Glitter = *shine brilliantly* .... : Glimmer = *to shine faintly*

Gloomy = *sad* .... : Cheerful

Glory = *exalted fame disgrace,* ..... : Ignominy = *abject insult/obloquy*

Glean = *to gather by picking up bit* : Scatter *by bit*

Glut = *excessive, abundance of, supply* ... : Scarcity = *acute/inordinate shortage*

Gnostic = *one who is having knowledge about something* .... : Agnostic = *one who is not knowledgeable about something*

Gobble = *to eat in large morsels* ... : Nibble = *to eat by biting small pieces*

Gradual = *in slow pace or steps* ... : Abrupt = *suddenly*

Gluttonous = *one who eats voraciously* .... : Abstemious = *abstain from much eating and drinking*

Grace = *politeness in behaviour* ... : Disgrace = *Insulting behaviour*

Grateful = *obliged* .... : Ungrateful, Ingrate

Gravameu (of changes) .... : Quintescence (of firhus)

Gravitate = *fall down to the lowest level* : Levitate = *to rise up to float in air*

Gregarious = *living in flocks or herd* .... : Recluse = *living in solitude; secluded*

Grieve = *lament* .... : Rejoice = *to feel delight*

Groan = *make low sound as in pain* .... : Moan = *make low sound as in intense pleasure*

Guilt = *act of sin crime* .... : Innocence = *fact of free from guilt*

H

Hallow = *show deep respect* .... : Denigrate = *ruin respect unfairly*

Harmony = *state of pleasant understanding with others* .... : Disharmony = *absence of harmony*

Haphazard = *disorderly* .... : Orderly

Hasten = *to quicken* .... : Retard = *to slow down*

Heaven .... : Hell

Heckle = *to hoot* .... : Applaud = *to praise, approbate*

Heed = *to pay attention to advice* . : Ignore = *to disregard advice*

Hegemony = *state of predominating influence on others* .... : Subservience = *state of being in subordination*

Heinous = *reprehensive (act)* .... : Venial = *pardonable (act)*

Hell .... : Heaven

Heresy = *action/opinion contrary to religious beliefs* .... : Conformism = *act of conforming to accepted belief*

Heterodoxy = *holding unorthodox doctrine* .... : Orthodoxy = *holding accepted doctrine*

Heterogeneous = *not uniform*	: Homogeneous = *uniform*
Hinder = *put obstacle in progress* .	: Facilitate
Hindsight	: Foresight
Hide	: Display
Honorable = *worthy of honour*	: Abject = *cast away; mean; worthless*
Honoured	: Abashed; dishonoured
Hostile = *not favourable*	: Favourable
Hubris = *extreme arrogance; insolence*	: Humility = *humbleness*
Humble = *not proud*	: Rude, Proud
Humility	: Hubris, Pride
Hypocrisy = *not practising what one preaches*	: Sincerity = *honesty in practising what one preaches*
Hygienic	: Unhygienic

I

Iconoclast = *breaker of accepted.. or beliefs*	: Conformist = *follower of norms accepted norms or beliefs*
Identical twins = *twins having identical gender and resembling appearance*	: Fraternal twins = *twins of different or same gender but not having resemblance in appearance*
Ignoble = *dishonourable*	: Honourable = *noble; illustrious*
Ignominy = *public disgrace; infamy*	: Glory = *renown; exalted; triumphant honour*
Ignorant = *without knowledge*	: Knowledgeable = *possessing knowledge; intelligent*
Ignore = *disregard; set aside*	: Heed = *to attend to; to observe*
Illegible = *writing which cannot be clearly read*	: Legible = *which can be clearly read*
Illegitimate = *unlawful*	: Legitimate = *lawful; having the legal status of those born in wedlock*
Illicit = *not permitted; unlawful; unlicensed*	: Licit = *permitted*
Immaculate = *spotlessly clean*	: Maculate = *spotted by stains; flemished*

Word	Antonym
Immense = *too large to measure*	Limited, Measurable
Immerge	Emerge
Immerse	Emerse
Immigrant	Emigrant
Imminent = *impending*	Remote (chance) = *distant*
Immune = *protected from harm*	Susceptible = *prone to harm*
Impair = *damage the condition of something, e.g., health*	Improve, Repair
Impartial	Biased
Impassioned = *filled with passion*	Impassive = *devoid of passion*
Impede = *to retard progress*	Expedite = *to increase the pace of progress*
Impenitence = *not regretting*	Atonement = *regretting for sins*
Impertinent = *rude*	Polite = not rude
Impotent	Potent
Improvident = *not taking care for future needs*	Provident = *taking care for future needs*
Impertinent = *intrusive; interfering*	Pertinent = *relevant; appropriate*
Imprudent = *wanting foresight or discretion*	Prudent = *discreet*
Inadvertently = *failing to turning attention to something; unintentionally*	Deliberately = *intentionally*
Implicate = *to ensnare in accusation*	Explicate = *to lay open or explain the meaning of*
Implicit = *implied*	Explicit = *conclusion; distinctly stated*
Implore = *beg for something tearfully*	Spurn = *reject to accept scornfully*
Impoverish = *make poor*	Enrich = *make rich*
Improvement	Deterioration
Impulsive = *impetuous, hasty*	Thoughtful, Considered
Inapt = *inappropriate*	Apt = *appropriate, suited to situation*
Inclement = *unkind, unfavourable, troublesome*	Clement
Include = *enclose; to reckon as a part*	Exclude = *to shutout; to except; to thrust out*

Incorporate = *to embody* .... : Eliminate = *remove; cancel;*
.... *got rid of*

Incriminate = *to charge with crime* : Absolve = *to set free; pardon*

Indifferent = *without importance*.... : Curious = *inquisitive*

Indigent = *poor* .... : Wealthy; rich

Inept = *unfit; irritant; futile*............. : Deft = *handy; clever*

Indigenous = *native* .... : Exogenous = *derived externally*

Indulge = *to yield to the wishes of* : Abstain, Refrain, Abjure

Inexorable = *not able to be made to*: Exorable = *who can be made to*
yield .... *yield*

Inferior = *of low quality* .... : Superior = *higher in place,*
.... *rank or excellence*

Inflate = *to make swell by* .... : Deflate = *to make flat by*
introducing air inside .... *removing air from its within*

Influx = *flow into something*.......... : Efflux = *flowing out*

Influent = *inflowing; exerting* .... : Effluent = *flowing; liquid industrial*
influence .... *waste*

Infuriate = *enrage, anger*............... : Pacify = *to calm*

Ingress = *come in* .... : Egress = *go out*

Ingenuous = *simpleton* .... : Cunning, Wily

Inhale = *breathe in* .... : Exhale = *breathe forth*

Inherit .... : Bequeath, Demise

Iniquitous = *wicked, perverse;*....... : Righteous = *morally upright;*
unjust .... *unjust*

Innocuous = *harmless* .... : Ferrocious = *ravage;*

Insane = *of unsound mind*............. : Sane = *of sound mind*

Insipid = *tasteless*.......................... : Delectable = *delightful*

Insist (upon) = *to speak*................. : Desist = *refrain*
emphatically; persist in pressing ...
for an act or confiscation

Intelligible = *able to be understood*: Un-intelligible; *not comprehensible*

Inferior = *lower in any respect;* ...... : Superior = *higher in status; poor*
in quality .... *rank or excellence*

Insinuate = *to hint; to enter gently*. : Elicit = *to draw forth; to* ....

Integrate = *to bring together in a* .. : Dis-integrate = *to break up*
whole

Intensity = *to make intense*	Abate = *to lessen intensity*
Interested = *be curious in something*	Un-interested = *not interested*
Interest = *concern for self-gain*	Dis-interest = *having no concern intention/scheme for self-gain; free from bias*
Interior = *inner*	Exterior = *outer*
Intimacy = *close relationship*	Alienation, Estrangement = *break up of relationship*
Intrepid = *undaunted; without fear*	Pusillanimous = *cowardly*
Intrinsic = *inward*	Extrinsic = *external; foreign*
Introvert = *a person interested mainly in his own inner states and processes*	Extrovert = *a person interested mainly in the world external to himself*
Intrude = *to enter uninvited or welcome*	Protrude, Extrude = *to project; to thrust or push out or forward; to expel*
Invest = *insuperable*	Divest = *disinvest*
Invincible = *who cannot be subdued; to lay out for profit*	Vincible = *capable of being conquered*
Invoke = *call a rule in application*	Revoke = *cancel a rule in operation*
Irenic, Eirenic = *which promotes peace; tending to create peace*	Polemic = *given to disputing controversial*
Irritate	Pacify

J

Jabber = *chatter; indistinct or idle talk*	Breviloguy = *speak in short*
Jaded, Blase = *bored with over-eating*	Insatiated = *not fully satisfied or satiated*
Jealous = *one who feels resentment over other's success*	Magnanimous = *long/kind-hearted*
Jeer = *to shout derisively*	Extol = *to praise*
Jinx = *that brings bad luck*	Mascot = *that brings good luck*
Jitter = *nervousness*	Elation = *feeling of high spirit*
Jolt = *shake roughly*	Lull = *to quiet down*

Word	Antonym
Jovial = *pleasantly humorous*	Splenetic, Mirthless = *joyless; cheerless*
Jubilant = *exultant, rejoice; triumph*	Depressed = *dispirited*
Judicious = *showing judgement*	Injudicious Iniquitous = *wicked; unjust; unreasonable*
Jumble = *mixed in unravelling mass*	Unravel = *to disentangle*
Just = *justified*	Unjust

K

Word	Antonym
Keen = *very curious; eager*	Indifferent = *apathetic*
Kempt = *combed (hairs)*	Unkempt = *uncombed*
Kindle = *to light up; to arouse passions; to provoke*	Extinguish; to put out fire
Kitsch = *cheap quality of art/ literature*	Classic = *superb quality of art/ literature*
Knave = *crooked person deceitful fellow*	Simpleton = *a weak or foolish person*
Knowledge = *information; instruction*	Ignorance = *want of knowledge*

L

Word	Antonym
Laconic = *expressing in few words*	Garrulous, Prolix = *talkative*
Laity = *layman*	Cogniscenti = *a group of people who have a great knowledge and understanding of a particular subject, especially one of the arts*
Lament = *to express sorrow*	Rejoice; *show jubilant attitude*
Languid = *lacking in vigour*	Vigorous = *full of spirit, liveliness*
Latent = *not openly visible*	Patent = *lying open*
Later = *after the usual time*	Sooner = *before the usual time*
Latter	Former
Lax = *loose/not strict in observance*	Strict, Astere
Laxity = *state of carelessness; inattention or going beyond control*	Control = *order; rule*
Laud = *to praise publicly*	Decry = *to lament*
Lavish = *spending in great amount*	Parsimoniously = *miserly spending*
Legible	Illegible

Legitimate .... : Illegitimate

Lenient = *not strict* .... : Strict, Rigid

Lithe = *supple, flexible* .... : Rigid, Stiff

Lessee = *one who takes on lease* : Lessor = *one giving on lease*

Lethargic = *sluggish* .... : Vivacious = *lively active*

Levitate = *raise in air* .... : Gravitate = *to be attracted; move by force of gravitation*

Levity = *absence of seriousness in behaviour* : Solemnity, Earnestness

Liability .... : Assets

Liable = *subject to suffer/obligation to be fulfilled for avoiding financial loss* : Exempt = *free from obligation*

Liberal = *generous; noble-minded* : Conservative = *averse to change*

Liberate = *to set free* .... : Enslave = *to reduce to slavery*

Libertine = *who behaves in lewd manner* ... : Prude = *who is shocked by what is in lewd*

Liberty = *freedom to act, not binding* : Compulsion = *state of being compulsory*

Licit = *lawful; permissible* .... : Illicit = *unlawful*

Likely = *possible to occur* .... : Unlikely = *not likely*

Limber = *flexible* .... : Stiff = *rigid*

Limited .... : Unlimited, Immense

Limp = *lacking stiffness* .... : Stiff

Link = *to connect* .... : Delink

Lively = *full of life* .... : Torpid = *lacking energy*

Loath = *hate, dislike* .... : Felicitate

Lofty = *sublime, high-sounding in contents* : Base = *low in quality*

Logical = *in accordance with reasonability* .... : Absurd, Illogical = *improper*

Loquacious = *talkative* .... : Taciturn = *brief in speaking*

Loud = *making great sound* .... : Muted = *suppressed loudness*

Loyal = *faithful to allegiance* .... : Storm, Agitate, Jolt

Ludicrous = *laughably absurd* .... : Solemn = *deeply sincere*

Lustre = *shine* .... : Dullness = *faintness*

M

Maculate = *spotted*	: Immaculate = *spotlessly clean; unblemished*
Magnanimous = *large hearted*	: Parvanimous = *small hearted in showing kindness*
Magnify = *to make large*	: Reduce, Diminish = *to make small*
Majority = *larger than half of total* .	: Minority = *less than half of total*
Make	: Mar = *spoil*
Maladroit	: Dextrous
Malafide	: Bonafide
Malevolent	: Benevolent
Malfeasance	: Beneficence
Malignant	: Benignant
Manifest = *clearly obvious*	: Obscure = *not visible*
Masochist = *one who takes pleasure in pain or humiliation inflicted on him or her* ...	: Sadist = *one who takes pleasure by inflicting pain or humiliation on others*
Mandatory = *ordered by authority to obey* ...	: Optional = *given choice to act on others*
Marooned = *left on desolate island*	: Stranded = *left aground on sea shore, unable to go ahead*
Mascot = *bringer of good luck*	: Jinx = *bringer of bad luck*
Mature	: Immature, Fledgeling
Maverick = *independent minded in taking decision* ...	: Docile = *who can be taught to do as desired*
Meagre = *much less in quantity*	: Plentiful = *abundance*
Malancholy	: Bliss
Meliorate = *make better*	: Exacerbate = *make condition even more worse*
Melliferous = *carrying honey and hence sweet* ..	: Acerbic = *bitter; astringent*
Mellifluous = *sweet as honey*	: Discordant, Cacophonous
Mercenary = *motivated by gain/profit earning*	: Voluntary = *motivated by self-desire*

Merit .... : Demerit

Messy, Sloppy = *disordered* .... : Tidiness = *neatly arranged*

Metamorphosis = *change in physical form* : Stasis = *no change in state*

Meticulous .... : Flippant

Mild = *gentle, not harsh* .... : Severe = *harsh*

Minnow = *small fish like veryinsignificant person* .... : Triton = *very large size, influential person among minnows; resourceful*

Miraculous = *strange as act of god* : Mundane = *ordinary*

Misanthrope = *one who hates mankind* .... : Philanthrope = *one who likes mankind*

Miser = *one who hates spending money* .. : Generous = *one who lavishly spends money*

Misogynest = *one who hates women folk* : Philogynist = *one who likes womenfolk*

Mitigate = *to lessen the gravity of something* . : Aggravate = *one who makes the gravity worse*

Moan = *lament; complaint* .... : Groan = *utter in distress or disapprobation*

Modest = *humble about one's own importance* : Immodest, Egotist

Modesty .... : Egotism

Mollify = *to appear the anger* .... : Enrage = *to provoke one's anger*

Mondaine = *fashionable woman* ... : Slut = *woman who is untidy, dirty in habits and appearance (slut = woman who is untidy; dirty in habits and appearance)*

Monopoly = *control over market by seller* : Monopsony = *control over market by purchaser*

Monotheism = *belief in one god* .... : Pantheism = *belief in all religions gods*

Morose = *bad mood* .... : Cheerful = *spirited mood*

Mortal = *liable to die* .... : Immortal

Motivate = *stimulate someone to do* : Demotivate *something*

Mourn = *to lament* .... : Rejoice

Mundane = *worldly* .... : Spiritual = *transcending worldly matters; metaphysical*

Munificent = *generous* .... : Stingy

Murky (water) .... : Pellucid, limpid (water)

Mute = *silent* .... : Vociferous = *shouting*

Myopic = *short-sighted* .... : Clairvoyant = *far-sighted*

N

Nadir = *the lowest position in a path of sphere* ..... : Zenith = *the highest point*

Native = *one who belongs to a place by birth* .... : Alien = *one who belongs to another place*

Negate = *to deny, nullify* .... : Affirm = *firmly accept or declare*

Negative .... : Positive, Affirmative

Negligent = *careless* .... : Chary, Careful

Novice = *inexperienced* .... : Expert, Veteran

Nepotism = *favouritism granted to relatives* .... : Fairness = *justice done in decisions*

Nibble = *to bite gently or by small bites* . : Gobble = *devour; to swallow in lumps*

Niggardly .... : Generous

Nightmare = *frightening experience or dream* : Nostalgia = *longing to experience or remembering happy moments of past life*

Nocturnal = *active by night* .... : Diurnal = *active by the day-time*

Noisy .... : Quiet

Non-conformist .... : Conformist

Normal = *usual in extent normal* ... : Enormous = *out or beyond extent in size, cruelty, loss, etc.*

Novel .... : Trite = *cliche*

O

Object = *express dissent* .... : Subscribe (to) = *express consent to a program by signing in its favour*

Objective = *free from personal opinion* ...... : Subjective = *based on personal opinion*

Obnoxious = *unpleasant, annoying* : Pleasant

Obscene = *indecent* .... : Decent

Obverse = *front side of coin* .... : Reverse = *back side*

Obvious = *clearly visible* .... : Obscure, Vague = *hazy*

Occident = *countries of the west*... : Orient = *countries of the east*

Occupy = *take possession of a place* : Vacate

Offensive = *attacking, disagreeable* : Inoffensive, Defensive

Ominous = *of frightening omen* ..... : Auspicious = *indicating favourable omen*

Omnipotent = *all powerful* .... : Impotent = *devoid of power*

Opaque = *not transparent* .... : Translucent, Transparent = *see able through*

Optimist = *one who hopes for the best* .... : Pessimist = *one who does not have hopes for something good to happen*

Orthodox .... : Heterodox

Orderly .... : Haphazard

Outlandish = *belonging to another land & so unfamiliar* : Familiar

Outrageous = *grossly unpleasant* . : Flattering = *which pleases*

Outstanding = *extraordinary in nature* ...... : Commonplace = *that which is found everywhere*

Overt = *openly* .... : Covert = *in a concealed manner*

Own = *to accept as belonging to oneself* .. : Disown = *not accept as one's own*

P

Pacify = *make calm* .... : Provoke, Infuriate, Irritate, Enrage

Palliate = *alleviate* .... : Aggravate

Pantheon = *a memorial for all the illustrious persons, temple of all Gods* . : Monotheon

Parity .... : Disparity

Parochial .... : Catholic

Parsimonious .... : Lavish

Partial = *biased to someone* .... : Impartial = *not biased*

Patriot = *one who is loyal to his or her own country* ... : Traitor = *one who is disloyal to his/her own country*

Passionate = *moved by passion* ... : Impassive = *imperturbable*

Passive .... : Active
Peccadillo = *minor offence* .... : Felony = *serious offence*
Patience .... : Impatience
Peevish = *querulous, fretful* .... : Jovial, Genial
Penury = *extreme poverty* .... : Affluence = *wealthiness, Richness*
Perdition = *state of ruination of soul* : Salvation = *deliverance of soul*
Perennial = *perpetual* .... : Deciduous = *shedding all the leaves together at a certain period*
Perfidious = *unfaithful; treacherous*: Faithful = *loyal*
Perfunctory = *(work) done in trivial manner* .... : Meticulous = *careful about perfection in work*
Perpetual = *lasting forever* .... : Transitory, Temporary = *lasting for a short period*
Persuade = *make one agree to do something as desired; prevail upon* : Dissuade = *discourage*
Pertinent = *relevant to the subject* : Impertinent = *irrelevant*
Petty = *lacking importance* .... : Important
Phantom = *ghost, unreal in existence* : Real
Placid = *undisturbed* .... : Agitated, Ebulient
Plebeian = *undisturbed strata* .... : Elite = *people of the highest strata society*
Plentiful .... : Meagre
Plausible = *seemingly credible* ..... : Dubious = *doubtful*
Polite = *humble* .... : Rude, Insolent, Impertinent
Polemic .... : Irenic
Politic = *prudent, expedient sagacious* .... : Impolitic = *inexpedient, imprudent*
Posterior .... : Anterior
Posterity = *succeeding generation* : Ancestry = *prceding generation*
Postpone = *defer to a later time* .... : Prepone = *advance to earlier time period*
Potent .... : Impotent
Pour = *to make liquid flow down in stream* .... : Trickle = *to flow down (liquid) in drops*
Pragmatic = *based on practicality*. : Dogmatic = *based on rules/ principles; disapproving*

Praise	Criticize
Predator = *an animal which preys on another*	Prey = *an animal which is killed by another animal for food*
Predecessor = *one who has preceded office/instituter by someone*	Successor = *one who other in another*
Premiere	Finale
Premium = *price to be paid over and above the normal price*	Discount = *deduction in price to be paid by a customer*
Prescribe = *recommend*	Proscribe = *prohibit as outlaw*
Preserve = *to save stock*	Squander = *waste away*
Prey	Predator
Privilege = *special advantage*	Disadvantage = *lacking advantage*
Proactive = *act forward*	Retroactive = *act later in response*
Probity = *upright honesty*	Improbity = *dishonesty*
Proud	Ashamed
Profane = *irreverent*	Sacred, Holy = *reverent*
Profound = *having depth*	Superficial, Shallow = *of no depth*
Profuse = *pouring abundantly*	Scanty
Progenitor = *who gives birth*	Progeny = *who is produced/born*
Progress = *move ahead*	Regress = *go back to early state*
Prolix = *lengthy in duration of speech*	Succinct
Prolong	Curtail
Promiscuous = *unselective*	Selective, Discriminating
Promulgate = *to bring into effect*	Abrogate = *repeal, revoke*
Propriety = *state of being proper/appropriate*	Impropriety
Propitiate, Appease = *to make pleased*	Antagonize = *to displease*
Prospective = *effective from a future date*	Retrospective = *effective from back date*
Prostrate	Erect, Upright
Protract = *lengthen in duration*	Curtail
Protector = *one who protects*	Protege = *one who is protected*

Protrude = *to enter forward* .... : Intrude = *to enter inside*

Proud .... : Humble

Provide = *to give, supply* .... : Deprive = *to take away from possessing, deny possession*

Provident = *careful for providing future needs* ... : Improvident

Provoke = *instigate* .... : Pacify = *calm down*

Provincial .... : Cosmopolitan

Pursue = *chase to catch* .... : Evade = *to avoid from being caught*

Prudent = *wise to be practical in approach* ... : Imprudent, Unwise

Pungent = *sharp in smell or taste* . : Bland = *lacking taste*

Pull = *drag towards oneself* .... : Push = *drag away from oneself*

Punctilious = *meticulous* .... : Flippant

Pusillanimous = *faint-hearted, fearful* ...... : Intrepid, Brave = *who is not lacking courage*

Q

Quaint = *pleasantly unusual due to being old fashioned* : Modern; *one who keep in rogue*

Qualified = *restrict with a condition* : Unqualified, Absolute = *unconditional*

Quash = *to declare illegal or invalid* : Uphold = *to declare valid*

Quell = *to suppress* .... : Fan, Provoke = *to instigate*

Querulous = *complaining* .... : Genial = *cordial in nature*

Quiet = *silent* .... : Clamorous, Clamant = *shouting*

Quixotic = *impractical* .... : Practical

R

Radical = *having roots* .... : Superficial = *being on surface*

Rapacious = *greedy* .... : Generous = *not greedy*

Rarely .... : Frequently

Rash .... : Discreet, Cautious

Rear .... : Front

Rearguard = *guard standing in the back* : Vanguard = *guard standing in front*

Receive = *take what is given* .... : Deliver = *to give something to someone*

Reciprocal = *mutual in exchanging; give something in return* : Unilateral = *one-sided*

Recluse = *one who lives in solitude* : Gregarious = *living in group/flock*

Rectitude = *moral uprightness* ...... : Turpitude = *morally depraved*

Reduce .... : Magnify

Refrain = *abstain from doing something* .... : Indulge = *involve in doing something*

Refined .... : Crude

Regressive = *going back in reducing quantity or to the statue quo ante* .. : Progressive = *going forward in increasing quantity or improving condition*

Regret = *feel sorrow* .... : Rejoice = *feel joy*

Relenting .... : Adamant

Recluse = *secluded* .... : Gregarious = *fond of the company of others*

Regular = *bound by religious rules* : Secular = *not following religious rules*

Rejoice = *take delight express* .... : Grieve, Lament, Mourn = *to sorrow*

Religious .... : Profane

Relinquish = *to give up* .... : Retain = *to hold in possession*

Reluctant = *unwilling* .... : Enthusiastic = *filled with zeal*

Replenish .... : Exhaust

Replete = *fill up with* .... : Deplete = *diminish/reduce e.g. stock*

Resilient = *flexible; elastic* .... : Rigid = *stiff; unfeasible*

Resist = *oppose pressure* .... : Yield = *surrender to pressure*

Repulsion = *driving away* .... : Attraction = *drawing to wards*

Rescind = *repeal a law in force* ..... : Promulgate = *proclaim*

Resolute = *firm in opinion* .... : Wavering = *fluctuating in opinion; vacillating*

Restrain = *mandating not to do things* ..... : Constrain = *compelled by certain circumstances*

Retain = *hold back* .... : Relinquish = abandon; give up
.... cease to hold an office

Retard = *to slow down* .... : Hasten

Reticent = *keeping oneself silent* .. : Loquacious, Talkative

Retract = *to draw back* .... : Stretch = *to draw out*

Retreat = *move back* .... : Advance = *move ahead*

Retroactive = *acting fact ward* .... : Proactive = *acting forward*

Retrospective = *taking backward* .. : Prospective = *effective from a*
effect .... *future date*

Retrogress = *move back to inferior* : Progress = *move forward to*
condition .... *better condition*

Reveal = *to remove veil from;* .... : Conceal = *to hide (e.g a secret)*
disclose

Revoke = *to cancel, nullify* .... : Invoke, Promulagate

Revulsion = *repugnance* .... : Fascination = *attraction*

Righteous = *just; upright* .... : Iniquitous = *unjust*

Rigid = *stiff; inflexible* .... : Resilient, Flexible

Rude = *impertinent* .... : Polite = *city life*

Ruffle = *to disturb smoothness* ..... : Spruce, Preen = *to set in smooth*
.... *manner*

Rural = *of village life; rustic* .... : Urban = *of town life; city life*

Rustic = *uncouth in manner* .... : Urbane, Sophisticated

Remote, Distant .... : Imminent

Remote = *far away situated* .... : Vicinal = *nearby; in close*
.... *proximity*

S

Sad = *regretful* .... : *Mirthful, Cheerful*

Sacred = *pure* .... : Profane = *desecrate*

Sadist = *sexual perversion with* .... : Masochist = *sexual perversion*
passion .... *with pleasure in being*
.... *dominated or treated cruelly by*
.... *the other sex*

Sagacious = *practically wise* .... : Impractical/unwise = *foolish in*
.... *being practical as per situation*

Salient = *raised up so to be above* : Inconspicuous = *not visible else*

Salutary = *giving healthy effect*	Deleterious = *giving harmful effect*
Salvation = *saving of man from the penalty*	Perdition = *utter loss of power and happiness*
Sane = *of sound mind*	Insane = *of unsound mind*
Sanguine = *cheerful; hopeful*	Funereal = *mournful*
Scarcity	Abundance, Glut; over supply
Scanty	Profuse
Scatter = *spread*	Glean, Gather
Sceptic, Skeptic	Credulous
Scion	Doyen
Scrupulous = *careful about right or wrong in action*	Unscrupulous, Trifling = *not careful about right or wrong*
Scurrilous = *insultingly bad*	Decent = *nice*
Secluded = *removed apart from others*	Incorporated
Secular	Regular
Sediment = *matter settled on the bottom of liquid*	Scum = *matter forming layer on liquid surface*
Segregate = *separate from flock*	Congregate
Seize = *catch hold of*	Release = *set free*
Selfish	Unselfish, Altruist
Severe = *harsh*	Mild = *not harsh, gentle*
Shallow = *without depth*	Deep, Profound
Sham = *spurious*	Genuine = authentic
Sharp = pointed	Blunt = *not sharp*
Shove = *move something by pushing*	Tow = *drag (vehicle) by tying to a rope from backside*
Shrink = *make smaller in size*	Stretch = *make large in size; enlarge; expand*
Simplicity	Complexity
Sinistral = *on the left side, left-handed*	Dextral = *right-handed*
Skilful = *showing skill*	Clumsy = *not skilful*

Skirt = *move around a problem, avoiding it*	: Confront = *to meet a problem headlong*
Skirmish = *scuffle, minor fight*	: Armaggedon = *score of the final struggle between the powers of good and evil; a great war or battle of nations*
Slender = *thin*	: Plump = *rounded in shape*
Sling = *hang loosely by a strip*	: Cling = *hang tightly adhered to something*
Slipshod = *careless manner*	: Fastidious
Sloven = *one who is habitually untidy in appearance*	: Dandy = *one who is habitually careful about tidy appearance*
Sluggish = *slow in action*	: Active = *fast in action*
Slut = *habitually untidy woman,*	: *fashionable woman slattern*
Soar = *rise up vertically upward in speed*	: Swoop = *come down in speed*
Solemn	: Frivolous
Somber = *dull in colour*	: Bright, Mirthful
Soothe = *give comfort*	: Upset = *disturb*
Sororate = *marriage with wife's sister*	: Levirate = *marriage with husband's brother an ancient custom, in conformity with the Biblical times required in warranting circumstances*
Sorority = *sisterhood*	: Fraternity = *brotherhood*
Spartan = *living a life devoid of luxury*	: Voluptuary = *living a life full of luxury*
Spendthrift = *extravagant person*	: Thrift = *frugal person*
Specific = *of particular kind*	: Generalised = *of general kind*
Spirited = *lively*	: Dispirited, Dejected
Spiritual	: Mundane, Corporeal
Spontaneous = *occurring without pre-meditation*	: Pre-meditated = *happening with much deliberation beforehand*
Sporadic = *occurring at irregular intervals*	: Frequent = *occurring at regular intervals*

Spruced = *well groomed; fastidious*	Dishevelled, Ruffled; keeping loose hair
Spurious = *counterfeit*	Authentic = *genuine*
Sincere	Affected, Pretended
Squander	Conserve
Static = *in stationary state*	Dynamic = *in moving state*
Stationary	Moving
Steady = *in stable state*	Unsteady = *in unstable state*
Stiff = *rigid*	Lithe, Supple = *flexible*
Stingy, Niggard = *miser*	Generous = *liberal in spending*
Stoic = *unmoved even in adverse circumstances*	Capricious = *changing mood without any plausible reason*
Straight = *not bent*	Crooked = *bent*
Strange = *unfamiliar*	Familiar
Stretch = *extend outward*	Retract = *to draw back*
Strict	Lenient
Stringent = *strict; harsh*	Mild, Liberal
Stubborn = *haughty*	Tractable = *controllable*
Stupendous = *causing amazement*	Un-impressive *stounding*
Subdued = *suppressed*	Exuberant = *effusive; luxuriant; over flowing*
Subjection	Freedom
Subjective = *subject to personal opinion*	Objective = *not subject to personal opinion, based on objectivity*
Subjugate = *enslave*	En-franchise
Subvert, Undermine = *damage*	Fortify = *to make strong*
Susceptible (to)	Immune (from)
Superior	Inferior
Sublime	Ludicrous
Submerge	Emerge
Supple	Stiff
Successor	Predecessor
Succinct = *concise*	Loquacious, Prolix = *in detail; elaborate*

Surrender, appear .... : Abscond = *flee away*

Swoop = *sudden onslaught to come down with a sweeping rush* : Soar = *to rise to a great height*

Succumb = *to get defeated to pressure, injury or disease* .... : Survive = *to remain alive after an accident, or after someone else's death*

Symphony = *melodious sound* ...... : Cacophony = *noisy sound*

Sufficient = *adequate* .... : Deficient = *shortfall*

Sullen = *sulky* .... : Cheerful = *joyous*

Superior = *higher in status* .... : Inferior = *lower in status*

Superficial = *occurring on the Periphery only* .... : Deep, Radical, Profound

Supple = *flexible* .... : Rigid = *stiff*

Surfeit = *excessive in amount* .... : Deficient = *lacking in amount*

Surplus .... : Deficit

Survive = *outlive someone* .... : Succumb = *to yield to something and die*

T

Tawdry = *cheap in quality; showy without taste or worth* . : Elegant = *refined or luxurious*

Terminate = *end a process* .... : Originate = *start a process*

Terrestrial = *living on earth* .... : Celestial = *belonging to heaven*

Terrible = *frightening* .... : Delightful = *joyful*

Testate = *having made a will to demise property* ..... : Intestate = *having not made a will (before death)*

Timid, Timorous .... : Courageous, Bold

Thaw = *to melt by warmth* .... : Congeal = *to frost by cold to semisolid state*

Thrifty .... : Extravagant, Spendthrift

Thrive = *grow vigorously* .... : Languish = *lie in bad condition*

Traduce = *ridicule* .... : Praise

Traitor .... : Patriot

Transient = *of short duration* .... : Perpetual = *incessant; permanent*

Transparent .... : Opaque

Trice .... : Aeons
Trickle .... : Pour
Trifling, Flippant .... : Scrupulous, Punctilious
Trite .... : Novel
Triumph = *victory* .... : Defeat
Trivial = *having no importance* ...... : Serious
Trough .... : Crest
Trust .... : Distrust
Turmoil .... : Tranquil
Turpitude .... : Rectitude
Tyron = *novice* .... : Celebrity
Tiny .... : Gigantic

U

Ultra = *extreme* .... : Infra = *below*
Un-animous .... : Factious
Un-animity .... : Controversy
Uncouth .... : Couth
Underestimate .... : Exaggerate
Undermine .... : Fortify
Unfurl (a flag) .... : Furl
Unhygienic .... : Hygienic
Unilateral .... : Reciprocal
Unkempt .... : Kempt
Unwavering .... : Resolute
Upright .... : Erect, Prostrate
Usurp .... : Delegate
Utility .... : Futility

V

Vacant = *empty* : Occupied = *filled; captured; held*
Vacate = *to make or leave empty* .. : Occupy = *to held; to fill*
Vague = *indefinite; unclear* .... : Obvious, Clear
Vainglory = *too much pride* .... : Humility = *Humble*

Valedictory = *on the occasion of closing ceremony* : Inaugural, Salutatory = *on the ocasion of opening ceremony*

Valour = *courage* : Cowardice = *lacking courage*

Vanguard : Rearguard

Variable = *changing* : Fixed, Constant

Veil = *cover to hide* : Unveil = *uncover to expose*

Venial = *pardonable* : Heinous = *wicked in a high degree*

Veracious = *truthful* : Mendacious = *untruthful, lying*

Vertical = *standing upward* : Horizontal

Veteran = *person of long experience* : Tyro = *novice*

Viable = *capable of succeeding* : Unviable = *incapable of being successful*

Vigilant = *careful* : Careless

Vigorous = *full of strength* : Dull = *lacking viguor*

Vice = *bad habit* : Virtue = *good habit*

Vincible : Invincible

Vindictive = *revengeful* : Forgiving = *being able to forgive*

Virgin = *being near in close proximity with* : Remote = *being distant*

Virgin = *not defiled* : Defiled = *polluted; corrupted*

Virile = *of manly characteristics* : Effeminate = *having unmanly characteristics*

Virtue = *moral excellence* : Vice = *moral depravity*

Virtuous = *having good quality* : Vicious = *having bad quality*

Vis-á-vis = *face to face* : Dos-á-dos = *back-to-back*

Vivacious = Cheerful : Cadaverous = *looking like corpse*

Vociferous = *shouting; noisy* : Mute = *silent*

Voluble = *speaking much* : Taciturn = silent

Voluntary = *on one's own will volition* : Compulsory, Involuntary

Voluptuary = *sensual* : Spartan = *rigorous; frugal*

Vulgar = *indecent* : Refined = *sophisticated*

Vulnerable = *exposed to harm* : Protected = *safe from harm*

W

Wallow = *to lie in a comfortable place and enjoy it* .... : Welter = *to lie writhing in trouble/suffering*

Wane = *gradually decrease in size* : Wax = *gradually increase in the size of moon*

Wanton = *unrestrained in something bad* : Restrained

Warm .... : Cool

Wary (of) = *alert as to avoid danger* : Unwary = *not watchful against danger*

Wavering = *vacillating, changing mind* .... : Resolute = *firm in opinion/ decision*

Weal = *well-being* .... : Woe = *distress*

Weary = *tired* .... : Energetic = *full of energy*

Wild = *untamed* .... : Tame

Wily = *cunning* .... : Ingenuous, Straightforward = *artless, not crafty*

Wont = *accustomed (to)* .... : Unaccustomed *(to)*

Z

Zenith = *the highest point of career, path* .... : Nadir = *the lowest point*

OOO

Multiple Choice Questions' Answers

Choose the opposite words (out of the options given hereunder) for:

1. Abet
   (A) Reduce (B) Deter (C) Alleviate (D) Abscond
2. Abstemious
   (A) Absentism (B) Absolute (C) Gluttonous (D) Absurd
3. Acerbic
   (A) Bitter (B) Sweet (C) Melliferous (D) Cruel
4. Absolve
   (A) Disperse (B) Dissolve (C) Distribute (D) Incriminate
5. Zenith
   (A) Nadir (B) Abysmal (C) Wonder (D) Scintillating
6. Vice
   (A) Deputy (B) Virtue (C) Vicious (D) Crook
7. Valedictory
   (A) Valuable (B) Virtuous (C) Inaugural (D) Departing
8. Wane
   (A) Wax (B) Alleviate (C) Abate (D) Welter
9. Abject
   (A) Humiliating (B) Despicable
   (C) Honourable (D) Wax
10. Acclaim
    (A) Claim (B) Assert (C) Denounce (D) Curse
11. Arrogant
    (A) Mild (B) Absolute (C) Modest (D) Curse
12. Ameliorate
    (A) Better (B) Worse (C) Sweeten (D) Exacerbate
13. Analogy
    (A) Similarity (B) Difference (C) Anomaly (D) Absurdity
14. Arrogate
    (A) Arrogant (B) Credit (C) Usurp (D) Appreciate
15. Ascetic
    (A) Miser (B) Thrifty (C) Spendthrift (D) Epicure
16. Bequeath
    (A) Donate (B) Demise (C) Inherit (D) Bestow
17. Bete noire
    (A) Beloved (B) Likable (C) Hated (D) Cynosure

18. Classic
(A) Kitsch (B) Novel (C) Superb (D) Classified

19. Curious
(A) Agog (B) Anxious (C) Indifferent (D) Inquisitive

20. Elite
(A) Plebeian (B) Shining (C) Aristocrat (D) Lighted

21. Affluent
(A) Flowing (B) Static (C) Indigent (D) Prosperous

22. Effluent
(A) Indigent (B) Clotted (C) Influent (D) Stagnant

23. Eloquent
(A) Loquacious (B) Fluent (C) Dumb (D) Taciturn

24. Emerse
(A) Dip (B) Inundate (C) Immerse (D) Merge

25. Profound
(A) Deep (B) Superb (C) Shallow (D) Sallow

26. Provide
(A) Supply (B) Give (C) Arrange (D) Deprive

27. Resilient
(A) Elastic (B) Flexible (C) Rigid (D) Arrogant

28. Segregate
(A) Separate (B) Congregate (C) Gregarious (D) Grave

29. Sadism
(A) Masochism (B) Sad (C) Sorrow (D) Cruelty

30. Symphony
(A) Harmony (B) Melody (C) Cacophony (D) Strident

31. Weal
(A) Woe (B) Sympathy (C) Welfare (D) Wilful

32. Provoke
(A) Irritate (B) Stimulate (C) Pacify (D) Punish

33. Adamant
(A) Arrogant (B) Relenting (C) Sympathetic (D) Vicious

34. Albino
(A) Brunette (B) White (C) Black (D) Dark

35. Cleanse
(A) Emunge (B) Scour (C) Wash (D) Defile

36. Mundane
(A) Bland (B) Bald (C) Spiritual (D) Worldly

37. Novel
(A) Story (B) New (C) Trite (D) Novice

38. Dandy
(A) Sloven (B) Slattern (C) Slut (D) Dirty

39. Biased
(A) Disinterested (B) Prejudiced (C) Belligerent (D) Bullied

40. Catholic
(A) Christian (B) European (C) Parochial (D) Pantheism

41. Agoraphobia
(A) Fear of darkness (B) Fear of daylight
(C) Xenophobia (D) Claustrophobia

42. Myopia
(A) Blindness (B) Clairvoyance (C) Meteropia (D) Alopecia

43. Outstanding
(A) Egregious (B) Blatant (C) Flagrant (D) Commonplace

44. Garner
(A) Collect (B) Scatter (C) Disseminate (D) Gather

45. Squander
(A) Waste (B) Spend (C) Conserve (D) Throw

46. Soar
(A) Levitate (B) Ascend (C) Swoop (D) Descend

47. Generous
(A) Kind (B) Stingy (C) Generating (D) Gracious

48. Ruffle
(A) Spouce (B) Uncomb (C) Wet (D) Wilt

49. Perennial
(A) Annual (B) Daily (C) Deciduous (D) Monthly

50. Transient
(A) Temporary (B) Transitory (C) Perpetual (D) Evanescent

51. Benevolent
(A) Banal (B) Benign (C) Malevolent (D) Tyrant

52. Dissemble
(A) Pretend (B) Hide (C) Betray (D) Disclose

53. Intrepid
(A) Pusillanimous (B) Brave (C) Adventurous (D) Courageous

54. Auspicious
(A) Gracious (B) Merciful (C) Ominous (D) Kind

55. Blaspheme
(A) Blast (B) Reputable (C) Insulting (D) Revere

56. Cadaverous

(A) Vivacious (B) Corpulent (C) Deadly (D) Lifeless

57. Deliberate
(A) Intentional (B) Knowingly (C) Pre-meditated (D) Inadvertent

58. Dilettante
(A) Novice (B) Connoisseur (C) Cad (D) Novice

59. Scion
(A) Shoot (B) Young (C) Offspring (D) Doyen

60. Corpulent
(A) Fatty (B) Rotund (C) Emaciated (D) Cadaverous

61. Hubris
(A) Fatty (B) Rotund (C) Emaciated (D) Cadaverous

62. Inept
(A) Expert (B) Foolish (C) Skilled (D) Deft

63. Eirenic
(A) Ironic (B) Polemic (C) Syncretic (D) Peaceful

64. Judicious
(A) Honest (B) Mediator (C) Judging (D) Iniquitous

65. Latent
(A) Dormant (B) Hibernating (C) Patent (D) Hidden

66. Parsimonious
(A) Lavish (B) Poor (C) Miserly (D) Cautious

67. Laud
(A) Hail (B) Applaud (C) Shout (D) Decry

68. Exacerbate
(A) Acerbate (B) Meliorate (C) Annoy (D) Offend

69. Misogynist
(A) Philanthrope (B) Philander (C) Philogynist (D) Cynic

70. Nocturnal
(A) Diurnal (B) Naughty (C) Dreadful (D) Daily

71. Protege
(A) Supporter (B) Disciple (C) Subordinate (D) Protector

72. Succumb
(A) Surrender (B) Yield (C) Survive (D) Resist

73. Slipshod
(A) Fastidious (B) Haphazard (C) Loose (D) Dirty

74. Promulgate
(A) Pronounce (B) Declare (C) Abrogate (D) Defy

75. Monopoly
(A) Control (B) Superiority (C) Monopsony (D) Monarchy

ooo

Exercises on Antonyms

Test-1

Choose the most appropriate antonym out of the given options for the word (in bold) in the sentences:

1. He is **crazy** about cricket game.
(A) mad (B) cool (C) sane (D) shaky
2. He is temperamentally a **cedulous** person.
(A) suspicious (B) creditable
(C) unsuspecting (D) crude
3. It is a very **critical** moment in his life.
(A) hazardous (B) crucial
(C) precarious (D) unimportant
4. He was censured for his **culpable** act.
(A) criminal (B) heinous
(C) blameworthy (D) praiseworthy
5. He is trying to **cultivate** friendship with me.
(A) till (B) grow (C) neglect (D) improve
6. He is crazy about **accumulating** wealth.
(A) amassing (B) gathering
(C) filling (D) squandering
7. Police used force to **curb** violence.
(A) quell (B) check (C) block (D) encourage
8. He is very **curious** about his neighbours.
(A) desirous (B) inquisitive (C) indifferent (D) excited
9. **Current** practice of endogamous marriages is crumbling now.
(A) prevalent (B) running (C) obsolete (D) modern
10. He gave a very **curt** reply to my query.
(A) rude (B) brief (C) abrupt (D) polished
11. He followed **customary** practice of visiting neighbours occasionally.
(A) habitual (B) conventional
(C) uncommon (D) regular
12. He is **cynical** about his colleague's motives.
(A) insane (B) contemptuous
(C) distrustful (D) trusting
13. He deliberately **dallies** with his duties.
(A) procrastinates (B) fondles
(C) hastens (D) loiters
14. There is a **dearth** of doctors in hospitals.
(A) famine (B) abundance
(C) plethora (D) scarcity

15. Health gradually **decays** in old age.
(A) rots (B) degenerates
(C) decomposes (D) flourishes

16. She has acquired reputation for **deceit**.
(A) deception (B) fraud (C) honesty (D) distortion

17. **Deciduous** trees take on new leaves annually.
(A) permanent (B) shedding (C) evergreen (D) eternal

18. He is a man of **decisive** actions.
(A) determining (B) determined
(C) conclusive (D) prevaricating

19. He **affirmed** his intention to resign his job.
(A) offended (B) averred (C) denied (D) assented

20. A **decrepit** old man could hardly walk.
(A) weak (B) infirm (C) emaciated (D) vigorous

21. **Dedicated** workers are assets of a company.
(A) devoted (B) sacrificing (C) dallying (D) triffling

22. He is a scholar of **deep** knowledge.
(A) profound (B) abysmal (C) shallow (D) drowning

23. **Defective** machine hampered the progress of work.
(A) imperfect (B) faulty (C) flawless (D) abnormal

24. The meeting was **deferred** due to lack of quorum.
(A) postponed (B) put off
(C) held on schedule (D) yielded

25. He was in **defiant** mood.
(A) defeating (B) obedient (C) rebellious (D) decorous

26. **Deficit** in money withheld the work on the project.
(A) flaw (B) shortage (C) want (D) surplus

27. The **defiled** house was stinking.
(A) impure (B) sullied (C) impure (D) immaculate

28. He felt **degraded** with their remark.
(A) disgraced (B) deprived (C) reduced (D) exalted

29. The defeated team members wore a **dejected** expression.
(A) rejected (B) sad (C) despirited (D) elated

30. The guests were treated with **delectable** dinner.
(A) delightful (B) tasteful (C) charming (D) disagreeable

31. Factory chimney spewed **delectable** dinner.
(A) lamless (B) pernicious (C) stinking (D) unpleasant

32. It was a **deliberate** action.
(A) careful (B) intentional
(C) premeditated (D) impulsive

33. He has a **delicate** sense of smell.
(A) crude (B) exquisite (C) fragile (D) delightful

34. She takes great **delight** in teasing me.
(A) charm (B) joy (C) satisfaction (D) distress

35. Oh! God, **deliver** me from these boring people.
(A) throw (B) liberate (C) enthrall (D) save

36. He **demurred** to accept the post offered to him.
(A) wavered (B) hesitated (C) refused (D) agreed

37. The **demure** girl sat aloof.
(A) sober (B) hesitant (C) indecorous (D) arrogant

38. People **denounce** politicians as morally corrupt.
(A) declare (B) announce (C) condemn (D) commend

39. He **denied** me what was my due.
(A) refuse (B) withheld (C) allowed (D) repudiated

40. We all should **deplore** the present state of morality.
(A) bemoan (B) denounce (C) rejoice (D) applaud

41. One earnestly **desires** to join family get-together in festivals.
(A) yearns (B) craves (C) solicits (D) loathes

42. Polar regions are **desolate** place.
(A) sad (B) uninhabited
(C) populous (D) barren

43. Rescuers made a final **desperate** attempt to save the child.
(A) reckless (B) hopeless (C) hopeful (D) intolerable

44. He has become **despondent** about his failing health.
(A) dependent (B) despairing
(C) happy (D) encouraged

45. He is now **destitute** of resources due to reckless squandering.
(A) deprived (B) needy (C) impoverished (D) affluent

46. He could not get a job yet, due to his **desultory** attempts.
(A) distressing (B) fitful (C) consistent (D) pertinent

47. He **detected** a thief lurking behind the house in dark.
(A) descried (B) discovered (C) overlooked (D) missed

48. He is a devout Hindu.
(A) sincere (B) holy (C) pious (D) irreverent

49. He is a **dextrous** artist.
(A) deft (B) clever (C) inept (D) right-handed

50. This creeper is **dextrorse**.
(A) right-handed (B) climbing from right to left
(C) climbing straight up (D) sinistrorse right

51. **Diffident** person shirks from taking responsibility.
(A) confused (B) defiant
(C) unconfident (D) self-confident

52. Narrow arteries are **dilated** to all blood flow.
(A) expanded (B) expatiated
(C) spread (D) constricted

53. The government adopts **dilatory** tactics in taking unpalatable decisions.
(A) procrastinating (B) deferring
(C) prompt (D) widening

54. He **discarded** old hat.
(A) rejected (B) cast aside (C) threw (D) retained

55. Hooting by audience **disconcerted** the orator.
(A) ruffled (B) discomfitted
(C) calmed (D) confused

56. Bereaved of elder brother, he was **disconsolate**.
(A) unhappy (B) inconsolable
(C) soothed (D) sad

57. There is stark **discrepancy** in what you preach and what you practise.
(A) gap (B) contrariness
(C) consistency (D) discreetness

58. He brought **disgrace** on his family with his misdeeds.
(A) insult (B) ignominy (C) respect (D) honour

59. His petty quibblings **disgusted** me.
(A) delighted (B) relished (C) offended (D) annoyed

60. A gust of wind **dishevelled** his hairs.
(A) tidied (B) disarrayed (C) hanged (D) loosened

61. Stashed pot of valuables was **disintered** from the courtyard's underground.
(A) burried (B) exhumed (C) dug out (D) extracted

62. He is **disinterested** in their dispute.
(A) impartial (B) un-interested
(C) having selfish motive (D) indifferent

63. He was in **dismal** mood.
(A) sinister (B) melancholic
(C) gay (D) annoyed

64. He **dismantled** machine's parts for packing.
(A) broke (B) knocked down
(C) separated (D) assembled

65. Deadlock in negotiation **dismayed** both sides.
(A) grieved (B) disheartened
(C) encouraged (D) pained

66. Wind **dispersed** the cloud in the sky.
(A) dispelled (B) gathered (C) blew (D) drove away

67. His disposition towards meticulousness in work is appreciable.
(A) liking (B) proclivity (C) unwillingness (D) mentality

68. He **disregarded** my advice.
(A) ignored (B) heeded (C) disrespected (D) mistreated

69. She **dissembled** crookedness with ingenuous pretentions.
(A) betrayed (B) concealed (C) dispersed (D) dismantled

70. I **dissuated** him from leaving the job.
(A) persuaded (B) deterred (C) discouraged (D) dissipated

71. His stomach **distended** with flatulence.
(A) extended (B) protruded (C) bloated (D) shrunk

72. **Distinction** in height helps us identify the twins.
(A) clarity (B) confusion (C) difference (D) resemblance

73. The boy was reading the story of a damsel in **distress**.
(A) agony (B) comfort (C) danger (D) safety

74. **Diurnal** cacophony on city roads subsides in late evening.
(A) daytime (B) nocturnal (C) daily (D) morning

75. Social and cultural **diversity** is the uniqueness of our country.
(A) divergence (B) dis-similarity
(C) difference (D) uniformity

76. Compassion is **divine** virtue in a person.
(A) supreme (B) sacred (C) mundane (D) religious

77. **Docile** workers readily follow the instructions.
(A) submissive (B) meek (C) intractable (D) stubborn

78. Pet is a **domesticated** animal.
(A) domestic (B) tamed (C) household (D) wild

79. He is sitting with **dreary** face.
(A) fearful (B) gloomy (C) dreaded (D) cheerful

80. He is a **droll** person.
(A) comically humorous (B) serious
(C) boring (D) whimsical

81. He is a person with **dusky** complexion.
(A) shadowy (B) swarthy
(C) blond (D) twilight

82. He made an **earnest** appeal to people to help him.
(A) urgent (B) arrogant (C) fervent (D) triffling

83. It is our weakness to run after **earthly pleasures**.
(A) divine (B) mundane
(C) ordinary (D) worthless

84. His **egotism** has alienated all his friends.
(A) egoism (B) self-conceit
(C) humility (D) selfishness

85. The sun **emerged** from behind the clouds.
(A) came out (B) emanated (C) immerged (D) mixed up

86. Hordes of technocrats **emigrate** to U.S.A. every year.
(A) leave own country to settle in foreign countries
(B) immigrate (C) move (D) flee

87. He soon rose to **eminence** in his field of expertise.
(A) exclusiveness (B) prominence
(C) reputation (D) obscurity

88. He is **encumbered** with numerous obligations.
(A) enmeshed(B) burdened(C) hampered (D) disburdened

89. His arrogant behaviour **infuriated** me.
(A) incensed (B) pacified (C) fired (D) provoked

90. Social system has still **enslaved** womenfolk.
(A) bonded (B) imprisoned
(C) emancipated (D) suppressed

91. Joys of childhood are **ephemeral**.
(A) temporary (B) permanent
(C) shortlived (D) long lasting

92. **Epicurean** leaders of present time are in sharp contrast to Gandhian leaders.
(A) indulgent in luxury (B) sensuous
(C) ascetic (D) licentious

93. I **esteem** him for his honesty.
(A) commend(B) respect (C) disdain (D) support

94. The universe is **eternal**.
(A) unchanging (B) perpetual (C) enduring (D) transitory

95. Triffling with patients' treatment is against the professional **ethics**.
(A) beliefs (B) honesty
(C) immorality (D) principles of morality

96. The minister tried to **evade** reporter's questions.
(A) dodge (B) confront (C) escape (D) elude

97. Adversaries always tend to **exaggerate** one's weaknesses.
(A) extenuate (B) magnify (C) overstate (D) extend

98. He was **exalted** to venerable position by the people.
(A) elevated (B) depreciated
(C) downgraded (D) praised

99. The boy is endowed with **exceptional** intellect.
(A) special (B) peculiar (C) average (D) outstanding

100. He is reputed to be easily **excitable**.
(A) stimulated (B) placid (C) infuriated (D) provoked

101. The old woman began to **execrate** all those who were teasing her.
(A) denounce (B) imprecate (C) damn (D) bless

102. Cool breeze **exhilarated** that morning walkers.
(A) inspired (B) exhorted (C) cheered up (D) depressed

103. Moneylenders charge **exorbitant** interests on loans.
(A) prevailing (B) usurious (C) fair (D) unusual

104. He ordered his staff to **expedite** the work.
(A) hasten (B) move
(C) procrastinate (D) ensnare

105. He is an **expert** in this field.
(A) experienced (B) greenhorn
(C) knowledgeable (D) connoisseur

106. He expressed his **explicit** opinion.
(A) open (B) unequivocal
(C) confused (D) ambiguous

107. His remark was **extraneous** to the topic at hand.
(A) extrinsic (B) extra (C) intrinsic/pertinent (D) rare

108. He is an **extravagant** person.
(A) expensive (B) spendthrift
(C) immoderate (D) thrifty

109. This is the story of **fabulous** exploits of an adventurer.
(A) marvellous (B) fictitious (C) factual (D) historical

110. The hall is adorned with **factitious** flowers.
(A) fictional (B) artificial (C) real (D) factual

111. Fiction writer needs a **fecund** mind.
(A) prolific (B) fruitful (C) effete (D) lazy

112. He made a **fervent** appeal for support.
(A) feverish (B) fiery
(C) burning (D) dispassionate

113. He is a person of extremely **fickle** mind.
(A) capricious (B) stable (C) capacious (D) fictitious

114. The servant's **fidelity** towards his master is perfect.
(A) fealty (B) belief (C) disloyalty (D) confidence

115. He extended a **flimsy** excuse for his failure.
(A) thin (B) shoddy (C) loose (D) convincing

116. He is my bitter **foe**.
(A) adversary (B) feud (C) friend (D) fiend

117. Lack of generosity is his notable **foible**.
(A) failing (B) character (C) forte (D) flaw

118. Speeches shall be **followed** by dinner.
(A) accompanied (B) succeeded
(C) preceded (D) ensued

119. He is feeling **forlorn** of own people in this distant city.
(A) sad (B) in company of
(C) desolate (D) hopeless

120. The **former** of the two suggestions was acceptable.
(A) prior (B) past (C) latter (D) ancient

121. A **fortuitous** incident changed his life.
(A) fortunate (B) incidental (C) accidental (D) deliberate

122. He is a man of **frail** body constitution.
(A) fragile (B) brittle (C) delicate (D) robust

123. **Fresh** vegetables are available in abundance.
(A) new (B) raw (C) unfaded (D) stale

124. She is worried about her **forward** daughter.
(A) contrary (B) arrogant (C) tractable (D) frowning

125. He is very **frugal** in spending money.
(A) miser (B) prudont (C) penurious (D) lavish

126. He made a **futile** attempt to appease his foe.
(A) vain (B) fruitless (C) effectual (D) frivolous

127. **Gallant** soldier captured enemy post single handed.
(A) galloping (B) chivalrous (C) valorous (D) cowardly

128. Clouds are **gathering** in the sky Indicating rainfall.
(A) accumulating (B) collecting
(C) dispersing (D) frittering

129. **Gaudy** decoy looks vulgar.
(A) showy (B) garish (C) immodest (D) sober

130. Kids were frolicking in **gay** spirit.
(A) miserable (B) jolly (C) wanton (D) showy

131. **Germane** facts were collected to reach the conclusion.
(A) genuine (B) relevant (C) inept (D) inapt

132. **Giant** stature of a woman makes her unattractive.
(A) great (B) monstrous (C) huge (D) petite

133. His career prospect seems to be **gloomy**.
(A) shady (B) dark (C) bright (D) hopeless

134. He is sitting with **glum** face.
(A) morose (B) dark (C) sorrowful (D) cheerful

135. His social service brought **glory** to her.
(A) wonder (B) fame (C) grace (D) obloquy

136. Human-beings are generally **gregarious** people.
(A) reclusive (B) seclusive (C) social (D) un-social

137. He **grieves** over the loss in business.
(A) laments (B) weeps (C) rejoices (D) desecrate

138. Ordinary people **hallow** saints.
(A) honour (B) venerate (C) consecrate(D) desecrate

139. Bad weather **hampered** progress of the work.
(A) hindered (B) furthered (C) interferred (D) delayed

140. The group, though looked cohesive, lacked **harmony**.
(A) symmetry (B) melody (C) concord (D) discord

141. A **hasty** decision usually makes one repentant.
(A) precipitate (B) testy (C) deliberated (D) quick

142. He never **heeds** sane advice.
(A) listens (B) cares (C) worries (D) ignores

143. He was punished for his **heinous** offence.
(A) sinful (B) feral
(C) reprehensible (D) admirable

144. He is **humble**, despite his high rank.
(A) arrogant (B) polite (C) meek (D) submissive

145. He is **ignorant** of what is happening around him.
(A) oblivious (B) unknown (C) aware (D) illiterate

146. He was censured for his **ignoble** conduct.
(A) honourable (B) ignominious
(C) inferior (D) infamous

147. Breaking out of war with hostile country is **imminent**.
(A) impending(B) possible (C) remote (D) impossible

148. Innoculation renders a child **immune** to diseases.
(A) impunity (B) exempt (C) resistant (D) susceptible

149. His **impassionate** appeal moved people.
(A) emotional (B) impassive(C)tranquil (D) inflamed

150. An **impecunious** person was unable to procure basic needs.
(A) penniless (B) poor (C) wealthy (D) indigent

151. He was feared due to his **imperious** behaviour.
(A) unnecessary (B) perilous (C) overbearing (D) submissive

152. His **impertinent** behaviour annoyed me.
(A) irrelevant (B) brazen (C) insane (D) polite

153. He is known always to take **impetuous** decisions.
(A) rash (B) emotional (C) careful (D) studied

154. A country is left **impoverished** by war it fights.
(A) reduced to poverty (B) bereft
(C) enriched (D) poor

155. The boy got punishment for his **impudent** behaviour.
(A) bold (B) arrogant (C) brazen (D) courteous

156. His habit of lying is **acquired** since childhood.
(A) inherent (B) natural (C) cultivated (D) congenital

157. Dissatisfaction **incites** anger.
(A) stimulates(B) instigates(C) subsides (D) encourage

158. The crowd was **instigated** by inflammatory speech to resort to violence.
(A) provoked (B) exhorted (C) deterred (D) urged

159. The police **inculpated** him with unlawful activity.
(A) exonerated (B) incriminated
(C) ensnared (D) indicted

160. He is **indif ferent** towards politics.
(A) attracted (B) unconcerned
(C) concerned (D) similar

161. This plant is **indigenous** to India.
(A) autochthonous (B) aboriginal
(C) alien (D) natural

162. The **implacable** creditor refused to give more time to return money, despite entreaties.
(A) cruel (B) inexorable (C) merciful (D) flexible

163. He **improvised** his act directly on the stage.
(A) extemporize (B) rehearsed
(C) provided (D) prepared

164. Rain water **ingressed** into houses in low-lying areas.
(A) immersed(B) entered (C) egressed (D) progressed

165. People somehow got rid of **iniquitous** despot.
(A) unjust (B) cruel (C) hostile (D) righteous

166. **Inordinate** delay in the train's arrival irked the passengers.
(A) disorderly (B) excessive (C) unreasonable (D) moderate

167. **Inquisitive** mind keeps on asking why.
(A) prying (B) peeking (C) curious (D) uninterested

168. An **intrepid** person does not hesitate to venture.
(A) anxious (B) fearless (C) shaky (D) timid

169. The **irascible** old man was easily provoked to anger.
(A) testy (B) irritating (C) calm (D) rash

170. The spy was in **jeopardy** of being discovered.
(A) danger (B) hazard (C) chance (D) safety

171. He is in **jolly** mood.
(A) sportive (B) jovial (C) melancholy(D) playful

172. She **ravelled** the knot like a Gordian knot.
(A) tangled (B) unravelled (C) revolved (D) complicated

173. They pursued their goal in **lackadaisical** manner.
(A) lacking (B) listless (C) unconcerned (D) lively

174. Spectators **lauded** their home team for winning the game.
(A) extolled (B) celebrated (C) lamented (D) shouted

175. She **lavished** praise on him.
(A) lashed (B) heaped (C) grudged (D) reserved

176. **Lax** laws engenders sense of impunity in offenders.
(A) rigid (B) strict (C) lenient (D) loose

177. He ...... his friend until entire fortune was exhausted.
(A) sucked (B) sponged on (C) treated (D) befooled

178. A **libertine** person is despicable.
(A) free (B) licentious(C) prudish (D) pure

179. It was a **lifeless** performance.
(A) dead (B) animate (C) dull (D) living

180. Gymnast's daily practice keeps his muscles **limber**.
(A) stiff (B) lithe (C) bending (D) loose

181. His body was **limp** with exhaustion.
(A) loose (B) drooping (C) tired (D) erect

182. One can see the bottom of the **limpid** pool.
(A) pellucid (B) lucid (C) calm (D) opaque

183. **Lineage** of a race horse determines its worth.
(A) age (B) pedigree
(C) posterity (D) performance

184. In the absence of meaningful engagements, time **lingers**.
(A) fleets (B) lengthens (C) tarries (D) stays

185. An incompetent person becomes **malevolent** towards successful people.
(A) injurious (B) malicious (C) benevolent (D) selfish

186. **Malign** people in high position without substance.
(A) vilify (B) abuse (C) praise (D) despise

187. He is suffering from **malignant** tumour.
(A) malevolent (B) malicious (C) pernicious (D) benignant

188. The holiday was **marred** by bad weather.
(A) damaged (B) impaired (C) spoilt (D) enhanced

189. The lawyer **marshalled** facts before arguing the case in the court.
(A) ordered for (B) arranged in order
(C) combined (D) scattered

190. He is a **mendacious** person.
(A) false (B) veracious (C) lying (D) untrue

191. Mostly the non-government organizations, though profess to work for poor people, are **mercenary**.
(A) profit-seeking (B) venal
(C) voluntary (D) dishonest

192. He is **meticulous** about his physical appearance.
(A) finical (B) fearful (C) methodical (D) careless

193. A **moderate** change in the existing law is required.
(A) mild (B) excessive (C) radical (D) harsh

194. He leads a **modest** life.
(A) modern (B) moderate (C) pretentious (D) unassuming

195. The need to take tough stand against corruption is a **moot** point.
(A) doubtful (B) debatable (C) indisputable (D) major

196. **Morbid** condition of economy is the cause of concern.
(A) deadly (B) bad (C) sick (D) healthy

197. Rejected by voters in election, many small parties are in **moribund** state.
(A) discarded (B) dying (C) vivacious (D) closure

198. His death was **mourned** by his colleagues.
(A) deplored (B) lamented
(C) remembered (D) rejoiced

199. He **mumbled** his views on the subject of discussion.
(A) articulated (B) muted (C) muttered (D) uttered

200. She is so **naive** as to believe in anyone.
(A) novice (B) simpleton (C) crafty (D) nonsense

201. His wife keeps on **nagging** at him all day.
(A) pricking (B) hectoring (C) comforting (D) complaining

202. He **nibbled** at the apple he was eating.
(A) bite (B) gorged (C) gulped (D) scratched

203. He gave the restaurant waiter a **niggardly** tip.
(A) poor (B) stingy (C) miser (D) generous

204. The accused was pronounced guilty, defence lawyer's brilliant arguments **notwithstanding**.
(A) failure (B) despite (C) due to (D) without

205. He is a **novice** in politics.
(A) tyro (B) experienced
(C) fool (D) new

206. **Obnoxious** smell forced us to cover our nose.
(A) annoying (B) odious (C) offensive (D) delightful

207. New models of cars become **obsolete** in a few years.
(A) old (B) outdated (C) in vogue (D) antique

208. Dark clouds look **ominous**.
(A) portentous (B) threatening (C) propitious (D) harmful

209. Public anger against price-rise of petrol is **palpable**.
(A) obvious (B) evident
(C) perceptible (D) imperceptible

210. An amount of one rupee is a **paltry** sum these days.
(A) petty (B) contemptible
(C) significant (D) inconsiderable

211. He **paraded** his medal and prizes proudly.
(A) marched (B) flaunted (C) concealed (D) promenaded

212. Checking corruption in the country is **paramount**.
(A) supreme (B) most important
(C) unimportant (D) superior

213. Grief is **patent** on her face.
(A) unconcealed (B) latent
(C) dim (D) obscure

214. The old man was sitting in a **pensive** mood.
(A) sorry (B) grieving (C) thinking (D) thoughtless

215. It is a **perennial** fruit-bearing plant.
(A) throughout the year (B) seasonal
(C) perpetual (D) eternal

216. His **perfidious** friend ditched him.
(A) faithful (B) disloyal (C) perfect (D) false

217. He does his job in **perfunctory** manner.
(A) professional(B) functional (C) indifferent (D) diligent

218. Mountaineering is a **perilous** adventure.
(A) injurious (B) risky
(C) safe (D) disadvantageous

219. The building **perished** in the earthquake.
(A) ruined (B) survived (C) decayed (D) disappeared

220. The shrine witnesses **perpetual** stream of pilgrims.
(A) unending (B) discontinuous
(C) permanent (D) temporary

221. **Persistent** incidents of violence in the city make people afraid of moving out freely.
(A) insistent (B) steady (C) sporadic (D) tenacious

222. A **perspicacious** person does not easily get befooled.
(A) astute (B) transparent
(C) imperceptive (D) dim

223. The import of what he said in his speech was **perspicuous**.
(A) indistinct (B) lucid (C) paque (D) bright

224. He was **persuaded** to perjure in the court.
(A) agreed (B) induced (C) dissuaded(D) coaxed

225. Do not try to **pervert** my statement.
(A) distort (B) correct (C) mislead (D) misuse

226. A hypochondriac is suffering from **phantom** feeling of pain in abdomen.
(A) real (B) imaginary (C) ghost (D) illusory

227. He is a man of **phlegmatic** disposition.
(A) humorous(B) placid (C) passionate(D) passive

228. The devotee leads a life full of **piety**.
(A) pain (B) devotion (C) veneration (D) irreverence

229. His **piteous** cry for help moved us.
(A) reverent (B) pathetic (C) delightful (D) pious

230. The political leaders **pillory** each other in public fora.
(A) push (B) ridicule publicly
(C) approbate (D) laugh at

231. His slogans are full of **platitudes**.
(A) cliche (B) novelty (C) repetitions (D) trivial

232. He gave a **plausible** explanation of his failure to accomplish the assigned task.
(A) applaudable (B) truthful (C) specious (D) untrue

233. People of **plebeian** taste can't appreciate abstract art works.
(A) sophisticated (B) vulgar
(C) popular (D) trite

234. The power breakdown **plunged** the whole city into darkness.
(A) stooped (B) submerged (C) emerged (D) soared

235. His **poignant** remorse was cathartic.
(A) severe (B) pricking (C) sincere (D) mild

236. She was walking carefully **poising** a water jug on her head.
(A) balancing (B) controlling (C) disbalancing (D) stabilizing

237. **Polemical** views of bigots are threat to social harmony.
(A) uncompromising (B) controversial
(C) eirenic (D) argumentative

238. To joust with a potent person is not a **politic** act.
(A) shrewd (B) expedient (C) tactless (D) clever

239. People's outrage over rising hardships due to high inflation **portends** doom for the government.
(A) augurs (B) forebodes (C) threatens (D) foretells

240. Judgement of this age should be left to **posterity**.
(A) descendants (B) ancestry (C) priority (D) future

241. Several **potent** arguments were put forward to prove the point.
(A) weak (B) powerful (C) cogent (D) useful

242. His plan was unacceptable because it was not **practicable**.
(A) practical (B) feasible (C) unattainable (D) worth

243. He is a **practical** politician.
(A) sensible (B) unwise (C) practising (D) practicable

244. Job tenure in private companies is **precarious**.
(A) secure
(B) unsure because of depending on other's mercy
(C) unsteady (D) dangerous

245. Many a tribal society is still mired in **primitive** traditions.
(A) primany (B) pristine (C) old (D) modern

246. He is highly regarded because of his impeccable **probity**.
(A) venality (B) rectitude (C) obediency (D) sincerity

247. A **prodigal** person is likely to be impoverished in due course of time.
(A) improvident (B) frugal
(C) proud (D) extraordinary

248. A precocious child possesses **prodigious** talent.
(A) extraordinarily marvellous (B) commonplace
(C) proven (D) progressing

249. Harsh retort by the son **ruffled** his father.
(A) upset (B) untidied (C) smoothed (D) soothed

250. Tyrants are **ruthless**.
(A) compassionate (B) cruel
(C) adamant (D) ferocious

251. Holy shrines are **sacred** to the devotees.
(A) pious (B) blasphemous
(C) pure (D) venerable

252. **Sagacious** patriarch is a source of prudent advice.
(A) sapient (B) practical (C) illustrious (D) foolish

253. **Salient** features of a machine determine its price.
(A) solid (B) outstanding
(C) basic (D) unimportant

254. The chief organizer delivered his **salutatory** speech.
(A) valedictory (B) welcoming (C) favourable (D) beneficial

255. The criminals committed the crime with complete **sangfroid**.
(A) composure (B) discomfiture
(C) confusion (D) easiness

256. The boy passed **scurrilous** remark on girls passing-by.
(A) obscene (B) jocular (C) decent (D) crude

257. He has a **queer** notion about life in U.S.A.
(A) different (B) odd (C) usual (D) questionable

258. **Radical** change in polity is needed to check rampant corruption.
(A) root (B) basic (C) superficial (D) drastic

259. He failed to **redeem** his pawned watch due to want of money.
(A) reclaim (B) ransom (C) forfeit (D) abandon

260. It is very difficult to handle a **refractory** child.
(A) hard (B) obstinate (C) obedient (D) rude

261. The party refused the return of the **renegades** into party fold.
(A) apostates (B) adherents (C) sticklers (D) traitors

262. **Repentance** cleanses the sinner's soul.
(A) remorse (B) sorrow (C) impenitence (D) regret

263. He **repudiated** charges made against him.
(A) disowned (B) enforced (C) accepted (D) contradicted

264. Dispersal of clouds **revealed** the sun in the sky.
(A) shrouded (B) divulged (C) unveiled (D) concealed

265. The river takes a **sinuous** path through the valley.
(A) side (B) straight (C) flexuous (D) circuitous

266. People are **skeptical** about government's sincerity to curb corruption.
(A) shaky (B) confident (C) doubtful (D) cynic

267. A **somber** passage way led to the large hall.
(A) gloomy (B) doleful (C) dusky (D) bright

268. The **volube** spokesman kept on speaking to the chagrin of the listeners.
(A) succinct (B) verbose (C) strident (D) loud

269. Only a few lucky ones could **survive** in the disaster.
(A) succour (B) remain alive
(C) succumb (D) win

270. It is not wise to **squander** precious resources.
(A) spend (B) preserve (C) dissipate (D) splurge

271. He is **steadfast** in his faith.
(A) staunch (B) firm (C) wavering (D) constant

272. He unleashed vicious compaign to **tarnish** my reputation.
(A) blacken (B) blemish (C) brighten (D) exalt

273. His position in the team is **tenuous**.
(A) slender (B) strong (C) attenuated(D) tender

274. She took out frozen stuff from refrigerator and kept on the table to let it **thaw**.
(A) warm (B) deliquesce (C) melt (D) freeze

275. It is not good to **traduce** someone's character.
(A) malign (B) abuse (C) praise (D) expose

276. **Treason** is an unforgivable crime.
(A) loyalty (B) sedition (C) treachery (D) patriotism

277. He was forgiven for **venial** offence.
(A) vicious (B) pardonable
(C) felonious (D) serious

278. His **wanton** disregard of others' sentiments is not appreciable.
(A) willful (B) reckless
(C) lewd (D) unintentional

279. This town has **warm** climate throughout the year.
(A) hot (B) moderately hot
(C) cold (D) cool

280. The wet log got **warped** on getting dried up.
(A) bent (B) straightened
(C) twisted (D) flat

281. His **wayward** son has become incorrigible.
(A) willful (B) obedient (C) astray (D) capricious

282. He looked **weary** after long hours of work.
(A) tired (B) interested
(C) energetic (D) sad

Test-2

Choose the correct option for antonyms of the given words:

1. Impeccability
(A) Faultlessness (B) Sin
(C) Wrongfulness (D) Rightness

2. Immaculate
(A) Clean (B) Spotless (C) Tainted (D) Defective

3. Vivacious
(A) Lively (B) Energetic (C) Animated (D) Inanimated
4. Exonarate
(A) Aquit (B) Exculpate (C) Punish (D) Release
5. Amass
(A) Gather (B) Exhaust (C) Fritter (D) Collect
6. Pedant
(A) Learned (B) Charlatan (C) Attach (D) Fool
7. Kudos
(A) Criticism (B) Approbation
(C) Applause (D) Appreciation
8. Entice
(A) Allure (B) Attract (C) Repulse (D) Feign
9. Noisome
(A) Pleasant (B) Noxious (C) Distasteful (D) Foul
10. Benevolence
(A) Beneficence (B) Charity (C) Malevolence (D) Arrogance
11. Annoint
(A) Consecrate (B) Desecrate (C) Purify (D) Paint
12. Zenith
(A) Nadir (B) Depth (C) Acme (D) Pinnacle
13. Zealous
(A) Apathetic (B) Enthusiastic (C) Passionate (D) Dull
14. Youthful
(A) Young (B) Senile (C) Aged (D) Dotard
15. Yield
(A) Surrender (B) Repent (C) Submit (D) Resist
16. Compliant
(A) Obedient (B) Submissive (C) Intractable (D) Dutiful
17. Yearn
(A) Loathe (B) Crave (C) Long (D) Wish
18. Adore
(A) Worship (B) Revere (C) Scorn (D) Venerate
19. Worldly
(A) Mundane (B) Temporal (C) Spiritual (D) Base
20. Womanly
(A) Virile (B) Effeminate (C) Feminine (D) Masculine
21. Wither
(A) Shrivel (B) Decay (C) Refresh (D) Fade

22. Interest
(A) Indifference (B) Liking (C) Choice (D) Attraction

23. Thrive
(A) Flourish (B) Prosper (C) Decay (D) Grow

24. Wilful
(A) Intentional (B) Fortuitous (C) Meditated (D) Desired

25. Contemplate
(A) Pender (B) Reflect (C) Ignore (D) Cogitate

26. Wax
(A) Wane (B) Enlarge (C) Amplify (D) Reduce

27. Waver
(A) Flicker (B) Vacillate (C) Fickle (D) Stay firm

28. Want
(A) Abundance (B) Paucity (C) Privation (D) Penury

29. Wander
(A) Rove (B) Linger (C) Traipse (D) Ramble

30. Vulgar
(A) Unrefined (B) Refined
(C) Of common people (D) Crude

31. Vivid
(A) Vague (B) Lively (C) Bright (D) Animated

32. Virulent
(A) Malevolent (B) Benign (C) Spiteful (D) Wicked

33. Vengeance
(A) Retribution (B) Forgiveness
(C) Revenge (D) Reprisal

34. Venal
(A) Mercenary (B) Corrupt (C) Upright (D) Saleable

35. Veil
(A) Conceal (B) Cloak (C) Mask (D) Bare

36. Vapid
(A) Stale (B) Insipid (C) Stimulating (D) Banal

37. Vanish
(A) Evanesce (B) Appear (C) Disappear (D) Dissolve

38. Vainglory
(A) Humility (B) Conceit (C) Vanity (D) Arrogance

39. Erect
(A) Crooked (B) Upright (C) Straight (D) Unbent

40. Unkempt
(A) Untidy (B) Rumpled (C) Preened (D) Ruffled

41. Unintelligible
(A) Lucid (B) Vague (C) Ambiguous (D) Indistinct

42. Unfold
(A) Furl (B) Spread (C) Open up (D) Unwrap

43. Ultimate
(A) Final (B) Last (C) Latest (D) Foremost

44. Triumph
(A) Victory (B) Conquest (C) Defeat (D) Win

45. Trifling
(A) Frivolous (B) Trivial (C) Petty (D) Serious

46. Trite
(A) Novel (B) Commonplace
(C) Hackneyed (D) Stale

47. Trepidation
(A) Boldness (B) Fearlessness
(C) Fright (D) Dread

48. Traduce
(A) Extol (B) Malign (C) Vilify (D) Revile

49. Touchy
(A) Snappish (B) Testy (C) Stolid (D) Peevish

50. Thaw
(A) Solidify (B) Melt (C) Liquefy (D) Dissolve

51. Thankful
(A) Grateful (B) Obliged (C) Obligated (D) Ungrateful

52. Testify
(A) Refute (B) Attest (C) Endorse (D) Witness

53. Terrify
(A) Embolden (B) Intimidate (C) Horrify (D) Appal

54. Tenacious
(A) Lax (B) Steadfast (C) Pertinent (D) Persistent

55. Temperate
(A) Extreme (B) Moderate (C) Restrained (D) Controlled

56. Temerity
(A) Audacity (B) Timidity
(C) Hardihoodness (D) Recklessness

57. Tardy
(A) Punctual (B) Sloth (C) Slow (D) Delayed

58. Tangible
(A) Palpable (B) Tactile
(C) Perceptible (D) Untouchable

59. Deft
(A) Adroit (B) Dextrous (C) Inept (D) Proficient

60. Survive
(A) Live (B) Continue (C) Continued (D) Succumb

61. Succinct
(A) Garrulous (B) Curt (C) Terse (D) Brief

62. Subtle
(A) Subliminal (B) Obvious
(C) Imperceptible (D) Indirect

63. Subside
(A) Relent (B) Aggravate (C) Decline (D) Decrease

64. Submissive
(A) Deferential (B) Yielding (C) Compliant (D) Intractable

65. Stop
(A) Start (B) Begin (C) End (D) Commence

66. Speak
(A) Talk (B) Utter (C) Hush (D) Tell

67. Corporal
(A) Somatic (B) Corporeal (C) Physical (D) Spiritual

68. Solemn
(A) Grave (B) Sedate (C) Cheerful (D) Staid

69. Indigent
(A) Impoverished (B) Impecunious
(C) Destitute (D) Affluent

70. Stern
(A) Strict (B) Stringent (C) Lenient (D) Harsh

71. Scanty
(A) Meagre (B) Plentiful (C) Sparse (D) Scarce

72. Savage
(A) Wild (B) Ferocious (C) Kind (D) Cruel

73. Sagacious
(A) Prudent (B) Reckless (C) Judicious (D) Foresighted

74. Sag
(A) Raise (B) Bend (C) Prolapse (D) Buckle

75. Sacred
(A) Holy (B) Divine (C) Profane (D) Pious

76. Rigid
(A) Stiff (B) Supple (C) Inflexible (D) Unbending

77. Libertine
(A) Licentious (B) Profligate (C) Righteous (D) Immoral

78. Preposterous
(A) Sound (B) Ridiculous (C) Farcial (D) Absurd

79. Reward
(A) Recompense (B) Wages
(C) Prize (D) Award

80. Revile
(A) Honour (B) Traduce (C) Asperse (D) Malign

81. Retreat
(A) Recede (B) Retract (C) Withdraw (D) Advance

82. Retard
(A) Impede (B) Accelerate (C) Decelerate (D) Slow down

83. Restraint
(A) Liberty (B) Constraint (C) Check (D) Regulate

84. Reluctant
(A) Averse (B) Loath (C) Disinclined (D) Disposed

85. Regal
(A) Royal (B) Imperial (C) Plebeian (D) Majestic

86. Sham
(A) Real (B) Counterfeit
(C) Fictitious (D) False

87. Readable
(A) Legible (B) Illegible (C) Distinct (D) Clear

88. Raze
(A) Construct (B) Demolish (C) Wreck (D) Refined

89. Raw
(A) Coarse (B) Crude (C) Rough (D) Refined

90. Ravage
(A) Protect (B) Pillage (C) Sack (D) Plunder

91. Raucus
(A) Strident (B) Hoarse
(C) Harmonious (D) Discordant

92. Rapture
(A) Bliss (B) Exaltation (C) Delight (D) Woe

93. Rankle
(A) Redolence (B) Stink (C) Stench (D) Reck

94. Rancour
(A) Ill-will (B) Spite
(C) Malice (D) Benevolence

95. Raging
(A) Fierce (B) Mild (C) Intense (D) Acute

96. Radical
(A) Root (B) Fundamental
(C) Shallow (D) Ouintessential

97. Rabid
(A) Sober (B) Frenzied (C) Violent (D) Raving

98. Quell
(A) Crush (B) Suppress(C) Stiffle (D) Foment

99. Queer
(A) Odd (B) Strange (C) Familiar (D) Outlandish

100. Quash
(A) Validate (B) Nullify (C) Annul (D) Cancel

101. Quandary
(A) Plight (B) Predicament
(C) Dilemma (D) Certainty

102. Provident
(A) Frugal (B) Prodigal (C) Thrifty (D) Sparing

103. Provide
(A) Deprive (B) Endow (C) Bestow (D) Afford

104. Supercilious
(A) Meek (B) Overbearing
(C) Haughty (D) Disdainful

105. Protract
(A) Retract (B) Spread (C) Expand (D) Elongate

106. Propensity
(A) Proclivity (B) Predisposition
(C) Aversion (D) Tendency

107. Propel
(A) Halt (B) Actuate (C) Impel (D) Drive

108. Propagate
(A) Transmit (B) Relay (C) Spread (D) Hold back

109. Prolific
(A) Fecund (B) Effete (C) Productive (D) Fertile

110. Prodigious
(A) Usual (B) Marvellous
(C) Remarkable (D) Astonishing

111. Primordial
(A) Modern (B) Pristine (C) Quaint (D) Primitive

112. Pretend
(A) Be honest (B) Profess (C) Feign (D) Affect

113. Precarious
(A) Dependent on mercy (B) Unsafe
(C) Perilous (D) Secured

114. Postpone
(A) Defer (B) Prepone (C) Delay (D) Adjourn

115. Phlegmatic
(A) Passionate (B) Impassive (C) Sluggish (D) Lazy

116. Philanthrope
(A) Benevolent (B) Humane
(C) Altruist (D) Misanthrope

117. Petty
(A) Significant (B) Pattry (C) Trivial (D) Trifling

118. Pester
(A) Chafe (B) Annoy (C) Bother (D) Console

119. Pertinent
(A) Relevant (B) Extraneous
(C) Germane (D) Apropos

120. Perspicacious
(A) Discerning (B) Understanding
(C) Unknowing (D) Wise

121. Perspicuous
(A) Transparent (B) Limpid (C) Opaque (D) Visible

122. Persist
(A) Cease (B) Persevere (C) Endure (D) Continue

123. Persecute
(A) Harass (B) Torment (C) Harry (D) Help

124. Perpetual
(A) Ephemeral (B) Eternal (C) Unceasing (D) Everlasting

125. Penitent
(A) Remorseful (B) Contrite
(C) Repentant (D) Remorseless

126. Parsimonious
(A) Miser (B) Generous (C) Stingy (D) Niggardly

127. Pacify
(A) Agitate (B) Lull (C) Calm (D) Compose

128. Overbearing
(A) Humble (B) Domineering
(C) Imperious (D) Dominant

129. Outdated
(A) Obsolete (B) Old-fashioned

(C) Haute couture (D) Outmoded

130. Ostracize
(A) Banish (B) Excommunicate
(C) Admit (D) Exile

131. Onerous
(A) Facile (B) Arduous (C) Sisypheous(D) Taxing

132. Offer
(A) Proffer (B) Tender (C) Deny (D) Propose

133. Offend
(A) Outrage (B) Flatter (C) Provoke (D) Irritate

134. Obvious
(A) Obscure (B) Patent (C) Manifest (D) Apparent

135. Obtain
(A) Acquire (B) Possess (C) Attain (D) Forfeit

136. Obdurate
(A) Callous (B) Stubborn (C) Tender (D) Tough

137. Nurture
(A) Cherish (B) Rear (C) Cheer (D) Neglect

138. Novice
(A) Expert (B) Greenhorn
(C) Caddie (D) Neophyte

139. Novel
(A) New (B) Unique (C) Original (D) Trite

140. Nervous
(A) Upset (B) Rattled (C) Flustered (D) Tranquil

141. Friendly
(A) Amicable (B) Congenial (C) Amiable (D) Hostile

142. Negligent
(A) Lax (B) Indifferent
(C) Meticulous (D) Remiss

143. Nebulous
(A) Hazy (B) Fuzzy (C) Clouded (D) Distinct

144. Spruced
(A) Unkempt (B) Tidy (C) Preened (D) Elegant

145. Sloppy
(A) Slovenly (B) Slut (C) Dirty (D) Smart

146. Native
(A) Alien (B) Aborigine
(C) Indigenous (D) Autochthon

147. Narrow-minded
(A) Cosmopolitan (B) Provincial
(C) Parochialism (D) Catholic

148. Murky
(A) Gloomy (B) Obscure (C) Dark (D) Clear

149. Muster
(A) Garner (B) Collect (C) Scatter (D) Marshall

150. Mumble
(A) Mutter (B) Whisper (C) Stammer (D) Shout

151. Monotonous
(A) Humdrum (B) Tedious (C) Boring (D) Exciting

152. Mar
(A) Spoil (B) Impair (C) Make (D) Damage

153. Mad
(A) Sane (B) Insane (C) Crazy (D) Demented

154. Luscious
(A) Delicious (B) Delectable (C) Tasteless (D) Tasty

155. Loathsome
(A) Delightful (B) Abominable
(C) Odious (D) Unpleasant

156. Linger
(A) Tarry (B) Flit (C) Stay (D) Delay

157. Limber
(A) Supple (B) Flexible (C) Loose (D) Stiff

158. Liberate
(A) Emancipate (B) Deliver
(C) Enthral (D) Enfranchise

159. Liable
(A) Answerable (B) Amenable
(C) Likely (D) Exempt

160. Lethargic
(A) Active (B) Sluggish (C) Lazy (D) Dull

161. Legitimate
(A) Rightful (B) Lawful (C) Illicit (D) Licit

162. Learned
(A) Erudite (B) Scholarly (C) Pedantic (D) Ignorant

163. Laud
(A) Praise (B) Commend
(C) Extol (D) Criticise

164. Lament
(A) Laud (B) Deplore (C) Regret (D) Keen

165. Knack
(A) Ineptitude (B) Talent (C) Aptitude (D) Propensity

166. Kindle
(A) Ignite (B) Inflame (C) Arouse (D) Extinguish

167. Keen
(A) Astute (B) Blunt (C) Acute (D) Sharp

168. Joyous
(A) Melancholy (B) Mirthful (C) Blithe (D) Jovial

169. Jeer
(A) Scoff (B) Sneer (C) Fleer (D) Laud

170. Intrinsic
(A) Extrinsic (B) Inherent (C) Innate (D) Inborn

171. Intentional
(A) Deliberate (B) Contemplated
(C) Pre-meditated (D) Accidental

172. Insult
(A) Honour (B) Affront (C) Outrage (D) Indignity

173. Inquisitive
(A) Uninterested (B) Prying
(C) Curious (D) Inquiring

174. Innate
(A) Inborn (B) Congenital (C) Natural (D) Acquired

175. Detrimental
(A) Deleterious (B) Harmful (C) Injurious (D) Salutary

176. Inhibit
(A) Contain (B) Restrain (C) Bridle (D) Encourage

177. Inflate
(A) Distend (B) Dilate (C) Swell (D) Deflate

178. Just
(A) Iniquitous (B) Fair (C) Impartial (D) Proper

179. Frail
(A) Decrepit (B) Vulnerable
(C) Robust (D) Weak

180. Indolent
(A) Slothful (B) Sluggish (C) Torpid (D) Zestful

181. Indebted
(A) Un-obligated (B) Obliged
(C) Beholden (D) Grateful

182. Imply
(A) Connote (B) Denote (C) Mean (D) Assert

183. Implore
(A) Solicit (B) Entreat (C) Bestow (D) Importune

184. Impertinent
(A) Polite (B) Brazen (C) Impudent (D) Rude

185. Impair
(A) Improve (B) Mar (C) Spoil (D) Damage

186. Immerse
(A) Dunk (B) Sink (C) Submerge (D) Emerge

187. Immense
(A) Minuscule (B) Enormous
(C) Humongous (D) Vast

188. Immaculate
(A) Spotless (B) Tainted (C) Unblemished (D) Clean

189. Imitation
(A) Replica (B) Simile (C) Prototype (D) Magnette

190. Imitate
(A) Mimic (B) Ape (C) Simulate (D) Pioneer

191. Imbibe
(A) Exude (B) Drink (C) Assimilate (D) Eat

192. Imbecile
(A) Dullhead (B) Nincompoop
(C) Idiot (D) Clever

193. Imaginative
(A) Prosaic (B) Inventive (C) Visionary (D) Clairvoyant

194. Illusive
(A) Real (B) Misleading
(C) False (D) Unreal

195. Elusive
(A) Escaping (B) Unrealising
(C) Slipping (D) Apprehensive

196. Allusive
(A) Direct (B) Indirect (C) Hinting (D) Indicating

197. Ignorant
(A) Unaware (B) Familiar
(C) Oblivious (D) Un-informed

198. Ignominious
(A) Exalted (B) Abject (C) Despicable (D) Ignoble

199. Ideal
(A) Fantastic (B) Utopian (C) Impractical(D) Practical

200. Idea
(A) Notion (B) Impression
(C) Knowledge (D) Concept

201. Honesty
(A) Dishonesty (B) Sincerity
(C) Integrity (D) Uprightness

202. Hideous
(A) Attractive (B) Ugly (C) Unattractive (D) Repulsive

203. Holy
(A) Divine (B) Pious (C) Hallowed (D) Impious

204. Hobby
(A) Pastime (B) Vocation (C) Avocation (D) Occupation

205. Hire
(A) Employ (B) Enlist (C) Engage (D) Fire

206. Hide
(A) Dissemble (B) Betray (C) Disguise (D) Cloak

207. Latent
(A) Dormant (B) Inactive (C) Invisible (D) Patent

208. Hesitation
(A) Conviction (B) Scruple (C) Suspense (D) Doubt

209. Hesitate
(A) Demur (B) Waver (C) Falter (D) Resolve

210. Abet
(A) Connive (B) Assist (C) Thwart (D) Collude

211. Acme
(A) Apex (B) Pinnacle (C) Vertex (D) Base

212. Hearty
(A) Cordial (B) Earnest (C) Warm (D) Cool

213. Cheerful
(A) Dispirited (B) Animated (C) Exhilarated (D) Elated

214. Forlorn
(A) Sad (B) Desolate
(C) Disconsolate (D) Exulted

215. Healthy
(A) Wholesome (B) Salutary (C) Salubrious (D) Noxious

216. Hatred
(A) Dislike (B) Ill-will (C) Loathing (D) Affection

217. Hate
(A) Loathe (B) Abominate (C) Admire (D) Abhor

218. Scurry
(A) Scamper (B) Scoot (C) Sprint (D) Lurch

219. Expedite
(A) Hasten (B) Accelerate (C) Dawdle (D) Quicken

220. Harmony
(A) Accord (B) Concord (C) Discord (D) Unison

221. Hamper
(A) Hinder (B) Obstruct (C) Thwart (D) Expedite

222. Hallow
(A) Dishonour (B) Exalt (C) Glorify (D) Consecrate

223. Guile
(A) Wile (B) Craftiness (C) Chicanery (D) Innocence

224. Grow
(A) Bloom (B) Snowball (C) Shrink (D) Burgeon

225. Grief
(A) Joy (B) Woe (C) Distress (D) Anguish

226. Govern
(A) Rule (B) Submit (C) Reign (D) Command

227. Gorgeous
(A) Ugly (B) Grand (C) Dazzling (D) Magnificent

228. Fade
(A) Wither (B) Shrivel (C) Decay (D) Enliven

229. Glut
(A) Teen (B) Swarm (C) Overflow (D) Deplete

230. Dismal
(A) Sullen (B) Sad (C) Gay (D) Dreary

231. Confer
(A) Deny (B) Bestow (C) Award (D) Grant

232. Fuzzy
(A) Hazy (B) Blurred (C) Obscure (D) Lucid

233. Imminent
(A) Impending (B) On the anvil
(C) Ulterior (D) In the offing

234. Futile
(A) Fruitful (B) Vain (C) Worthless (D) Useless

235. Fury
(A) Wrath (B) Rage (C) Fierveness (D) Calmness

236. Furtive
(A) Clandestine (B) Surreptitious
(C) Unhidden (D) Secret

237. Brawl
(A) Melee (B) Skirmish (C) Strife (D) Peace

238. Frail
(A) Fragile (B) Delicate (C) Sturdy (D) Dainty

239. Formidable
(A) Unimpressive (B) Imposing
(C) Forbidding (D) Awesome

240. Formal
(A) Conventional (B) Ceremonious
(C) Proper (D) Informal

241. Forbid
(A) Permit (B) Ban (C) Prohibit (D) Disallow

242. Foe
(A) Friend (B) Enemy (C) Adversary (D) Antagonist

243. Capricious
(A) Fitful (B) Fickle (C) Unstable (D) Steady

244. Drooping
(A) Sagging (B) Limp (C) Prolapsing (D) Stiff

245. Ferocious
(A) Savage (B) Wild (C) Brutal (D) Innocuous

246. Famous
(A) Renowned (B) Infamous (C) Unknown (D) Eminent

247. Familiar
(A) Intimate (B) Acquainted
(C) Conversant (D) Unfamiliar

248. Feign
(A) Fake (B) Pretend (C) Malinger (D) Be honest

249. Foible
(A) Fraility (B) Strength (C) Peccadillo (D) Defect

250. Front
(A) Face (B) Facade (C) Visage (D) Rear

251. Extend
(A) Protrude (B) Project (C) Manhandle (D) Retract

252. Exhaust
(A) Replenish (B) Drain (C) Empty (D) Deplete

253. Excite
(A) Arouse (B) Incite (C) Stimulate (D) Lull

254. Eternal
(A) Everlasting (B) Perpetual (C) Transient (D) Endless

255. Evade
(A) Confront (B) Avert (C) Avoid (D) Parry

256. Erroneous
(A) Fallacious (B) Mistaken (C) Wrong (D) Accurate

257. Colossal
(A) Gargantuan (B) Gigantic
(C) Humongous (D) Tiny

258. Involve
(A) Engross (B) Engage (C) Occupy (D) Keep away

259. Elegant
(A) Unrefined (B) Polished (C) Refined (D) Cultured

260. Dissipate
(A) Conserve (B) Squander (C) Diffuse (D) Dwindle

261. Disperse
(A) Scatter (B) Collect (C) Disseminate (D) Sprinkle

262. Disgrace
(A) Odium (B) Dignity (C) Obloquy (D) Disrepute

263. Disdainful
(A) Regardful (B) Contemptuous
(C) Scornful (D) Disgraceful

264. Disavow
(A) Repudiate (B) Acknowledge
(C) Reject (D) Disown

265. Disaster
(A) Fortune (B) Calamity (C) Catastrophe (D) Misfortune

266. Din
(A) Hush (B) Voice (C) Hum (D) Clamour

267. Dextrous
(A) Deft (B) Adroit (C) Proficient (D) Clumsy

268. Deprive
(A) Restitute (B) Bereave (C) Strip (D) Snatch

269. Deliver
(A) Enslave (B) Emancipate
(C) Liberate (D) Rescue

270. Delicious
(A) Delectable (B) Savoury
(C) Unpalatable (D) Tasty

271. Decrepit
(A) Strong (B) Infirm (C) Rickety (D) Dilapidated

272. Decorate
(A) Garnish (B) Adorn (C) Deface (D) Beautify

273. Decent
(A) Comely (B) Seemly (C) Decorous (D) Vulgar

274. Daunt
(A) Deter (B) Intimidate (C) Dishearten (D) Encourage

275. Daring
(A) Timorous (B) Intrepid (C) Bold (D) Brave

276. Dandy
(A) Fop (B) Coxcomb (C) Sloven (D) Fashionable

277. Damnable
(A) Commendable (B) Execrable
(C) Outrageous (D) Evil

278. Zig-zag
(A) Meandering (B) Curved (C) Straight (D) Flexuous

279. Crave
(A) Hanker (B) Long (C) Desire (D) Dislike

280. Contrary
(A) Obedient (B) Stubborn (C) Wilful (D) Perverse

281. Contemplate
(A) Ponder (B) Disregard (C) Reflect (D) Think

282. Confess
(A) Confute (B) Refute (C) Admit (D) Accept

283. Compassionate
(A) Cruel (B) Benign (C) Kind (D) Merciful

284. Commendation
(A) Applause (B) Praise
(C) Condemnation (D) Approbation

285. Circumspect
(A) Vigilant (B) Wary (C) Provident (D) Heedless

286. Exhume
(A) Disinter (B) Excavate (C) Digout (D) Bury

287. Brag
(A) Vaunt (B) Swagger (C) Boast (D) Be modest

288. Banish
(A) Harbour (B) Exile (C) Deport (D) Oust

289. Banal
(A) Hackneyed (B) Trite
(C) Humdrum (D) Stimulating

290. Austere
(A) Lenient (B) Stern
(C) Harsh (D) Strict

291. Abandon
(A) Desert (B) Discard
(C) Relinquish (D) Acquire

292. Assemble
(A) Gather (B) Congregate
(C) Disperse (D) Collect

293. Ascend
(A) Soar (B) Rise
(C) Climb (D) Descend

294. Anxiety
(A) Nonchalance (B) Concern
(C) Apprehension (D) Disquiet

295. Board
(A) Embark (B) Alight
(C) Mount (D) Ride

ooo

Unit- 3
Sentence Correction

Parts of Speech

In English language, certain words acquire different meanings when they are used in different grammatical positions.

For example:

Ashok was scolded for his bad *play*. (noun)

Ashok *played* the game well. (verb)

In both these cases, the meaning of the word 'play' changes depending upon its usage as a noun (play) or a verb (played). This shows that the word gets its meaning by the function it performs. The different functions of a word are called the **PARTS OF SPEECH**.

Parts of Speech in English Language

English language, traditionally, has **eight parts of speech.** But in **modern grammar, two more have been added.** Thus, we have **ten parts of speech**, which can be categorised as:

Group A – *Open-class items*

- *i)* ***Noun*** – John, room, question, play
- *ii)* ***Adjective*** – happy, new, small, round
- *iii)* ***Adverb*** – really, quickly, slowly, then, there
- *iv)* ***Verb*** – search, play, grow, look, has, be, do

Group B – *Closed-system items*

- *i)* ***Article*** – the, a, an
- *ii)* ***Demonstrative*** – that, this
- *iii)* ***Pronoun*** – he, they, anybody, one, which
- *iv)* ***Preposition*** – of, at, in, without, in spite of

v) ***Conjunction*** – and, when, that, although

vi) ***Interjection*** – oh, ah, ugh, phew, alas

Group A consists of the parts of speech which grow in number and are indefinitely extendable. It is not possible to draw a list of all the nouns in English. New items are constantly being created and added to the list of already existing nouns, adjectives, adverbs and verbs. ***Group B,*** on the other hand, consists of those items which cannot normally be extended by the creation of additional terms.

Parts of Speech and Sentence Correction

A sentence is the smallest meaningful unit of a language. ***The Parts of Speech are the elements of a sentence.*** Very often, it is in these small constituent elements of language that major sentential errors occur. A bottom-up approach to the study of the language can help us tackle and master the sentence correction section. For this, it is essential to break up the language into its smallest constituent parts and try to understand each one of them separately.

Nouns

In traditional grammar, **nouns are defined as names of persons, places, animals and things, feelings, emotions, thoughts, attitude(s),** etc. Non-material nouns are also discussed under the category of abstract nouns. However, the broadest classification of nouns is between **countable** and **non-countable**. There is a great overlapping between the categories of non-countable and abstract nouns. But at times, the non-countable nouns assume countable characters.

For example:

Countable Nouns	*Non-countable Nouns*
Buy an evening paper.	Wrap the parcel in brown paper.
He's had many odd experiences.	This job requires experience.
I've had many difficulties.	He's not had much difficulty.

Nouns may be **singular** (dog, cat, house) or **plural** (dogs, cats, houses). A few nouns have the **same singular** and **plural** forms (deer, sheep, furniture). Some nouns are always used in their **plural** forms (scissors, trousers, pants, spectacles). Nouns which name a group of people or things are called **collective nouns** (bunch, band, mob, troop, herd, etc.), and those which name individuals, persons, unique places, or things are called **proper nouns** (India, John, the Suez Canal, etc.). The names of genre or species are called **common nouns** (book, sugar, water, pen, cow, etc. Feelings, emotions, ideas, thoughts, etc. are given the name of **non-material** or **abstract nouns** (anger, happiness, love, hatred, etc). We shall discuss the different kinds of nouns a little later. Let us first determine what are countable and non-countable nouns.

Countable Nouns		***Non countable Nouns***
Singular	***Plural***	
Apple	Apples	Water
Table	Tables	Air
Cow	Cows	Sand
Copy	Copies	Grief

Proper Nouns	***Common Nouns***	***Collective Nouns***	***Abstract Nouns***
Sita	Pen	Army	Anger
Jaipur	Paper	People	Hatred
Qutub Minar	Cow	Class	Joy

Parts of speech that also function as nouns

Some words in a given situation may take up the function of a part of speech. **Not only pronouns but also adjectives and verbs function as nouns, at times.**

For example:

Bangladesh is a *poor* (adjective) country.

The *poor* (noun) should be treated with sympathy.

The secretary *conducted* (verb) the meeting.

He was rewarded for his good *conduct* (noun).

Children *play* (verb) and enjoy.

The *play* (noun) enacted last night impressed the audience.

Pronouns

'Pro' means 'instead of' and 'nomen' means 'noun'. Hence **a pronoun is a word that stands in place of a noun**. The noun that the pronoun stands in place of is called its **antecedent**. For example:

The doctor called the patient in. Then the doctor examined the patient.

We should write this as:

The doctor called the patient in. Then *he* examined *him*.

'He' is the pronoun for 'doctor' while 'him' is the pronoun for its antecedent 'patient'.

The pronouns belong to the closed-system category of the parts of speech. Like their antecedent nouns, they are singular (I, he, she, it, this) and plural (they, we). 'Your' functions as singular as well as plural depending on the antecedent noun for which it is used. **There are eight categories of pronouns:**

Personal Pronouns – I, you, he, she, it, they

Possessive Pronouns – my, mine, him, his, her, its, their, theirs, your, yours

Demonstrative Pronouns – this, that, these, those

Interrogative Pronouns – who, whose, which, what, whom, why

Indefinite Pronouns – anybody, somebody, nobody, none either, each, one

Reflexive Pronouns – yourself, yourselves, himself, herself, itself, themselves

Reciprocal Pronouns – (Showing two people do the same thing)

For example: Mohan and Radha like each other.

Relative Pronouns – (Introducing relative clause)

For example: who(m), that, which, when, why, where, whose.

Adjectives

The word 'Adjective' comes from the Latin word meaning 'added to'. **Adjective is a word added to a noun and tells us more about the person or thing named in the noun.** For example: a lazy girl, a strong boy, a cruel master, a happy wife, a big ship, etc.

The words, 'lazy', 'strong', 'cruel', 'happy', 'big' say something about the nouns – girl, boy, master, wife, ship.

Adjectives can function as 'pre-modifiers' as well as 'post-modifiers', i.e. *they may be placed before or after a noun.*

For example:

We are a *small* family.

Here 'small' is a *pre-modifier* as it is placed before the noun, 'family'.

The house is *small.*

Here 'small' is a *post-modifier* as it is placed after the noun, 'house'.

Degrees of Comparison of Adjectives

There are **three degrees of comparison of adjectives**, i.e., **Positive, Comparative and Superlative.**

(a) **Positive** – This is the simplest form of the adjective. For example: He is a *strong* man.

(b) **Comparative** – This is used when two persons or things are being compared. For example: He is *stronger* than his father.

(c) **Superlative** – This is used when more than two persons or things are being compared. For example: He is the *strongest* boy of the class.

Examples of the degrees of comparison of Adjectives

Positive	*Comparative*	*Superlative*
Good	better	best
Late	later	latest
Old	older/elder	oldest/eldest
Many/Much	more	most
Easy	easier	easiest
Difficult	more difficult	most difficult
Harmful	more harmful	most harmful
Beautiful	less beautiful	least beautiful
Little	less	least
Far	farther	farthest
Thin	thinner	thinnest

Verbs

Words that express an action, a process, a position or state of being are called verbs.

For example: go, run, read, grind, clarify, be, being, deploy, remember, stay, is, etc.

Verbs have different forms to indicate the time when actions take place. These forms are called Tenses. There are three principal forms of tenses:

Simple Present Tense : Asha talks.

Simple Past Tense : Asha talked.

Simple Future Tense : Asha will talk.

Other forms of tenses include the following :

Present Continuous Tense	: Asha is talking.
Past Continuous Tense	: Asha was talking.
Future Continuous Tense	: Asha will be talking.
Present Perfect Tense	: Asha has talked.
Past Perfect Tense	: Asha had talked.
Future Perfect Tense	: Asha will have talked.
Present Perfect Continuous Tense	: Asha has been talking.
Past Perfect Continuous Tense	: Asha had been talking.
Future Perfect Continuous Tense	: Asha will have been talking.

The *subject of the verb is the word or group of words that performs the action of that verb.* In the above sentences, 'Asha' is the subject of the verb 'talk'. Similarly, *the object of the verb is the word or group of words that receive the action of the verb.* In the sentence, 'The horse hit the girl', 'the girl' is the object of the verb 'hit'.

A verb that requires an object to complete its meaning is called a Transitive Verb.

For example:

The patient needs exercise.

'Exercise' *is the object of the verb* 'needs' and this object is necessary to complete the meaning of 'The patient needs ....'.

A verb that does not need an object to complete its meaning but makes complete sense by itself is called an Intransitive Verb.

For example:

The boy cried.

The verb 'cried' *does not need an object to complete its meaning.*

Verbs like *is, am, are, was, were, will be, shall be, appear, seem* and *look are 'Incomplete Verbs'*. They need 'complements' to complete their meaning.

For example:

The boy *is* smart.

The word 'smart' is needed to complete the meaning of 'The boy is.......'

In the above sentence 'smart' is a **complement** and 'is' is a **linking verb** (or **incomplete verb**)

(A) **Finite form of the verb 'be'** – 'am', 'is', 'are', 'was', and 'were' are the finite forms of the verb 'be'.

For example:

I *am* leaving.

He *is* crying.

We *are* going.

In the above sentences, the word 'am', 'is' and 'are' are governed by the **person** and **number** of the subject **(I, he or we).**

(B) **Non-finite forms of the verb 'be'** – 'being', 'been' are the non-finite forms of the verb, 'be'.

The following sentences show that these forms of 'be' are not governed by the person and number of the subject.

You *will be* coming.

You *have been* beaten.

She *is being* scolded.

We *are being* abused.

Adverbs

An adverb is a word that adds something to the meaning of a verb, an adjective or an adverb.

For example:

Lizards crawl *fast.*

'Fast' is the adverb that adds something to the meaning of the verb 'crawl'.

He is *very* handsome.

'Very' is the adverb that adds something to the meaning of the adjective 'handsome'.

Handle it *very* delicately.

'Very' is the adverb that adds something to the meaning of the adverb 'delicately'.

An adverb can modify a phrase or a sentence too.

For example:

He is *just* in time.

'Just' modifies the phrase 'in time'.

Unfortunately, she missed the bus.

'Unfortunately' modifies the sentence, 'she missed the bus'.

Prepositions

A preposition is placed before a noun or a pronoun showing relationship with some other word.

For example:

The rat is *under* the table.

'Under' shows the relationship between the 'table' and the 'rat'.

The boy ran *after* the dog.

'After' shows the relationship between the 'boy' and 'ran'.

Prepositions can be classified as follows:

(A) **Simple Prepositions**

These prepositions are simple and short words that are elementary, i.e., they are not derived from any other word.

For example: in, on, with, out, under, till, down, off, since, of, through, etc.

(B) **Compound Prepositions**

These prepositions are compound words that are made up of words using prefixes.

For example: about, around, into, before, inside, beneath, upto, etc.

(C) **Phrasal Prepositions**

Phrasal prepositions begin and end with prepositions.

For example: at the top of, by virtue of, in case of, in favour of.

(D) **Participle Prepositions**

These prepositions are *present participles* in form but are actually prepositions.

For example: considering, permitting, concerning, owing, during, needing, etc.

Conjunctions

Conjunctions are *linking devices.* A conjunction is a word that joins words, phrases or sentences.

For example:

Bread *and* butter make a healthy breakfast.

Leave it *or* take it.

They may come in between the words/groups to be linked or in the beginning. For example:

Before she came in, I had finished working on the project.

Although it sounds well, I should show it to the boss before finally approving it.

Interjections

Interjections are *words of exclamations.* They express powerful emotions, like feelings of joy or pain, wonder, disgust, pity or fear.

For example:

Alas! What a pity that he has missed his target again!
Oh! How beautiful!

Note: Each interjection is followed by a sign of exclamation(!)

Exercises

A

Different kinds of mistakes appear in the following sentences. Rewrite them correctly. Answers are given at the end of the exercises.

(a) Make a list of the content of this box.

(b) What is the criteria of selection?

(c) The staff is having a party this evening.

(d) We lived in Hyderabad since 1987.

(e) I am begging your pardon.

(f) It is harder to be an honest man than to be a successful man.

(g) My loud voice made the asleep students wake up.

(h) Mathematics is more harder than Economics.

(i) That is the man which sold his car.

(j) My brother often is angry with me.

B

Correct the following sentences by putting the appropriate punctuation marks or proper verbs, adjectives, pronouns, prepositions, articles, adverb forms, etc.

(a) I have met him fifteen years ago.

(b) The colleges are closed in the whole of May.

(c) I can concentrate and study well in the night.

(d) Myself, Dr. William De-Souza.

(e) Will see you soon.

(f) Ram has more confidence.

(g) There are no any books for sale.

(h) He has left for Delhi last week.

(i) Bread and butter are everyone's need.

(j) Oh, what a pity.

How to Use Articles Correctly

Articles are **noun markers** as they signal the appearance of a noun. Usually, articles appear immediately before the noun or before some words or phrases that appear between the article and noun.

Kinds of Articles

There are three kinds of articles. The words **A, An,** and **The** are known as **Articles**. **A** and **An** are **indefinite articles**. They are also known as **countable articles** as they are used before the nouns that can be counted. **The** is a **definite article** which is also known as an **uncountable article**. The word **some** is also an uncountable article. *It is used before the nouns that cannot be counted.* We shall clarify more about countable and uncountable articles separately with the help of various examples.

Simple Examples of Article Usage

(a) A table, a nice table, a beautiful picture, a black cat, an umbrella, an inkpot, an owl, etc. are all examples of **indefinite article usage**.

(b) We met a strange man near *the* hospital. *The* man was wearing a red turban.

Both 'hospital' and 'man with a red turban' take the **definite article** 'the' before them as they indicate definiteness. The hospital about which the speaker is referring to is already known to the listener. It is, therefore, a particular hospital about which a reference is being made. The speaker uses 'the' before 'man' which implies that he was the same man whom he met near the hospital. Thus, both hospital and man take 'the' before them.

(c) We use 'some' to indicate that the number of things, articles or persons under reference is not known or cannot be counted.

For example:

Give me *some* sugar to make tea for *some* visitors.

Conditions for using Indefinite Articles - A and An

A is used before countable nouns giving consonant sounds and **an** is used before countable nouns that give vowel sounds. The following examples will clarify it.

A man, a book, a chair, a classroom, an umbrella, an inn, an anchor, an idea, an honest person, an honourable man, an orange, etc.

Therefore, you must remember that **an** is used **before a noun beginning with a vowel sound. But it is not used before a noun merely beginning with a vowel.** For example: Words like 'honest' or 'honourable' though they do not start with a vowel, yet they take 'an' before them, as these words start with vowel sounds.

Similarly, to use **an** before a word (noun) beginning with a vowel but not producing a vowel sound will be incorrect.

For example, to say 'an union' or 'an uniform' will be incorrect as both the words do not start with a vowel sound. Let us learn some rules to use articles.

Conditions for using A and An

A and **An** can be used under the following conditions:

- **A** is used with singular countable nouns, such as 'a man, a woman, a boy, a chair, a library, a classroom, a teacher, a job, a city, etc.
- **An** is also used to display similar situations, such as 'an idea, an umbrella, an elephant, an inkpot, etc.
- **A** or **an** are never used with plural and uncountable nouns. For example, it is wrong to say 'a water, a milk, an oil, a paint, a polish, etc.
- There is another rule when you can use **a** or **an.** If the uncountable noun is preceded by a *quantifier* such as 'a gallon of gas, an ounce of salt, a pack of ice-cream, etc., you can use **a** or **an** as required. If you can remember the above rules broadly, you are not likely to make mistakes in the use of the countable articles 'a' and 'an'.

Conditions for using The

The definite article, **The** can be used before every common noun whether countable or uncountable, but we must keep in mind the following conditions:

- We use the definite article **the** to refer back to a noun that has already been mentioned before. We have already provided a good example earlier. Let us try to understand it with another example. '*I met a woman in the street, last night. The woman was wearing a black dress. I saw her again this morning wearing the dress and walking swiftly towards the playground.*' When I said 'I met a woman' she was not known to me before. But second time, when I mentioned the same woman and the same dress I had already talked about, I used 'the' before both 'woman' and 'dress'.

- We use **the** in a context known to the speaker (writer/speaker, etc.) and the listener as mentioned in the above example. Let us examine the same example again. '*I met a woman in the street last night. The woman was wearing a black dress. I saw her again this morning wearing the dress and walking swiftly towards the playground.*' We used 'the' before 'street' and 'playground', as the listener as well as we knew it well which street and playground are being referred to. Thus, 'the' is used in a context known to both the listener and the speaker. It is a kind of identification made to something already known or which is already in the minds of the listener and the speaker.

Conditions where The **is not to be used**

- You should not use the definite article **the** without any purpose, as is quite customary with most people for whom English is a second language. For example, 'I met the strange man in the street.' In this case, the correct sentence would be, 'I met *a* strange man in *the* street.'

- No articles are used before a proper noun, such as the names of countries and cities.

- When we mention countable nouns referring to a class, we do not use the definite article. We also do not use the definite article when we refer to uncountable nouns that possess a 'general meaning.' For example, 'Europeans eat a lot of apples in their breakfast', would be correct, but to say that 'Europeans eat a lot of the apples ...' would be incorrect.

Exceptions to the Rule

- But there are exceptions to these rules. When we refer to the large regions, we use the definite article, such as 'the U.K.' or 'the USA', or refer to the names of the rivers, such as 'the Ganges', 'the Yamuna'. In the same way, we use 'the' before names of mountain ranges, such as 'the Himalyas', etc. We use a definite article before the single entities also, such as 'the sky', 'the sun', 'the earth', 'the equator', etc.
- No articles are used before common nouns except when a special function is denoted. For example, '*She went to bed'. It means, 'She went to sleep.*' But if we say, '*She went to the bed,' it would mean 'she reached the bed.*' Another example, '*Ramesh is at school',* But if we say, '*We shall meet him at the school',* would simply refer to the meeting place, i.e. the school.

Exercises

Note: *Please rewrite the following sentences by inserting or dropping articles wherever necessary. Look at the answers only when you have finished the exercises.*

1. There is the dirt on the door.
2. Give him the glass of the milk and put a sugar in it.
3. Give him some ink to write the letter.
4. She gave me books last night.
5. The good student is never late for the lessons.
6. The banana has the sweet taste.
7. She always likes to read the books in restaurant.
8. Please give her the food and the cup of milk.
9. An door of living room is wide open.
10. A youngest son is at the college now.
11. The birds can fly very high in sky.
12. The horses are animals.
13. The girls wear the beautiful dresses.
14. The children love the sweets.
15. She has pen and a piece of paper.
16. The Indian sheep give us a good wool.
17. The bread is made with the flour, sugar and the milk.

18. She wants the doll with blue eyes.
19. A car she drives often makes a loud noise.
20. Please write your name legibly on blackboard.

Structure of Varied Sentences

When we speak or write, we use a group of words that makes a sentence.

For example:

John is going to school.

Sheela has finished her work.

However, if we use the same group of words as under, it does not make a sentence.

To is John school going.

Sheela her work has finished.

Do the above sentences make any sense? Certainly not. Therefore, until we use words in a certain fixed pattern or order, with proper punctuation, it will not make any sense. Let us examine what a sentence is.

A sentence is a group of words arranged in a certain fixed pattern or order based on grammar which conveys a complete meaning as well as complete sense.

Every sentence must have a subject and a predicate, which essentially contain a finite verb. A subject is a person or thing we are speaking about. The words that tell something about the subject, together form a predicate. Hence, each sentence has two parts.

For example:

Subject	*Predicate*
Birds	fly.
My brother	has passed the exams.
The old man	had no son.

In this chapter, we shall discuss broadly two categories of sentences — **Sentence Patterns** and **Sentence Structures**.

Sentence Pattern

A sentence may contain any or all of the following **five elements,** such as, **subject, verb, object, (direct and indirect), complement** and **adverbial.**

1. Subject

We may call it the *heart of a sentence.* It is the most essential part of a sentence. It is mainly **a word** or a **group of words** about which the sentence is.

Usually, a sentence begins with a subject.

For example:

Prakash has a good memory.

Borrowed garments never fit well.

Sometimes, a subject can be put at the end of a sentence too.

Down went *the Royal Convoy.*

Sweet are the uses of *adversity.*

Certain sentences start with a verb and the subject is omitted.

For example:

Sit down. (The subject 'you' is left out.)

Thank you. (The subject 'I' is left out.)

2. Verb

It is the second most important element of a sentence. Each sentence must contain at least a **finite verb**. For example:

She *is singing.* ('She' is **a subject**, and 'is singing', **a verb.**)

How old *are* you?

Please *lend* me your pen.

How beautiful you *look*!

3. Object

Most transitive verbs take an **object**. *Transitive* means *passing over. Transitive verbs* are those verbs that denote an action which *passes over* from the doer (subject) to an object. These objects are of two kinds: **Direct object** and **Indirect object**.

(a) Direct Object

It is a word, a phrase or a clause affected by a verb.

He teaches *English.*

He gave a *book.*

No one knew how to make a *beginning.*

I said that I would never understand *that.*

In order to identify a direct object, better ask a question beginning with 'what' 'who' or 'why', etc. It will immediately help you know the object. For example:

He gave, what? The answer is – 'book'.

No one knew, what? The answer is – 'how to make a beginning'.

(b) Indirect Object

It is a person or thing for whom or which the action is performed.

For example:

He gave *me* a book.

He teaches *us* English.

In order to identify an indirect object, you may ask a question for whom the action is being performed.

For example:

To whom was the book given? Answer is 'me'. Hence, '*me*' is the indirect object. It should be remembered that **an indirect object always precedes a direct object.**

The teacher gave *me* a prize.

The mother told *us* a story.

Who teaches *you* mathematics?

4. Complement

A sentence is usually complete with a subject, verb and object, but sometimes, it does not make complete sense even if these elements are present in a sentence. In that case, we add some words to make complete sense. The words which complete the sense function as a **complement**.

For example:

The boys made Rama *captain.*

She made him *laugh.*

The baby seems *happy.*

The cup is full *up to the brim.*

The rose smells *sweet.*

5. Adverbial

An adverbial phrase, adverb or adverb clause used in a sentence is known as an **adverbial**. There may be more than one adverbial in a sentence, such as:

She runs *quickly.*

I have done well *on the whole.*

Since you have done this, *I shall punish you.*

Thus, a sentence is made up of ***five elements*** only. With the addition of each element, a sentence becomes relatively more narrative and it conveys clear and multiple information. Most of the sentence construction errors are natural and connected with the five elements. Let us examine what a sentence structure is.

Sentence Structure

Sentences are of three types — ***Simple, Compound*** *and* ***Complex.***

Simple Sentence

It has only one **finite verb. In other words, a simple sentence consists of a subject and a predicate.**

The Moon was bright.
(subject) (predicate)

They played football.
(subject) (predicate)

Compound Sentence

A compound sentence consists of two or more than two simple sentences. For example:

'The moon was bright and *we could see our way'.* This sentence has two main clauses. Each has a finite verb. Both of them are linked with *'and'.* Such sentences may have more than two simple sentences, but each sentence must have a finite verb. For example:

The moon was bright, the sky was clear and *we could see our way.*

The sun set and *the night came on.*

Men may come and *men may go* but *I stay on forever.* In the above compound sentences, each clause is independent and makes complete sense.

Complex Sentence

It has one main clause and one or more than one subordinate clause.

For example:

I returned home as *I was tired.*

(main clause) (subordinate clause)

Clauses

In the above sentence, there are two finite verbs, which means two clauses. 'I returned home' is the main clause. It makes complete sense. Therefore, it is independent in itself. '*As I was tired*' is a dependent or subordinate clause because it does not make complete sense. **A subordinate clause may be a noun clause, adjectival clause or an adverbial clause.** Let us discuss these three types of clauses.

Subordinate Noun Clause

It performs the role of a noun in a complex sentence. It can occur in the following positions:

(a) The subject of a verb: *What he said* was true.

(b) The object of a verb: No one knows *who he is.*

(c) The object to a preposition: There is no meaning in *what you say.*

(d) The complement to a verb: This is exactly *what everyone can understand.*

(e) In apposition to a noun or pronoun: The report *that he had submitted* is false.

Subordinate Adjectival Clause

Its function is that of an **adjective**, i.e., to tell something about a noun or pronoun. For example:

The house *we lived in* has been sold.

He is the boy *who stood first* in the class.

Subordinate Adverbial Clause

It performs mainly the function of an **adverb** adding to the meaning of the verb. See the following examples.

Don't talk *while she is singing.*	(Adverb of time)
You may put it *where you like.*	(Adverb of place)
Write it down *lest you forget all about it.*	(Adverb of purpose)
He will succeed *as he works hard.*	(Adverb of cause)

I will do this *if I am allowed.*	(Adverb of condition)
He worked so hard *that he was quite tired.*	(Adverb of effect)
He was so weak *that he could not even walk.*	(Adverb of result)
Ram is honest *although he is poor.*	(Adverb of contrast)
He likes you more *than (he likes) me.*	(Adverb of comparison)
Even if it rains I shall come.	(Adverb of concession)
Men will reap *as they sow.*	(Adverb of manner)

Phrases

A phrase *is a combination of words that make some sense but not complete sense.* It may also contain non-finite verbs (not affected by a person and number of the subject) such as, *'in the corner*', '*on the table*', and 'a *smiling* face', 'a *good looking* person', etc.

Like a clause, a phrase may also function as a noun, an adjective or an adverb. Remember that a phrase will either *have a subject or an object.* It will never have both. In case it has both, it will not be treated as a phrase but will be known as a **clause. Phrases are of three types, such as noun phrase, adjectival phrase and adverbial phrase.**

Noun Phrase

Your mother will not do this for you.

Our duty is to serve *our country.*

He wants *to go home.*

Adjectival Phrase

He is a *good looking* man.

She has a ring *made of gold.*

I like to see a face *with a smile on it.*

Adverbial Phrase

I have done well *on the whole.*

She left *at sunrise.*

He fell *to the ground.*

A phrase may include a non-finite verb at times but never a finite verb.

Non-finite verbs are of three types: The Infinitive, The Gerund and The Past Participle.

I. The Infinitive

It is usually preceded by 'to' and functions as a noun/pronoun in a sentence. **In short, the infinitive is a verb + noun.** For example:

To err is human.

Birds love *to sing.*

They always tried *to find* fault with me.

The speaker is about *to begin.*

II. The Gerund

It is that form of a verb, that ends in '-ing' and works as a verb + noun.

Sleeping is necessary for health.

Seeing is believing.

I like *reading* poetry.

III. Past Participle

It is the form of verb which usually ends in -ed, -d, -t, -en or -n. It is also known as Verbal Adjective.

For example:

A *retired* officer lives nearby.

A *failed* candidate, a *faded* rose, a *fallen* city, etc.

While using past participle, we must remember the following:

(a) **If a verb is transitive (having an object), the past participle will never be used in active voice, but only in passive.**

Iron is a metal *dug out* of the earth.

(b) If the **verb is intransitive, past participle is not used** at all. In case, it is used as a participle, it must precede a noun and should not be followed by it.

For example:

The *departed* guest, the *dead* horse, an *abandoned* house, etc.

(c) It is sometimes used to express some permanent habit, state, or character. For example:

A well *read* man, an out *spoken* lady, a *broken* heart, etc.

Exercises

Please identify the right clauses in the following sentences. Answers are provided at the end of the exercises. Read the examples carefully to enable you to answer the questions.

1. Don't talk *while she is singing*. (Adverb clause of time/purpose)
2. Keep it in mind *lest you should forget* all about it. (Adverb clause of time/purpose/place)
3. He thinks *because he is rich,* he can buy justice. (Adverb clause of purpose/cause or reason)
4. I'll live, *where you live*. (Adverb clause of time/place).
5. *As you sow,* so shall you reap. (Adverb clause of purpose/manner)
6. You can pass *provided you work hard.* (Adverb clause of manner/ condition)
7. She is younger *than she looks*. (Adverb clause of degree or comparison/ manner/condition)
8. He was so tired *that he could hardly walk.* (Adverb clause of manner/result)
9. *Even if I fail* I shall not give up hope. (Adverb clause of purpose/ contrast or supposition)
10. *Why she told a lie* is not clear. (Noun clause/Adverb clause)
11. No one knows *who she is*. (Noun clause/Adjective clause)
12. This is the place *where I was born*. (Noun clause/Adverb clause)
13. He is a man *whom we all respect.* (Adjective clause/Adverb clause)
14. He saves money *so that he may grow rich*. (Noun clause/Adjective clause)
15. He is as foolish *as lazy he is*. (Noun clause/Adverb clause)
16. He is energetic *although he is old.* (Adjective clause/Adverb clause)
17. I hate such men *as are false to their friends*. (Noun clause/Adjective clause)
18. Pay attention *to what your teacher says*. (Noun clause/Adjective clause)
19. Do *as you like*! (Adverb clause/Noun clause)
20. She began to pray *that God might forgive her*. (Noun clause/ Adverb clause)

Agreement of Verb with Subject

The verb should agree with its subject in number and person as well.

Rule-1

(a) ***A singular subject takes a singular verb and a plural subject is followed by a plural verb form.*** **This is called the Subject-Verb Agreement.**

For example:

Deepak is reading a storybook.

There is a playground beside the main school building.

Boys are playing football.

There are twenty boys in my class.

The stars shine in the night.

(b) ***Two or more singular subjects joined by 'and' take a verb in the plural.***

For example:

Kapil and Shyam are friends.

He and I are classmates.

Mohan and his sister have gone to school.

(c) ***If two singular nouns, joined by 'and' refer to the same person or thing, the verb is singular.***

For example:

The great orator and poet is dead.

The Secretary and Treasurer is absent.

Notice that the verb 'is' used only once when the two nouns refer to the same person. If different persons are referred to, a plural verb will be used for the nouns.

The orator and the statesman are dead.

(d) ***If two singular nouns joined by 'and' express one idea, the verb is singular.***

For example:

Slow and steady wins the race.

Truth and honesty is the best policy.

Curry and rice is my favourite food.

(e) ***The verb is usually singular, when 'each' or 'every' follows a singular subject. Or, if a singular subject is preceded by 'each' or 'every', the verb is usually singular.***

For example:

Every man, woman and child was happy.

Each day and night is pleasant in the spring.

Every boy and girl was present in the meeting.

Rule-2

When two subjects are joined with 'as well as' or together with, the verb should agree with the first subject.

For example:

The house, with its furniture, was burnt.

The captain, with all his men, was drowned.

Hari, as well as Anil, likes music.

Sita, and not you, has solved this problem.

Rule-3

(a) **Two or more singular subjects connected by *or, nor, either... or, neither... nor, not only....but also, take a verb in the singular.***

For example :

Ram or Shyam is to blame.

Either Sita or Leela was singing a song.

Neither Raman nor Balu was present.

Not only Ram, but also Sohan was present there.

(b) **If one of the subjects is in the plural, verb must be in *plural and the plural subject must be placed next to the verb.***

For example:

Gopi or his friends have done this.

Either Shyam or his parents were given a prize.

Neither Ali nor his friends are present.

(c) ***When two subjects are joined by 'or or 'nor' and indicate different persons, the verb agrees with the subject nearest to it.***

For example:

Either he or I am mistaken.

Neither Daleep nor you are guilty.

But such sentences can be put in a better way as –

Neither Daleep is guilty nor you are.

Rule-4

Either, neither, each, every, every one, and many a, must always be followed by a verb in the singular.

For example:

Either of the two boys has done this.

Neither of the two boys has done this.

Each of the boys was clever.

Every boy and every girl was given a prize.

Every one of them has told a lie.

Many a boy has not done his duty.

Rule-5

A collective noun (like committee, assembly, congress, jury) may take a singular or a plural verb. If the collection is thought of as a whole, a singular verb is used, but if the individuals or members of the group are thought of separately, a plural verb is used.

For example:

The committee have decided this.

The jury has given its verdict.

Note: 'The committee have decided this' means 'the members of the committee have decided this'. Similarly:

'The jury has given its verdict' means 'the members of the jury are not divided in their verdiot'.

Rule-6

(a) ***Some nouns, which are plural in form but singular in meaning, take a singular verb.***

For example:

No news is good news.

Mathematics is a difficult subject.

The wages of sin is death.

(b) ***Some nouns, which are singular in form but plural in meaning, take a plural verb.***

For example:

According to the present market rate, twelve dozen cost rupees one hundred.

Rule-7

(a) ***When the plural noun is the name of one thing (say, a book or a country), it takes a singular verb.***

For example:

The Arabian Nights is a storybook.

The United States has a big army.

(b) ***When the subject of a verb is a relative pronoun, the verb must agree with the number and person with the antecedent of the relative pronoun.***

(Antecedent means – A thing coming before something else).

For example:

I, who am your friend, will help you through thick and thin.

You, who are my friend, should not blame me.

He, who is my friend, should stand by me.

She is one of the bravest women that have ever lived.

Rule-8

The verb must always be made to agree with its proper subject instead of with the noun near it.

For example:

The *quality* of these mangoes *is* good.

The *behaviour* of the children *was* praiseworthy.

Rule-9

The case of 'each' and 'none' is slightly complicated. 'None' is not always singular, it could be either singular or plural, depending upon the context in which it is used.

For example:

None of the horses *were* injured.

None of the food *was* eatable.

None of the glasses *were* dirty.

The above sentences give the impression of many glasses or the condition of all the glasses; whereas the sentence 'none of the glasses was dirty' has the effect of individualising each glass.

In case of 'each', the word takes a singular verb, when it is subject of a sentence, acting as a pronoun as in 'Each was given ninety seconds to paint a doll.'

But when 'each' is used as an addition to a subject, it takes a plural verb as in 'We each were given ninety seconds to paint the doll.'

Rule-10

(a) ***If a subject consists of a collective noun (noun + of + plural noun) such as 'bunch of keys', it will take a singular verb.***

For example:

The bunch of keys is lost.

A herd of cattle grazes in his fields.

(b) ***If a collective noun is used as a subject and indicates a single unit, it is appropriate to use a singular verb.***

For example:

The team *is* unhappy at the remarks of the coach.

However, when we say, 'The members of the team *were* unhappy with the remarks of the coach,' we will use a plural verb.

(c) **There is a subtle difference in the use of the phrases 'a number of' and 'the number of'.**

In the sentence, 'A large number of books were ordered by the library', the phrase, 'a number of' is clearly plural. However, the expression 'the number of' is distinctly singular, such as 'The number of library members has been declining over the years'.

Rule-11

(a) ***A singular verb is needed after 'one of + plural noun', and a plural verb is needed after 'more than one of + plural noun'.***

For example:

Ram is one of those students who rarely sings.

Here is one of the pens that were lost.

Concluding Remarks

The basic thing in **sentence correction** is to see whether the subject and the verb are in agreement. If they do not agree, the first part of detecting the error has already been done. If you find that there is no error in the subject-verb agreement, you need to check the tenses of all the finite verbs.

Exercises

Supply an appropriate verb at the missing place in each of the following sentences.

1. No news........................good news.
2. She is one of the best members that ....ever lived.
3. The chief, with all his men,..........massacred.
4. Justice, as well as mercy,................it.
5. Each of the sisters.............clever.
6. The quality of the mango..........not good.
7. Neither of the men..........very tall.
8. *Gulliver's Travels*..........written by Swift.
9. The wages of sin............death.
10. According to the present market rate, twelve dozen ....rupees one hundred.
11. The fleet................set sail.
12. The military.....................called out.
13. The crew................large.
14. The crew......................taken prisoners.
15. He and I.................well.
16. You and he.................birds of the same feather.
17. Either he or I..................mistaken.

18. Neither you nor he.............to blame.

19. Ram or his brothers............done this.

20. No nook or corner................left unexplored.

Tenses and Parallel Constructions

A tense is usually described as a form of verb, which indicates the time of an action. But this is only half the truth. ***A tense in its real sense is a grammatical category, which expresses much more than the time of an action.*** It tells about the aspects (progressive, perfect, the mood, conditions, completion, non-completion of an action, process, etc,. Though there are several rules regarding the uses of tenses, it is pertinent to discuss a single rule, which can help one to avoid errors in the use of tenses.

Rule

If a sentence starts with a particular tense, the same tense should be carried forward in the rest of the sentence. In other words, all the finite verbs in a single sentence must have the same tense. For example:

> 'When she *is* given any responsibility, she *carries* it out to the best of her abilities and always *did* her work in time too.'

In this sentence, the first two clauses have present indefinite tense while the tense in the last clause is in past tense, which is incorrect. In order to correct it, the same tense should be used throughout.

For example:

> When she *is* given any responsibility, she *carries* it out to the best of her abilities and always *does* her work in time too.

Another example:

> Subhash will be *relaxing* in a pleasant climate in Simla while we *perspire* in the scorching heat of Delhi.

The rule says that the future continuous tense used In the first part of the sentence should continue till the end.

> Subhash will be *relaxing* in a pleasant climate in Simla while we will be *perspiring* in the scorching heat of Delhi.

Exceptions to the Rule

1. **The use of past perfect**

   When two events take place in past, one followed by the other, the previous event will take a verb in past perfect while the later will take a verb in the simple past.

For example:

The train had left the station when we reached the platform.

The patient had already died before the doctor arrived.

2. The difference in time

When there is a definite difference in time between now and then or when action is clearly shown to precede the other in terms of a definite time frame, a present tense verb can sometimes be used to refer to events occurring in past or future. For example:

Last year, he could not pass, but this year, he is doing well.

John tells me that there was an accident last night.

Rules about Parallel Sentences

Several devices are used to join sentences. In compound sentences, the coordinate clauses are linked by conjunctions while in complex sentences, the subordinators function as linking devices to connect the subordinate clauses to the main clause.

Parallel construction sentences are those compound or complex sentences that contain clauses/phrases expressing a series of actions set off from one another by commas or conjunctions.

Too busy to pack her things herself, Jessica made a list of things to be taken, ordered a packed lunch, went into the *street calling a taxi.* (Incorrect)

In this sentence, four actions are mentioned:

Made a list of things, ordered a packed lunch, went into the street, calling a taxi

The first three actions are in simple past but the fourth action is in present continuous tense. According to the rules of parallel construction sentence, all phrases of a sentence must have similar phrase structures. Therefore, the verb in the last part of the sentence should be in the past tense.

Too busy to pack her things herself, Jessica made a list of things to be taken, ordered a packed lunch, went into the *street and called a taxi.* (Correct)

The same rule can be illustrated by using a few more examples.

The shorter the speech is, people understand it easily.

This sentence is incorrect, as the phrase in the second part of the sentence does not match the structure of the first part. It should be:

> The shorter the speech, the easier it is (for the people) to understand it.

Rule-1

In parallel sentences with single words or phrases, one should not mix the forms.

For example:

> Rahul likes to swim, playing cricket and go out with friends in the evening.

This sentence is an example of the mixed forms, hence it does not contain parallel construction. In order to correct it, one should write it as follows:

> *Rahul likes to swim, to play cricket and to go out with friends in the evening.*

Parallel Construction with Clauses

As with phrases, the rules of parallel construction apply to clauses as well.

For example:

> Pramila was happy caring for her family, looking after her parents and to watch television.

To make it a correct sentence with parallel construction, it should be written as:

> *Pramila was happy when she was caring for her family, when she was looking after her parents and watching television.*

If the voice of the two clauses in a sentence is different, then also the sentence is incorrect.

For example:

> The collector liked the proposal and
> *it was supported by the MLA too.* (Incorrect)

It should be written as:

> The collector liked the proposal and
> *the MLA supported it too.* (Correct)

A Note for the Examinees

Both the errors, pertaining to tenses and parallel constructions, are easy to locate. When you go through a sentence for the first time and see a series of actions or two/three clauses constructed in a similar fashion, you know that it is a parallel construction. Therefore, what you have to do is to find out where the form differs and mark the one which has a similar construction to that of the other phrases/clauses. If the sentence does not appear to be in the form of a parallel construction, find out whether all the finite verbs possess the same tense. In case they do not, see if there is a clear-cut variation in terms of the time gap. If such a variation does not exist and the verbs do not match, check up the options to determine whether there is an option which has a similar tense. This is, in fact, the right answer.

Exercises

Correct the following sentences. Answers are given at the end of the exercises.

1. When John is given any assignment he does it timely and completed it in all respect.
2. Ram gave the staff a luxurious party giving them expensive gifts too.
3. When the boss reached office all the clerks are playing cards.
4. The principal started praising his school, showing the photographs appreciated its garden too.
5. The members of the committee found him not guilty, he was acquitted by the jury too.
6. Children are happy to watch T.V., play cricket and visiting their friends.
7. Major Singh caught the enemy soldiers, tied them with ropes and bringing them to the quarterguard.
8. The writer writes story, types it and posted it.
9. The university offers courses in literature providing for improvement in language proficiency too.
10. When the inspector arrived the constables are smoking and gossiping.
11. The servant started cleaning the floor, watering plants and scrubbed the utensils.

12. The painter draws the sketch, mixes the colours and applied them too.
13. The head of the department submitted a proposal, it was supported by the dean too.
14. My friend did not see me for many years when I met him last week.
15. He was extremely annoyed when I reported the matter to him and has fired me.

Errors in The Use of Pronouns

A proper use of pronouns in English is of great value. ***A pronoun is a word that comes in place of a noun.*** There are various kinds of pronouns, such as **personal pronouns** (*I, me, you, yours, he, him, she, her*), **possessive pronouns** (*my, mine, ours, hers, their, his, yours*), **demonstrative pronouns** (*this, that, those, these*), **interrogative pronouns** (*who, whose, which, what*) and **reflexive pronouns** (*yourself, yourselves, himself, herself, itself, themselves*). **There are another kind of pronoun known as indefinite pronouns.** We call them indefinite as they reflect indefiniteness when referring to an object, person or a thing (anybody, anyone, anything, everyone, everybody, somebody, something, someone, no one, nobody, neither, either and nothing) etc. Pronouns used with nouns and doing the work of adjectives are known as **possessive adjectives**. For example: 'This is *his* book.' 'These are *your* books.' Let us examine and try to understand the rules that govern the use of pronouns in English.

Rule-1

Indefinite pronouns always use a singular verb. *When any one of the above referred to indefinite pronouns acts as a subject of a sentence or a clause, it requires a singular verb.* For example:

Nobody says that he was present in the meeting.

Everyone is ready to leave.

Everyone has boarded the bus.

Rule-2

There are good chances to commit errors when two pronouns are used in a sentence as objects. *It becomes more difficult and confusing as well when one of these pronouns is 'I'.* For example:

She requested me and my son to come to the theatre.

Both the above sentences are incorrect. The correct form will be as follows:

She requested my son and me to come to the theatre.

It is also correct to say, 'My son and I were requested (by her) to come to the theatre.'

Rule-3

Sometimes a pronoun has a double reference and it becomes difficult at that time to say whom the pronoun refers to.

For example:

(i) Some teachers maintain strict discipline in the class and their students dislike it.

In this case, it is not quite clear to whom the pronoun 'it' refers to? Does it refer to 'strict discipline' or the fact that 'some teachers maintain strict discipline'. This sort of confusion needs to be sorted out by rewriting the sentence correctly. Its correct form could be:

Some teachers keep strict discipline in the class and their students don't like that sort of discipline.

There can be more examples of that kind where confusion may occur because of an ambiguous sentence by the wrong use of a pronoun. For example:

(ii) Sheela and Meera went to school early in the morning but she could not deposit her fees.

In the above case, it is difficult to know who that 'she' is? Therefore, to make it clear it would be correct to say:

Sheela and Meera went to school but Meera (or Sheela) could not deposit her fees.

(iii) Similarly, when someone says:

Lalita and Lucy are good friends but she is so arrogant at times, that she soon starts fighting.

To clarify such a confusing statement, one has to be prudent and make its meaning clear. It would be correct to state:

Lalita and Lucy are good friends but Lalita is so arrogant at times that she soon starts fighting.

Rule-4

Pronouns should agree in person and number. It can easily be clarified with the help of a good example.

It would be wrong to state 'One should do their work regularly.' The correct form will be, 'One should do one's work regularly.' Let us examine one more example in this context:

> Susheel is a bachelor who is in quest of a good girl for him. So he often tries to look for a good girl whom he could marry. But whenever he meets them, he is unable to decide which of the girls he should choose.

This example has one great error. It is the use of 'them', which does not coincide with the noun, 'Susheel', which is singular in number. Therefore, in place of 'them' one should use 'a girl.'

A Final Word About Pronouns

Once you have analysed the subject-verb agreement and the tenses, you then need to see the pronouns and check for the following:

(a) What does the pronoun refer to? Is the antecedent of the pronoun clear?

(b) Does the pronoun agree in person and number with its antecedent? If you feel that the pronoun does not agree with its antecedent, check the options to see which of them corrects the error. If you are able to locate it, it means you have solved the problem. If the antecedent is pretty clear, then you have to check the options for a pronoun case. If everything seems all right, it could be a problem of a dangling or misplaced modifier. So let us study all that in the following chapter. For the time being, we shall examine the different types of errors (relating to pronouns) in this chapter.

1. Errors in Pronoun Subject-Object

Check if a pronoun is the subject or the object of a verb or preposition.

For example:

How could he blame she and he for the accident? (Incorrect)
How could he blame her and him for the accident? (Correct)

Another example:

All of us — Ravi, Meera, Alice, and me were on time. (Incorrect)
All of us — Ravi, Meera, Alice, and I were on time. (Correct)

2. Errors with 'who', 'whom' as an object

She did not know who I meant. (Incorrect)
She did not know whom I meant. (Correct)

They discussed for hours whom was better suited. (Incorrect)
They discussed for hours who was better suited. (Correct)
I really did not know who should I blame. (Incorrect)
I really did not know whom I should blame. (Correct)
She did not know who she should complain to about the electricity failure. (Incorrect)
She did not know whom she should complain to about the electricity failure. (Correct)

3. Errors relating to Pronoun Subject-Verb Agreement

It is important to understand that a pronoun and its verb agree in number. To eliminate such errors, one should remember that *the following are singular in number:*

anything	anyone	either	each	everyone	everything
neither	no one	nothing	what	whatever	whoever
either...or	neither...nor				

The following are plural in number:

both a few many several others

A few examples:

Meeta was away from the class but a few was there. Incorrect)
Meeta was away from the class but a few were there. (Correct)
Either of them are permitted to attend the function. (Incorrect)
Either of them is permitted to attend the function. (Correct)
Everyone from this class have to report to the Principal. (Incorrect)
Everyone from this class has to report to the Principal. (Correct)
Neither of them are good at debate. (Incorrect)
Neither of them is good at debate. (Correct)
No one from the invitees have come to attend the ceremony. (Incorrect)
No one from the invitees has come to attend the ceremony. (Correct)
Neither she nor he were able to give a good and proper presentation. (Incorrect)
Neither she nor he was able to give a good and proper presentation. (Correct)

However, if the noun immediately preceding the verb is plural, you need to use a plural verb.

For example:

Either her mother or her brothers is coming to attend the function. (Correct)

Either her mother or her brothers are coming to attend the function. (Correct)

4. Errors relating to Possessive Pronoun Agreement

Please remember that a possessive pronoun agrees in person and number as well.

For example:

Those of us who are interested in it should inform their director. (Incorrect)

Those of us who are interested in it should inform our director. (Correct)

If anyone remains absent, tell the director about them. (Incorrect)

If anyone remains absent, tell the director about him. (Correct)

Some of you will be required to clean their own room. (Incorrect)

Some of you will be required to clean your own room. (Correct)

Everyone of them should check in his own room. (Incorrect)

Everyone of them should check in their own room. (Correct)

5. Errors in the position of Relative Pronouns

Please keep in mind that a relative pronoun refers to the word preceding it. In case the meaning of the sentence is not clear, take it that the pronoun is placed in a wrong position.

For example:

She did not permit to enter the house the naughty children. (Incorrect)

She did not permit the naughty children to enter the house. (Correct)

Mixed Exercises on the Errors of Pronouns

Correct the mistakes and rewrite the sentences. Answers are given at the end of the exercises.

1. She is not so poor as me.
2. Satish and me are good friends, but at time Satish gets annoyed with them.
3. No one from the relatives have come to attend the function.
4. Please tell him not to forget to bring mine books.
5. Some of you will require to clean their own room.
6. Reema is as old as her.
7. Please don't leave the house without waiting for Prakash and you.
8. I have two of mine houses in the colony adjoining to your.
9. When did him leave to join the new college?
10. All of us — Mohan, Jatin, Shyam and me — did not reach home on time.
11. She did not know who I meant.
12. I want to know if you have seen a shirt of me.
13. One must try to do his work regularly.
14. She did not permit to enter the house the naughty children.
15. Neither he nor she were able to give a good presentation.
16. Either her mother or her brothers is coming to attend the function.
17. He was allowed to park the truck inside the building, which was quite convenient.
18. She really did not know who should she blame.
19. Everyone of us checked their rooms in the hotel around 2 p.m.
20. Those of us who love to visit the park should inform their hostel warden.

- Sentence errors take various forms. One of these areas is the placement of modifiers. Such errors result when there is some ambiguity in the meaning of a sentence.

Misplaced Modifiers

A Modifier is a word, phrase or a clause that adds to the meaning of other words in a sentence. A modifier must have unambiguous relation with other words and be placed as closely as possible to the word it modifies. A modifier placed before the word it modifies is called **pre-modifier** and the modifier placed after it is called a **post-modifier**.

There are certain rules, which need to be observed in the placement of the modifiers.

Rule-1

Modifiers must be placed as close as possible to the word they modify. Special care needs to be taken while using **the adverbial and adjectival phrases.**

For example:

Wanted a tutor for a student, M.A. in English literature. (Incorrect)

The intended meaning is:

Wanted a tutor, M.A. in English literature, to teach a student. (Correct)

Another example:

Wanted a maidservant for a baby, 26 years old. (Incorrect)

The intended meaning is not that a maidservant is required for a 26 years old baby, but it is:

Wanted a 26-year-old maidservant to look after a baby. (Correct)

Rule-2

A phrase beginning with 'As' should never be left unrelated i.e., the corresponding noun/pronoun must be stated after the adjectival phrase.

For example:

As a collector, the tension in the town is a concern.

'As a collector' is a phrase, it must refer to someone. The correct form of the sentence would be:

As a collector, *I am* concerned about the tension in the town.

Another example:

As a teacher, *I am* concerned about the absence of some students from the college.

Rule-3

If there is more than one noun/pronoun in a sentence, then the modifying participle should attach itself to the one which is nearest to it.

The problem occurs when the noun/pronoun to which the modifier is intended to refer is not placed next to the modifier.

For example:

While walking home, the traffic made him halt for more than an hour.

Appropriate changes are required in the above sentence to clarify the meaning.

While *he was* walking home, the traffic made him halt for more than an hour.

or

While walking home, *he was made to* halt for more than an hour due to heavy traffic.

Another example:

While driving the car, the police inspector ordered him to stop.

In this sentence, it appears as if the police inspector were driving the car. The intended meaning, however is:

While *he was* driving the car, the police inspector ordered him to stop.

or

While driving the car, *he was ordered by* the police inspector to stop.

These examples make it very clear that a modifier must have a noun or pronoun to go with it. For correcting the sentences with errors of this kind, an appropriate noun/pronoun needs to be placed at the right place.

Let us take another example:

Starting from the railway station, the university can be reached in half an hour.

The modifier 'Starting from the railway station' must be followed by a noun or pronoun to answer the question 'who starts from the railway station?' The error therefore, lies in the second part of the sentence. It would require an addition of a noun/pronoun like visitors/people/one/you, etc.

Starting from the railway station, *the visitors/people/you/one* can reach the university in half an hour.

If the modifier in a sentence given for correction is underlined, it has to be revised.

Starting from the railway station, the university can be reached within half an hour.

If the modifier is in the form of a non-finite phrase, the correct sentence should be the one which changes a non-finite verb into a finite verb with a subject of its own. Changing the phrase into a clause can do this.

If you start from the railway station, the university can be reached within half an hour.

It is just an example of the error of a misplaced modifier. The above mentioned rules are helpful in finding a correct alternative.

Exercises

Correct the following sentences.

1. Wanted a match for a beautiful girl, twenty-five years old.
2. Wanted a nurse for a baby, 20 years old.
3. As a teacher, the privatisation of education is a concern.
4. As a reviewer, increasing sex and violence in films is a concern.
5. As a political activist, falling moral standards in politics is a concern.
6. While preparing for interview, Mr. Bose gave me certain tips.
7. While visiting the homes of the victims, the public forced him to announce the relief measures.
8. Starting from the market, the secretariat can be reached in twenty minutes.
9. Starting from the college, the university office can be reached in twenty minutes.
10. As a journalist, entry of MNCs in print media is a concern.
11. As a conscientious citizen, rising crime rate disturbs.
12. While reading a book, the students stormed into the library.
13. While taking the examination, Dr. Roy reached his pockets.
14. Wanted a psychiatric doctor for a private clinic.
15. He bought a fresh basket of fruits.

Comparatives

- **Sentences or clauses that indicate some kind of comparison are called COMPARATIVES.** To make comparisons, we often use words like — 'than', 'like', 'as though', 'similar to'. The usage of comparatives is also ruled by certain basic rules.

Rule-1

While comparing two dissimilar things, it is important to bear in mind that we compare certain items having similar qualities or attributes. It can be clarified with the help of a pronoun or a modifying clause.

For example:

It is *as hot as* yesterday. (Incorrect)

The correct form of the sentence would be:

It is *as hot as it was* yesterday. (Correct)

We can give another example of this kind, such as:

The cotton of Japan is *superior to Egypt.*

It is incorrect, because, it reflects the comparison between 'cotton' and 'Egypt' and not between 'cotton of Japan' and 'cotton of Egypt'. The correct sentence would be:

The *cotton of Japan is superior to* the cotton *of* Egypt.

Rule-2

Don't compare a thing with the class it belongs to.

For example:

Roses smell sweeter than any flowers.

It is incorrect because smell and flowers are compared.

The correct sentence would be:

Roses smell sweeter than any *other flowers do.*

It is correct because the smell of roses and that of the flowers is being compared. One more example will clarify it further.

Gold is more expensive than any metals. (Incorrect)

Gold is more expensive than any *other metal.* (Correct)

Rule-3

Comparative constructions must not be ambiguous. They should be clear and easy to understand.

For example:

He hates television as much as his wife.

It is an ambiguous sentence which may mean that 'he hates television and his wife both', or 'he hates television and his wife also hates television'. Therefore, to make the meaning more clear, one must say:

He hates television as much as *he hates his wife.*

or

He hates television as much as *his wife does.*

Rule-4

We must be careful to use expressions like 'as good as'* and *'if not better than':

For example:

Mangoes are as cheap, if not cheaper than they were last year. (Incorrect)

The correct form of this sentence would be:

Mangoes are as cheap *as they were last year,* if not cheaper. (Correct)

Concluding Remarks

While looking for an error in comparatives, we need to keep in mind that a sentence comparing two things or a sentence having the words such as, 'as' 'than', 'like', etc., have been used correctly.

For example:

There were twice as many casualties in the riots this year than in the year before.

It simply compares two different things (number of casualties with the year). *So it is incorrect. The correct sentence would be*:

There were twice as many casualties in the riots this year than *those* in the year before.

Exercises

Fill up the blanks with the appropriate adjectives (comparative/ superlative).

Example: Which is the ...of the two. (good)
Which is the *better* of the two.

1. He is the ....boy in the class. (lazy)
2. He has seen.......days. (happy)
3. What is the ......news from America? (late)
4. It was the ....moment in my life. (proud)
5. Iron is ....than any other metal. (useful)

6. Mohan is........than any other student. (clever)
7. The population of Mumbai is.......than that of Delhi. (great)
8. Your coffee is not.........than mine. (good)
9. The houses of the rich are...............than those of the poor. (large)
10. Sheela is the ....of the three. (clever)
11. He is the................of all men in the village. (wise)
12. She is the ....student in the class. (smart)
13. He ran.................than everyone in the class. (fast)
14. She is the ....of all her sisters. (thin)
15. Gold is ....than silver. (cost)

- An idiom is a phrase or a group of words used to convey some special meaning that cannot be easily understood through a dictionary. ***An idiom can be defined as a set of words or a language, which has some specific character and which is peculiar to a country, district or group of people.*** Many phrasal verbs such as 'look after' or 'run over', are idiomatic. They convey special meanings and are frequently used when one communicates to the other. Most idioms are formed with the help of prepositions. The use of such idioms is conventional. ***There are no rules or assumptions to determine the correctness of an idiomatic expression except that it is used conventionally by some people and carries a special meaning in a particular situation.***

The simplest way to know the correctness of an idiomatic expression is to play by the ear. If you go on using the language correctly and encounter idiomatic expressions in between, it would become easier for you to know which idiom is correct at a particular situation. Only then you can play by the ear. Otherwise, there is no logical way to find out whether a particular idiom is correct or incorrect.

Some of the most common idiomatic expressions that at times may confuse you, are given below. Please go through them very carefully and try to understand them with the help of their usage on different occasions, and consult a good dictionary that gives the meanings of such expressions.

The Phrasal Verbs

Verbs preceded or followed by prepositions are known as phrasal verbs. These phrasal verbs are of two kinds — ***inseparable*** and ***separable. Inseparable verbs*** are generally formed by two words out of which one word is a preposition. ***Separable verbs*** are formed by a

verb + pronoun + preposition. The phrasal verbs that are formed by a **verb + preposition**, are ***inseparable.*** It will be grammatically wrong to separate them as by doing so, their meaning will be changed. Some common inseparable phrasal verbs (idiomatic expressions) that may be helpful in enriching your language have been given on the following page.

Phrasal Verbs (Inseparable verbs)	***Meanings***
Above board	Open, (frank) without deception
Agree with	Be of the same opinion
Appeal to	Make an earnest request
Arrange for	To settle or to adjust
Ask for	To invite trouble
Attend to	To give care and thought
Babble out	Talk mistaken or not understood
Back up	To support
Bear against	Having (a grudge) in the heart or mind.
Better of	To overcoming or winning
Blow out	To exhaust itself
Cry out	Crying until emotionally relieved
Call on	Pay a short visit
Care for	Look after
Clear up	Become clear
Direct to	To speak or to put address
Die away	Lose strength
Dig into	To push hard
Drop off	To become fewer or less
Drive hard	To put pressure on someone
Give in	To yield
Go back	Extend backwards in space or time
Hold up	Stop by use of threat or force
Look after	To take care
Pull up	Check, reprimand
Pull down	Weaken (of illness)
Run down	Knock down or collide
Send for	Ask or order to come

The *separable verbs* have also idiomatic meanings and are called phrasal verbs. They are separated (or joined) by a pronoun, a noun, a conjunction or a preposition, but they also form idiomatic expressions. A list of separable verbs (idioms), for the reference of the readers, is given below:

Phrasal Verbs (Separable verbs)	*Meanings*
Air it out	Expose
Argue it for	Give reasons for
Ask for it	Behaving to get in trouble
Back it up	Support
Bear it away	Carry it on/carry it off
Break it down	Divide, analyse and classify
Be up and about	Be out of bed and become alert
Bring it about	Cause to change direction
Bring it up	To educate, to call attention
Carry it forward	To transfer it to the head of a new page
Catch it up	Overtaking
Clear it away	Take it away, get rid of
Close it down	Stop production, shut it down
Cut it out	Remove by cutting
Draw it up	Bring it to stop
Fill it up	Make it, or become quite full
Find it out	To detect a wrongdoing
Finish it up	Eat up (dinner/lunch/breakfast) completely
Get down to	To start work earnestly
Give it away	Handing over
Get it done	Complete it
Get it off	Save from punishment or penalty
Hand it over	To give it to, to surrender
Leave it out	To omit, fail to consider
Lock it up	Make safe by placing in custody
Look it up	Raise the eyes, search for, pay a call
Make it up	To complete, supply, invented or composed
Make it out	Write out, to complete it, managed to see
Mix it up	To confuse or maladjusted

Pass out	To faint, leaving college having passed
Pay it back	To return
Pick it up	To break up, recover
Pick it out	Make out, choose, distinguish from objects
Point it out	To indicate, to identify, call attention
Put it away	Give up, renounce
Round them off	Bring to a satisfactory conclusion
Round it up	Driving together, bring to a whole number
Set it up	To establish
Take it out	Accept as compensation
Take it in	To receive in place of actual payment
Take it all	Considering everything
Talk it over	Discuss it
Talk it out	Persuade to do/not to do
Think it over	Reflect upon, consider further
Think it out	Consider carefully
Try it on	Put on garments
Try it out	Use it, experiment with it
Turn them away	Refuse to look at it, turning it to different direction
Turn them down	Refuse to consider it
Turn it off	Stop the flow (of gas)
Turn them over	Fall over, change the position of
Wear them out	Exhaust or tire out
Wind it up	Handle, raise it by doing or handling
Wipe it out	Clean the sides of it
Wipe it away	To remove by wiping
Work it in	Find a place for, introduce into
Work it out	Calculate, devise, to develop, to find a solution

Errors Relating to Idiomatic Usage

It has been observed that we often use idiomatic expressions incorrectly. There is no reason for doing so except that it happens on account of lack of reading the right material and not giving attention to the language properly. In order to provide the reader an idea how we often make mistakes in relation to the use of idiomatic expressions, some examples are given below. ***These examples will help you understand that a***

verb when followed by an appropriate preposition or adjective, becomes an idiom. These prepositions or adjectives have been interwoven into the language with the passage of time. Therefore, they are used conventionally. ***Thus, no particular rule or canon can be provided to identify or explain why a particular adjective or a pronoun is used to make an idiom.*** Idioms are therefore, the legacy of a country, people or a particular language. The reader is advised to consult a standard dictionary when he/she is in doubt.

1. **Agree with** something means to be willing to accept or to allow something.

   She agrees to my views. (Incorrect)

   She *agrees with* my views. (Correct)

2. **Appeal to** means an earnest appeal/request.

   The mother appealed with the principal to pardon her son. (Incorrect)

   The mother *appealed to* the principal to pardon her son. (Correct)

3. **Arrange for** means to settle or to adjust, to make plans in advance.

   Sheela has arranged a car to receive them at the airport. (Incorrect)

   Sheela has *arranged for* a car to receive them at the airport. (Correct)

4. **Babble out** stands for talking in a way that is difficult to comprehend.

   She often babbles so nothing is clear to me when she talks. (Incorrect)

   She often *babbles out* so nothing is clear to me when she speaks. (Correct)

5. **Back up** means to support.

   Seema is my good friend. She always backs me on when I need her help. (Incorrect)

   Seema is my good friend. She always *backs me up* when I need her help. (Correct)

6. **Back down** conveys the sense of giving up a claim.

   Although she promised to continue as a president of the company, she backed out in the last meeting. (Incorrect)

Although she promised to continue
as the president of the company,
she *backed down* in the last meeting. (Correct)

7. **Bear against** means to have (grudge) in the heart or mind.

   Please don't bear any grudge for
   your friends for nothing. (Incorrect)

   Please don't *bear any grudge against*
   your friends for nothing. (Correct)

8. **Bent on** gives the meaning of having determination.

   I am bent to attain very good
   marks in my final examination. (Incorrect)

   I am *bent on (upon)* attaining very
   good marks in my final examination. (Correct)

9. **Better of** implies the sense of overcoming or winning.

   His cowardice got the better in him. (Incorrect)

   His cowardice got the *better of* him. (Correct)

10. **Bound for** means to get ready to start (destination).

    This train is bound to Delhi. (Incorrect)

    This train is *bound for* Delhi. (Correct)

11. **Call off** means to call away.

    The strike has been called out. (Incorrect)

    The strike has been *called off.* (Correct)

12. **Care about** means to feel interest, anxiety or sorrow.

    She does not care much for what
    happened to me in the hotel. (Incorrect)

    She does not *care much about*
    what happened to me in the hotel. (Correct)

13. **Depend upon** (**on**) means to rely on or need.

    One's good health depends at
    one's good habits. (Incorrect)

    One's good health *depends upon*
    one's good habits. (Correct)

14. **Deprive of** means to take away from.

She was deprived in books when she was in high school. (Incorrect)

She was *deprived of* books when she was at high school. (Correct)

15. **Ease off** means to give relief to the body or mind from pain, discomfort or anxiety.

Can I ease you from your anxiety so that you may think properly? (Incorrect)

Can I *ease you off your* anxiety so that you may think properly? (Correct)

16. **Escape from** means to get free or get away.

The parrot has escaped away from its cage. (Incorrect)

The parrot has *escaped from* its cage. (Correct)

17. **Excuse from** means to get free from a duty or requirement.

You are excused to attending the classes. (Incorrect)

You are *excused from* attending the classes. (Correct)

18. **Fall flat** means failing to have the intended effect.

The function was managed so badly that it fell down at the end. (Incorrect)

The function was managed so badly that it *fell flat* at the end. (Correct)

19. **Find out** means to detect any wrongdoing or error.

She was found while stealing the papers. (Incorrect)

She was *found out* while stealing the papers. (Correct)

20. **Finish up** means to eat up completely.

The boy was so hungry that he finished his whole meal. (Incorrect)

The boy was so hungry that
he *finished up* his whole meal. (Correct)

Common Expressions in English

These expressions are often used either in writing or during conversation. You must keep in mind that these words are framed in such a way that unless you use them correctly they will not provide the desired or appropriate meanings. Some of them are given on the following pages, with their meanings and uses as well.

As a consequence of
It means **as a result of**. He was expelled from the college *as a consequence* of his misconduct.

As good as
It means **the same thing as**. She is *as good as* her brother.

As long as

It means **on condition that**. You will get your pocket money *as long as* you behave well.

At the most

It indicates **some limit or to an (some) extent**. *At the most* he can attain the position of a principal but not of a director.

At any cost

It means **by using all sorts of ways and means**. We want to fulfil that mission *at any cost.*

As soon as

It means **soon**. *As soon as* she comes home we all will leave.

Better than

It involves **a kind of comparison** between two things, persons, etc. Hari is *better than* Mohan in many respects.

In line with

It denotes some sort of **similarity or equality**. Your decisions are *in line with* mine.

Not only ...but also
It is a phrase that is **used to stress that one more thing or quality or whatever, besides the previous one is also there.** She *not only attended the party, but also sang* a song at the request of the host.

Not so much .....as
It is also used to show some sort of **comparison between two things**

but in a negative manner. For example: She *does not possess so much enthusiasm towards work as* you had reported to me. There is *not so much water in the lake as* you had described.

Responsible for

It relates to **someone's liability towards work, or commitment or a person**. It can be used in a positive or in a negative sense. For example: She was *responsible for ruining* his life and future. She worked very hard to help him. Therefore, eventually she was *responsible for making* his career.

Auxiliary Verbs that Make Idioms

When sentences start with verbs like **have, make, take** and **do,** you may make mistakes, as it is tricky to use them correctly. Let us examine them separately to learn more about them.

Phrases starting with 'take'	***Their usage***
Take a test	*Take a test* to know whether you are really good at work.
Take it normally	*Take it normally.* Please don't mind what he said.
Take it coolly	*Take my word coolly.* Please don't misunderstand me.
Take to (one's) heel	*Taking to heels* at the sight of the police, the thieves were finally caught.
Take notice of	*Take notice of* all what is said to you right now.
Take it well	*Take my advice well,* for it will help you in future.
Take a shower	*Take a shower* right now, for it is very hot.
Take it out	*Take out* these dirty stains from my shirt.
Take down	*Take down* the entire speech and make a report.
Take into account	*Take Deepak into account* as he is highly trustworthy.
Take over	*Take over* from him all the household duties.

Sentences starting with 'do'	*Their usage*
Do your duty	*Do your duty* well.
Do exercise	*Do exercise* regularly to help you build your body.
Do your best	*Do your best* to improve your performance.
Do as told	*Do what you are told* and don't argue.
Do good	*Do good* to others if you want to live happily.
Do some shopping	*Do some shopping* in line with our requirements.
Do take it well	*Do take well* his advice; it will help you a lot.
Do keep silence	*Do keep silence* as it is always required here.
Do no harm	*Do no harm* to the poor for they are often unhappy.
Do your job	*Do your job* well if you want to progress.

Phrases starting **with 'make'**	*Their usage*
Make believe	*Make believe* that Shyam is your best friend until I come back to help you.
Make noise	*Making noise* in the library is not permitted.
Make off	*Make off* to reach the railway station on time.
Make out	*Make out* a cheque worth Rupees one thousand.
Make for	*Make for* the market right now.
Make offer	*Make an offer* to him to sell the house.
Make up	*Make up* the sum we need in the theatre.
Make over	*Make over* this place as your study room.

Phrases taking **the verb 'have'**	*Their usage*
Have breakfast	*Have some breakfast* before you leave home.
Have a bath	*Have a bath* right now.
Have fun	*Have fun* with your friends.
Have a lesson	*Have a lesson* on this topic.

Have a party	*Have a tea party* tonight.
Have a programme	*Have a nice programme* tonight.
Have a class	*Have a class* tonight.
Have a picnic	*Have a picnic* with your girl friend.
Have a drink	*Have a drink* right now.

Test Exercises on this Chapter

Let us take two tests on the material that we have gone through in this chapter. Remember that your good habit of reading will always help you to identify the mistakes hidden in a sentence. Please correct the following sentences keeping in view what you have learnt from the language material given in this chapter as well as in other chapters. Don't read the answers given at the end of the exercises until you have finished them.

Exercises

Test 1

1. The manager of the company appealed with the director to wait for some time before taking any decision in that matter.
2. It is never advisable to bear any grudge for your friends on flimsy matters.
3. A couple of captives escaped away from the Central Jail last night around twelve.
4. The principal excused Rohit to attending the classes, as he was sick for many days.
5. Sheela was found by her mother when she was stealing money from the chest.
6. As the beggar was extremely hungry, he finished the food in a few minutes.
7. Don't take grudges against your brother for no solid reasons against him.
8. You must make it coolly as such unusual happenings do happen in every family.
9. Take out the details of the project very carefully before you intend to submit it.
10. Go, take a picnic with your friends during the coming Deepawali break.

11. I advise you to take fun at times than to remain doleful all the time.
12. Their plans to visit the Taj during last summer fell down as none of them had any idea what route or how much money was involved in the journey to the Taj city.
13. Meera has arranged a car to receive her uncle from the airport.
14. He is bend to attending the party even if he is not invited.
15. The workers of the factory have called out the strike.
16. She cares much for her mother though she is seriously ill.
17. I shall depend at you to look after my house when I am out of station.
18. When she left home in the night, she was deprived to taking any money with her.
19. He can easily ease me from my problems if he likes.
20. She is not so much good in physics than in mathematics.

Test 2

1. Sitting on the ground a letter was written by her.
2. Ganesh was married with Sheela.
3. He who you helped has turned a union leader.
4. All his hairs are grey.
5. Teacher's room was locked and the teachers had to remain outside.
6. This kind of books are not liked by me.
7. His daughters are beautiful but his sons ugly.
8. The electric bulb was hot to be touched.
9. The M.L.A. had interviewed of the Governor.
10. She is true to her words.
11. The fort is built of bricks, not of stones.
12. He ran ten miles race.
13. One of the passengers' daughter got hurt.
14. He wants two breads.
15. It was him who broke the chair.
16. Five hundred miles are a long distance.
17. All except him had run away.

18. She need not to come to office.
19. She is not selfish, nor I am.
20. She spoke very hasty.
21. Call his anything else than a stupid.
22. God may bless you.
23. If you study hard, then you will pass.
24. She tried to quickly cross the road.
25. She is junior than me.
26. Her problem is the same like yours.
27. The clerk copied the letter word to word.
28. What for is Mumbai famous?
29. After 1979, the use of eggs has increased each year.
30. Bangalore is very popular among the people of India.
31. See these phrases in standard dictionary.
32. I am enclosing a cheque of Rs.100.
33. She would like to discuss about what to do next.
34. On every Sunday afternoon she plays tennis.
35. London is far from Delhi.
36. Unless you do not study hard, you will not get good marks.
37. Gopal does not dare come here.
38. Have you ever gone to Mumbai?
39. He wants to know as to why he has been detained.
40. She is a student in the University of Jaipur.
41. As it was raining they decided to stay indoor.
42. He arrived in Mumbai on 15th of December.
43. We shall supply you everything you need.
44. He will phone you again in ten minutes.
45. He could hardly believe in his eyes.
46. It is childish to complain against rules.
47. Does your country import something?
48. He sent for the doctor because I am ill.
49. They have each their problems.
50. Will she have to pay custom duty?

Exercises

Test. 1

A part of a sentence or the entire sentence is underlined in each of the following sentences. Five alternatives are given beneath each sentence to replace the underlined part. You may choose the best alternative out of the five. These exercises are given to help you know more about the common mistakes that one often commits while writing or speaking English. The problems test the ability to recognise correct and effective expressions. Please follow the requirements of Standard Written English Grammar and choose the words and sentence construction in line with that. While choosing the answers, do not change the meaning of the original sentence. Answers are given at the end of the tests.

1. A good physician investigates not only about patients' physical health, but about their mental health as well.
   - (a) but about their mental health too.
   - (b) but about their mental health also.
   - (c) but also about their mental health.
   - (d) but as well as their mental health.
   - (e) but about mental health too.
2. The main reason of his failing was quite evident to those whom he had brought into the project.
   - (a) to those whom he had brought
   - (b) to them whom he had brought
   - (c) to the ones whom he had brought
   - (d) to those who he had brought
   - (e) to those who he had brought
3. She is the kind of person who I think would be capable of making these kind of remarks.
   - (a) who I think would be capable of making these kind of
   - (b) who I think would be capable of making these kinds of
   - (c) who I think would be capable of making this kind of
   - (d) whom I think would be capable of making these kinds of
   - (e) whom I think would be capable of making this kind of
4. She rose to state that in her opinion, she thought, the rule should be referred back to the President for amendment.

(a) in her opinion she thought the rule should be referred back

(b) she thought the rule should be referred back

(c) she thought that it must be referred back

(d) in her opinion the rule should be referred

(e) the rule should be referred

5. Whoever objects to she going to the theatre should say it immediately.

 (a) objects to her going into

 (b) objects to me going to

 (c) objects to hers going to

 (d) objects to her going to

 (e) objects to she going to

6. Vinaya, the President of the Club and who is also a member of the finance committee, will accompany the foreign dignitary.

 (a) who is also a member of the finance committee

 (b) who is as well as a member of the finance committee

 (c) since he is a member of the finance committee

 (d) a member of the finance committee

 (e) who is a member of the finance committee as well

7. Because they cooperated with one another, they divided up the work on the report, which had been assigned.

 (a) with one another, they divided up the work on the report which had been assigned.

 (b) with one another, they divided the work on the report which had been assigned.

 (c) they divided up the work on the report which was assigned.

 (d) they divided the work on the assigned report.

 (e) they divided up the work on the assigned report.

8. On account of continual wind, the clouds scattered and it resulted that it did not rain.

 (a) As the wind continued, the clouds scattered which resulted in no rains.

(b) It did not rain because the clouds scattered on account of continued wind.

(c) On account of continual wind, the clouds got scattered and it stopped raining.

(d) On account of continued wind, the clouds scattered and resulted in not raining.

(e) As the wind continued and the clouds scattered as a consequence it stopped raining.

9. Besides him, there were many people, who did not approve of her odd demeanour.

(a) There were many people besides him, who did not approve of her odd demeanour.

(b) Besides him, who did not approve of her odd demeanour, there were many people.

(c) Besides many people he was also there who did not approve of her odd demeanour.

(d) Many people as well as he were there who did not approve of her odd demeanour.

(e) Besides many people, he was also there who did not approve of her odd demeanor.

10. The taxi, driven by an experienced driver with an outdated engine, must be sent to the workshop.

(a) driven by an experienced driver, must be sent to the workshop with an outdated engine.

(b) driven by an experienced driver, with an outdated engine, must be sent to the workshop.

(c) with an outdated engine driven by an experienced driver, must be sent to the workshop.

(d) having an outdated engine and driven by an experienced driver must be sent to the workshop.

(e) fitted with an outdated engine though driven by an experienced driver must be sent to the workshop.

11. Having managed his home for many years, she understood his family better.

(a) Because she managed his home for years she understood his family better.

(b) As she managed his home for many years, she understood his family better.

(c) Having managed his home for many years she could understand his family better.

(d) For many years she managed his home, so she understood his family better.

(e) Managing his home for many years she was able to understand his family better.

12. Since she was living in Mumbai for many years she was reluctant to move to a smaller city.

    (a) As she was living in Mumbai for many years she was reluctant to move to a smaller city.

    (b) Since she lived in Mumbai for many years she was reluctant to move to a smaller city.

    (c) As for many years she lived in Mumbai, she was reluctant to move to a smaller city.

    (d) Since she had been living in Mumbai for many years, she was reluctant to move to a smaller city.

    (e) She lived in Mumbai for many years she was reluctant to move to a smaller city.

13. The Principal, who was very kind spoke to the student and he was very rude.

    (a) who was very kind he spoke to the student who

    (b) was a kind person and he spoke to the student who

    (c) spoke to the student kindly and the student

    (d) a kind person, spoke to the student who

    (e) who was a kind person spoke to the student and he

14. Dharmpal had never done it if he would have known that it would hurt his parents.

    (a) would have never done it if he had

    (b) had done it never if he would have

    (c) would have not have done it if he had

    (d) would never do it if he would have

    (e) had never done it if he had

15. If she is desirous to get admission in school, she should submit their applications before the closing date, which is June 20th.

    (a) submit their application
    (b) submit her application
    (c) submit their applications in
    (d) submit an application
    (e) submit their application in

16. A good mill owner not only needs to know his workers thoroughly, but requires to know their families well.

    (a) but requires to find out
    (b) but needs to find out
    (c) but also requires to know
    (d) but requires to see
    (e) but requires to meet

17. As a small boy, my mother took me to Benaras to visit that holy place.

    (a) My mother took me, as a small boy, to Benaras to visit that holy place.
    (b) My mother took me to Benaras, as a small boy, to visit that holy place.
    (c) As a small boy, my mother took me to Benaras to visit that holy place.
    (d) A small boy, my mother took me to Benaras to visit that holy place.
    (e) When I was a small boy, my mother took me to Benaras to visit that holy place.

18. Too busy to pack her things herself, Sheela made a list of articles to be taken with her, ordered a working lunch, went to the corner of the next building calling a taxi.

    (a) left to the corner of the next building calling a taxi.
    (b) went to the corner of the next building and to call a taxi.
    (c) went to the next building calling a taxi.
    (d) went to the corner of the next building and called a taxi.
    (e) went to the next building and called a taxi.

19. The shorter the speech is, it is not only welcoming, but people understand it easily too.

    (a) but they understand it easily too.

    (b) but people understand the speech easily.

    (c) but people understand it easily.

    (d) but people understand it easily as well.

    (e) but people understand it also easily.

20. The collector liked the proposal and it was supported by the MLA too.

    (a) it was supported too by the MLA.

    (b) the MLA supported it too.

    (c) it was supported by the MLA as well.

    (d) it was supported by the MLA.

    (e) it was supported also by the MLA.

Test. 2

1. Beautifully re-varnished, John displayed the antique chair in his den.

    (a) Beautiful re-varnished, John proudly displayed the antique chair in his den.

    (b) Beautifully re-varnished. John proudly displayed the antique chair in his den.

    (c) John displayed the beautifully re-varnished antique chair in his den.

    (d) An antique and beautifully re-varnished in his den John displayed the chair.

    (e) John, beautifully antique and re-varnished chair displayed in his den.

2. The most important food energy source of most of the population of the world are grains.

    (a) of most of the population of the world are grains.

    (b) for most of the population of the world are grains.

    (c) for most of the population of the world are grain.

(d) for most of the population of the world is grain.

(e) for the most of the population of the world are grains.

3. The probability of massive earthquakes are regarded by most of the residents of the area with a mixture of disbelief and caution.

   (a) are regarded by most of the residents of the area with

   (b) is regarded by most of the residents of the area with

   (c) are regarded with most residents of the area with

   (d) is regarded by most residents of the area with

   (e) are regarded by most residents of the area by

4. Everyone in the hall except the small kid and me were injured as the roof fell down.

   (a) except the small kid and me was injured

   (b) except the small kid and me were injured

   (c) except the small kid and me had been injured

   (d) except the small kid as well as me were injured

   (e) except me and the small kid were injured

5. Neither Sheela's cousins nor her mother like the guests' arrogant disposition.

   (a) Neither Sheela's cousins nor her mother liked

   (b) Sheela's cousins as well as her mother did not like

   (c) Neither Sheela's cousins nor her mother likes

   (d) Neither Sheela's mother nor her cousins likes

   (e) Neither Sheela's cousins and her mother does not like

6. Every candidate of the Congress Party except Malik and he lost the party elections.

   (a) except Malik and his

   (b) except Malik and him

   (c) except Malik and himself

   (d) except Malik and he

   (e) except his as well as Malik

7. If I were him, I would laid that book on the table and keep it away from the kitchen.

(a) If I were he, I would lay

(b) If I was he, I would laid

(c) If I were him, I would have laid

(d) If I were he, I would lay

(e) If I was him, I would lay

8. In this commentary, the writer imply that everyone who likes his idea must still accept its principal theory.

(a) the writer imply that everyone who likes his idea must still accept its principal theory.

(b) the writer implies that everyone who likes his idea must still accept his principal theory.

(c) the writer imply that everyone whom his idea is liked must also accept its principal theory.

(d) the writer implies that everyone who like his idea must also accept his principal theory.

(f) the writer implies that everyone who likes his idea should also accept his principal theory.

9. If she would have paid attention, she would have not needed to be directed again.

(a) she had have paid attention,

(b) she had paid attention,

(c) she paid attention,

(d) would have paid attention,

(e) she would pay

10. He is not and does not intend to play again for the county cricket.

(a) is not and does not intend to play

(b) is not playing and does not intend to play

(c) is not and will not play

(d) has not and does not play

(e) has no intention nor he will play

11. The engine of the machine runs quieter when he added a heavier transmission fluid to it.

(a) engine of the machine runs quiet

(b) engine of the machine ran quieter

(c) engine of the machine ran more quietly

(d) engine of the machine will run quietly

(e) engine of the machine ran quietly

12. Sheetal believes that her academic achievement is better or at least as good as Meena's.

(a) is better or at least as good as Meena's.

(b) is as good or better than Meena's.

(c) is better or at least as good as Meena's academic records.

(d) at least is as good as Meena's.

(e) is better or at least as good as Meena.

13. His fortitude is as great as any other person in defending his country.

(a) as great as any other person.

(b) as great as other person

(c) great like any other person

(d) as that of any person

(e) as great as that of any other person

14. Pradeep not only likes to work hard but believes others to do hard work.

(a) but believes that others should also work harder.

(b) but thinks that others to do hard work also.

(c) but considers that others to do hard work also.

(d) but also believes others to do hard work.

(e) but believes others to do hard work.

15. Our current Finance Minister must be honoured on account their boosting up the country's economy.

(a) on account his boosting up the country's economy.

(b) on account of their boosting up the country's economy.

(c) on account of his mates boosting up the country's economy.

(d) the reason being his boosting up their country's economy.

(e) the account of his boosting up the country's economy.

16. Despite his harsh criticism of the competition, the Captain reached the stage to take the trophy.

(a) Despite his harsh criticism of the competition,

(b) The competition was criticised yet,

(c) Harshly criticising such competitions always,

(d) In spite of criticising such competitions,

(e) Criticising very harshly all competition,

17. Considering a diagnosis on the basis of insufficient or deceptive evidence is neglecting years of dedicated medical training.

(a) Considering a diagnosis on the basis of insufficient or deceptive evidence

(b) To consider a diagnosis just to see insufficient or deceptive evidence

(c) In view of an insufficient or deceptive evidence considering a diagnosis

(d) Considering a diagnosis because of insufficient and deceptive evidence

(e) In considering a diagnosis just because of insufficient or deceptive evidence

18. While many members of the Party may feel powerless to influence the Secretary about the policy matters, it is truly effective to write to him with an opinion.

(a) it is truly effective to write to him with an opinion.

(b) writing to the Secretary with an opinion is actually effective.

(c) to write to the Secretary with an opinion is effective.

(d) writing of an opinion to the Secretary may be effective.

(e) writing as an opinion to the Secretary may be effective.

19. Dr Radhakrishnan was a professor of Philosophy at the University of Madras, at the same time also one of India's greatest President.

(a) at the same time also one of India's greatest President.

(b) and at the same time was also one of India's greatest Presidents.

(c) at the same time as he was India's great President.

(d) at the same time was also one of India's greatest Presidents.

(e) being one of India's greatest president at the same time.

20. Having been asked by the magistrate to pay the fine, Nitin was still not required by it to pay.

(a) Nitin was still not required by it to pay.

(b) Nitin was further not required by it to pay the fine.

(c) Nitin was never required to pay the fine.

(d) Nitin was still not required to pay.

(e) Nitin was hardly required by it to pay.

Test. 3

Miscellaneous Sentences

The area of the error is indicated in each case.

Subject and verb must always agree

1. Her cat, along with her dog and the goldfish, don't permit her to take long trips.

(a) along with her dog and the goldfish , don't permit

(b) as well as her dog and goldfish, doesn't permit

(c) together with her dog and goldfish, are not permitting

(d) accompanied by her dog and goldfish, don't permit

(e) in addition to her dog and goldfish, don't permit

Pronouns must agree with the words they refer to

2. The teacher said that everyone will bring home-made foodstuff from their home.

(a) that everyone will bring home-made foodstuff from their home.

(b) that everyone must bring home-made foodstuff from his home.

(c) that everyone must bring homemade foodstuff from one's home.

(d) that everyone must bring homemade foodstuff from her home

(e) that all of us must bring homemade foodstuff from their home.

Pronouns must be in the correct case

3. The judges were requested to award the scholarships to whomever got the highest marks.

   (a) to award the scholarships to whomever got the highest marks.

   (b) to award the scholarships to whomever gets the highest marks.

   (c) to award the scholarships to whoever got the highest marks.

   (d) to award the scholarships to whom got the highest marks.

   (e) to award the scholarships to whose marks were high.

Tenses (verb) must reflect the sequence of events

4. When he opened the hood of his van and saw smoke coming from the engine, he realised that he forgot to add engine oil.

   (a) realised that he forgot to add engine oil.

   (b) realised that he forgets to add engine oil.

   (c) realised that he forgot to add some engine oil.

   (d) realised that he had forgotten to add engine oil.

   (e) had realised that he forgot to add engine oil.

A pronoun modifying a gerund must be in the possessive case

5. She disapproves of you insisting that the books were misplaced on purpose.

   (a) She disapproves of you that the books were misplaced on purpose.

   (b) She disapproves of you insisting that the books were purposely misplaced.

   (c) She disapproves of your insisting that the books were misplaced on purpose.

(d) She does not approve of you insisting that the books were misplaced purposefully.

(e) She disapprove of your insisting that the books were misplaced on purpose.

Comparisons must be logical

6. A teacher's physical impact including gestures, body and facial impressions is as important as listening to his lectures.

   (a) A teacher's physical impact including gestures, body and facial impressions is

   (b) A teacher's physical impact gestures, facial impressions and body carriage are

   (c) A teacher's physical, body and facial impressions are

   (d) To examine a teacher's physical impact and body and facial impressions are

   (e) Examining a teacher's physical, body and facial impressions are

Modifiers must stay close to home

7. By leading trump, the proposal was defeated flatly by the defenders.

   (a) By leading trump, the proposal was defeated flatly by the defenders.

   (b) By leading trump, the defenders defeated the proposal flatly.

   (c) The defenders flatly defeated the proposal by leading trump.

   (d) The proposal, by leading trump, was defeated flatly by the defenders.

   (e) Flatly, the proposal was defeated by the defenders by leading trump.

Sentence fragments don't cut it. (When a sentence does not contain a subject or verb *it is not a complete sentence no matter how long a phrase it contains.)*

8. The lovesick girl was very doleful as the boy who she loved and who had left her for another girl.

   (a) the boy who she loved and who had left her for another girl.

   (b) the boy whom she loved and whom had left her for another girl.

   (c) the boy whom she loved and who had left her for another girl.

(d) the boy whom she loved had left her for another girl.

(e) the boy who she loved had left her for another girl.

Run-on sentences don't make it. (The following sentence is an example of a run-on sentence. *It is a sentence that contains two independent clauses which are not joined properly.)*

9. At the outset, Sadhana was the group's leader, <u>later on it occurred to the group that</u> Seema was more capable and more agile.

   (a) later on it occurred to the group that

   (b) that was not the better thing to reckon with

   (c) but the group came to realise that

   (d) the group concluded, however, that

   (e) then the group decided that

We don't start a sentence with 'Because'

10. <u>Because she does not agree with you</u> it does not indicate that she does not like you.

   (a) Because she does not agrees with you

   (b) If she does not agrees with you

   (c) Because you and she does not agree with

   (d) When she does not agree with you

   (e) That she does not agree with you

Choose the right word. (Don't get trapped by making a needless change unless you *have a good reason for it.* Faulty diction is often a big problem.)

11. <u>The unlawful students were expedited from one place to the other</u> for reformation.

   (a) The unlawful students were expedited from one place to another

   (b) From one place to another the unlawful students were expedited

   (c) The unlawful students were expedited to another place

   (d) The unlawful students were extradited from one place to another

   (e) The unlawful students from one to another place were expedited

Wordy answer choices are no solutions. *Please don't choose answers just because they sound 'important'.*

12. If one starts drinking at an early age, it is possible that he will go on drinking in future.
    (a) it is possible that he will go on drinking in future.
    (b) it is possible that he will go on drinking forever.
    (c) he will probably go on drinking more and more.
    (d) it is hard to stop him from drinking more in future.
    (e) he is likely to continue drinking.

Misplaced Modifiers. Misplaced modifiers come in several forms. A few examples are given below.

(i) Remember that when a sentence begins with a *participial phrase*, it is supposed to modify the noun or pronoun that immediately follows it.

13. Coming out of the office Satish's valuables was robbed.
    (a) Coming out of the office, Satish's valuables was robbed.
    (b) Coming out of the office, Satish was robbed of his valuables.
    (c) In coming out of the office, Satish's valuables were robbed.
    (d) While Satish left the office someone had robbed him of his valuables.
    (e) Satish was coming out of the office, someone robbed his valuables.

(ii) When a *participial phrase* is preceded by a preposition, it must modify the noun or pronoun.

14. On leaving the office Satish's valuables were robbed.
    (a) On leaving the office Satish's valuables were robbed.
    (b) While Satish left the office he was robbed of his valuables.
    (c) When Satish came out of the office someone robbed his valuables.
    (d) As Satish left the office, his valuables were robbed.
    (e) On leaving the office, Satish was robbed of his

(iii) A close relative of a misplaced modifier is a *dangling modifier.* It can be identified in an easy way.

15. Before designing a building, the owner of the building must be considered.

(a) Before designing a building the owner of the building must be considered.

(b) The owner of the building must be considered before designing the building.

(c) Before designing a building, the architect must consider its owner.

(d) The owner needs to be consulted before any building is designed.

(e) When a building is designed, it is necessary that its owner must be considered.

Test Paper

1. The number of people jogging in city parks, in playgrounds, and even in the streets, <u>is at least five times what they were</u> five years ago.

   (a) is at least five times what they were

   (b) are at least five times what they had been

   (c) is at least five times more what it was

   (d) are at least five times what it was

   (e) is at least five times than what the numbers were

2. For some children, <u>accepting parental discipline that they consider unfair, constitute</u> a necessary impediment.

   (a) accepting parental discipline that they consider unfair, constitute

   (b) acceeding to parental discipline which they consider unfair, constitute

   (c) accepting parental discipline that one considers unfair, constitute

   (d) to accept parental discipline what they consider unfair, constitute

   (e) accepting parental discipline which they consider unfair, constitutes

3. <u>To protest their being underpaid in comparison to other city agencies, a strike was called by the paramedical workers.</u>

   (a) To protest their being underpaid in comparison to other city agencies, a strike was called by the paramedical workers.

(b) To protest them being underpaid in comparison with other city agencies, the paramedical workers called a strike.

(c) To protest their being comparatively underpaid with other city agencies, a strike was called by the paramedical workers.

(d) To protest their being underpaid in comparison with the workers of other city agencies, the paramedical workers called a strike.

(e) The paramedical workers called a strike to protest them being underpaid in comparison with other city workers.

4. The parties have an agreement in principle, <u>and because there is no</u> signed contract does not mean that they cannot do business immediately.

    (a) and because there is no

    (b) and there being no

    (c) so an absent

    (d) so the lack of a

    (e) therefore no

5. The committee rejected the proposal for several reasons, <u>the chief among which were the cost of borrowing the money.</u>

    (a) the chief among which were the cost of borrowing the money

    (b) the chief among which was the cost of borrowing the money

    (c) the chief of which was the cost of borrowing money

    (d) the chief were the cost of borrowing the money

    (e) with the cost of borrowing money being the one of them

6. To be fair, it was Finance Minister P. Chidambaram who suggested the changeover on the grounds that "Vibrancy of the equity market <u>must be extended to the debt market on moving to a screen-based trading platform".</u>

    (a) must be extended to the debt market on moving to a screen-based trading platform".

    (b) ought to be extended to the debt market by moving to a screen-based trading platform".

    (c) must extend to the debt market on moving to a screen-based trading platform".

(d) must have been extended to the debt market on moving to a screen-based trading platform".

(e) need to be extended to the debt market on moving to a screen-based trading platform".

7. The employment contracts of most high-level managers contain so-called Golden Parachute clauses, under which the executive is guaranteed substantial compensation if their firms ever fall victim to a hostile takeover.

(a) clauses, under which the executive is guaranteed

(b) clauses that guarantee the executives

(c) clauses, guaranteeing that these executives

(d) clause, under which the executive is guaranteed of

(e) clause that guarantee the executive of

8. *Mahabharat* has often been described as a great story told greatly.

(a) *Mahabharat* has often been described as a great story told greatly.

(b) *Mahabharat* has been described as a great story often told greatly.

(c) Often told greatly, *Mahabharat* has been described as a great story.

(d) Told greatly, *Mahabharat* is often described as a great story.

(e) A great story, *Mahabharat* is often described as greatly told.

9. The portfolio, which was apparently left inadvertent at home, contained three completed watercolours, including several uncompleted sketches.

(a) left inadvertent at home, contained three completed watercolours, including several uncompleted sketches.

(b) left inadvertently at home, contained three completed watercolours, including several uncompleted sketches.

(c) inadvertently left at home containing three completed watercolours, including several uncompleted sketches.

(d) left inadvertently at home with three completed watercolours and several uncompleted sketches.

(e) inadvertently left at home, contained three completed watercolours and several uncompleted sketches.

10. Although the stock market offers the possibility of great personal gain, you must understand that to invest in stocks is accepting the risk of financial ruin as well.

(a) is accepting the risk of financial ruin as well.

(b) is to accept the risk of financial ruin as well.

(c) is to accept the risk as well as financial ruin.

(d) are accepting the risk of financial ruin as well.

(e) Are to expect the risk of financial ruin as well.

11. Political games are played over river waters in the north too. Only last week, the President seeked the Supreme Court's opinion on whether law makers in Punjab are right in rejecting an agreement to share Sutlej waters with Haryana.

(a) seeked the Supreme Court's opinion on whether law makers in Punjab are

(b) seeked the Supreme Court's opinion on whether law makers in Punjab have the

(c) sought the Supreme Court's opinion on whether law makers in Punjab were

(d) sought the Supreme Court's opinion on whether law makers in Punjab are

(e) sought the Supreme Court's opinion to know whether the law makers in Punjab were

12. Concrete is an artificial material made from a mixture of Portland cement, water, fine and coarse aggregates, having a small amount of air.

(a) having a small

(b) having added a small

(c) adding a small

(d) and a little

(e) and a small

13. Although today it is easy to make perfumes with synthetic ingredients, they used to make the classic fragrances from flowers only and other natural essences.

(a) they used to make the classic fragrances from flowers only

(b) the classic fragrances used to be made only from flowers

(c) the classic fragrances used to be made by them only from flowers

(d) the classic fragrances ought to be made from flowers only

(e) only flowers were used for making the classic fragrances

14. Americans give pride of place to the value of individual liberty, and we find especially unintelligible the infliction of suffering on the innocent.

(a) especially unintelligible the infliction of suffering

(b) especial unintelligible the fiction of suffering

(c) especially unintelligible suffrage that is inflicted

(d) especially unintelligible the suffering that is inflicted

(e) specially illegible infliction of suffering

15. The revelation that Shakespeare wrote certain of his plays expressly for Queen Elizabeth I lends credence to the theory that the dark lady of the sonnets was not Shakespeare's mistress nor any other woman the playwright had romanced but, in fact, the Queen herself.

(a) not Shakespeare's mistress nor any other woman the playwright had romanced

(b) neither Shakespeare's mistress or any other woman the playwright had romanced

(c) neither Shakespeare's mistress nor any other woman the playwright had romanced

(d) not Shakespeare's mistress or any other woman the playwright had romanced

(e) not Shakespeare's mistress neither any other woman he had romanced

16. Many travellers state unequivocally that the streets in Delhi are more beautiful than any other city.

(a) that the streets in Delhi are more beautiful than any other city.

(b) that the streets in Delhi are more beautiful than those in any other city.

(c) that Delhi streets are more beautiful than in any other city.

(d) that unlike any other city, Delhi streets are more beautiful.

(e) that the streets of Delhi are more beautiful than the streets in any other city.

17. Assigning additional work to an already overburdened worker, one made often by inept managers, it increases the risk that the worker will become totally alienated and cease being productive altogether.

    (a) one made often by inept managers, it increases the risk

    (b) one often made by inept managers, increases the risk

    (c) a mistake often made by inept managers, the risk rises

    (d) a mistake often made by inept managers, increases the risk

    (e) which is often done by inept managers, the risk is increased that

18. Although the reaction to initial marketing surveys was not favourable, the growing acceptance by consumers seem to indicate the product will ultimately be very popular.

    (a) seem to indicate the product will ultimately be very popular

    (b) seem to indicate the ultimate popularity of the product

    (c) seems to indicate that the product will ultimately be very popular

    (d) are indicating that the product will ultimately be very popular

    (e) seems to be an indication as to the ultimately popularity of the product

19. The number of illiterate adults in the United States is rising, but it is probably only temporary.

    (a) rising, but it is probably only temporary

    (b) rising, but it is only temporary

    (c) rising, but it is temporary only

    (d) rising, but the increase is probably only a temporary one

    (e) rising, although the increase may only be temporarily

20. The prospects of rich countries to discover the virtue of altruism seems quite slim at the moment.

    (a) to discover the virtue of altruism seems

    (b) discovering the virtue of altruism seem

(c) having discovered the virtue of altruism seems

(d) on discovering the virtue of altruism seem

21. Fidel Castro found it simple to seize power, but maintaining it difficult.

(a) maintaining it difficult

(b) its maintenance difficult

(c) difficult to maintain it

(d) difficulty was experienced in maintaining it

(e) difficulty in as much as maintaining it was concerned

22. Results of the recent study make it mandatory that the Medical Superintendent rejects implementation of the experimental procedure.

(a) rejects

(b) should reject

(c) reject

(d) must reject

(e) will reject

23. The *munshi* told me that the lawyer's office closes at 5:00 P.M.

(a) The *munshi* told me that the lawyer's office closes at 5:00 P.M.

(b) The *munshi* told me that the lawyer's office closed at 5:00 P.M.

(c) The *munshi* had told me that the lawyer's office had closed at 5:00 P.M.

(d) The *munshi* told me that lawyer's office would have to close at 5:00 P.M.

24. Smart investors saw early that the compact disc, on which music is recorded in a digital code to be read by a laser, would soon become the most common form of recorded music, eventually replacing records and tapes altogether.

(a) music, eventually replacing

(b) music, and eventually replacing

(c) music that eventually replaces

(d) music by eventually replacing

(e) music to eventually replace

25. Tibetan rugs are so expensive because the weaver still pursues his art as they have for centuries, by hand-dyeing all their wool and then knotting each thread individually to achieve a unique pattern for every piece.

(a) the weaver still pursues his art as they have

(b) the weaver still pursues his art as he has

(c) weavers still pursue their art as they have

(d) weavers still pursue their art as was done

(e) the weaver still pursues his art as has been done

26. The exclusive Taj restaurant has been popular with business customers because of its excellent service, responsive management, and because its parking facilities are extensive.

(a) because of its excellent service, responsive management, and because its parking facilities are extensive.

(b) because of its excellent service, responsive management, and because their parking facilities are extensive.

(c) because of its service, which is excellent, management, which is responsive, and because of parking facilities which are extensive.

(d) because of its excellent service, responsive management and extensive parking facilities.

(e) because of its excellent service, responsive management and its extensive parking facilities.

27. Since they shared so much when they were growing up, Neena and Juhi have cultivated a very special friendship and even now confide their most intimate thoughts only to one another.

(a) to one another

(b) one with the other

(c) one with another

(d) each to the other

(e) to each other

28. A survey of business schools concludes that female students are more concerned about job discrimination than male students.

(a) female students are more concerned about job discrimination than male students

(b) female students are more concerned about job discrimination than male students are.

(c) female students, as opposed to male students, are more concerned about job discrimination

(d) female students are more concerned about job discrimination than male students are concerned

(e) female students are more concerned about job discrimination than their male counterparts.

29. <u>To lack self-discipline is to lack</u> any true commitment to the goals one has set.

(a) To lack self-discipline is to lack

(b) To be lacking in self-discipline is to lack

(c) To lack self-discipline must be to lack

(d) Lacking self-discipline is to be lacking

(e) Lacking self-discipline is the lack of

30. Married women raising young children do not respond to social stresses <u>as poorly as unmarried women do.</u>

(a) as poorly as unmarried women do.

(b) as much as unmarried women do

(c) as poorly as unmarried women

(d) as much as unmarried women have

(e) as well as unmarried women

31. They pay attention to small details, eliminate problems at the source and <u>trimming anything resembling excess, whether it is</u> work, code or material.

(a) trimming anything resembling excess, whether it is

(b) trim anything resembling excess, whether it is

(c) trim anything resembling excess, whether it was

(d) trim anything resembling excess, whether it be

(e) trim resembling anything in excess

32. <u>In spite of forbidden by Church law to marry, it was not unusual for a priest during the Middle Ages to sire a family</u>.

(a) In spite of forbidden by Church law to marry, it was not unusual for a priest during the Middle Ages to sire a family.

(b) Forbidden by Church law to marry, it was quite normal for a priest during the Middle Ages to sire a family.

(c) Though they were forbidden by Church law to marry, it was usual for him during the Middle Ages to sire a family.

(d) Although they were forbidden by Church law to marry, it was not unusual for priests during the Middle Ages to sire families.

(e) They were forbidden by Church law to marry, but it was not usual for priests in the Middle Ages to sire families.

ooo

Unit- 4

Active and Passive Voice

Active and passive voice questions are quite common in English sections of various exams. The difference between active and passive voice is that in active voice, subject performs the action denoted by the verb, while in passive voice, the subject is acted upon by the verb. To understand this, read the following examples carefully:-

Active Voice	Passive Voice
1. I'm drinking milk.	1. Milk is being drunk by me.
2. I drink water.	2. Water is drunk by me.
3. He ate banana.	3. Banana was eaten by him.
4. They were flying kites.	4. Kites were being flown by them.
5. She teaches us math.	5. Math is taught to us by her.
6. Anuj drives the car.	6. The car is driven by Anuj.
7. Shilpa was writing a letter.	7. A letter was being written by Shilpa.
8. They were playing tennis.	8. Tennis was being played by them.
9. Which movie are you watching?	9. Which movie is being watched by you?
10. Who helped you in your homework?	10. By whom were you helped in your homework?/ Who were you helped by in your homework?
11. We will maintain silence.	11. Silence will be maintained.
12. Someone killed him.	12. He was killed.
13. I won the first prize.	13. The first prize was won by me.
14. Somebody has stolen my car.	14. My car has been stolen.
15. Switch on the light.	15. Let the light be switched on.
16. Nobody can foretell the future.	16. The future cannot be foretold.
17. Who took my jacket?	17. By whom was my jacket taken?/ Who was my jacket taken by?
18. I wrote that book.	18. That book was written by me.

19. They made the topper the class monitor.	19. The topper was made the class monitor.
20. They cut the tree down.	20. The tree was cut down by them.
21. Someone helped her.	21. She was helped.
22. To my surprise, they knew her.	22. To my surprise, she was known to them.
23. Someone kept ice in the ice-box.	23. Ice was kept in the ice-box.
24. I want someone to throw these vegetables.	24. I want these vegetables to be thrown out.
25. They found him in a café.	25. He was found in a café.
26. Since he had not done the homework, the teacher sent him out of the class.	26. Since the homework hadn't been done by him, he was sent out of the class by the teacher.
27. People should do it.	27. It should be done. ('by people' is understood.)
28. Do it.	28. Let it be done.
29. Tell everyone.	29. Let everyone be told.
30. Hear this.	30. Let this be heard.
31. People should not make fun of him.	31. He should not be made fun of.
32. We will close the gate at five.	32. The gate will be closed at five.
33. We caught the thief on the road.	33. The thief was caught on the road.
34. I think she has made a mistake.	34. I think a mistake has been made by her.
35. One should not tell lies.	35. Lies should not be told.
36. Let us not leave the class.	36. It is suggested that we do not leave the class.
37. Please come here.	37. You are requested to come here.
38. We have to do it.	38. It has to be done.
39. There is a lot to accomplish.	39. There is a lot to be accomplished.
40. Prepare to leave.	40. Be prepared to leave.
41. Don't do it! (order)	41. You are ordered not to do it!
42. It looks sharp.	42. It is sharp when looked at.
43. We have to get it.	43. It has to be gotten by us.
44. I had to do it.	44. It had to be done by me.
45. Someone must help her.	45. She must be helped.
46. Someone stole our umbrellas.	46. Our umbrellas were stolen.
47. There is no way someone can reach the top.	47. There is no way the top can be reached.

48. Did they say it? — 48. Was it said by them?

49. Did she punish him? — 49. Was he punished by her?

50. We were playing Ludo. — 50. Ludo was being played by us.

51. She has been singing. — 51. Singing has been being done by her.

52. We had been swimming. — 52. Swimming had been being done by us.

Have you read the given examples carefully? More than once? Good. Now you are supposed to use your knowledge to solve the following practice exercise:

Practice Exercise

Change from active voice to passive voice. *(The correct answers have been provided in the appendix.)*

1. I did it.
2. I do it.
3. I was doing it.
4. I shall do it.
5. I have done it.
6. Lekha was typing the essay.
7. Priyanka madam taught us Math.
8. Roshan did my homework.
9. We should not tease the animals in the cage.
10. Our company manufactures shoes.
11. We must help poor people.
12. Finish the work.
13. Shut the door.
14. I'm to inform my brother.
15. Someone must inform my brother.
16. A little spark caused the fire.
17. Please stop talking.
18. Nina knows Tina.
19. Why did you join this class?
20. The police arrested the wrong doers.
21. People believe that the God is omnipresent.
22. Let us eat it now. (suggestion)
23. I will have completed the project by that time.
24. You should not let your parents down.
25. Mohit told me that the teacher punished Rajesh.
26. The great leader's sudden demise shocked the nation.
27. Who took my chocolate?
28. Read out the order.
29. Someone broke her heart.
30. Everyone should respect the law of the land.
31. No one can do it.
32. Who beat you?
33. Switzerland manufactures fine quality cheese.
34. Someone must bring the keys.
35. Let me have it. (request)
36. Those boys play football.
37. World knows the great scientist.
38. People were teasing the poor animal.
39. That dog looks fierce.
40. Who taught you dancing?
41. The mob punished the culprit.

42. Lemon tastes sour.
43. The constable caught the thief red-handed.
44. Nobody was following me.
45. No one can cross the mountain-range.
46. No one has crossed the mountain-range.
47. People are laughing at me!
48. There is a lot to do.
49. We have a lot to do.
50. No one can dispute it.
51. I had eaten the ice-cream.
52. Rajan had done it.
53. Please rescue the poor animal.
54. We should cross the ditch from that side.
55. People must care for everyone.
56. Punish the criminal.
57. Can you forgive me?
58. They may forgive me this time.
59. My horse will win the race.
60. Who could have done this?
61. We could have won the match!
62. She would have done it.
63. I should have done it.
64. Humans make mistakes.
65. Drop the curtain.
66. They had been jogging.
67. I have been cooking.

Passive to Active Voice

1. It couldn't be done by her.
2. Pending bills must be paid immediately.
3. The question remained unanswered by the speaker.
4. He was left behind (by them).
5. Banana is sweet when tasted.
6. The sword is sharp when looked at.
7. The rod was red hot when looked at.
8. Are his whereabouts known?
9. We may be allowed to go out.
10. The poor must be helped (by us).
11. She was caught stealing from her father's drawer (by her mother).
12. That man must be helped by onlookers.
13. If we wear these clothes, we will be laughed at.
14. Is the speaker known to everyone?
15. He was given a glass of water by the host.
16. The Sun God is worshipped in that country.
17. The child was rescued by our brave army men.
18. His hunger for money can't be satiated by any amount.
19. By whom were you taught singing?
20. Children were taken to a safer place by their mother.
21. She was made to wait for an hour (by her friend).
22. The pets should not be made to suffer (by their owners).
23. A good life is deserved by everyone.
24. He wasn't replied to by her.
25. Rice is grown in Chhattisgarh.
26. Sriniwas is the tallest boy in the class when looked at.
27. The bill was passed by the majority.
28. It couldn't have been done better.
29. The peak of this mountain is unreachable.

OOO

Unit- 5

Direct and Indirect Speech

Just like active and passive voice questions, direct and indirect speech questions are frequently asked in various competitive exams. Let's understand the difference between direct and indirect speech. When you tell what someone has said using the exact words that person used, you are using direct speech. (*'He said, "I'm not going."'* is an example of direct speech.) On the other hand, when you tell what someone has said using your own words, you are using indirect speech. (*'He said he wasn't going.'* is an example of indirect speech.) Let's take some examples:-

1. Direct speech: Ram said to me, "I took your pen."
   Indirect speech: Ram told me that he had taken my pen.
2. Direct speech: Ravi said, "I want to leave."
   Indirect speech: Ravi said that he wanted to leave.
3. Direct speech: He says, "I jog."
   Indirect speech: He says that he jogs.

(Note: We generally don't use past tense for describing the routine actions.)

4. Direct speech: I told him, "You are my best friend."
   Indirect speech: I told him that he was my best friend.
5. Direct speech: He said to me, "I love flying."
   Indirect speech: He told me that he loved flying.
6. Direct speech: She said, "I've read that book."
   Indirect speech: She said that she had read that book.
7. Direct speech: She said, "I will sing."
   Indirect speech: She said that she would sing.
8. Direct speech: She said, "I was writing letters."
   Indirect speech: She said that she had been writing letters.
9. Direct speech: He said, "The earth is round."
   Indirect speech: He said that the earth is round.

(Note: Since it's a universally accepted, everlasting truth that the earth is round, you don't need to use past tense here.)

10. Direct speech: She said to me, "I have tasted it."
    Indirect speech: She told me that she had tasted it.
11. Direct speech: He said, "Then I recited the poem but she didn't."
    Indirect speech: He said that then he recited the poem but she didn't.
12. Direct speech: Hari said, "Honey is sweet."
    Indirect speech: Hari said that honey is sweet. *(Again, a universal truth)*
13. Direct speech: She said to me, 'Jump."
    Indirect speech: She told me to jump.
14. Direct speech: He said, "I will do it."
    Indirect speech: He said that he would do it.
15. Direct speech: She said to me, "Who is calling me?"
    Indirect speech: She asked me who was calling her.
16. Direct speech: The policeman said to him, 'Stop the car."
    Indirect speech: The policeman told him to stop the car.
17. Direct speech: He said, "Nepal is a sovereign nation."
    Indirect speech: He said that Nepal is a sovereign nation.
18. Direct speech: She said, "Please convey my message."
    Indirect speech: She requested him to convey her message.
19. Direct speech: The inspector said to the thief, "Hands up.'
    Indirect speech: The inspector ordered the thief to put his hands up.
20. Direct speech: She said, "May you live long!"
    Indirect speech: She wished that I might live long.
21. Direct speech: He said, "Let's play football every day."
    Indirect speech: He suggested that we should play football every day.
22. Direct speech: He said to his dad, "Please buy me a chocolate."
    Indirect speech: He requested his dad to buy him a chocolate.
23. Direct speech: His boss said to him, 'Go and finish the report."
    Indirect speech: His boss ordered him to go and finish the report.
24. Direct speech: "I'm a student," she tells people.
    Indirect speech: She tells people that she is a student.
25. Direct speech: They said to me, "We were trying to help you."
    Indirect speech: They told me that they had been trying to help me.
26. Direct speech: Rajkumar said, "Einstein was a great scientist."
    Indirect speech: Rajkumar said that Einstein was a great scientist.
27. Direct speech: The doctor said, "We must drink pure water to stay healthy."
    Indirect speech: The doctor said that we must drink pure water to stay healthy.

28. Direct speech: I told him, "Vikas can not come."
Indirect speech: I told him that Vikas couldn't come.
29. Direct speech: She said to me, "I will visit my mother."
Indirect speech: She told me she would visit her mother.
30. Direct speech: "You must do it," Ravina said to him.
Indirect speech: Ravina told him that he would have to do it.
31. Direct speech: She told me, "While I was studying, my brother was playing."
Indirect speech: She told me that while she was studying, her brother was playing.
32. Direct speech: Son said to his mother, "I'm hungry."
Indirect speech: Son told his mother that he was hungry.
33. Direct speech: A passenger said to me, "Do you know that place?"
Indirect speech: A passenger asked me if I knew that place.
34. Direct speech: I said to her, "What are you up to?"
Indirect speech: I asked her what she was up to.
35. Direct speech: The waiter said to me, "Please try our signature dish."
Indirect speech: The waiter requested me to try their signature dish.
36. Direct speech: Kumar said, "I congratulate you on your victory."
Indirect speech: Kumar congratulated me on my victory.
37. Direct speech: We said, "Hurray! We have won."
Indirect speech: We exclaimed with joy that we had won.
38. Direct speech: She said to me, "I don't know him."
Indirect speech: She told me she didn't know him.
39. Direct speech: Dad said to me, "Don't disturb your sister now."
Indirect speech: Dad told me not to disturb my sister then.
40. Direct speech: "Leave at once," the owner said to the shabby stranger.
Indirect speech: The owner ordered the shabby stranger to leave at once.
41. Direct speech: Student said, "Good Morning, teacher."
Indirect speech: Student wished his teacher good morning.
42. Direct speech: The poor man said, "May God make me rich."
Indirect speech: The poor man prayed that God might make him rich.

Practice Exercise

If you have read the above examples carefully, please try answering the following questions. *(The correct answers have been provided in the appendix.)*

1. He said, "Nobody is doing anything wrong."

2. The child said, “My father came home late.”
3. Shweta said to him, “Do you love your wife?”
4. She said, “I cannot go with them.”
5. Kirti said to us, “Hey! I saw a tiger in the forest!”
6. “I apologise,MrPandey,” said the hotel manager.
7. Nina said, “Congratulations, Ashish. You have done well.”
8. The guest asked, “Where is the main entrance to the hotel?”
9. They said, “We will be there.”
10. “I was writing a letter when it happened,” she said.
11. The principal said to Vijay, “If you don’t behave properly, you shall be rusticated from the school.”
12. The general said, “I will make sure that the enemy does not cross the border.”
13. He said, “What a lovely picture!”
14. His mother said to him, “Finish your food.”
15. His mother said to him, “Have you finished your food?”
16. She said to me, “Thank you for your help.”
17. Rohit said to his friends, “Let’s swim.”
18. The teacher said to the principal, “Sir, can I leave early today?”
19. The teacher said to the principal, “Sir, please allow me leave early today.”
20. He said, “Oh my God, I have won!”
21. Lokesh said, “The best player could not get into the semi-finals. It’s a pity.”
22. His mother said, “May God be with you.”
23. Reena said to me, “I won’t come tomorrow.”
24. The man said to me, “What can we do about it?”
25. He said to his friends, “You should not go there.”
26. The teacher said to the student, “Get out.”
27. The beggar said to us, “I have eaten nothing since yesterday.”
28. The soldiers said, “Long live the king.”
29. “Who attacked you?” he said to me.
30. She said to her servant, “Take the dog out for a walk.”
31. He said to me, “It is impossible.”
32. She said to me, “I have never been to a circus ever before.”
33. He said to her, “I love you.”

34. Veena said to me, "Sheela told Neela about you."
35. My friend said to me, "We are going for a movie. Will you join us?"
36. Soni said, "Rajesh, can you lend me some money?"
37. "Good evening, Colonel," the soldier said.
38. My colleague Shikha said to me, "I was followed by a man."
39. The manager said, "Alas! We have committed a blunder!"
40. The patientcried, "Ouch! It hurts."
41. Shiva said to the class, "The earth is round."
42. Nurse said, "The patient is no more."
43. He said, "How magnificent this palace is!"
44. "Rinku," said his father, "bring your aunty a glass of water."
45. She said to me, "I was playing tennis when Geet arrived."
46. She said to me, "I was playing tennis."
47. She said to me, "I had been playing tennis since years."
48. The judge said to the minor criminal, "Your apologies are being accepted this time."
49. Her mother said to her, "Who is this boy?"
50. The speaker said, "Swami Vivekananda was a great scholar."
51. The customer, Mrs Yogi, said, "Who am I speaking to?"
52. "I had been to London," he said.

Please express the following sentences in direct speech:

1. He asked me who I had been trying to contact.
2. She said her mother was ill.
3. She says her mother is ill.
4. I told him I couldn't attend the party.
5. They said they had worked together for years.
6. We told them that we couldn't help them.
7. He asked me who the most intelligent student in our class was.
8. Neha said that she had been studying for her exams.
9. Shashank says that he is in love with that girl.
10. Amřita told me that she didn't like Shashank.
11. Amrita told me that she could never like Shashank.
12. Billy says he is fed up with the system.
13. Billy said that he was fed up with the system.
14. The farmer asked them who they were.

15. Her mother said she prays to God every day.
16. He says he lives in a skyscraper.
17. The boy told his father that he hadn't been lying.
18. The teacher told the class that the sun rises in the east.
19. The student wished the teacher a good afternoon.
20. She said she hadn't done it.
21. She told me that she wouldn't be able to attend the morning prayers.
22. Vishakha asked me if I could dance.
23. We exclaimed with joy that our team had won the match.
24. They exclaimed with sorrow that they had lost the match.
25. She proposed that we should go to Nainital.
26. She told me that Sohan had left Delhi.
27. She told me that Sohan had been living in Mumbai for the last three years.
28. The coach told the team that if they wanted to win the match, they should practice hard.
29. They said they were going there on a trip.
30. The teacher told him to shut up.
31. The teacher asked him if he would shut up.
32. His friend requested him to speak slowly.

ooo

Unit- 6

Idioms and Phrases

Definition

Idiom consists in a set of words for an expression, which bears no direct meaning on the words employed. Thus, idiom carries a peculiar meaning which cannot be construed from the meaning of individual words contained in the idiom. To reiterate, if one attempts to determine the meaning of the idiom by analysing the words constituting the idiom and finding out the individual meaning of the analysed words, the resultant interpretation will be insensible.

For example, 'To talk turkey'.

Phrase is a set of words for an expression whose meaning can be interpreted from the meanings of the individual words composing the phrase.

For example, 'Gird up one's loins'.

Phrasal Verbs

Back down	–	concede defeat
Back off	–	withdraw from action
Back out	–	withdraw from promise/commitment
Back up	–	spare copy of necessary data
Blow someone	–	kill by firing gun away
Blow off	–	lose temper and give into one's feelings
Blow over	–	pass off without serious consequences
Blow someone up	–	explode
Break down	–	lose emotional control suddenly, sudden functional failure of a machine/equipment.
Break away	–	escape from control or separate from group
Break in	–	enter forcibly

Break into	–	suddenly burst into anger, laughter, singing; to enter by force; to interrupt (a conversation); to begin suddenly (break into a run); to use part of, unwillingly e.g. to break into the money one has saved
Break off	–	suddenly snap relationship
Break out	–	sudden happening of fire, hostilities, war, curfew etc.
Break up	–	item-wise accounting, disperse a crowd
Break with	–	act in contravention of tradition /customs
Breathe down	–	to keep too close a watch on what someone is someone's neck doing e.g. Indian students cannot work properly when the Britishers are breathing down their necks all the time
Breathe last	–	to die
Breathe into	–	i. to take into the lungs e.g. He became ill after breathing in a lot of coal dust ii. to listen to closely. She breathed in every word he was saying.
Call back	–	to summon back; recall; revoke; retract
Call for	–	demand
Call down	–	make one appear before someone
Call off	–	cancel (e.g. demonstration, meeting etc.)
Call in question	–	challenge; throw doubt on
Call to order	–	ask audience to keep silence (e.g. in a meeting)
Call upon	–	go to meet/visit
Call up	–	summon from beneath, or from another world
Carry away	–	take away
Carried away	–	lose self control; to get excited. Martha got so carried away while arguing with her boss as she resigned presently
Carry forward	–	take the figures or data on the next page to continue further; balance in accounting is carried forward
Carry off	–	take away by force
Carry on	–	continue with what one is doing

Carry out – perform a task

Carry over – keep something to use elsewhere

Carry through – bring a task to completion

Check in – arrival at a hotel or at airport for stay or travel

Check into – enter occupancy in hotel register

Check out – enter vacating time in hotel register

Check on – verify

Check up – investigate; examine

Clear away – remove from a place

Clear off – go away from a place

Clear up – be cured of symptoms

Close up – feel blocked, choked

Close on – gradually get nearer to (closely on the heels of the enemy)

Close around – surround

Close down – shut business/shop

Come across – meet by chance

Come around – recover from shock

Come down (upon) – criticize

Come forward – come ahead to accept a challenge or responsibility, so as to rise to the occasion

Come about – happen, to take place

Come back – return; revival; retort

Come before – be presented to someone for consideration, discussion and judgement.

Come off – succeed; take place; happen.

Come on – start doing something

Come out – emerge

Come through – to arrive as expected

i. Have your examination results come through yet? (with) to do what is needed or expected.

ii. I knew that in the end John would come through with the money we needed to survive a risk.

iii. John was so ill as gloomy prognostications were made about him, but despite he (John) survived

Come up – appear unexpectedly as of a problem

Come up against – to encounter a difficulty or confront opposition, e.g. The workers came up against their employer's willingness to pay higher wages despite waranting situations

Cut in – interrupt

Cut off – break connection

Cut out – stop machine's operation; cut out a niche = found a suitable job.

Cut up – behave in unruly manner; cause a person to be emotionally upset.

Cut down – cause to fall by cutting.

Draw back – not to take action because one feels unsure or nervous.

Draw in – come close as of an occasion.

Draw out – become longer in coming of an occasion; hours of day light become longer in spring.

Drop behind – fall back and be left

Drop by or in – visit to meet someone

Drop off – fall

Drop out – cease to take part; e.g. school dropout.

Get across – manage to make idea or proposal known to someone

Get away – escape

Get down to – give serious attention to task/business

Get off – be acquitted of charges/punishment

Get over – recover from a problem; surmount

Get around – manage to deal with a problem

Get through – make contact on telephone

Get up – rise from seat

Give away – hand over prizes etc.

Give in – surrender, yield to demands

Give out – stop working due to weariness; emit

Give up	–	cease making effort any longer due to losing hope; abandon.
Go about	–	carry out a work; pursue.
Go against	–	oppose
Go ahead	–	proceed
Go along with	–	agree to
Go at	–	tackle something
Go back on	–	fail to keep promise/assurance
Go down	–	be defeated in contest; be remembered in history.
Go for	–	to assail; to set out to secure; to go to secure or fetch
Go into	–	investigate
Go off	–	explode as a bomb, gunfire
Go on	–	continue
Go out	–	be extinguished (of a fire or lights)
Go through	–	pass through difficult time/search or examine a document carefully
Go with	–	agree to someone
Go without	–	suffer lack of something
Hand (something) down	–	pass over to successor
Hand (someone) off	–	push
Hand (something) out	–	disseminate information (press statement); award punishment.
Hand over	–	pass to someone else
Hold down	–	succeed in keeping; stop a vehicle
Hold off	–	fail to occur, resist a challenge or attack
Hold on	–	wait, stop
Hold out	–	resist difficult situation
Hold for	–	continue to demand
Hold over	–	postpone something
Hold up	–	delay progress
Keep off	–	be away from
Keep on	–	continue to do

Keep up	–	continue progress
Keep up with	–	keep oneself aware of
Keep someone up	–	keep someone awake
Keep something up	–	continue a course of action
Knock down	–	dismantle
Knock out	–	make unconscious
Lay down	–	formulate rules, conditions
Lay off	–	discharge from work
Lay out	–	spread to full extent
Let down	–	fail to support
Let in	–	allow to come
Let off	–	set free
Let out	–	allow (an opportunity) to escape; to release a person from his unpleasant situation
Let up	–	lessening of intensity; relax one's efforts
Live for	–	regard as the most important in one's life
Live in/at	–	reside
Live off	–	depend on as source of income
Live through	–	survive unpleasant experience
Live in with	–	live with someone without marriage
Look after	–	take care
Look back	–	stop progressing
Look down upon	–	treat with disdain
Look in	–	examine
Look on	–	watch without getting involved
Look out	–	be vigilant for possible danger
Make good	–	to compensate for; to provide restitution or reporation.
Make off	–	to run away; depart hastily.
Make off with	–	to carry away; steal
Make out	–	to write out or complete; to establish/prove (e.g. as a liar); to comprehend; to imply; to suggest (informally meaning for managing or succeeding)

Make over	–	to remodel; alter; to make over a dress/page; to transfer or convey the title deeds of the property
Make up	–	the way anything is arranged, composed or constituted; mental qualities; an actor's materials for personating a part or a woman's cosmetics; to invent
Make up for	–	to compensate for; to make good
Pass by	–	go without notice; hardly aware that it was happening
Pass off	–	happen
Pass out	–	lose consciousness; passing out ceremony for cadets after completing the training
Pass over	–	ignore, avoid
Pick on	–	Single out for unkind remark or treatment
Pick out	–	select from a heap
Pick up	–	gain speed, collect someone from a place
Play about	–	behave in a casual manner
Play down	–	try to lessen the gravity of something happened; belittle.
Play on	–	exploit someone's weak point
Pull back	–	withdraw from doing something
Pull down	–	demolish
Pull off	–	succeed in achieving
Pull out	–	withdraw from a group
Pull through	–	come out of a problem
Put aside	–	keep reserved for future use
Put down	–	suppress rebellion, riot by force
Put off	–	cancel a meeting etc., postpone
Put on	–	become heavier by gaining weight
Put through	–	subject to unpleasant experience
Put up	–	offer a fight or resistance, present a matter for discussion
Put up with	–	tolerate
Run across	–	meet by chance
Run after	–	chase

Run away	–	escape
Run down	–	become weak due to illness
Run into	–	collide
Run off	–	abscond
Run out	–	exhaust
Run over	–	knock down and crush
Set about	–	start doing something; begin a task; informally, attack with blows or words
Set against	–	be in opposition
Set apart	–	keep separate
Set aside	–	keep reserved for some purpose; to rescind an order or cancel or reject a verdict sentence; superseding the judgement of a lower court by an appellate court
Set back	–	delay in progress
Set forth	–	begin a journey; state or describe; present or declare.
Set off	–	explode
Show off	–	display one's ability boastfully; to draw attention by displaying prominently one's accomplishments
Show forth	–	exhibit; expound
Show up	–	expose fault, misdeed etc.; disagree, discredit embarrass or humiliate
Sit in	–	demonstrate in protest
Sit on	–	delay in dealing with something
Sit up	–	be alert
Sit down	–	get ready to start working
Take off	–	be airborne; to embark on a travel
Take (clothes) off	–	remove
Take on	–	accept responsibility etc.
Take over	–	take under control
Take up	–	accept, such as a challenge
Touch down	–	descend on the ground
Touch off	–	ignite or make explode

Touch up – make improvement to spruce up

Touch on – mention a subject briefly

Touch at – stay at a place for brief period

Turn against – be hostile

Turn up – come to a place

Turn away – send back

Turn down – reject

Turn off – stop machine's operation

Turn on – start machine's operation

Turn out to be – become known

Turn over – hand over control

Turn around – change for better

Walk away with – steal

Walk away from – abandon responsibility

Walk over – a race where only one competitor appears, resulting in his easy or unopposed victory

Walk out – the act of walking out; to indicate disapproval; a sudden industrial strike.

Phrases

A

A priori – an opinion is a priori when it is framed on the basis of theoretical knowledge, principles, premises, or deductive reasoning rather than actual experience.

A fortiori – a conclusion, opinion which is having greater conviction, certainty than even the one which formed the basis of the latter conclusion.
* If I cannot do this, a fortiori, neither can you do it.

A la carte – as per the chart or list or menu.
* This hotel serves food items a la carte and charges as per each item.

A la table d'hote – as per fixed rate for a full meal in a hotel.
* Some hotels provide meals a la table d'hote to its customers irrespective of one's diet.

Aces up one's sleeve – a winning plan kept reserved for timely use.

Achilles heels – a vulnerable point in an otherwise redoubtable structure; the great and bold Greek hero in the Trojan war, Achilles was feld by his mother Thetis in his infancy stage on the heel while dipping into the Styx (infernal river) to make him invulnerable.
* Runaway inflation is the Achille's heels in our well thought economic planning.

At odds – at variance

Ad hoc – for the purpose at hand.
* Central government granted ad hoc money for relief work in the food affected areas.
* Ad hoc appointments are made in an office to meet the sudden extra load of work.
* The country should frame some coordinated policy instead of ad hoc measures to combat poverty and unemployment in the country.

Ad interim – temporary measure pending final solution.
* The government announced ad interim pay hike for employees to give partial respite from price rise pending final decision about the exact quantum of enhancement.
* The court ordered ad interim injunction against government orders.

Ad verbatim – word by word
* He narrated ad verbatim the argument between him and his friend

Much ado about nothing –a lot of fuss over some petty matter.
* Most of the persons entrusted with arrangement of function tend to make much ado about nothing, instead of contributing something silently on the occasion.

(Act) against one's better judgement – Act foolishly.

Agent provocateur – a secretly insinuated person into a group to provoke them to commit crime.
* An unscrupulous group acted as agents provocateurs to foment trouble in population already divided on communal lines.

* Pakistan is alleged to employ agents provocateurs to create an atmosphere of insecurity amongst people of a particular community.

Aide memoir – a brief note on salient points of a text which helps one's memory to recollect it when desired.
* The assistant prepared aide memoir of speech.

Alive and kicking – still living in good health and activated.
* He is still alive and kicking at the age of sixty.

All hell broke loose – widespread chaos erupted suddenly.

Alter ego – a second self; counterpart; double.
* He became my alter ego.
* The alter egos of a political boss followed his suit in resigning their posts in the government

Amicus curiae – friend (Ami) of the court, who advises court of helps in its proceedings.

* The court appointed a social worker as its amicus curiae to report on the plight of slumdwellers.

Arm-in-arm – with the arm of one person being passed through the bent arm of the other.

* Protestors walked arm-in-arm on the street.

At hand – very near, about to occur.
* The final exam is at hand

At home with – be comfortable with

A propos – In reference to; to the purpose; appropriately.

At par/Below par/ – equal/below/above in value to Above par something else

At one's wit's end – at the end of intelligence/ingenuity.
* A person confronted with several problems simultaneously, was at his wit's end to solve them satisfactorily.

At the end of one's tether –a rope, chain which is used to fasten a cattle to restrict its movements, is called tether. It is used in sentences, like "Tether cow to graze." "Tether a balloon with string to the doorknob". This phrase indicates that one's resources, or strength, or patience is almost exhausted.
* An indigent person was at the end of his tether.
* A salaried person reaches the end of his tether by the month end.

At the helms of – be in a position of controlling situation

B

Back and forth – to and fro.
* Move back and forth

back to back – one behind another.
* They were sitting back to back.

(on) Back foot – on defensive position against accusation.

Back against the wall – in desperate situation.
*All round criticism pushed him with his back against the wall.

Back to square one – return to the starting point.

Back in reckoning – recover one's lost position.

Turn one's back on – to ignore someone.

Balmy days – happy days in life.

Bated breath – held up breathing in anxiety, excitement or impatience.
* He waited for his son's returning home with bated breath.

Bay for blood Hold – hanker for revenge.

/Keep someone at bay keep someone or something some distance away.

Beck and call – ready to obey
* He keeps himself at his boss's beck and call.

Bear in mind – to remember

Bear the brunt of – suffer major cousequence of some injurious action.

Bear grudge – harbour enmity or resentment
* He bears grudge against me.

Beat about the bush – to discuss a matter without coming to point.

Bete noire (French) – the person or thing one dislikes most.
* Poor people are bete noire of sophisticated strata of population.

Beyond the pale – outside the bounds of civilized behaviour.
* Conduct beyond the pale attracts criticism.

Bids one's time – wait for opportune time.
* He bides his time to settle score with his adversaries.

Blaze the trail – do something new in such a way as others follow that. Literally, it means marking out trees in a path for others to follow.
* He blazed the trail in a new branch of science.

Blockbuster – (block + buster) Block means a wide space in a city. A city is divided into many blocks of residential areas.

Bust – to knock, to hit, viz. bust in the nose. Therefore, blockbuster means a powerful thing like a bomb which can knock or destroy the whole block of a city. For that matter, a movie, or a speech which is so effective as to attract the whole city or to impress the whole audience, may be called a blockbuster movie, or speech.
* Rajnikant's films mostly turn into blockbuster movies. (Greatly demanding and successful)

* The new economic measures to control black money may prove blockbusters (highly effective).

* His extempore speech was a real blockbuster.

Go berserk – become uncontrolled in a state of frenzy.

Blanket ban – complete prohibition

Draw blank – be unsuccessful in one's attempt

Blow the whistle – to expose wrong doing against someone.

* He blew whistle against wrong doings going on in his office.

Blow by blow – (describe) events as had happened one by one in logical sequence.

Blow hot and cold – vacillate between hot temper and cool one.

Bog down – be trapped in difficulty

Body blow – severe setback
* Suffer a body blow

Bolt from the blue – sudden and unexpected event causing surprise
* Chinese attack on our country was a bolt from the blue

Bone of contention – source of continuous disagreement

Bonne bouche – literally, "Good mouth". It means supremely dainty.
* Each dish was a bonne bouche.

Bon hommie – Bon – good, hommie – man, people, so, geniality.

* Undying bon hommie (warm nature) radiates from him.

* Christmas bon hommie is enjoyed by all.

* The bon hommie of a family reunion is a nostalgic experience.

Bon vivant – (life – viva) So, one who enjoys a good life.

* He is a prodigious worker and a bon vivant.

* Bon vivants revel in sumptuous food

Bon voyage – It means good journey.
* All of us bade him bon voyage and happy, safe return.

Booby prize – award given to the competitor who finishes last i.e., to the lowest score

(to) Boot – besides, over and above, something extra.

* I swapped my pen with that of my friend and paid him Rs. 5 to boot.

This means that I exchanged my pen with a costlier pen of my friend, and paid him Rs. 5 in addition to my pen, so as to compensate the difference in prices of the two pens.

* He is essentially a scholar, and a musician to boot.

		* Mr. Birla, a businessman, was a member of parliament to boot.
Bone of contention	–	a contentious matter; cause for dispute.
Brace oneself up	–	to prepare for making efforts to achieve something.
		* The party in power is bracing itself up for winning next election to continue in powers.
Break the ice	–	start talking by breaking initial hesitation in relationship with strangers or enemy
Breathe down	–	keep close watch over someone; to stress the someone's neck importance of it
Bring something home	–	to stress the importance of it impress upon
Bring someone to book	–	to punish/to take someone to task for failure or wrong action
Bury hatchet	–	to stop quarrelling and become friendly.
By all means	–	yes, of course; certainly.
By no means	–	not to inquire into private matters impertinently.
Breathe last	–	to die
By and by	–	gradually
By the way	–	incidently
By and large	–	on the whole
By hook or by crook	–	to achieve something through any means.

C

Carpe diem	–	Carpe – fruit, diem – day. So (enjoy) the fruit of today (without having any concern for the next day).
		* Improvident persons believe in carpe diem –they wallow in their present even if it spells disaster for future.
Carp and cavil	–	to raise objection on trivial issues.
		* The losing team began to carp & cavil on referee's decision in the match.

* Opposition parties carp and cavil even at well intended measures of the government.

Carte blanche – also, charta blanche – Blank Cheque. So, it means allow exercise of full discretionary power.

Casus beli – beli – belligerence, anything which is used as excuse for conflict or war.

* In our country, the religion has been freely and wantonly used as casus beli between people of different ethnic groups.

* Even a minor tiff becomes a casus beli between Israel and the Palestinians.

Catch one's breath – to stop running or talking so as to recover from breathlessness.

Cause celebre – an incident, case or a topic which has attracted wide attention of public.

* Shah Bano case on divorced muslim women's maintenance became a cause celebre in our country.

* A sensational case of moral depravity of a cabinet minister is a potential cause celebre.

Caveat emptor – the principle that the seller cannot be held responsible for the quality of his product unless guaranteed in a warranty (Let the buyer beware).

Caviare to the general – be too refined or delicate to be appreciated by ordinary people.

Carve a niche for oneself – earn a respectable position for oneself in one's field of work/study/research.

Call the shot – take initiative in something by revealing one's intentions.

Call a spade a spade – to speak the plain truth without being delicate or sensitive.

Call it a day – stop activity for the day and go to rest.

Call someone to order – to ask someone to stop disobeying the rules of a formal meeting.

Change one's stance – change one's previously taken stand on a matter.

(on) cloud nine – be extremely elated.

Cock a snook at – to give a damn by joining thumb to one's nose top with rest of the palm wide open.

* The kids cocked a snook at the back of the teacher when he was leaving the class.

* A few in the crowd cocked a snook at the policemen when ordered to disperse.

Cool one's heels – to be forced to wait.

Out in the cold – neglected.

Come a cropper – to fall heavily, to fail completely.

Having reached the final, the British have come a cropper against the more experienced German team.

Come home to roost – to take effect upon the person who has said them.

Come of age – to be matured *Our democracy has come of age

Come to blows – start fighting

Come to grips with – have a firm hold on something

Corpus delicti – corpse (careass) – corporeal, body, delicti means crime. In law, the basic element of a crime, as in murder, the death of the murdered person.

* The criminal tried to dispose of the corpus delicti before he escaped.

Corpus vile – worthless (vile) thing which can be risked by experimenting upon.

* Primates are the corpus vile for medical research.

* Education is a corpus vile which is always subjected to new ideas and fancies.

Coup d' etat – coup – blow, stroke. Therefore, it means a blow imparted to an established rule by using force and eventual capture of that institution.

* In many countries, the governments are very frequently overthrown by coup d' etat, and power captured and wielded by military junta.

Coup d' grace – blow of mercy, so, mercy killing, euthanasia. Also, any decisive, final blow.

* Relatives' right to decide giving coup d' grace to a patient afflicted with a terminal disease is a raging controversy.

* His action was coup d' grace for my faith in him.

Cri d' coeur – Coeur – heart, so, cry coming from the core of the heart. Heart-felt protestations, strong and forceful entreaty.

* His cri de coeur for my help moved me.

* His cri de coeur in his attempt to prove his innocence seems to be genuine.

Cross the Rubicon – Rubicon was a small river between Rome and a province of Roman Empire. Julius Caesar was provincial governor who came in conflict with central ruler over maintaining his own band of army, and eventually crossed the river with his army into Rome to overthrow the central ruler. Therefore, a step which sets the events proceed beyond point of no return; which commits one irrevocably to a cause of action; of which one can say that the 'die is cast' is explained by this phrase.

Cry in wilderness – futile exercise in advocating something to others.

* His all attempts to refurbish the image of his organisation ended in a cry in the wilderness.

Cul-de-sac – literally, it means "Bottom of the bag". Therefore, it means passage with no exit forward, i.e., closed at its one end.

* The clues led the investigator finally into a culde-sac.

Curriculum vitae – personal bio-data, autobiography.

* Applicants for a job are required to send brief curriculum vitae along with other information.

*An interesting curriculum vitae was written by the author.

Curry favour – To flatter to gain favour.

* Bureaucrats are ever eager to curry favour with their political boss.

Cut Gordian knot – When you are unable to untie a complicated knot despite a prolonged effort, you are likely to lose patience and snap the thread instead. In this way, you seek a sudden solution to a complicated problem.

* Alexander-the-Great cut (rather than united) the Gordian knot tied by Gordian the ancient king of Phrygia, who tied a knot in conformity with the prophecy that it was to be undone only by the person who was to rule Asia.

* The rampant corruption has become a Gordian knot. * To import technologies in preference to developing indigenous know-how is akin to cutting the Gordian knot.

D

Damocle's sword – A danger continuously hanging over one's head like a sword.

* Damocle's sword of glut and the consequent descending prices is vexing the blue chips of industry.

Damp squib – (something) failing to impress

Dance attendance upon –Behave obsequiously, be at one's beck and call.

* An opportunist will dance attendance upon you till you are useful to him.

Dance to someone's tunes – Act at someone's behest

* An uxorious man will dance to his wife's tune and do nothing without her approval.

Dark horse – A virtually unknown person who suddenly comes in prominence.

* A veteran was defeated by a dark horse in the election.

Day in and day out – Everday without fail; continuously.

De facto – By fact, in actuality, for all practical purposes.

* There exists a de facto state of war between Israel and Palestinians.

De jure – By right; according to law * Pt. Nehru was a de jure litterateur to boot.

Deja vu – in any of the arts, unoriginal material, old stuff; an illusion of having experienced before something that is really being experienced for the first time; a form of paramresia (psych.)

* A film on British Raj, which has been newly produced, is just a deja vu for us.

Dernier cri – The last word; the latest fashion.

*The 3-piece suit is dernier cri in winter garment

* These particular shoes are dernier cri.

Demier resort – Final/last resort/stay/refuge

* Shimla is the dernier resort in my current itinerary.

Dog in the manger – a person who does not let someone use something even if not needed by him.

Down-to-earth – (be) realistic in approach or thinking

* A down-to-earth person

Down but not out – disappointed at failures but not surrendered

(Take a) dig at – criticize someone for his failure

Double entendre – a word or expression having two meanings – one of which is risque indelicacy or impropriety; off colour.

* A risque strong

(In the) doldrums – in stagnant situation, in state of inactivity

Double speak – speak in two veins making himself ambiguous

Double standard – use a rule unfairly for different people

Dressing down – give a reprimand

* Give a dressing down to him

Dribs and drabs – Miserably small amounts spread over a period of time; bit by bit

* Tax collected in dribs and drabs by way of income tax is too insufficient to support even the expenses of the income tax department.

Ducks and drakes – It is used "to play ducks and drakes". It means pastime of ricocheting flat stones on still surface of water. So, to throw away heedlessly, or squander, is what it means. *Private teaching shops are playing ducks and drakes with the students' career.

E

Eminence grise – "Grey eminence" also. It means a confidant of the person in power, who exercises power unofficially.

* The eminence grise sons and daughters of ministers don't hesitate even to humiliate senior bureaucrats, but one day each of them proved himself or herself the nemesis for his or her father.

Esprit d' corps – (vigour and spirit in a body) devotion to the organization to which one belongs.

* The esprit d'corps of the entire regiment dropped when its captain was hit by a bullet of the enemy.

*The esprit d' corps, obedience, and acceptance of responsibility are the essence of an employee * A man with esprit d' corps puts his country before his own self.

(Take) exception to – express strong objection because of being offended.

* He took exception to my remarks against him.

(Look) eye-to-eye – (be) in full agreement

* They look eye-to-eye on this matter.

In the eye of storm – be in the centre of controversy

(To) Eat a humble pie – be humiliated

Eat the cake & have it too – try to gain both ways

F

Fait accompli – A situation of something already done or accomplished, and is no longer worth arguing against its merits or demerits.

* He made emergency purchasing of stationery and got approval fait accompli.

Far cry – A distant goal. * Even after forty years since independence, emancipation of womenfolk in our society is a far cry.

Faux pas – Blunder, embarrassing act against etiquette.

* The whole plan or strategy to counter enemy attack ended in a fiasco due to a minor faux pas.

* His unpleasant remark in the tea party was a faux pas.

Femme fatale – A woman (femme) who seduces men

In fine fettle – in very good condition of health

(Play) first fiddle – To take leading part. * This scientist played first fiddle in the development of nuclear capability of our country.

(Play) second fiddle – To take subordinate position or role to the one who plays the first fiddle.

* He plays second fiddle to his elder brother and faithfully obeys him.

* A junior officer is always expected to play second fiddle to his senior.

* An uxorious husband plays second fiddle to his wife's wishes.

Fire first salvo – start a fight

(Be) Fit as fiddle – To be in extremely good health without any problem whatsoever.

* After recovering from past illness, he is now fit as fiddle.

Fits and starts – Move ahead, then suddenly stop, and again move and so on.

* He completed his education in fits and starts due to financial reasons.

* War against terrorism is going on in fits and starts for quite some time.

Fight shy – avoid something to face, keep away from

Fly-by-night – (business) not reliable and liable to bust overnight

*Foreign Institutional Investors (F.I.I.s) follow the principle of fly-by-night share business.

Fool's paradise – state of illusory happiness

Foot in mouth – making an embarrassing blunder (remark)

For the asking – (get something) with little effort

(Pick up) the gauntlet – To accept a challenge (gauntlet is the glove with loose wrist portion which a wicket-keeper or a fencer uses in the arena. So when a player or, for that matter, any contestant picks up his gauntlet, it is taken as his accepting the challenge of the opponent.)

Throw the gauntlet – To issue challenge to one's opponent (when a contestant throws a gauntlet on the ground in front of his opponent, it is open for him to accept the challenge, or to turn his back and accept defeat).

Run the gauntlet – To get through an array of hostile opponents in the way who are all out to oppose, criticise, harm.

* The government has to run the gauntlet of press criticisms.

G

Get hold of – catch

Get one's deserts – (desert dervied from 'to deserve') To receive reward or punishment as one deserves by dint of one's action.

* Judge awarded to each according to his desert.

* Praising someone beyond just desert is but flattery.

* He won appointment on grounds of deserts rather than through family connection.

Get out of hand – be uncontrolled

Gird up one's loins – be ready to fight or face what might come upon someone

Get off the ground – start

* The match just got off the ground

Give a damn – reject scornfully

Give and take – mutual compromise on helping each other

Go abegging – (something) be available, but not wanted by people

* Party tickets for election go abegging because of bad prospect of the party winning elections.

Go to dogs – become very bad

* The state of education in government schools has gone to the dogs

Go whole hog – do something with full energy

* He went whole hog to achieve success

H

Have no truck with – have no dealings with someone

Happy-go-lucky	–	cheerful, without caring for the future
Hand to mouth	–	manage to live on scanty resources available just to meet bare needs
Hands down	–	easily
		* They won the match hands down
(at) hand	–	be very near to happen
		* Exams are at hand
Hands off	–	not involved
		* Keep oneself hands off the controversy
Hand in hand	–	together
		* Mob were moving ahead hand-in-hand
(On) hand	–	be available
Hands in glove	–	work secretly in association with someone
Hang fire	–	Delay in execution
		* The courts' verdicts on the millions of cases are hanging fire for years together.
		* The young man is hanging fire about his marriage for the last several years.
Hang in the air	–	Be in incomplete situation
		* He left the task hung in the air.
Hang in balance	–	be uncertain in outcome
		* The prisoners' fate hung in the balance.
		* Have one's head in the cloud – have one's thought far away.
On one's heels	–	to flee from a place
Herculean task	–	a task requiring great strength and effort.
High and dry	–	be in a position of without resources
Hit below the belt	–	to criticise or deal a foul blow in an unfair manner
		*The common people are often hit by the government below the belt on economic issues.
To the hilt	–	to the maximum extent

Hobson's choice	–	Hobson used to give horse to others on hire. But, he used to force a customer to take the first horse in queue and did not allow him to choose one from the lot. The customer was left with no choice other than to "take or leave it". It means "a compelling situation of accepting one of the two equally detestable or injurious alternatives *Monopoly business forces the commodity on customers as Hobson's choice. * Under-employment is Hobson's choice for an unemployed person as he has to either accept it or suffer penury. * A conquered army is left with Hobson's choice of either accepting defeat or face annihilation. * Developing countries are constrained to accept foreign aids with strings as Hobson's choice.
Hoist with one's own petard	–	Caught or injured by what one intended as a trick for others.
Hold fast	–	keep tightly secured
Hold good	–	be valid as of a condition, argument
Hold back	–	hesitate to do something
Hold one's ground	–	refuse to budge
Hold water	–	be sound in logic (about a theory, idea etc.)
No holds barred	–	a fight in which any tactic, howsoever unfair, is used.
On the horns of a dilemma	–	Faced with a choice between things that are equally undesirable.

I

Ill at ease	–	feel uncomfortable
Inter alia	–	Among other things * Progress of our country depends upon, inter alia, the industrial growth and generation of employment opportunities. * Success of a project depends, inter alia, upon the quantity and quality of the persons who will execute it.

Inter se – Amongst themselves

* They resolved the differences inter se.

* All the species breed inter se.

In the offing – (offing – the part of off-shore sea which is visible from the shore, and is, therefore, not far. So, this phrase means something not far off and is likely to reach or apear in a short while.

* A change in the cabinet of ministers is in the offing.

In toto – In full, in totality

* He accepted my proposal in toto.

In the pink of health – in good health

In shambles – in chaotic condition

Ins and outs – all the details of something

Ipso facto – (literally, by the very fact itself.) It means 'by the nature of the act or fact itself'.

* Cheating in examination ipso facto is a crime.

* Indecent behaviour ipso facto deserves deprecation.

J

Jack of all trades – a person who does or tries to do many things without expertise in any trade

Joust with – to cross swords with

K

Keep someone posted with – keep informed of the latest situation

Keep someone at arm's length – keep a distance and not make intimacy with someone

Keep abreast of – be in up-to-date knowledge of something

Kick up a row – start an acrimonious quarrel

Kick someone upstairs– remove from powerful post by giving promotion to higher but powerless position

L

(For a) lark – (to do something) for amusement

Laissez faire – Let (people) do (as they choose).

* Business community has long been demanding laissez faire in industries.

* Mob indulged in laissez faire vandalism.

* Laissez faire religious practice is the antithesis of fundamentalism.

Leaps and bounds – Rapidly

* Economy is growing leaps and bounds

Leave in the cold – desert someone

Leave in the lurch – To abandon someone who deserves help and assistance.

* His friends left him in the lurch when he lost his fortune and needed their help.

Lese majeste – Crime against king, i.e., ruler, therefore, it means treason.

* In despotic regime, criticism of government is tantamount to lese majeste.

Live on the edge – be in a precarious condition

Lock horns with – engage in conflict with someone

Look askance at – take with suspicion

* The opposition parties look askance at every measure of welfare by the government.

Look with jaundiced eyes – Treat in a prejudiced manner

M

Magnum opus – magnum – big, great, opus – work. So, great work of an artist.

* The Discovery of India is the magnum opus of Pt. Jawaharlal Nehru.

Make good – become rich and successful

Make do with – manage with limited means

Make or break – do or die

Make no bones of – do not hesitate to tell something unpleasant

Make hay while sun shines – make good use of opportunities; take advantage of favourable conditions

Neck and neck – close to each other in competition

Make up one's mind – to make a firm decision

Modus operandi – Way of action/accomplishment of a task.

* To develop concord initially and then deprive of the belongings is the standard modus operandi of local thugs.

Modus vivendi – Temporary solution to a problem worked out, pending the final and permanent solution.

*Modus vivendi was set up between the belligerent parties pending final and permanent agreement of truce or armistice. * "No war" agreement between India and Pakistan would be a modus vivendi which would give a reprieve from spending huge resources on defence. *He worked out a satisfactory modus vivendi (workable agreement) with his life. *Well-intending relatives and friends made him to strike a modus vivendi with his wife, and save the family from ruin.

N

Nip in the bud – (Nip – to sever, to snap, to bite, to cut) Nip off flower buds. Nip off a proposal. There is a nip in the winter air (– a biting cold).

So, 'nip in the bud' means to snap, check, halt something harmful in the very incipient stage. * The rebellion was nipped in the bud by the troops loyal to the government. * It is always prudent to nip a potential administrative problem, or a social, or communal problem in the bud.

Nip & tuck – So close running that the lead or advantage shifts from one contestant to the other alternately. So, a very close contest.

* They ran nip and tuck. *It was a nip and tuck tournament for both the teams.

* These two students always compete nip and tuck with each other, and nobody can guess who will beat whom in the end.

Noblesse oblige – One's nobility or high position obliges him to conduct himself in generous, honourable, and responsible manners. Duty of a person occupying high position.

*Noblesse oblige prohibits one from freely mixing with common people.

* Noblesse oblige of judges demand their above suspicious image in the eyes of the litigants.

Nom d' plume – Additional name used with one's proper name for special effects

* Urdu poets used to assume a nom de plume viz "Dard", "Rahi", etc.

Non sequitur – An inference wrongly drawn from a valid premise. It does not follow inference from premise. * The veiled suggestion to ignore or wink at the widespread corruption because it is global phenomenon, is non-sequitur. (widespread corruption is true & hence a valid premise, but to ignore it on that account is a wrong inference).

Nouveau riche – Newly acquired wealth, devoid of commen surate education, culture or sophistication. *Inferiority complex of nouveau riche made him desirous of fame and respect through wealth.

* Honest public servants have to suffer a grim tribulation when their children too have to

compete with their nouveau riches peers in daily life from buying ice-cream to wearing jeans.

Nuts and bolts – basic detail of something

O

Obiter dictum – Incidental remark; a statement not essential to the main argument.

Odds and ends – miscellaneous articles

Odd man out – Distinguishable from the lot. * A man of his own ideology, he is odd man out of his colleagues.

Of no avail – without getting benefit

Of late – lately, recently

* Daytime is getting warmer of late

Off hand – (deal) in non-caring manner

Off the cuff – spontaneous, unprepared, informal.

* He gave an off the cuff discourse on the topic of discussion.

Off the hook – spared from charges or punishment

Off the mark – get started

Off and on – intermittently, not continuously

Off the track – away from the right path

(sit) On fence – wait for opportune moment to decide on whom to take side with, or avoid taking sides

On the rampage – engaged in violence and looting

On the rocks – in a difficult situation, fighting for existence

On the anvil – (anvil is the block of iron on which smith works.) Therefore, it means something is in the process of being prepared.*Proper fiscal discipline with avoidance of profligacy in economic policies will ensure that successful economic policy is on the anvil.

On one's mettle – On one's best of ability in the face of a challenge *He was put on his mettle by the new challenges in his task * He is on his mettle in the field of literature.

On one's own accord – voluntarily, on one's own volition

Out of the blue – unexpectedly, without warning

Out of order – not being in working order

Of sorts – of inconsequential quality.

* He is a poet of sorts. * He is a student of sorts. * He is an M.P. of sorts.

Out of sorts – in bad mood * He is feeling out of sorts.

Out and out – completely

Once in a blue moon – very rarely

* He is seen once in a blue moon

On the tenterhook – be in suspense

Over and above – in addition to what you get

P

Palmy days – Happy and prosperous period of one's life

Papier mashe/mache – A figure moulded in glued pulp. Hence, unreal, artificial and easily demolished.

*Papier mache aristocracy. * A papier mache crisis was tauted to gain support in its favour. * A papier mache hero, trepid from within.

* A papier mache magnanimity will give way to selfishness at the very first opportunity.

*A papier mache facade of harmony will crumble at the slightest jerk.

Pass muster – To pass inspection or examination, hence, found to be satisfactory.

* These excuses will not pass muster.

* Variety of music of sorts pass muster under the name of experiments in this art.

Pass the buck – To shift responsibility on others. * One tends to pass the buck to others for a blunder one commits, but does not hesitate to arrogate others' achievement to himself.

Per se – As such, in itself, intrinsically. *Envy per se is not always bad, because it may be the primus mobile for one's diligent effort to emulate a success, which has caused him envy. * Mere pronouncement of equality before law of the land per se is not enough; its implementation is what that matters.

Personae dramatis – Participants in an actual event. * The personae dramatis of this new movie contain great names of film industry.

* All the personae dramatis in our freedom struggle were accomplished personalities in their respective discipline.

Persona non grata – It means an unacceptable person. * Government declared two officers of a diplomatic mission as persona non grata.

Pip at the post – To defeat at the last moment near the goal post. *The runner-up in the race pipped the front runner at the post.

* Those who slogged for the whole year were pipped at the post by those who never read but had the gumption common sense and initiative of cheating in examinations.

Play to the gallery – Aim to gain popularity by satisfying the people's whims.

Play footsie with – Indulge in intimacy covertly and sometimes with duplicity.

* Politicians play footsie with criminals.

Play down – to treat a serious matter in light manner.

Play safe – be careful in doing something

Play possum – Pretend asleep or dead. * It is difficult to get response from one who is playing possum.

Play truant – be absent from school or workplace

Pour or vent one's spleen upon – To release violently one's latent spite, malignant feelings of anger upon someone (who is made the target of attack).

		* His countrymen poured their spleen at his failure by excommunicating him. *The people vent their spleen at the goverment for its failure to maintain law and order.
Pride of place	–	the most prominent position
Prima donna	–	The leading person who leads others. Hence, a persona who cannot work under someone else, or as a team-mate. * We are looking for team-mate, rather than prima donna.
Prima facie	–	At face value *His arguments seem prima facie valid.
Pro tem or Pro tempore	–	for temporary period
Put paid to	–	To destroy, demolish * This failure put paid to his pretension to be a good student.
Put someone through their paces	–	Test someone's physical mental ability/skill. *The players were put through their paces in adverse condition. *Test pilot put the new planes through their paces.
Pyrrhic victory	–	A victory won at great cost. *The Second World War proved a pyrrhic victory for the Allied countries – millions of lives and stupendous amount of resources were lost in the war.
Put one's best foot forward	–	start something confidently and impressively

Q

Quacks and midget	–	Pseudo experts and those of no consequence in a matter which needs trained and expert hands * Due to the non-availability of medical facilities in remote villages, quacks and midgets rule the roost. * Entry of quacks and midgets in industries requiring sophisticated technologists and experts is a potential hazard.
Queer the pitch	–	To make a mess of, to botch up a smooth process. * His pyrotechnical speech queered

the pitch for ongoing peace negotiation. * A parochial leader is enough to queer the pitch of communal harmony.

Quid pro quo – Something taken or given in return for something else given or taken.*Exchange of quids for quos. * You cannot expect to get prompt service in certain government offices without a quid pro quo. *Bilateral deal between India and a rich nation like USA would ensure the rich party a large quid for minor quo. *It is a folly to grant an increase in status and salary of an employee without insisting upon commensurate quid pro quo.

(on the) Qui vive – Who are you? A sentry on guard challenges with this sentence. "Qui vive" is the equivalent call of a French guard. Hence, this phrase means "To be alert, or be on the look-out for something dangerous."

* A suspicious person is always on the qui vive for his own safety from any possible deceitful action of others around him. *A cautious worker is always on the qui vive for possible errors.

R

Raise cains over – To make noise over something * The boss raised cains over the late coming of his staff.

* The kids were raising cains.

Rap and rend – To seize by hook or by crook * Expedient politicians rap and rend electoral victory and ministerial berth.

Take the rap – To take punishment * He took the rap for the lapses of his subordinates.

Raison d' etre – Reason for, or justification for, existence.

* Work seems to be her raison d' etre.

Raring to go – be excited to start something

Reach nadir – go to the bottom of downfall; time of the greatest depression, despair etc. *With this failure, she reached the madir of her career.

Res Judicata	–	A point/legal point that has been finally decided by the court, and cannot be re-opened, de novo at least between the same two parties.
Ride roughshod over	–	To trample, put down ruthlessly. *He rode roughshod over opponents. * Biased occupants of gubernatorial assignments ride roughshod over constitutional propriety.
Rigor mortis	–	Rigidity of body after death. * A deadbody undergoes rigor mortis in certain hours after death
Rise to occasion	–	to act according to the exigent need of the time
Rub shoulder with	–	be in company of an important person
Rub someone the wrong way	–	to make someone angry
Rule the roost	–	To have full control * The criminals now rule the roost in Indian polity.
(Give) a run for one's money	–	give a tough fight in competition
Run-of-the-mill	–	Constituting an ordinary fair sample; not selected * The quality of our body politic has, of late, been vitiated by the run-of-the-mill politicians who now rule the roost.
Run to seed	–	To exhaust vitality, cease growing, deteriorate extremely. * Let his mind run to seed. * The old man has run to seed.
Be on the run	–	keep fleeing to avoid to be caught
Run with the hare and hunt with the hound	–	have your cake and eat it; to be in advantage both ways by remaining with both sides in a fight; try to remain friendly with both sides in a dispute.
Run from pillar to post	–	to go from one person to another in an attempt to be heard about problems

S

Salad days – in young days

Savoir faire – (Savoir – learning, knowledge; faire – to do) ability to act in society in elegant fashion or according to the demand of the situation on the spur of the moment.

*Lacking in savoir faire, he creates a disharmony with whomsoever he deals.

* Savoir faire is the cardinal virtue for a diplomat.

Scylla & charybdis – An unfortunate situation in which both the alternatives are equally injurious.

* Caught between scylla and charybdis, he was forced to choose between his wife and the child in a difficult delivery.

* The teacher was at a loss in deciding how to make the students understand the subject; he was obviously caught between the Scylla of abstruseness of the subject, and Charybdis of inaccuracy stemming from over-simplification of the matter.

(be in the) Saddle – be in full control of situation

Sold like hot cake – sold quickly because of being in great demand

Settle account with – take revenge

Send shudders down one's spine – To frighten over the possible danger.
* A narrow escape from road accident sent shudders down the motorist's spine.

Short change – To cheat by giving less than what is due.

* Cashier shortchanged him by ten rupees.

* People are shortchanged by pseudo religious saints

Short shrift – (1) A brief respite from work, a limited lease of life. * The salesman in a big shop hardly gets a short shrift during working hours. * Only a short shrift is allowed to students between the two sittings of examinations. *

The doctor pronounced short shrift for a few months only to a cancer patient.

(2) Little consideration, summary dismissal. * The insolent head of the department gives short shrift to every suggestion by his juniors/ subordinates.

* He gave short shrift to the silly suggestions.

* Unfortunately, culture and education in our country get short shrift by the policy makers.

Shot in arm – A boost in one's morale

* Indian sports need shot in the arm.

Sine die – (A meeting or assembly) adjourned for an indefinite period. That means this is adjourned indefinitely but not cancelled.

Sine qua non – Indispensable, condition

* A good stock or repertoir of vocabulary is sine qua non for command on English language.

* Journals are sine qua nons for a researcher.

* Diplomat's savoir faire is a virtue sine qua non.

Slip of tongue – speak a wrong thing unwittingly

Smell rat – suspect foul play

(At) snail's pace – move at slow speed

Sotto voce – In low voice, undertone.

* Musicians play the finale sotto voce. * Uninterested in the solemn rites, a group of people indulged solecistically in gossiping sotto voce in the back seats.

Sow wild oats – To commit offences which may be ascribed to youthful exuberance.

* Youngsters are wont to sow their wild oats.

Spick and span – Spotless, immaculate, spruced, unblemished. * A spick and span car is its owner's pride. *She keeps her house spick and span.

Spill the beans – cause embarrassment, or to spoil a plan by indiscreetly divulging the secrecy.

Stand a treat – pay the bills for hotel (food) and entertainment for others. * He stood a treat to his pals.

Stand in good stead – To place in advantageous position, to assist. * His hard labour throughout the year stood him in good stead in examinations.

* The non-aligned policy stood the country in good stead

* Your ancestors cannot stand you in good stead if you do not have the ability of your own.

* Without regular stint with the studies, your talent alone cannot stand you in good stead during the course of your educational career.

Status quo ante – In the same state or condition as it was before effecting any change. *The troops were ordered to go to their status quo ante position as per the armistice agreement.

Stick to one's guns – To be firm in one's stand in the face of stiff opposition.

* The industrial employees stuck to their guns on their main demand.

Stand by someone – give support in need.

Storm in a teacup – make serious of a trivial matter.

Suo moto – On one's own initiative, without external prompting. * The government suo moto took the decision to raise the salary of judges. * A court can suo moto take congnizance of government's order which is ultra vires of its constitutional powers.

T

Take someone for ride – To beguile him, deceive him by a giving high hopes.*Promises made on the eve of an election are designed to take the constituents for a ride.

* Utopian vision of 21st century as oracled by our new government of computers and hi-fi technologies has successfully taken the whole population for a ride.

Take in one's stride – To pass over an obstacle without any difficulty. * A fortitudinous person takes all trials and tribulations of life in his usual strides.

Talk turkey – Talk bluntly *The chairman talked turkey to the board members and warned them of the company's bleak future.

Throw tantrum – Display violent emotions. * On being denied what he wanted to purchase, the child threw tantrums in the shop itself.

Thumb rule – A premise based on experience and, hence, never to fail. * It is a thumb rule that a kid should never be burdened heavily with his studies.

Tip of the the iceberg – a part of whole which is visible

Through and through – completely, thoroughly

Throw in the towel – to accept defeat; admit that one is defeated.

Tit for tat – retaliate in the same manner

Tongue in cheek – casual (remark), not to be taken seriously.

* He made a tongue-in-cheek remark on my misdemeanour.

Tower of babel – utter chaos where no one listens to others

Treasure trove – (A find, discovery) which becomes a source of income. *Alfred Nobel's discovery of explosive mixture became his treasure trove and further paved the way for Novel price.

* Industrial growth world over turned the oil wells into a treasure trove for the Arabs.

Trials and tribulations– endurance in a suffering.

*Out of this trial and tribulation will be born a new freedom and glory for all mankind – Churchill. * The epic 'Trials and Tribulations in Abject Poverty' is the manifestation of unfaltering faith of our poor mass in their hope for future. * 'The trial and tribulation of South African blacks' is the epic saga of their fight against injustice.

Trigger-happy – ready to open fire from gun at the slightest provocation * A trigger-happy hoodlum is found to suffer punishment under the law.

Triton amongst minnows – One who appears giant among the small ones around it.

* Ashark is a triton amongst the minows in the sea.

Trojan horse – During legendary ten-year war between Greeks and City of Troy. Greek soldiers had been hidden inside a huge wooden horse before the rest of the Greek army made a retreat. The wooden horse was dragged by the people of Troy inside the fortified city, and then the hidden Greek army suddenly came out and opened the gate of the fort of the City of Troy. The main bulk of Greek army forced its way into the city, which resulted in the defeat of the City of Troy. Hence, it means a trick, ploy, ruse implanted into the enemy camp to destroy it.

*The international level of financial espionage involves the use of someone as Trojan horse to beat the rivals.

Turn turtle – overturn upside down

Tweedledum and Tweedledee – Two persons or things only nominally different; a nearly identical pair.

* Changing Chief Ministers, rather than policy, is akin to replacing tweedledums with tweedledees.

(It takes) two to tango – nothing is possible to do where at least two are needed.

U

Ultra vires – Beyond one's power or authority. * He acted ultra vires in deciding an issue which was not within his powers. *An ultra vires contract.

Up and coming – Enterprising, promising, advancing. *Up and coming entrepreneurs get all the help from the government. * An up and coming organization is expanding its business very rapidly.

Up in arms – To rise unitedly against someone. *The majority of trade unions were up in arms against decreasing the interest on PF deposits.

Upset applecart – spoil a plan

Under duress – (to do something) under threat or pressure

Up to the mark – as per expectations

* His performance is not up to the mark.

Ups and downs – good and bad times in life; vicissitudes

V

Volte face – To turn face, turn about of one's opinion/stand. * He made a volte face and turned hostile to his associates.

Vox populi – Vox – voice, populi – people. So, voice of the people or popular opinion.

* Vox populi is the main guiding factor, the government's decisions.

W

Wax and wane – Wax – to increase gradually, wane – to decrease gradually. * Waxing and waning of the moon is alternate.

Whipping boy – Someone/something to whom or which onus of every lapse is attributed unjustly.

* Opposition parties are used as whipping boys by the government for disrupted sessions of the parliament.

Willy nilly – Helplessly, inevitably. *Everybody treads willy nilly the trodden path in his social obligations without any effort to improve upon it. *The world is drifting willy nilly towards disaster.

(Take) wind out of one's sails	–	To outmanoeuvre, to pre-empt one's attempt, to make ineffective. *The runaway inflation takes wind out of economic planner's sails, and everything goes awry. *The army's blitz took wind out of the enemy's sails.

Y

Yeoman's service	–	To do some useful and efficient help who is in need. * Dr. Ambedkar did a Yeoman's service to the nation and the downtrodden people by including several provisions in the constitution to help raise their lot.

OOO

Exercises on Idioms & Phrases

A given phrase (in bold) can be replaced with one of the options mentioned thereunder. Identify which option is the most appropriate.

1. Emancipation of women from social bondage is **a far cry**.

   (A) Protested widely

   (B) A matter of crying for women

   (C) A distant goal to achieve

   (D) A matter to shout on the offenders

2. Play **ducks and drakes with** serious matters of concern.

   (A) Treat carelessly

   (B) Hide one's face from

   (C) Be concerned with

   (D) Play game of throwing stones in water

3. Eveyone **plays second fiddle** to the matriarch in the family.

   (A) Be second in the race

   (B) Be second in importance

   (C) Support

   (D) Have no importance

4. He had a feeling of **deja vu** on his trip to the hill-station after a lapse of two decades.

   (A) Dejection

   (B) Nothing new

   (C) Seeing the same things

   (D) Great enjoyment of seeing attractive things

5. He was asked by the employer to submit his fresh **curriculum vitae.**

   (A) Bio-data

   (B) Games he plays

   (C) Curriculum of studies

   (D) Details of what he can do

6. The spectre of ghost **sent shudders down his spine.**
   - (A) Threatened him
   - (B) A chill within his body
   - (C) Jolted his soul
   - (D) Made him unable to stand on his feet

7. My adversary **poured his spleen at** me in his speech.
   - (A) Showered his praise on me
   - (B) Expressed desire to forgive and forget old enmity
   - (C) Vented his accumulated anger against me
   - (D) Spit on me

8. Poor people in this country compromise with fate and work out **a modus vivendi** with the rigours of poverty.
   - (A) A way how to live with
   - (B) Surrender before poverty
   - (C) A way of living happily
   - (D) A scape from poverty

9. A new law to deal with corruption in public life **is in the offing**.
   - (A) Very far in future
   - (B) In impossible position to control corruption
   - (C) In people's imagination far from reality
   - (D) Soon coming

10. The food minister acted as a **dog in the manger** by refusing to distribute rotting grains in open sky.
    - (A) Custodian of property as a dog protects his master's house
    - (B) A faithful and trusted dog
    - (C) A person who neither uses himself nor lets others use
    - (D) A miser

11. His all-out efforts to make a plan successful **came a cropper**.
    - (A) Proved to be a grand success
    - (B) Failed miserably
    - (C) Became a problem for him

(D) Cropped up another problem

12. A politician can't ignore a **vox populi**.

    (A) People's problems

    (B) Threat of becoming unpopular

    (C) Chance to become popular

    (D) Popular demand of people

13. An emotionally charged person finally **broke down**.

    (A) Became hopeless

    (B) Became disappointed

    (C) Fell down on the ground

    (D) Began to weep

14. He **got down** to his task after taking meals.

    (A) Left doing the task

    (B) Gave it to someone else to do

    (C) Started doing or completing his task

    (D) Went to sleep

15. The unending spell of price rise **upset the applecart** of the economy.

    (A) Spoilt the health of the economy

    (B) Overturned people's budget

    (C) Ruined nation's economy

    (D) Disturbed the health of the economy

16. The governments tend to **play down** the challenge posed by the separatists.

    (A) Defeat the challenge

    (B) Fight the challenge

    (C) Make light of a serious matter

    (D) Play hide and seek with the problem

17. **Carry off**.

    (A) Continue with work

    (B) Lose self-control

(C) Perform a task

(D) Take away by force

18. **Check in.**

(A) Verify some facts

(B) Investigate a crime

(C) Stay in a hotel

(D) Fill up a blank cheque

19. **Come down upon.**

(A) Fall on someone

(B) Sleep on bed

(C) Criticize someone

(D) Throw someone on the ground

20. **Give up.**

(A) Lose hope of

(B) Give something to someone

(C) Give awards to someone

(D) Give nothing to someone

21. **Turn around.**

(A) Bend something

(B) Go in opposite direction

(C) Change in situation for better

(D) Change in situation for bad

22. **Black sheep.**

(A) Sheep of black colour

(B) Sheep having black patches on skin

(C) One who brings infamy for his whole social group

(D) Sheep which hides itself in its herd.

23. **White paper.**

(A) Paper of white colour

(B) Paper without anything written on it

(C) Paper on which something is written in invisible ink

(D) Official paper giving information of public matters

24. **Grey eminence**.

(A) On which grey colour is predominant

(B) An eminent person in grey area

(C) An infamous person

(D) A person who exercises power on behalf of another in power

25. **Be at beck and call of someone**.

(A) Be ready to call on someone

(B) Be ready to help someone

(C) Be ready to obey someone

(D) Be ready to be called by someone

26. He is **in fine fettle**.

(A) in good health

(B) in fine tune with others

(C) in good agreement with someone

(D) ready to play tune on a musical instrument

27. He has **carved a niche** for himself in the society.

(A) Draw a line

(B) Earned infamy

(C) Earned a place of respect

(D) Dig a hole for keeping valuables

28. He spoke in **double entendre** which was quite in bad taste.

(A) Double standards

(B) Ambiguous words

(C) Using words of two seemingly different meanings

(D) Double intentions

29. He made a **foot-in-mouth** remark in the meeting.

(A) Foolish

(B) Embarrassing blunder

(C) Suck foot in one's mouth

(D) Wrong

30. Leaders tend to **run with the hare and hunt with the hound** in a matter of social conflict.

(A) Do two impossible tasks simultaneously.

(B) Avoid taking sides in a conflict.

(C) Run behind a hare with hounds.

(D) Save hare from being killed by a hound.

31. He is a **trigger-happy** person

(A) Happy to walk with gun

(B) Happy to kill wild animals

(C) Happy to fire a weapon

(D) Apt to open fire at the slightest provocation

32. Their relationship is **on the rocks** due to differences.

(A) Depends upon rocking performance

(B) In a bad state with the possibility of breaking down

(C) In hardship

(D) As hard to break as a rock.

33. A problem befell him **out of the blue**.

(A) Unexpectedly

(B) While he was living happily

(C) Once in a while

(D) Very rarely

34. The impending court verdict in his case **kept him on tenter hooks**.

(A) Kept him in constant worries

(B) Kept him in a state of suspense about what would happen

(C) Kept him an hooked to it

(D) Kept him in uncertain situation

35. He asserted that he **had no trucks with** terrorists.

(A) Did not supply truckload of arms to terrorists.

(B) Did not drive trucks belonging to terrorists.

(C) Did not have any relations with terrorists.

(D) Did not travel together with terrorists.

36. Our team proved **damp squib** in the international matches

(A) dampened the spirit of opponent teams

(B) kept their spirit high

(C) lost hopes of winning

(D) failed to impress with their performances

37. Mother Teresa will always be remembered for her **yeoman's service** to this country.

(A) Notable contribution

(B) Service in yeoman company

(C) Religious work

(D) Converting people to Christianity

38. Humiliating electoral defeat **took wind out of the opposition party's sails**.

(A) Blew up sails off the opposition party's boat

(B) Thoroughly demoralised the opposition party

(C) Wind took the opposition party's boat off the course

(D) Thoroughly destroyed the party's unity

39. The I.I.T.s **have now acquired pride of place** in the world.

(A) Have become proud of their achievements or popularity

(B) Have become a matter of pride to get admitted to

(C) Have become a place to be proud of

(D) Have earned prominence.

40. Promises made by parties on the election eve are meant **to take voters for a ride**.

(A) To take voters on a trip to pilgrimmage.

(B) To promise distribution of cycles to voters in lieu of casting votes in the party's favour.

(C) To befool voters with false promises which they never intend to fulfil.

(D) To give voters the right to free ride in trains.

41. Regular studies **stand students in good stead** at the time of exams.

(A) Make students stand a good chance to succeed.

(B) Place them in an advantageous position.

(C) Place them in good chance to succeed without studying at the time of examinations.

(D) Stand students to lose at the examinations.

42. Unprecedented success in election gave a **shot in arm** to the party.

(A) Was wounded due to violence in election

(B) Party was wounded due to several leaders leaving the party because of losing prominence in the party

(C) Election was preceded by violence

(D) Party's morale got a boost.

43. The criminal's accomplice **spilled the beans** to the police which was investigating the crimes.

(A) Dilvulged the secrets

(B) Complained against the criminal

(C) Threw the beans in dustbin

(D) Vomitted the beans after eating

44. Babri Masjid demolition **queered the pitch** of communal harmony in the country.

(A) Dug out the pitch to prevent the game

(B) Made a smooth ground for communal harmony

(C) Facilitated communal harmony

(D) Disturbed the atmosphere of communal harmony.

45. A **dark horse pipped the front runner** at the post in a race.

(A) A dark-coloured horse pushed the horse running ahead of it in a race.

(B) A not-so-probable winner went ahead of the frontrunner at the last moment of a race to win the first place

(C) A dark horse won the race easily

(D) A probable winner lost the race to a front runner.

46. Ramcharit Manas is **magnum opus** of Hindu religious epic.

(A) voluminous book

(B) a great work of literature

(C) a great work of creation

(D) the most revered book.

47. Relief materials reach the victims of food in **dribs and drabs**.

(A) Intermittently in small amounts which is insufficient

(B) In sufficient quantity to meet the needs

(C) In excess of what is needed

(D) In the form of unusable materials.

48. He is my bete noire.

(A) Dearest person

(B) Most trusted friend

(C) The most hated person

(D) The best bet

49. We are forced to **willy nilly** take the rising cost of living in our stride.

(A) Wilfully accept calmly as a matter of fact

(B) Unwillingly accept calmly as a matter of fact

(C) Accept, whether you like it or not, as an inevitable fact

(D) Accept without protest and try to overcome this problem.

50. He was ready to help me, but made a **volte face** when time came to help me.

(A) Turned his face in another direction

(B) Suddenly changed his mind

(C) Turned his head upside down

(D) Made a somersault.

ooo

Some Idioms Categorised

1. Miscellaneous Idioms

I couldn't agree with you more: I entirely agree with you

- 'People are obsessed with celebrities. Don't you think it is funny?'
  'I couldn't agree with you more.'

I'm sick of it

If you are sick of something, you don't like it anymore.

- I don't know why she should behave so rudely. I'm sick of it.
- I'm sick of eating the same stuff for lunch every day.

You made it big

To *make it big* is to become highly successful.

- I can't believe that she earns a six figure salary. She's made it big!

Back to the grind

To be back to the grind is to get back to work.

- 'OK everybody, lunch break is over. Now get back to the grind.'

I blew it: I missed my opportunity

'Did you get that job?'
'No mate, I blew it.'

Pie in the Sky: an unrealistic dream

- Her dreams of becoming a famous writer ended up just being a pie in the sky.

A hidden agenda

When somebody has a hidden agenda, they have a secret motive for doing something.

- It would be foolish of us to believe everything that she says. I really suspect that she has a hidden agenda.

Half-baked

If something is half-baked, it hasn't been properly thought out or planned.

- It was a half-baked plan, so nobody was surprised when it failed.

Hang in there / hang on in there

This is usually said to encourage people who are in a difficult situation.

- Hang in there. Things should get better soon.

Hard to come by

If something is hard to come by, it is difficult to find.

- Writers of his caliber are hard to come by.

Hot under the collar

If you are hot under the collar, you are angry or annoyed about something.

- She was hot under the collar when she heard that they had lost that contract.

Bored to death

When you are bored to death you are so bored.

- I've nothing to do. I'm bored to death.

You've got to be kidding: you must be joking

- 'Mom, can I wear this short skirt to the party?'

  'You've got to be kidding baby. You're a 15 year old girl. You shouldn't wear clothes of that kind.'

Sick and Tired

When you are sick and tired of something, you no longer find it interesting or exciting.

- I'm sick and tired of my job. I must find something better.

Call it a day

To call it a day is to stop working.

- It's already 10 pm. Let's call it a day.

Get on one's nerves

To get on somebody's nerves is to annoy them.

- Your radio is starting to get on my nerves. You had better turn it down.

  Her constant nagging is getting on my nerves.

Couch potato

A person who sits in front of the TV all day long

- If you don't want to get a big fat belly, you must stop being a couch potato.

Get foot in the door / have foot in the door.

To get your foot in the door is to accept even a small job hoping that you would be able to get a promotion before long.

- It's not easy to find a job in these troubled financial times, so I'm considering even a lower position. At least, I'll have my foot in the door.

Give somebody a hard time

To give somebody a hard time is to make it difficult for them.

Be realistic and stop giving me a bad time. I can't do anything about it.

Make up one's mind

To make up one's mind is to come to a decision.

- I can't make up my mind. Can you help me decide which phone I should buy?

Go Dutch

To go Dutch is to pay your own share.

- I don't feel very comfortable when others pay for me. I prefer going Dutch.

Go/sell like hot cakes

When something sells like hot cakes, it sells really well.

- Her latest book is selling like hot cakes.

Sell someone short

To sell somebody short is to describe them as less impressive than they really are.

- He tends to sell himself short and that is his main fault.

2. Body Idioms

A large number of idioms are formed with the names of body parts. Here is a list of them.

Best foot forward

To put your best foot forward is to do your very best

- If you put your best foot forward you'll succeed in the interview.

First-hand

To experience something first hand is to experience it yourself

- The ideal candidate should have first-hand knowledge of accounting procedures.

Pull your hair out

To pull your hair out is to be very worried about something

- She has an interview tomorrow and she is pulling her hair out.

Have a free hand

When you have a free hand you have the power to do what you want.

- She made it clear right from the beginning that she must have a free hand.

Have a hand in something

- To have a hand in something is to be involved in it.
- My husband has a hand in running my website.

Have the upper hand

To have the upper hand is to have power and control over someone or a situation.

- In India upper castes still have the upper hand.

Be caught red handed

To get caught red-handed is to get caught while doing something illegal or wrong.

- He was caught red-handed while trying to encash a forged check at the bank

To be hand in glove

When two people are hand in glove, they have an extremely close relationship.

- The manager and his secretary work hand in glove.

Heartbroken

When you are heartbroken you are suffering from overwhelming sorrow, grief or disappointment.

- He was heartbroken when he found out that he had failed the test.

Heartwarming

Something that generates a feeling of happiness

- The story of the teenager who saved his friends from drowning was very heartwarming.

Rap someone's knuckles

To rap someone's knuckles is to give him a light punishment so that he wouldn't repeat the same offence.

- He got his knuckles rapped for talking too much in the class.

Break a leg

It is a phrase used to wish someone good luck

- So it is your debut tonight. Break a leg.

Pull someone's leg

To pull someone's leg is to subject him / her to a playful joke or hoax.

- Don't believe what he says. He is just pulling your leg.

Many a slip between cup and lip

Used to imply that things can wrong at any time

- They thought that they had won the contract, but in the end the client refused to sign the papers. There's many a slip twixt cup and lip.

To cross someone's mind

A thought that comes to mind briefly

- Let me tell you what just crossed my mind.

To have a big mouth

Used to refer to a person who talks too much, especially about things that should be secret

- She didn't look amused when I told her that her husband was having an affair with one of his colleagues. Me and my big mouth!

Your hands are tied

When your hands are tied, something prevents you from doing what you would normally have the power to do.

- I really want to help you, but my hands are tied.

Your heart goes out to (someone)

When your heart goes out to someone, you feel great sympathy for them.

- My heart goes out to the families of the kids who died in the mishap.

Have your heart in the right place

To have your heart in the right place is to have right intentions.

- He might come across as an arrogant guy, but I'm sure he has his heart in the right place.

Your heart isn't in it

If your heart isn't in something you're doing, you don't really want to do it or you make numerous mistakes.

- Your heart isn't in it. If it was, you wouldn't make so many silly mistakes.

A head start

If you have a head start, you start doing something ahead of others.

- He started preparing for the exams months in advance and that sort of gave him a head start.

Skeleton in the closet / cupboard

To have a skeleton in the closet is to hide a shocking secret about yourself.

- Almost all of us have a skeleton in the closet.

Have a thick skin / be thick skinned

If you have a thick skin you don't get upset when people criticize you.

- Most of our politicians are thick skinned.

By the skin of your teeth: If you do something by the skin of your teeth, you only just manage to do it.

- He escaped from the burning building by the skin of his teeth.

Get your teeth into something

To get your teeth into something is to get completely involved in it.

- He did really well on the TOEFL test after he got his teeth into learning English.

Jump down someone's throat

To jump down someone's throat is to react angrily to something that they say or do.

- You may not have liked what I said, but that doesn't mean that you've to jump down my throat.

Have a green thumb

If you have a green thumb, you are very good at gardening.

- Look at her garden. Beautiful, isn't it? She really has a green thumb.

Toe the line

To toe the line is to conform to certain rules and regulations

- You will have to learn to toe the line, if you want to get on in this organization.

The tip of your tongue

When something is at the tip of your tongue, it is known to you, but you just can't remember it at the moment.

- Her name is on the tip of my tongue.

A slip of the tongue

Used to refer to something that you say which you didn't mean to say

- Be careful what you say. Just one slip of the tongue is enough to land you in trouble.

Be tongue tied

The feeling that people experience when they can't seem to find the right words to say

- I knew I should I have said something to make her comfortable, but I was completely tongue tied.

3. Building Idioms

Here is a list of idioms about buildings.

To bank on something/someone

When you bank on somebody you are certain that they will be there for you when you need their help.

- You can bank on Ravi. He will never let you down.

To be banging/hitting your head against a brick wall.

To bang your head against a brick wall is to have to keep asking somebody to do something they don't want to do.

- I can't get them do their homework. It is like banging my head against a brick wall.

Like a ton of bricks

When something (for example, a piece of news) hits you like a ton of bricks, you are deeply affected by it.

- The news of her sudden demise hit me like a ton of bricks.

To burn your bridges

To burn your bridges is to do something that would make it impossible for you to return to your previous position.

- Changing jobs is fine, but one must not burn one's bridges.

Rome wasn't built in a day.

It takes a great deal of time to accomplish something great.

- It took him quite some time to establish himself as a successful publisher but that was hardly surprising. Rome wasn't built in a day.

Build castles in the air

To build castles in the air is to have daydreams.

- I don't think that Rohan will make a successful entrepreneur. He doesn't work hard. He only builds castles in the air.

To be in the doghouse

To be in the doghouse is to be in real trouble.

He was in the dog house when his wife found out that he was having an affair with one of his colleagues.

To hold the fort

To hold the fort is to take care of an office or store while the person in charge of that is away.

- When my boss is away on business tours, I hold the fort.

Close to home

When something is close to home, it affects you emotionally and personally.

- What the palmist said about my past life hit close to home. He seemed to know everything about me.

Make oneself at home

To make yourself at home is to behave as if you were at your own home.

- I always ask my guests to make themselves at home.

House of cards: A poorly thought out plan / action

- The ceasefire agreement between the two countries was no stronger than a house of cards and quickly fell apart.

Put one's own house in order

To put one's own house in order is to organize one's private affairs.

- She should put her own house in order before telling me what to do.

To bring the house down

To bring the house down is to cause a lot of applause by delivering a splendid performance.

- She brought the house down with her hilarious performance.

People who live in glass houses shouldn't throw stones

Do not criticize other people when you are as bad as they are.

Run-of-the-mill: Something very ordinary

- I'm tired of watching these run-of-the-mill programs on TV.

To go through the roof

To go through the roof is to become very angry.

- When she discovered that her son had been suspended from college, she went through the roof.

To hit the roof

To hit the roof is to become angry.

- He hit the roof when he found out that his son had lost a lot of money in gambling.

A tower of strength

A person who provides strong and reliable support

- She had been my tower of support all through these years of pain and suffering.

The writing on the wall

This idiom refers to the likelihood that something bad will happen.

- The ruling party should have seen the writing on the wall and taken measures to improve its public image before facing the electorate.

To climb the wall

To climb the wall is to be so bored that you become frustrated.

- The waiting was so boring that she soon found herself climbing the wall.

4. Colour Idioms

Black out: loss of electricity; sudden loss of memory

- Yesterday's black out was due to unexpected problems with electricity production.
- He blacked out for few minutes when he was hit on the head.

Go green with envy

To go green with envy is to be very jealous of objects belonging to other people.

Susie will go green with envy when she sees your new car.

Be yellow: Be a coward

- He is not the kind of guy you can depend on when you are in trouble. He's yellow.

Red tape

Delay in public affairs because there is too much attention to rules

- A lot of people want to adopt babies. It is the red tape that discourages them.

Black sheep: Person of bad character

- James was neither brilliant nor hardworking. His Dad always treated him like a black sheep.

Roll out the red carpet: Give the best treatment

- Mr. Mathews is going to take over as the next chairman. Be sure to roll out the red carpet when he arrives.

Green belt: The countryside around a city

- They have just purchased a new home in the green belt.

Black and white

When something is black and white, it is clear, simple and understandable.

- The situation is not as black and white as you think.

Feel blue: To feel blue is to be depressed

- I'm feeling rather blue these days. Have you got something to cheer me up?

White lie: A small insignificant lie

- He had to tell a white lie to escape his mother's punishment.

Give the green light

To give the green light is to approve a project.

- The civil authority has given the green light on the project.

5. Money Idioms

Put your money where your mouth is

To put your money where your mouth is to practice what you preach.

- If these so-called social activists are really interested in eradicating poverty they must put their money where their mouth is.

Pots of money: Lot of money

- He can buy just about anything he wants. His wife has got pots of money.

Throw money around / money to throw around

To throw money around is to spend it carelessly on unnecessary things.

- He doesn't have to work. He's already got plenty of money to throw around.

Hit pay dirt: Find something very profitable

- They have hit pay dirt with their new multi-level marketing system.

Pay through the nose

To pay through the nose is to pay too much money for something.

- I had to pay through the nose to get my car repaired.

Pay top dollar

To pay top dollar is to pay a lot of money for something.

- Employers are starting to realize that if they want to retain talent, they will have to pay top dollar.

A pretty penny

When something costs you a pretty penny, it is very expensive.

- That necklace cost me a pretty penny.

Dirt poor: Extremely poor

- She may be dirt poor, but she is honest.

As poor as church mice: Very poor

- We were as poor as church mice when we first arrived in Mumbai searching for a job.

To hold the purse strings

To hold the purse strings is to control a family's or company's money

- He may be the only earning member of his family, but it is his wife who holds the purse strings.

To tighten the purse strings

To tighten the purse strings is to reduce expenditure.

- If we want to buy an apartment we'll have to tighten the purse strings a bit.

Filthy rich: Extremely rich

- She is filthy rich and that's why he married her.

Rob Peter to pay Paul

Borrow money from one person to pay back money borrowed from another person.

- You can't rob Peter to pay Paul. If that is your policy you will never be out of debt.

Strike it rich

When a business strikes it rich, it becomes highly profitable.

- She struck it rich in the garments business.

Have your fingers in the till

To have your fingers in the till is to steal money from the place where you work

- He lost his job because he had his fingers in the till.

6. Animal Idioms

To be a chicken / to be chicken livered

If you are a chicken you are a coward.

- I can't believe that she went scuba diving last week. She is such a chicken.

To be like a dog with two tails

When you are like a dog with two tails, you are very happy.

- When he found out that he'd won the first prize, he was like a dog with two tails.

Gone to the dogs

When a business goes to the dogs it becomes less successful than it was.

- The country has gone to the dogs since they won the election.

Like a fish out of water

When you are like a fish out of water, you are uncomfortable.

- When she started talking about her male friends, he looked like a fish out of water.

Something is fishy

When something is fishy, it is suspicious.

- There was something fishy in the way he answered my questions.

To be a fly on the wall

To want to be somewhere secretly, so that you can overhear what is said

- I would love to have been a fly on the wall when they discussed their secret plans.

To be as sly as a fox: To be very clever or cunning

- He managed to escape before the police arrived. He is a sly old fox.

To get someone's goat

When something gets your goat, it really upsets you.

- The whole time I was performing she kept herself busy talking on her phone. She really got my goat.

Wouldn't say boo to a goose

Used to describe a person who is very timid or nervous

- He is not assertive enough to be a successful manager; he wouldn't say boo to a goose.

To not give a hoot

To not give a hoot is to not care at all

- He doesn't give a hoot about what others say.

A dark horse

This expression is used to describe a person who has skills not known to others.

- I was surprised when he sat down to play the piano. I didn't know that he could. He is a real dark horse.

To eat like a horse

To eat like a horse is to eat a lot.

- If you eat like a horse you will never lose weight.

Straight from the horse's mouth

When you hear something straight from the horse's mouth, you hear it from the person actually involved.

- The rumour is true. John is going to marry his longtime girlfriend. I heard it straight from the horse's mouth.

Mutton dressed (up) as lamb

Used to describe an older woman who wears clothes that are more suitable for a much younger woman

- You must stop wearing those miniskirts if you don't want to look like mutton dressed up as lamb. Don't forget that you are fifty-five.

To pull a rabbit out of the hat

To pull a rabbit out of the hat is to surprise everyone by doing something clever

- He really pulled a rabbit out of the hat by winning that business contract.

A wolf in sheep's clothing

Someone who is dangerous but pretends to be harmless

If I were you I wouldn't trust him. He's a real wolf in sheep's clothing.

7. Food Idioms

Eat dirt

To eat dirt is to accept bad treatment without complaining.

- He was such a bad boss that he would bully his employees and make them eat dirt.

Eat humble pie

To eat humble pie is to admit your mistake and apologize

- I had to eat humble pie when he proved that I was wrong.

Eat like a pig

Used to refer to a person who has bad table manners or who eats too much

- John has terrible table manners. He eats like a pig.

Eat one's words

To eat one's words is to take back something you have said

- I told him that I was a better singer than him but had to eat my words when he proved me wrong.

To want someone's head on a platter

To be very angry with someone

- She was so angry with her biographer that she wanted his head on a platter.

Suck up

To suck up to somebody is to try to gain favour by being extra nice to people in power

- I don't quite like her. She is always sucking up to the rich and the famous.

8. Entertainment idioms

To make a clown of yourself

To make a clown of yourself is to make yourself appear foolish or stupid.

- He tried everything he could to impress her and in the process made a clown of himself.

To be in the limelight

To be in the limelight is to be the centre of attention.

- I know quite a few socialites who will gladly do just about anything to keep themselves in the limelight.

Museum piece

If something is referred to as museum piece, it is very old-fashioned.

- It is true that my desktop computer is a museum piece but I don't want to throw it away.

A dog and pony show

An event organized with the sole objective of gaining approval for a product or service.

- We are going to stage a dog and pony show for the media this afternoon. We want to show them how amazing our new line of kitchen appliances is.

The show must go on

This is an idiom we use to mean that an event or activity must continue even if there are problems or difficulties.

- He wasn't feeling well; still he went to work. After all, the show must go on.

To run the show

To run the show is to be in charge of an organization or activity.

- When he joined the firm, he had a modest job profile but now he is running the show.

To sing your heart out

To sing your heart out is to sing with more passion or intensity.

- He only had a small audience but that didn't prevent him from singing his heart out.

To be star-studded

A star-studded event is one that is attended by lots of famous people.

- The award show was a star-studded event.

To steal the show

To steal the show is to do something that will win the greatest praise.

- She stole the show with her marvelous performance.

ooo

Unit- 7
One Word Substitution

A

Able :

1. Ability to see something which can't be seen normally by others. **— Clairvoyance**
2. Ability to hear a feeble sound which can't be heard by others. **— Clairaudience**
3. Able to be controlled b y someone else. **— Dirigible**
4. Able to be (suitable for) eaten. **— Edible**
5. Able to produce the desired effect. **— Efficacious**
6. Able to achieve accomplishment. **— Effectual**
7. Able to mislead others in conclusion. **— Fallacious**
8. Able to produce offsprings excessively. **— Fecund**
9. Able to produce books excessively or ideas by using creativity, or fruits as by trees. **— Prolific**
10. Able to break down easily. **—Fragile**
11. Able to break due to excess pressure. **— Frangible**
12. Able to be bent around. **— Supple, Lithe, Limber**
13. Able to be bent from straight position. **— Flexible, Pliant**
14. Able to induce laughter. **— Hilarious**
15. Able to cause fire. **— Incendiary**
16. Able to make one forget unpleasant memories. **— Nepenthean**
17. Able to be perceived by sensory organs. **— Palpable**
18. Able to be perceived by ears. **— Audible**
19. Able to be preceived by touch. **— Tactile**
20. Able to feel emotions of pain or pleasure. **— Passible**
21. Able to produce pity. **— Pathetic**

22. Able to be seen through one side to the other. — **Transparent**
23. Able to be seen through one's intention/motive. — **Perspicuous**
24. Able to see through other's intention/motive. — **Perspicacious**
25. Able to be fit for drinking. — **Potable**
26. Able to grasp and hold things. — **Prehensile**
27. Able to sense foreboding about the future. — **Prescient**
28. Able to be persuaded. — **Suasive**
29. Able to suck in. — **Suctorial**
30. Able to induce sleep. — **Sleep-inducing**
31. Able to survive/succeed. — **Viable**

Again :

32. Again lapse into the world of crime after reformed.— **Recidivate**
33. Again happen. — **Recur**
34. Again become worse (condition). — **Exacerbate**
35. Again serve the same food. — **Rehash**
36. Again make a statement (repeat). — **Re-iterate**
37. Again slip into bad condition. — **Relapse**
38. Again and again repetition to memorise a lesson. — **Rote**
39. Again repeat a performance. — **Encore**
40. Again get the sound health after illness (restore health). — **Recuperate**
41. Again take back what was pledged. — **Redeem**
42. Again bring to the good condition. —**Refurbish**
43. Again bring back to the condition of being whole after scattering. — **Redintegrate**
44. Again provide something lost viz. home, limbs. — **Rehabilitate**
45. Again get back which was lost or deprived of. — **Restitution**
46. Again take up the form of a living person, i.e., reborn. — **Re-incarnate**
47. Again come to life after getting destroyed. — **Revive**
48. Again come or send back to one's homeland which one had earlier left for another country. — **Repatriate**

Animal :

49. Animal belonging to the class of cats. — **Feline**
50. Animal belonging to the class of dogs. — **Canine**

51. Animal belonging to the class of cow. — **Bovine**

52. Animal belonging to the class of horse. — **Equine**

53. Animal belonging to the class of goats. — **Capricorn**

54. Animal belonging to the species of sheeps. — **Ovine**

55. Animal belonging to the species of rats. — **Rodent**

56. Animal belonging to the species of snake. — **Reptile**

57. Animal belonging to the species of bear. — **Ursine**

58. Animal living both on land and in water. —**Amphibian**

59. Animal living on land only. — **Terrestrial**

60. Animal living in water only. — **Aquatic**

61. Animal living in sea only. — **Marine**

62. Animal living on trees. — **Arboreal**

63. Animal which feeds on flesh, meat. — **Carnivorous**

64. Animal which feeds on grass. — **Graminivorous**

65. Animal which feeds on shrubs. — **Herbivorous**

66. Animal insect or other invertebrate which feeds on tree branches. — **Phytophagous**

67. Animal devoid of horns. — **Pollard**

68. Animal with one horn only. — **Unicorn**

69. Animal which kills smaller animals to feed on. — **Predator**

70. Animal which is killed by larger animal for food. — **Prey**

71. Animal which feeds on the flesh of its own species. — **Cannibal**

Arranging Styles

72. Arrangement like that of petals of flower's bud before expansion. — **Aestivation**

73. Arrangement like that of chain. — **Catenation**

74. Arrangement like that of stars. — **Constellation**

75. Arrangement like that of a holy cross. — **Decussation**

76. Arrangement for marshalling the troops/army in such a position as a sweeping fire from along the length of a line of troops/army. — **Enfilade**

77. Arrangement like that of an oriented overgrowth of crystalline material upon the surface of another crystal of different chemical composition but similar structure. — **Epitaxy**

78. Arrangement in a set of (pairs in two each).

79. Arrangement like that of tiles on a slope of thatched roof. — **Imbrication**

80. Arrangement like that of a net. — **Reticulate**

81. Arrangement like that of an inverted pyramid or a spinning top. — **Turbinate**

82. Arrangement like that of spokes in a cycle wheel. — **Verticillate**

83. Artist who makes solid figures by cutting metals or stone. — **Sculptor**

84. Artist who makes portraits on plain sheets.— **Painter**

85. Artist who performs on stage, e.g., dancer or singer. — **Artiste**

86. Artist who entertains villagers by singing folk songs by moving from village to village. — **Minstrel**

87. Artist who produces music by whistling his mouth. — **Siffleur**

88. Artist who displays his physical feats on a rope or pole. — **Acrobat**

89. Artist who displays skill of walking on a horizontal tight rope. — **Funambulist**

90. Artist who teaches learners. — **Maestro**

91. Artist of exceptional ability. — **Virtuoso**

92. Artist who is expert in his field. — **Exponent**

93. Artist who entertains with songs of epic or heroic poems.— **Bard**

94. Artist who performs on swinging ladders from the roofs of tents in circus. — **Trapeze artist**

95. Art of writing in beautiful handwriting. — **Calligraphy**

96. Art of making maps. — **Cartography**

97. Art of making ornamental objects with wires of silver gold or other non-ferrous metals. — **Filigree**

98. Art of making various shapes by folding a piece of paper (especially referrring to the Japanese art of tradition). — **Origami**

99. Artificial limbs-making for fitting in place of amputated limbs in a body. — **Prosthetics**

Misellaneous

100. Attack someone from a hiding. — **Ambush**

101. Attack public property and damage it. — **Vandalise**

102. Attack public property and set it on fire. — **Arson**

103. Age of person when physical changes start taking place. — **Climacteric**

104. Advertising boards erected in public place. — **Hoardings**

105. Advertising messages written on walls. — **Graffiti**

B

106. Bad conditioned buildings which are in a partially ruined state. —**Dilapidated**

107. Bad conditioned state due to being old. — **Decrepit State**

108. Bad condition state in which something is shaking. — **Ramshakled**

109. Bad conditioned with loosely shaking joints. — **Rickety**

110. Bad conditioned habitation with thickly populated poor inhabitants in squalid houses. — **Slum**

111. Bag which is carried by sailors for keeping odds and ends, e.g., sewing needles, threads buttons etc., besides toiletries. — **Ditty bag**

112. Bag which is carried by travellers; soldier's bag used for rations, extra clothing etc. — **Haversack**

113. Bag which opens up in two equal halves from the middle. — **Portmanteau**

114. Bag which is hung on one's back with the help of two shoulder straps. — **Rucksack**

115. Bag for carrying by hanging it from shoulders. — **Sachel**

116. Bag of small size for packing small amount of something e.g. coffee. — **Sachet**

117. Bag which is made up of two parts each, slung on either side of animal's back. — **Pannier**

118. Bed which is raised on sides to prevent falling of babies. — **Crib**

119. Bed which is foldable on one side of it which is attached or fixed from the side wall. — **Bunk**

120. Bed which is of low height so as to be pushed under another bed when not in use. — **Truckle bed**

121. Bed which can be moved easely on its wheels attached to legs. — **Trundle bed**

122. Bed which is made of a cloth and its ends hanged with poles. — **Hammock**

123. Bending knees before deity in reverence. — **Genuflect**

124. Bending knees before someone in show of courtesy by women. — **Curtsy**

125. Bending one's head after taking out hat from head in a show of courtesy. — **Vail**

126. Bells which are set to produce attuned sound. — **Chime**

127. Bell made of heavy and flat metal piece and struck with hammer to produce loud sound used in stock exchanges. — **Gong**

128. Bell which is set at the roof-top of church. — **Knell**

129. Body part of head and chest portion. — **Bust**

130. Body part below neck and upward of abdomen. — **Thorax**

131. Body part without head, hands and legs. — **Torso**

132. Body part down the chest portion and upward of waist.— **Midriff**

133. Body part of buttocks and thigh together. — **Haunch**

134. Book written by an author whose identity is not known, doubtful or not recognized; uncanonical. — **Apocrypha**

135. Book of selected writings by various authors usually in the same literary form, of the same period or on the same subject. — **Anthology**

136. Book written by an author on his own life. — **Autobiography**

137. Book which is published after the death of its author. — **Posthumous**

138. Book written by an author on someone's life. — **Biography**

139. Buying a commodity in a market and immediately selling in another market at higher price to earn profit on account of differential happening consequently (e.g. between rupee and foreign exchange markets). — **Arbitrage**

140. Behaviour which is appropriate under a given situation.— **Conduct**

141. Behaviour which is appropriate to the status or class to which one belongs. — **Comportment**

142. Behaviour or conduct which is indicated on one's facial appearance. — **Demeanour**

143. Buildings and open land within the boundary of an educational institution. — **Campus**

144. Buildings and open land within the bundary of an office or business. — **Premises**

145. Broken piece of ceramic or metal. — **Shard**

146. Broken piece of glass with sharp edge. — **Shrapnel**

147. Broken piece of wood. — **Sliver**

148. Born-together babies who look alike. — **Identical twins**

149. Born-together babies who are different in looks. **— Fraternal twins**

150. Born-together babies of dog. **— Puppies**

151. Born-together babies of cats. **— Litters (kittens)**

152. Born-together babies of the birds. **— Brood**

153. Born-together babies from the hatching of the eggs of a bird. **— Clutch**

154. Book of film which becomes great success on commercial scale. **— Blockbuster**

155. Bundle of keys. **— Bunch**

156. Bundle of yarn, cotton. **— Bale**

157. Bundle of grapes hanging from one stem. **— Cluster**

158. Bundle of firewoods. **— Faggot**

159. Bundle of grass, hay, etc. **— Sheaf**

160. Bundle of stitching thread. **— Skein**

161. Bundle of personal belongings which is hung from shoulders of a person. **— Swag**

162. Bundle of currency notes. **— Wad**

163. Burial ground consisting of graves. **— Cemetery**

164. Burial place made underground as in church. **— Catacomb**

C

165. Capable of producing the desired effects. **— Efficacious**

166. Capable of accomplishing what is desired. **— Effectual**

167. Capable of listening to sound coming from very far which a normal person can't. **— Clairsonant**

168. Capable of seeing something very far. **— Clairvoyant**

169. Capable of misleading others to make erroneous conclusion. **— Fallacious**

170. Capable of producing children excessively. **— Fecund**

171. Capable of producing humour, making one laugh. **— Hilarious**

172. Capable of producing or starting a fire easily. **— Incendiary**

173. Capable of easily bent. **— Flexible**

174. Capable of moving around freely in doing work (human body). **— Supple**

175. Capable of making one forget unpleasant memory of sad events. **— Nepenthean**

176. Capable of affecting someone without making him aware of it. — **Subliminal**

177. Capable of seeing in darkness. — **Scotopiac**

178. Capable of being perceived by touch. — **Tangible, Palpable**

179. Careful about minor details in behaviour, work to be done etc. — **Punctilious**

180. Careful about details of doing something because of fear of committing some mistake. — **Meticulous**

181. Careful about doing something due to the concern of being morally wrong. — **Scrupulous**

182. Carriage on which a deadbody is transported to cremation ground. — **Hearse**

183. Compulsory recruitment of young people in armed forces at the time of war. — **Conscription**

184. Copy someone's voice is to. — **Mimic him**

185. Copy someone's mannerisms, in order to make fun on him. — **Caricature**

186. Copy someone's achievements by trying to make similar achievements. — **Emulate**

187. Charging for eatables itemwise on per plate basis. — **Charge a'la' carte**

188. Charging for eatables at fixed rate for full meal per person. — **Charge a' la' table d'hote**

189. Comparison of one thing with another for indicating similarity. — **Analogy**

190. Comparison of one thing with another for indicating differences. — **Disparity**

191. Clever trick employed to deceive others. — **Artifice**

192. Civilian area where soldiers are temporarily lodged away from their contonment. — **Billet**

193. Cultivation of crops. — **Agriculture**

194. Cultivation of flowers. — **Floriculture**

195. Cultivation of such plants in garden as flowers, fruits, vegetables and ornamental plants. — **Horticulture**

196. Cultivation of trees for wood. — **Silviculture**

197. Cultivation of vegetables for the home or market.— **Olericulture**

198. Cultivation of fruits. — **Pomiculture**

199. Custom of marrying outside one's clan. — **Exogamy**

200. Custom of marrying within one's own clan. **— Endogamy**

201. Custom of marrying and having only one wife. **— Monogamy**

202. Custom of marrying and having more than one wife.**— Polygamy**

203. Custom of woman being the head of the family. **— Matriarchy**

204. Ceremony in which medals and honours are bestowed upon winners. **— Investiture ceremony**

205. Child who acquires abilities of a matured person at an age earlier than usual. **— Precocious child**

206. Child of extraordinary ability or intelligence. **— Prodigy**

207. Child who has begun learning to walk on his feet. **— Toddler**

208. Child who has been kept under the tutelage of someone is his. **— Ward**

209. Child who has been found abandoned by parents. **— Foundling**

210. Cheat someone by assuming identity of another person. **— Impersonate**

211. Carriage upon which a deadbody is kept for taking it to cremation or burial ground. **— Hearse**

212. Celebration in which participants indulge in drinking wine and revelry. **— Bacchanalia**

213. Category of art or literature in classification of various types. **— Genre**

214. Category of animal species in classification of various types. **— Genus**

D

215. Daring and dangerous activity is. **— Adventure**

216. Deadbody of a human-being. **— Corpse, Cadaver**

217. Deadbody of an animal. **— Carcass**

218. Deficiency of blood in body is. **— Anaemia**

219. Discarding human body of a dead person by its soul. **— Metempsychosis**

220. Discarding of dead skin and wearing new skin in its place by some living being, e.g., snake. **— Ecdysis or Moulting**

221. Discarding of loaded goods or bundles on ship or aeroplane so as to reduce load to save the ship from sinking. **— Jettison**

222. Disease in which the backbone curves in the backward direction. **— Lordosis**

223. Disease in which the backbone curves forward a hunchbacked condition. — **Kyphosis**

224. Disease of hair-fall causing baldness (skin disease).— **Alopecia**

225. Display of a theme through still/motionless statues and scenery as is presented in Republic Day Parade in Delhi. — **Tableau**

226. Divine impulse or inspiration to do something creative is. — **Afflatus**

227. Deprive someone of his voting rights is to. — **Disenfranchise**

228. Daily traveller between home to workplace is. — **Commuter**

229. Disorder prevalent due to lack of governance is. — **Anarchy**

230. Disease which can spread from one to another is. — **Communicable disease**

231. Disease which can spread by touching infected person. — **Contagious disease**

232. Defect which is present in someone since birth is. — **Congenital defect**

233. Dramatic sudden turn of events which change the course further. — **Coup de theatre**

234. Disease which is prevalent in a specified locality or amongst people of a specified place. — **Endemic disease**

235. Disease which is prevalent in all parts of the world. — **Pandemic disease**

236. Disease which affected large population at the same time. — **Epidemic**

237. Date of equal day and night duration. — **Equinox**

238. Design on an ornament or surface made by engraving or indenting. — **Intaglio**

239. Design on an ornament or surface made by projecting out on the surface. — **Relief**

240. Decline in standards from seriousness to trivial state. — **Bathos**

241. Day on which eating meat is forbidden on religious grounds. — **Maigre day**

242. Drain pipe (a projecting spout) usually grotesquely carved, from a roof-gutter. — **Gargoyle**

243. Dress worn by actors which suits their role. — **Costume**

244. Dress which is worn on ceremonial occasions. — **Regalia**

245. Dress which is worn by persons of a particular profession.— **Robe**

246. Dress which is worn on occasions of mourning the death of someone. **— Weeds**

247. Dress worn on the occasion of marriage by a bride. **— Troussea**

E

248. Edge of upper end of hollow utensil. **— Brim**

249. Edge of rock's top. **— Brink, Precipice**

250. Edge of a cloth which is turned inward and stitched to prevent unravelling. **— Hem**

251. Edge at the top of two slopes joint, e.g., of a thatched roof. **— Ridge**

252. Edge at the lower end of a sloping roof. **— Eaves**

253. Entering of soul or spirit in a new body. **— Metempsychosis**

254. Excessively high flown exaggerated talking. **— Hyperbole**

255. Excessive accumulation of harmful thing which needs to be removed. **— Plethora**

256. Excessively talented child which is rare in a child of his age. **— Prodigy**

257. Extra text or write-up which is added at the end of a text or book is. **— Addendum**

258. Extra chart or table of data which is added at the end of a book or text is. **— Appendix**

259. Excessive sugar in blood due to sugar disease/diabetes is. **— Hyperglycaemia**

260. Event involving large scale destruction is. **— Apocalypse**

261. Economic independence enjoyed by an organization or society is. **— Autarchy**

262. Eater of meat of one's own species. **— Cannibal**

263. Expression to acknowledge the supernatural power of God to save us, viz., God is great!. **— Alleluia/Hallelujah**

264. Endless period of time. **— Eternity**

265. Evening of the day just before the day of important occasion. **— Eve**

F

266. Fear of dogs one abnormally suffers from **— Cynophobia**

267. Fear of snakes one abnormally suffers from. **— Ophidiophobia**

268. Fear of taking injection (of parenteral medicines).**— Tripanophobia**

269. Fear of number 13 due to superstitious belief. **— Triskaideka phobia**

270. Feeling pleasure on seeing others in distress. **—Schadenfreude**

271. Feeling pleasure in inflicting pain, insult on others. **— Sadism**

272. Feeling pleasure in getting humiliated, insulted by others (morbid gratifi- cation in suffering pain). **— Masochism**

273. Female singer who leads a group song. **— Prima-donna**

274. Female (usually elderly woman) attendant of young unmarried girl going out of house so as to keep watch on her. **— Chaperone**

275. Feeling fear of looking down from a height such as from a high-rise building. **— Acrophobia**

276. Feeling fear of being in an incommodious or closed room. **— Claustrophobia**

277. Feeling fear of seeing a deadbody. **— Necrophobia**

278. Feeling fear of darkness (morbid fear of the night or darkness). **— Nyctophobia**

279. Feeling about something to happen without any reason to think so. **— Intuition**

280. Feeling about something bad to happen/occur. **— Premonition/Presentiment**

281. Feel like someone else is feeling by keeping oneself in place of sufferer. **— Empathize**

282. Feel sorry for someone suffering. **— Sympathize**

283. Feeling about something happening at a distant place. **—Telepathy**

284. Fellow feeling and display of unity and loyalty shown by members of a professional group. **— Esprit d' corps**

285. Fort which is built on a high ground for defence from enemy's attack is. **— Acropolis**

286. Fighting in a public place and breach public peace is. **— Affray**

287. Fit an old model of machine with latest gadgets so as to make it resemble with latest model old machine. **— Retrofit**

288. Flat board of reasonable height of which the speech maker keeps his book, paper from which he reads while making speech. **— Lectern**

289. Flat board which is raised on a tripod to tack drawing paper on it for artist to sketch or paint portrait on the drawing paper.**— Easel**

290. Flat piece of metal which is used to play strings of musical instruments (strum). — **Plectrum**

291. Fluid secreted by flowers which is collected by bees for making honey. — **Nectar**

292. Foul smelling room due to lack of ventillation/due to dampness. — **Musty room/Fetid/Fusty room**

293. Foul smelling breath of someone's mouth. — **Halitosis**

294. Fleeing from place of residence on large scale due to inhospitable conditions. — **Exodus**

295. Free-thinker. — **Esprit fort**

296. Freeing someone from bondage of servitude. — **Enfranchise**

297. Food or drink having very pleasant taste is. — **Ambrosia**

298. False and defamatory statement made about someone. — **Calumny**

299. False and defamatory rumour spread about someone.— **Canard**

300. Freedom to act as one thinks fit. — **Carte blanche**

301. Final blow given to something which ends the life or process. — **Coup de grace**

302. Fragment of crisp eatables like biscuits, cake etc. — **Crumb**

303. Fragment of broken earthenwares. — **Shard**

304. Fragment of stone. — **Scree**

305. Fragment of broken or demolished building materials.— **Rubble**

306. Fragment of broken structure of something. — **Debris**

307. First show of a picture, film, or theatre. — **Premiere**

308. First-time appearance in a role of acting in a film or drama. — **Debut**

309. First-time or chance of doing something, e.g., making speech etc. — **Maiden chance**

310. Feeling of extreme happiness. — **Euphoria**

311. Feeling of extreme joyful excitement. — **Ecstasy**

312. Fact of having accomplished a work leaving others with no option but to accept it. — **Fait accompli**

G

313. Game of guessing what someone from his group is trying to tell him by gesturing without speaking a word. — **Charade**

314. Gathering of people for spiritual sermons, discussions, etc. — **Seance**

315. Gathering of people for performing religious activity of devotees on holy river's bank. — **Congregation**

316. Glass container in which water is filled to keep fish for show is. — **Aquarium**

317. Goddess of justice who punishes evil-doers. — **Nemesis**

318. Group of ships or aircrafts owned by someone is. — **Fleet**

319. Group of warships under navy. — **Armada**

320. Group of people collected at a place. — **Crowd**

321. Group of people indulged in unlawful activity. — **Mob**

322. Group of persons assembled to watch a programme. — **Spectators**

323. Group of young women moving together. — **Bevy**

324. Group of cattle. — **Herd**

325. Group of birds. — **Flock**

326. Group of sheep. — **Hirsel**

327. Group of young birds newly hatched together. — **Brood/clutch**

328. Group of disorderly crowd/mob consisting of lower classes. — **Rabble**

329. Group of geese. — **Gaggle**

330. Group or multitude of fishes moving together in water. — **Shoal**

331. Group of bees. — **Swarm**

332. Group of islands in vicinity to each other. — **Archipelago**

333. Group of people engaged in plotting against a ruler (originally formed by five unpopular ministers of Charles II and now refers to any small party for executing some secret design). — **Cabal**

334. Group of people moving together in a company for security, especially for crossing deserts. — **Caravan**

335. Group of singers who sing in church. — **Choir**

336. Group of hired persons to applaud in a meeting. — **Claque**

337. Group of people with similar knowledge or interest. — **Clique**

338. Group of followers of a person. — **Cohort**

339. Group of stars forming a fixed pattern in the night sky. — **Constellation**

340. Group of mourners who join a funeral procession. — **Cortege**

341. Group of persons who jointly operate a ship, aeroplane etc. — **Crew**

342. Group of attendants of a V.I.P. — **Entourage**

343. Group of officials attached to a V.I.P. — **Retinue**

344. Group of military officers who forcibly overthrow ruler and usurp power. — **Junta**

345. Group of experts who discuss a subject. — **Panel**

346. Group of reveller engaged in revelry. — **Rout**

347. Group of symptoms of a disease. — **Syndrome**

348. Group of three gods. — **Trinity**

349. Group of artists performing together. — **Troupe**

350. Group of three persons who jointly exercise powers. — **Triumvirate**

351. Group of criminals engaged in organized crime on large scale. — **Mafia**

352. Group of three persons jointly holding an office. — **Triumvirate**

353. Group of three persons performing in unison. — **Troika**

354. Group of three god-heads joined together each representing particular function, viz. Brahma, the creator, Vishnu, the preservator, and Mahesh, the destroyer. — **Trinity**

H

355. Habit of involuntary grinding of teeth in sleep. — **Bruxism**

356. Habit of walking in sleep. — **Somnambulism**

357. Habit of speaking in sleep. — **Somniloquism**

358. Habit of urinating in sleep. — **Enuresis**

359. Habit of lying (telling lies). — **Mythomania/mendacity**

360. Habit of drinking alcoholic stimulants. — **Dipsomania**

361. Habit of purchasing things without having need of them. (The compulsive urge for buying things). — **Oniomania**

362. Habit of striking together nails in rage or pain. — **Gnashing**

363. Habit of indulging in highfalutin talks. — **Megalomania**

364. Hard and thick skin caused by friction. — **Callus**

365. Habit of involuntary urination on bed during sleep. — **Enuresis**

366. Hairs of animals which are soft, and are used for making wool. — **Fur**

367. Hairs of animals which are hard, erect and are used for making brush. — **Bristles**

368. Habit which is in a person since his birth is. — **Innate habit**

369. Hairs which are mix of black and grey. — **Grizzly hairs**

370. Habit of a person which can't be reformed is. — **Incorrigible**

371. Helper of a golfer who carries golf clubs. — **Caddie**

372. Highest point of, or level of something. — **Apex**

373. Highest point of mountains. — **Summit, Peak**

374. Highest point of a structure. — **Vertex**

375. Highest point of elevation or achievement. — **Pinnacle, Zenith**

376. Hole dug in the ground by animal for dwelling. — **Burrow**

I

377. Indefinitely long period of time in the past; an age or one of a series of ages; eternity. — **Aeon**

378. Indefinite future (tomorrow). — **Manana**

379. Items of china wares/materials made of china. — **Crockery**

380. Items of materials used for eating, e.g., spoons, forks, etc. — **Cutlery**

381. Items of materials used for keeping or serving food in, and for cooking in kitchen. — **Utensils**

382. Items of materials used for writing. — **Stationery**

383. Imaginary feeling of existence of something. — **Illusion**

384. Imaginary images created in one's dream while in sleep. — **Phantasmagoria**

385. Impossible to be avoided. — **Unavoidable**

386. Impossible to be tamed. — **Indomitable**

387. Impossible to be stopped by struggling against it *Ineluctable destiny. — **Ineluctable**

388. Impossible to do without something because of being essential. — **Indispensable**

389. Incapable of being placated is. — **Implacable**

390. Incapable of being avoided is. — **Ineluctable**

391. Incapable of being defeated. — **Invincible**

392. Incapable of doing any mistake is. — **Inpeccable**

393. Incapable of failing or being unsuccessful is. — **Infallible**

394. Inferior quality of imitation of a literary work. — **Burlesque**

395. Insensitive to other's feelings. — **Callous**

396. Incarnation of God as ordinary human-being, discarding godly attributes for the good of mankind. — **Kenosis**

K

397. Kill someone for alleged offence without legal process, usually in a mob frenzy. — **Lynch**

398. Killing a terminally ill person to spare him of painful condition out of mercy on him. — **Euthanasia**

399. Killing of one's own father. — **Patricide**

400. Killing of one's own mother. — **Matricide**

401. Killing of one's own son or daughter. — **Filicide**

402. Killing of one's own brother. — **Fratricide**

403. Killing of one's own sister. — **Sororicide**

404. Killing of a very large number of people belonging to a particular ethnic group. — **Genocide**

405. Killing of human-beings. — **Homicide**

406. Killing of one's wife. — **Uxoricide**

407. Killing of a parent or a near relative or a revered person. — **Parricide**

L

408. Lying dormant/inactive is a state of. — **Dormancy**

409. Lying inactive during hot climate is. — **Aestivation**

410. Lying inactive during winter climate is. — **Hibernation**

411. Love amongst people of a religious faith is. — **Agape**

412. Love between two sexes which is intimate but devoid of erotic feelings (love between soul and soul without sensual desire). — **Platonic love**

413. Language of talking by a specified group of people, viz, hawkers. — **Cant**

414. Language of speech or reply having more than one meaning, and hence the speech or reply is not clearly understood is. — **Ambiguous**

415. Language of speech or reply giving two mutually contradictory ideas is. — **Ambivalent**

416. Loss of someone's appetite. — **Anorexia**

417. Loss of hairs, resulting in baldness caused by a nervous disturbance. — **Alopecia**

418. Loss of memory is. — **Amnesia**

419. Loss of ability to smell. — **Anosmia**

420. Living being which lives both in water as well as on earth is. — **Amphibian**

421. Living being which lives only on earth is. — **Terrestrial**

422. Living being which lives only in water is. — **Aquatic**

423. Living form of human being or animal. — **Incarnation**

424. Listening of sound made by heart, lungs, or other body organs with stethoscope is. — **Auscultation**

425. Look around oneself for anything suspect which may cause harm. — **Circumspect**

426. Look within oneself to realise one's own weaknesses or reasons for failures. — **Introspect**

427. Look back in the past to know what went wrong. — **Retrospect**

428. Look back in the past with fond memory of happy moments in life. — **Nostalgia**

429. Lamentation for the dead person. — **Dirge/Threnody**

430. Lamentation for the dead person by weeping. — **Keen**

431. Large-scale leaving of their homes by people. — **Exodus**

432. Large-scale emigration of people of a country to countries around the world. — **Diaspora**

433. Land beside a sea. — **Coast**

434. Land farther away from coast. — **Hinterland**

435. Land beside a river (river-bank). — **Riparian**

436. Leaving of a dead body by soul to take another living body. — **Metempsychosis**

M

437. Manner of speaking, pronouncing a word in peculiar manner, or other peculiar behaviour which makes someone distinctly identified with a community, race, or nativity; an old phrase or custom which has no relevance in the present day. — **Shibboleth**

438. Matter which has nothing to do with moral values is. — **Unmoral (Amoral)**

439. Matter which is against moral values is.— **Immoral**

440. Matter which is not concerned with whether morally right or wrong is. **— Amoral**

441. Medals which are hung from the shoulder of a military uniform. **— Epaulette (Epaulet)**

442. Medicine which is supposed to protect or prevent a disease or infection. **— Prophylactic**

443. Medicine which is taken to get relief from fever. **— Febrifuge/Antipyretic**

444. Medicine which has no physically creative effect, given to a patient for humour or gratification. **— Placebo**

445. Medicine which is supposed to be a cure for all diseases. **— Panacea**

446. Medicine which expels worms from patient's intestine. **— Anthelminthic (Anthelmintic)**

447. Medicine as cough syrup, e.g. codeine. **— Antitussive**

448. Medicine which makes one younger and prolongs life. **— Elixir**

449. Medicine which expels cough from chest/lungs. **— Expectorant**

450. Medicine which is prepared by the physician himself and is not available in other medicine shops (patented medicine). **— Nostrum**

451. Male attendant of elderly woman (dancing partner). **— Gigolo**

452. Main substance of a virtue/quality which determines someone's or something's nature. **— Essence**

453. Main substance of a speech or text. **— Gist**

454. Main substance of accusation against someone. **— Gravamen**

455. Moneylender who charges unreasonably high interest.**— Usurer**

456. Model of full-size human being to display new clothes in shops. **— Mannequin**

457. Model of something in miniature size (wax or clay) for the sculptor to copy. **— Maquette**

458. Moneylender who lends money by keeping valuables as deposits to ensure return of loan with interests. **— Pawnbroker**

459. Most attractive item of something, such as a variety entertainment programme, or a substantial course of meal at dinner (feast); the best item. **— Piece de resistance**

460. Memory of dreadful past which keeps haunting the sufferer. **— Nightmare**

461. Memory loss in which a person fails to recognise familiar things or persons, either partially or totally. **— Agnosia**

462. Memory loss due to ageing. — **Senility**

463. Memory loss due to mental disorder. — **Dementia**

464. Monster who spews fire and has body of a serpent and head of a lion. — **Chimera**

465. (Migrate) Enter a foreign country, with the intention to live there permanently. — **Immigrate**

466. Migrate from one's own country to go and live in another country. — **Emigrate**

N

467. Narrow passage passing through rows of buildings, park or garden is. — **Alley**

468. Narrow passage passing through rows of sitting chairs is.— **Aisle**

469. Naked saint who does not wear clothes as a religious practice. — **Gymnosophist**

O

470. Object belonging to early time which becomes valuable in present time due to its age is. — **Antique**

471. Object of art made by skilled artists. — **Artefact (Artifact)**

472. Ointment which has softening, relaxing or soothing effect on skin. — **Emolient**

473. Object of irrational reverence; a belief in charms. — **Fetish**

474. Object which is used by witches to cause bad luck to someone. — **Hoodoo**

475. Object which is considered by a clan as their identity; superstitious respect as an outward symbol of an existing intimate unseen relation. — **Totem**

476. Object of value which is preserved as prized possession by successive generations in a family. — **Heirloom**

477. Objects which are having historical values and ought to be preserved by successive generations. — **Heritage**

478. Obsessive compulsive habit of drinking alcohol. — **Dispomania**

479. Obsessive compulsive habit of stealing. — **Kleptomania**

480. Obsessive compulsive habit of lying or exaggerating to an abnormal extent. — **Mythomania**

481. Obsessive compulsive habit of setting something on fire. — **Pyromania**

482. Outer protective layer of a tree. — **Bark**

483. Outer protective layer of banana, orange etc., which is easily removed/stripped off. **— Peel**

484. Outer protective layer of fruits which are thick and not stripped off (such as of watermelon). **— Rind**

485. Official who holds the post at present. **— Incumbent**

486. Official who had held the post before the present one (incumbent). **— Predecessor**

487. Official who holds the post after the present one. **— Successor**

488. Object which is preserved for the memory of a dead person – usually the personal effects of the dead person. **— Memorabilia**

489. Object which is preserved for the memory of past event/days. **— Memento**

490. Object which is preserved for the memory of a place visited where it was brought from. **— Souvenir**

491. Object which is preserved as a memory of person who has given it. **— Remembrance**

492. Object made of clay. **— Terracotta**

493. Object made of clay or metal resembling strange face of human or animal and used as drain outlet projected from roof. **— Gargoyle**

P

494. Pardon granted by the government to the person convicted for crime against the State is. **— Amnesty**

495. Person who receives and sells stolen goods. **— Fence**

496. Person who lives in caves. **— Troglodyte**

497. Person who is hired to insinuate himself in mob to provoke them to resort to violence. **— Agent provocateur**

498. Person who is holding a post without having official power to exercise/act. **— Functus officio**

499. Person who is used to enhance someone's virtue by contrasting with that of the very person former is called the latter person's. **— Foil**

500. Person who does duty as a substitute of someone during absence is called. **— Locum tenens**

501. Person who inherits or is entitled to inherit an ancestor's property is called. **— Heir**

502. Person who has become feebleminded due to old age. **— Dotard**

503. Person who does not have faith in a particular religion, especially Christianity/Islam, is called. **—Infidel**

504. Person who is simpleton, free from craftiness in dealing; a naive young woman on the stage. **— Ingenue**

505. Person who has become famous with popular achievements and admired by people. **— Legend**

506. Person who has been abandoned by his society and discarded. **— Outcast**

507. Person who lives away from people, or seclusion from society, in an isolated place. **— Recluse**

508. Person who is always ready to come forward to help people in distress. **— Samaritan**

509. Person who takes pleasure in secretly peeping into private affairs of others; a sexual pervert who derives sexual gratification from watching other's sexual acts or objects; a peeping tom. **— Voyeur**

510. Person who derives pleasure by getting hurt by others. **— Masochist**

511. Person who pretends to possess great wisdom. **— Wiseacre**

512. Person who cracks facetious jokes. **— Wag**

513. Person who is castrated in early age so as to grow into a sexless adult. **— Eunuch**

514. Plant (animal) which possesses the organs of both male and female. **— Hermaphrodite**

515. Person who has the misleading appearance of a female. **— Androgyne**

516. Person who belongs to a place since the earliest time is. **— Aborigine of that place**

517. Person who belongs to a place since his birth is. **— Native**

518. Person who flees to evade arrest is. **— Fugitive**

519. Person who flees from workplace or school without permission to evade work or class is a. **— Truant**

520. Person who argues to defend someone's controversial conduct is his. **— Apologist**

521. Person who has left/renounced his belief in party and harbouring rancour against it. **— Renegade**

522. Person who has renounced his belief in his party, religion, or principle and abandoned it without harbouring rancour against it. **— Apostate**

523. Person who renounces his old association or party for personal gain. — **Turncoat**

524. Person who decides about something or someone on his free will is. — **Arbiter**

525. Person who lives a life of extreme self-discipline by denying himself worldly conforms (as a monk does). — **Ascetic**

526. Person who kills a political leader is. — **Assassin**

527. Person who rules with his own absolute power is. — **Autocrat**

528. Person who carries someone's letter to deliver to another person is. — **Bearer**

529. Person who helps others by giving money is. — **Benefactor**

530. Person who receives money as help from others.— **Beneficiary**

531. Person who is fond of reading books, lover or collector of books, is. — **Bibliophile**

532. Person who habitually talks excessively. — **Blabbermouth**

533. Person who is fond of living in a good lifestyle. — **Bon vivant**

534. Person who behaves in amusingly ridiculous manner.— **Buffoon**

535. Person who pretends to be a qualified doctor. — **Quack**

536. Person who pretends to be learned. — **Charlatan**

537. Person who parades/shows off his knowledge. — **Pedant**

538. Persons who are considered to have knowledge about a specified subject. — **Cognoscenti**

539. Person who has acquired expert knowledge in a matter of art is. — **Connoisseur**

540. Person who has equal share with others in property inherited from ancestor is a. — **Coparcener**

541. Person who habitually doubts a belief or existence of something in absence of proof. — **Sceptic**

542. Person who habitually doubts the intention of everyone behind his action, as being surely motivated by self-gain. — **Cynic**

543. Person who is excessively attentive towards his fashionable, stylish appearance. — **Dandy/Fop**

544. Person who is fond of eating without choice of food. — **Glutton/Gourmand**

545. Person who is fond of eating choice food and possesses knowledge about dishes. — **Gourmet**

546. Person who is young and handsome. — **Adonis**

547. Person who excessively boasts about oneself. — **Braggart**

548. Person who spends lot of time sitting in chair watching television. **— Couch potato**

549. Person who is so pessimistic that he always prophesies about impending disaster. **— Cassandra**

550. Person who parades his superior moralistic behaviour. **— Prig**

551. Person who has different standards of behaviour – what he preaches, he does not practise himself. **— Hypocrite**

552. Person who is physically deformed and mental and suffers from defective due to development due to failure of secretion of thyroid gland. **— Cretin**

553. Person who is the natural successor to the ancestral property. **— Heir**

554. Person (or some event) who/which publicly announces something important to come or happen. **— Herald**

555. Person who holds or practises belief which is contrary to religious orthodoxy. **— Heretic**

556. Person living in solitude like a saint for religious practices. **— Hermit**

557. Person who is rowdy and violent trouble-maker. **— Hooligan, Hoodlum**

558. Person who is kept captive for fulfilment of demands of money or conditions. **— Hostage**

559. Person who joins discussion for resolution of dispute between two contenders. **— Interlocutor**

560. Person who acts in the negotiation between two parties for a deal. **— Intermediary**

561. Person who keeps his thoughts within oneself, and does not talk much. **— Introvert**

562. Person who speaks out his thoughts freely. **— Extrovert**

563. Person who has received an award for something. **— Laureate**

564. Person who is educated in a subject of literature. **— Litterateur**

565. Persons belonging to the class of litterateur. **— Litterati**

566. Persons belonging to the class of glamorous profession like cinema, fashion etc. **— Glitterati**

567. Person who is cunning, crafty, and unscrupulous person. **— Machiavellian**

568. Person (rich patron) who generously spends to support activities of art and literature. **— Maecenas**

569. Person who is wealthy and influential businessman. **— Magnate/Tycoon**

570. Person who is very strict about observance of discipline. **— Martinet**

571. Person who sacrifices his life for a lofty cause. **— Martyr**

572. Person who does massage. **— Masseur**

573. Person who does hair-cut. **— Barber/Coiffeur**

574. Person who is expert in cooking. **— Cook/Cordon bleu**

575. Person who does washing of kitchen utensils. **— Scullion**

576. Person (or living organism) which lives at the expense of other person (or organism). **— Parasite**

577. Person who has lost hope in his future. **— Pessimist**

578. Person who is hopeful for his future. **— Optimist**

579. Person who has lost hope or is dejected. **— Despondent**

580. Person who is capable of attracting people to come behind him to wherever he goes. **— Pied Piper**

581. Person who makes new changes in something existing. **— Innovator**

582. Person who is first to explore something new. **— Pioneer**

583. Person who makes a new path for others to follow.**— Trailblazer**

584. Person who helps to give a new direction to fashion. **—Trend setter**

585. Person who hunts to kill animals unauthorisedly in a protected jungle or sanctuary. **— Poacher**

586. Person who is converted to a new religion after deserting own one. **— Proselyte**

587. Person who gets protection of a superior person is his. **— Protege**

588. Person who is the seniormost member of a prominent family. **— Doyen**

589. Person who is the youngest member of a prominent family. **— Scion**

590. Person who spends recklessly. **— Spendthrift, Prodigal**

591. Person who spends judiciously. **— Thrift**

592. Person who (or organization which) undertakes to meet expenses of an event or a good cause. **— Sponsor**

593. Person who is cruel but equally coward. **— Dastard**

594. Person who makes first appearance in a role. **— Debutant**

595. Person who has cultivated interest in fine arts but in a superficial way and without serious purpose. — **Dilettante**

596. Person who sets up a business or enterprise. — **Entrepreneur**

597. Person who is considered a perfect symbol of highest quality of virtue. — **Paragon**

598. Person who is considered the most popular symbol of a particular field of activity. — **Icon**

599. Person or thing which is considered a symbol of good luck for an event like sports, organization etc. — **Mascot**

600. Person who has committed unpardonably serious crime on account of his wickedness and cruelty, and punished for his crime by forfeiture of lands etc. — **Felon**

601. Person who is engaged or betrothed to be married to a woman is her. — **Fiance**

602. Person who is engaged/betrothed to be married to a man is — **Fiance**

603. Person who betrays his own country. — **Traitor**

604. Person who helps enemy country which is at war with his own country. — **Fifth columnist**

605. Person who is rewarded with the power to rule his country in lieu of his help to the invading enemy to conquer it. — **Quisling**

606. Person who harms or destroys the very person who made him powerful; a person who destroys his own creator. — **Frankenstein**

607. Person who entertains spectators with his fight-to-finish with another person or animal (bull) in an arena. — **Gladiator**

608. Product which belongs to a place because it is produced in that place is. — **Indigenous**

609. Person who is substituted for someone in his role. — **Surrogate**

610. Person who is a habitual flatterer in order to please someone. — **Sycophant**

611. Person who is habitually servile to obey someone in order to please him. — **Toady**

612. Person who is strict in matters of discipline. — **Martinet**

613. Person who is a professional bull-fighter in a game of bull-fight. — **Matador**

614. Person who comes forward to help someone in distress. — **Samaritan**

615. Person who lives in cave. — **Troglodyte**

616. Person who is loyal to one's own country. — **Patriot**

617. Person who does not drink wine. — **Teetotaler**

618. Person who suddenly acquires wealth or prominence and becomes arrogant. — **Upstart**

619. Person without home and job and so wandering from place to place. — **Vagabond/Vagrant**

620. Person who suffers from anxiety of getting ill and always trying to find out symptoms in his body, especially abdomen. — **Hypochondriac**

621. Person who is over-concerned with his health. — **Valetudinarian**

622. Person who aspires to emulate another's success, or attain eminence in some area, often vainly. — **Wannabe actor**

623. Person who just failed to become something he would have been, such as a poet, because of defect of character and circumstances, and suffered frustration. — **Poet manque**

624. Person who is fearless is. — **Intrepid**

625. Person who deliberately intimidates those who are weaker. — **Bully**

626. Person who is capable of finding a source of underground water by tapping ground with a divining rod. — **Dowser**

627. Person who has won laurels, awards in any field for distinct achievements. — **Laureate**

628. Person who has the superiormost status amongst members of a group of equals. — **Primus inter pares**

629. Person who takes note of speech/dictation; a copying secretary. — **Amanuensis**

630. Person who practises his profession in unprofessional manners, e.g., a lawyer, doctor, etc.; an unscrupulous practitioner in any business or profession. — **Shyster**

631. Person who cannot be pleased with entreaties. — **Inexorable person**

632. Person who can't do any wrong. — **Impeccable person**

633. Person who cannot be conquered. — **Invincible person**

634. People of a country or race who have scattered throughout the world to live there. — **Diaspora**

635. Person who accompanies old woman when she goes out of house. — **Gigolo**

636. Person who is habitually dirty in appearance, dressing, etc. —**Sloven**

637. Person who is reserved in speaking and hence talks less.
— Reticent person

638. Person who does not react to provcations; not easily excited by other's actions/utterances. **— Phlegmatic person**

639. Person who acts against established practices in social or religious matters; against worship of images. **— Iconoclast**

640. Person who remains calm in both pain and pleasure.
— Stoic person

641. Person who hates women. **— Misogynist**

642. Person who hates mankind. **— Misanthrope**

643. Person who habitually flirts with women. **— Philander**

644. Person who loves mankind and generously helps people in need.
— Philanthrope/Philanthropist

645. Person who is self-centred or selfish. **— Egoist**

646. Person who has tendency to talk about himself and his abilities.
— Egotist

647. Person who habitually works with his left hand. **— Sinistral**

648. Person who is strictly vegetarian. **— Vegan**

649. Person who belongs to the same age as another one is his.
— Contemporary

650. Person who does not feel gratefulness for other's help in times of need. **— Ingrate**

651. Person who believes in enjoying life and indulges in good food and other enjoyments of life. **— Epicure**

652. Person who helps a criminal in committing crime is his.
— Accomplice

653. Person who lives on alms received by begging. **— Mendicant**

654. Person who belives that everything depends on luck. **— Fatalist**

655. Person who assumes false identity of someone else in order to deceive others. **— Impostor**

656. Person of supernatural powers who is considered as agent of god for spreading god's message to people. **— Prophet**

657. Person of supernatural power who reveals occult phenomena to the people. **— Oracle**

658. Person who dies without demising his properties through a will.
— Intestate

659. Person who does not appreciate someone's good work is.
— Inappreciative (person)

660. Person who can't be met by someone needing his help. **— Inapproachable by someone**

661. Person who is a voracious eater is a. **— Glutton**

662. Person who writes inscriptions on a monument's walls (murals) in beautiful and decorative letters, or manuscripts of high aesthetic values. **— Calligrapher**

663. Person who is a police informer. **— Nark**

664. Person who talks arrogantly/an annoying child. **— Brat**

665. Person whose honesty, integrity can be easily purchased by bribe is a. **— Venal person**

666. Person who sells his services for earning money is a. **— Mercenary**

667. Piece of wood or paper used for kindling a fire. **— Spill/Fidibus**

668. Place where grains are stored. **— Granary**

669. Place where horses are kept. **— Stable**

670. Place (a large cage) where birds are kept. **— Aviary**

671. Place where wild animals are kept in their natural environs. **— Sanctuary**

672. Place where coins are legally fabricated or invented out of metals (non-ferrous metals). **— Mint**

673. Place where goods are stored. **— Depot**

674. Place where food articles are stored. **— Pantry**

675. Place where animals' hides are processed for making leather. **— Tannery**

676. Place where wine is produced. **— Brewery**

677. Place where soldiers are housed. **— Cantonment**

678. Place where soldiers are kept in civilian area with authorisation. **— Billet**

679. Place where milk and milk products are produced. **— Dairy**

680. Place where aeroplanes are kept when not in use. **— Hangar**

681. Place where people do physical exercises for fitness. **— Gymnasium**

682. Place where orphan children are kept and looked after. **— Orphanage**

683. Place where tourists go for enjoyment. **— Resort**

684. Place where antiques are kept. **— Museum**

685. Place where valuable papers, files, articles are kept stored for future use. **— Archive**

686. Place where travellers take rest. — **Inn**

687. Place which is difficult to reach to is. — **Inaccessible place**

688. Place of study or training in a particular field of knowledge is. — **Academy**

689. Plant which belongs to a place since the earliest times; or pertaining to ideas unrelated to a person's train of thoughts which come into the mind. — **Autochthon**

690. Place where someone can live or stay is. — **Accommodation**

691. Place where important documents are kept for perservation is. — **Archive**

692. Place under control of an emperor. — **Empire**

693. Place under control of the Nature of creator of the world. — **Realm**

694. Place under control of a legal authority. — **Jurisdiction**

695. Place under one's command. — **Domain**

696. Place where a saint lives in solitude for religious purposes. — **Hermitage**

697. Place where large number of people stay by sharing a large room. — **Dormitory**

698. Place in a town where people of minority community inhabit, e.g. Jews quarters in Italian or other atics where they are confined. — **Ghetto**

699. Place where ill persons or needy, homeless ones are accommodated as charity. — **Hospice**

700. Place where people assemble to meet at appointed time. — **Rendezvous**

701. Place of stay made of ice blocks where Eskimos live. — **Igloo**

702. Place of stay where priests and nuns live. — **Monastery**

703. Place where pigs are kept. — **Stye**

704. Place where dogs are kept. — **Kennel**

705. Place where lions live or are kept. — **Den/Lair**

706. Place where farm animals are kept. — **Pen**

707. Place behind kitchen where dirty kitchenware is washed. — **Scullery**

708. Place in desert where water is available. — **Oasis**

709. Place where secret meeting is held by thieves, robbers, spy agents, etc. — **Assignation**

710. Place where lovers meet secretly. — **Tryst**

711. Place where people assemble at a pre-fixed timing by coming from different areas, usually for gossipping. — **Rendezvous**

712. Place where wild animals are kept for exhibiting. — **Menagerie**

713. Place where dead bodies are kept before being taken away for cremation. — **Mortuary**

714. Place where deadbodies are cremated. — **Crematorium**

715. Platform, usually made of bamboo, which is used to keep a deadbody on. — **Bier**

716. Platform on which a clergy in church stands to deliver sermon or raised structure for preachers to preach or the auctioneer's desk. — **Pulpit**

717. Platform on which religious offerings/sacrifices are made.— **Altar**

718. Platform on which public leaders stand to address electorates in elections; or election proceedings take place. — **Hustings**

719. Platform, usually decorated with flowers, on which deadbody lies in state. — **Catafalque**

720. Person who helps someone in committing an act of crime is his. — **Accomplice**

721. Person who is expert in an activity is an. — **Ace**

722. Person who performs gymnastic feats on a tight rope or erect pole, a rope dancer; a person who makes sudden changes or reversals in his opinions, relationships. — **Acrobat**

723. Person who is uncontrollably habituated to something injurious is an. — **Addict**

724. Person who remains faithful to his party or religion is an.— **Adherent**

725. Person who travels in space aboard a spacecraft is an. — **Aeronaut**

726. Person who appreciates the beauty of art is. — **Aesthete**

727. Person who is fond of a specific sporting activity or past time, such as bull-fighting, cricket, cinema etc. — **Aficionado**

728. Person who is related to someone by being descendant from the same male ancestor is. — **Agnate**

729. Person who is ignorant of the fact whether God exists or not is an. — **Agnostic**

730. Person who is believer of the existence of God is. — **Theist**

731. Person who is disbeliever of the existence of God is. — **Atheist**

732. Person who is an assistant to a public leader is. — **Aide**

733. Peson who is an assistant to a senior officer is. — **Subordinate**

734. Person who is an assistant to a criminal is. — **Henchman**

735. Person having white skin and hairs and pink eyes due to lack of skin pigment is an. — **Albino**

736. Person who belongs to other country/place than where he is living is an. — **Alien**

737. Person who is about to achieve adulthood. — **Adolescent**

738. Person who is opposed to someone is his. — **Adversary/Antagonist**

739. Person who insinuates into mob to provoke them to resort to violence. — **Agent provocateur**

740. Person who gives alms in charity. — **Almoner**

741. Person who belongs to noble section of society by birth. — **Aristocrat**

742. Person who wilfully indulges in setting public property on fire in violence. — **Arsonist**

743. Person who indulges in wilful looting or destroying of public property in mob violence. — **Vandal**

744. Person who moves from place to place to entertain people by composing and reciting epic or traditional folklores. — **Bard**

745. Person who rules with absolute authoritarian powers.— **Autocrat**

746. Person who rules with cruelty on people. — **Despot/Tyrant**

747. Person who is ill-reputed to indulge in promiscuous amorous relationships with serveral women. — **Casanova, Don Juan**

748. Person who is inspired with lofty but impractical ideas/ideals. — **Don Quixote**

749. Person who introduces a stage show to the audience before actors' performance so as to explain the theme or to laud the talented actors presented in the stage show. — **Compere**

750. Person who acts as an agent of a foreign business.— **Comprador**

751. Person who types text for publishing. — **Compositor**

752. Person who officially holds investigation into the cause of death of a person in doubtful circumstances. — **Coroner**

753. Person who is broad-minded and not prejudiced to provincialism in attitude. — **Cosmopolite/Cosmopolitan**

754. Person who is obsequiously servile to someone in power is his. — **Courtier**

755. Person who is in charge of taking care of antiques, animals in zoo, etc. — **Curator**

756. Person who exploits people's sentiments, passions, or emotions to win their following. — **Demagogue**

757. Person who advocates peaceful solution to problems with another country. — **Dove**

758. Person who advocates war as a solution to nation's problems with another country. — **Hawk**

759. Person who does menial, dull, hard work routinely. — **Drudge**

760. Person who indulges in odd patterns of behaviour. — **Eccentric**

761. Person who is wont to behave unpredictably. — **Freak**

762. Person who sells small wares like button, needles, ribbons, and other dress materials. — **Haberdasher**

763. Person who sells his professional skill as a writer, journalist, etc. by writing in someone's favour. — **Hack**

764. Person who exhibits characters of both the sexes. — **Hermaphrodite, Epicene**

765. Person who exhibits feminine character which is unmanly. — **Effeminate**

766. Person who is partly male and partly female having the toughness of a man and softness of a female. — **Androgyne**

767. Person who attacks cherished beliefs, or traditional and established values by denouncing as being superstitious. — **Iconoclastic**

768. Person who is so popular as to symbolise the society he belongs to. — **Icon**

769. Person who receives and entertains invited guests. — **Host**

770. Person who is ignorant. — **Ignoramus**

771. Person who lacks professional knowledge of a given subject as opposed to experts in that field. — **Laity/layman**

772. Person who practises idol worship. — **Idolator**

773. Person who deceives by assuming the character or identity or name of someone else. — **Impostor**

774. Person who organizes public entertainment programmes. — **Impresario**

775. Person who rises in revolt against lawful government and engages in armed struggle. — **Insurgent**

776. Person who is adept in wits, jokes and pranks which is entertaining to people. — **Jester**

777. Person who does not have any principle and is having base nature. — **Knave, Scoundrel**

778. Person who is playfully mischievous. — **Rogue, Rascal**

779. Person who is habitually lazy and so lags behind others in any activity. — **Laggard**

780. Person who works as a substitute for someone during his absence as his assistant; a temporary substitute for a doctor or a clergy. — **Locum tenens**

781. Person who holds the view that a ruler must act beyond the principle of morality in order to stay in power; political expediency is placed above morality. — **Machiavelli**

782. Person who is symbol of greed for money. — **Mammon**

783. Person who lives on begging as some sect's saints practise. — **Mendicant**

784. Person who does something for others, viz., a soldier who fights for foreign country against its enemy for money. — **Mercenary**

785. Person who is self-willed, does what he thinks right, and is not guided by anyone else. — **Maverick**

786. Person whose body size is extremely below normal. — **Midget, Pygmy, Dwarf**

787. Person who abnormally hates mankind in general. — **Misanthrope**

788. Person who abnormally hates womenfolk in general. — **Misogynist**

789. Person who indulges in creating public disorder. — **Miscreant**

790. Person who is habitually stupid. — **Moron**

791. Person who is habitually ill-tempered, gloomy. — **Morose**

792. Person who is habitually enarmoured with his own looks. — **Narcissus**

793. Person who is all powerful. — **Omnipotent**

794. Person who knows everything. — **Omniscient**

795. Person who adheres to traditional beliefs and conventions. — **Orthodox**

796. Person who is discarded by his own caste men, society.— **Outcast**

797. Person who is treated as untouchable by society. — **Pariah**

798. Person of ordinary class who becomes a rich person, influential or powerful without concomittant sophistication. — **Parvenu, Neorich, Upstart**

799. Person who holds honorary position in a set-up, or who supports a venture, organization as a distinguished person. — **Patron**

800. Person who takes to walk on road or pavement while going from a place to another place. — **Pedestrian**

801. Person who is welcome in company by others. — **Persona grata**

802. Person who is not welcome by others. — **Persona non grata**

803. Person who belongs to a group of robbers engaged in looting ships on high sea. — **Pirate**

804. Person in authority who is invested with full powers of acting or taking actions as he deems fit. — **Plenipotentiary**

805. Person who is sent to damnation by God for the sins committed by him. — **Reprobate**

806. Person who advocates radical change in a rotten system. — **Revolutionary**

807. Person who fights for protecting his religion from infidels. — **Crusader**

808. Person who indulges in unlawful activities, e.g., murder, robbery, playing pander for another. — **Ruffian**

809. Person who indulges in underhand damaging activities in one's own camp or by stealthily entering another camp. — **Saboteur**

810. Person who takes pleasure in inflicting pain on others. — **Sadist**

811. Person who takes pleasure in misery of others. — **Schadenfreude**

812. Person, creature or thing, whose presence assures good luck. — **Mascot**

813. Person who lives a life devoid of luxury on his own volition. — **Spartan**

814. Person who practises his profession as a lawyer by indulging in unfair means. — **Shyster**

815. Person who earns salary without doing commensurate job. — **Sinecurist**

816. Person who shows deep antipathy to foreigners or to foreign things. — **Xenophobe**

817. Person who is habitually dirty. — **Sloven**

818. Person who is well-known in social circle, and takes part in social gatherings. — **Socialite**

819. Person who is handicap with inability to control movements of limbs due to cerebral palsy. — **Spastic**

820. Person who takes possession of public land and starts living there due to having no place of his own to live in. — **Squatter**

821. Person who works as an agent for selling property, rail or games ticket for monetary gains. — **Tout**

822. Person who sells goods which are banned. — **Trafficker**

823. Person who lends money on premium rates of interest.— **Usurer**

824. Person who portrays bad character roles in cinema. — **Villain**

825. Person who has imaginative thinking and capacity to plan for the future. — **Visionary**

826. Person who enjoys gratification by looking at amorous activities or others, or by peeping into other's private affairs. — **Voyeur**

827. Person who is a vagabond. — **Waif**

828. Person who is adept in making facetious jokes. — **Wag**

829. Person who is a skilled fighter and takes part in war. —**Warrior**

830. Person who pretends to have great wisdom. — **Wiseacre**

831. Past student/students (male) of a college, school, or university is its. — **Alumnus/Alumni**

832. Past student/students (female) of a college, school, etc. is its. — **Alumna/Alumnae**

833. Person's close friend who is very much like him in his ego. — **Alter Ego**

834. Person who is concerned with the well-being of others instead of oneself is. — **Altruist**

835. Person who is a new entrant to a party or religion. — **Neophyte**

836. Person who is beginner in learning an art or work is. — **Callow**

837. Person who is a new hand in doing a job is. — **Novice/Tyro**

838. Person who is not expert in a field of art or music is.— **Amateur**

839. Person who is yet inexperienced in his job. — **Greenhorn**

840. Person who uses both his hands with equal ease in doing something is. — **Ambidextrous**

841. Person who is friendly in manners is. — **Amiable**

842. Person's earlier social background which is used to judge his character is his. — **Antecedent**

843. Phobia of height. — **Acrophobia**

844. Phobia of being present in open or public place.— **Agoraphobia**

845. Phobia of being present in a congested place.— **Claustrophobia**

846. Pot in which scented glues, agarbatti (incense) is burnt. — **Censer**

847. Pot in which flowers are kept in a room. — **Vase**

848. Politician who seeks to get elected from a constituency away from his home-place is. — **Carpetbagger**

849. Practice of marrying one's deceased brother's widow.— **Levirate**

850. Prayer for the repose of the soul of dead person. — **Requiem**

851. Prayer to God to save from crisis. — **Hosannah**

852. Prayer to be chanted in morning hours. — **Matins**

853. Prayer to be chanted in evening hours. — **Vespers**

854. Process of development of an organism by going through various stages of life. — **Evolution**

R

855. Rebirth of a dead one in new living human form.— **Reincarnation**

856. Recover health gradually after illness. — **Convalesce**

857. Remove a mistake or defect. — **Rectify**

858. Remove the cause of grievance. — **Redress**

859. Remove objectionable portion from a written text. — **Expunge**

860. Remove wrong notions about something from one's mind. — **Disabuse**

861. Rubbing of oil for purifying or consecrating someone is. — **Anointment**

862. Range of one's knowledge or understanding. — **Ken**

863. Remembering one's happy moments of past life. — **Reminiscence**

864. Remembering old days with sentimental longing for.— **Nostalgia**

865. Remaining/left-over portion of a felled tree. — **Stump**

866. Remaining portion of an used-up thing, such as pencil, cigarette, candle etc. — **Stub**

867. Reason of someone or something being in existence in this world. — **Raison d' etre**

868. Revival of old art, culture, fashion once again. — **Renaissance**

869. Recruitment of able-bodied persons compulsorily in army for defending the country. — **Conscription**

870. Rigidity of body occurring after the death. — **Rigor mortis**

S

871. Search for underground source of water by occult method of poking stick on the ground. — **Dowse**

872. Search for missing thing by turning around things all over a place. — **Rummage**

873. Search for usable materials in a heap or garbage. — **Scavenge**

874. Search for something in dark by moving hands all around to feel for it. — **Grope**

875. Search someone's body and pockets for objectionable things kept concealed. — **Frisk**

876. Shallow bed of a river through which we can cross it on feet. — **Ford**

877. Silent expression of one's emotions through body movement and facial expression. — **Pantomime**

878. Singer, usually a folk singer, who moves from village to village to entertain people. — **Minstrel**

879. Singer who tours villages to entertain people with songs on epics. — **Bard**

880. Skin which has become hard and insensitive due to constant friction or pressure on it. — **Callus**

881. Skin of dead animal which is removed to make leather. — **Hide**

882. Skin of animal with fur grown on it. — **Pelt**

883. Skin layer formed over a wound which finally falls down after wound is healed. — **Scurf**

884. Skin surrounding the edges of nails. — **Cuticle**

885. Story in which hidden message needs to be interpreted to reveal it is. — **Allegory**

886. Story which has no definite source as to who had said it is. — **Apocryphal story**

887. Substance that causes allergic reaction in one's body is. — **Allergen**

888. Someone who becomes centre of attention of all those present there is. — **Cynosure of all eyes**

889. Someone (or something) vehemently disliked by a person is his. — **Anathema**

890. Someone who is utterly hated by a person is his. — **Bete noire**

891. Someone who is untouchable for others in the society is a. — **Pariah**

892. Someone or something which suddenly appears like a ghost. —**Apparition**

893. Someone or something which represents direct opposite of something else is. — **Antithesis**

894. Something used to attract others so as to kill or trap is. **— Bait**

895. Something/someone used as a ploy to distract attention of someone else so as to deceive is. **— Decoy**

896. Something that is handed down by predecessor is. **— Legacy**

897. Something made from cross-breeding of two different species. **— Hybrid**

898. Something, viz., food, art etc., which does not suit the taste of common people and is appreciated only by those who are of refined taste and knowledge is called. **— Caviar to general or ordinary people**

899. Something which is passed on to successor. **— Legacy**

900. Something which is passed on to heir. **— Inheritance**

901. Something which is precious and so is preserved by people. **— Heritage**

902. Something produced magically by holy man in a gathering of devotees to impress upon them. **— Apport**

903. Song which is sung to mourn the death of someone. **— Dirge, Elegy**

904. Song which is sung in praise of someone. **— Encomium**

905. Song which is sung in praise of country, school, etc. **— Anthem**

906. Song which is sung in church by a group of singers (Choir). **— Carol**

907. Song which is sung by women on the occasion of marriage ceremony. **— Epithalamium**

908. Song which is sung to put a baby to sleep. **— Lullaby**

909. Sound of a heavy body falling on the ground. **— Thud**

910. Sound of horse's hoofs hitting the ground while running. **— Clop**

911. Sound of unoiled, loose joints of furniture, hinges etc. **— Creak**

912. Sound of sea waves hitting the shores and scattering of water. **— Splash**

913. Sound of forced walking through sticky mud produced upon taking legs out of mud. **— Squelch**

914. Sound produced by firing of machine gun. **— Staccato**

915. Sound produced by swift swinging of slender stick through the air. **— Swish**

916. Sound produed by releasing of stretched strings of musical instruments. **— Twang**

917. Sound produced by fast rotating wheels of a machine. **— Whir**

918. System of governance in which power is exercised by people. **— Democracy**

919. System of governance in which power is exercised by wealthy persons. **— Plutocracy**

920. System of governance in which rule is exercised by holy man. **— Theocracy**

921. System of governance in which power is exercised by officers. **— Bureaucracy**

922. System of governance in which a single person exercise power. **— Autocracy**

923. System which is under control of the government. **— Dirigible system**

924. System which is not under control of the government, and enjoys freedom of action decision etc. **— Laissez faire**

925. Shape of waxing or waning moon resembling a curved sickle. **— Crescent**

926. Shedding of old skin by a reptile, such as snake is. **— Ecdysis**

927. Shouting of crowd demanding once more of an artist's good performance. **— Encore**

928. Shouting of crowd to greet/acclaim someone. **— Hail**

929. Shouting of crowd wishing long life of a leader.**— Viva (long live!)**

930. Shouting of crowd expressing surprise. **— Wow**

931. Self-centered person is an. **— Egocentric**

932. Sardines, olives or any other wheat served before a meal or after soup. **— Hors d'oeuvre**

933. Subject over which one has complete knowledge. **— Province**

934. Successful venture or slogan which becomes popular and is joined by all and sundry. **— Bandwagon**

935. Stage during critical period in one's life when body functions, viz., fertility in women start declining. **— Climacteric**

936. Story which is in circulation through successive generations about a person, place, or heroic deeds. **— Legend**

T

937. Taking out working parts of a defunct machine so as to fit them in another similar machine requiring these parts. **— Cannibalise**

938. Teaching institution (school, college, or university) which one has passed from is his. **— Alma mater**

939. Terrifying experience in the past which keeps one haunting in present. — **Nightmare**

940. Tunnel or cave which is artificial and made in parks etc. — **Grotto**

941. Test of innocence through which a suspect is subjected. — **Ordeal**

942. Transmigration of a soul from the body of a dead person to another body, whether that of a human being or of an animal. — **Metempsychosis**

943. Taking up a new life again in another form. — **Reincarnation**

944. Town's residential area, usually away from the market area. — **Uptown**

945. Town's market and business area – usually in the centre of the town. — **Downtown**

946. Time period in the long past – even before the great deluge which is supposed to have destroyed the world. — **Antediluvian**

947. Travelling by taking free lifts in passing vehicles en route. — **Hitch-hiking**

948. Travel planning and deciding on the routes to be taken in journey. — **Itinerary**

949. Tail or trunk of animal which can catch hold of something. — **Prehensile (tail or limb)**

U

950. Unfit to take part in contest due to injury or not fulfilling conditions stipulated (out of the competition). — **Hors concours**

951. Uprising of people against someone in authority due to injustice. — **Revolt**

952. Uprising of people against the government in order to overthrow it. — **Rebellion**

953. Uprising of troops against their own command. — **Mutiny**

954. Use of words in a sentence starting with same letter is. — **Alliteration**

955. Underground prison cell in a fort; the principal tower in a castle. — **Dungeon**

966. Unpredictable animal which causes damages without reason. — **Rogue animal**

957. Unpredictable weather which causes damages unexpectedly. — **Freak weather**

958. Walk arrogantly with stiff body as display of arrogance. **— Strut, Swagger**

959. Washing of hands and feet for religious performance. **— Ablution**

960. Waterfall which comes down in stages of rock surfaces. **— Cascade**

961. Waterfall which falls down headlong; a sheep cascade; an opaque condition of the lens of the eye **— Cataract**

962. Weak spot in an otherwise strong body is its. **— Achilles heel**

963. Word formed from combining from the initial letters or a group of letters of words in a set phrase. **— Acronym**

964. Woman having light complexion of skin and light colour of hairs is called a. **— Blonde**

965. Woman having dark-coloured hairs is called a. **— Brunette**

966. Woman whose husband lives away from home frequently or for prolonged periods; a woman who is separated, divorced or lives apart from her husband. **— Grass widow**

967. Woman warrior with tall and stout physique. **— Amazon**

968. Woman who is the head of the family. **— Matriarch**

969. Woman of dirty habits who is dressed shabbily. **— Slut**

970. Word or sentence which has been formed by re-arranging letters of another word or sentence is. **— Anagram**

971. Words written about the person on the tombstone over his grave. **— Epitaph**

972. Word which is unoffending and, therefore, substituted for a harsh, offending one. **— Euphemism**

973. Words related to a particular subject (e.g. legal term or medical term)which require special explanation listed in alphabetical order. **— Glossary**

974. Words with same spelling and pronunciation. **— Homonyms**

975. Words with same pronunciation but different spellings. **— Homophones**

976. Word which is the same when it is read backward.**— Palindrome**

977. Woman who is quarrelsome and bad tempered; a malignant man; a devil. **— Shrew**

978. What is sure to happen is. **— Inevitable**

979. What is likely to happen soon is. **— Imminent**

980. What is beyond doubt is. — **Indubitable**

981. What is directly opposite in nature or quality of something is its. — **Antithesis**

982. What is unfailing to be effective in delivering is. — **Infallible**

983. What is spotless. * Immaculate character. — **Immaculate**

984. What is so essential that it can't be avoided. — **Indispensable**

985. What can't be harmed. — **Invulnerable**

986. What can't be described in words. — **Ineffable**

987. Woman who is very attractive and seductive; one who leads man into difficult, dangerous or disastrous situations. — **Femme fatale**

988. Woman who lends her womb to another woman's foetus due to inability to deliver a child. — **Surrogate**

989. Woman who has round and plump body, and full bosomed. — **Buxom**

990. Woman who has manly courage. — **Virago**

991. Woman who attracts men, exploits & ruins them. — **Vampire**

992. Woman of loose morals or untidy. — **Trollop**

993. Woman of quarreling nature. — **Shrew**

994. Woman who is engaged to be married to a person is his. — **Fiancée**

995. Woman who sings and has very sweet melodious voice. — **Nightingale**

996. Woman who bewitches men to ruin them. — **Circe**

997. Woman oftenly aged one, who accompanies young woman or girl going out of home. — **Chaperone**

998. Woman who is a mistress of a gangster. — **Moll**

999. Woman who is very foxy in character; an ill-tempered or quarrelsome woman. —**Vixen**

1000. Woman who is habitually dirty in manners of living, dressing, etc. — **Slut/Slattern**

1001. Woman who remained unmarried. — **Spinster**

1002. Woman who is married but has not borne a child — **Nullipara**

1003. Woman who has borne a child for the first time. — **Primipara**

1004. War which was fought between good and evil and was fierce and disastrous. — **Armageddon**

ooo

Test on One Word Substitution

1. A country which comprises a number of islands instead of a large tract of territory is called ....
2. Habitual flatterer is called ....
3. Habitual servile to a person is his ....
4. Habitually suspicious to be suffering from imaginary ailments is a ....
5. Habitually over-concerned with one's health is a ....
6. A person who suffers from morbid fear of open, vast space, or market-place, and does not like to go there is said to suffer from ....
7. A person who is fearful of crowds is ....
8. A person who is fearful of closed space ....
9. A professional bull-fighter who earns by entertaining spectators with his fighting a ferocious bull is called a ....
10. A person who shows courtesy and considerate behaviour towards women in distress in public place and needs help, is a .... person.
11. A person who helps anyone in distress and needs help, is a ....
12. A person who substitutes himself or herself in place of another one in his or her role is his or her ....
13. A person who just failed to become what he wanted to be, say a doctor, is a ....
14. A person who deliberately pretends to be like someone, say an actor, by acting or adopting mannerisms, as he, too, wants to become like him is a ....
15. Process of development of a life or object coming into existence by going through various stages of changes is called ....
16. Process of a living organism undergoing change to different form is a ....
17. Woman of quarreling nature is called ....
18. A person with exceptional ability to hear from a distance which is not audible to common people is a ....
19. A delicate material which easily breaks down is called a .... material.
20. Our bones are hard and capable to bear impacts, but these, too, can break due to forceful impact, because our bones are ....

21. The policy of government control over business activities in the country is called ....
22. The policy of government's non-interference in business activities in the country is called ....
23. Something which is not fit for eating is ....
24. Something which is not fit for drinking is not ....
25. A land which is capable of producing sufficient crops is a .... land.
26. A woman who is capable to or has produced many children is a .... woman.
27. A woman who has grown old and is now incapable of bearing child is an ....
28. A writer who has written several books, and is capable of writing many more books is a .... writer.
29. A bomb which, when exploded, causes fire is called an .... bomb.
30. Time is a great healer – it makes one forget bereavement of one's most lovable person, because time is the most effective ....
31. A seductive and attractive woman who bewitches men is a ....
32. A woman who is habitually dirty in her living manners is called a ....
33. A man who is habitually dirty in his living manners is called a ....
34. A word with such spelling as to be the same when it is read from right to left, is called ....
35. An unoffending word which is used to substitute an offending word without change in meaning is called an .... for offending word.
36. Learning by cramming the lessons is called learning by ....
37. Crowd shouts .... in unison for demanding a performer or singer for more of his or her performance.
38. The patient's condition becoming worse again after improvement is called .... of the bad condition.
39. An inveterate criminal vows to shun crime after punishments, but he .... to the world of crime once again.
40. Bringing back the unity amongst people is to .... them.
41. Bringing back the lost or obsolete art or culture is called its ....

42. Style of writing in which author uses words in a sentence which start with the same letter is called ....
43. Fearful foreboding of unpleasant occurrence is called ....
44. A medicine which induces sleep is a .... medicine.
45. An unpredicted storm which suddenly hits a place is called a .... storm.
46. Born again as another living body is to ....
47. To return the loan and take back what was pledged in return is to .... it.
48. Underground prison cell in a fort of yore is ....
49. A regime which is dominated by rich people is called ....
50. A regime which is dominated by people belonging to uncultured, lower strata of society is called ....
51. Animal which has only one horn on its head is an ....
52. The process of moulting skin by a snake is called ....
53. An untouchable of the society is called ....
54. A person's most hated person is his ....
55. A shape of a sickle is called a .... shape.
56. Arranging in pairs is called ....
57. A man who eats flesh of humans is called a ....
58. Evening just before an important day is called .... of that day.
59. Hair on the back of an animal which is hard and erect is called ....
60. Main substance of accusation against someone is called the .... of charges.
61. Grinding of teeth during sleep is called ....
62. A period of time which seems to be endless is ....
63. Inspiration of doing something is called ....
64. Taking away rights to vote is called ....
65. Migration of the soul after death of a person into the body of another one born is called ....
66. A very close friend of yours in your ....
67. What is used to allure someone is called ....
68. What is used to distract attention is called ....
69. The person who has passed out of an institution is called its ....

70. The women who have passed out of a woman's college are called its ....

71. The institution / college from which you have received your education is your ....

72. Staying place of the nuns and priests is called ....

73. Staying place of a saint is called ....

74. The house of Eskimos is called ....

75. The washing room behind the kitchen where dishes are washed and cleaned is called ....

76. The person who is very fond of his wife is .... person.

77. The mother who is very fond of her kids is a .... mother.

78. The part of a town where minority community inhabits is called ....

79. The practice of marrying out of one's own community is called ....

80. Putting troops in a civilian area like schools, etc. when they are away from their base is to .... them in such a place.

81. Valuable objects which are preserved by successive generations in a family is called ....

82. Compulsory recruitment of young persons in army at the time of war is called ....

83. Matured child at an early age is a .... child.

84. An extraordinary skilled worker is a .... worker.

85. A person who likes to enjoy life is a ....

86. An artificial cave made in a place like park for entertainment purpose is a ....

87. Artistic objects made of clay are called ....

88. A lover of some kind of sport is .... of that sport.

89. The starter item in a feast which is taken as an appetizer is called ....

90. The most attractive item in a feast is called ....

91. Criminal who flees from one place to another in order to avoid arrest is a ....

92. One who habitually absents himself from the place where he is supposed to be, like a worker from his workplace, or a student from his school, is called a ....

93. Honour-killing of a girl by her brother is called ....

94. The soft covering of banana is called its ....
95. Sharp-edged pieces of a broken glass or an exploded bomb is called ....
96. The written work of an author which is published after the death of the author is called ....
97. An elderly woman who used to accompany a young girl going out of her home to market or in a social function and is supposed to keep watch on her is called ....
98. A young boy who accompanies an elderly lady while going out of house, and is supposed to be in her attendance is called ....
99. Sentimental longing of past happy days in one's life is called ....
100. The happiest period in one's life is called ....
101. A person who cleans utensils and dirty kitchenware is called.............
102. A person who is wise enough to see through the bad intention of someone in touch is a .... person.
103. A person of clean intention whose motive is easily known to others is a .... person.
104. The main area of a town where markets and offices are located is called ....
105. A story which carries hidden moral message which can be revealed by interpreting it is called ....
106. What can be perceived by being tough is ....
107. A limb of animal usod to catch something is called .... limb.
108. A person without a fixed place of stay is a ....
109. Onc who is an expert in making maps is a ....
110. Growing fruits is called ....
111. The day of equal day and night is called an ....
112. Kid who has just started to learn walking on his feet is called a ....
113. Consecration of a deity by rubbing it with oil is called .... of the deity.
114. One who pretends to be a learned person is a ....
115. A piece of wood taken out of a log is ....
116. All the equal partners of a property are ....

117. The area of one's knowledge is his ....
118. The group of persons who are knowledgeable about a subject is ....
119. One who has doubting habit, and does not believe in something without covincing proof is a ....
120. One who is new in a job is a ....
121. The river-side area is called ....
122. Migration of people from their homes in a large number is called .... of people.
123. One who is not choosy in eating and takes whatever he gets is called .... person.
124. Spreading out of inhabitants of a place all over the world is called ....
125. One who is in a habit of impressing others by demonstrating his knowledge is a ....
126. Weeping of women on death of someone in the family is to ....
127. Medicine which is supposed to protect us from getting affected with a disease is a .... medicine.
128. Morbid fear of seeing a deadbody is ....
129. Small pieces of a broken ceramic ware is called ....
130. A person hired to clap in a gathering for someone is called a ....
131. The mourners who join a funeral procession are called ....
132. A number of symptoms appearing in a disease is called .... of the disease.
133. Hearing body sounds with the help of stethoscope or other medical instruments is called ....
134. Hairfall resulting in baldness is called ....
135. Inability to feel smell of things is called ....
136. Peculiar style of speaking to announce what a hawker is selling is called his ....
137. Inability to bear lights and hence liking to remain in dark place is called ....
138. Folding paper-sheet into various figures is an art called ....
139. Aversion to food caused by mania of losing body weight in order to maintain good figures is called ....
140. The campus of a building is called its ....

141. Inactivity in a living-being during the winter season is called ....

142. Travelling daily between home and office is called ....

143. A communicable disease which spreads by touching an infected person is called .... disease.

144. The system of keeping a patient infected with contagious disease aloof from others to check disease from spreading is called ....

145. An attempt to do something for the first time is called .... attempt.

146. Remains of the ruin of something damaged is called ....

147. Remains of the ruin of a demolished building is called ....

148. Broken pieces of stone is called ....

149. Inaugural show of a film is called its ....

150. No amount of entreaties and prayers can please the god of death because Yamraj is said to be ....

151. The strongest army is ....

152. The feeling that you have seen a ghost in the darkness is an ....

153. Mercy killing of someone in an unbearable condition is called ....

154. Medals and laurels which are hung on the uniform of a military officer are called ....

155. Something considered an object of irrational reverence is to make .... of it.

156. An item given by a person to you which you preserve as a memory of the person who gave it to you is called ....

157. An item preserved by you as a token of a place visited from where you had brought it is called ....

158. Uncontrolled physical urge for something is called one's .... to it.

159. Product which is produced locally is called .... product.

160. Free hand granted to someone to take a decision as he deems fit is to grant him ....

161. Narrow path through rows of chairs is called ....

162. Narrow passage passing through rows of buildings, or through a park, garden, etc. is called ....

163. Thickened skin on toes which is caused by constant friction of shoes is called ....

164. Crowd of fishes which swim together in the sea is called ....

165. Bees collect .... from flowers to turn it into honey.

166. A sudden feeling coming to one's mind without any apparent reason is called ....

167. A feeling coming to one's mind about something bad which is imminent to happen is called ....

168. A natural reaction in response to an external stimulus is called ....

169. What is not concerned with matters of morality is ....

170. Buildings, monuments, etc. which are important and needed to be preserved for posterity are called ....

171. A person who had held the office earlier to the present one is called the latter's ....

172. A new entrant to a party or religion is called ....

173. An unselfish person who puts others' interest above his own is called an ....

174. One who is adept in using his left hand is called ....

175. Information about a person's past activities which helps determine his character is called his ....

176. Important documents are safely kept in a place called ....

177. A patch of greenery which indicates the presence of water in a desert is called ....

178. The staying place of dogs, where dogs are kept is called ....

179. A natural successor to ancestral property is called ....

180. An event which is considered indicative of something important imminent arrival is called..................

181. A young and handsome person is called ....

182. A person who is very conscious of his good appearance, and, therefore, keeps himself dressed up is called ....

183. One who does not observe orthodox religious practices is called ....

184. A go-between who facilitates two negotiating parties reach an agreement is called ....

185. One who excessively boasts about himself is a ....

186. One wears a good look by dyeing one's .... hairs.

187. Lying inactive before eruption of a volcano is called it's lying ....

188. An opinion expressed in mutually contradictory language is an.................opinion.

189. One who has white skin and white hairs due to acute lack of melanin in his skin is called ....

190. One who has black hairs and black skin due to excessive melanin under skin is called ....

191. The killer of a public leader is called ....

192. One who leads a life which is very simple and devoid of even minimal luxury is called ....

193. An insidious cruel person is called ....

194. One who enjoys music even though he is not a connoisseur of it is called ....

195. One who commits unforgivable serious sin is called a ....

196. One who destroys his own creator is a ....

197. The sufferings undergone by someone in order to prove his innocence are called ....

198. The stickler of discipline is called a ....

199. One who does not drink wine is a ....

200. One who lives in caves is called ....

Choose the appropriate option out of the given ones which fits in the meaning of the word mentioned at the top of the options:

201. Slattern
   (A) A woman who is habitually dirty and looks untidy.
   (B) A man who is habitually dirty and looks shabby.
   (C) A boy who has dirty manners.
   (D) A person of loose morals.

202. Cognoscenti
   (A) The people who are knowledgeable in a specified area of knowledge.
   (B) The people who are able to recognize the problems faced by the society.
   (C) A person who travels without being recognized in order to study the problems faced by general people.
   (D) An expert who is knowledgeable in many areas of knowledge.

203. Nepenthes

(A) A medicine which helps people forget the unpleasant memories.

(B) A medicine which makes one forget death of a family member in due course of time.

(C) A wine which makes a drunkard forget worries.

(D) A drink which makes a drinker forget everything which he does not want to remember.

204. Charlatan

(A) A cheat who does not spare anyone from cheating.

(B) A person who advertises his knowledge and skill about a subject.

(C) A quack who pretends to have great knowledge.

(D) A fool who behaves as if he were a learned person.

205. Prodigious

(A) Extraordinary in talent before attaining the age of maturity.

(B) Having the tendency to behave as a monster.

(C) Having the tendency to waste money recklessly on unnecessary showmanship.

(D) (Something) regarded as extraordinary in importance.

206. Chaperon

(A) A person who flatters others for obtaining something.

(B) A servant who accompanies his master wherever he goes.

(C) An old woman who accompanies a young girl when she goes out to some place.

(D) A young boy who accompanies a woman wherever she goes out of her house.

207. Metamorphosis

(A) A process of undergoing change in some form.

(B) A situation is which someone undergoes degeneration into a bad shape.

(C) A change from unsatisfactory situation to that of an improved one.

(D) A situation in which any change in the condition of something is not possible.

208. Renaissance

(A) Revival of an art after vanishing in the past.

(B) Rebirth of dead person in another life.

(C) The soul of a dead person leaving the body to take another body of the person who has been just born

(D) The cycle of birth and death which occurs alternately.

209. Fugitive

(A) A boy who escapes from his school in order to avoid his classes.

(B) A boy who escapes from his house and loiters in mark and parks to pass time.

(C) A criminal who escapes from captivity and avoids being arrested.

(D) A criminal who surrenders to the court on his own volition.

210. Scullery

(A) A room where food is cooked in the running trains.

(B) A room where the dirty utensils are washed and cleaned for re-use.

(C) A person who washes the dirty utensils in a feast, and keeps the cleaned plates on the dining table.

(D) A hall where food is cooked and the dirty plates are cleaned.

211. Posthumous

(A) An author whose book is published after his death.

(B) A book which is published after its author's death.

(C) An author whose last book is published before his death.

(D) A book that is published before its author's death.

212. Effete

(A) (A woman) unable to bear a baby due to overage or weakness.

(B) (A woman) who has never borne a baby.

(C) (A woman) who has borne many babies.

(D) (A woman) capable of bearing a baby.

213. Crescent

(A) In the shape of a curved moon (in its first quarter).

(B) In the shape of a moon.

(C) In the shape of a curve.

(D) In the shape of a sickle.

214. Heirloom

(A) The prized possession of a family which is preserved by successive generations.

(B) The property obtained by a heir.

(C) Succession of heirs from generation to generation.

(D) A group of heirs who share the property of an ancestor.

215. Legacy

(A) Anything left by the predecessor to be handed over to the successor.

(B) The office of a legate.

(C) The property bequested by an ancestor.

(D) The legal office held by someone.

216. Valetudinarian

(A) A person who is very concerned about his bad health.

(B) A person who suffers from bad health.

(C) A person who suffers from imaginary health problems.

(D) A person who has become invalid due to ill health.

217. Archipelago

(A) An island country in the midst of a sea.

(B) A country comprising a number of islands.

(C) A group of islands in the midst of a sea.

(D) A large-sized island in a sea.

218. Prolific

(A) Capable of producing much or many, highly productive.

(B) Spreading in all the directions by growing.

(C) Rapidly spreading in all the directions by growing.

(D) Spreading in the forward direction.

219. Prolix

(A) Unnecessarily lengthy (speech or writing).

(B) Existing for a long time.

(C) Extended to a long period.

(D) Flowing forward like a liquid.

220. Martinet

(A) A strict person who does not tolerate indiscipline.

(B) A disciplined person.

(C) A person who oversees discipline in the armed forces.

(D) A person who does not like excessive discipline.

221. Fop

(A) Dandy.

(B) Handsome person.

(C) Fashion lover.

(D) Fail.

222. Frankenstein

(A) A person who is frank in dealings.

(B) A monster.

(C) A monster who destroys its own creator.

(D) An ungrateful person who deceives the very person who has helped.

223. Hearse

(A) A horse-driven carriage.

(B) A carriage to carry a deadbody to the burial ground.

(C) A carriage to carry the people from one place to another.

(D) A stand for holding candles which is kept in a room.

224. Cortège

(A) The people who attend a funeral of a dead person.

(B) The procession of the mourners accompanying a funeral procession.

(C) The decoration of a pandal for a celebration.

(D) A group of people who move together to go to a place.

225. Altruist

(A) A truthful person.

(B) A person who always speaks the truth.

(C) A person who truly thinks about the good for others instead for himself.

(D) A selfish person.

226. Samaritan

(A) A resident of a desert.

(B) A person who helps people in distress.

(C) A person who actively fights for a public cause.

(D) A resident of samaristan.

227. Teetotaler

(A) A person who drinks tea too much.

(B) A person who does not drink tea at all.

(C) A person who drinks all types of drinks.

(D) A person who does not take alcoholic drinks at all.

228. Heretic

(A) A person who does not believe in religion.

(B) A person who does not obey religious command.

(C) A person who does not follow religious rituals.

(D) A person who holds opinions contrary to the established religious doctrines.

229. Dastard

(A) A wicked person.

(B) A cruel person.

(C) A coward.

(D) A cruel but coward person who commits mean acts of cruelty causing harm to innocent persons.

230. Memorabilia

(A) The objects preserved because of their associations with memorable persons or events.

(B) Remembrance of important events.

(C) Something fit for keeping in memory.

(D) A momorable event or occurrence.

231. Herald

(A) A person who announces official information to people with beating of drums for attracting their attention.

(B) A messenger who announces the imminent disastrous event.

(C) A messenger who brings forth happy news to people.

(D) An event which indicates another event to happen soon.

232. Hibernation

(A) The state of inactivity during the winter season.

(B) The state of inactivity during the summer season.

(C) Laziness caused by acute hot climate.

(D) Staying indoors in the rainy days and enjoy leisure.

233. Diaspora

(A) Dispersal of people to different places in search of job.
(B) People of a country spreading throughout the world.
(C) People of a country who have spread in various parts of the world to settle there.
(D) People of a country who have been driven out of the country.

234. Anorexia
(A) Inability to eat due to nausea.
(B) Inability to eat due to upset stomach.
(C) Aversion from eating due to anxiety of putting on weight and get fatter and unattractive body figure.
(D) Inability to eat due to psychological aversion from eating.

235. Bulimia
(A) An abnormal desire for eating and feeling of constant hunger.
(B) Greediness of food.
(C) A habit of excessive eating.
(D) Abnormal feeling of hunger.

236. Ordeal
(A) Passing through torturous test, in order to prove innocence by an accused person
(B) Painful experience of punishment.
(C) Torturous punishment given to an accused.
(D) Order to punish an accused.

237. Oasis
(A) A patch of greenery in a desert.
(B) A matter of hope in an all-round atmosphere of gloom.
(C) An island in ocean with no easy access.
(D) A patch of fertile land surrounded by infertile land.

238. Heritage
(A) Historical places.
(B) Ancient monuments.
(C) Valuable structural wonders of the past which are considered worth preserving in their pristine form.
(D) Inherited property of ancestors by the heirs.

239. Dilettante
(A) An expert of specific form of art.
(B) A person who is not expert in, but merely enjoys, a specific form of art.

(C) A person who does not understand any form of art.

(D) A person who contributes money liberally to promote art.

240. Nectar

(A) A sweet drink.

(B) Honey produced by bees.

(C) The flower juice which is sucked by bees for making honey.

(D) An essence used to flavour drinks.

241. Premonition

(A) Intuition.

(B) A feeling of an event before it happens.

(C) A feeling of some bad occurrence which is imminent to happen soon.

(D) Feeling bad about something.

242. Ascetic

(A) A person who has become a saint.

(B) A person who lives a life like a saint.

(C) A person who lives a life devoid of luxury.

(D) A saint who lives on mountains.

243. Palindrome

(A) A race course for cycling competitions.

(B) A person who runs in the backward direction.

(C) A word which reads same when letters are reversed.

(D) A habit of running fast even if there is no urgency.

244. Ghetto

(A) A cave in a mountain.

(B) A ruined fort.

(C) The part of a town which is inhabitated by people of the minority community.

(D) The part of a village where the untouchables live.

245. Eternity

(A) A period of time with no beginning or end.

(B) An endless period.

(C) A very very long period.

(D) A life without death.

246. Precocious

(A) Maturing earlier than the normal time.

(B) Knowing before happening.

(C) Growing at a faster rate than usual.

(D) Having preconditions.

247. Sliver

(A) A piece of wood.

(B) A piece of torn cloth.

(C) A piece of broken glass.

(D) Splinter of wood, mental, glass etc.

248. Cartographer

(A) Photographer.

(B) Chart maker.

(C) Map maker.

(D) Photobin.

249. Redeem

(A) To buy back pledged materials.

(B) To restore.

(C) To retain.

(D) To fulfil a promise.

250. Grotto

(A) Artificial cave.

(B) Tunnel.

(C) Castle.

(D) Large cave.

251. Autochthon

(A) A native person.

(B) Aborigine.

(C) Indigenous flora of a place.

(D) Self-dependent.

252. Cant

(A) Chant prayer.

(B) Hawkers' peculiar manner of speaking.

(C) A speech which is not clear to others.

(D) Jargon.

253. Debris

(A) Scattered remains of a broken glass.

(B) Scattered remains of a vehicle involved in an accident.

(C) Scattered remains of a demolished building.

(D) Scattered garbage.

254. Fallacious

(A) Misleading.

(B) False.

(C) Insincere.

(D) Liable to fail.

255. Debutante

(A) An actor who acts in a film for the first time.

(B) An actress who acts for the first time in career.

(C) First-time screening of a new film.

(D) A person who takes part in a debate.

256. Proselyte

(A) A person who has parted with his religion and adopted another religion.

(B) A person who has deserted his party.

(C) A person who refuses to fulfil his promise.

(D) A person who changes his opinion for selfish gains.

257. Pioneer

(A) One who opens up a new area of knowledge.

(B) One who guides research.

(C) One who invents something.

(D) One who is expert in a field of knowledge.

258. Scion

(A) A young shoot of a plant.

(B) A young person of a notable family.

(C) A young bird.

(D) A young ruler.

259. Thrift

(A) To float on water.

(B) Miser.

(C) One who spends money carefully.

(D) One who spends money recklessly.

260. Mascot

(A) Symbol of good luck.

(B) Puppet.

(C) Ghost.

(D) Emblem.

261. Apocrypha

(A) Hidden secret.

(B) Book written by unknown author.

(C) Cryptic remark.

(D) Secret knowledge.

262. Paragon

(A) A model of excellence.

(B) Rival.

(C) Unparalleled quality.

(D) The most important person.

263. Toady

(A) Behaving like a toad.

(B) Subservient.

(C) Sycophant.

(D) Greedy person.

264. Matins

(A) Morning-time prayer.

(B) Subservient.

(C) Sycophant.

(D) Greedy person.

265. Matador

(A) Bull fighter.

(B) Gatekeeper in hotels.

(C) One who gives life defending the country from the enemy.

(D) A person who displays his adventurous skill.

266. Vagabond

(A) Vagrant.

(B) Worthless person.

(C) Lazy person.

(D) Touring.

267. Minstrel

(A) A singer.

(B) A folk singer who goes from village to village for singing.

(C) A folk singer.

(D) A drama actor.

268. Entrepreneur

(A) A person who starts a business.

(B) One who enters in a risky field of activity.

(C) A businessman.

(D) One who takes risk of doing something with uncertain outcome.

269. Quisling

(A) A traitor.

(B) Fifth columnist.

(C) One who sides with an enemy against his own country.

(D) One who sacrifices his life for his country.

270. Plutocracy

(A) The rule by experienced leaders.

(B) The rule by aristocrats.

(C) The rule by highly educated leaders.

(D) The rule by rich persons.

ooo

Exercise on One Word Substitution

Give single word each which will appropriately subsititute each of the following :

1. One who takes pleasure in tormenting others.
2. One who feels pleasure to see someone in misery.
3. One who feels sexual pleasure in tormenting himself.
4. One who takes pleasure in prying into others' private affairs.
5. A companion of someone who behaves ridiculously to make his (some one's) behavior look more dignified.
6. An animal which feeds on whatever is available.
7. The sharp-edged pieces of broken material.
8. Simultaneous purchase and sale of the same securities, commodities or foreign exchange in different markets, with a view to profiteering from the differential in prices.
9. A book of an author which is published after his death.
10. Drawing similarity of two different things.
11. Drawing dis-similarity of two different things.
12. Never-ending period of time.
13. Evening prayer.
14. A female with dirty habits.
15. A male with dirty habits.
16. One who thinks about himself only.
17. One who thinks about others.
18. One who helps anyone who is in need of help.
19. Casting off of intugement by snakes.
20. Casting off of dead and dried leaves by trees in which place new leaves grow afresh.
21. A storm which suddenly builds up without any apparent cause.
22. Migration of the soul from a deadbody upon death to another living body.
23. Re-birth after death.
24. Old and obsolete form of art or culture becoming popular again.
25. Artificial leg which is fitted in place of amputated leg of a person.
26. The song which makes a baby sleep.
27. Public speech praising someone.
28. Educational institution of ex-students is their..........

29. A person who risks his life in fighting with men or animals in the arena for people's entertainment.
30. A person who starts his own business.
31. A person who is an influential businessman in a particular field of business.
32. An animal which eats meat of its own species.
33. An artist who makes various figures from a sheet of paper.
34. A person who makes stamp collection.
35. A tree which starts giving fruits earlier than usual time.
36. A baby who has just started to learn walking.
37. A disease which spreads by touch.
38. Snatching someone's voting rights.
39. Tricks used to deceive others.
40. Sense of self well-being which makes one feel satisfied.
41. Remains of a demolished house.
42. Doing something for the first time.
43. Grinding teeth in one's sleep.
44. River-side area of a place.
45. Medals and decorations displayed on a uniform.
46. Walking space passing through rows of seats in an auditorium.
47. Artefacts made of clay.
48. One who does not believe in something without proof.
49. One who claims to be a learned person.
50. A saint who lives in an isolated place to practise religious meditations.
51. What is vehemently hated by someone is his...........
52. A cow belongs to which animal species?
53. A grass-eating animal is called..................
54. Large boards which are used for advertising.
55. Social practice of marrying within one's own community.
56. Physical problems caused by medical treatments are called...........
57. One who gets frightened on seeing a deadbody.
58. One who suffers from involuntary urination on the bed during sleep.
59. A man who accompanies an elderly woman.
60. Valuables which are kept preserved by successive generations of a family.

61. Using less harsh words to avoid unpleasantness associated with harsh words.
62. Writings on tombstone.
63. Prison cell made in the basement of a fort.
64. Tough time undergone to prove one's innocence.
65. A moral story to convey an useful lesson.
66. Hard skin caused by regular friction on the spot.
67. The most popular symbol of a particular field.
68. The youngest member of a prominent family.
69. The part of a town inhabited by the minority community.
70. Erect and hard hair which is used for making brush.

Unit- 8

Synthesis

In simplest terms, combining two or more simple sentences to form a simple, complex or compound sentence is called synthesis. Some examples of synthesis are following:-

Forming A Simple Sentence

1. I'm coming to your home. I want to meet you.
   I'm coming to your home to meet you.
2. Hari bought a new pen. He wanted to use it to write his paper.
   Hari bought a new pen to write his paper.
3. She completed her homework. She closed the book.
   Having completed her homework she closed the book.
4. She helped me. I finished my work.
   I finished my work with her help.
5. I didn't wait. I was in a hurry.
   Being in a hurry I didn't wait.
6. He accepted it. He was guilty.
   He accepted to have been guilty.
7. He resisted. He was tempted to laugh.
   He resisted his temptation to laugh.
8. Priyanka left for Chennai. Her mother also left with her.
   Priyanka and her mother left for Chennai.
9. Premlata plucked a flower. She wanted to put it into her vase.
   Premlata plucked a flower to put into her vase.
10. Manish sold his vintage car. He sold it for money.
    Manish sold his vintage car for money.
11. He was determined. He would win the race.
    He was determined to win the race.

12. I went to stationery. I wanted to buy a book.
    I went to stationery to buy a book.
13. I bought a book. I bought a pen also.
    I bought a book and a pen.
14. My brother bought a new watch. He wanted to give it to me.
    My brother bought a new watch to give it to me.
15. My rival brought his medal along. He wanted to make me jealous.
    My rival brought his medal along to make me jealous.

Forming A Complex Sentence

1. The reason is. I'm not ready.
   The reason is that I'm not ready.
2. Please say. You will come.
   Please say that you will come.
3. Please pay attention. Our host is saying something.
   Please pay attention to what our host is saying.
4. Everyone knew. He was lying.
   Everyone knew that he was lying.
5. The fact cannot be denied. He is a liar.
   The fact that he is a liar cannot be denied.
6. I cannot say. Is he a liar?
   I cannot say whether he is a liar.
7. Nobody can predict. Will it rain?
   Nobody can predict whether it will rain./Nobody can predict if it will rain.
8. I know. He is capable of doing it.
   I know that he is capable of doing it.
9. She was aware. He was ill.
   She was aware that he was ill.
10. He was trapped. The police knew.
    The police knew that he was trapped.
11. I have no idea. How could he run so fast?
    I have no idea how he could run so fast.
12. It is true. She can't run.
    It is true that she can't run.
13. The Prime Minister said. We will be a developed nation.
    That Prime Minister said that we would be a developed nation.

14. The Prime Minister couldn't say. Shall we be a developed nation?
    The Prime Minister couldn't say whether we should be a developed nation.

15. There is no way to know. What does he do?
    There is no way to know what he does.

Forming A Compound Sentence

1. He was tired. He had been running.
   He was tired for he had been running.

2. No one can eat it. It should be thrown out.
   It should be thrown out because no one can eat it.

3. He won the race. He was rewarded.
   He won the race so he was rewarded.

4. She is smart. She is beautiful, too.
   She is not only smart but beautiful too.

5. Don't touch the cauldron. You'll burn your hand.
   Don't touch the cauldron otherwise you'll burn your hand.

6. Ranjan is a good actor. Ranjan will be a star one day.
   Ranjan is a good actor so he will be a star one day.

7. Ranjan is a good actor. Ranjan is an arrogant man.
   Ranjan is a good actor but an arrogant man.

8. Ranjan is a good actor. Ranjan is a down to earth man.
   Ranjan is a good actor yet a down to earth man.

9. We must plan a trip. We are getting bored.
   We are getting bored so we must plan a trip.

10. She could have done it. She didn't do it.
    She could have done it but she didn't do it.

11. She couldn't have done it. She didn't do it.
    She didn't do it because she couldn't have done it.

12. Run fast. You'll lose the race.
    Run fast or you'll lose the race.

13. Don't hurry. You'll ruin everything.
    Don't hurry or you'll ruin everything.

14. Don't be silly. Don't be stupid.
    Be neither silly nor stupid.

15. She stopped writing. She could have finished the test.
    She stopped writing otherwise she could have finished the test.

Practice Exercise

A) Form simple sentences by combining the given sentences:
(The correct answers have been provided in the appendix.)

1. He is too ill. He cannot attend the meeting.
2. He is very soft-spoken. He cannot be a politician.
3. She was bored. She went out to play.
4. He entered the arena. He saluted the king.
5. She was in a hurry. She asked her husband to drive fast.
6. People were willing to hear the popular leader. They waited for him.
7. People were bent on disturbing the leader. They hooted.
8. She wasted her time. It was foolish of her.
9. She studied meticulously. It was wise of her.
10. A gentleman knocked at the door. He was old.
11. A young lady entered the room. She was naughty.
12. Sheela is a noted surgeon. She works in the general hospital.
13. Rama is a popular singer. He sings patriotic songs.
14. Rajni will pass the exam. We can be sure about that.
15. He will fail the test. I'm sure.
16. He was given a big hand. He did so much for the society.
17. People hate him. He is a rude fellow.
18. India is our motherland. It must be defended.
19. Friends' Colony is the best colony. It should be kept clean.
20. He was talking. His voice was loud.
21. She is too tall. She won't like this car.
22. He is too proud. He won't talk first.
23. Srikant is a famous painter. He lives in Shimla.
24. Srikant is a novice. He is struggling hard.
25. His contribution was acknowledged. I'm aware of it.
26. His contribution remains unknown. I'm sad about it.
27. She dropped her purse. She dropped her mobile as well.
28. She participated in the quiz. Her friend also participated in the quiz.
29. The dance program ended. The viewers proceeded for the magic show.
30. I have three pairs of shoes. They are under the cupboard.

31. She has a sweet voice. She doesn't like to sing.
32. Seema was lying. Anyone could see it.
33. His heart is too big. It cannot hate anyone.

B) Form complex sentences by combining the given sentences:
(The correct answers have been provided in the appendix.)

1. Nobody can tell. Will it be too hot?
2. Anyone can guess. Will it rain?
3. She told me. He likes me.
4. He didn't tell me. She hates me.
5. I have forgotten. Where had we parked the car?
6. I remember very well. Where had we met first?
7. Major had been informed. Enemy was about to attack.
8. General could not be informed. The enemy was retreating.
9. We can be sure. The train will arrive on time.
10. Everyone knows. He is a scientist.
11. Very few know. He is a sportsman.
12. The allegations are absurd. He stole the watch.
13. People are wondering. Did he steal the diamond?
14. The fact remains. This river is hard to cross.
15. The facts remain. This mountain has been climbed before.
16. The students were heard saying. The teacher was to remain absent for a while.
17. We were enjoying the snacks. The snacks were crunchy.
18. He will take bus no. 8. Bus no. 8 stops in his village.
19. He has diabetes. He can't eat sweets.
20. She has a good nature. Everyone likes her.
21. He is very cruel. Everyone despises him.
22. He is a CEO. He still eats in general canteen.
23. Raj is rich. Raj is stupider.
24. Hurry up. We will miss the train otherwise.
25. He burned the midnight oil. Otherwise he could not have passed with flying colours.
26. Athlete's coach guided him. Athlete acted on his guidance.
27. He hurried. He didn't want to be late
28. He finished his homework. He didn't want to be punished.

29. She dances nicely. Her friend dances equally nicely.
30. He did not study sufficiently. He would have scored good marks.
31. Rohan is intelligent. No other student in the class is as intelligent.
32. Our hopes were. He will hit the ball.
33. It is too hot. No one can step outside.
34. The police reached the crime scene. The thief had gotten away.
35. I know my neighbours. They live in the adjacent quarter.
36. He died in France. He had been there for twelve years.

C) Form compound sentences by combining the given sentences:
(The correct answers have been provided in the appendix.)

1. He is not a liar. His friend is not a liar.
2. She isn't bad. Her brother isn't bad.
3. She is poor. Her brother is poor.
4. It might rain. It might hail.
5. We may find a hut. We may find a cave.
6. He is still playing. He cannot complete his homework in time.
7. His train was late. He missed the exam.
8. I miss her a lot. I barely ever see her.
9. He is a bright student. He doesn't study hard.
10. Prithvi missile can be launched from the land. Prithvi missile can also be launched from the sea.
11. She can swim. He can swim.
12. He can't swim. She can't swim.
13. He is rich. He is a miser.
14. She is smart. She is active also.
15. He is not smart. He is not active.
16. We were getting late. We stayed till the end of the party.
17. Sumit drank a glass of water. Sumit walked on.
18. Sit still. Your father will scold you.
19. She wastes time. She will fail.
20. She is in the meeting. She can't meet anyone.
21. He came from nowhere. He ate all the food.
22. One should not complain. One should not cry.
23. You are good. Your friend is good.

ooo

Unit- 9

Reading Comprehension Strategy

Reading Comprehension (RC) questions measure your ability to read with understanding, insight and discrimination. These types of questions explore your ability to analyze a passage from several perspectives. They also test your power to recognize

- Explicit statements
- Implicit statements
- Facts and Half truths

In order to score better in these types of questions, you have to be an effective reader. Speed and accuracy in solving the questions are important. You must manage your reading speed to solve the questions in limited time.

Reading Speed

To perform better than the rest of the examination takers, one very significant factor is good reading speed. However, do remember that RCs are not only about reading quickly, they are about understanding them, too.

Here are a few factors that influence the reading speed.

A. Increase the number of words you read in a single glance. Avoid word by word reading.

B. Do not try to pronounce words, as this is not a test for your speaking skill.

C. Stay focused. If you are regressing multiple times, it indicates you are not focused.

D. Use your finger effectively to point at the text you are reading. If your hand movement is slow, it affects your reading speed also. Move your hand with uniform speed. Underline key words while reading.

Improve Vocabulary

Though you do not need to interpret the meaning of every single word in the passage, a good vocabulary is always an asset. Try to interpret the meaning of unfamiliar words based on surrounding context.

Eclectic Reading

Read a lot to improve your grip over RC. Read editorials of the newspaper etc., regularly. After that, note down the summary of the article. Then read it again and list the points that you have missed, if any. This will definitely help your reading, grasping and comprehending abilities.

An important point to remember is to make yourself comfortable with reading articles of different genres that you otherwise don't like to read. That is the key to success in RC.

Types of Questions

1. **Main Idea Question**

   The main idea or the central idea is the one thing that you can say about the passage. It is the 'subject' of the passage. Avoid all other details.

   For example, if someone asks you "What did you do on Friday?" You may answer that you went to watch an IPL match. That's the main thing. Describing every ball, over by over, are the details.

A. Opening and closing sentences

   The opening and closing sentences of the paragraph are essential sentences, which may, many a time, give the essence of the passage. In a well written passage, they can point out the main idea or central theme.

B. Look for repetitive ideas

   Sometimes, it could happen that using the opening and closing sentences, you are not able to ascertain the main idea in the passage. In such a case, you must look for that idea or thought that is being repeated throughout the passage.

C. Implied main idea

   In this case, after thoroughly reading the entire passage, try and answer the following questions

   - Who or what is the author talking about?
   - What are the distinctive features of the subject that are being conveyed?
   - What message does the author want to give?

Note: Your answer should neither be too specific nor too broad. The central theme must be specific to the passage and include all the essential elements of the passage.

2. **Contextual Meaning Question**

   In this type of a question, you may be asked the meaning of a certain phrase that has been used in the passage in a certain context, or an analogy based on an aspect discussed in the passage etc.

3. **Explicit Question**

   Explicit means being clearly and precisely expressed and questions that test you on ideas and thoughts that are unequivocally explained in the passage are called Explicit Questions. Read with concentration, spot the keywords in the paragraph and identify the particular topic in which it is mentioned. You should not go wrong with such questions.

4. **Implicit question**

   Here the answers will not be given directly, like in the explicit questions. You will have to read between the lines and try and understand the ideas and draw conclusions that the author is trying to put forth. You have to try and understand all the hidden meanings and draw inferences behind an idea.

5. **Application to Other Situation Question**

   Questions like "With which of the following statements would the author most likely agree/disagree?". "The author's contention would be strong/weak if which of the following is true?" come under this type.

   In cases like these, put yourself in the author's shoes and try to gauge his pulse. This would be the easiest way. Also, in these type of questions, being able to predict and anticipate the author's motives is highly important. There may sometimes be questions that ask you to complete the passage or find a suitable conclusion for it.

6. **Tone/mood Based Questions**

   The tone of a passage, very simply, is what the author feels about the matter at hand; it would also encompass his style of writing. There is a subtle difference between the tone and the mood.

   The tone is what the author feels, mood is what the author wants his audience to feel. A mood is created by the author, but is something that he wants you, the reader to feel.

   A few points that help you calibrate the tone and mood of the passages are as follows:

   - Look at the word choice and connotations. Analyze the phrases.

How is the author expressing his ideas? Does he use many metaphors, or lay out facts without opinion?

- How do you feel when you are reading it? What emotions come naturally to you?

7. **Organization of The Passage Type Questions**

In this type of questions, you would be asked questions about the passage that are based on the arrangement and methodology in which the idea is put across. You may also be asked what the continuing passage will discuss. Understand the main idea of the entire passage and choose an option that is in sync with entire passage and also comes immediately after the next paragraph.

Approaches to Reading

1. **Scanning**

Scanning is a method of reading a particular article or passage in which an individual is searching for specific facts (words, dates etc.) related to a particular subject. For example, searching for a word in dictionary is similar to scanning.

2. **Skimming**

Skimming is used to quickly identify the main ideas of a text, when an individual has a large amount of text to be read in less time. This is an appropriate technique when high levels of comprehensions are not required. For example, reading the headlines in a newspaper and extracting the information is similar to skimming.

3. **3M method**

Whenever you read an article identify the following: What Is the *message*? What is the *method* of writing? What is the *mood* of the passage?

Finally here are some approaches that may help you in answering reading comprehension based questions.

- Analyze each passage carefully before answering the accompanying questions. As with any kind of thoughtful reading, look for clues that will help you understand less explicit aspects of the passage.
- Whenever you are reading a paragraph, understand what the *message* is and the *method* in which it is stated. Also interpret the *mood* or tone of the passage. What methods (chronological order, statistics etc.) are used to organize the paragraph.

- Note transitions from one idea to the next, and examine the relationships among the different ideas or parts of the passage. For example, are they contrasting or complementary? Consider the points the author makes, the conclusions drawn, and how and why those points are made or conclusions are drawn.
- Read each question carefully and be certain that you understand exactly what is being asked. Always read all the answer choices before selecting the best answer. Be careful not to be misled by answer choices that are only partially true or only partially satisfy the problem posed in the question.

ooo

Exercise

Read the following passages and answer the questions that follow.

Passage 1

When one thinks about China, one imagines a container ship brimming with cartons of toys, clothing, iPhones, and other goods bound for the world's consumer markets, whose populations power China's economic engine. That view couldn't be more wrong.

The Chinese government runs various programmes to encourage domestic consumption. Although millions of peasants live on subsistence wages, millions more Chinese are moving to urban centres and achieving a recognizably middle-class lifestyle. Consider just a few data points that give evidence of China's unexpectedly fast-paced move towards a more balanced, consumer-driven economy: In a variety of consumer categories—including such items as shoes, consumer electronics, and jewellery—China already ranks as the number one or number two market in the world market. The combined flow of shipping containers between Asia & North America & Asia and Europe is already less than the flow among Asian nations—with much of the latter consisting of goods imported to China. Domestic demand accounts for most sales of Chinese-produced air conditioners, motorcycles, trucks, and steel.

Adoption rates of new technologies among the rising middle class exceed those of nearly every other developing country. China has 400 million internet users, most with broadband access. Mobile telephony is ubiquitous in urban areas, and most of its consumers have leapfrogged landlines.

China's cities are growing so quickly that the country now has more urban centres than most Western nations do. For instance, China has about 90 cities with a middle-class population of 250,000 or more; the U.S. and Canada together have fewer than 70. According to projections, by 2020 China will have 400 cities with at least 2,50,000 middle-class inhabitants—and 50 of those cities will have more than 1 million middle-class inhabitants. And by then it is expected to have 800 cities whose residents' real disposable incomes are greater, on average, than those of Shanghai's residents today.

Chinese companies are already recognized as among the world leaders in numerous B2B technologies, including wind-turbine blades, solar panels, high-speed rail equipment, steam boilers, port terminal cranes, and electric-transmission equipment.

1. Which statement best summarizes the passage?

   A. China has achieved tremendous growth, in recent years and is moving towards a more balanced, consumer-driven economy.

B. China develops low-cost goods that are then exported to various countries, so it can never compare with the West.

C. China has a huge population and by 2020, it is expected to have 400 cities with more than 2,50,000 middle-class inhabitants.

D. Chinese government is determined to increase the domestic consumption and reduce exports.

2. What is the meaning of the word 'ubiquitous' used in the passage?

A. Rarely found B. Omnipresent

C. Innovative D. Technically advanced

3. According to the passage, Chinese companies are recognized as world leaders in the following except

A. Steam boilers

B. Solar Panels

C. Air Conditioners

D. Electric-transmission equipment

4. About how many cities in China have more than 2,50,000 middle class population?

A. 70 B. 90

C. 400 D. 800

5. As per the passage, the flow of shipping containers is higher

A. between Asia and North America

B. between Asia and Europe

C. among Asian nations

D. between Europe and North America

6. According to the author in the first paragraph, what can be inferred from the visualization about China ?

A. China only exports good.

B. China transports products through ships.

C. China makes good money from exports.

D. China produces small items like toys and clothes.

7. According to the passage, China is ranked in the top few consumer markets for all of the following products except?

A. Electronics B. Footwear

C. Ornaments D. Information technology

Passage 2

October 1 to 7 is designated as World Wildlife Week. What does this entail? This is a chance for us to take a look at what we have done to the environment and how much we have damaged animal habitat.

Look out of your window. Do you see something missing? The house sparrow which was a rather common sight is hardly spotted these days, thanks to human encroachment and urban lifestyles that do not give these feathered friends a chance.

If this is the fate of a species that co-existed with humans, imagine the chance of the ones that need their own habitat. We humans threaten species with our growing population and urbanization. Many species of animals and plants are listed in various degrees of the "endangered" category.

The reasons for the decline in their number are many and humans are responsible for most; the main being, loss of habitat due to human encroachment or imbalance in the ecosystem. Poaching is another grave threat that resulted in putting many a species like the Royal Bengal Tiger and the Asian Elephant species in the 'endangered' category. While the former was hunted for its skin and supposed medicinal properties, the latter was targeted for its tusks. Meanwhile, the horns of the rhinoceros have high commercial value and hence these animals are heartlessly hunted. Another reason is the extinction of one species leads to the endangerment of a dependent species. Dr. Manimozhi, the Zoo biologist, quotes the example of the Dodo in Madagascar, the disappearance of which led to the subsequent extinction of the Calvaria tree species as it depended on these birds to germinate its seeds.

And if you thought that we humans are safe, well you are wrong. "Every organism is inter-dependent," says Dr. Manimozhi. "Thus with the extinction of one species after the other, the ecological balance will be upset leading to calamities like earthquakes and other environmental problems. Of course, it will take time, but in due course it will become a reality."

"The government is doing its bit in terms of forest protection, wildlife regulations and conservation. We have to understand that this is everybody's problem. We need to co-operate with the government and do our bit — co-existing with nature, promoting sustainable development and not over-exploiting resources."

8. According to the author, which of the following animals would need a habitat of their own?

   A. Tiger B. Sparrow

   C. German shepherd dog D. Cow

9. According to Dr Manimozhi, "Will human beings be affected by extinction of species?"
   A. Yes, they will be immediately affected
   B. No, humans will not be affected at all
   C. Yes, but may not be immediately affected
   D. Cannot say anything
10. Which of the following may not be useful to save environment?
   A. Plant trees and build a bird feeder in your backyard
   B. Recycle stuff and avoid use of non biodegradable material
   C. Paint walls green
   D. Do not buy leather bags as it would encourage animal hunting
11. According to the passage, which of the following about Dodo can be said?
   A. Poaching is a threat to this animal
   B. The calavaria trees depend on this bird for the sprouting of its seeds.
   C. It survives on Calavaria tree
   D. Urbanization resulted in extinction of this species
12. Which of the following best explains the author's tone?
   A. Indifference   B. Daunting
   C. Concern   D. Empathy
13. When the author says "feathered friends" what does he refer to?
   A. Rising houses   B. Flies
   C. Sparrows   D. Extinct species

Passage 3

Three art movements which contributed to the development of abstract art were Romanticism, Impressionism and Expressionism. Artistic independence for artists was advanced during the 19th century. Patronage from the church diminished and private patronage from the public became more capable of providing a livelihood for artists.

Romanticism was an artistic, literary and intellectual movement that originated in the second half of the 18th century in Europe, and gained strength in reaction to the Industrial Revolution. In part, it was a revolt against aristocratic social and political norms of the Age of Enlightenment and a reaction against the scientific rationalization of nature. It was embodied most strongly in the visual arts, music, and literature, but had a major impact on historiography, education and natural history. The movement validated strong emotion as an authentic source of aesthetic experience, placing new emphasis on emotions as trepidation, horror, terror and awe—especially that which is experienced in confronting the sublimity of untamed nature and its picturesque qualities, both new aesthetic categories.

Impressionism was a 19th-century art movement that originated with a group of Paris-based artists whose independent exhibitions brought them to prominence during the 1870s and 1880s. Characteristics of Impressionist paintings include relatively small, thin, yet visible brush strokes; open composition; emphasis on accurate depiction of light in its changing qualities; common, ordinary subject matter; the inclusion of movement as a crucial element of human perception and experience; and unusual visual angles. The development of Impressionism in the visual arts was soon followed by analogous styles in other media which became known as Impressionist music and Impressionist literature. The term "Impressionism" can also be used to describe art created in this style, but not during the late 19th century.

Expressionism was a modernist movement, initially in poetry and painting, originating in Germany at the beginning of the 20th century. Its typical trait is to present the world solely from a subjective perspective, distorting it radically for emotional effect in order to evoke moods or ideas. Expressionist painters explored the bold use of paint surface, drawing distortions and exaggerations, and intense colour. Expressionists produced emotionally charged paintings that were reactions to and perceptions of contemporary experience; and reactions to Impressionism and other more conservative directions of late 19th century painting. The Expressionists also drastically changed the emphasis on subject matter in favour of the portrayal of psychological states of being. Expressionist artists sought to express meaning or emotional experience, rather than physical reality. Expressionism was developed as an avant-garde style – the first of its kind, before the First World War. The style then extended to a wide range of the arts, including painting, literature, theatre, dance, film, architecture and music. The term is sometimes suggestive of emotional angst. In a general sense, painters such as Matthias Grünewald and El Greco are sometimes termed expressionist, though in practice the term is applied mainly to 20th-century works. The Expressionist emphasis on individual perspective has been characterized as a reaction to positivism and other artistic styles such as naturalism and impressionism.

14. Which of the following characterizes the 19th Century artists?

    A. Support from the church increased

B. A lot of colour and contortions were prominent in the paintings

C. Physical actuality had more importance in the paintings

D. Bread and butter for the painters came from non – theological sources

15. Nature was an inspiration to which kind of painters?

A. Romanticists B. Impressionists

C. Expressionists D. Both A and B

16. Which of these abstract art forms was a result of the rebellion against the nobility?

A. Romanticist B. Impressionist

C. Expressionist D. All the three

17. From the passage, what do you understand of the phrase 'avant-garde'?

A. Drab and usual

B. Something happening before a war

C. Original and daring

D. Amalgamation of music, literature, theatre etc.

18. In the same way that unusual angles and movement were salient features of the Impressionist artists, what was the main feature of an Expressionist painter?

A. Fine brush strokes

B. Science and its discoveries

C. Industrial revolution

D. Anxiety and apprehensions relating to emotions

19. According to the passage the painters Matthias Grünewald and El Greco belonged to which time?

A. 20th Century B. Before the 20th Century

C. Modern age D. Impressionist period

20. In an art class, the teacher asked a group of students to draw a flower vase. One particular student chose to depict the flower vase when the Sun was shining on it partially at its top-left. The student showed a beautiful transition from the lustrous to the dull portions of the vase. Which art form was it that he was portraying?

A. Romanticist B. Impressionist

C. Expressionist D. All the three

21. Which of the following is not mentioned as a character of Expressionist?
   A. They reflect the personal opinion of the subject not the object of thought.
   B. It expresses the emotional experience.
   C. It uses intense colour
   D. It depicts varied visual angles
22. What does the word patronage mean?
   A. Livelihood B. Idea
   C. Concept D. Support or encouragement

Passage 4

It is well known that Mahatma Gandhi, had to pass through the ordeal of being locked up many times. But what is much less known is that he linked suffering and its exaltation with the asceticism of Sufi traditions, i.e., the acceptance of pain as a necessary stage in a human being's spiritual development. In search of tranquility, he regarded the time spent behind prison bars as a crowning achievement.

Bodily hardships provided mental strength to Gandhi. To a friend in New York, he explained that "when the conviction goes deeper than the intellect, you will brave all danger and risks and live the true life, and you will at once find that it is its own reward." He felt privileged to receive the same sentence of six years simple imprisonment in the 1922 sedition case against him, as had been given to Bal Gangadhar Tilak in 1908. His attitude vindicated Lord Krishna's comforting words in the Gita: "Even here, in this life, the universe is conquered by those whose mind is established in equanimity"; confirmed the Biblical verse — Patriots and reformers all over the world have had the capacity to put up with pain when they take it up in the true spirit. Gandhi, for one, was a seeker of the pure spirit of fearlessness or tapasya.

Gandhi expected all others in the civil resistance movement to do the same — to know as much as possible about jails. They had to fight for their rights, face the worst, deny themselves the privilege of being let off, and in the process stimulate the public to win Swaraj. Therefore, instead of fretting over jail, Gandhi exhorted satyagrahis to brave the attendant risks, such as uttermost penury, loss of all possessions, and lathi blows, and not be either contaminated or dissipated by worldly gains.

23. What does the word "penury" in the passage mean?
   A. punishment B. hardship
   C. poverty D. imprisonment

24. According to the passage, Gandhiji's attitude confirmed all aspects of the given Biblical verse except:
   A. Praying regularly instead of only when in need
   B. Having patience when faced with distress
   C. Having a positive attitude
   D. Fretting over incarceration
25. According to the passage, Bal Gangadhar Tilak was incarcerated for the offence of
   A. Theft B. Sedition
   C. Disobedience D. Misappropriation
26. All the following have been referred in the passage except
   A. Sufi tradition B. Bhagavad Gita
   C. Bible D. Ramayana
27. According to the passage, what was the message of Gandhi to his followers?
   A. Suffering is universal
   B. Imprisonment leads to success
   C. Hardship teaches endurance
   D. Stop worrying about imprisonment and fight for freedom
28. In the passage, what does the word "equanimity" mean?
   A. Tolerate pain B. Composure
   C. Unyielding D. Happiness

Passage 5

When a catastrophe strikes, analysts typically blame some combination of powerful mechanisms. An earthquake is traced to an immense instability along a fault line; a stock market crash is blamed on the destabilizing effect of computer trading. These explanations may well be correct. But systems as large and complicated as the Earth's crust or the stock market can break down not only under the force of a mighty blow but also at the drop of a pin. In a large interactive system, a minor event can start a chain reaction that leads to a catastrophe.

Traditionally, investigators have analyzed large interactive systems in the same way as they analyze small orderly systems, mainly because the methods developed for small systems have proved so successful. They believed they could predict the behavior of a large interactive system by studying its elements separately and by analyzing its component mechanisms individually. For lack of a better theory, they assumed that in large interactive systems the response to a disturbance is proportional to that disturbance.

During the past few decades, however, it has become increasingly apparent that many large complicated systems do not yield to traditional analysis. Consequently, theorists have proposed a "theory of self-organized criticality": many large interactive systems evolve naturally to a critical state in which a minor event starts a chain reaction that can affect any number of elements in the system. Although such systems produce more minor events than catastrophes, the mechanism that leads to minor events is the same one that leads to major events.

A deceptively simple system serves as a paradigm for self-organized criticality: a pile of sand. As sand is poured one grain at a time onto a flat disk, the grains at first stay close to the position where they land. Soon they rest on top of one another, creating a pile that has a gentle slope. Now and then, when the slope becomes too steep, the grains slide down, causing a small avalanche. The system reaches its critical state when the amount of sand added is balanced, on average, by the amount falling off the edge of the disk.

Now when a grain of sand is added, it can start an avalanche of any size, including a "catastrophic" event. Most of the time, the grain will fall so that no avalanche occurs. By studying a specific area of the pile, one can even predict whether avalanches will occur there in the near future. To such a local observer, however, large avalanches would remain unpredictable because they are a consequence of the total history of the entire pile. No matter what the local dynamics are, catastrophic avalanches would persist at a relative frequency that cannot be altered: Criticality is a global property of the sand pile.

29. The passage provides support for all of the following generalizations about large interactive systems EXCEPT:
    - A. They can evolve to a critical state
    - B. They do not always yield to traditional analysis
    - C. They make it impossible for observers to make any predictions about them
    - D. They are subject to the effects of chain reactions
30. According to the passage, the criticality of a sand pile is determined by the
    - A. Size of the grains of sand added to the sand pile
    - B. Number of grains of sand the sand pile contains

C. Rate at which sand is added to the sand pile

D. Balance between the amount of sand added to and the amount lost from the sand pile

31. It can be inferred from the passage that the theory employed by the investigators mentioned in the last sentence of the second paragraph would lead one to predict that which one of the following would result from the addition of a grain of sand to a sand pile?

A. The grain of sand would never cause anything more than a minor disturbance

B. The grain of sand would usually cause a minor disturbance, but would occasionally cause a small avalanche

C. The grain of sand would usually cause either minor disturbance or a small avalanche, but would occasionally cause a catastrophic event

D. The grain of sand would invariably cause a catastrophic event

32. Which one of the following best describes the organization of the passage?

A. A common misconception is elaborated and its consequences that describe a detailed example of one of these consequences is then given

B. A general principle is stated and supported by several examples; an exception to the rule is then considered and its importance evaluated

C. A number of seemingly unrelated events are categorized: the underlying processes that connect them are then detailed

D. A traditional method of analysis is discussed and the reasons for its adoption are explained; an alternative is then described and clarified by means of an example

33. Which one of the following is most analogous to the method of analysis employed by the investigators mentioned in the second paragraph?

A. A pollster gathers a sample of voter preferences and on the basis of this information makes a prediction about the outcome of an election

B. A historian examines the surviving documents detailing the history of a movement and from these documents reconstructs a chronology of the events that initiated the movement

C. A biologist observes the behavior of one species of insect and from these observations generalizes about the behavior of insects as a class

D. An engineer analyzes the stability of each structural element of a bridge and from these analyses draws a conclusion about the structural soundness of the bridge

34. In the passage, the author is primarily concerned with
    A. arguing against the abandonment of a traditional approach
    B. illustrating the superiority of a new theoretical approach
    C. reconciling conflicting points of view
    D. describing the evolution of a radical theory

Passage 6

Oil spills can have serious effects on marine life, as highlighted by the photos of dead birds which regularly appear in the news after such an event. Such images fuel the perception of widespread and permanent environmental damage after every spill, and an inevitable loss of marine resources with serious economic repercussions. A science-based appraisal of the effects reveals that whilst damage occurs and may be profound at the level of individual organisms, populations are more **resilient** and natural recovery processes are capable of repairing the damage and returning the system to normal functions. The first stage on the road to recovery is usually a well conducted clean-up operation but in some specific habitats aggressive clean-up methods can cause more harm than good and then it is better to let natural cleaning processes take their course.

Many spill impacts have been documented in the scientific and technical literature, and although not all the effects of oil pollution are completely understood, an indication of the likely scale and duration of damage can usually be deduced from the information available. However, it can be difficult to present a balanced view of the realities of spill effects, given the often highly charged and emotional nature of a spill and its aftermath. The scientific community can become polarized into opposing camps with one side intent on quantifying every aspect of damage, and the other emphasizing the capacity of the environment to recover naturally. The simple reality is that sometimes significant damage occurs, sometimes not and the aim of these pages is to draw together what general information is known about spill effects and their longevity.

The marine ecosystem is highly complex and natural fluctuations in species composition, abundance and distribution are a basic feature of its normal function. The extent of damage can therefore be difficult to detect against this background variability. Nevertheless, the key to understanding damage and its importance is whether spill effects result in a downturn in breeding success, productivity, diversity and the overall functioning of the system. Spills are not the only pressure on marine habitats; chronic urban and industrial contamination or the exploitation of the resources they provide are also serious threats.

35. What does the author mean by the word resilient when he says that populations are resilient?

    A. Recover readily from adversity

    B. Immune to any damages

    C. Multiply frequently in times of calamities

    D. Adopt to normal life quickly

36. Which analogy, best describes the clean-up process for some specific habitats elucidated in the last line of the first paragraph of the passage?

    A. A young singer stops singing, because his voice cracks naturally and quits his career as a musician

    B. A patient not taking pills to cure himself of a sickness because the human body has the power to cure itself naturally

    C. A painter brings to paint with more vibrant colours to make his paintings look better, disregarding his natural abilities

    D. An advocate begins to take bribes from his clients in order to survive as the cost of living has increased

37. According to the passage, why is it difficult to give an equitable view of the actualities in an oil spill?

    A. There is a huge media glare after each oil spill

    B. There is a lot of economic and marine life damage

    C. There is generally an outburst of feelings and emotions, during and after a spill

    D. Too many birds are killed and there is ambiguity about the numbers

38. Which of the following is true as per the passage?

    A. Oil spills along with other factors pose a threat to the development and growth of marine life

    B. After an oil spill, the areas should be left to recover by themselves because cleaning them up does more harm than good

    C. Oil spills are not as harmful as they are portrayed

    D. All the scientists are against using cleaning processes after oil spills

39. Which of the following, if true, adds weight to the information given by the author?

A. There is no account of any of the oil spills in history, which makes it difficult to assess the damage done

B. The scientific community is always biased and will not be able to come to a conclusion in regard to oil spills

C. There are not many distinctions and differences in the types of marine animals

D. The ability of a single entity to recover is lesser than the ability of a group to recover

40. Pick the odd word in the following group of words.

A. Nautical B. Maritime

C. Terrestrial D. Marine

41. Which of the following is not mentioned in the passage as a cause that would affect environments of sea or ocean dwelling creatures?

A. Pollution that resulted from leakage of oil

B. Industrial effluents released into seas and oceans

C. Misuse and exploitation of the resources given by sea

D. Increased motor vehicle fishing activity on the seas

42. Which of the following best explains the many pictures of carcass taken after the spill?

A. Overrate the loss of life

B. Underestimate the extent of spill

C. Give exact picture of the extent of damage to the ecology and economy

D. Apathetic to the accident

Passage 7

When a rattlesnake shakes its tail, does it hear the rattling? Scientists have long struggled to understand how snakes, which lack external ears, sense sounds. Now, a new study shows that sound waves cause vibrations in a snake's skull that are then "heard" by the inner ear.

In humans, sound waves traveling through the air hit the eardrum, causing the movement of tiny bones and vibrations of tiny hair cells in the inner ear. These vibrations are then translated into nerve impulses that travel to the brain. Snakes have fully formed inner ear structures but no eardrum. Instead, their inner ear is connected directly to their jawbone, which rests on the ground as they slither. Previous studies have shown that vibrations travelling through the ground—such as the footsteps of predators or prey—cause vibrations in a snake's jawbone, relaying a signal to the brain via that inner ear.

It was still unclear, however, whether snakes could hear sounds traveling through the air. So, biologists in Denmark took a closer look at one particular type of snake, the ball python (Python regius). They used electrodes attached to the reptiles' heads to monitor the activity of neurons connecting the snakes' inner ears to their brains. Each time a sound was played through a speaker suspended above the snake's cage, the researchers measured whether the nerve relayed an electrical pulse (the snakes showed no outward response to the sounds). The nerve pulses were the strongest, the researchers found, with frequencies between 80 and 160 hertz—around the frequency for the lowest notes of a cello, though not necessarily sounds that snakes encounter often in the wild.

The snakes don't seem to be responding to vibrations that these sounds cause in the ground, since these vibrations were too weak to cause nerve activity when they weren't accompanied by sound in the air, the researchers found. However, when the researchers attached a sensor to the snake's skull, they discovered that the sound waves were causing enough vibration in the bone—directly through the air—for the snakes to sense it.

Scientist Young calls the work "extremely nice," but he notes that the team studied only one species of snakes. "Given that there are almost 3000 types of snakes, the next question would be how this differs between them." Some snakes, he notes, are known to be better at sensing vibrations through the ground, so their ability to sense sound waves in the air might be reduced. Since many sounds are too weak to cause ground-borne vibrations that snakes can sense, having both abilities helps them detect a wider range of noises. Some salamanders and frogs lack eardrums, too, he notes, and they may listen in the same way as snakes do. Young also says that there are probably other ways that snakes are sensing vibrations in the air and on the ground. "We know snakes have some special sense organs in their skin and their head that likely react to vibrations. And we have some evidence that they detect vibration along the length of their body," he says. "This is unlikely to be the final word on how snakes sense sound and vibrations."

43. Which of the following best explains the organization of the last paragraph?
    - A. New evidence is introduced to support a traditional point of view
    - B. A summary of the material in the preceding paragraphs is presented, and conclusions are drawn
    - C. Previous study is appreciated but with certain limitations and suggestions for future study are given
    - D. A methodology for future study is elaborated

44. According to scientist Young what could be the immediate next course of study for biologists in Denmark?
   A. Study the other varieties of snakes
   B. Study at various frequencies of sound
   C. Study the eardrums of Salamanders
   D. Study the ability of snakes to hear through skin
45. According to the previous studies, a snake could sense a sound travelling through ground only if?
   A. it is slithering.
   B. its jaw is on the ground.
   C. the intensity of sound is between 80-160 Hz
   D. the electrodes are attached to inner ear.
46. What is main conclusion of the studies conducted by the biologists from Denmark?
   A. Vibrating skulls help snakes hear
   B. It is difficult to study the behavioral response of snakes
   C. Jawbone helps the snakes to hear
   D. Laboratory environment is different from the life in the wild
47. The passage discusses all of the animals that do not have a eardrum except?
   A. Python regius
   B. Salamander
   C. Frog
   D. Ball regions
48. The scientists of Denmark who studied Ball Python, would most likely agree with which of the following?
   A. Snakes do not react to sound waves through air
   B. Snakes react to only sound waves that cause vibrations through ground
   C. Snakes may not be able to react to certain weak signals through ground but when coupled with air vibrations they may respond
   D. Sound travels the fastest on air than any other medium
49. According to the passage, a snake may hear
   A. by sensing the vibrations
   B. by detecting vibrations through skin
   C. by sensing vibrations through air or ground
   D. All the above.

Passage 8

The probable origin of the government is a question of fact, to be settled, not by conjecture but by history. Its answer is to be sought amidst such traces as remain to us of the history of primitive societies. Facts have come down to us from that early time in fragments, many of them having been revealed only by inference, and having been built together by sagacious ingenuity of scholars much as complete skeletons have been reared by inspired naturalists in the light of the meagre suggestions of only a fossil joint or two. As those fragments of primitive animals have been kept for us sealed up in earth's rocks, so fragments of primitive institutions have been preserved, embedded in the rocks of surviving law or custom, mixed up with the rubbish of accumulated tradition, crystallized in the organization of still savage tribes, or kept curiously in the museum of fact and rumour swept together by some ancient historian. Limited and perplexing as such means of reconstructing history may be, they repay patient comparison and analysis as richly as do the materials of archaeologist and the philologist. The facts as to the origin and early history of government are at least as available as the facts concerning the growth and kinship of languages or the genesis and development of arts and sciences. At any rate, such light as we can get from the knowledge of the infancy of society thus meagrely afforded us is better than that which might be derived from any a priori speculations founded upon our acquaintance with our modern selves, or from any fancies, how learnedly so ever constructed, that we could weave as to the way in which history might plausibly be read backwards.

50. The author would consider which of the following in reconstructing history?
    - A. Fragments of information available from archaeological excavations
    - B. A world-wide analysis of the works of early historians
    - C. A world-wide survey on traces of every primitive tribe
    - D. Study of the oldest available documentation
51. According to the author, what can be inferred about 'facts that have come down' so far?
    - A. They are not completely real as they are inferred from meagre information
    - B. They are the fictitious products of creative geniuses
    - C. Law makers and sociologists have conspired together to draft books according to their convenience

D. Little effort has been put in reconstructing history

52. Which of the following would be the best agreeing with the author's feeling about the task of reconstructing history?

    A. It requires ingenuity and patience to infer from the fragments of available information

    B. Only little information can be available by traditional methods

    C. Guesswork and retracing steps to past from future is equally as useful as starting from the primitive methods of studying history

    D. It is not an easy task but the benefits are high once accomplished.

53. What does the word conjecture mean?

    A. Guess work B. Trace

    C. Evidence D. Familiar things

Passage 9

Earliest ancestors and chimpanzees share a common ancestor (around 5-7 million years ago). Therefore, understanding chimpanzee hunting behavior and ecology may tell us a great deal about the behavior and ecology of those earliest hominids.

In the early 1960s, when Jane Goodall began her research on chimpanzees in Gombe National Park (Tanzania), it was thought that chimpanzees were herbivores. In fact, when Goodall first reported meat hunting by chimpanzees, many people were extremely skeptical. Today, hunting by chimpanzees at Gombe and other locations in Africa has been well documented. We now know that each year chimpanzees may kill and eat more than 150 small and medium-sized animals, such as monkeys (red colobus monkey, their favorite prey), but also wild pigs and small antelopes.

Did early hominids hunt and eat small and medium-sized animals? It is quite possible that they did. We know that colobus-like monkeys inhabited the woodlands and riverside gallery forest in which early hominids lived 3-5 Million years ago. There were also small animals and the young of larger animals to catch opportunistically on the ground. Many researchers now believe that the carcasses of dead animals were an important source of meat for early hominids once they had stone tools to use (after 2.5 million years ago) for removing the flesh from the carcass. Wild chimpanzees show little interest in dead animals as a food source, so scavenging may have evolved as an important mode of getting food by hominids. Before this time, it seems likely that earlier hominids were hunting small mammals as chimpanzees do today and that the role that hunting played in the early hominids' social lives was probably as complex and political as it is in the social lives of chimpanzees.

54. Which of the following is not a food for Wild Chimpanzees?

A. Red colubus monkey B. Wild pigs

C. Small antelopes D. Animal Carcasses

55. In the first paragraph, the author is attempting to

A. generalize the behaviour of chimpanzees

B. establish an analogy between hominids and chimpanzee

C. study the specific traits of chimpanzee ancestors

D. compare and contrast the traits of hominids and other animals.

56. The author may most likely agree to which of the following about early hominids being carnivorous animals?

A. Once the stone tools developed Hominids survived only on dead meat

B. They were highly uninterested in eating dead meat.

C. It is believable that they did hunt and eat small and medium sized animals.

D. All the above.

57. Which of the following explains why people were skeptical about Jane Goodall's initial reports on Chimpanzees?

A. As indicated by the canons people believed that Chimpanzees were not carnivorous and now they were not willing to accept any counter statements

B. Jane Goodall was female intern from a London University and her statements were contradicting the earlier held beliefs.

C. Chimpanzees were heavily built and not as fast as a tiger, so it is believed that they will not be able to attack any animal for prey.

D. Hunting by Chimpanzees was never reported earlier by any of the Primatologists.

58. What is the main purpose of the passage?

A. Food habits of all primates

B. Amiability of Chimpanzees and their eating habits not known to the world

C. Understanding the behavior of early hominids from the behavior of Chimpanzees

D. Origin of stone tools and their application in food hunt of animals

59. Which of the following is one of the ways in which stone tools were put to use by hominids?

A. Removing flesh from a corpse

B. Digging for agriculture

C. Kill prey

D. Discover light

60. Which of the following best explains the organization of the third paragraph?

A. Criticizing a well established theory

B. Analyzing a current debate

C. A question is posed and explained

D. Contrasting two types of behaviors

Passage: 10

Asia may be leading the world in terms of economic recoveryfrom the recent global crisis, but in one critical area it remains a laggard: employment of women. A recent report by the International Labor Organization and the Asian Development Bank, "Women and Labor Markets in Asia: Rebalancing for gender equality," makes out a strong case for effective policy interventions in this important segment of the labor market, for two main reasons—the untapped economic potential and the effect on meeting the region's development goals. The finding that the Asia and Pacific region loses up to $47 billion annually because of the limited access given to women for employment and another $16-30 billion as a result of gender gaps in education drives home the magnitude of the social opportunities lost.

But it is not merely the missed growth in incomes that matters. Deeper still lie stubborn differentials that persist between the genders in various attributes of employment—the type of jobs and the regularity of incomes, for instance—reducing women to serve as the "buffer workforce." South Asia is home to the highest percentage of women in vulnerable employment: 84.5 per cent in 2009, compared with the global average of 52.9 per cent. This vulnerability is exacerbated by the high and rising informalisation

of the workforce. The strong link between informal employment and poverty calls for urgent policy interventions to break the vicious cycle. Of the interventions suggested by the ILO and the ADB, two are crucial: better-designed public employment programmes that factor in gender sensitivity and a mechanism to provide for social security. The immediate and long-term effects of these two measures will be highly beneficial. For example, the study provides persuasive evidence that India's Mahatma Gandhi National Rural Employment Guarantee Scheme has been successful in bringing in unskilled women agricultural workers to this public works programme as private wages for women are lower in the farm sector. Such public works-based solutions, howsoever effective they may be, can only be interim measures. In the long term what matters are coordinated policies that eradicate gender bias in employment. Rising India has everything to gain—economically, socially, and morally—by quickly initiating a process that will empower the women in the workforce.

61. What could be the suitable title of the passage?
    - A. Poverty in Asian women
    - B. Economical development of India
    - C. Providing employment opportunities to unskilled women
    - D. Empowerment of Asia's women

62. Which of the following is not implied in the passage?
    1. Rural employment schemes are temporary solutions
    2. Removing the gender bias towards men by the employers is the complete solution
    3. Work ambience has to be made comfortable for women to work

    A. 1 only B. 2 only
    C. 3only D. 1 & 2

63. Which of the following primary concerns expedite the need for intervention?
    - A. Women work resources are not being tapped
    - B. Women are not educated enough to get jobs
    - C. Tax allowances are high for women; hence the government is losing money
    - D. The inclination shown towards men over women in various issues

64. What could be the main purpose behind writing the first passage?
    - A. To disprove an erroneous assumption
    - B. To discuss a problem
    - C. To debate over the complexities behind a policy
    - D. To enlighten about a solution to a persistent issue

65. According to the author, which of the following is the reason for Rising India to fall back upon?
    - A. Poor policy making

B. Failed employment schemes

C. An irrational preference towards a particular gender in recruitment process

D. A better designed public employment scheme

66. Which of the following, if true would relieve author's concerns?

A. Enrollment figures from schools which show an increasing trend of female literacy rate

B. Interviews with married men indicating that they are now doing some household tasks

C. Creation of new jobs specifically for women

D. A study reporting recruitments sans inequality

67. The passage states which of the following as true about Asia

A. Women were restricted to domestic jobs

B. Utilizing the potential of women workforce can promote the region's growth

C. It resisted employment to women as it would radically change women's roles in the family

D. Families with employed women are above poverty line

68. According to the author Mahatma Gandhi Rural Employment Scheme is

A. A highly successful and beneficial scheme for skilled women

B. Does not give jobs to men

C. Provides social security for all the village women wage workers across the nation

D. Provides a temporary solace to given crisis but not a complete solution

69. What does the word exacerbate mean?

A. To aggravate the issue

B. To solve the problem

C. To calm down a disorderly state

D. To provide temporary relief

70. Wages given to women ___________ lower than that given to men.

A. has been B. is

C. are D. was

ooo

Unit- 10

Parajumbles

Parajumble questions have jumbled sentences that you need to rearrange in a logically coherent manner. These questions may have 4 or 5 individual sentences jumbled, or it may have a single sentence split and jumbled. When it comes to rearranging these questions you have clues or strategies to follow. You have to also simultaneously look at the options.

Approach to Solve Parajumble Questions

- Read through all the sentences and get an overall 'feel' of the passage.
- Understand what the main point, or subject of the paragraph is.
- Identify mandatory pairs – a pair of sentences that are together for sure.
- Identify if any of the options has that pair.

It will be useful if you check for 'definite pairs' –sentences that have a logical connection to the other and cannot exist in any other sequence.

- **Check for names, proper nouns, pronouns and demonstrative pronouns**

Many-a-times, you can identify a 'definite pair' with the help of names, proper nouns and pronouns. Personal pronouns such as he, she, it, him, her, they, you, your etc.. refer to a person, place or thing etc. So, always identify the noun that connects to the pronoun, as a pronoun is generally used after the noun.

Example:

(i) It is true, of course, that the two of **them** had their differences, which neither kept particularly secret.

(ii) As a recent biographer of **Jawaharlal Nehru**, I have been somewhat disconcerted to discover that my admiration for my subject immediately prompts people to assume that I must dislike his formidable deputy, **Sardar Vallabhbhai Patel.**

(iii) However, **they** overcame them and successfully handled all the issues during the tough times of the partition of India.

(iv) In fact, I count myself among the doughty **Sardar's** fans, and am at somewhat of a loss to account for the presumed incompatibility of these two inclinations.

A. (i), (ii), (iii), (iv) B. (ii), (iv), (i), (iii)

C. (iv), (i) ,(iii), (ii) D. (iii), (i), (iv), (ii)

The above sentence discusses about two leaders Jawaharlal Nehru and Sardar Vallabhbhai Patel. It is clearly evident that sentence (ii) is the first sentence of the paragraph in the correct order, because it has the complete names of the leaders. Also it introduces the biographer which relates to the pronoun 'I'. Next is sentence (iv). There is a smooth flow of ideas from (ii) to (iv) and, hence, they are 'definite pairs'.

Also notice the usage of short names and pronouns in the later sentences of the paragraph instead of the full names. The third sentence in the passage is (i). It again has a definite link to the idea put forward in sentence (iv). The last sentence is (iii).

So, the answer is option B. Hence, names and pronouns are a great help in sorting out the order.

- **Transition Words**

  Transition words make the shift from one idea to another very smooth. They organize and connect the sentences logically. Observing the transition words found in a sentence can often give you a clue about the sentence that will come before/after that particular sentence. A few transition words are - in addition, likewise, moreover, similarly, consequently, hence, otherwise, subsequently, first of all, to begin with, at the same time, for now, for the time being, in time, later on, meanwhile, next etc.

  In the example above, 'however' has been used as a transition word. In the paragraph above, disagreements between the leaders have been discussed. The concluding line though specifies that the leaders rose above their differences when the country needed them the most. This is why the word 'however' is used – to specify two diverse points.

- **Obvious openers and closers**

  Look out for sentences which would definitely be the opening or closing sentences in a parajumble.

Example:

(i) **His** idea was that the sun was stationary at the centre and that the earth and the planets move in circular orbits around the sun.

(ii) **Then** two astronomers - Johannes Kepler, and Galileo Galilei started publicly to support the Copernican theory, despite the fact that the orbits it predicted did not quite match the ones observed.

(iii) A simple model was proposed in 1514 by a Polish priest, **Nicholas Copernicus**.

(iv) Nearly a century passed before this idea was taken seriously.

A. (iii), (i), (iv), (ii) B. (iii), (iv), (ii), (i)

C. (i),(ii), (iii), (iv) D. (iii),(ii), (iv), (i)

Here, it is obvious that the first sentence in this para jumble is sentence (iii). The pronoun 'his' in sentence (i) refers to 'Nicholas Copernicus'. So the next one is sentence (i). The first statement speaks about a model and the next gives more information about the model. The answer is Option A.

- **Cause and effect relation**

  In many instances, a cause and an effect may be discussed, making it a 'definite pair'. Transition words coupled with the idea behind the passage will make it very easy for you to spot a definite pair. The cause would be stated first, followed by its repercussions.

- **Idea and example**

  If there are two sentences, one containing an idea and another giving examples of the same idea then the sentence containing the idea should come before the sentence containing the examples. But they need not necessarily be one after the other.

Example:

(i) Russia possesses the largest stockpiles of weapons of mass destruction in the world.

(ii) 489 missiles carrying up to 1,788 warheads and 12 submarines carrying up to 609 warheads form a looming threat.

(i) will come before (ii) in this case, even though there might be sentences in between.

- **Chronology**

  Another very important pointer towards spotting 'definite pairs' is to understand the chronology of events that is discussed in the passage.

  Words like first, secondly, thirdly, again, also, present, future, past, earlier, now, then etc. help you recognize the pairs quickly.

Example:

(i). I have to admit, **though**, that **they** pose a lot many practical problems.

(ii) **Secondly**, their short life - **they** tend to lose freshness very quickly and need to be cooked and eaten as soon as they are picked.

(iii) **First**, there is a lot of plucking and cleaning that needs to be done.

(iv) Leafy greens of all kinds are great for health - low in calories and fat, high in protein.

Focus on the words 'though' 'secondly', 'they', 'first' to identify definite pairs. The answer is (iv), (i), (iii), (ii)

ooo

Exercise

The constituent phrases of a sentence are jumbled up. Read the jumbled phrases carefully and then select the most appropriate sequence to make the sentence meaningful.

1. (i) the top-secret contingency plan for a "runaway bride" scenario has been dubbed "Operation Pumpkin",

   (ii) while simultaneously attempting to preserve Prince William's option to pursue and dramatically win her back

   (iii) in a desperate attempt to generate a moving security cordon around the escaping future Queen,

   (iv) and if put into effect would see hundreds of operatives switch tasks

   A. (i), (ii), (iii), (iv) B. (i), (iv), (iii), (ii)

   C. (i), (iii), (ii), (iv) D. (iv), (iii), (ii), (i)

2. (i) from the big things like mission and vision,

   (ii) brand is caring about your business at every level and in every detail,

   (iii) no matter how small

   (iv) to your people, your customers, and every interaction anyone is ever going to have with you,

   A. (i), (ii), (iv), (iii) B. (ii), (iv), (i), (iii)

   C. (ii), (i), (iv), (iii) D. (iii), (i), (ii), (iv)

3. (i) when it delved into the dark centre of the Earth's shadow

   (ii) The moon's bright white glow

   (iii) during the century's longest and darkest lunar eclipse

   (iv) turned crimson brick red

   A. (iii), (i), (ii), (iv) B. (i), (ii), (iv), (iii)

   C. (iii), (iv), (ii), (i) D. (ii), (iv), (i), (iii)

4. (i) Chelsea Clinton and chef Mario Batali among others –

   (ii) flogged stuff either designed or customized by Sir Jony and designer Marc Newson

(iii) and attended by actress Meg Ryan, guitarist the Edge,

(iv) The Sotheby's gala – co-sponsored by U2 rock star Bono

A. (i), (ii), (iv), (iii) B. (iv), (iii), (i), (ii)

C. (iv), (iii), (ii), (i) D. (iv), (ii), (i), (iii)

5. (i) The scheme invokes a new approach

(ii) for both pregnant women and sick neonates

(iii) and elimination of out-of-pocket expenses

(iv) to healthcare, placing, for the first time, utmost emphasis on entitlements

A. (i), (ii), (iii), (iv) B. (i), (iv), (iii), (ii)

C. (i), (iii), (ii), (iv) D. (iv), (iii), (ii), (i)

6. (i) companies scramble to build unique assets or capabilities

(ii) from leaking out to competitors

(iii) in their quest for upstream competitive advantage,

(iv) and then construct a wall to prevent them

A. (i), (ii), (iv), (iii) B. (ii), (iv), (i), (iii)

C. (ii), (i), (iv), (iii) D. (iii), (i), (iv), (ii)

7. (i) the Chairman of the electricity board said that the power plant should receive

(ii) to ensure uninterrupted

(iii) coal upto 1000 tonnes daily

(iv) supply of power for the city

A. (ii),(i), (iv), (iii) B. (i),(iii), (ii), (iv)

C. (iv), (i), (iii), (ii) D. (ii), (iv), (i), (iii)

8. (i) world-wide dive and sail, which operates across the country

(ii) was quick to reassure clients, via its website and on social media,

(iii) and sends nearly 50 people a month on scuba diving trips,

(iv) that the majority of tourist areas are unaffected.

A. (ii), (i), (iv), (iii) B. (iv), (i), (iii), (ii)

C. (i), (iii), (ii), (iv) D. (ii), (iv), (i), (iii)

9. (i) as Asia's natural-born allies,

(ii) have a pivotal role

(iii) Japan and India,

(iv) to play in preserving stability and helping to safeguard vital sea-lanes in the wider Indo-Pacific region

A. (iii), (i), (ii), (iv) B. (i), (iv), (iii), (ii)

C. (iv), (i), (iii), (ii) D. (ii), (iv), (i), (iii)

10. (i) the sudden crash of a Boeing 737 airliner

(ii) and the need to create awareness among the smaller, regional airlines

(iii) has turned the focus back on air safety

(iv) about ensuring that international standards are followed in aircraft maintenance.

A. (i), (iii), (ii), (iv) B. (i), (ii), (iii), (iv)

C. (iv), (iii), (ii), (i) D. (i), (ii), (iv), (iii)

11. (i) as we all know, the world trade bill

(ii) but they became deadlocked over the details in the past few days

(iii) and there remains so much disagreement that it needs several more weeks of negotiations to close the gaps

(iv) needs the consensus of majority of the diplomats

A. (i), (iii), (ii), (iv) B. (i), (iv), (iii), (ii)

C. (iv), (iii), (ii), (i) D. (i), (iv), (ii), (iii)

12. (i) particularly the humiliations of a century before Mao's irrationalities took over.

(ii) his extraordinary powers to summarize his views on statecraft in short pithy sentences

(iii) and the pains he has taken to bone up on China's troubled background,

(iv) are evident as is his deep knowledge of European history

A. (ii),(i), (iv), (iii) B. (i),(iii), (ii), (iv)

C. (iv), (i), (iii), (ii) D. (ii), (iv), (iii), (i)

13. (i) as the latter was not only his loyal companion

(ii) there was a time when man had very close ties with the horse

(iii) which could traverse any type of terrain

(iv) but also his dependable mode of transport,

A. (ii), (i), (iv), (iii) B. (i), (iii), (ii), (iv)

C. (iv), (i), (iii), (ii) D. (ii), (iv), (i), (iii)

14. (i) the anticipation is that e-commerce will have a terrific Thanksgiving week —

(ii) for that matter

(iii) and booming sales for the entire holiday season,

(iv) regardless of weather,

A. (i), (iii), (ii), (iv) B. (i), (iii), (ii), (iv)

C. (iv), (i), (iii), (ii) D. (i), (iv), (ii), (iii)

15. (i) Japan is already doing more for India than any other economic partner of this country:

(ii) as illustrated by the Japanese-financed Western Freight Corridor, the Delhi-Mumbai Industrial Corridor, and the Bangalore Metro Rail Project.

(iii) and is playing a key role in helping India to improve its poor infrastructure,

(iv) it is the largest source of aid,

A. (iii), (i), (ii), (iv) B. (i), (iv), (iii), (ii)

C. (iv), (i), (iii), (ii) D. (ii), (iv), (i), (iii)

Rearrange the following jumbled sentences into a coherent paragraph.

16. (i) We are indeed close, but not quite there.

(ii) And this prevented us from getting to the finish line.

(iii) Over the last few days, we stopped making the tough political calls.

(iv) We managed to make progress in a large number of very difficult areas.

A. (iii), (i), (ii), (iv) B. (i), (iv), (iii), (ii)

C. (iv), (iii), (ii), (i) D. (ii), (iv), (i), (iii)

17. (i) The problem does not entirely lie with garbage collection agencies, who are doing their best to lift all the refuse.

(ii) One proposed solution has been incineration of the waste to make it more compact and manageable.

(iii) Rather, the thousands of tonnes of solid and liquid waste generated every day by the gargantuan population of these thriving Indian cities pose the conundrum with respect to waste disposal: where will it all go?

(iv) Waste disposal is the bane of many a new-age city, and bustling metros.

A. (iii), (i), (ii), (iv) B. (i), (ii), (iv), (iii)

C. (iv), (i), (iii), (ii) D. (ii), (iv), (i), (iii)

18. (i) Its aim was to remove from dance, any external associations, so that dancers could concentrate on pure movement and pure pattern.

(ii) Abstract dance was the name of specific style of ballet, devised in the 1920s and developed at the Bahamas.

(iii) Ballroom dancing, for example, is concerned with the pleasure, the movement and the pattern making given to the dancers, and not with some external 'programme'.

(iv) In the wider sense, a great deal of dance is 'abstract'.

A. (iv), (ii), (i), (iii) B. (ii), (i), (iv), (iii)

C. (ii), (iv), (iii), (i) D. (ii), (iv), (i), (iii)

19. (i) The Greeks usually carried with them affection for the government they left behind and sacred fire from the altar of the parent city.

(ii) They established compacts of government for themselves, set up altars of their own, sought not only new soil to till but also political and religious liberty.

(iii) In a way, the American colonization differed from that of the ancients.

(iv) But thousands of the immigrants who came to America disliked the state and disowned the church of the mother country.

A. (iv), (ii), (iii), (i) B. (iii), (i), (iv), (ii)

C. (i), (iii), (ii), (iv) D. (iii), (i), (ii), (iv)

20. (i) Consecutively, this helps them develop into more efficient and effective leaders and managers.

(ii) This way, the trainees get the actual knowledge of the performance of the organization, beginning from the peak to the base of the administration ladder.

(iii) This is accomplished by a rotational guidance of all the subdivisions, and it gives an exposure to all the vital operations and activities of the organization.

(iv) The leadership development training programmes are intended to present the trainees with a general idea about the various operations that are going on in the organization.

A. (iv), (iii), (ii), (i) B. (i), (ii), (iii), (iv)

C. (iii), (ii), (iv), (i) D. (iii), (i), (ii), (iv)

21. (i) What were the 'boundary conditions' at the beginning of universe?

(ii) Science seems to have uncovered a set of laws that within the limits set by the uncertainty principle, tells us how the universe will develop with time, if we know its state at any one time.

(iii) But how did he choose the initial stage or configuration of the universe?

(iv) These laws may have originally been decreed by God, but it appears that he has since left the universe to evolve according to them and does not now intervene in it.

A. (ii), (iii), (i), (iv) B. (i), (iii), (iv), (ii)

C. (ii), (i), (iii), (iv) D. (ii), (iv), (iii), (i)

22. (i) Akbar moved to the eastern parts of the Safavid Empire where he was raised by his uncle Mirza Askari.

(ii) He spent his youth learning to hunt, run, and fight, but he never learned to read or write.

(iii) Although this did not hinder his search of knowledge as it is said whenever he use to go to bed, there would be somebody reading for the king.

(iv) This lifestyle of his childhood made him a daring, powerful and a brave warrior but he remained illiterate throughout his life.

A. (i), (ii) , (iv), (iii) B. (i), (iii), (iv), (ii)

C. (i), (ii), (iii), (iv) D. (ii), (i), (iii), (iv)

23. (i) Then, maybe they notice that a googol plus one is also a number, and they realize that although the names for numbers run out, the numbers themselves never do.

(ii) Yet to mathematicians, the idea that there are infinitely many numbers is just the beginning of an answer.

(iii) For children, the answer might be a million— that is, until they discover a billion, or a trillion, or a googol

(iv) How many numbers are there?

A. (iii), (i), (ii), (iv) B. (iv), (iii), (ii), (i)

C. (iii), (ii), (iv), (i) D. (iv), (iii), (i), (ii)

24. (i) This may yet happen, but rather than resolving the question, research on the genetic makeup of indigenous varieties has created more divergent estimates.

(ii) Debate exists regarding the number of distinct cultivars varieties inhabiting Greece.

(iii) With the advent of genetic testing, it seemed reasonable to assume that a consensus would be reached.

(iv) Until recently, it was common to hear estimates in excess of 300.

A. (ii), (iv), (iii), (i) B. (iv), (ii), (i), (iii)

C. (iii), (iv), (i), (ii) D. (i), (ii), (iii), (iv)

25. (i) One of them is that their symbols are nearly identical.

(ii) The Hindu zodiac, being sidereal, does not maintain this seasonal alignment but there are still similarities between the two systems.

(iii) The Hindu zodiac uses the sidereal coordinate system which makes reference to the fixed stars.

(iv) The Tropical zodiac however, is divided by the intersections of the ecliptic and equator which shift in relation to the backdrop of fixed stars at a rate of 1° every 72 years.

A. (iii), (ii), (i), (iv) B. (iv), (iii), (ii), (i)

C. (iii), (iv), (ii), (i) D. (iv), (iii), (i), (ii)

26. (i) But now, the Indian Railways has extended the e-ticketing concept to four trains under Western Railway.

(ii) Life just became a lot simpler for the train traveller.

(iii) All one has to do is take the e-ticket print-out along with a photo ID card before hopping onto the train.

(iv) Earlier, one had to book a ticket on the internet and wait for it to be delivered home.

A. (iv), (i), (ii), (iii) B. (ii), (iv), (i), (iii)

C. (ii), (i), (iv), (iii) D. (iv), (iii), (ii), (i)

27. (i) And getting to where they live, within a human lifetime, is as close to utterly impossible as I can imagine.

(ii) The biggest dilemma is that if there are paradise civilizations like the Pandoran culture, they are non-technological and, therefore, cannot communicate with us.

(iii) This incident leaves me to wonder if people can get this wrapped up in a fantasy about extra terrestrial life, what would happen if the real thing came along?

(iv) It was reported that a 42-year-old Taiwanese man with a history of heart problems died of a stroke while getting overly excited watching "Avatar."

A. (i), (ii), (iii), (iv) B. (iv), (iii), (ii), (i)

C. (ii), (i), (iv), (iii) D. (iv), (iii), (i), (ii)

28. (i) No other poet has so profoundly influenced Malayalam poetry, in recent times, as Changampuzha did.

(ii) He remains a cult figure!

(iii) This year marks the birth centenary of one of the most revered and adulated of all Malayalam poets — Changampuzha Krishna Pillai.

(iv) Sixty-four years after his death, his powerful poetry continues to mesmerize the Malayalee minds.

A. (ii), (i), (iii), (iv) B. (iv), (iii), (i), (ii)

C. (iii), (i), (iv), (ii) D. (i), (iv), (iii), (ii)

29. (i) Taking up a metaphysical stance is both unavoidable and has profound consequences for human life.

(ii) However, while all metaphysical reasoning is speculative, it is far from inconsequential.

(iii) Spending time discussing them may seem speculative and inconsequential.

(iv) Why should anyone bother about metaphysical questions?

A. (iv), (iii), (ii), (i) B. (i), (ii), (iii), (iv)

C. (ii), (iii), (iv), (i) D. (iv), (iii), (i), (ii)

30. (i) The idea of studying modern social problems in a methodical way emerges in the late 19th, early 20th century through the writings of scholars such as Karl Marx, Max Weber, Sigmund Freud and especially, Emile Durkheim and W.E.B. Du Bois.

(ii) This was, after all, a time, when the dark side of modernity was starting to become more apparent.

(iii) People were poor and ragged and often left homeless in the streets, upward mobility through education was reserved mostly for rich, white women and working class men, and the rural, small town edges of the great, new 20th century cities seemed to be finally wearing off.

(iv) It's not difficult to imagine why.

A. (i), (ii), (iii), (iv) B. (i), (iii), (ii), (iv)

C. (iii), (i), (ii), (iv) D. (i), (iv), (ii), (iii)

ooo

APPENDIX

Answers of The Exercises

Unit-2

Synonyms and Antonyms

SYNONYMS

Multiple Choice Questions Answers

1. (D)	2. (B)	3. (D)	4. (A)	5. (A)	6. (C)
7. (A)	8. (A)	9. (A)	10. (A)	11. (A)	12. (C)
13. (B)	14. (A)	15. (C)	16. (C)	17. (C)	18. (A)
19. (C)	20. (B)	21. (C)	22. (D)	23. (A)	24. (B)
25. (A)	26. (D)	27. (C)	28. (C)	29. (A)	30. (B)
31. (B)	32. (A)	33. (B)	34. (B)	35. (B)	36. (C)
37. (A)	38. (B)	39. (B)	40. (C)	41. (C)	42. (D)
43. (C)	44. (D)	45. (C)	46. (C)	47. (A)	48. (C)
49. (A)	50. (A)	51. (B)	52. (B)	53. (C)	54. (D)
55. (A)	56. (C)	57. (B)	58. (B)	59. (D)	60. (D)
61. (A)	62. (B)	63. (A)	64. (D)	65. (A)	66. (B)
67. (A)	68. (A)	69. (D)	70. (B)	71. (B)	72. (A)
73. (D)	74. (A)	75. (B)	76. (B)	77. (B)	78. (B)
79. (A)	80. (C)	81. (B)	82. (B)	83. (B)	84. (A)
85. (A)	86. (C)	87. (D)	88. (A)	89. (C)	90. (C)
91. (B)	92. (C)	93. (B)	94. (A)	95. (C)	96. (B)
97. (D)	98. (B)	99. (D)	100. (C)	101. (C)	102. (A)
103. (C)	104. (B)	105. (D)	106. (D)	107. (B)	108. (D)
109. (B)	110. (B)	111. (A)	112. (A)	113. (C)	114. (D)
115. (D)	116. (B)	117. (A)	118. (B)	119. (B)	120. (C)
121. (C)	122. (B)	123. (A)	124. (C)	125. (A)	126. (B)
127. (A)	128. (A)	129. (C)	130. (C)	131. (A)	132. (C)
133. (A)	134. (B)	135. (B)	136. (B)	137. (B)	138. (B)
139. (A)	140. (B)	141. (A)	142. (C)	143. (A)	144. (C)
145. (B)	146. (C)	147. (D)	148. (C)	149. (A)	150. (A)
151. (B)	152. (B)	153. (A)	154. (B)	155. (D)	156. (A)
157. (C)	158. (B)	159. (B)	160. (A)	161. (B)	162. (A)
163. (B)	164. (A)	165. (B)	166. (D)	167. (C)	168. (B)

169. (C)	170. (A)	171. (B)	172. (B)	173. (D)	174. (B)
175. (B)	176. (A)	177. (A)	178. (D)	179. (A)	180. (C)
181. (D)	182. (B)	183. (C)	184. (A)	185. (B)	186. (B)
187. (B)	188. (C)	189. (B)	190. (D)	191. (C)	192. (A)
193. (B)	194. (C)	195. (C)	196. (D)	197. (B)	198. (A)
199. (D)	200. (A)	201. (B)	202. (C)	203. (C)	204. (C)
205. (D)	206. (B)	207. (D)	208. (B)	209. (C)	210. (A)
211. (B)	212. (C)	213. (B)	214. (B)	215. (B)	216. (B)
217. (A)	218. (C)	219. (A)	220. (D)	221. (B)	222. (A)
223. (C)	224. (D)	225. (D)	226. (D)	227. (B)	228. (B)
229. (B)	230. (B)	231. (D)	232. (A)	233. (B)	234. (A)
235. (C)	236. (A)	237. (B)	238. (A)	239. (C)	240. (D)
241. (B)	242. (A)	243. (B)	244. (B)	245. (A)	246. (C)
247. (C)	248. (B)	249. (B)	250. (C)	251. (D)	252. (A)
253. (B)	254. (C)	255. (A)	256. (D)	257. (A)	258. (B)
259. (C)	260. (C)	261. (C)	262. (B)	263. (B)	264. (A)
265. (A)	266. (B)	267. (D)	268. (C)	269. (D)	270. (C)
271. (C)	272. (D)	273. (B)	274. (A)	275. (B)	276. (A)
277. (B)	278. (A)	279. (C)	280. (D)	281. (A)	282. (D)
283. (D)	284. (C)	285. (C)	286. (A)	287. (C)	288. (B)
289. (D)	290. (B)	291. (C)	292. (C)	293. (D)	294. (C)
295. (C)	296. (D)	297. (B)	298. (B)	299. (A)	300. (C)
301. (A)	302. (B)	303. (C)	304. (D)	305. (B)	306. (D)
307. (C)	308. (B)	309. (A)	310. (D)	311. (A)	312. (B)
313. (C)	314. (C)	315. (C)	316. (C)	317. (D)	318. (D)
319. (A)	320. (B)	321. (A)	322. (A)	323. (A)	324. (D)
325. (D)	326. (B)	327. (C)	328. (C)	329. (B)	330. (C)
331. (D)	332. (B)	333. (A)	334. (B)	335. (D)	336. (A)
337. (C)	338. (D)	339. (D)	340. (C)	341. (C)	342. (A)
343. (D)	344. (B)	345. (A)	346. (B)	347. (A)	348. (C)
349. (B)	350. (C)	351. (D)	352. (A)	353. (B)	354. (B)
355. (A)	356. (A)	357. (A)	358. (C)	359. (A)	360. (D)
361. (B)	362. (A)	363. (B)	364. (C)	365. (B)	366. (B)
367. (A)	368. (A)	369. (B)	370. (B)	371. (C)	372. (B)
373. (B)	374. (C)	375. (C)	376. (A)	377. (B)	378. (B)
379. (B)	380. (B)	381. (B)	382. (B)	383. (A)	384. (C)
385. (A)	386. (A)	387. (A)	388. (B)	389. (B)	390. (B)
391. (C)	392. (B)	393. (A)	394. (C)	395. (A)	396. (B)
397. (C)	398. (A)	399. (A)	400. (B)	401. (B)	402. (B)
403. (B)	404. (B)	405. (D)	406. (B)	407. (C)	408. (A)
409. (B)	410. (B)	411. (B)	412. (A)	413. (A)	414. (A)
415. (B)	416. (B)	417. (B)	418. (C)	419. (C)	420. (A)

421. (B)	422. (B)	423. (A)	424. (B)	425. (B)	426. (A)
427. (A)	428. (C)	429. (B)	430. (B)	431. (A)	432. (A)
433. (B)	434. (B)	435. (A)	436. (A)	437. (C)	438. (A)
439. (B)	440. (B)	441. (D)	442. (A)	443. (C)	444. (A)
445. (D)	446. (A)	447. (B)	448. (C)	449. (B)	450. (A)
451. (D)	452. (B)	453. (A)	454. (B)	455. (A)	456. (B)
457. (A)	458. (B)	459. (A)	460. (A)	461. (B)	462. (A)
463. (A)	464. (B)	465. (C)	466. (A)	467. (B)	468. (C)
469. (A)	470. (A)	471. (B)	472. (A)	473. (C)	474. (A)
475. (B)	476. (B)	477. (B)	478. (C)	479. (B)	480. (A)
481. (B)	482. (C)	483. (A)	484. (B)	485. (A)	486. (C)
487. (A)	488. (B)	489. (C)	490. (C)	491. (A)	492. (B)
493. (A)	494. (C)	495. (A)	496. (A)	497. (C)	498. (B)
499. (A)	500. (A)	501. (C)	502. (C)	503. (A)	504. (A)
505. (B)	506. (B)	507. (A)	508. (B)	509. (A)	510. (B)
511. (A)	512. (B)	513. (C)	514. (B)	515. (A)	516. (B)
517. (B)	518. (A)	519. (B)	520. (A)	521. (B)	522. (C)
523. (B)	524. (B)	525. (A)	526. (B)	527. (B)	528. (A)
529. (B)	530. (C)	531. (B)	532. (A)	533. (C)	534. (C)
535. (B)	536. (C)	537. (A)	538. (A)	539. (A)	540. (D)
541. (B)	542. (C)	543. (B)	544. (B)	545. (C)	546. (B)
547. (B)	548. (A)	549. (B)	550. (B)	551. (A)	552. (C)
553. (B)	554. (A)	555. (C)	556. (D)	557. (B)	558. (B)
559. (A)	560. (C)	561. (A)	562. (B)	563. (C)	564. (B)
565. (A)	566. (A)	567. (B)	568. (A)	569. (B)	570. (B)
571. (A)	572. (B)	573. (B)	574. (C)	575. (B)	576. (B)
577. (A)	578. (C)	579. (B)	580. (B)	581. (B)	582. (A)
583. (B)	584. (B)	585. (B)	586. (A)	587. (B)	588. (B)
589. (A)	590. (B)	591. (B)	592. (B)	593. (A)	594. (A)
595. (A)	596. (B)	597. (D)	598. (A)	599. (B)	600. (B)
601. (A)	602. (A)	603. (B)	604. (A)	605. (A)	606. (B)
607. (A)	608. (A)	609. (A)	610. (C)	611. (C)	612. (C)
613. (C)	614. (B)	615. (B)	616. (C)	617. (A)	618. (B)
619. (C)	620. (C)	621. (A)	622. (B)	623. (B)	624. (A)
625. (B)	626. (A)	627. (A)	628. (A)		

Test-1

1. (C) See Archaic
2. (C) See Assignation
3. (C) See Assent
4. (B) See Aborigine
5. (A) See Abandon
6. (B) See Abate
7. (A) See Abstain
8. (A) See Confess

9. (B) See Apposite
10. (B) See Apraise
11. (B) See Exhort
12. (A) See Conspicuous
13. (D) See Anthem (it means song of praise for country, institution, etc. Requiem means songof lamentation for the dead person)
14. (B) See Aroma
15. (A) See Obstinate
16. (D) See Avert
17. (A) See Indict
18. (A) See Abject
19. (A) See Usurp
20. (C) See Aquit
21. (A) See Levitate
22. (A) See Franchise
23. (A) See Abscond
24. (C) See Vitriolic
25. (A) See Deft
26. (B) See Hug
27. (A) See Adjourn
28. (B) See Distraught
29. (A) See Fealty
30. (B) See Awesome
31. A-D See Abrade
32. A-B See Accuse
33. A-D See Ancestor
34. A-B See Autocrat
35. A-D See Absurd
36. A-C See Ancestor
37. A-B See Aborigine
38. A-B See Discard
39. A-B See Abysmal
40. A-C See Adroit
41. A-C See Affirm
42. A-B See Admirer
43. A-C See Amends
44. A-B See Announcer
45. A-B See Appropriate
46. A-C See Arrogant
47. A-B See Aspect
48. A-B See Absorb
49. A-B See Affect
50. A-C See Awkward
51. (C) See Admirer
52. (B) See Affix
53. (A) See Agitate
54. (D) See Abscond
55. (B) See Admire
56. (D) See Allegiance
57. (B) See Avert
58. (A) See Alone
59. (D) See Abundant
60. (A) See Adulterate
61. (D) See Abound
62. (A) See Abstain
63. (C) See Acclimatise
64. (D) See Alibi
65. (B) See Annoy
66. (D) See Anger
67. (A) See Apotheosis
68. (D) See Austere
69. (B) See Awesome
70. (A) See Atrabilious

Test-2

1. (C) See Bequeath
2. (A) See Beat
3. (C) See Bogus
4. (C) See Burn
5. (C) See Buckle
6. (B) See Bundle
7. (A) See Bump
8. (C) See Boundary
9. (C) See Babel
10. (A) See Backtrack
11. (B) See Bad Smelling
12. (C) See Boredom
13. (A) See Block
14. (C) See Brat
15. (A) See Benumb
16. (A) See Bark
17. (C) See Bait
18. (C) See Banish
19. (A) See Beat
20. (B) See Beg
21. A-B See Behaviour
22. B-D See Beg
23. A-C See Backtrack
24. A-B See Bias
25. (A) and (B)
26. (A) and (B)
27. A-D See Bigot
28. A-B See Bundle
29. A-C See Bad Smelling
30. B-D See Baffle
31. (C) See Bable
32. (D) See Bundle
33. (C) See Boycott
34. (B) See Bounce
35. (D) See Bundle
36. (D) See Adulterate
37. (D) See Bias
38. (C) See Beat
39. (B) See Baron
40. (D) See Forbid

Test-3

1. (C) See Curse
2. (A) See Caress
3. (D) See Compensate
4. (B) See Cadaverous
5. (A) See Catholic
6. (C) See Cautious
7. (C) See Chatter
8. (D) See Cry
9. (A) See Cant
10. (B) See Contempt
11. (C) See Calm
12. (A) See Collect
13. (C) See Contempt
14. (C) See Caprice
15. (A) See Chant
16. (D) See Cringe
17. (B) See Cheat (v)
18. (A) See Clique
19. (D) See Crawl
20. (C) See Crave

21. (C) See Credit
22. (C) See Catch
23. (C) See Caper
24. (D) See Cheat
25. (C) See Chew
26. (C) See Chide
27. (B) See Circadian
28. (A) See Climax
29. (B) See Cruel
30. (D) See Hiatus
31. (A) See Clean
32. (B) See Clean
33. (C) See Classify
34. (A) See Clever
35. (C) See Closeness
36. (C) See Clot
37. (D) See Cogitate
38. (C) See Confine
39. (C) See Confiscate
40. (B) See Consult
41. A-B See Continuously
42. B-C See Contemporary
43. A-C See Coward
44. A-B See Cringe
45. A-C See Cadaverous
46. A-C See Cant
47. A-D See Caress
48. B-D See Chatter
49. A-B See Create
50. B-D See Congenital
51. (D) See Crack
52. (B) See Criticize
53. (D) See Chatter
54. (A) See Catch
55. (B) See Cheat
56. (D) See Clique
57. (B) See Classfiy
58. (A) See Class
59. (C) See Clever
60. See Collect

Test-4

1. (A) See Devise
2. (C) See Devour
3. (C) See Dull
4. (A) See Damage
5. (B) See Dull
6. (A) See Danger
7. (C) See Drink
8. (D) See Deadbody
9. (B) See Droop
10. (C) See Dazzle
11. (C) See Demise
12. (D) See Delve
13. (D) See Debris
14. (B) See Dominance
15. (C) See Declare
16. (A) See Decorate
17. (D) See Decrepit
18. (C) See Dregs
19. (B) See Defame
20. (C) See Defector

21. (A) See Defect
22. (B) See Degenerate
23. (A) See Dormant
24. (C) See Dilemma
25. (D) See Digout
26. (B) See Difference
27. (A) See Dip
28. (C) See Dilly-dally
29. (C) See Disaster
30. (C) See Disbelief
31. A-C See Disguise
32. A-B See Disobey
33. A-B See Disgorge
34. A-C See Discard
35. A-D See Disclose
36. A-B See Discourage
37. A-D See Disobedient
38. A-C See Disorderly
39. A-B See Dodge
40. A-C See Dress
41. (D) See Dazzle
42. (D) See Dull
43. (D) See Domain
44. (B) See Denounce
45. (A) See Demonstrate
46. (D) See Deride
47. (A) See Desire
48. (C) See Determination
49. (B) See Discard
50. (D) See Disappointment

Test-5

1. (B) See Example
2. (A) See Eager
3. (C) See Extenuate
4. (A) See Protract
5. (D) See Eject
6. (C) See Extravagant
7. (B) See Effective
8. (A) See Enthusiasm
9. (C) See Explain
10. (A) See Essential
11. (D) See Equality
12. (C) See Extinquish
13. (A)
14. (B) See Scarecrow
15. (C) See Flagrant
16. (D) See Extraordinary
17. (C) See Examine
18. (A) See Essential
19. (D) See Equality
20. (C) See Ephemeral
21. (D) See Educe
22. (C) See Heave
23. (C) See Exude
24. (A) See Emphasize
25. (C) See Ape
26. (A) See Mime
27. (C) See Transgress
28. (C) See Infiltrate
29. (B) See Eradicate
30. (A) See Extempore
31. A-C See Keen
32. C-D See Ephemeral

33. B-D See Inveigle
34. A-D See Boost
35. A-C See Belch
36. A-D See Enshrine
37. A-B See Paradigm
38. A-D
39. A-D
40. A-C
41. (D)
42. (A)
43. (A)
44. (B) See Elevate
45. (D) See Encounter
46. (D)
47. (A)
48. (C) See Essential
49. (A)
50. (D)

Test-6

1. (C) See Facetious
2. (A) See Foretell
3. (B) See Face
4. (B) See Frighten
5. (B) See Face
6. (B) See Free
7. (D) See Foretell
8. (A) See Friend
9. (C) See Fake
10. (D) See Foster
11. (C) See Forbid
12. (A) See Flexuous
13. (B) See Fake
14. (C) See Falter
15. (D) See Fare
16. (A) See Follower (Henchmen is plural of Henchman, Cohort is plural)
17. (C) See Failure
18. (D) See Fastidious
19. See Flatter
20. (C) See Flag
21. (B) See Fight
22. (C) See Famous
23. (D) See Fatal
24. (A) See Foresight
25. A-C See Face
26. B-C See Fare
27. A-B See Frighten
28. A-D See Foretell
29. B-D See Facetious
30. A-B See Foster
31. A-B See Free
32. A-C See Friend
33. B-D See Fluxuous
34. (C) See Flag
35. (D) See Flexuous
36. (A) See Forbid
37. (D) See Famous
38. (A) See Falter
39. (B) See Fake
40. (A) See Fight

Test-7

1. (D) See Garbage for explanation
2. (C) See Gaze
3. (A) See Genocide
4. (B) See Genocide
5. (C) See Garbage
6. (C) See Get rid of
7. (A) See Gorge
8. (D) See Guide
9. (A) See Impious
10. (C) See Impassive
11. (A) See Invincible
12. (C) See Indecent
13. (D) See Gaze
14. (D) See Instigate
15. (A) See Gradation
16. (C) See Inserted
17. (C) See Grind
18. (B) See Irritation
19. (C) See Interject
20. (C) See Growl
21. (C) See Instruction
22. (C) See Harass
23. (D) See Inkling
24. (C) See Inkling
25. (D) See Innovate
26. (C) See Injurious
27. (A) See Healthful
28. (C) See Herd
29. (A) See Hide
30. (C) See Hint
31. (B) See Hesitate
32. (C) See Holy
33. (C) See Hurl
34. (A) See Idea
35. (A) See Intrusive
36. (C) See Impinge
37. (D) See Impinge
38. (D) See Imprison
39. (C) See Inclination
40. (D) See Infer
41. (C) See Indemnify
42. (D) See Indiscriminate
43. (D) See Insert
44. (C) See Inform
45. (B) See Inherent
46. (B) See Injurious
47. (D) See Involved
48. (C) See Guide
49. (D) See Growl
50. (C) See Harass

Test-8

1. (A) Immaculate is used for spotless, clean dress, consummate means perfect, Divine means sacred.
2. (C) Compatible means capable of existing together, congruous means resembling in shape of parts, consonant means being in harmony of sound.
3. (B) Vivacious means full of vigour.

4. (A) Exonerate means declare free from charges, Exculpate means declare free from criminal offence, Acquit means declare free by a court, Release means set free from captivity.
5. (D) Indict means accuse of wrong doing. Means call to court for answering indictment, Incriminate means charge of involvement in an act of crime.
6. (A) Acquire means come to possess as property, assets; Gain profit, etc. Gather means to collect by picking up as flowers.
7. (A) Affiction means to cause pain by diseases, injury, ordeal means trial to prove innocence as an ordeal by fire, Disaster means natural calamity, viz., flood, earthquake.
8. (C) Quack is an unqualified practitioner, charlatan is a pretender to have knowledge, Hypocrite is a person who professes to have qualification which he does not possess himself. Pedant is a person who makes excessive show of his knowledge.
9. (C) Aver means to assert with confidence, Avouch means to assert with full responsibility, Avow means to declare openly, Vouch means to confirm something to be true.
10. (A) Lark means to have fun.
11. (B) Kudos means praise, Admire means to praise for wonderful job, Appreciate means to praise in high estimation of person.
12. (C) Playground on ice is called Rink.
13. (A) Invade means attack enemy's territory, Assault means to attack to injure, harm.
14. (C) Ascribe is to give credit, Impute is used for questionable intention, Assign is to allot duty, reason.
15. (A) Seduce means to lead away on wrong path. All other words are related to the meaning of 'get attracted towards'.
16. (B)
17. (C) Malinger means pretend illness to bunk classes etc.
18. (B) Poisonously harmful is noxious. Abnoxious means having offending smell as is Noisome & Foul.
19. (A) Benefactor helps with money to the needy, samaritan helps people in distress, Attruist keeps others' interests above his own interest.
20. (C) Clean is to wash or remove dirt, cleanse is to purify from the guilt of sin, Anoint is to wash with oil for consecration of deity.

21. (D) Climax is used for interest, Peak for mountain, Zenith for planet's orbit of movement.

22. (D) Order is official, Decree is court's order, ordain is holy or divine order, Enjoin is order with emphasis on compliance.

23. (B) Constrain means to compel to do something. Coerce means compel by threatening, Restrain means compel someone not to do something, and Exact means compel to comply with as repayment of loan, payment of fine, etc.

24. (A) Dissemble means to hide one's emotional feelings, Conceal means to hide from others' view, Cloak means to hide by putting under cover, Camouflage means to hide by painting in colour of surroundings so that detection is diffcult.

25. (A) Show contempt by ignoring or dismissing something means to snub, scoff is to laugh at disdainfully, Sneer is to smile disdainfully, Scorn means to treat someone contemptuously.

26. (D) Pioneer is one who is first in a field of enterprise.

27. (A) Indomitable is what can't be subdued, Invincible is what can't be defeated, Unwavering means not flickering.

28. (C) Premonition means feeling anxiety over future event, Presentiment means feeling of something bad to happen, Prescience is fore-knowledge of what will happen. Apprehension mens fear of coming evil.

29. (C) Deleterious is injurious to health.

30. (B)

31. (B) Badger means annoy with persistent nagging.

32. (C) Indemnify means to ensure to make up for possible loss caused by one's action, compensate means make up for the loss, Recompense means to pay as reward for services or help rendered.

33. (C) Snarl means to growl in anger, Purr means to make sound as by a cat, Grumble is to make indistinct guttural voice as in discontent.

34. (C)

35. (B) Balk means hesitate or refuse to move forward due to some problem ahead, Jib means to move backward instead of forward, Dither means hesitate due to fear or threat.

36. (A)

37. (A)

38. (D) Interpret means explain the meaning of, Infer means to derive by reasoning, Deduce means to conclude from something else, Construe means to assign a particular interpretation.

39. (D) Salutary means causing beneficial effect, Salubrious means health promoting climate, Sanitary means health promoting cleanliness, Wholesome means conducive to general well-being.

40. (C)

41. (D)

42. (D)

43. (C)

44. (B) Incite is used for provoking to do something unlawful as by one's internal urge, Instigate is used when someone provokes, Arouse means stir someone to action, Foment means to promote the growth of or to allow the development of something undesirable, viz., to foment dissatisfaction.

45. (C)

46. (B)

47. (C)

48. (B) Carnage means killings of a great number of people, Genocide means killing deliberately of people belonging to particular racial group, Pogrom means organised killings.

49. (D)

50. (C) Grind means to reduce to fine particles, Comminute means to break into small particles, Pulverise means to reduce to powder, Triturate means to reduce to powder by rubbing.

Test-9

For explanations, go to the synonyms of the chosen option as mentioned in comprehensive list synonymous words.

1. (A)	2. (A)	3. (C)	4. (A)	5. (A)	6. (A)
7. (C)	8. (A)	9. (B)	10. (A)	11. (B)	12. (A)
13. (C)	14. (A)	15. (C)	16. (A)	17. (A)	18. (A)
19. (A)	20. (C)	21. (C)	22. (A)	23. (B)	24. (C)
25. (A)	26. (D)	27. (C)	28. (B)	29. (B)	30. (C)
31. (A)	32. (C)	33. (D)	34. (A)	35. (C)	36. (C)
37. (D)	38. (C)	39. (C)	40. (B)	41. (A)	42. (A)

43. (B)	44. (B)	45. (A)	46. (B)	47. (C)	48. (A)
49. (B)	50. (B)	51. (D)	52. (B)	53. (C)	54. (A)
55. (C)	56. (C)	57. (C)	58. (C)	59. (A)	60. (C)
61. (C)	62. (C)	63. (A)	64. (B)	65. (B)	66. (A)
67. (B)	68. (C)	69. (A)	70. (C)	71. (C)	72. (A)
73. (D)	74. (C)	75. (C)	76. (B)	77. (B)	78. (B)
79. (A)	80. (A)	81. (C)	82. (A)	83. (C)	84. (A)
85. (A)	86. (C)	87. (C)	88. (B)	89. (C)	90. (D)
91. (D)	92. (B)	93. (A)	94. (A)	95. (D)	96. (D)
97. (C)	98. (C)	99. (C)	100. (D)	101. (D)	102. (A)
103. (C)	104. (C)	105. (A)	106. (A)	107. (B)	108. (A)
109. (D)	110. (C)	111. (B)	112. (A)	113. (D)	114. (C)
115. (B)	116. (C)	117. (A)	118. (C)	119. (D)	120. (B)
121. (C)	122. (B)	123. (C)	124. (C)	125. (B)	126. (C)
127. (C)	128. (C)	129. (A)	130. (B)	131. (A)	132. (C)
133. (A)	134. (C)	135. (C)	136. (C)	137. (B)	138. (A)
139. (C)	140. (C)	141. (A)	142. (C)	143. (D)	144. (B)
145. (A)	146. (C)	147. (A)	148. (D)	149. (C)	150. (C)
151. (A)	152. (B)	153. (B)	154. (C)	155. (A)	156. (A)
157. (C)	158. (C)	159. (A)	160. (D)	161. (A)	162. (A)
163. (C)	164. (C)	165. (C)	166. (A)	167. (B)	168. (C)
169. (D)	170. (A)	171. (C)	172. (B)	173. (B)	174. (B)
175. (B)	176. (C)	177. (A)	178. (B)	179. (B)	180. (D)
181. (D)	182. (C)	183. (B)	184. (D)	185. (C)	186. (D)
187. (C)	188. (B)	189. (A)	190. (C)	191. (B)	192. (D)
193. (C)	194. (A)	195. (C)	196. (D)	197. (B)	198. (A)
199. (B)	200. (A)	201. (D)	202. (B)	203. (C)	204. (B)
205. (D)	206. (C)	207. (D)	208. (C)	209. (C)	210. (D)
211. (C)	212. (B)	213. (D)	214. (D)	215. (C)	216. (D)
217. (C)	218. (D)	219. (C)	220. (D)	221. (C)	222. (D)
223. (C)	224. (B)	225. (C)	226. (B)	227. (D)	228. (C)

229. (C)	230. (D)	231. (B)	232. (D)	233. (C)	234. (C)
235. (D)	236. (B)	237. (D)	238. (D)	239. (B)	240. (B)
241. (C)	242. (D)	243. (B)	244. (D)	245. (B)	246. (D)
247. (D)	248. (C)	249. (B)	250. (B)	251. (B)	252. (C)
253. (D)	254. (C)	255. (C)	256. (C)	257. (D)	258. (D)
259. (B)					

Test-10

1. (B) See Journey
2. (A) See Ruse
3. (C) See Kind
4. (C) See Lewd
5. (D) See Rude
6. (A) See Jut out
7. (C) See Risk
8. (C) See Kill
9. (C) See Ridicule
10. (A) See Lament
11. (A) See Laugh
12. (A) See Revenge
13. (A) See Lawyer
14. (B) See Laziness
15. (C) See Retaliate
16. (B) See Limp
17. (C) See Rich
18. (A) See Look
19. (C) See Retrench
20. (B) See Loud
21. (D) See Repair
22. (C) See Loyalty
23. (A) See Reprimand
24. (C) See Malice
25. (C) See Relic
26. (A) See Mark
27. (B) See Rehabilitation
28. (A) See Marvel
29. (C) See Reason
30. (D) See Masacre
31. (C) See Mire
32. (B) See Quarrelsome
33. (C) See Mistake
34. (C) See Quack
35. (D) See Motive
36. (C)
37. (B) See Nonsense
38. (B) See Novice
39. (B) See Pierce
40. (C) See Overture
41. (B) See Nascent
42. (C) See Object
43. (C) See Occurrence
44. (B) See Omen
45. (A) See Outdated
46. (C) See Ominous
47. (A) See Opposite
48. (C) See Order

49. (A) See Politic
50. (D) See Peak
51. A-B See Journey
52. A-C See Regard
53. A-C See Kind
54. A-D See Lewd
55. A-C See Rude
56. A-C See Justify
57. A-D See Ridiculous
58. A-B See Kneel
59. A-B See Ridicule
60. A-D See Lament
61. A-D See Laugh
62. A-C See Retract
63. A-C See Lazy
64. A-B See Lazy
65. A-B See Resurrect
66. B-C See Lonely
67. A-D See Revolt
68. B-C See Look
69. A-B See Request
70. A-C See Look
71. A-C See Replace
72. A-B See Loot
73. A-C See Relieve
74. A-B See Malice
75. A-D See Regret
76. B-D See Mark
77. B-C See Recede
78. A-B See Marvel
79. A-C See Rebuff
80. A-C See Mercenary
81. A-B See Memento
82. (D) See Quibble
83. A-B See Miserable
84. A-D See Praise
85. B-C See Mysterious
86. A-B See Property
87. A-C See Pride
88. A-B See Obstacle
89. A-C See Poverty
90. A-B See Perplex
91. A-C See Peep
92. A-B See Perplex
93. B-D See Order
94. A-B See Pillar
95. B-C See Potpourri
96. A-B See Powerful
97. A-D See Prayer
98. A-B See Precedence
99. A-C See Prevaricate
100. A-B See Property
101. (D) See Journey
102. (C) See Ploy
103. (D) See Kind
104. (D) See Learned
105. (B) See Rude
106. (D) See Lamentation
107. (B) See Risk
108. (C) See Kneel
109. (C) See Ridicule
110. (B) See Lament
111. (D) See Laugh
112. (D) See Reverence
113. (C) See Lawyer
114. (D) See Laziness

115. (D) See Restore
116. (C) See Limp
117. (B) See Revolt
118. (A) See Look
119. (D) See Request
120. (C) See Loud
121. (A) See Repentance
122. (D) See Lure
123. (B) See Relevant
124. (C) See Malodoraous
125. (D) See Recrimination
126. (A) See Mark
127. (A) See Rebound
128. (C) See Mash
129. (D) See Rebuke
130. (B) See Memento
131. (D) See Memento
132. (B) See Quarrel
133. (D) See Miser
134. (D) See Praise
135. (C) See Motivate
136. (A) See Prize
137. (D) See Principle
138. (D) See Pretend
139. (B) See Prevaricate
140. (A) See Persuade

Test-11

1. (C) See Sacrilege
2. (C) See Writhe
3. (B) See Sad/Alone
4. (D) See Wreckage
5. (A) See Sarcastic
6. (B) See Wicked
7. (C) See Satire
8. (C) See Warning
9. (B) See Seclude
10. (B) See Vagabond
11. (D) See Serious
12. (C) See Unrestrained
13. (C) See Shine
14. (B) See Ubiquitous
15. (A) See Shrink
16. (C) See Twist
17. (C) See Shy
18. (B) See Turning Point
19. (C) See Similarity
20. (A) See Trim
21. (C) See Speech
22. (A) See Steal
23. (C) See Threat
24. (A) See Stimulate
25. (D) See Stub
26. A-C See Will
27. A-D See Writhe
28. A-B See Sad
29. A-C See While away
30. B-C See Scatter
31. A-D See Weird
32. C-D See Scrap
33. A-C See Upheaval
34. B-D See Servile
35. A-B See Unrestrained
36. C-D See Shake

37. A-B See Upset
38. A-B See Similarity
39. A-D See Sink
40. B-D See Understanding
41. B-C See Slap
42. C-D See Treasury
43. B-C See Smell
44. B-D See Tie
45. A-B See Speech
46. A-B See Spontaneous
47. B-C See Stay
48. B-D See Theft
49. A-B See Tarnish
50. A-C See Tear
51. (D) See Sad
52. (B) See Waver
53. (B) See Scatter
54. (C) See Wander
55. (D) See Scrape
56. (A) See Verify
57. (D) See Scream
58. (D) See Shake
59. (A) See Weird
60. (D) See Shameless
61. (C) See Untidy
62. (A) See Shelter
63. (A) See Try
64. (B) See Sink
65. (C) See Uncommunicative
66. (A) See Trim
67. (A) See Smile
68. (D) See Tremble
69. (B) See Spin
70. (D) See Tolerate
71. (A) See Spoils
72. (D) See Throw
73. (D) See Tear
74. (D) See Talkative
75. (B) See Strike

ANTONYMS

Multiple Choice Questions' Answers and Their Explanations

1. (B) 2. (C) 3. (C) 4. (D) 5. (A) 6. (B) 7. (C)
8. (A) 9. (C) 10. (C) 11. (C) 12. (D) 13. (C) 14. (B)
15. (D) 16. (C) 17. (D) 18. (A) 19. (C) 20. (A) 21. (C)
22. (C) 23. (D) 24. (C) 25. (C) 26. (D) 27. (C) 28. (B)
29. (A) 30. (C) 31. (A) 32. (C) 33. (B) 34. (A) 35. (D)
36. (C) 37. (C) 38. (A) 39. (A) 40. (C) 41. (D) 42. (B)
43. (D) 44. (C) 45. (C) 46. (C) 47. (B) 48. (A) 49. (C)
50. (C) 51. (C) 52. (C) 53. (A) 54. (C) 55. (D) 56. (A)
57. (D) 58. (B) 59. (D) 60. (C) 61. (A) 62. (D) 63. (B)
64. (D) 65. (C) 66. (A) 67. (D) 68. (B) 69. (C) 70. (A)
71. (D) 72. (C) 73. (A) 74. (C) 75. (C)

Explanations

1. Abet = help someone to commit crime
   Deter = discourage someone from doing something by threatening reprisal; so, Help is opposite of Discourage
2. Abstemious = not indulging in over-eating
   Gluttonous = devouring everything in excessive amount
3. Acerbic = bitter
   Melliferous = carrying honey, sweet
4. Absolve = set free from charges
   Incriminate = set charges against someone
5. Zenith = highest point in sky above our head
   Nadir = lowest point
6. Vice = evil habits
   Virtue = righteous conduct
7. Valedictory = related to saying goodbye
   Inaugural = making the beginning of an event
8. Wax = gradual increase in size of moon every night
   Wane = gradual decrease in size
9. Abject = utterly humiliating
   Honourable = causing honour
10. Acclaim = praise openly
    Denounce = condemn publicly
11. Arrogant = one who makes unwarranted claims, superiority
    Modest = one showing humble estimation of oneself
12. Ameliorate = make the condition better
    Exacerbate = make the condition bitter, *i.e.,* worse
13. Analogy = comparison of similar features of two things
    Anomaly = deviation from usual feature
14. Arrogate = usurp credit which belongs to someone else
    Credit = recognize credit of someone
15. Ascetic = person who practises self-denial to pleasures of life
    Epicure = person who believes in enjoying pleasurable things in life
16. Bequeath = to hand down property to someone by an act of will
    Inherit = to get property of one's ancestor as a right to heir
17. Bete noir = an object of intense hate
    Cynosure = an object of utmost attraction
18. Classic = (something, especially art, literature) of highest class
    Kitsch = (art, literature) having little value

19. Curious = be eager to know about something
Indifferent = have to interest about something

20. Elite = people belonging to highest class of society
Plebeian = people belonging to comon class of society

21. Affluent = prosperous, wealthy person
Indigent = poor person

22. Effluent = (water, etc.) flowing out (prefix Ex to fluent)
Influent = flowing in a place

23. Eloquent = speaking out fluently and forcefully
viz. He gave an eloquent speech
Taciturn = reserve in speech

24. Emerse = to come out (Ex + merge)
Immerse = to go in (In + merge)

25. Profound = of great depth; *viz.* He has a profound knowledge; a profound grief
Shallow = of little depth

26. Provide = make available to someone
Deprive = deny the privilege of having something

27. Resilient = returning to earlier position, flexible
Rigid = refusing to shift, bend

28. Segregate = separate things into groups, separate something from others of a group
Congregate = to come together, assemble

29. Sadism = enjoy one's act of cruelty on others
Masochism = enjoy sufferings inflicted on oneself by others

30. Symphony = harmonious combination of different sounds
Cacophony = harsh discordant combination

31. Weal = well-being, prosperity, and happiness *viz.* A work for people's weal
Woe = distress, trouble; Indescribable woe

32. Provoke = incite
Pacify = to make calm

33. Adamant = refusing to yield
Relenting = soften one's temper

34. Albino = a person whose skin lacks in melanin, causing white skin, hairs, eyebrows, etc.
Brunette = person with dark hairs, eyes and skin

35. Cleanse = to clean for religious, spiritual purpose; cleanse one's soul of sins

Defile = to make a sacred place dirty

36. Mundane = belonging to worldly things
Spiritual = belonging to soul, not physical or worldly things
37. Novel = having newness
Trite = boring due to being repeated many times
38. Dandy = a person who is very careful about his physical appearance, neat dress, caressed hairs etc
Sloven = a person who is habitually negligent of his appearance, dress, cleanliness
39. Biased = prejudiced
Disinterested = unbiased due to having no personal interest
40. Catholic = wideness of one's attitude
Parochial = narrow in attitude
41. Agoraphobia = morbid dread of open space, marketplace
Claustrophobia = morbid dread of closed, congested place
42. Myopia = lacking the power to see in distant future, lacking foresight
Clairvoyance = having super-power to see in distance
43. Outstanding = standing above others in good quality
Commonplace = having nothing special to mention
44. Garner = to pick up grains and collect
Disseminate = scatter
45. Squander = spend extravagantly
Conserve = to save by spending judiciously
46. Soar = rise up straight in sky at great speed
Swoop = to come down at great speed to attack on prey
47. Generous = giving out something with open hand
Stingy = reluctant to give or spend, niggardly
48. Ruffle = disturb smoothness, neatness
Spruce/Preen = arrange neatly
49. Perennial = (plants) covered with green leaves throughout the year (per + ennial)
Deciduous = (plants) shedding leaves in a season every year, so as to take on new leaves afresh
50. Transient = staying for short duration
Perpetual = continuing forever
51. Benevolent = bene + volent = wishing well of others
Malevolent = male + volent = wishing evil of others
52. Dissemble = to hide inner emotion, attitude

Betray = to reveal inner emotion, attitude inadvertently through external facial or behavioural expression

53. Intrepid = one who is fearless (In + trepid)
Pusillanimous = one who is faint hearted (pisillus = petty +anium = spirited)

54. Auspicious = favourable due to propitious luck
Ominous = inauspicious

55. Blaspheme = speak irreverentially against
Revere = show respect

56. Cadaverous = like a corpse, looking pale and lifeless
Vivacious = full of life and zeal

57. Deliberate = carefully thought about, intentional
Inadvertent = unintentional

58. Dilettante = a person who enjoys art, music for having interest in it
Connoisseur = a person who is conversant with intricate knowledge of art, music and so he enjoys it

59. Scion = young shoot of a tree, young person of a well-known family or group
Doyen = senior person of family or group

60. Corpulent = of bulky body
Emaciated = of lean and thin body

61. Hubris = full of arrogant pride
Humility = full of humbleness

62. Inept = without aptitude for a particular task, lacking skill
Deft = skillful

63. Eirenic or Irenic = (activity) promoting peace and harmony
Polemic = promoting controversy

64. Judicious = doing justice
Iniquitous = characterised by gross injustice

65. Latent = hidden from sight
Patent = openly visible

66. Parsimonious = stingy, showing miserliness
Lavish = spending or living luxuriously

67. Laud = praise someone for doing good
Decry = to speak disparagingly, denounce

68. Exacerbate = make condition worse
Meliorate = Ameliorate

69. Misogynist = Miso = hate, gyny = female

Philoginist = Philo = like, gyny = female

70. Nocturnal = (activity) done during night
    Diurnal = done during day time
71. Protege = a person who is under protection of someone powerful
    Protector = a person who protects
72. Succumb = to yield to disease, injury, etc., *i.e.,* to die
    Survive = remain alive after an accident, injury
73. Slipshod = untidy, sloppy
    Fastidious = critical to untidiness, sloppiness
74. Promulgate = put a law into operation
    Abrogate = to repeal a law
75. Monopoly = control of seller on market
    Monopsony = control of buyer on market

Exercises on Antonyms

Test-1

1. (B)	2. (A)	3. (D)	4. (D)	5. (C)	6. (D)
7. (D)	8. (C)	9. (C)	10. (D)	11. (C)	12. (D)
13. (C)	14. (B)	15. (D)	16. (C)	17. (C)	18. (D)
19. (C)	20. (D)	21. (D)	22. (C)	23. (C)	24. (C)
25. (B)	26. (D)	27. (D)	28. (D)	29. (D)	30. (D)
31. (A)	32. (D)	33. (A)	34. (D)	35. (C)	36. (D)
37. (C)	38. (D)	39. (C)	40. (C)	41. (D)	42. (C)
43. (C)	44. (C)	45. (D)	46. (C)	47. (C)	48. (D)
49. (C)	50. (D)	51. (D)	52. (D)	53. (C)	54. (D)
55. (C)	56. (C)	57. (C)	58. (D)	59. (A)	60. (A)
61. (A)	62. (C)	63. (C)	64. (D)	65. (C)	66. (B)
67. (C)	68. (B)	69. (A)	70. (A)	71. (D)	72. (D)
73. (D)	74. (B)	75. (D)	76. (C)	77. (C)	78. (D)
79. (D)	80. (B)	81. (C)	82. (D)	83. (A)	84. (C)
85. (C)	86. (B)	87. (D)	88. (D)	89. (B)	90. (C)
91. (D)	92. (C)	93. (C)	94. (D)	95. (C)	96. (B)
97. (A)	98. (C)	99. (C)	100. (B)	101. (D)	102. (D)
103. (C)	104. (C)	105. (B)	106. (D)	107. (C)	108. (D)
109. (C)	110. (C)	111. (C)	112. (D)	113. (B)	114. (C)
115. (D)	116. (C)	117. (C)	118. (C)	119. (B)	120. (C)
121. (D)	122. (D)	123. (D)	124. (C)	125. (D)	126. (C)
127. (D)	128. (C)	129. (D)	130. (A)	131. (D)	132. (D)
133. (C)	134. (D)	135. (D)	136. (B)	137. (C)	138. (D)

139. (B)	140. (D)	141. (C)	142. (D)	143. (D)	144. (A)
145. (C)	146. (A)	147. (C)	148. (D)	149. (B)	150. (C)
151. (D)	152. (D)	153. (D)	154. (C)	155. (D)	156. (A)
157. (C)	158. (C)	159. (A)	160. (C)	161. (C)	162. (C)
163. (B)	164. (C)	165. (D)	166. (D)	167. (D)	168. (D)
169. (C)	170. (D)	171. (C)	172. (B)	173. (D)	174. (C)
175. (C)	176. (B)	177. (C)	178. (C)	179. (B)	180. (A)
181. (D)	182. (D)	183. (C)	184. (A)	185. (C)	186. (C)
187. (D)	188. (D)	189. (D)	190. (B)	191. (C)	192. (D)
193. (C)	194. (C)	195. (C)	196. (D)	197. (C)	198. (D)
199. (A)	200. (C)	201. (C)	202. (B)	203. (D)	204. (C)
205. (B)	206. (D)	207. (C)	208. (C)	209. (D)	210. (C)
211. (C)	212. (C)	213. (B)	214. (C)	215. (B)	216. (A)
217. (D)	218. (C)	219. (B)	220. (B)	221. (C)	222. (C)
223. (A)	224. (C)	225. (B)	226. (A)	227. (C)	228. (D)
229. (C)	230. (C)	231. (B)	232. (B)	233. (A)	234. (C)
235. (D)	236. (C)	237. (C)	238. (C)	239. (A)	240. (B)
241. (A)	242. (C)	243. (B)	244. (A)	245. (D)	246. (A)
247. (B)	248. (B)	249. (D)	250. (A)	251. (B)	252. (D)
253. (D)	254. (A)	255. (B)	256. (C)	257. (C)	258. (C)
259. (C)	260. (C)	261. (B)	262. (C)	263. (C)	264. (A)
265. (B)	266. (B)	267. (D)	268. (A)	269. (C)	270. (B)
271. (C)	272. (D)	273. (B)	274. (D)	275. (C)	276. (D)
277. (C)	278. (D)	279. (D)	280. (B)	281. (B)	282. (C)

Test-2

1. (B)	2. (C)	3. (D)	4. (C)	5. (C)	6. (B)
7. (A)	8. (C)	9. (A)	10. (C)	11. (B)	12. (A)
13. (D)	14. (C)	15. (D)	16. (C)	17. (A)	18. (C)
19. (C)	20. (A)	21. (C)	22. (A)	23. (C)	24. (B)
25. (C)	26. (A)	27. (D)	28. (A)	29. (B)	30. (B)
31. (A)	32. (B)	33. (B)	34. (C)	35. (D)	36. (C)
37. (B)	38. (A)	39. (A)	40. (C)	41. (A)	42. (A)
43. (D)	44. (C)	45. (D)	46. (A)	47. (B)	48. (A)
49. (C)	50. (A)	51. (D)	52. (A)	53. (A)	54. (A)
55. (A)	56. (B)	57. (A)	58. (D)	59. (C)	60. (D)
61. (A)	62. (B)	63. (B)	64. (D)	65. (A)	66. (C)
67. (D)	68. (C)	69. (D)	70. (C)	71. (B)	72. (C)
73. (B)	74. (A)	75. (C)	76. (B)	77. (C)	78. (A)
79. (B)	80. (A)	81. (D)	82. (B)	83. (A)	84. (D)

85. (C)	86. (A)	87. (B)	88. (A)	89. (D)	90. (A)
91. (C)	92. (D)	93. (A)	94. (D)	95. (B)	96. (C)
97. (A)	98. (D)	99. (C)	100. (A)	101. (D)	102. (B)
103. (A)	104. (A)	105. (A)	106. (C)	107. (A)	108. (D)
109. (B)	110. (A)	111. (A)	112. (A)	113. (D)	114. (B)
115. (A)	116. (D)	117. (A)	118. (D)	119. (B)	120. (C)
121. (C)	122. (A)	123. (D)	124. (A)	125. (D)	126. (B)
127. (A)	128. (A)	129. (C)	130. (C)	131. (A)	132. (C)
133. (B)	134. (A)	135. (D)	136. (C)	137. (D)	138. (A)
139. (D)	140. (D)	141. (D)	142. (C)	143. (D)	144. (A)
145. (D)	146. (A)	147. (D)	148. (D)	149. (C)	150. (D)
151. (D)	152. (C)	153. (A)	154. (C)	155. (A)	156. (B)
157. (D)	158. (C)	159. (D)	160. (A)	161. (C)	162. (D)
163. (D)	164. (A)	165. (A)	166. (D)	167. (B)	168. (A)
169. (D)	170. (A)	171. (D)	172. (A)	173. (A)	174. (D)
175. (D)	176. (D)	177. (D)	178. (A)	179. (C)	180. (D)
181. (A)	182. (D)	183. (C)	184. (A)	185. (A)	186. (D)
187. (A)	188. (B)	189. (C)	190. (D)	191. (A)	192. (D)
193. (A)	194. (A)	195. (D)	196. (A)	197. (B)	198. (A)
199. (D)	200. (C)	201. (A)	202. (A)	203. (D)	204. (B)
205. (D)	206. (B)	207. (D)	208. (A)	209. (D)	210. (C)
211. (D)	212. (D)	213. (A)	214. (D)	215. (D)	216. (D)
217. (C)	218. (D)	219. (C)	220. (C)	221. (D)	222. (A)
223. (D)	224. (C)	225. (A)	226. (B)	227. (A)	228. (D)
229. (D)	230. (C)	231. (A)	232. (D)	233. (C)	234. (A)
235. (D)	236. (C)	237. (D)	238. (C)	239. (D)	240. (D)
241. (A)	242. (A)	243. (D)	244. (D)	245. (D)	246. (C)
247. (D)	248. (D)	249. (B)	250. (D)	251. (D)	252. (A)
253. (D)	254. (C)	255. (A)	256. (D)	257. (D)	258. (D)
259. (A)	260. (A)	261. (B)	262. (B)	263. (A)	264. (B)
265. (A)	266. (A)	267. (D)	268. (A)	269. (A)	270. (C)
271. (A)	272. (C)	273. (D)	274. (D)	275. (A)	276. (C)
277. (A)	278. (C)	279. (D)	280. (A)	281. (B)	282. (B)
283. (A)	284. (C)	285. (D)	286. (D)	287. (D)	288. (A)
289. (D)	290. (A)	291. (D)	292. (C)	293. (D)	294. (A)
295. (B)					

ooo

Unit-3

Sentence Correction

Parts of Speech

A

(a) Make a list of the contents of this book.
(b) What is the criteria for selection?
(c) The staff are having a party this evening.
(d) We have been living in Hyderabad since 1987.
(e) I beg your pardon.
(f) It is hard to be an honest man than to be a successful man.
(g) My loud voice made the sleeping students wake up.
(h) Mathematics is harder than Economics.
(i) That is the man who sold his car.
(j) My brother is often angry with me.

B

(a) I met him fifteen years ago.
(b) The colleges remain closed in the whole of May.
(c) I can concentrate and study well during the night.
(d) I'm Dr. William De-Souza.
(e) I'll see you soon.
(f) Ram has much confidence.
(g) There are no books for sale.
(h) He left for Delhi last week.
(i) Bread and butter is everyone's need.
(j) Oh, what a pity!

The Articles

1. There is dirt on the door.
2. Give him a glass of milk and put some sugar in it.
3. Give him some ink to write a letter.
4. She gave me the books last night.
5. A good student is never late for the lessons.
6. A banana has a sweet taste.
7. She always likes to read (some) books in a restaurant.
8. Please give her food and a cup of milk.
9. The door of living room is wide open.
10. The youngest son is at college now.
11. Birds can fly very high in the sky.
12. Horses are animals.
13. Girls wear beautiful dresses.
14. Children love sweets.
15. She has a pen and a piece of paper.
16. Indian sheep give us good wool.
17. Bread is made with flour, sugar and milk.
18. She wants a doll with blue eyes.
19. The car she drives often makes a loud noise.
20. Please write your name legibly on the blackboard.

Sentences

1. Adverb of Time
2. Adverb of Purpose
3. Adverb of Cause/Reason
4. Adverb of Place
5. Adverb of Manner
6. Adverb of Condition
7. Adverb of Degree
8. Adverb of Result
9. Adverb of Contrast/Supposition
10. Noun Clause
11. Noun Clause
12. Adverb Clause
13. Adjective Clause
14. Noun Clause
15. Adverb Clause
16. Adverb Clause
17. Adjective Clause
18. Noun Clause
19. Adverb Clause
20. Noun Clause

Subject-Verb Agreement

1. is, 2. have, 3. was, 4. allows, 5. is, 6. was, 7. was, 8. is, 9. is, 10. cost, 11. has, 12. were, 13. was, 14. were, 15. are, 16. are, 17. am, 18. is, 19. have, 20. was

Tenses

1. When John is given any assignment, he does it in time and completes it in all respects.
2. Ram gave the staff a luxurious party and gave them expensive gifts too.
3. When the boss reached office all the clerks were playing cards.
4. The principal started praising his school, showing the photographs and appreciating its garden too.
5. The members of the committee did not find him guilty and the jury acquitted him too.
6. Children are happy to watch T.V., to play cricket and to visit their friends.
7. Major Singh caught the enemy soldiers, tied them with ropes and brought them to the quarterguard.
8. The writer wrote a story, typed it and posted it.
9. The university offers courses in literature and provides for improvement in language proficiency too.
10. When the inspector arrived, the constables were smoking and gossiping.
11. The servant started cleaning the floor, watering the plants and scrubbing the utensils.
12. The painter draws the sketch, mixes the colours and applies them too.
13. The head of the department submitted a proposal; the dean too supported it.
14. My friend had not seen me for many years when I met him last week.
15. He was extremely annoyed and fired me when I reported the matter to him.

Pronouns

1. She is not so poor as I am.
2. Satish and I are good friends, but at times Satish gets annoyed with me.
3. No one from the relatives has come to attend the function.
4. Please tell him not to forget to bring my books.
5. Some of you will require to clean your own room.
6. Reema is as old as she.
7. Please don't leave the house without waiting for Prakash and him.

8. I have two of my houses in the colony adjoining to yours.
9. When did he leave to join the new college?
10. All of us — Mohan, Jatin, Shyam and I did not reach home on time.
11. She did not know whom I meant.
12. I want to know if you have seen a shirt of mine.
13. One must try to do one's work regularly.
14. She did not permit the naughty children to enter the house.
15. Neither he nor she was able to give a good presentation.
16. Either her mother or her brothers are coming to attend the function.
17. He being permitted to park his truck inside the building was quite convenient.
18. She really did not know whom she should blame.
19. Everyone of us checked in our rooms in the hotel around 2 p.m.
20. Those of us who love to visit the park should inform our hostel warden.

Modifiers

1. Wanted a match for a beautiful 25-year-old girl.
2. Wanted a 20-year-old nurse, for a baby.
3. As a teacher, I'm concerned about the privatisation of education.
4. As a reviewer, I'm concerned about the increasing sex and violence in films.
5. As a political activist, I'm concerned about the falling moral standards in politics.
6. While I was preparing for the interview, Mr. Bose gave me certain tips.
7. While he was visiting the homes of victims, the public forced him to announce the relief measures.
8. Starting from the market, one can reach the secretariat in twenty minutes.
9. If one starts from the college, the university office can be reached in twenty minutes.
10. As a journalist, I am disturbed with the entry of MNCs in print media.
11. As a conscientious citizen, I am disturbed with the rising crime rates.
12. While I was reading a book, the students stormed into the library.
13. While he was taking the examination, Dr. Roy reached into his pockets.

14. Wanted a doctor, experienced in psychiatry for a private clinic.
15. He bought a basket of fresh fruits.

Comparatives

1. laziest, 2. happier, 3. latest, 4. proudest, 5. more useful, 6. cleverer, 7. greater, 8. better, 9. larger, 10. cleverest, 11. wisest, 12. smartest, 13. faster, 14. thinnest, 15. costlier.

The Phrasal Verbs

Test 1

1. appealed to, 2. grudge against, 3. escaped from, 4. excused Rohit from, 5. found out, 6. finished up, 7. have grudges against, 8. take it coolly, 9. make out, 10. have a picnic, 11. have fun, 12. fell flat, 13. arranged for, 14. bent upon, 15. called off, 16. care for, 17. depend upon, 18. deprived of, 19. ease me off, 20. physics as.

Test 2

1. Sitting on the ground, she wrote a letter.
2. Ganesh was married to Sheela.
3. He whom you helped has turned a union leader.
4. All his hair is grey.
5. The teacher's room was locked and they had to remain outside.
6. This kind of book is not liked by me.
7. His daughters are beautiful but his sons are ugly.
8. The electric bulb was too hot to be touched.
9. The MLA had an interview with the Governor.
10. She is true to her word.
11. The fort is built of bricks, not of stone.
12. He ran a ten mile race.
13. The daughter of one of the passengers got hurt.
14. He wants two slices of bread.
15. It was he who broke the chair.
16. Five hundred miles is a long distance.
17. All except he had run away.
18. She need not come to the office.
19. She is not selfish, nor am I.
20. She spoke very hastily.
21. Call him anything else but a stupid.
22. May God bless you!
23. If you study hard, you will pass.
24. She tried to cross the road quickly.
25. She is junior to me.
26. Her problem is same as yours.
27. The clerk copied the letter word by word.

28. What is Mumbai famous for?
29. Since 1979, the use of eggs has increased each year.
30. Bangalore is very popular with the people of India.
31. Look up these words in a standard dictionary.
32. I am enclosing a cheque for Rs.100/-.
33. She would like to discuss what to do next.
34. Every Sunday afternoon she plays tennis.
35. London is a long way from Delhi.
36. Unless you study hard, you will not get good marks.
37. Gopal dare not come here.
38. Have you ever been to Mumbai?
39. He wants to know why he has been detained.
40. He is a student at the University of Jaipur.
41. As it was raining, they decided to stay indoors.
42. He arrived in Mumbai on the 15th of December.
43. We shall supply everything you need.
44. He will phone back in ten minutes.
45. He could hardly believe his eyes.
46. It is childish to complain about rules.
47. Does your country import anything?
48. He sent for the doctor because I was ill.
49. Each of them have their own problems.
50. Will she have to pay the customs duty?

Sentence Correction

Test 1

1. (c) 2. (a)

3.(b) is *correct, as an adjective* should agree in number with the noun *it modifies. 'Who' is the right choice.*

4. (e) Words *'she thought'* and *'back'* are not required.

5. (d) The correct use is the pronoun *'her'* and not she.

6.(d) Words like *'who is also,'* are superfluous.

7. (d) *It's the precise and* to the point expression.

8. (b) *It seems to be the most befitting expression*

9. (a) *It's the most appropriate and* to the point expression.

10. (b) *Two commas put after 'driver' and 'engine' provide better sense.*

11. (b) *It provides the best meaning and sense. Normally, we don't start a sentence with 'because'.*

12. (d) *Past perfect tense is* correct in this case.

13. (d) *It's a more precise and* to the point expression.

14. (a) *It makes the sentence past conditional,* which is the correct usage in this case.

15. (d) *As she is singular, it will* not take *'their'* application.
16. (c) '*not only'* is followed by *'but also'.*
17. (e) *It corrects the modifier as a small boy*, referring to *'my mother'* incorrectly.
18. (d) *Verb in the last clause/ sentence* should have the same tense.
19. (e) *'not only'* goes with *'but also'.*
20. (b) *Where it is possible, use active voice only.*

Test. 2

1. (c) It provides the best and the most accurate sense.
2. (d) It is not 'of' but *'for'* is correct. *'Is',* is the only correct form as it agrees with the number with its subject. Again, it is *'grain'* and not 'grains' which is acceptable.
3. (d) Is the only nearest correct form as it is not 'are' but *'is'* that agrees with the subject 'possibility.'
4. (a) *'Everyone'* is always considered to be a singular indefinite pronoun. Therefore, it will have *'was'* and not 'were'.
5. (c) is correct as there is a rule that when two dictinct words or phrases are joined by the correlative *'either...or, neither...nor,* or *not only...but also',* the number (singular or plural) of the word or phrase nearer to the verb decides the number of the verb. The verb 'liked' cannot be used as it changes the tense and the meaning of the sentence.
6. (b) is correct as *'except'* is a proposition so it should take an object *'him'* and not a subject 'he'.
7. (d) is correct because pronoun on both sides of the verb should be a subject. So the use of *'he'* is correct.
8. (b) is correct. The word *'writer'* being singular, will take a singular verb *'implies.'* Again, 'its' is a wrong choice as it refers to the author, so it should take *'his'* and not 'its.'
9. (b) is correct because the event of paying attention actually would have occurred earlier than her being directed for it again. Therefore, the event that was to take place earlier will have the verb *'had'* and the other one will have *'would have'.*
10. (b) is the correct answer. The sentence contains an example of an ellipsis (omission of a word or words from a sentence) in some form. It is the word *'playing'* after *'ic not'* that is missing.
11. (c) is correct. The error in the sentence is the use of the verb 'quieter' (the adjective form of quiet). The word 'quieter' modifies the verb *'runs'* therefore, it should take the correct form of the adverb

'more quietly, rather than 'quieter'.

12. (c) is the correct alternative. The word *'than'* is essential to be used as two items are being compared.
13. (e) is the correct answer because it clearly shows comparison between his fortitude and that of any other person's fortitude.
14. (d) is correct as *'not only'* takes *'but also'* in the next clause.
15. (a) is the only correct form as it takes the correct pronoun *'his'* instead of 'their' which is misplaced.
16. (a) is the only correct choice as it makes logical sense.
17. (a) is the most suitable choice as it is a clear expression in itself.

    Therefore, there is no error in the sentence.
18. (b) is the correct answer. The original sentence is not logical. It implies that one should write to the Secretary who has an opinion. The answer 'b' eliminates this ambiguity.
19. (d) is the only correct option. The original sentence runs two distinct ideas together. 'B' separates the two ideas and puts it in such a way that both have equal weight.
20. (d) is the correct choice as it does not take 'by it' which is not required in the sentence.

Miscellaneous Exercises

Test. 3

1. (b) is the only correct answer as the verb 'don't' doesn't match with the subject *'her cat',* which is in singular.
2. (c) is the correct answer as it refers to each one's home (one's home). *'Everyone'* being singular in number must take a singular pronoun which it refers to. Although (b) also looks to be correct, but (c) is more accurate than (b) as *'everyone'* has a neutral gender, so *'one's home'* is more correct.
3. (c) is the correct answer as the correct pronoun to be used is *'whoever'* and not 'whomever'.
4. (d) is the correct answer as adding the engine oil should have preceded than to realising that he forgot to add engine oil. The event that took place first will have *'had'* and the second clause will simply be in the past tense.
5. (c) is the only correct answer as it has the pronoun *'your'*, (modifying the gerund *'insisting'*) in possessive case.
6. (e) seems to be the only nearest correct answer. The sentence as it is there, makes a comparison between *impact* and *listening*, which is grammatically incorrect. In fact *'examining'* is closer to

'listening' therefore (e) is the only correct answer under the circumstances.

7. (c) is the only correct choice as it corrects the error of the misplaced modifier.

8. (d) is the only correct alternative as it makes complete sense. The underlined portion of this sentence is a fragment because it contains a subject *(boy)* but no verb to act as a predicate for the subject. Besides *'whom'* is the correct possessive pronoun than 'who' which is just an error to do use.

9. (c) is the only correct alternative. The portion of the sentence before the comma is an independent clause which can work as a complete sentence. So is the case with the part after the comma. A comma by itself is not sufficient to separate two independent clauses. It therefore requires a coordinating conjunction such as *and, but, yet, or, nor*, etc. The choice (c) provides such a conjunction.

10. (e) is the only correct choice as none of the other choices can act as the subject of the sentence. In fact, the omission of *'The fact'* from the choice 'e' is another example of an ellipsis. Please omit 'it' when joining the clauses.

11. (d) In this sentence, the word 'expedited' has been incorrectly used as it means 'speed up' or 'hastened.' The proper word to choose in the context is *'extradited',* which means to surrender from one place to another. Thus, choice 'd' is correct.

12. (e) is correct. It is an example of unnecessary wordy original sentence. While you shorten a wordy sentence, you must remember that you don't change the meaning of the sentence. In view of that, the choice (e) is the only correct choice. It not only reduces the size of the sentence, but also doesn't change its meaning.

13. (b) is the correct choice under the rule.

14. (e) Under the circumstances and keeping in view the rule it is the only correct option.

15. (b) is the correct choice under the rule.

Test Paper

1. (c), 2. (e), 3. (d), 4. (d), 5. (c), 6. (b), 7. (b), 8. (a), 9. (e), 10. (b), 11. (c), 12. (e), 13. (b), 14. (a), 15. (c), 16. (b), 17. (d), 18. (c), 19. (d), 20. (b), 21. (c), 22. (a), 23. (b), 24. (a), 25. (c), 26. (e), 27. (e), 28. (b), 29. (a), 30. (a), 31. (d), 32. (d).

ooo

Unit-4
Active and Passive Voice

Practice Exercise

1. It was done by me.
2. It is done by me.
3. It was being done by me.
4. It shall be done by me.
5. It has been done by me.
6. The essay was being typed by Lekha.
7. Math was taught us by Priyanka madam.
8. My homework was done by Roshan.
9. The animals in the cage should not be teased.
10. Shoes are manufactured by our company.
11. Poor people must be helped.
12. Let the work be finished.
13. Let the door be shut.
14. My brother is to be informed by me.
15. My brother must be informed.
16. The fire was caused by a little spark.
17. You are requested to stop talking.
18. Tina is known to Nina.
19. Why was this class joined by you?
20. The wrongdoers were arrested by the police.
21. It is believed that the God is omnipresent.
22. It is suggested that we should eat it now.
23. The project will have been completed by me by that time.
24. Your parents should not be let down.
25. It was told to me by Mohit that Rajesh was punished by the teacher.
26. The nation was shocked by sudden demise of the great leader.
27. By whom was my chocolate taken?
28. Let the order be read out.
29. Her heart was broken.
30. The law of the land should be respected.
31. It cannot be done.
32. By whom were you beaten?

33. Fine quality cheese is manufactured in Switzerland.
34. The keys must be brought.
35. I may be allowed to have it.
36. Football is played by those boys.
37. The great scientist is known to the world.
38. The poor animal was being teased (by people).
39. That dog is fierce when looked at.
40. By whom were you taught dancing?/ By whom was dancing taught you?/Who were you taught dancing by?
41. The culprit was punished by the mob.
42. Lemon is sour when tasted.
43. The thief was caught red-handed by the constable.
44. I was not being followed.
45. The mountain range cannot be crossed.
46. The mountain range has not been crossed.
47. I'm being laughed at!
48. A lot is to be done.
49. A lot has to be done.
50. It cannot be disputed.
51. The ice-cream had been eaten by me.
52. It had been done by Rajan.
53. You are requested to rescue the poor animal.
54. It is suggested that the ditch should be crossed from that side.
55. Everyone must be cared for.
56. Let the criminal be punished.
57. Can I be forgiven by you?
58. I may be forgiven this time.
59. The race will be won by my horse.
60. By whom could this have been done?
61. The match could have been won by us!
62. It would have been done by her.
63. It should have been done by me.
64. Mistakes are made by humans.
65. Let the curtain be dropped.
66. Jogging had been being done by them.
67. Cooking has been being done by me.

Passive to Active Voice

1. She couldn't do it.
2. People must pay pending bills immediately.
3. The speaker didn't answer the question.
4. They left him behind.
5. Banana tastes sweet.
6. The sword looks sharp.
7. The rod looked red hot.
8. Does anyone know his whereabouts?
9. Please let us go out.
10. We must help the poor.
11. Her mother caught her stealing from her father's drawer.
12. Onlookers must help that man.

13. If we wear these clothes, people will laugh at us.
14. Does everyone know the speaker?
15. The host gave him a glass of water.
16. That country worships the Sun God.
17. Our brave army men rescued the child.
18. No amount can satiate his hunger for money.
19. Who taught you singing?
20. Children's mother took them to a safer place.
21. Her friend made her wait for an hour.
22. The owners should not make their pets suffer.
23. Everyone deserves a good life.
24. She didn't reply to him.
25. Chhattisgarh grows rice.
26. Sriniwas looks the tallest boy in the class.
27. The majority passed the bill.
28. Nobody could have done it better.
29. Nobody can reach the peak of this mountain.

ooo

Unit-5

Direct and Indirect Speech

Practice Exercise

1. He said that nobody was doing anything wrong.
2. The child said that his father had come home late.
3. Shweta asked him whether he loved his wife.
4. She said she couldn't go with them.
5. Kirti exclaimed with excitement that she had seen a tiger in the forest.
6. The hotel manager apologised to Mr.Pandey.
7. Nina congratulated Ashish, saying that he had done well.
8. The guest asked where the main entrance to the hotel was.
9. They said they would be there.
10. She said she was writing a letter when it happened.
11. The principal told Vijay that if he didn't behave properly, he would be rusticated from the school.
12. The general said that he would make sure that the enemy didn't cross the border.
13. He exclaimed with wonder that the picture was very lovely.
14. His mother told him to finish his food.
15. His mother asked him if he had finished his food.
16. She thanked me for my help.
17. Rohit suggested his friends that they should swim.
18. The teacher asked the principal if he could leave early that day.
19. The teacher requested the principal to allow him to leave early that day.
20. He exclaimed with joy that he had won.
21. Lokesh said that it was a pity that the best player could not get into the semi-finals.
22. His mother prayed that God might be with him.
23. Reena told me that she wouldn't come the next day.
24. The man asked me what we could do about it.

25. He advised his friends that they should not go there.
26. The teacher ordered the student to get out.
27. The beggar told us that he had eaten nothing since the previous day.
28. The soldier wished that the king might live long.
29. He asked me who had attacked me.
30. She ordered her servant to take the dog out for a walk.
31. He told me that it was impossible.
32. She told me that she had never been to a circus ever before.
33. He told her that he loved her.
34. Veena told me that Sheela had told Neela about me.
35. My friend told me that they were going for a movie and asked if I would join them.
36. Soni asked Rajesh if he could lend her some money.
37. The soldier wished the Colonel a good evening.
38. My colleague Shikha told me that she had been followed by a man.
39. The manager exclaimed with regret that they had committed a blunder.
40. The patient cried and exclaimed with pain that it hurt.
41. Shiva told the class that the earth is round.
42. Nurse told that the patient was no more.
43. He exclaimed with wonder that the palace was very magnificent.
44. Rinku's father told him to bring his aunty a glass of water.
45. She told me that she was playing tennis when Geet arrived.
46. She told me that she had been playing tennis.
47. She told me that she had been playing tennis since years.
48. The judge told the minor criminal that his apologies were being accepted that time.
49. Her mother asked her who that boy was.
50. The speaker said that Swami Vivekananda was a great scholar.
51. The customer, Mrs Yogi, asked who she was speaking to.
52. He said that he had been to London.

Indirect to Direct Speech

1. He said to me, "Who have you been trying to contact?"
2. She said, "My mother is ill."
3. She says, "My mother is ill."
4. I said to him, "I cannot attend the party."
5. They said, "We have worked together for years."

6. We said to them, "We cannot help you."
7. He said to me, "Who is the most intelligent student in your class?"
8. Neha said, "I have been studying for my exams."
9. Shashank says, "I'm in love with that girl."
10. Amrita said to me, "I don't like Shashank."
11. Amrita said to me, "I can never like Shashank."
12. Billy says, "I'm fed up with the system."
13. Billy said, "I'm fed up with the system."
14. The farmer said to them, "Who are you?"
15. Her mother said, "I pray to God every day."
16. He says, "I live in a skyscraper."
17. The boy said to his father, "I haven't been lying."
18. The teacher said to the class, "The sun rises in the east."
19. The student said to the teacher, "Good afternoon."
20. She said, "I haven't done it."
21. She said to me, "I won't be able to attend the morning prayers."
22. Vishakha said to me, "Can you dance?"
23. We said, "Wow! Our team has won the match!"
24. They said, "Oh no! We have lost the match!"
25. She said to us, "Let's go to Nainital."
26. She said to me, "Sohan has left Delhi."
27. She said to me, "Sohan has been living in Mumbai for the last three years."
28. The coach said to the team, "If you want to win the match, you should practice hard."
29. They said, "We are going there on a trip."
30. The teacher said to him, "Shut up."
31. The teacher said to him, "Will you shut up?"
32. His friend said to him, "Please speak slowly."

ooo

Unit-6

Idioms and Phrases

Exercises on Idioms & Phrases

1. (C)	2. (A)	3. (B)	4. (C)	5. (A)	6. (B)
7. (C)	8. (A)	9. (D)	10. (C)	11. (B)	12. (D)
13. (D)	14. (C)	15. (D)	16. (C)	17. (D)	18. (C)
19. (C)	20. (A)	21. (C)	22. (C)	23. (D)	24. (D)
25. (C)	26. (A)	27. (C)	28. (C)	29. (B)	30. (B)
31. (D)	32. (B)	33. (A)	34. (B)	35. (C)	36. (D)
37. (A)	38. (B)	39. (D)	40. (C)	41. (B)	42. (D)
43. (A)	44. (D)	45. (B)	46. (C)	47. (A)	48. (C)

Unit-7

One Word Substitution

Exercises on Idioms & Phrases

1. (C)	2. (A)	3. (B)	4. (C)	5. (A)	6. (B)
7. (C)	8. (A)	9. (D)	10. (C)	11. (B)	12. (D)
13. (D)	14. (C)	15. (D)	16. (C)	17. (D)	18. (C)
19. (C)	20. (A)	21. (C)	22. (C)	23. (D)	24. (D)
25. (C)	26. (A)	27. (C)	28. (C)	29. (B)	30. (B)
31. (D)	32. (B)	33. (A)	34. (B)	35. (C)	36. (D)
37. (A)	38. (B)	39. (D)	40. (C)	41. (B)	42. (D)
43. (A)	44. (D)	45. (B)	46. (C)	47. (A)	48. (C)

Test on One Word Substitution

1. Archipelago
2. Sycophant
3. Toady
4. Hypochondriac
5. Valetudinarian
6. Agoraphobia
7. Ochlophobic
8. Claustrophobic
9. Matador
10. Chivalrous
11. Samaritan
12. Surrogate
13. Doctor manque
14. Wannabe
15. Evolution
16. Metamorphosis
17. Shrew
18. Clairsonant
19. Fragile
20. Frangible
21. Dirigible
22. Laissez-faire
23. Inedible
24. Potable
25. Fertile
26. Fecund
27. Effete
28. Prolific
29. Incendiary
30. Nepenthes
31. Femme fatale
32. Slut or slattern
33. Sloven
34. Palindrome
35. Euphemism
36. Rote

37. Encore
38. Relapse
39. Recidivate
40. Redintegrate them
41. Renaissance
42. Alliteration
43. Presentiment
44. Soporific
45. Freak
46. Re-incarnate
47. Redeem
48. Dungeon (mortgage or pledge)
49. Plutocracy
50. Plebeianism
51. Unicorn
52. Ecdysis
53. Pariah
54. Bete noire
55. Crescent
56. Gemination
57. Cannibal
58. Eve
59. Bristle
60. Gravamen
61. Bruxism
62. Eternity
63. Afflatus
64. Disenfranchise
65. Metempsycosis
66. Alter ego
67. Bait
68. Decoy
69. Alumnus
70. Alumnae
71. Alma mater
72. Monastery
73. Hermitage
74. Igloo
75. Scullery
76. Uxorious
77. Doting
78. Ghetto
79. Exogamy
80. Billet
81. Heirloom
82. Conscription
83. Precocious
84. Prodigious
85. Bon vivant
86. Grotto
87. Terracotta
88. Aficionado
89. Hors d'oeuvre
90. Piece d'resistance
91. Fugitive
92. Truant
93. Sororicide
94. Peel
95. Shrapnel
96. Posthumous
97. Chaperon
98. Gigolo
99. Nostalgia
100. Palmy days
101. Scullion
102. Perspicacious
103. Perspicuous
104. Downtown
105. Allegory
106. Tactile
107. Prehensile
108. Vagabond
109. Cartographer
110. Pomoculture
111. Equinox
112. Toddler
113. Anointing
114. Charlatan
115. Sliver
116. Coparceners
117. Ken
118. Cogniscenti
119. Sceptic or
120. Novice Skeptic

121. Riparian
122. Exodus
123. Omnivorous
124. Diaspora
125. Pedant
126. Keen
127. Prophylactic
128. Necrophobia
129. Shard
130. Claque
131. Cortege
132. Syndrome
133. Auscultation
134. Alopecia
135. Anosmia
136. Cant
137. Photophobia
138. Origami
139. Anorexia nervosa
140. Cynosure of Premises
141. Hibernation
142. Commuting
143. Contagious
144. Quarantine
145. Maiden
146. Debris
147. Rubble
148. Scree
149. Premiere
150. Inexorable
151. Invincible
152. Illusion
153. Euthanasia
154. Epaulettes
155. Fetish
156. Memorabilia
157. Souvenir
158. Addiction
159. Indigenous
160. Carte blanche
161. Aisle
162. Alley
163. Calus
164. Shoal
165. Nectar
166. Intuition
167. Premonition
168. Instinct
169. Unmoral
170. Heritage
171. Predecessor
172. Neophyte
173. Altruist
174. Sinistral
175. Antecedents
176. Archive
177. Oasis
178. Kennel
179. Heir
180. Herald
181. Adonis
182. Dandy/Fop
183. Heretic
184. Intermediary
185. Braggart
186. Grizzled
187. Dormant
188. Ambivalent
189. Albino
190. Brunette
191. Assassin
192. Ascetic
193. Dastard
194. Dilettante
195. Felon
196. Frankenstein
197. Ordeal
198. Martinet
199. Teetotaler
200. Troglodyte

201. (a) 202. (a) 203. (a) 204. (c) 205. (a) 206. (c) 207. (a)
208. (a) 209. (c) 210. (b) 211. (b) 212. (a) 213. (a) 214. (a)

215. (a) 216. (a) 217. (b) 218. (a) 219. (a) 220. (a) 221. (a)
222. (c) 223. (b) 224. (b) 225. (c) 226. (b) 227. (d) 228. (d)
229. (d) 230. (a) 231. (a) 232. (a) 233. (c) 234. (c) 235. (a)
236. (a) 237. (a) 238. (c) 239. (b) 240. (c) 241. (c) 242. (b)
243. (c) 244. (c) 245. (a) 246. (a) 247. (d) 248. (c) 249. (a)
250. (a) 251. (c) 252. (b) 253. (b) 254. (a) 255. (b) 256. (a)
257. (a) 258. (b) 259. (c) 260. (a) 261. (b) 262. (a) 263. (c)
264. (a) 265. (a) 266. (a) 267. (b) 268. (a) 269. (c) 270. (d)

Exercise on One Word Substitution

1. Sadist
2. Schadefreude
3. Sado masochist
4. Voyeur
5. Foil
6. Omnivorous
7. Shrapnel
8. Arbitrage
9. Posthumous
10. Analogy
11. Disparity
12. Eternity
13. Vespers
14. Slut
15. Sloven
16. Selfish
17. Altruist
18. Samaritan
19. Ecdysis
20. Shed
21. Freak storm
22. Metempsycosis
23. Re-incarnation
24. Renaissance
25. Prosthesis
26. Lullaby
27. Encomium
28. Alma mater
29. Gladiator
30. Entrepreneur
31. Tycoon
32. Cannibal
33. Origamist
34. Philatelist
35. Precocious tree
36. Toddler
37. Contagious disease
38. Dis-enfranchise
39. Artifice
40. Euphoria
41. Rubble
42. Maiden
43. Bruxism
44. Riparian
45. Epaulette
46. Aisle
47. Terracotta
48. Skeptic
49. Charlatan
50. Hermit
51. Bete noire
52. Bovine
53. Graminivorous
54. Hoarding
55. Endogamy
56. Iatrogenic problems
57. Necrophobist
58. Eneuresis
59. Gigolo
60. Heirloom
61. Euphemism
62. Epitaph
63. Dungeon
64. Ordeal
65. Allegory
66. Sclera
67. Icon
68. Scion
69. Ghetto
70. Bristle

Unit-8

Synthesis

Exercises on Idioms & Phrases

(A) Forming Simple Sentences

1) He is too ill to attend the meeting.
2) He is too soft-spoken to be a politician.
3) Being bored she went out to play.
4) Entering the arena he saluted the king.
5) Being in a hurry, she asked her husband to drive fast.
6) Willing to hear the popular leader people waited for him.
7) Bent on disturbing the leader, people hooted.
8) It was foolish of her to waste her time.
9) It was wise of her to study meticulously.
10) An old gentleman knocked at the door.
11) A naughty young lady entered the room.
12) Sheela, a noted surgeon, works in the general hospital.
13) Rama, a popular singer, sings patriotic songs.
14) We can be sure that Rajni will pass the exam.
15) I'm sure that he will fail the test.
16) He was given a big hand for doing so much for the society.
17) People hate him for being a rude fellow.
18) India, our motherland, must be defended.
19) Friends' Colony, the best colony, should be kept clean.
20) He was talking loudly.
21) Being too tall she won't like this car.
22) Being too proud he won't talk first.
23) Srikant, a famous painter, lives in Shimla.
24) Srikant, a novice, is struggling hard.
25) I'm aware of his contribution being acknowledged.
26) I'm sad about his contribution remaining unknown.
27) She dropped her purse as well as mobile.

28) She and her friend participated in the quiz.
29) The dance program having ended, the viewers proceeded for the magic show.
30) I have three pairs of shoes under the cupboard.
31) Inspite of having a sweet voice, she doesn't like to sing.
32) Anyone could see that Seema was lying.
33) His heart is too big to hate anyone.

(B) Forming Complex Sentences

1) Nobody can tell if it will be too hot.
2) Anyone can guess if it will rain.
3) She told me that he likes me.
4) He didn't tell me that she hates me.
5) I have forgotten where we had parked the car.
6) I remember very well where we had met first.
7) Major had been informed that enemy was about to attack.
8) General could not be informed that the enemy was retreating.
9) We can be sure that the train will arrive on time.
10) Everyone knows that he is a scientist.
11) Very few know that he is a sportsman.
12) The allegations that he stole the watch are absurd.
13) People are wondering if he stole the diamond.
14) The fact remains that this river is hard to cross.
15) The fact remains that this mountain has been climbed before.
16) The students were heard saying that the teacher was to remain absent for a while.
17) We were enjoying the snacks that were crunchy.
18) He will take bus no. 8 that stops in his village.
19) He can't eat sweets because he has diabetes.
20) Everyone likes her because she has a good nature.
21) Everyone despises him because he is very cruel.
22) Though he is a CEO, he still eats in general canteen.
23) Raj is more stupid than he is rich.
24) If you do not hurry up, we will miss the train.
25) If he hadn't burned the midnight oil, he couldnot have passed with flying colours.
26) Athlete acted as his coach guided him.
27) He hurried, lest he should be late.
28) He finished his homework lest he should be punished.
29) She dances as nicely as her friend does.
30) If he had studied sufficiently, he would have scored good marks.
31) No other student in the class is as intelligent as Rohan is.
32) Our hopes were that he would hit the ball.
33) It is so hot that one can step outside.

34) When the police reached the crime scene, the thief had gotten away.

35) I know my neighbours who live in the adjacent quarter.

36) He died in France where he had been for twelve years.

(C) Forming Compound Sentences

1. Neither he nor his friend is a liar.
2. Neither she nor her brother is bad.
3. She is poor and so is her brother.
4. It might either rain or hail.
5. We may find either a hut or a cave.
6. He is still playing, so he cannot complete his homework in time.
7. His train was late so he missed the exam.
8. I barely ever see her, so I miss her a lot.
9. He is a bright student but doesn't study hard.
10. Prithvi missile can be launched not only from the land but also from the sea.
11. She can swim and so can he.
12. He can't swim nor can she. / Neither he nor she can swim.
13. He is rich but miser.
14. She is not only smart but also active.
15. He is neither smart nor active.
16. We were getting late yet we stayed till the end of the party.
17. Sumit drank a glass of water and walked on.
18. It still or your father will scold you.
19. She wastes time so she will fail.
20. She is in the meeting so she can't meet anyone.
21. He came from nowhere and ate all the food.
22. One should neither complain nor cry.
23. You are good and so is your friend.

OOO

Unit-9

Reading Comprehension Strategy

1. A	2. B	3. C	4. B	5. C	6. C
7. D	8. A	9. C	10. C	11. B	12. C
13. C	14. D	15. A	16. A	17. C	18. D
19. B	20. B	21. D	22. D	23. C	24. D
25. B	26. D	27. D	28. B	29. C	30. D
31. A	32. D	33. C	34. B	35. A	36. B
37. C	38. A	39. D	40. C	41. D	42. A
43. C	44. A	45. B	46. A	47. D	48. C
49. D	50. C	51. A	52. D	53. A	54. D
55. B	56. C	57. D	58. C	59. A	60. C
61. D	62. C	63. A	64. B	65. C	66. D
67. B	68. D	69. A	70. C		

ooo

Unit-10

Parajumbles

1. B	2. C	3. D	4. B	5. B	6. D
7. B	8. C	9. A	10. A	11. D	12. D
13. A	14. C	15. B	16. C	17. C	18. B
19. B	20. A	21. D	22. A	23. D	24. A
25. C	26. B	27. B	28. C	29. A	30. D

ooo